INTERNET OF THINGS

Technologies, Architectures, Security, Governance, AI and Smart Applications

INSIGHT PUBLICA®

Nadakkavu, Kozhikode, Kerala, 673011
www.insightpublica.com
e-mail: insightpublica@gmail.com
Title: **INTERNET OF THINGS**
Author: **Dr. Mahalingam Palaniandi**
(English)
First Edition: July 2026
Printed and Published by
InsightinPublica Printers & Publishers Pvt. Ltd.
ISBN 978-93-7853-126-2
₹1400

First published 2026
Printed for academic and educational use

INTERNET OF THINGS

Technologies, Architectures, Security, Governance, AI and Smart Applications

A Comprehensive Academic and Professional Reference for the Connected Digital World

Dr. Mahalingam Palaniandi
National University of Science and Technology,
Oman, 2026

INSIGHT PUBLICA®

Dr. Mahalingam Palaniandi

Dr. Mahalingam Palaniandi is an academic and researcher with over 30 years of experience in higher education, IT leadership, curriculum development, and applied research. He currently serves as Assistant Professor at the College of Advanced Technology, National University of Science and Technology, Muscat, Oman. He holds a Ph.D. in Computer Science, with specialization in Storage Area Networks and Security.

His research and teaching interests span Artificial Intelligence, Cloud Computing, the Internet of Things, Smart City Systems, Cognitive Psychology, Network Security, and emerging digital technologies. He is the author of six textbooks published in India and has contributed three international book chapters published by IGI Global, USA, Springer, Singapore, and BP International, UK. He has also published more than twenty journal and conference papers in reputed venues, including IEEE and Scopus-indexed publications.

Recognized with academic and teaching awards, including the Best Inspirational Teacher Award in 2024, Dr. Palaniandi has dedicated his academic journey to shaping young minds and nurturing the next generation of technologists. He strongly believes in bridging emerging technology with effective teaching and learning, and has worked throughout his career to make complex concepts accessible, engaging, and relevant to students' lives. Mentoring students and guiding their research and career journeys remain, for him, among the most rewarding aspects of academic life.

An active IEEE member, international peer reviewer, and Ph.D. thesis evaluator, Dr. Palaniandi is committed to advancing quality education, meaningful research, and technology-driven academic development across Oman and India.

To my father and mother –
whose unwavering love, sacrifice, and faith
planted in me everything I have ever grown into.
This work is yours as much as it is mine.

- *Dr. Mahalingam Palaniandi*

Declarations

During the preparation of this book, selected digital and AI-based tools were used to support the writing and production process. Grammarly was used for grammar checking and language refinement. ChatGPT (OpenAI) and Claude (Anthropic) were used in selected cases for idea structuring, cross-checking case study references, improving clarity, and supporting content review.

All figures, diagrams, and illustrations in this book represent the author's own conceptual design, developed to meet the specific content and pedagogical requirements of each chapter. The author used image editing and diagramming tools such as Canva, together with AI-assisted tools including Napkin AI, Claude, and ChatGPT, to support the structuring, layout, positioning, and visual refinement of these author-conceived figures. All visual content was conceived, directed, reviewed, and finalised by the author.

All AI-assisted and AI-supported content used in this book has been carefully reviewed, edited, verified, and finalised by the author. Technical specifications, product names, platform references, and brand names mentioned in this book are used only for educational, academic, and referential purposes. Wherever applicable, such information has been checked against the respective official websites or reliable technical sources. The responsibility for the final content, academic interpretation, organization, and presentation of this book rests entirely with the author.

CONTENTS

Part IV
Security, Governance, and Future Directions

Preface

The Internet of Things has emerged as one of the most influential technological developments shaping the connected digital world. It is no longer confined to research laboratories, industrial automation systems, or futuristic predictions. Today, IoT is deeply embedded in homes, hospitals, factories, cities, farms, transport systems, energy grids, classrooms, and public infrastructure. Sensors capture real-world conditions, gateways connect diverse devices, cloud platforms process large volumes of data, artificial intelligence converts data into meaningful insights, and actuators transform digital decisions into physical actions. Through this transformation, the boundary between the physical and digital worlds is becoming increasingly narrow.

This book, Internet of Things: Technologies, Architectures, Security, Governance, AI and Smart Applications, has been written as a comprehensive academic and professional reference for understanding IoT in a systematic, technically sound, and future-ready manner. The purpose of this book is not only to introduce IoT as a collection of smart devices or communication protocols, but also to explain it as a complete technological ecosystem. This ecosystem brings together embedded systems, sensors, actuators, wireless communication, cloud computing, data analytics, cybersecurity, governance, artificial intelligence, and real-world applications.

IoT is a truly multidisciplinary field involved with many technologies enable to achieve the connected world. A good understanding of IoT requires knowledge of how sensors capture physical reality, how microcontrollers process signals, how gateways connect constrained devices to IP-based networks, how data moves through protocols such as MQTT, CoAP, LoRaWAN, Zigbee, BLE, Wi-Fi, and 5G, how cloud and edge platforms manage connected devices, how analytics and machine learning extract value from data, and how security and governance protect individuals, systems, and organisations. This book has been designed to bring these dimensions together in one coherent and practical reference.

The book begins with the foundations of IoT. It introduces the meaning, evolution, characteristics, enabling technologies, deployment levels, application domains, ecosystem stakeholders, and standardisation landscape of IoT. These chapters provide the conceptual foundation required to understand how IoT differs from traditional internet systems and earlier machine-to-machine communication models. They also explain the physical layer of IoT, including transducers, sensors, actuators, microcontrollers, single-board computers, communication modules, device identity, and energy management in constrained devices.

The next part of the book focuses on IoT architecture, communication, and system design. It examines the evolution from vertical M2M systems to horizontal IoT ecosystems. It explains three-layer, five-layer, seven-layer, and four-tier reference architectures, along with the functional blocks that form a complete IoT platform. The communication chapter provides a structured explanation of IoT protocol stacks, including link-layer, network-layer, transport-layer, application-layer, and management protocols. The system design chapter connects theory with practice by presenting a complete methodology for designing IoT systems, from purpose specification and requirement analysis to prototyping, application development, deployment, and continuous improvement.

The middle part of the book deals with IoT data, platforms, analytics, and applications. IoT systems create value not simply by collecting data, but by converting raw signals into information, knowledge, decisions, and actions. For this reason, the book explains data serialisation, ingestion, storage, stream processing, batch processing, Lambda and Kappa architectures, edge computing, fog computing, cloud IoT platforms, time-series databases, data lakes, APIs, analytics hierarchies, machine learning pipelines, and data governance. These concepts are then connected to major application domains such as smart homes, smart buildings, smart cities, industrial IoT, connected healthcare, smart agriculture, energy management, retail, logistics, and supply chain systems.

The later chapters address trust, security, governance, and the responsible management of IoT systems. As connected systems expand into critical infrastructure and personal environments, security and governance can no longer be treated as optional additions. They are essential design requirements. This book therefore examines IoT vulnerability categories, attack surfaces, authentication, authorisation, encryption, secure boot, public key infrastructure, over-the-air updates, privacy by design, incident response, connectivity management, device lifecycle management, compliance, operational governance, and multi-stakeholder data sharing. These topics are essential for building IoT systems that are not only functional, but also reliable, secure, accountable, and socially responsible.

The concluding part of the book looks ahead to the emerging future of IoT. Digital Twins, 5G and next-generation connectivity, Edge AI, Blockchain, Green IoT, sustainability, and intelligent automation are changing the way IoT systems are designed, deployed, and operated. Special attention is given to the convergence of Artificial Intelligence and IoT. AI and Machine Learning are no longer external tools applied after data collection.

This book is intended for a wide range of readers, including students, educators, researchers, engineers, IT professionals, system architects, policymakers, entrepreneurs, self-learners and whoever want to know more about IoT. Readers who are new to IoT will find step-by-step explanations, practical examples, diagrams, definitions, and structured frameworks. Experienced practitioners will find architecture models, protocol comparisons, deployment patterns, governance frameworks, and future technology roadmaps. Researchers and educators will find a broad reference that connects established IoT knowledge with emerging developments in AIoT, Digital Twins, Edge AI, cybersecurity, and sustainability.

How to Use This Book

This book may be used in different ways depending on the reader's background and purpose. Readers who are new to IoT may follow the chapters in sequence, beginning with the foundations and gradually moving towards architecture, communication, data platforms, applications, security, governance, and AI-enabled IoT. Practitioners and system designers may focus on the architecture, protocol selection, deployment, security, and governance chapters as a professional reference for real-world projects. Researchers and educators may use the diagrams, tables, case examples, standards reference, and structured explanations to support teaching, curriculum development, and applied research. Policymakers and decision-makers may find the chapters on applications, governance, security, sustainability, and emerging trends useful for understanding the wider impact of connected systems. Thus, the book is designed not only for formal study, but also for professional consultation, self-learning, and strategic technology planning.

Writing a book of this scope has been both a professional responsibility and a personal academic journey. IoT is not a narrow subject that can be understood from a single viewpoint. It requires the ability to think across hardware, software, networks, data, intelligence, security, management, society, and ethics. My experience in teaching, academic leadership, research, curriculum development, and technology practice has repeatedly shown me that learners and professionals need a book that explains not only what IoT is, but also how IoT systems are designed, secured, deployed, governed, and evolved.

I am deeply grateful to the many students, colleagues, researchers, practitioners, and institutions whose questions, discussions, feedback, and professional experiences have enriched my understanding of this field. I also acknowledge the wider academic and technical community whose standards, research papers, documentation, frameworks, and innovations have built the foundation on which this book stands. Any textbook on IoT necessarily carries an intellectual debt to the engineers, scientists, educators, standards bodies, and industry professionals who have advanced this remarkable field.

I sincerely thank the Management of the National University of Science and Technology, Muscat, Oman, and the NU Executives for their continuous support, encouragement, and academic inspiration for scholarly and professional works of this nature. I also express my sincere appreciation to my students, colleagues, friends, and family members for their constant encouragement, understanding, and support throughout the preparation of this book.

My special thanks are also due to Insight Publica, Kerala, for their professional, transparent, and supportive publishing services, and for their cooperation in bringing this academic work to publication.

The Internet of Things will continue to evolve. Devices will become smaller, networks faster, analytics more intelligent, systems more autonomous, and governance more important. The future of IoT will not be defined only by the number of connected devices, but by how responsibly, securely, intelligently, and sustainably those devices serve human needs. I hope this book helps readers understand the present architecture of IoT, appreciate its interdisciplinary richness, and prepare for the next generation of connected intelligent systems.

Welcome to Internet of Things: Technologies, Architectures, Security, Governance, AI and Smart Applications.

Dr. Mahalingam Palaniandi

Assistant Professor, College of Advanced Technology

National University of Science and Technology

Muscat, Oman

www.nu.edu.om

2026

Part I

Foundations of the Internet of Things

Chapter 1

Introduction to the Internet of Things

Chapter 1 establishes the conceptual foundation of the Internet of Things as a large-scale, interconnected ecosystem that extends digital intelligence into the physical world. It examines the evolution of IoT from RFID, ubiquitous computing, traditional internet systems, and machine-to-machine communication into a modern architecture of connected devices, platforms, data, services, and intelligent applications. The chapter defines the essential characteristics that distinguish IoT systems, including connectivity, identity, data generation, distributed intelligence, communication, scalability, layered architecture, and security. It also introduces the enabling technologies that make IoT possible, such as sensors, actuators, cloud computing, big data analytics, artificial intelligence, machine learning, and wireless connectivity. In addition, the chapter presents IoT deployment levels, major application domains, ecosystem stakeholders, standardisation bodies, and the key challenges and opportunities shaping the future of connected systems. Overall, this chapter provides the intellectual and technical base for understanding IoT not as a single technology, but as a multidisciplinary digital infrastructure that integrates devices, networks, data, intelligence, governance, and real-world value creation.

Opening Scenario: A Morning Counted

It is 6:47 a.m. on an ordinary Wednesday. A commuter in Singapore wakes not to the alarm she set the night before, 6:38 a.m., but nine minutes later, because a sensor on her wrist detected that she was in light sleep at 6:38, passed that observation to an algorithm running on a cloud server two time zones away, and the algorithm instructed her phone to delay the alarm. No human decision was made. No direct intervention occurred. A small piece of data, a short wireless transmission, a brief computation, and a physical outcome: she woke at a better moment in her sleep cycle.

She leaves the bedroom and the lights adjust automatically, not because she pressed a switch, but because a motion sensor above the door detected her movement and a local controller evaluated the room's ambient light level against a threshold. In the kitchen, the coffee maker started brewing at 6:30 based on a schedule that was automatically shifted forward nine minutes when the alarm was delayed. The thermostat reduced heating at 6:00 a.m. because a geofencing algorithm detected that her phone was still within the building's perimeter and would, at the normal time, have been moving toward the door. The building's energy management system logged all of these events along with 847 other sensor readings collected in the same minute from across the 12-floor residential block.

On the street, a sensor array embedded in the pavement counted her footstep as she walked to the bus stop, one of 2.3 million pedestrian events recorded on that block that month, used to optimise traffic light timing. The bus she boarded was tracked in real time by the city's public transport authority, its location broadcast every four seconds to passengers' phones. The overhead panel reporting the next bus's arrival time was itself an IoT device: a display fed by a data stream, not a timetable.

By the time she reached her desk at 8:12 a.m., she had been subject to, and benefited from, interactions with approximately 60 connected devices. None required her direct attention. None were what most people would call a computer. All were part of the Internet of Things. The chapter's opening question: if the majority of internet traffic already flows between machines rather than between humans, and if the majority of connected devices are already things rather than people, what does that mean for the engineers, architects, and policy makers who must design, build, and govern these systems? The answer is the subject of this book.

1.1 What Is the Internet of Things?

The Internet of Things is not primarily a technology; it is a paradigm shift in how physical reality relates to the digital world. Its essence is deceptively simple: physical objects, equipped with sensors and communication capability, become active participants in information systems rather than passive subjects of human observation. A temperature sensor that transmits a reading without human initiation, a motor that reports its vibration signature to a maintenance platform, a shipping container that announces its location at every port, each is an instance of the same idea. The physical world has acquired, in effect, a data layer.

1.1.1 Historical Origins

The intellectual lineage of IoT begins, by convention, with Kevin Ashton. In 1999, working as a brand manager at Procter and Gamble, Ashton coined the phrase 'Internet of Things' to describe a proposal he was developing: equipping physical objects in the supply chain with RFID (Radio Frequency Identification) tags so that inventory systems could track them automatically, without human data entry. He used the phrase in a presentation to senior Procter and Gamble management to argue that if computers had tools to gather information about the physical world without relying on humans to enter data, they could track and manage things far more accurately. Ashton later reflected: 'If we had computers that knew everything there was to know about things, using data they gathered without any help from us, we would be able to track and count everything, and greatly reduce waste, loss, and cost.'

The conceptual precursors extend further back. In 1982, researchers at Carnegie Mellon University connected a Coke vending machine to the ARPANET, the precursor to the internet, enabling remote queries about the machine's inventory and the temperature of its drinks, making it arguably the first internet-connected physical appliance.

Mark Weiser's 1991 paper 'The Computer for the 21st Century', published in Scientific American, articulated the concept of ubiquitous computing: the idea that computation would eventually recede into the background of physical environments, embedded in everyday objects and transparent to users. Weiser's vision required computational capability to be distributed across many small, inexpensive devices, precisely what the subsequent decades of silicon miniaturisation, battery technology improvement, and wireless protocol standardisation eventually delivered.

The trajectory from Ashton's coinage to the present was shaped by several enabling developments that matured simultaneously in the 2000s and 2010s: the cost of MEMS (Micro-Electro-Mechanical Systems) sensors fell from dollars to cents per unit; low-power wireless standards (IEEE 802.15.4, Bluetooth Low Energy) were standardised; cloud computing eliminated the need for organisations to own their own server infrastructure; and mobile network coverage extended to the point where virtually any geography could be served by cellular-connected IoT devices. By 2010 the number of internet-connected devices exceeded the number of people on earth for the first time. By 2025, the number of connected IoT devices had grown to about 21.1 billion globally, equivalent to roughly two to three IoT devices per person, with forecasts projecting around 39 billion connected IoT devices by 2030 (IoT Analytics, 2025).

1.1.2 Definitions

The term 'Internet of Things' has attracted a proliferation of definitions, which itself reflects the breadth of the phenomenon. Three institutional definitions provide a useful triangulation. The International Telecommunication Union's Recommendation ITU-T Y.2060 (2012) defines the IoT as 'a global infrastructure for the information society, enabling advanced services by interconnecting (physical and virtual) things based on existing and evolving interoperable information and communication technologies.' This definition emphasises the infrastructure character of IoT; it is not a single product or application but an interconnection fabric, and its reliance on standard, interoperable communications protocols.

ISO/IEC 30141 (2018), the international IoT reference architecture standard, defines the IoT as 'an infrastructure of interconnected entities, people, systems and information resources together with services which processes and reacts to information from the physical world and virtual world.' This definition adds the important dimension of things-plus-people: the IoT is not a machine-only network but a sociotechnical system in which human actors, organisations, and regulatory frameworks are integral components. The IETF, through RFC 7228 and related documents, approaches IoT from a network engineering perspective, focusing on the constrained node classes that characterise IoT devices and the protocol adaptations required to serve them.

For the purposes of this textbook, we adopt a working definition that synthesises the above: the Internet of Things is an interconnected system of physical objects embedded with sensors, actuators, and communication capability that enables these objects to collect, exchange, and act on data, connecting the physical world to digital information systems at scale. Three elements are essential to this definition: physical embedding (the intelligence is in the object, not attached to it), autonomous communication (the object initiates data exchange without direct human instruction), and system integration (the object's data creates value only when integrated with other objects, platforms, and applications).

Key Insight: Three Essential Elements of the IoT Working Definition. Physical embedding — intelligence resides within the object, not in an attached device. Autonomous communication — the object initiates data exchange without direct human instruction. System integration — an object's data creates value only when integrated with other objects, platforms, and services. A deployment that satisfies all three qualifies as IoT; one that lacks any of them is either a sensor, a remote-control device, or a standalone data logger.

Internet of Things

An interconnected system of physical objects embedded with sensors, actuators, and communication capability that enables these objects to collect, exchange, and act on data, connecting the physical world to digital information systems at scale. Three essential properties: physical embedding of intelligence; autonomous communication without direct human instruction; and system integration that derives value from aggregated data across devices, platforms, and applications.

1.1.3 IoT vs. the Traditional Internet vs. M2M

IoT is often conflated with both the traditional internet and the older concept of M2M (Machine-to-Machine) communication. Understanding the distinctions clarifies IoT's scope and the engineering challenges it presents. The traditional internet was designed for and by human users: web browsers, email clients, and social media applications are all human-initiated, human-interpreted exchanges. IoT inverts this: the majority of connected devices have no user interface, generate data continuously without human initiation, and transmit to other machines rather than to human readers.

M2M communication predates the IoT concept and describes bilateral machine communication, typically a sensor reporting to a server or a controller sending commands to an actuator, using cellular or wired links. M2M systems were typically vertical: proprietary protocols, vendor-specific platforms, and point-to-point data flows. IoT extends M2M in three important ways: it uses internet-standard protocols (IP, MQTT, CoAP) enabling horizontal integration across systems; it connects device data to cloud platforms, analytics engines, and third-party applications; and it operates at a scale that M2M systems, designed for specific bilateral connections, cannot accommodate. Where M2M created silos, IoT creates ecosystems.

1.2 Eight Fundamental Characteristics of IoT Systems

An IoT system is distinguishable from a generic networked system by a cluster of eight fundamental characteristics. These characteristics are not independent, they interact and reinforce each other, but together they constitute a definitional fingerprint. A deployment that possesses all eight characteristics is, without ambiguity, an IoT system; one that lacks several may be M2M, industrial SCADA, or a traditional sensor network, each with a distinct engineering tradition. The characteristics also function as a design checklist: for each characteristic, the system designer must make explicit choices about how it will be satisfied.

1.2.1 Connectivity

Connectivity is the foundational characteristic: an IoT device must be able to communicate with other devices, gateways, platforms, or applications over a network. What distinguishes IoT connectivity from traditional networking is its heterogeneity – IoT deployments routinely combine multiple radio technologies (Zigbee for local mesh, LoRaWAN for wide-area coverage, LTE-M for mobile assets) within a single system, and must manage the interaction between these networks at the gateway layer. Connectivity also encompasses the concept of intermittent connectivity: many IoT devices sleep between transmissions, connect briefly to send data, and disconnect again. Platforms and protocols must handle this gracefully. MQTT's persistent session mechanism and LoRaWAN's confirmed uplink are both connectivity-layer solutions to the intermittency problem.

1.2.2 Identity

Every IoT device must have a unique and persistent identifier (a hardware address (MAC, IMEI, EUI-64), a logical identifier (URI, UUID), or a platform-registered device ID) to enable management, data attribution, and security policy enforcement at scale. Identity is not merely a technical address: it is the foundation of accountability. When a sensor reports an anomalous reading, the system must be able to determine which physical device generated it, where that device is located, what firmware version it is running, and when it was last calibrated. Without robust identity infrastructure, backed by certificate-based authentication rather than shared passwords, device spoofing, data injection, and fleet management errors become impossible to detect or correct.

1.2.3 Data

IoT systems continuously generate large volumes of structured and unstructured data. The value of this data derives not from individual readings but from patterns extracted across time and across device populations: a single temperature reading is a number; ten million temperature readings from 50,000 devices over six months is a model of how a building behaves. IoT data has distinctive properties that distinguish it from conventional enterprise data: it is time-series in nature (a reading at a specific moment, not a static record), it is generated at high frequency and often at high volume, and it degrades in value quickly: a real-time alert is far more valuable than the same alert delivered an hour later. These properties drive the need for time-series databases, stream-processing architectures, and edge analytics, all addressed in Chapter 6.

1.2.4 Intelligence

IoT systems incorporate analytic and decision-making capability ranging from simple threshold rules at the device level to machine-learning models at the cloud platform level. Intelligence is what transforms raw IoT data into autonomous action: a temperature sensor alone is not intelligent; a thermostat that adjusts heating based on occupancy prediction derived from historical sensor patterns is. The intelligence dimension of IoT is expanding rapidly: TinyML: the deployment of machine-learning inference on microcontrollers with kilobytes of RAM is enabling classification and anomaly detection at the device edge without cloud connectivity. This trend toward distributed intelligence, treated in depth in Chapter 10, fundamentally changes the architecture of IoT systems by reducing their dependence on cloud round-trips for every decision.

1.2.5 Communication

IoT devices employ a diverse set of communication protocols selected to match the power, range, and bandwidth constraints of each deployment context. No single protocol serves all IoT scenarios: a wearable medical device has different communication requirements from a smart city parking sensor, which has different requirements from an industrial motor controller. The selection of the right protocol stack (from link layer (Zigbee, BLE, LoRaWAN) through transport (UDP, DTLS) to application (MQTT, CoAP)) is one of the first and most consequential engineering decisions in any IoT project. Chapter 4 provides the comprehensive treatment of IoT communication protocols and a practical selection framework.

1.2.6 Scalability

IoT architectures must accommodate growth from pilot (tens of devices) to production (millions of devices) without fundamental redesign. Scalability in IoT has two dimensions. Horizontal scalability at the platform layer means that as device count grows, additional platform compute and storage resources can be added without architecture change: the reason why cloud IoT platforms (AWS

IoT Core, Azure IoT Hub) use auto-scaling infrastructure. Hierarchical network scalability means that the network topology, device to gateway to edge to cloud, distributes load across tiers rather than concentrating it at a single broker. A system that works perfectly with 100 devices but requires a complete re-architecture at 100,000 devices has failed the scalability requirement, regardless of its initial performance.

1.2.7 Architecture

IoT systems are not monolithic. They follow a layered architecture that distributes processing, storage, and communication across the tier best suited to each function. The canonical four-tier IoT architecture (device, gateway, edge, cloud) is the subject of Chapter 3. At the device tier, processing is constrained to what a microcontroller can do locally: filtering, threshold evaluation, and data compression. The gateway tier aggregates device data, performs protocol translation (Zigbee to MQTT, for example), and provides the first IP connectivity boundary. The edge tier hosts analytics and inference workloads that require proximity to the data source for latency reasons. The cloud tier provides long-term storage, fleet management, AI model training, and integration with enterprise systems.

1.2.8 Security

IoT systems present an enlarged attack surface relative to traditional networks. Unlike conventional IT endpoints, laptops and servers that receive regular security patches and are protected behind firewalls, IoT devices are often physically accessible, manufactured with minimal security provisions, deployed for years without firmware updates, and connected to both operational technology (OT) and information technology (IT) networks simultaneously. Security in IoT cannot be added retrospectively; it must be designed into every layer of the system from the outset, from hardware secure elements and secure boot to protocol-layer authentication (mTLS), encrypted transport (DTLS, TLS 1.3), and access control at the platform layer. Chapters 8 and 9 treat IoT security and governance in depth.

Table 1.1 maps all eight characteristics across IoT, the traditional Internet, and M2M communication, showing how IoT synthesises and extends both predecessor paradigms.

Table 1.1: IoT vs. Traditional Internet vs. M2M: Eight Characteristics Comparison

Characteristic	Traditional Internet	M2M	IoT
Connectivity	Wired and wireless, human-initiated sessions	Bilateral, proprietary, point-to-point	Heterogeneous multi-radio, intermittent, multi-hop mesh
Identity	IP address + domain name (human-memorable)	IMSI/MSISDN (carrier-assigned)	EUI-64, URI, X.509 certificate per device
Data	Human-authored content, documents, media	Telemetry between specific endpoint pairs	High-volume, time-series, multi-source streams
Intelligence	Human interpretation; browser/app logic	Rule-based responses at server	Distributed: edge ML, cloud AI, TinyML
Communication	HTTP/TCP, standardised web protocols	Vendor-proprietary protocols	Layered: 802.15.4/BLE/ LoRa + IPv6 + MQTT/ CoAP
Scalability	Horizontal web scale (CDN, load balancer)	Limited to bilateral pairs; poor horizontal scale	Designed for millions of devices; hierarchical tiers
Architecture	Client-server, browser-server	Controller-device point-to-point	Multi-tier: device, gateway, edge, cloud
Security	HTTPS/TLS, password auth, PKI for servers	SIM-based; often no mutual auth	mTLS per device, DTLS, secure boot, OTA updates

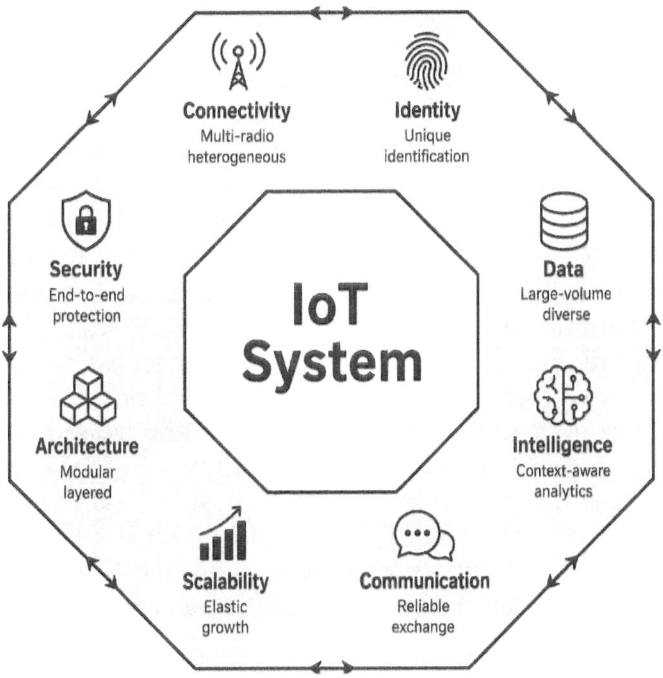

Figure 1.1: The eight fundamental characteristics of IoT systems.

1.3 Enabling Technologies

The Internet of Things did not arise from a single invention. It emerged from the simultaneous maturation of six previously distinct technology trajectories, each of which was necessary but not sufficient on its own. The confluence of these trajectories in the 2010s created the conditions for IoT's rapid expansion: sensors became cheap enough to deploy by the thousands, wireless protocols became efficient enough to run on coin-cell batteries for years, cloud platforms became accessible enough for any organisation, and artificial intelligence became powerful enough to extract actionable insight from the data streams these sensors generated. Understanding these enabling technologies as an interdependence map, each reinforcing the others, is the conceptual foundation for everything that follows in the book.

1.3.1 RFID (Radio Frequency Identification)

RFID is the technology that inspired the phrase 'Internet of Things' and remains one of its most widely deployed components. An RFID system consists of a reader that emits radio waves and a tag, attached to a physical object, that responds with a unique identifier. Passive RFID tags have no battery: they harvest energy from the reader's field and transmit their ID code in response. Active RFID tags carry their own power source and can transmit over longer distances. The fundamental IoT contribution of RFID is identity assignment to physical objects: a pallet of goods, a hospital asset, a library book, or an airline bag acquires a digital identity that supply chain and logistics systems can track without human data entry.

RFID operates at multiple frequency bands with different range and data-rate characteristics. Low-frequency (125-134 kHz) RFID achieves short range (under 10 cm) and is used in access control cards and animal tagging. High-frequency (13.56 MHz) RFID, standardised under ISO/IEC 14443, underlies contactless payment cards and NFC (Near Field Communication) smartphone interactions. Ultra-high frequency (860-960 MHz) RFID, standardised under ISO/IEC 18000-63 (EPC Gen2), achieves read ranges of 1-12 metres and is the dominant standard in retail and logistics. Walmart's mandate in 2003 that its top 100 suppliers adopt RFID was a watershed moment that drove down tag costs and established RFID as an industrial standard. Today passive UHF RFID tags cost less than five US cents each.

1.3.2 Sensors and Actuators

Sensors are the perceptual layer of IoT: the interface through which digital systems observe the physical world. The diversity of sensor types reflects the breadth of physical phenomena that IoT systems must monitor. Temperature and humidity sensors (resistive, thermistor, or capacitive) are the most ubiquitous IoT sensor type, present in every smart building, weather station, and cold-chain logistics system. Motion and proximity sensors (PIR, ultrasonic, radar) underpin building security, occupancy detection, and retail analytics.

Gas and chemical sensors (electrochemical, optical, MEMS-based) monitor air quality, detect hazardous gases in industrial environments, and measure CO2 levels in smart buildings. Accelerometers and gyroscopes, MEMS inertial measurement units, are embedded in every wearable device, vehicle telematics unit, and industrial vibration monitor. Optical sensors, ranging from simple photodiodes to megapixel camera arrays, provide the rich environmental perception needed for smart city surveillance, agricultural drone imaging, and automated visual inspection systems.

The cost reduction enabled by MEMS (Micro-Electro-Mechanical Systems) manufacturing technology has been the single most important enabling factor for dense IoT sensor deployment. MEMS fabricates microscopic mechanical structures (cantilevers, membranes, proof masses) on silicon wafers using processes derived from semiconductor manufacturing. This allows an accelerometer, microphone, or pressure sensor to be fabricated as a single chip the size of a grain of rice, costing cents rather than dollars. The accelerometer in every smartphone: a device that in 1990 would have cost hundreds of dollars and occupied a cubic centimetre of board space, today costs under fifty US cents and occupies less than two square millimetres.

Actuators are the IoT effector layer: devices that translate digital commands into physical action. Electric motors, solenoid valves, relay switches, servo mechanisms, LED lighting controllers, and display panels are all actuators in IoT deployments. The combination of sensors (perceiving physical state) and actuators (changing physical state) enables closed-loop control: sense-decide-act cycles that operate autonomously without human intervention. A smart irrigation system that senses soil moisture and opens or closes a valve is a minimal closed-loop IoT system. An autonomous manufacturing robot that senses workpiece position, processes visual data, and operates multiple actuated joints simultaneously is a complex one.

1.3.3 Cloud Computing

Cloud computing transformed IoT from a technically interesting concept into an economically viable industry by eliminating the requirement for IoT system builders to own and operate their own server infrastructure. Before cloud computing, connecting a sensor to a data platform required purchasing servers, co-locating them in a data centre, and managing the full software stack. AWS (launched 2006), Microsoft Azure (2010), and Google Cloud (2011) replaced this model with on-demand, pay-per-use compute and storage that scales from a single device to millions without infrastructure investment.

In the IoT context, cloud platforms provide five core services that are impractical to operate at the device or gateway level. Long-term time-series storage retains sensor readings for months or years, enabling trend analysis that is impossible at shorter time horizons. Horizontal compute scaling allows platforms to ingest tens of thousands of device connections per second without the bottlenecks of fixed infrastructure. Machine-learning training uses the accumulated historical data of an entire device fleet to build inference models that are then deployed back to edge devices.

Integration APIs connect IoT data to enterprise systems (ERP, CRM, and maintenance management platforms) where its operational value is realised. Global availability ensures that devices in any geography connect to the same platform endpoint, simplifying multi-region fleet management. Chapter 6 examines major cloud IoT platforms in depth, including AWS IoT Core and Microsoft Azure IoT Hub (Note: Google Cloud IoT Core was discontinued in August 2023; Chapter 6, Section 6.5.3 covers migration paths and current alternatives).

1.3.4 Big Data and Analytics

IoT is one of the primary generators of the data volumes that define the 'big data' era. A single industrial IoT deployment (a factory with 2,000 sensors each sampling at 1 Hz) generates over 172 million data points per day. A smart city with 100,000 connected sensors generates billions. The volume, velocity, and variety of IoT data challenge conventional database architectures: relational databases optimised for transactional consistency are poorly suited to storing and querying billions of time-stamped sensor readings.

Time-series databases (InfluxDB, TimescaleDB, Apache IoTDB) are purpose-built for IoT data, optimised for high-ingest writes and time-range queries (return all temperature readings from sensor group A between 09:00 and 17:00 yesterday). Stream-processing frameworks (Apache Kafka, Apache Flink, AWS Kinesis) process IoT data in real time as it arrives, enabling alerts and automated responses within milliseconds. The analytics hierarchy progresses from descriptive (what happened?), through diagnostic (why did it happen?), predictive (what will happen?), to prescriptive (what should we do?), each level delivering higher operational value but requiring more sophisticated models and larger training datasets. Chapter 6 addresses the full data management and analytics stack.

1.3.5 Artificial Intelligence and Machine Learning

Artificial intelligence provides the intelligence dimension of IoT: the capacity to extract non-obvious patterns from sensor data and act on them autonomously. Supervised learning models trained on labelled historical sensor data detect anomalies, classify events, and predict failures: a vibration signature that precedes a bearing failure by 72 hours, a power consumption pattern that identifies a malfunctioning HVAC unit, a visual inspection model that detects surface defects on a production line. Unsupervised learning identifies natural clusters in device populations without labelled data, useful for fleet segmentation and baseline behaviour modelling.

The most significant recent development for IoT AI is TinyML: the deployment of trained machine-learning inference models directly on microcontrollers with kilobytes of RAM, without cloud connectivity. Frameworks such as TensorFlow Lite for Microcontrollers and Edge Impulse enable keyword recognition, gesture detection, and anomaly detection on processors with under 100 KB of flash and less than 10 mW of power consumption. TinyML inverts the traditional cloud-centric IoT architecture: instead of transmitting all sensor data to the cloud for analysis, the device processes data locally and transmits only the result (an alert, a classification, a compressed summary), dramatically reducing bandwidth consumption, latency, and cloud processing cost. Chapter 11 examines AI and Machine Learning with IoT in depth, while Chapter 10 introduces AIoT and Edge AI as emerging IoT trends.

Practical Note: TinyML Tools for IoT. Edge Impulse (edgeimpulse.com) is the leading development platform for TinyML on constrained IoT devices, supporting Arduino Nano 33 BLE Sense, ESP32, and STM32 targets. TensorFlow Lite for Microcontrollers (TFLM) provides the inference runtime. Anyone with an ESP32 board can train a keyword recognition or gesture detection model in Edge Impulse, export it as a TFLM library, and deploy it in under one hour — with no cloud round-trip required at inference time. Chapter 10 introduces the Edge AI and TinyML direction, and Chapter 11 expands the AI/ML implementation pipeline, tools, and deployment models.

1.3.6 Wireless Connectivity: 5G, LPWAN, and Wi-Fi

Wireless connectivity is the circulatory system of IoT: the medium through which sensor data flows from physical device to digital platform. The diversity of IoT connectivity requirements (from sub-metre asset tracking to multi-kilometre agricultural sensing) has produced a corresponding diversity of wireless standards, each optimised for a different point in the power-range-data-rate design space.

5G (Fifth Generation cellular), whose New Radio (NR) standard was published by 3GPP in Release 15 (2018), adds three capabilities relevant to IoT beyond 4G LTE: Ultra-Reliable Low Latency Communication (URLLC) with sub-1 ms latency for industrial control and autonomous vehicle applications; massive Machine-Type Communication (mMTC) supporting up to one million device connections per square kilometre for dense IoT deployment; and enhanced Mobile Broadband (eMBB) for high-bandwidth IoT applications such as 4K video surveillance. The two IoT-specific 5G modes, NB-IoT (Narrowband IoT) and LTE-M, are embedded in the 5G standard and provide low-power, long-range cellular connectivity for battery-operated sensors with global coverage through existing cellular infrastructure.

LPWAN (Low-Power Wide Area Network) technologies (LoRaWAN, Sigfox, NB-IoT) address the gap between short-range, low-power technologies like Zigbee (under 100 m) and power-hungry cellular: they achieve kilometres of range at ultra-low power consumption (device battery life measured in years), at the cost of very low data rates (tens to hundreds of bytes per message). This trade-off is perfectly suited to the majority of IoT sensing applications: a soil moisture sensor, a water meter, or a waste bin fill-level sensor transmits fewer than 100 bytes every 15 minutes and must last 10 years on a primary battery. Chapter 4 provides the complete protocol treatment.

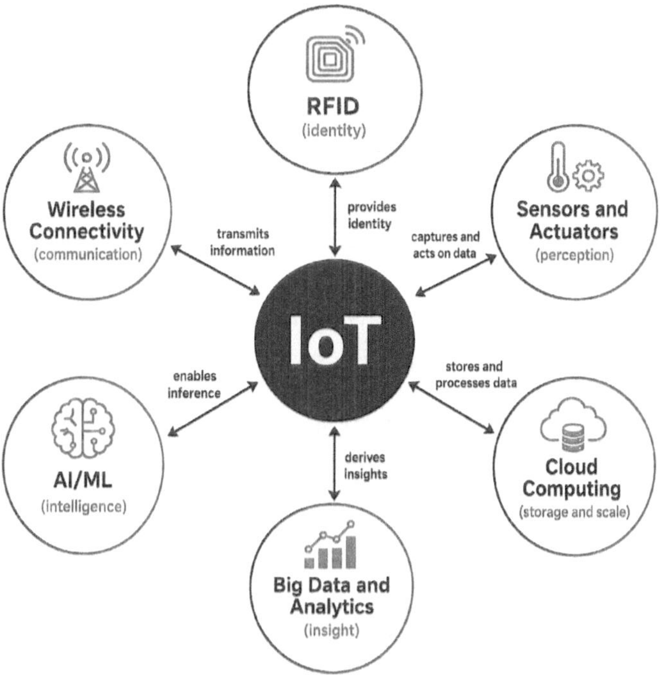

Figure 1.2: Enabling Technologies Interdependence Map.

Table 1.2: Enabling Technologies Overview

Technology	Function in IoT	Maturity Level	Chapter Reference
RFID	Assigns digital identities to physical objects via radio	Mature (ISO 18000, EPC Gen2)	Ch. 1
Sensors and Actuators	Perceives physical state; effects physical action	Mature (MEMS, miniaturised)	Ch. 2
Cloud Computing	Scalable storage, compute, and API platform	Mature (AWS, Azure, GCP)	Ch. 6
Big Data and Analytics	Time-series storage, stream processing, analytics	Mature (InfluxDB, Kafka)	Ch. 6
AI / Machine Learning	Pattern recognition, prediction, TinyML inference	Rapidly evolving	Ch. 11
Wireless Connectivity	Device-to-platform communication fabric	Mature and evolving (5G, LoRaWAN)	Ch. 4

1.4 IoT Levels: A Deployment Taxonomy

Not all IoT deployments are equally complex. A smart thermostat that adjusts temperature based on its own sensor is architecturally simpler than a smart city platform that processes millions of readings from thousands of heterogeneous devices and feeds real-time decisions to a network of actuators across an urban area. The IoT Levels taxonomy used in this textbook provides a systematic classification of IoT deployments by their data processing location, networking architecture, and intelligence distribution. Understanding which level a proposed deployment occupies helps engineers identify the right technology choices and helps readers understand why the same general concept of 'IoT' requires radically different engineering solutions at different scales.

1.4.1 Level 1: Single Device, Local Action

At Level 1, a single IoT device processes data locally and takes immediate action without network involvement. The device contains both the sensor (or sensors) and the decision logic, and its outputs (physical actuation or local display) occur entirely within the device itself. A smart thermostat that adjusts a room's temperature based on its own temperature sensor, without connecting to a cloud platform, is a Level 1 IoT device. A standalone industrial safety relay that detects an overcurrent condition and opens a circuit breaker within milliseconds is a Level 1 system. Level 1 systems have the lowest complexity, the lowest cost, and the lowest failure-mode surface; their limitation is that their intelligence is fixed at design time and cannot be updated or contextualised by data from other devices or external sources.

1.4.2 Level 2: Single Device with Local Storage

Level 2 adds local data logging to the single-device model. The device captures and stores sensor readings in local memory (an SD card, on-device flash, or EEPROM) for later retrieval, but does not maintain a live network connection. A standalone environmental data logger deployed in a remote location without cellular coverage, recording temperature and humidity readings at five-minute intervals for retrieval via USB when a technician visits the site, is a Level 2 system. The key distinction from Level 1 is temporal: Level 2 creates a historical record, enabling trend analysis that requires data from multiple time points, but the analysis occurs offline, not in real time.

1.4.3 Level 3: Single Device with Cloud Connection

Level 3 is the canonical 'simple IoT' deployment: a single device transmits its data to a cloud platform for storage, remote access, and analysis. A connected weather station that publishes temperature, humidity, pressure, and rainfall data to an MQTT broker every minute, from which a web dashboard reads and displays current conditions, is a Level 3 system. The cloud provides historical analytics, remote access, and alerting that the device itself cannot. The key limitation of Level 3 is that all intelligence resides in the cloud: every decision requires a cloud round-trip, which introduces latency and creates a hard dependency on network availability. A Level 3 system that loses network connectivity also loses all analytics and alerting capability.

1.4.4 Level 4: Multi-Device with Local Gateway

Level 4 introduces a local gateway that aggregates data from multiple devices before forwarding to the cloud. The gateway performs protocol translation (converting Zigbee mesh transmissions to MQTT over Wi-Fi, for example), data aggregation (combining readings from ten soil sensors into a single averaged payload), and local buffering (storing readings during network outages and replaying them on reconnection). A factory floor deployment with 50 vibration sensors transmitting via IEEE 802.15.4 to a gateway that forwards aggregated data to an Azure IoT Hub is a Level 4 system. The gateway reduces upstream bandwidth requirements, improves resilience during network outages, and enables the use of constrained link-layer protocols that cannot connect directly to the internet.

1.4.5 Level 5: Multi-Device with Edge Intelligence

Level 5 extends Level 4 by adding significant local analytics and decision-making capability to the gateway or edge node. Rather than forwarding raw data to the cloud for analysis, the edge device processes data locally and transmits only results, alerts, or compressed summaries. A predictive maintenance deployment where the edge node runs a machine-learning model that analyses vibration signatures in real time and triggers a maintenance alert when bearing degradation is detected, without a cloud round-trip, is a Level 5 system. Edge intelligence provides three advantages over Level 4: latency (decisions in milliseconds rather than seconds), bandwidth efficiency (transmitting kilobytes of results rather than megabytes of raw data), and resilience (continued operation during cloud connectivity loss).

1.4.6 Level 6: Distributed Multi-Tier System

Level 6 represents the full hierarchical IoT architecture: devices, edge nodes, fog layer, and cloud, with distributed intelligence at each tier. A smart city platform with thousands of heterogeneous sensors (environmental, traffic, parking, and waste management) district-level edge inference nodes, a city-level fog layer correlating data across districts, and a national cloud platform for long-term storage, model training, and regulatory reporting is a representative Level 6 deployment.

Level 6 systems require a complete IoT architecture competency: network design, edge-cloud orchestration, data governance across jurisdictions, security at every tier, and operational management of a heterogeneous device fleet. The engineering depth addressed throughout this textbook provides the prerequisites for designing and operating Level 6 deployments.

Table 1.3: IoT Levels Comparison

Level	Data Processing	Storage	Networking	Intelligence	Example	Typical Scale
1	Single device	On-device flash / register	None required	Hardcoded rules	Smart thermostat (offline)	1 device
2	On-device flash / SD card	Local storage	Local retrieval only	None	Remote environmental logger	1 device
3	Cloud platform	Cloud database	internet (cellular/Wi-Fi)	Cloud ML/ rules engine	Connected weather station	1 device
4	Cloud via gateway	Cloud + local buffer	Multi-hop (mesh to gateway)	Cloud analytics	Factory sensor network	10s - 100s
5	Edge node + cloud	Edge cache + cloud	Constrained mesh + backhaul	Edge ML + cloud training	Predictive maintenance	100s - 1000s
6	Distributed tiers	Edge + fog + cloud	Multi-tier heterogeneous	Distributed AI at every tier	Smart city platform	1000s - millions

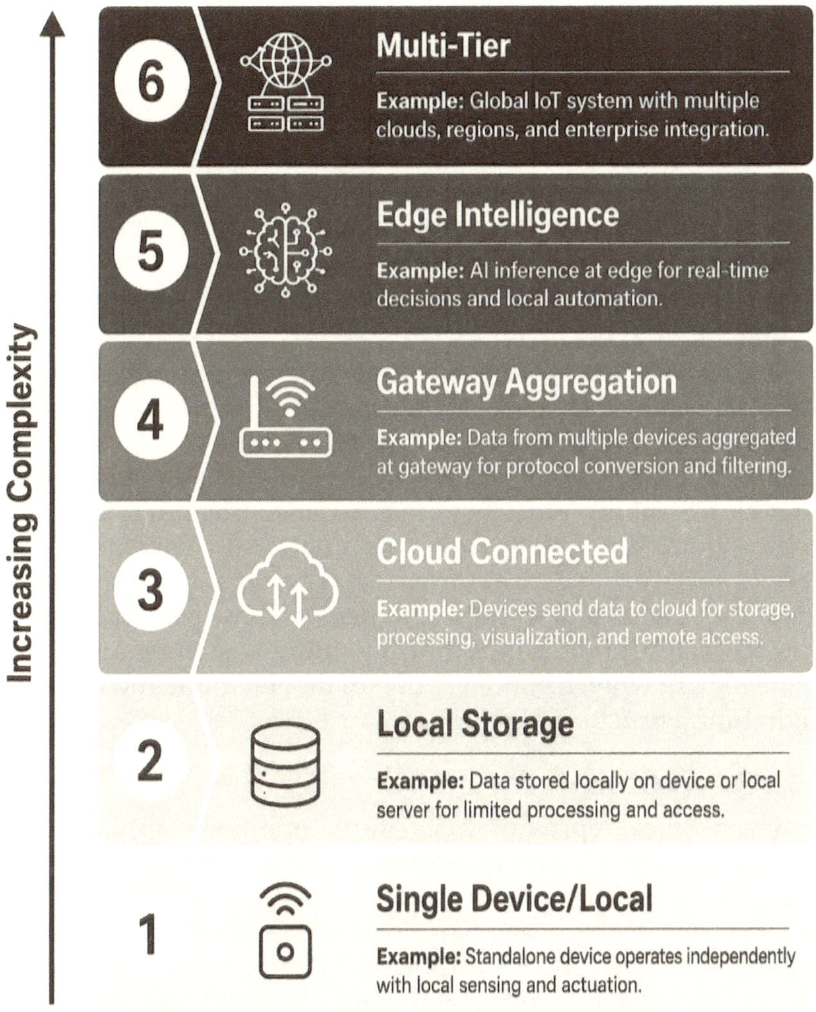

Figure 1.3: IoT Levels Hierarchy: Six-level deployment taxonomy from single-device local action to distributed multi-tier systems.

1.5 IoT Application Domains

The Internet of Things is not a single market; it is a cluster of distinct application domains, each with its own scale, regulatory environment, data characteristics, and engineering requirements. This section provides a structured overview of the seven most significant domains, offering sufficient depth to make each concrete and meaningful without duplicating the comprehensive treatment in Chapter 7. The purpose here is breadth: to give the reader a map of the territory before the book provides the engineering detail.

1.5.1 Smart Home and Building Automation

The smart home and building automation domain is the largest IoT market by device volume. Connected appliances, smart lighting, automated climate control, video doorbells, smart locks, and energy monitoring systems collectively represent billions of deployed devices globally. The defining characteristic of this domain is the transition from remote control: the user operating a device from their phone instead of a physical switch, to autonomous optimisation: a home or building that adjusts its own behaviour based on occupancy patterns, weather forecasts, energy pricing signals, and user preferences without explicit instruction.

Singapore's smart housing and utilities initiatives illustrate the scale achievable when public agencies coordinate IoT-enabled building and utility management. HDB's Smart Hub and Smart Estate initiatives demonstrate how sensor data can support estate operations, energy efficiency, maintenance planning, and service optimisation. In parallel, Singapore's national smart metering initiatives have expanded electricity and water monitoring through advanced meters and smart water meters. These programmes show how IoT can support public housing, utility visibility, and resource management when technology deployment is aligned with national digital-infrastructure planning.

1.5.2 Smart Cities

Smart cities represent IoT's most ambitious application: the instrumentation of urban infrastructure to optimise traffic flow, public services, energy consumption, environmental quality, and citizen safety at city scale. Barcelona's Superblock programme embedded sensors in street furniture to monitor air quality, noise levels, and pedestrian density. Singapore's Virtual Singapore initiative created a dynamic 3D city model fed by real-time IoT data from across the island. Masdar City in Abu Dhabi was designed from the ground up as a sensor-instrumented sustainable city, with every building, vehicle route, and utility system connected to a central management platform.

The engineering challenge of smart cities is not sensor deployment; it is integration. A smart city is an IoT system of systems: multiple independently operated subsystems (traffic management, waste management, water utility, environmental monitoring) that were procured from different vendors at different times, using different protocols and data formats, must be integrated into a unified operational picture. The governance challenge is equally significant: data collected by a city's sensor network about its citizens' movements and behaviours must be managed under data protection frameworks that were not designed with city-scale continuous monitoring in mind.

1.5.3 Industrial IoT (IIoT)

Industrial IoT, also referred to as IIoT (Industrial Internet of Things), extends connectivity and analytics into manufacturing, energy production, mining, and logistics. The primary value proposition of IIoT is predictive maintenance: using sensor data to predict equipment failure before it occurs, reducing unplanned downtime and extending asset lifetime. A turbine manufacturer that can predict bearing failure 72 hours in advance transforms an unplanned shutdown (costing tens of thousands of dollars per hour) into a scheduled maintenance event. Bosch, Siemens, and GE have all built IIoT platforms (Bosch IoT Suite, Siemens MindSphere, GE Predix) specifically to capture this value across their own equipment fleets and those of their customers.

IIoT deployments have distinctive requirements that differentiate them from consumer IoT: deterministic latency (control loop closure in under 10 ms in some industrial applications), functional safety certification (IEC 61508 for safety instrumented systems), and the operational technology (OT) security model inherited from decades of SCADA and DCS practice. The integration of IP-connected IoT sensors with legacy OT infrastructure (Modbus, PROFIBUS, CAN) is one of the most common and challenging engineering tasks in IIoT deployment.

1.5.4 Healthcare and Wearables

Healthcare IoT encompasses remote patient monitoring, smart medical implants, clinical asset tracking, and ambient assisted living. The clinical value of continuous remote monitoring, detecting atrial fibrillation from a smartwatch ECG, monitoring blood glucose in real time from a subcutaneous sensor, tracking a Parkinson's patient's tremor severity through an accelerometer wristband is well established and growing. The Apple Heart Study (2019), conducted with over 400,000 Apple Watch users, demonstrated that PPG-based irregular rhythm notification could identify atrial fibrillation with 84 percent positive predictive value: a result that accelerated regulatory approval of consumer-grade cardiac monitoring as a medical device.

Healthcare IoT presents the most complex regulatory and privacy environment of any IoT domain. Health data is a special category under GDPR Article 9, requiring explicit consent or a specific legal basis for processing. Medical devices connected to patients are subject to the EU Medical Device Regulation (MDR 2017/745) and FDA 510(k) or De Novo clearance processes. The combination of intimate personal data, life-safety consequences of device malfunction, and complex regulatory requirements means that healthcare IoT deployments require more governance investment per device than any other domain.

1.5.5 Agriculture and Environment

Precision agriculture uses IoT sensor data to optimise inputs (water, fertiliser, pesticide) at sub-field resolution, reducing cost and environmental impact while maintaining or improving yield. Soil moisture and temperature sensors, crop cameras, drone imaging platforms, and weather station networks feed algorithms that recommend irrigation schedules, planting dates, and input application rates. The John Deere Operations Center, which aggregates data from millions of connected machines, is one of the largest agricultural IoT platforms in the world, providing fleet operators with per-machine productivity data and enabling yield map analysis that correlates inputs with outputs at field-parcel resolution.

LoRaWAN is the dominant link-layer technology for agricultural IoT because its long range (10-15 km in rural line-of-sight conditions), ultra-low power, and low per-message cost match the requirements of sensors distributed across fields that may cover hundreds of hectares with no mains power available. Environmental monitoring extends this model to watershed monitoring, wildfire detection networks (temperature, humidity, and smoke sensors in forested areas), flood warning systems, and ocean monitoring buoy networks.

Regional Example: Smart Agriculture in Oman and the GCC. *The Gulf Cooperation Council faces a critical combination of food security pressure and extreme water scarcity. In Oman, smart irrigation IoT deployments over date palm plantations and vegetable farms in the Batinah and Salalah regions use soil moisture and salinity sensor networks — connected via LoRaWAN gateways to cloud dashboards — enabling farmers to reduce irrigation water consumption by 20-30% while maintaining yields. Similar programmes in the UAE and Saudi Arabia are scaling these deployments as part of national food security strategies, demonstrating that precision agriculture IoT is directly applicable to arid-climate production environments and not limited to temperate-region farming models.*

1.5.6 Energy and Utilities

Smart metering is the most widely deployed IoT application in the utilities sector: by 2023, over 300 million smart electricity meters were installed in Europe and North America, enabling half-hourly or sub-hourly consumption data, remote connect/disconnect, and demand-response signalling. Smart meters are the infrastructure foundation for the smart grid: the bidirectional electricity network that integrates distributed renewable generation (solar panels, wind turbines), flexible demand (EV charging, heat pumps), and grid-scale storage (batteries, pumped hydro) into a dynamically balanced system.

IoT in energy extends beyond metering to grid monitoring (fault detection, equipment condition monitoring), demand-response automation (adjusting industrial loads in response to grid frequency signals), and renewable energy asset management (monitoring wind turbine blade condition via vibration sensors, predicting solar panel degradation from performance data). The energy transition creates substantial new IoT demand: integrating the billions of distributed energy resources expected by 2030 into a stable grid requires sensing and control infrastructure at a scale that did not exist a decade ago.

1.5.7 Transport and Logistics

Vehicle telematics (the real-time collection of vehicle position, speed, fuel consumption, driver behaviour, and diagnostic data) is one of the oldest and most mature IoT application domains, with commercial deployments dating to the mid-1990s. Fleet management platforms used by logistics companies, bus operators, and emergency services track hundreds of thousands of vehicles simultaneously, optimising routes, scheduling maintenance, and monitoring regulatory compliance (driver hours, emissions). The connected vehicle is evolving beyond telematics toward Vehicle-to-Everything (V2X) communication: vehicles sharing real-time data with each other, with roadside infrastructure, and with traffic management platforms to improve safety and flow.

Cold-chain logistics illustrates the value of IoT monitoring in supply chains requiring temperature-controlled transport. Pharmaceutical supply chains, fresh food distribution, and vaccine logistics must maintain prescribed temperature ranges throughout transit; a cold-chain breach that spoils a shipment of vaccines can represent millions of dollars of loss and, in the case of vaccination campaigns, public health consequences. IoT temperature loggers with cellular connectivity provide real-time visibility across the entire chain, enabling intervention before a breach becomes a spoilage event.

The breadth of these seven domains illustrates both IoT's transformative potential and the engineering challenge it presents: the same body of knowledge must serve the engineer building a smart home thermostat and the architect designing a national smart city platform. Chapter 7 revisits each domain with the technical depth, deployment architectures, and case studies that this introductory overview necessarily defers.

Before examining specific technologies, protocols, and architectures in subsequent chapters, it is important to understand the commercial and organisational landscape within which IoT systems are built and deployed. Section 1.6 maps the IoT ecosystem value chain: the full set of stakeholders whose coordinated work is required to deliver any IoT deployment from concept to production.

1.6 The IoT Ecosystem and Value Chain

The Internet of Things is not a single technology or a single company's product; it is a multi-stakeholder ecosystem in which each participant depends on the others to deliver value to the end user. A connected temperature sensor in a hospital ward generates value only when a silicon vendor has manufactured the sensing element, a module maker has integrated it with a wireless radio, a connectivity provider has activated the SIM or radio profile, a platform vendor has ingested and stored the readings, a system integrator has connected the platform to the hospital's patient management system, and a clinical application developer has built the dashboard that the nursing staff actually use. Remove any one of these stakeholders and the value chain fails.

Understanding this value-chain interdependence is essential for anyone who will work within the IoT ecosystem; whether as a hardware engineer, connectivity architect, platform developer, system integrator, or deployment manager. The sections that follow map each stakeholder tier and explain its role, capabilities, and dependencies.

1.6.1 Device and Component Manufacturers

At the base of the IoT value chain are the companies that manufacture the physical hardware. Silicon vendors design and fabricate the microcontrollers, system-on-chip (SoC) devices, radio transceivers, and sensor ASICs that are the building blocks of every IoT device. STMicroelectronics, Nordic Semiconductor, Silicon

Labs, Texas Instruments, and Espressif are among the most prominent IoT silicon vendors, each serving different points in the power-performance-cost spectrum. Sensor manufacturers such as Bosch Sensortec, TE Connectivity, and Sensirion supply the MEMS and electrochemical sensing elements that give IoT devices their perception capability. Module manufacturers (u-blox, Quectel, Sierra Wireless) integrate silicon components into certified radio modules that device makers can drop into their products without managing the complexity of radio regulatory certification.

1.6.2 Connectivity Providers

Connectivity providers supply the network infrastructure through which IoT devices communicate. Mobile Network Operators (MNOs) (Vodafone, Deutsche Telekom, Verizon, SingTel) provide cellular coverage for IoT devices using LTE-M, NB-IoT, and legacy 2G/3G technologies, along with SIM management and billing infrastructure. IoT-specialist MVNOs (Mobile Virtual Network Operators) and connectivity management platform providers such as KORE Wireless, Twilio, and Eseye operate by reselling MNO capacity with value-added management services tailored to IoT fleet management. LPWAN network operators (including The Things Network (community LoRaWAN), Actility's ThingPark, and legacy Sigfox) provide wide-area low-power connectivity for deployments that cannot afford cellular costs or do not need cellular data rates.

1.6.3 IoT Platform Vendors

IoT platform vendors provide the software infrastructure that sits between device connectivity and business applications: device management, data ingestion, rule engines, APIs, and developer tooling. The hyperscaler platforms (AWS IoT Core, Microsoft Azure IoT Hub, and Google Cloud IoT) leverage the compute and storage infrastructure of their parent cloud services, attracting customers already committed to those ecosystems.

Independent IoT platform vendors (PTC ThingWorx, Siemens MindSphere, Software AG Cumulocity, and Bosch IoT Suite) offer deeper vertical specialisation, particularly in industrial IoT contexts where operational technology (OT) integration and domain-specific analytics matter more than cloud-native developer experience. The platform layer has consolidated significantly since 2015, when over 300 IoT platforms were counted; many smaller vendors were acquired or discontinued as the market recognised that undifferentiated platform functionality would be commoditised by hyperscaler offerings.

1.6.4 System Integrators

System integrators are the companies that assemble device, connectivity, platform, and application components into working, deployed IoT solutions for end customers. They are typically the primary commercial interface for enterprise customers who lack the internal expertise to evaluate and integrate the full technology stack. Major global system integrators (Accenture, Capgemini, IBM Global Services, Wipro) have established IoT practice groups. Regional and specialist integrators serve specific verticals: a smart building integrator combines building automation expertise with IoT platform skills; a precision agriculture integrator combines agronomic knowledge with sensor deployment and data analytics capability. The system integrator's margin derives from their ability to reduce the deployment risk that individual technology layers cannot eliminate on their own.

1.6.5 Application Developers and Independent Software Vendors

Application developers and Independent Software Vendors (ISVs) build domain-specific software that transforms IoT platform data into business outcomes. A predictive maintenance SaaS product that ingests vibration sensor data from Azure IoT Hub and delivers maintenance recommendations to a facility manager's mobile app is an ISV application built on top of a platform layer. The ISV's value lies in domain expertise, understanding which vibration patterns precede which failure modes in which machine types, rather than in IoT infrastructure. The platform-as-a-service model has dramatically reduced the cost of building IoT applications by abstracting away device management, connectivity, and data storage concerns, enabling small software teams to build sophisticated vertical applications without owning any IoT infrastructure.

1.6.6 End Users and Operators

End users and operators are the organisations and individuals who deploy IoT systems to address operational challenges or create new services. They span the full spectrum from a homeowner installing a smart thermostat to a multinational corporation deploying 500,000 connected asset trackers across a global logistics network. End users are the primary source of IoT demand and the ultimate judges of whether a deployment delivers value. Their requirements, expressed in terms of operational outcomes rather than technical specifications, drive the entire upstream value chain. A municipality that wants to reduce fleet fuel consumption by 15 percent creates demand for vehicle telematics hardware, cellular connectivity, a fleet management platform, and analytics applications that was not present before the municipality articulated that requirement.

1.6.7 Regulators and Standards Bodies

Regulators and standards bodies shape the IoT ecosystem by setting the rules within which all other participants must operate. Spectrum regulators (the ITU-R at the international level, Ofcom in the UK, FCC in the US, and national telecommunications authorities elsewhere) allocate the radio frequency bands that IoT wireless technologies use, set power limits, and enforce duty-cycle restrictions. Product safety regulators require that IoT devices meet electromagnetic compatibility (EMC) and radio equipment directive standards before they can be placed on market.

Data protection authorities enforce GDPR and equivalent national regulations on how IoT systems may collect, store, and process personal data. Security regulators are increasingly moving from voluntary guidance to binding requirements: the EU Cyber Resilience Act (2024) imposes mandatory security obligations on IoT product manufacturers as a condition of EU market access. Chapter 9 provides the comprehensive governance and regulatory treatment.

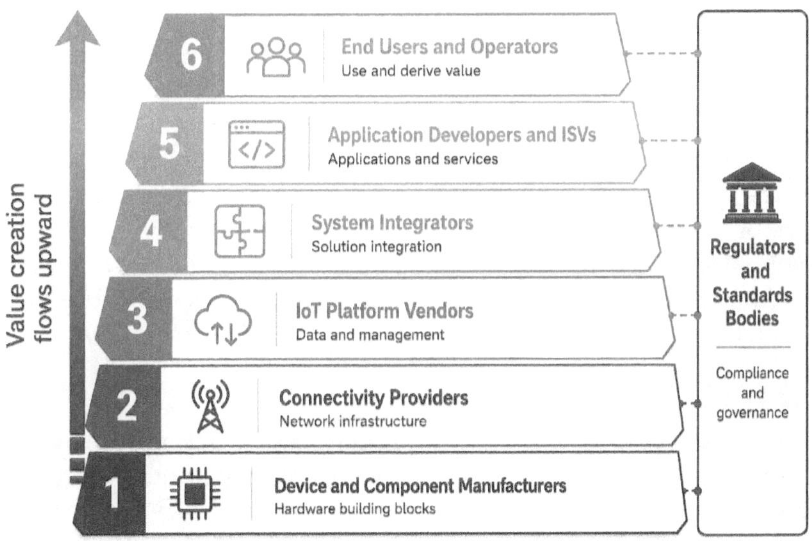

Figure 1.4: IoT Ecosystem Stakeholder Map: Key actors across the IoT value chain, from device manufacturers and connectivity providers to platform operators, system integrators, and end users.

1.7 Standards and Standardisation in IoT

Interoperability is the central technical challenge of IoT at scale. A world moving toward nearly 39 billion connected IoT devices by 2030 from thousands of manufacturers, operating across dozens of wireless technologies and as many cloud platforms, can only deliver seamless integration if participants agree on common standards at every layer of the protocol stack. Without standards, every connection between any two IoT components requires a custom integration effort: a proposition that is economically unsustainable at the scale IoT demands. The history of IoT standardisation is, in part, a history of fragmentation followed by gradual convergence: the market has produced dozens of competing standards at every layer, and the engineering and commercial costs of that fragmentation have created pressure toward consolidation that is now delivering results in some domains while others remain contested.

1.7.1 IEEE

The Institute of Electrical and Electronics Engineers is the primary standards body for IoT physical and link-layer protocols. IEEE 802.15.4 (Low-Rate Wireless Personal Area Networks) is the foundational standard for constrained IoT radio communication, underpinning Zigbee, Thread, 6LoWPAN, and WirelessHART. IEEE 802.11 (Wi-Fi) governs the highest-bandwidth IoT link-layer option. IEEE 802.15.1 covered early classic Bluetooth (subsequently withdrawn); Bluetooth Low Energy (BLE), introduced in Bluetooth 4.0 (2010), is governed by the Bluetooth SIG Core Specification, not an IEEE standard. The IEEE P2510 standard, published in 2019, addresses data quality and trust in IoT sensor data: a governance dimension that earlier IoT standards neglected. The IEEE Standards Association's IoT initiative coordinates IoT-relevant work across multiple IEEE working groups and publishes the IEEE Internet of Things Journal, one of the field's primary academic venues.

1.7.2 IETF

The Internet Engineering Task Force (IETF) is the primary body for IoT network-layer and application-layer protocol standards. Multiple IETF working groups have produced RFCs that are now fundamental to IoT infrastructure: the 6LoWPAN working group produced RFC 4944 and RFC 6282 (IPv6 header compression over 802.15.4); the ROLL working group produced RFC 6550 (RPL routing for low-power lossy networks); the CoRE working group produced RFC 7252 (CoAP), RFC 7641 (CoAP Observe), and RFC

8613 (OSCORE); and the ACE working group produced RFC 9200, adapting OAuth 2.0 for constrained IoT devices.

The IETF's consensus-based, open-participation process, any engineer can submit a draft and participate in working group discussions, has made it the most trusted source of IoT internet-layer standards. All RFCs are freely available at www.rfc-editor.org, making the IETF standards corpus accessible to device manufacturers and platform developers worldwide.

1.7.3 ITU-T

The International Telecommunication Union's standardisation sector (ITU-T) provides IoT framework standards that align national telecommunications regulatory frameworks with emerging IoT architectures. ITU-T Recommendation Y.2060 (2012) was the first internationally agreed definition and vocabulary for IoT, establishing the terminological foundation on which subsequent standards could build. The Y.4000 series of recommendations (IoT frameworks, smart sustainable cities, digital twin standards) extends this foundation to specific application contexts. The ITU's role is particularly important in developing economies where ITU recommendations carry regulatory weight and influence national IoT strategies and spectrum allocation decisions.

1.7.4 ETSI

The European Telecommunications Standards Institute (ETSI) is the primary IoT standards body in the European Union context. ETSI EN 303 645 (Cyber Security for Consumer Internet of Things: Baseline Requirements, v2.1.1, 2020) established 13 baseline security provisions for consumer IoT devices, including the prohibition of universal default passwords, a mandatory vulnerability disclosure policy, and a requirement that all software components remain updatable throughout the product lifecycle.

EN 303 645 has had significant regulatory impact beyond its technical scope: it was adopted as the technical basis for the UK's Product Security and Telecommunications Infrastructure (PSTI) Act 2022 and directly informed the security requirements of the EU Cyber Resilience Act. ETSI SmartM2M is the European counterpart to the oneM2M global partnership and has been central to aligning European IoT service layer standards with international frameworks.

1.7.5 oneM2M

oneM2M is a global partnership of eight regional standards development organisations — the seven founding partners from 2012 (ARIB, ATIS, CCSA, ETSI, TIA, TTA, and TTC) plus TSDSI (Telecommunications Standards Development Society, India), which joined in 2015 that develops horizontal IoT service layer standards. The oneM2M architecture defines a Common Service Layer (CSL) that sits between IoT applications and the underlying network and device layers, providing standardised interfaces for device management, data management, group management, and security.

The CSL abstraction is designed to allow application developers to write IoT applications once and deploy them over any compliant device and network infrastructure: the horizontal interoperability vision that fragmented IoT markets have consistently struggled to deliver at scale. oneM2M TS-0001 (Release 4, 2021) is the current core functional architecture specification.

1.7.6 W3C Web of Things

The World Wide Web Consortium's Web of Things (WoT) Working Group addresses semantic interoperability: the ability of systems to understand not just what a device is sending but what that data means. The W3C WoT Thing Description (TD) specification, adopted as a W3C Recommendation in April 2020, defines a JSON-LD-based metadata format that describes a device's properties (readable data values), actions (invocable operations), and events (asynchronous notifications), along with their data schemas and protocol bindings. A device that exposes a Thing Description can be automatically integrated by any WoT-compliant platform without prior custom configuration: a level of plug-and-play interoperability that has historically required proprietary device drivers and integration code.

1.7.7 Regulatory Frameworks

Beyond technical standards, IoT is increasingly shaped by legal and regulatory frameworks that mandate security, privacy, and safety properties. The EU General Data Protection Regulation (GDPR, 2016/679) governs the collection and processing of personal data by IoT systems operating in or targeting EU residents, requiring lawful basis for processing, data minimisation, purpose limitation, and breach notification within 72 hours.

The EU Cyber Resilience Act (CRA, 2024) imposes security-by-design obligations on manufacturers of products with digital elements, including IoT devices, sold in the EU market, with mandatory vulnerability disclosure and OTA update capability requirements. The US NIST Cybersecurity Framework and the NIST IR 8259 series provide voluntary IoT security guidance that is increasingly referenced in procurement specifications and national regulatory guidance. Chapter 9 provides the comprehensive governance and compliance treatment of these frameworks.

Table 1.4: Key IoT Standards Bodies and Selected Standards

Standards Body	Primary IoT Domain	Key IoT Standards
IEEE	Physical and link layer	802.15.4, 802.11, Bluetooth Core Spec (BLE), P2510
IETF	Network and application layer	RFC 6550 (RPL), RFC 7252 (CoAP), RFC 8613 (OSCORE)
ITU-T	Framework and vocabulary	Y.2060 (IoT overview), Y.4000 series
ETSI	Security and service layer	EN 303 645 (consumer IoT security), SmartM2M
oneM2M	Service layer architecture	TS-0001 Functional Architecture
W3C WoT	Semantic interoperability	Thing Description (TD) Recommendation 2020
OASIS	Application protocols	MQTT v5.0, AMQP v1.0
LoRa Alliance	LPWAN	LoRaWAN Specification v1.0.4/v1.1
GSMA	Cellular IoT	IoT Security Guidelines, eSIM/eUICC SGP.02

The Internet of Things is shaped by international standards, regulatory frameworks, and industry guidelines that support interoperability, security, governance, and responsible deployment. Table 1.5 provides a consolidated view of selected standards and frameworks referenced throughout this book and shows how they relate to the major themes of IoT design and operation.

Table 1.5: International Standards and Frameworks Alignment

Standard / Framework	Main Focus	Relevant Chapters	Importance for IoT
ITU-T Y.2060	Foundational definition of IoT as a global infrastructure for the information society	Ch. 1, 3	Provides a broad conceptual foundation for understanding IoT as an interconnected infrastructure of physical and virtual things.
ISO/IEC 30141	IoT reference architecture	Ch. 1, 3, 9	Supports structured architectural thinking by defining common viewpoints, entities, domains, and interactions in IoT systems.
ISO/IEC 20924	IoT vocabulary and terminology	Ch. 1, Glossary	Promotes consistent use of technical terms across academic, professional, and standards-based discussions.

IEEE 802.15.4	Low-rate wireless personal area networks	Ch. 3, 4	Provides the foundation for several low-power wireless IoT communication technologies used in constrained environments.
IETF IPv6, 6LoWPAN, RPL, CoAP, DTLS, OS-CORE	Internet-layer and application-layer communication for constrained devices	Ch. 4, 8	Enables constrained IoT devices to communicate securely and efficiently using Internet-based protocols.
MQTT and AMQP	Message-oriented communication	Ch. 4, 5, 6	Supports publish-subscribe messaging, telemetry exchange, and scalable device-to-cloud communication.
oneM2M	Common IoT service layer and interoperability	Ch. 3, 6, 9	Helps connect heterogeneous devices, applications, and platforms through standard service-layer functions.
ETSI EN 303 645	Consumer IoT cybersecurity baseline	Ch. 8, 9	Provides widely recognised security requirements for consumer IoT products, including password security, vulnerability handling, secure updates, and data protection.
NIST IR 8425	Consumer IoT cybersecurity capabilities	Ch. 8, 9	Defines cybersecurity outcomes for consumer IoT products and supports secure product design, procurement, and evaluation.
EU Cyber Resilience Act	Cybersecurity requirements for products with digital elements	Ch. 8, 9, 10	Strengthens product-lifecycle cybersecurity expectations for connected hardware and software, including vulnerability handling and security updates.
GDPR and privacy-by-design principles	Personal data protection and privacy governance	Ch. 7, 8, 9, 11	Guides responsible handling of personal, location, health, behavioural, and operational data generated by IoT systems.
NIST FIPS 203, 204, and 205	Post-quantum cryptography standards	Ch. 8, 10	Provides a future-facing cryptographic reference for long-life connected systems that may need protection against future quantum-era security threats.

1.8 Challenges and Opportunities

The Internet of Things offers extraordinary potential, but it does not exist without cost or complication. Interoperability gaps, security vulnerabilities, operational complexity, data quality problems, energy constraints, and regulatory fragmentation are all real, consequential challenges that engineers, architects, and system operators encounter in practice. Alongside each challenge, however, progress is measurable and accelerating: new standards are converging, lightweight security mechanisms are maturing, regulatory frameworks are raising the floor, and edge intelligence is alleviating the data burden. This section examines six major challenge domains and the corresponding opportunities that the field's response to them is creating.

1.8.1 Interoperability and Fragmentation

The most persistent structural challenge in IoT is fragmentation: hundreds of competing protocols, proprietary platforms, and incompatible data formats that make integration between systems expensive, slow, and fragile. The smart building opening scenario is a microcosm of an industry-wide pattern: every vertical has its own protocol preferences, every vendor has its own data model, and every new deployment requires a custom integration effort that could have been avoided with prior standardisation. Estimates from the IoT Analytics 2023 market report suggest that integration costs account for 30 to 40 percent of total IoT deployment cost in enterprise projects.

The opportunity is real and accelerating. The Matter protocol, developed by the Connectivity Standards Alliance and released in 2022, has brought Apple, Google, Amazon, Samsung, and over 200 other companies behind a single smart home interoperability standard: an alignment that would have seemed implausible a decade earlier. W3C WoT Thing Descriptions are being adopted by industrial IoT platforms to enable semantic interoperability at the gateway layer. oneM2M compliant service layer deployments are growing in Asia and Europe. The direction of travel is toward convergence; the pace is slower than the market would prefer, but the structural incentives for interoperability are increasingly aligned.

1.8.2 Security and Privacy at Scale

IoT expands the cybersecurity attack surface to every physical object. The 2016 Mirai botnet attack demonstrated the consequences with brutal clarity: 600,000 compromised consumer IoT devices (cameras, routers, DVRs) were weaponised to generate a 1.2 Tbps distributed denial-of-service attack against Dyn's DNS infrastructure, taking major internet services offline for hours. The compromised devices all shared a common vulnerability: they used default factory credentials that their owners had never changed, and their manufacturers had provided no mechanism to update their firmware. Constrained IoT devices, by definition, cannot run the full security stacks that protect conventional computing endpoints.

Key Insight: Lessons from Mirai. *Mirai's destructive power came not from technical sophistication but from scale and systemic neglect. Default credentials were a known problem that manufacturers had not addressed and regulators had not mandated fixing. The EU Cyber Resilience Act (2024) directly prohibits universal default passwords that cannot be changed — a regulatory response to exactly this class of attack. This illus-*

trates a key IoT security principle: most large-scale IoT security failures are failures of economics and incentives, not failures of available technical knowledge.

The opportunity comes from both technology and regulation. Lightweight security standards (DTLS 1.3, OSCORE, LwM2M certificate management) provide security properties appropriate for constrained devices without the overhead of full TLS and PKI. Hardware security elements (secure enclaves, Trusted Execution Environments, Physical Unclonable Functions) are being integrated into IoT microcontrollers at modest cost increments. Regulatory mandates (ETSI EN 303 645, the EU CRA, the UK PSTI Act) are raising the floor: manufacturers who sell devices with default credentials or without update capability will face legal consequences, not just reputational ones. Chapter 8 provides the comprehensive technical treatment of IoT security.

1.8.3 Scalability and Operational Complexity

Managing a fleet of millions of heterogeneous IoT devices (each with its own firmware version, failure history, connectivity state, and security certificate expiry date) is an operational challenge without precedent in IT management. The tools and processes developed for managing hundreds of servers do not scale to managing millions of embedded devices with ten-year operational lifetimes, limited connectivity, and physical inaccessibility. An IoT operator who needs to patch a critical vulnerability across a fleet of 500,000 field-deployed devices faces a logistical problem that no enterprise IT team has previously had to solve.

Connectivity Management Platforms (CMPs), Zero Touch Provisioning (ZTP), and OTA firmware update frameworks are systematically addressing this challenge. LwM2M's standardised firmware update object, the GSMA's eSIM/eUICC remote provisioning standards, and cloud-native fleet management APIs are reducing the per-device management cost toward the economics required for million-device deployments. Chapter 9 addresses IoT fleet management and operational governance in depth.

1.8.4 Data Volume, Quality, and Value

IoT generates more data than most organisations have the infrastructure, skills, or budget to process meaningfully. A 2022 IDC study estimated that only 2 percent of IoT data generated is ever analysed: the remainder is discarded at the gateway or never retrieved from device storage. The data quality challenge is equally significant: raw sensor readings are noisy, subject to drift, affected by environmental interference, and occasionally erroneous. An analytics model trained on uncleaned IoT data will inherit its defects and produce unreliable outputs.

Edge computing and AI at the edge are the primary responses to the data volume challenge. By processing data locally and transmitting only results (an anomaly flag, a compressed statistical summary, an inference output) edge intelligence reduces the data-to-cloud firehose while increasing the signal-to-noise ratio of transmitted data. TinyML enables inference on microcontrollers that previously could only forward raw data. Chapter 6 addresses data management and analytics; Chapter 10 addresses AIoT and Edge AI as emerging trends; and Chapter 11 addresses AI and Machine Learning with IoT in depth.

1.8.5 Energy and Sustainability

Battery-powered IoT devices impose hard constraints on protocol design, processing capability, and update frequency. A device that requires a battery change every six months is economically and operationally unviable when deployed by the millions in infrastructure locations. Conversely, an IoT industry that deploys billions of devices (each containing a battery, a microcontroller, various sensors, and a radio) creates a substantial environmental footprint in manufacturing, operation, and end-of-life disposal.

LPWAN technologies with decade-long battery lives, energy harvesting from solar, kinetic, and thermoelectric sources, and aggressive duty-cycling firmware are dramatically improving the energy economics of IoT deployment. Green IoT: the design of IoT systems that minimise energy consumption and environmental impact throughout their lifecycle is emerging as a recognised design discipline rather than an afterthought. Chapter 10 examines sustainability in IoT in the context of emerging applications.

1.8.6 Regulatory Complexity

IoT deployments frequently span multiple jurisdictions, each with different regulations governing radio spectrum use, data protection, product liability, and sector-specific safety standards. A cold-chain monitoring deployment that tracks pharmaceutical shipments across 15 countries must comply with 15 different data protection regimes, use frequency bands approved in each jurisdiction, and meet the medical device regulatory requirements of each market. The compliance overhead for global IoT deployments can equal or exceed the engineering cost.

The European Union's proactive regulatory framework (GDPR, NIS2, the Cyber Resilience Act, and the AI Act) is, despite its compliance burden, creating a de facto global baseline standard in the same way that GDPR shaped global data protection practice after 2018. Organisations designing IoT systems to meet EU requirements find that their products are competitive in most global markets without additional regulatory work. The opportunity in regulatory complexity is the emergence of clear, internationally influential frameworks that provide predictable compliance targets rather than a fragmented patchwork of inconsistent national requirements.

The connected morning described at the opening of this chapter (the sleep tracker, the adaptive thermostat, the smart city street) rests on an engineering foundation that spans link-layer radio protocols (Chapter 4), layered system architectures (Chapter 3), cloud platforms and analytics (Chapter 6), security and governance (Chapters 8 and 9), and domain applications (Chapter 7). Each challenge identified in Section 1.8 has a corresponding technical treatment in a later chapter: interoperability in Chapters 3 and 4; security in Chapter 8; operational scalability in Chapter 9; data management in Chapter 6; energy and sustainability in Chapter 10; regulatory complexity in Chapter 9. The chapters that follow provide the engineering depth that transforms the morning vignette from a vivid narrative into a technically comprehensible, practically buildable, and responsibly governed system.

1.9 Chapter Summary

This chapter has introduced the Internet of Things as a paradigm shift in the relationship between the physical and digital worlds: a transition from networks of human users to networks in which physical objects (embedded with sensors, actuators, and communication capability) become autonomous participants in information systems. The opening scenario of a connected morning in Singapore established the personal and immediate relevance of IoT before the chapter moved to its technical and conceptual foundations.

Section 1.1 traced the historical lineage of IoT from Kevin Ashton's 1999 coinage at Procter and Gamble through the Carnegie Mellon internet-connected Coke machine and Mark Weiser's vision of ubiquitous computing, to the present day in which about 21.1 billion connected IoT devices in 2025 and around 39 billion forecast by 2030. Three institutional definitions from ITU-T Y.2060, ISO/IEC 30141, and the IETF were presented and synthesised into the working definition used throughout the book. The critical distinction between IoT, the traditional internet (designed for human users), and M2M communication (proprietary bilateral machine links) was established.

Section 1.2 identified the eight fundamental characteristics that define an IoT system: Connectivity (heterogeneous multi-radio networks with intermittent connection patterns), Identity (persistent per-device identifiers enabling management and security), Data (high-volume time-series streams with rapid value decay), Intelligence (distributed analytics from device-level rules to cloud AI), Communication (protocol diversity matched to deployment constraints), Scalability (architectural design for million-device fleets from pilot inception), Architecture (multi-tier device-gateway-edge-cloud hierarchy), and Security (designed-in protection at every layer). Table 1.1 mapped these characteristics across IoT, traditional Internet, and M2M to demonstrate IoT's synthesis of both.

Section 1.3 examined the six enabling technologies whose simultaneous maturation created IoT: RFID (digital identity for physical objects), sensors and actuators (perception and effector layers), cloud computing (scalable data infrastructure), big data and analytics (time-series processing and insight extraction), AI and machine learning (intelligence including TinyML edge inference), and wireless connectivity (5G, LPWAN, and Wi-Fi spanning the full power-range design space). The enabling technologies were presented as an interdependence map in which each technology reinforces the value of the others.

Section 1.4 introduced the six-level IoT deployment taxonomy, progressing from Level 1 (single device, local action) through Levels 2-5 (increasing connectivity, storage, gateway aggregation, and edge intelligence) to Level 6 (distributed multi-tier systems with intelligence at every tier). The taxonomy provides a practical classification tool that helps engineers identify appropriate technology choices and helps readers understand why IoT requires radically different engineering solutions at different scales.

Section 1.5 surveyed seven major IoT application domains: smart home and building automation (largest by device volume, transitioning from remote control to autonomous optimisation), smart cities (IoT systems of systems at urban scale), Industrial IoT (predictive maintenance, process optimisation, OT-IT integration), healthcare and wearables (remote monitoring and clinical applications with complex regulatory requirements), agriculture and environment (LoRaWAN-based sparse wide-area deployments), energy and utilities (smart metering and smart grid infrastructure), and transport and logistics (fleet telematics, cold-chain monitoring, and connected vehicles).

Section 1.6 mapped the IoT ecosystem value chain from device and component manufacturers at the base through connectivity providers, platform vendors, system integrators, and application developers to end users and operators at the apex, with regulators and standards bodies as a framing constraint across all tiers. The multi-stakeholder nature of the ecosystem explains why IoT deployment requires organisational and commercial competencies alongside technical skills.

Section 1.7 surveyed the principal standards bodies shaping IoT: IEEE (physical and link layers), IETF (network and application layer protocols), ITU-T (framework standards and vocabulary), ETSI (consumer IoT security and EU regulatory alignment), oneM2M (service layer architecture), and W3C WoT (semantic interoperability). The EU regulatory framework (GDPR, CRA, NIS2) was identified as an increasingly influential global baseline for IoT security and privacy requirements.

Section 1.8 addressed six categories of IoT challenges alongside the opportunities that progress toward addressing each of them has created: interoperability and fragmentation (addressed by Matter, W3C WoT, oneM2M convergence), security and privacy at scale (addressed by lightweight security standards and regulatory mandates), scalability and operational complexity (addressed by CMPs and ZTP), data volume and quality (addressed by edge AI and TinyML), energy and sustainability (addressed by LPWAN and energy harvesting), and regulatory complexity (addressed by EU framework convergence). The section closed by returning to the opening morning scenario and mapping each IoT interaction to the chapter and topic that explains its engineering foundation.

Chapter 2

IoT Hardware: Sensors, Actuators, and Platforms

Chapter 2 examines the physical foundation of IoT systems by explaining how real-world conditions are sensed, measured, converted, processed, and acted upon through hardware components. It introduces transducers as the critical interface between the physical and digital worlds, and provides a structured treatment of major sensor categories, including thermal, mechanical, optical, chemical, electromagnetic, and environmental sensors. The chapter also explains actuators as the response mechanism of IoT systems, showing how digital commands are converted into physical actions through relays, motors, solenoids, valves, thermal devices, and other control elements. In addition, it presents the hardware platforms used to build IoT nodes, including microcontrollers, single-board computers, communication modules, and embedded development boards. The chapter further discusses device roles, addressing, identity, power constraints, and energy management strategies that are essential for reliable IoT deployment. Overall, this chapter provides the hardware-level understanding required to design IoT devices that can sense accurately, communicate efficiently, operate reliably, and support intelligent connected applications.

Opening Scenario: The Invisible Custodian

A pharmaceutical logistics company ships temperature-sensitive vaccines in refrigerated containers across a 4,000 km road-and-air supply chain from a manufacturing facility in Hyderabad to distribution hubs in Muscat. Each container carries a battery-powered IoT monitoring unit no larger than a paperback book. Inside that unit (invisible to the driver, the cargo handlers, and the airline ground crew) are a resistance temperature detector (RTD) measuring container temperature to within 0.1 degrees Celsius, a MEMS accelerometer detecting shock events, a MEMS pressure sensor logging altitude and cabin pressure during the flight, a 3000 mAh lithium primary cell as the power source, an STM32L microcontroller sleeping at 1.1 microamperes between its scheduled 90-second duty cycles, and a LoRa radio that wakes for 2 seconds to transmit and then sleeps for the remaining 88.

When the container passes through a desert transfer point in Oman and the internal temperature climbs 1.8 degrees Celsius above the permitted upper bound of 8 degrees Celsius, the accelerometer simultaneously records a 3.1G shock event: the container was set down too hard on hot tarmac. The microcontroller, still within its 90-second duty cycle window, detects both threshold crossings, activates a solenoid-controlled cooling bypass valve for 45 seconds, logs the event with a cryptographic timestamp, wakes the LoRa radio, and transmits a 47-byte alert packet to the nearest LoRaWAN gateway.

The gateway forwards the alert to a cloud platform via cellular backhaul within 8 seconds. A quality assurance engineer in Hyderabad receives a push notification with the container ID, GPS coordinates, temperature excursion magnitude, shock event severity, and corrective action taken.

The entire sequence (sensing, decision, actuation, transmission, relay) takes 11 seconds. The vaccines are undamaged. The driver receives a dashboard alert on his tablet. The quality assurance team has a complete, cryptographically signed data log. This chapter explains how every component of that invisible custodian works: the physics of the sensors, the electrical characteristics of the actuator, the architecture of the microcontroller platform, the energy arithmetic that makes years of battery life possible, and the addressing scheme that lets the cloud platform identify this specific container out of 12,000 in the fleet.

2.1 Transducers: The Physical-Digital Interface

Everything in an IoT system begins at the physical interface between the digital world and the physical world. This interface is a transducer: a device that converts one form of energy into another. In IoT, two conversion directions dominate: physical phenomenon to electrical signal (sensing), and electrical signal to physical phenomenon (actuation). Both sensors and actuators are therefore transducers. A temperature sensor converts thermal energy into a voltage or resistance change; an electric motor converts electrical energy into mechanical rotation. The engineering discipline that designs these interfaces, instrumentation engineering, is the physical foundation on which all subsequent IoT layers depend.

2.1.1 Active vs. Passive Transducers

Transducers are classified by whether they generate their output signal independently or require an external excitation source. Active transducers generate their own electrical output directly from the sensed physical phenomenon, without requiring an external power supply. A thermocouple, for example, exploits the Seebeck effect: the temperature difference between its two junctions produces a small voltage (typically 40-60 microvolts per degree Celsius) directly, without requiring any power supply at the sensing junction. A piezoelectric sensor generates a charge when mechanically stressed — squeeze the crystal, get a voltage. Active transducers are inherently suited to energy-harvesting applications because they generate power from the phenomenon they measure.

Passive transducers change an electrical property (resistance, capacitance, or inductance) in response to the sensed phenomenon, but require external excitation (a voltage or current source) to convert that property change into a measurable signal. A thermistor is a passive transducer: its resistance changes with temperature, but the measurement circuit must supply a known current and measure the resulting voltage to determine resistance. A capacitive humidity sensor changes its dielectric constant with relative humidity, requiring an external AC excitation source and a capacitance measurement circuit.

The vast majority of IoT sensors are passive transducers. This is an important design consideration: passive sensors require the microcontroller's ADC and associated signal conditioning circuitry to produce a usable digital reading, adding to the hardware complexity and current draw of the IoT node. Choosing sensors with integrated digital interfaces (I2C, SPI), which package signal conditioning on-chip, is the dominant strategy for reducing node complexity in production IoT designs.

2.1.2 Sensor Classification by Physical Parameter

IoT sensors are most usefully classified by the physical parameter they measure, since this classification directly determines selection criteria and deployment context. Five primary categories encompass the overwhelming majority of IoT sensing applications. Thermal sensors measure temperature, heat flux, and thermal conductivity: the most ubiquitous IoT sensing need, present in every cold-chain logistics system, HVAC controller, and industrial process monitor. Mechanical sensors measure displacement, force, pressure, acceleration, vibration, and flow — fundamental to industrial condition monitoring, wearables, and process control.

Optical sensors detect light intensity across the electromagnetic spectrum from ultraviolet through infrared, enabling presence detection, ambient light sensing, spectroscopic analysis, and machine vision. Chemical sensors detect gas concentrations, humidity, pH, and specific analyte presence — central to air quality monitoring, industrial safety, and environmental sensing. Electromagnetic sensors detect magnetic fields, proximity, and position using inductive or magnetic effects, used in contactless switches, motor position feedback, and NFC-based identification.

DEFINITION: Transducer

A device that converts one form of energy into another. In IoT, the dominant conversion directions are: physical phenomenon to electrical signal (sensing) and electrical signal to physical phenomenon (actuation). Active transducers generate their output directly from the sensed phenomenon without external power; passive transducers change an electrical property that requires external excitation to measure. Both sensors and actuators are transducers.

2.1.3 Signal Conditioning

The raw electrical output of most transducers cannot be directly processed by a microcontroller's analogue-to-digital converter (ADC). A thermocouple produces millivolts; a thermistor produces a resistance change; a piezoelectric sensor produces an electrical charge. Before any of these signals reach a microcontroller, they must be conditioned: amplified to match the ADC input range (typically 0 to 3.3 V), filtered to remove high-frequency noise and anti-aliasing artefacts, and linearised where the sensor transfer function is nonlinear — thermistors, for example, have an exponential resistance-temperature relationship that must be compensated in firmware using the Steinhart-Hart equation or a lookup table.

Dedicated signal conditioning ICs significantly reduce this design burden. The MAX31856 (universal thermocouple amplifier with cold-junction compensation) and ADS1115 (precision 16-bit ADC with programmable gain amplifier) integrate amplification, filtering, and conversion in a single package. MEMS sensors with digital output interfaces, I2C or SPI, integrate signal conditioning on-chip and deliver pre-processed digital readings directly to the microcontroller, eliminating discrete analogue circuitry from the IoT node design and substantially reducing development effort.

Key Insight: Digital vs. Analogue Sensor Interfaces. When selecting IoT sensors, prefer devices with digital output interfaces (I2C, SPI, UART) over purely analogue sensors wherever the accuracy requirements permit. Digital sensors integrate signal conditioning, ADC, and often temperature compensation on-chip, reducing node hardware complexity, eliminating analogue noise pickup on PCB traces, and simplifying firmware. Analogue sensors remain essential for high-speed sampling (vibration analysis above audio frequencies), specialised electrochemical applications, and ultra-low-cost nodes where every component cost must be minimised.

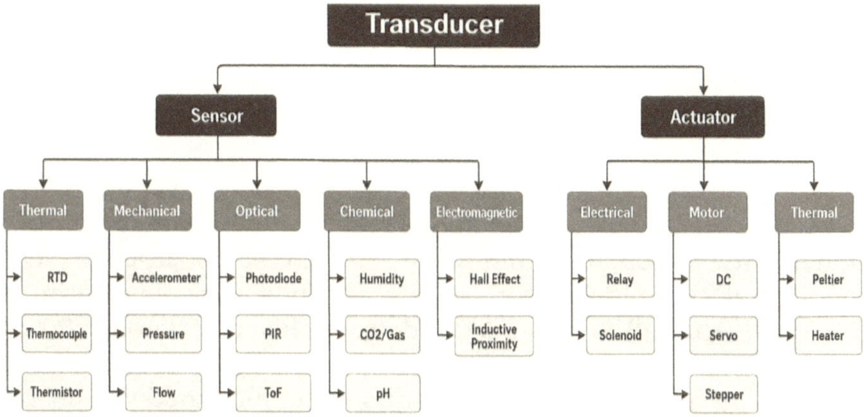

Figure 2.1: Sensor Classification Taxonomy Tree.

2.2 Sensor Technology

Selecting the right sensor for an IoT deployment requires evaluating multiple performance parameters simultaneously: accuracy, resolution, power consumption, interface type, long-term stability, and cost. Before surveying individual sensor types, it is useful to establish this selection criteria framework explicitly, since it applies across all sensor categories and forms the basis for Table 2.1.

Six key parameters are especially important in sensor selection: measurement range, accuracy, resolution, power consumption, interface type, and long-term stability. Measurement range defines the minimum and maximum values the sensor can reliably measure: a soil temperature sensor needs -10 to +60 °C; a pharmaceutical cold-chain sensor needs -20 to +15 °C; a furnace sensor may require 0 to 1,200 °C. These requirements immediately eliminate certain sensor technologies. Accuracy is the maximum systematic error between the sensor's reading and the true value, typically expressed as ±a fixed value or percentage of full scale. Resolution is the smallest detectable change in the measured quantity, limited by the analogue noise floor and the ADC bit depth.

Response time determines how quickly the sensor tracks changes in the measured quantity, critical for shock detection (microseconds) but largely irrelevant for ambient temperature monitoring (seconds). Power consumption determines battery lifetime in wireless sensor nodes and is often the primary selection criterion after accuracy for battery-powered IoT deployments. Interface type (analogue voltage, resistance, I2C, SPI, UART, or 4-20 mA current loop) determines the hardware integration effort with the target microcontroller.

2.2.1 Temperature Sensors

Temperature is the most commonly measured physical quantity in IoT. Three principal sensing technologies serve different points in the accuracy-cost-range trade-off space.

Thermocouples exploit the Seebeck thermoelectric effect: two dissimilar metal wires joined at one end produce a voltage proportional to the temperature difference between the hot junction (sensing tip) and the cold junction (reference). The K-type thermocouple (Chromel-Alumel) is the most widely deployed, covering -200 to +1,372 °C with a sensitivity of approximately 41 μV/°C. Thermocouples require cold-junction compensation: the cold junction temperature must be independently measured and subtracted, and signal amplification before the signal can be digitised.

The MAX31856 IC integrates cold-junction compensation and a programmable-gain amplifier, providing a digital SPI output with 0.0078 °C resolution. Thermocouples are the standard choice for high-temperature industrial IoT applications (furnace monitoring, kiln control, and turbine exhaust sensing) where thermistors and RTDs cannot survive the operating temperature range.

Resistance Temperature Detectors (RTDs), standardised under IEC 60751, use the predictable linear increase in platinum resistance with temperature. The Pt100 (100 ohms at 0 degrees Celsius) is the standard industrial RTD, offering accuracy of plus or minus 0.1 to 0.3 degrees Celsius across -200 to +600 degrees Celsius. RTDs require a precision current source and a high-resolution ADC (typically 24-bit) to achieve their rated accuracy, making them more expensive to interface than thermistors or digital sensors. They are the gold standard for pharmaceutical cold-chain monitoring, calibration laboratories, and industrial process control where measurement traceability is mandated.

Thermistors (thermally sensitive resistors) use semiconductor oxides whose resistance changes dramatically with temperature.

NTC (Negative Temperature Coefficient) thermistors decrease in resistance as temperature rises, with high sensitivity near room temperature (typically -3 to -5 percent per degree Celsius) but a strongly nonlinear (exponential) response. The Steinhart-Hart equation characterises the resistance-temperature relationship and is implemented in firmware to linearise readings. Thermistors are inexpensive, sensitive in the -40 to +125 degrees Celsius range, and compatible with direct ADC measurement using a voltage divider circuit, making them the dominant choice for battery-powered consumer and building IoT applications where laboratory accuracy is not required.

Digital temperature sensors integrate the sensing element, signal conditioning, ADC, and digital interface on a single chip. The DHT22 provides temperature (plus or minus 0.5 degrees Celsius accuracy) and relative humidity via a single-wire serial interface. The Bosch BME280 provides temperature (plus or minus 0.5 degrees Celsius), humidity (plus or minus 3 percent RH), and barometric pressure (plus or minus 1 hPa) via I2C or SPI, consuming only 3.6 microamps in weather monitoring mode. The DS18B20 provides plus or minus 0.5 degrees Celsius accuracy via 1-Wire interface and is uniquely suited to multiple-sensor daisy-chaining on a single GPIO pin. Digital sensors dominate new IoT designs because they eliminate discrete analogue conditioning circuitry entirely.

2.2.2 Humidity Sensors

Relative humidity (RH) measurement in IoT is almost exclusively accomplished by capacitive humidity sensors. A capacitive sensor uses a polymer or metal oxide dielectric layer that absorbs or releases water molecules in proportion to ambient relative humidity, changing the capacitance of the sensor element. The Sensirion SHT31 offers plus or minus 2 percent RH accuracy across 0 to 100 percent RH with an I2C interface and 2 microamps average current in single-shot measurement mode: a standard choice for building automation and weather station IoT nodes. The DHT22 (AM2302) offers plus or minus 2 to 5 percent RH accuracy at lower cost but with a proprietary single-wire protocol and slower response time.

Resistive humidity sensors use a hygroscopic material whose resistance changes with humidity. They are less accurate (plus or minus 3 to 5 percent RH typical) and more prone to contamination and long-term drift than capacitive types, but cost less, appropriate for coarse monitoring applications where calibration can be performed infrequently. Temperature compensation is always required for accurate humidity measurement because the sensor's response is temperature-dependent; most digital humidity sensors integrate a temperature sensor for this purpose.

2.2.3 Motion and Presence Sensors

PIR (Passive InfraRed) sensors detect the thermal radiation emitted by warm bodies (humans, animals) passing through their field of view. A pyroelectric detector element responds to changes in infrared radiation: a stationary person at constant temperature produces no output; a person moving into or out of the detection zone creates a thermal gradient that generates a voltage pulse. PIR sensors require no active illumination, consume under 100 microamps in standby, and produce a simple binary (presence/no presence) output. The Panasonic AMG8833 advances this concept with an 8x8 thermopile array that produces a thermal image, enabling rudimentary person counting and thermal mapping.

MEMS accelerometers are the dominant technology for vibration monitoring, shock detection, and motion sensing in IoT. A MEMS accelerometer uses a microscopic proof mass suspended on silicon springs; acceleration deflects the mass and the deflection is measured capacitively. The STMicroelectronics LIS3DH provides three-axis acceleration measurement at up to 400 Hz sampling rate with 2G/4G/8G/16G selectable range and an I2C/SPI interface, consuming 11 microamps at 1 Hz in low-power mode. The built-in activity/inactivity threshold detection allows the accelerometer to wake the host microcontroller on a threshold crossing, enabling interrupt-driven architectures that keep the MCU in deep sleep until a shock event occurs, critical for the cold-chain scenario's shock detection requirement.

2.2.4 Light Sensors

Ambient light sensors measure illuminance in lux, enabling IoT systems to adapt to lighting conditions. The Texas Instruments OPT3001 provides a 23-bit effective dynamic range from 1.2 millilux to 83 kilolux with an I2C interface and 1.8 microamps current consumption — suited to smart building lighting control and outdoor monitoring. Photodiodes and phototransistors provide analogue current or voltage outputs proportional to incident light, used in optical encoder position sensing, laser-based object detection, and fibre-optic receivers. Time-of-Flight (ToF) LiDAR sensors such as the STMicroelectronics VL53L1X use pulsed infrared laser ranging to measure distance from 1 mm to 4 m with 1 mm accuracy at up to 50 Hz, used in proximity detection, people counting, and robotic navigation.

2.2.5 Gas and Environmental Sensors

Gas sensing for IoT covers a wide range of analytes and sensing principles. Electrochemical sensors (used for CO, NO2, SO2, O3 detection) produce a current proportional to the analyte concentration at a working electrode; they are highly selective and accurate but have limited lifetimes (typically 2-3 years) and require careful temperature compensation. The Alphasense CO-B4 electrochemical sensor is a standard reference for urban air quality monitoring networks.

MQ-series resistive metal oxide sensors (MQ-2 for LPG/smoke, MQ-7 for carbon monoxide, MQ-135 for air quality index) use a heated tin oxide or zinc oxide element whose resistance changes in the presence of reducing or oxidising gases. They are inexpensive (under two US dollars) but require a 5V heater (consuming 150-300 mW: a significant power burden for battery operation), have poor selectivity (they respond to multiple gases), and drift over time. They are appropriate for fixed, mains-powered air quality monitors but unsuitable for battery-powered IoT nodes.

NDIR (Non-Dispersive InfraRed) CO2 sensors use the unique absorption of infrared light at 4.26 micrometres by CO2 molecules. The SenseAir S8 and MH-Z19 are widely used in smart building ventilation control: they achieve plus or minus 50 ppm accuracy across 0 to 5000 ppm CO2 with an UART or I2C interface, typically consuming 35-40 mA during measurement (a few seconds every minute in duty-cycled operation). PM2.5 and PM10 particulate matter sensors such as the Plantower PMS5003 use laser particle counting to measure airborne particle concentrations, with typical accuracy of plus or minus 10 micrograms per cubic metre, used in outdoor air quality monitoring and HVAC filtration control.

2.2.6 Proximity and Distance Sensors

Ultrasonic distance sensors (HC-SR04) emit a 40 kHz ultrasonic pulse and measure the time-of-flight of the echo to calculate distance. They operate from 2 cm to 4 m with approximately 3 mm resolution, are insensitive to ambient light and surface colour, and cost under two US dollars. They are the standard choice for waste bin fill-level detection, liquid level monitoring in tanks, and proximity detection in access control. IR proximity sensors (Sharp GP2Y0A21YK) use triangulation of a reflected IR beam to measure distance from 10 to 80 cm; they are faster than ultrasonic but affected by ambient light and surface reflectivity.

Capacitive proximity sensors detect the presence of conductive or dielectric objects (including human fingers) through a change in the sensor electrode's capacitance. They are used in touch interfaces, liquid level sensing through tank walls, and non-contact switch applications. Hall effect sensors detect magnetic fields and are used for contactless position sensing (door open/close detection, shaft rotation counting, linear position measurement), consuming microamps in standby mode with instant wake response to a magnet.

Table 2.1 provides a consolidated reference across all major sensor types covered in this section.

Table 2.1: IoT Sensor Type Comparison

Sensor	Operating Principle	Accuracy	Range	Interface	Power	Typical IoT Use Case
Thermocouple (K-type)	Seebeck thermoelectric	+-1-2 deg C	-200 to +1372 deg C	SPI (via MAX 31856)	~1 mW (amplifier)	Furnaces, industrial high-temp
RTD Pt100	Platinum resistance	+-0.1 deg C	-200 to +600 deg C	Analogue / 24-bit ADC	~5 mW (excitation)	Cold chain, calibration labs
Thermistor NTC	Semiconductor resistance	+-0.5 deg C	-40 to +125 deg C	Analogue (voltage divider)	<0.1 mW	Consumer IoT, HVAC, wearables
BME280 (temp+hum+pressure)	MEMS integrated digital	+-0.5 deg C, +-3% RH	-40 to +85 deg C	I2C / SPI	3.6 uA average	Weather station, smart building
DHT22	Capacitive humidity + thermistor	+-0.5 deg C, +-2-5% RH	-40 to +80 deg C	1-Wire serial	1.5 mA active	Indoor climate monitoring
PIR (AMG 8833)	Pyroelectric thermal	Binary / 8x8 thermal image	0 to 80 deg C (body)	I2C	80-200 uA	Occupancy, access control
MEMS Accelerometer (LIS3DH)	Capacitive proof mass	+-0.03 G resolution	+-2 to +-16 G	I2C / SPI	11 uA at 1 Hz LP	Vibration, shock, wearable motion
OPT3001 (ambient light)	Photodiode + ADC	+-0.01 lux	1.2 mlux to 83 klux	I2C	1.8 uA	Smart lighting control
VL53L1X (ToF LiDAR)	Time-of-flight infrared	+-1 mm	1 mm to 4 m	I2C	19 mA active	Proximity, people counting
SenseAir S8 (CO2 NDIR)	Non-dispersive infrared	+-50 ppm	400 to 5000 ppm CO2	UART / I2C	35 mA active	Smart ventilation, indoor air

PMS5003 (PM2.5)	Laser particle counting	+-10 ug/m3	0 to 500 ug/m3	UART	100 mA active	Outdoor air quality monitoring
HC-SR04 (ultrasonic)	Time-of-flight acoustic	~3 mm	2 cm to 4 m	Digital trigger/echo	15 mA active	Bin level, tank level, proximity

2.3 Actuators: Converting Digital Commands into Physical Action

Where sensors give an IoT system eyes and ears, actuators give it hands. An actuator is a device that converts an electrical signal, most often a digital command from a microcontroller or gateway, into a physical effect: rotating a shaft, opening a valve, switching a circuit, heating a space, or generating sound. The actuator completes the IoT feedback loop: the system senses a condition, processes it against a rule or model, and then acts on the physical world to correct, optimise, or respond to what it detected.

This section surveys the principal actuator categories encountered in IoT deployments, from the simplest electromechanical switches to sophisticated closed-loop servo systems, and explains the drive electronics and control strategies that connect microcontrollers to each actuator type.

DEFINITION: Actuator

A transducer that converts electrical energy into mechanical, thermal, acoustic, or optical energy, thereby producing a physical effect in response to a control signal. In IoT systems, actuators receive commands from microcontrollers, gateways, or cloud platforms and translate those commands into real-world actions.

Source: IEC 60050-151

2.3.1 Electromechanical Actuators: Relays and Solenoids

The relay is the most widely deployed actuator in industrial and building-automation IoT. A relay is an electrically operated switch: a small control current energises an electromagnet coil, which attracts a ferromagnetic armature and mechanically closes or opens a set of electrical contacts. The key value of a relay is galvanic isolation: the microcontroller circuit is physically separate from the switched load circuit, protecting low-voltage electronics from the high voltages and currents that industrial loads may carry.

Relay specifications relevant to IoT selection include coil voltage (typically 5 V or 12 V for MCU-compatible modules), coil current (5-150 mA, usually requiring a transistor or MOSFET driver because

GPIO pins source only 8-40 mA), contact rating (maximum load voltage and current (commonly 250 VAC / 10 A for general-purpose relays), switching speed (typically 5-15 ms) unsuitable for PWM), and mechanical lifetime (typically 10-100 million operations). Solid-state relays (SSRs) replace the mechanical contacts with thyristors or TRIACs, eliminating mechanical wear and contact bounce at the cost of higher on-state resistance and heat dissipation.

A solenoid actuator is a linear electromechanical device: an energised coil generates a magnetic field that pulls or pushes a ferromagnetic plunger along its axis. Solenoid valves are the dominant form in IoT: a solenoid coil drives a valve stem to open or close fluid flow (water, gas, compressed air). The pharmaceutical cold-chain unit introduced in the chapter-opening scenario uses a solenoid valve to inject nitrogen gas into the insulated container, suppressing temperature excursions when the passive phase-change material is exhausted. Solenoid valves are classified as normally open (NO, flow in de-energised state) or normally closed (NC, flow blocked when de-energised), a choice that defines fail-safe behaviour on power loss.

2.3.2 Electric Motors: DC, Servo, and Stepper

Electric motors convert electrical energy into rotational mechanical energy and are the actuator of choice wherever sustained or variable-speed rotation is required — pumps, fans, conveyors, valves with rotary stems, robotic joints, and camera pan-tilt units.

Brushed DC motors are the simplest: applying voltage across the terminals produces rotation; reversing polarity reverses direction. Speed is proportional to applied voltage and inversely proportional to load torque. IoT control of a DC motor uses an H-bridge driver (e.g. DRV8833, L298N) which switches four transistors to control direction, combined with pulse-width modulation (PWM) to control effective voltage and therefore speed. The duty cycle of the PWM signal, the fraction of each period for which the output is high, determines the average voltage and hence motor speed.

Servo motors add a closed-loop position feedback mechanism to a DC motor: a potentiometer or encoder measures the shaft angle, and a built-in controller adjusts drive current to maintain the commanded position. Hobby RC servos use a 50 Hz PWM signal with pulse width 1-2 ms to command angles from 0 to 180 degrees — widely used in IoT prototyping because a single GPIO pin and no external driver are required. Industrial servos use quadrature encoders for precision positioning in manufacturing and logistics automation.

Stepper motors divide a full rotation into discrete steps (typically 200 steps per revolution for a 1.8-degree step motor) by energising stator coils in sequence. Because each step is a fixed angular increment, stepper motors achieve precise open-loop position control without an encoder: the controller simply counts pulses. This makes steppers ideal for IoT applications requiring repeatable positioning: 3D printers, CNC valve actuators, medical infusion pumps, and automated laboratory equipment. Microstepping drivers (e.g. A4988, DRV8825) interpolate between full steps, achieving up to 1/32-step resolution and reducing mechanical resonance.

2.3.3 Thermal Actuators: Heaters, Coolers, and Peltier Devices

Thermal actuators produce or remove heat in response to electrical signals. Resistive heaters are the simplest: a high-resistance element (nichrome wire, PTC ceramic, printed carbon film) converts electrical power to heat with near-100% efficiency. Power (and therefore temperature) is controlled by PWM or phase-angle control (for AC elements). Temperature-feedback control invariably uses a PID controller, discussed in Section 2.3.5, to maintain a setpoint precisely.

Peltier devices (thermoelectric coolers, TECs) exploit the Peltier effect: when direct current flows through a junction of two dissimilar semiconductor materials (bismuth telluride is the most common), heat is transported from one face of the module to the other. The cold face can reach 40-70 degrees Celsius below ambient; the hot face must be heat-sinked to dissipate both the pumped heat and the electrical power consumed. Reversing current polarity reverses the direction of heat pumping, allowing a single TEC to both heat and cool: a critical capability in pharmaceutical cold-chain logistics where both maintaining cold (2-8 degrees Celsius for biologics) and preventing freezing (0 degrees Celsius lower limit) must be managed actively.

Peltier devices have coefficient of performance (COP) values of 0.3-0.7, far lower than compressor-based refrigeration, but their solid-state construction (no moving parts, no refrigerant, silent operation) makes them the preferred thermal actuator for space-constrained or vibration-sensitive IoT deployments such as medical sample transport, optical component temperature stabilisation, and portable diagnostic instruments.

2.3.4 Other Actuator Types

Piezoelectric actuators use the inverse piezoelectric effect: an applied voltage causes mechanical deformation of a piezoelectric crystal (PZT ceramic). Displacement is tiny (nanometres to micrometres) but achievable at very high frequency and with sub-micrometre precision. IoT applications include ultrasonic transducers (both transmitting and receiving), inkjet print heads, vibration motors in wearables, and precision micro-positioning in medical devices.

Electroacoustic actuators (loudspeakers, buzzers, and ultrasonic emitters) convert electrical signals to sound. Passive buzzers require an oscillating drive signal; active buzzers include an internal oscillator and respond to a DC on/off signal. IoT alarm, notification, and voice-interface applications routinely use small electromagnetic or piezoelectric speakers driven by PWM audio signals from a microcontroller DAC or I2S audio interface.

Pneumatic and hydraulic actuators use compressed fluid rather than direct electrical power to generate large forces or torques. In IIoT contexts, solenoid-controlled pneumatic valves are the standard interface between the digital control layer and large mechanical systems, pressing dies, clamping workpieces, actuating robot grippers. The IoT node controls the solenoid valve; the valve controls the high-power pneumatic or hydraulic circuit.

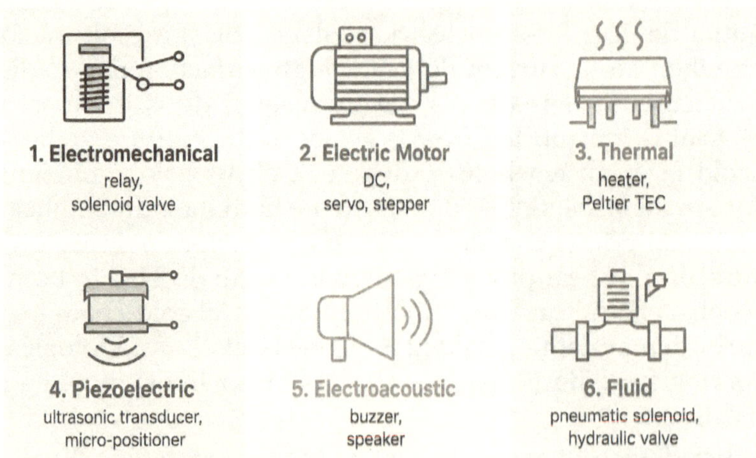

Figure 2.2: Actuator Taxonomy: Six principal actuator categories in IoT deployments, with representative device examples and applications.

2.3.5 Control Strategies: PWM and PID

Most actuators require analogue control (variable speed, variable temperature, variable position) rather than simple on/off switching. Two control mechanisms underpin virtually all IoT actuator control: pulse-width modulation (PWM) for power delivery, and proportional-integral-derivative (PID) control for closed-loop regulation.

Pulse-width modulation is a digital technique for approximating an analogue output voltage using a fixed-frequency square wave. The duty cycle D (0-100%) determines the time-average output voltage: V_avg = D x V_supply. A GPIO pin toggling at 1 kHz with 50% duty cycle delivers an average of 1.65 V from a 3.3 V supply. The load (motor, heater, LED) responds to the average power rather than the instantaneous switching — provided the PWM frequency is much higher than the load's thermal or mechanical time constant. Most microcontrollers include dedicated PWM hardware timers that generate the waveform independently of the CPU, allowing software to set duty cycle with a single register write.

A PID controller is a feedback control algorithm that continuously adjusts a control output to minimise the difference between a measured process variable and a desired setpoint. The three terms contribute independently: the Proportional term applies a correction proportional to the current error (large error produces large correction); the Integral term accumulates past errors and eliminates steady-state offset (the output increments until the error is truly zero); the Derivative term anticipates future error by responding to its rate of change (damping overshoot). Tuning requires selecting gains K_p, K_i, K_d appropriate to the system dynamics, commonly accomplished using the Ziegler-Nichols method or auto-tuning routines provided in embedded PID libraries.

In the pharmaceutical cold-chain unit, a PID controller running on the STM32L microcontroller reads the RTD temperature sensor at 1 Hz and adjusts the Peltier TEC duty cycle to maintain the 5 degrees Celsius setpoint. The integral term eliminates the steady-state offset that a proportional-only controller would exhibit under varying ambient temperature. The derivative term suppresses the overshoot that would otherwise occur when the system transitions from warming to active cooling after a door-open event.

TECHNOLOGY SPOTLIGHT: *Tech Spotlight: Closed-Loop Actuator Control on a Microcontroller*

The Arduino PID Library (Brett Beauregard, MIT licence) encapsulates a complete discrete-time PID algorithm in approximately 200 lines of C++. The library handles anti-windup (limiting integral accumulation when the output saturates), derivative kick suppression (applying the derivative term to the process variable rather than the error to avoid output spikes on setpoint changes), and adjustable sample time.

On an ESP32, the LEDC (LED Control) peripheral provides 16 independent PWM channels with up to 20-bit resolution at adjustable frequencies, accessible from both Arduino and ESP-IDF frameworks via a single API call: ledcWrite(channel, duty_cycle). Combining LEDC with the Arduino PID Library gives a complete closed-loop thermal controller in under 50 lines of application code: the STM32L cold-chain implementation uses an equivalent HAL TIM PWM output.

For motor control, Texas Instruments' DRV8833 dual H-bridge driver integrates decay-mode selection, over-current protection, and thermal shutdown in a 3 x 3 mm QFN package, handling motor currents to 1.5 A per channel while interfacing directly to 3.3 V MCU GPIO. The SPI-controllable DRV8434S extends this to 2.5 A with microstepping support for stepper motor IoT applications.

2.4 IoT Hardware Platforms: Microcontrollers, SBCs, and Modules

The processing core of an IoT node may range from a microcontroller with 256 KB of flash and no operating system to a full application processor running Linux with gigabytes of RAM. Selecting the right hardware platform is one of the earliest and most consequential architectural decisions in an IoT project: it determines power consumption, processing capability, connectivity options, software ecosystem, unit cost, and, ultimately, whether the deployment is technically and commercially viable.

This section surveys the principal hardware platform categories used in IoT: Arduino-family microcontroller boards for low-power sensing and actuation; ESP32 system-on-chip modules for Wi-Fi and Bluetooth-connected nodes; Raspberry Pi single-board computers for gateway and edge-intelligence roles; BeagleBone Black for industrial Linux-based control; and Nordic Semiconductor nRF52840 for ultra-low-power BLE and Thread mesh applications.

2.4.1 Arduino Family: Prototyping to Production

The Arduino platform, launched in 2005 at the Interaction Design Institute Ivrea, democratised embedded systems development by combining an open-source hardware design with a simplified C++ programming environment (the Arduino IDE) and an extensive library ecosystem. The platform remains the dominant choice for IoT prototyping and education, and several Arduino variants have crossed into production deployments.

The Arduino Uno (ATmega328P, 8-bit, 16 MHz, 2 KB SRAM, 32

KB flash) is the canonical entry platform — inexpensive, well-documented, and supported by thousands of libraries, but constrained in RAM and processing speed for complex IoT tasks. It lacks native connectivity: wireless capability requires a separate Wi-Fi or LoRa shield, adding cost and form-factor overhead. The Arduino Nano (same processor, smaller footprint, breadboard-compatible) and Nano Every (ATmega4809, improved peripherals) extend the low-end range.

The Arduino MKR family bridges prototyping and production with a standardised form factor (61.5 x 25 mm) and integrated connectivity. The MKR WAN 1310 embeds a SAMD21 Cortex-M0+ processor (32-bit, 48 MHz) with a Murata CMWX1ZZABZ LoRa module supporting LoRaWAN class A, B, and C operation, plus a LiPo battery charger and a cryptographic co-processor (ATECC608A) for TLS and key storage. This integrated design makes MKR WAN 1310 a production-viable LoRaWAN end node requiring only an antenna, battery, and sensors: the platform used in several commercial agricultural IoT deployments.

2.4.2 ESP32: Wi-Fi and Bluetooth in a USD 2 Module

The Espressif ESP32 system-on-chip, released in 2016, fundamentally changed the economics of connected IoT nodes. By integrating a dual-core Tensilica Xtensa LX6 processor (240 MHz), 520 KB SRAM, Wi-Fi 802.11 b/g/n, Bluetooth 4.2/BLE, and an extensive peripheral set (SPI, I2C, I2S, UART, ADC, DAC, PWM, touch sensing, hall-effect sensor) into a single chip priced below USD 2 in volume, ESP32 enabled a generation of low-cost connected products (smart plugs, energy monitors, occupancy sensors, irrigation controllers) that would previously have required a separate microcontroller and a separate Wi-Fi chipset.

The ESP32's ultra-low-power co-processor (ULP) allows the main cores to enter deep sleep (consuming as little as 10 microamperes) while the ULP continues monitoring GPIO or ADC inputs and can wake the main processor on a threshold event. This architecture supports battery-operated deployments with periodic sensor reporting: a node waking every 60 seconds, acquiring a sensor reading, transmitting over Wi-Fi, and returning to deep sleep can achieve multi-year operation from a 2,000 mAh LiPo battery.

The ESP-IDF (Espressif IoT Development Framework) provides a FreeRTOS-based RTOS environment with TLS 1.3, MQTT, HTTP/S, mDNS, OTA update, and provisioning libraries. Alternatively, MicroPython and the Arduino framework both support ESP32, lowering the barrier for rapid prototyping. The ESP32-S3 variant adds USB-OTG and hardware acceleration for neural network inference (supporting TensorFlow Lite operations), while the ESP32-C3 replaces the Xtensa core with a RISC-V core for reduced cost in single-core applications.

CASE STUDY: *Case Study: ESP32-Based Smart Agriculture Node — Maharashtra, India Aurangabad District, Maharashtra, 2022*

An agri-tech startup deployed 800 ESP32-based soil monitoring nodes across cotton farms in Maharashtra's Marathwada region, one of India's most water-stressed agricultural zones. Each node integrates a capacitive soil moisture sensor, a DHT22 temperature-humidity sensor, and a DS18B20 soil temperature probe, connected to an ESP32-WROOM-32E module mounted in an IP67-rated enclosure with an integrated 6 V/2 W solar panel and a 3,000 mAh LiPo battery.

The node firmware uses ESP-IDF's power management API to sleep between 15-minute reporting intervals, drawing an average of 180 microamperes. Sensor data is published over Wi-Fi to an AWS IoT Core MQTT broker using TLS mutual authentication with device certificates provisioned via the ATECC608A crypto-accelerator on each node. A custom irrigation-scheduling algorithm on AWS Lambda processes soil moisture telemetry and issues solenoid valve commands through a separate ESP32 gateway co-located with each pump house.

After one full kharif (summer) crop season, participating farms reported a 28% reduction in water consumption and an 18% improvement in yield compared to control plots using traditional flood irrigation. The unit hardware cost was USD 14.50 per node at production volumes, yielding a payback period of less than two seasons at regional water tariff rates.

2.4.3 Raspberry Pi: Linux at the Edge

The Raspberry Pi single-board computer (SBC), first released by the Raspberry Pi Foundation in 2012, delivers a full Linux computing environment on a credit-card footprint at low cost. The Raspberry Pi 4 Model B (Broadcom BCM2711, quad-core Cortex-A72 at 1.8 GHz, 1-8 GB LPDDR4, Gigabit Ethernet, dual-band Wi-Fi, Bluetooth 5.0, USB 3.0, dual micro-HDMI) is the most capable IoT platform below industrial single-board computers in both price and thermal envelope.

In IoT architectures, Raspberry Pi occupies the gateway and edge-intelligence tier rather than the constrained end-node tier. Running Raspberry Pi OS (Debian-based Linux), it can execute full Python, Node.js, or Java applications; run Docker containers; host MQTT brokers (Mosquitto), Node-RED visual programming environments, InfluxDB time-series databases, and Grafana dashboards; and connect to constrained end nodes via serial, I2C, SPI, USB, Zigbee USB dongles, or LoRaWAN concentrator HATs. This versatility makes Pi an extremely productive IoT gateway prototyping platform, though its power consumption (3-7 W) and lack of hardware watchdog (mitigated by third-party WDT HATs) limit suitability in power-critical or unattended industrial deployments.

The Raspberry Pi Zero 2 W (RP3A0, quad-core Cortex-A53, 512 MB, single-band Wi-Fi, BLE 4.2, consuming as little as 0.4 W in idle) extends the Pi family into battery-tolerant applications: wearable health gateways, portable diagnostic instruments, and low-volume embedded products where Linux application compatibility is required but the full Pi 4 form factor is excessive. The Raspberry Pi Compute Module 4 (CM4) allows the BCM2711 SoC to be embedded on custom carrier boards for production deployments, providing the Pi's software ecosystem in a production-grade hardware design.

2.4.4 BeagleBone Black: Industrial Linux Control

The BeagleBone Black (BBB), produced by BeagleBoard.org, is a single-board computer designed specifically for real-time industrial control applications. Its distinguishing feature is the dual PRU-ICSS (Programmable Real-time Unit and Industrial Communication Subsystem): two independent 200 MHz RISC cores that execute deterministically without OS scheduling latency, enabling microsecond-precision GPIO bit-banging, industrial fieldbus protocols (EtherCAT, PROFIBUS, EnDat encoder interfaces), and PWM generation beyond the resolution of Linux kernel timers.

The BBB's TI Sitara AM3358 SoC (Cortex-A8, 1 GHz) runs a full Debian Linux distribution with 512 MB DDR3 RAM and 4 GB eMMC flash. The 92-pin cape expansion headers expose four UARTs, two I2C buses, two SPI buses, eight PWM outputs, seven analog inputs (12-bit ADC at 1.8 V), and both PRU interfaces. Industrial IoT deployments use BeagleBone Black as a sub-station controller or local intelligence unit, reading Modbus RTU sensor networks on the UARTs, running control algorithms on the Cortex-A8, executing real-time output sequencing on the PRU, and forwarding aggregated data to an IoT platform via Ethernet or cellular modem.

2.4.5 Nordic nRF52840: Ultra-Low-Power BLE and Thread

The Nordic Semiconductor nRF52840 is the dominant system-on-chip for applications requiring ultra-low-power wireless connectivity with protocol flexibility. It integrates a 64 MHz ARM

Cortex-M4F processor (with hardware floating-point unit), 256 KB RAM, 1 MB flash, and a multi-protocol radio supporting Bluetooth 5.3 (including LE Audio and direction-finding), IEEE 802.15.4 (enabling Thread and Zigbee), ANT+, and 2.4 GHz proprietary protocols, all selectable in firmware without hardware changes.

The nRF52840's power architecture is tuned for coin-cell and energy-harvesting operation: the chip draws 4.6 mA during BLE advertising, 7.7 mA during BLE connection event transmission, and as little as 1.5 microamperes in system-off mode with a single GPIO wake-up source retained. Nordic's nRF5 SDK and the newer Zephyr RTOS-based nRF Connect SDK provide complete BLE, Thread, and Zigbee stacks, along with DFU (device firmware update), key-value storage, and cryptographic libraries.

The nRF52840 is the processor on the Arduino Nano 33 BLE Sense, the Adafruit Feather nRF52840, and the Nordic DK development board, all commonly used in academic and prototype IoT development. In production, the nRF52840 is embedded in wearable health monitors, asset-tracking tags, smart-building occupancy sensors, and Thread-based smart home devices (where it acts as a Thread router or end device within a Matter-over-Thread fabric).

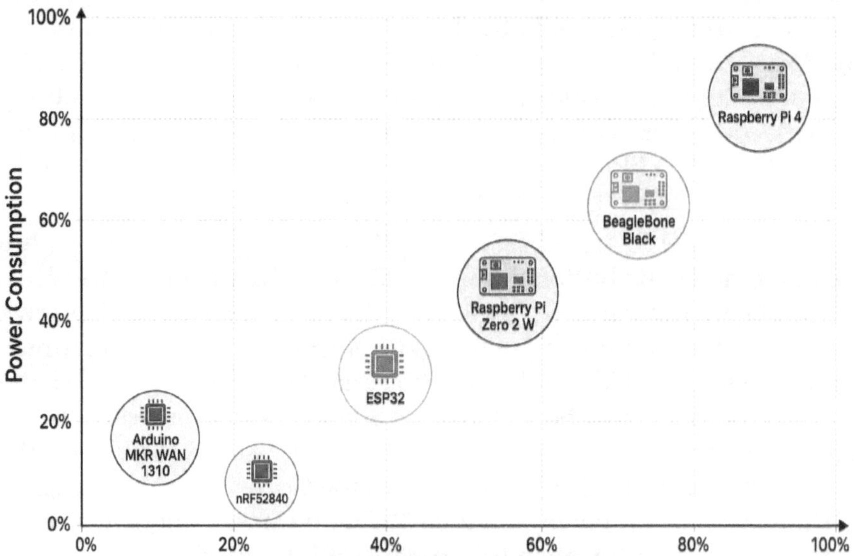

Figure 2.3: IoT Hardware Platform Comparison: Arduino MKR WAN 1310, ESP32, Raspberry Pi 4, BeagleBone Black, and Nordic nRF52840, key specifications and deployment roles across the IoT computing spectrum.

2.4.6 Platform Comparison and Selection Guidelines

Table 2.2 summarises the key specifications of the five platforms surveyed above across the dimensions most relevant to IoT deployment decisions: processor architecture, clock speed, memory, wireless connectivity, power consumption, operating system, unit cost, and primary IoT role. The table is intended as a rapid selection reference; design decisions should be validated against current vendor datasheets and availability.

Platform	Processor	Clock	RAM / Flash	Wireless	Power	OS / Framework	Unit Cost	Prim ary IoT Role
Arduino MKR WAN 1310	SAM D21 Cortex-M0+	48 MHz	32 KB / 256 KB	LoRa WAN	~3 mA active ~100 uA sleep	Bare metal / Arduino	~USD 35	LoRa WAN end node
ESP 32- WR OOM -32	Xtensa LX6 dual-core	240 MHz	520 KB / 4 MB	Wi-Fi + BLE	~180 mA Tx ~10 uA deep sleep	FreeRTOS / Arduino / MicroPython	~USD 2-5	Connected sensor / actuator node
Raspberry Pi 4 B	Cortex-A72 quad-core	1800 MHz	1-8 GB RAM / microSD	Wi-Fi + BT 5	3-7 W	Linux (Raspberry Pi OS)	~USD 55-75	IoT gateway / edge server
Raspberry Pi Zero 2 W	Cortex-A53 quad-core	1000 MHz	512 MB / microSD	Wi-Fi + BT 4.2	~0.4-2 W	Linux (Raspberry Pi OS)	~USD 15	Lightweight gateway / edge node
BeagleBone Black	Cortex-A8 + 2x PRU	1000 MHz	512 MB / 4 GB eMMC	Ethernet (no wireless built-in)	~2-3 W	Debian Linux	~USD 55	Industrial real-time controller
Nordic nRF 52840	Cortex-M4F	64 MHz	256 KB / 1 MB flash	BLE 5.3 + 802.15.4	~8 mA active ~1.5 uA system-off	Zephyr / bare metal	~USD 3-7 (module)	BLE/ Thread end node, wearable

Table 2.2: IoT Hardware Platform Comparison

Platform selection follows a hierarchy of constraints rather than a single criterion. Power budget is the first gate: applications that must operate from a coin cell or small battery for months are limited to the nRF52840 or a deeply-sleeping ESP32. Real-time determinism gates second: applications requiring microsecond-precision output control demand a bare-metal MCU or the BeagleBone Black PRU: a Linux-based SBC with its kernel scheduling jitter is unsuitable for hard real-time control loops.

Connectivity protocol determines the next constraint: LoRaWAN deployments favour the MKR WAN 1310 or a custom ESP32 with a LoRa module; BLE mesh or Thread favour the nRF52840; Wi-Fi-connected nodes favour the ESP32. Finally, software complexity governs the highest tier: when the application requires containerised services, Python ML inference, or complex data pre-processing pipelines, a Raspberry Pi gateway is appropriate regardless of power cost. Table 2.2 consolidates these selection criteria.

A common architectural pattern in production IoT deployments combines two platform tiers: constrained MCU end nodes (ESP32 or nRF52840) for power-efficient sensing and actuation, communicating via BLE, Zigbee, or LoRaWAN to a Raspberry Pi or BeagleBone gateway that handles protocol translation, local analytics, OTA update management, and cloud connectivity. This two-tier architecture maps directly to the Level 4 or Level 5 IoT taxonomy introduced in Chapter 1.

2.5 IoT Node Roles in System Architecture

Not every IoT device plays the same role in a deployment's communication topology. The IoT protocol and architecture community distinguishes at least three fundamental node roles (end node, gateway, and edge endpoint) each with distinct resource profiles, connectivity requirements, and software responsibilities. Understanding these roles is essential for hardware selection, because the correct hardware platform for a battery-powered end node differs fundamentally from the platform appropriate for a gateway that must maintain persistent connectivity to both a constrained wireless network and a cloud platform simultaneously.

2.5.1 End Nodes: Sensing and Actuation at the Edge

An IoT end node is a device that directly interfaces with the physical world through sensors and actuators. End nodes are characterised by constrained resources: limited RAM and flash, low clock speed, restricted power budget, and a single short-range or LPWAN radio. They do not route traffic for other devices and typically communicate with a single gateway or access point rather than maintaining mesh routing tables.

RFC 7228 (Terminology for Constrained-Node Networks, IETF 2014) classifies constrained nodes into three classes based on RAM availability: Class 0 devices have less than 10 KB of RAM and cannot practically run a full IP stack; they rely on proxies or gateways for protocol translation; Class 1 devices have approximately 10 KB of RAM and can run a lightweight IP stack (6LoWPAN, CoAP) but with restricted functionality; Class 2 devices have approximately 50 KB or more of RAM and can run full TCP/TLS stacks comparable to those used on standard internet hosts. The ESP32 (520 KB RAM) and nRF52840 (256 KB RAM) both qualify as Class 2, while many simpler sensor nodes built on ATmega328P (2 KB RAM) are Class 0.

DEFINITION: Constrained Node (RFC 7228)

An IoT device with severe limitations in resources such as RAM, processing speed, code flash, and energy budget that prevent direct participation in standard internet protocols without protocol adaptation or proxy assistance. RFC 7228 defines three classes (C0, C1, C2) based on RAM availability and full IP stack supportability.

Source: IETF RFC 7228, Bormann et al., 2014

End nodes in a well-designed IoT architecture communicate upward to gateways and do not need direct internet routing. This simplifies their security posture and reduces their radio duty cycle: an end node in a LoRaWAN deployment sends uplink messages at intervals from 1 minute to 24 hours, spending the vast majority of its operating life in sleep mode. The gateway provides the always-on presence, internet connectivity, and any time-sensitive downlink delivery.

2.5.2 Gateways: Protocol Translation and Local Aggregation

An IoT gateway is a device that bridges constrained end nodes to the wider internet or a cloud platform. Gateways serve several concurrent functions: protocol translation (converting LoRaWAN or Zigbee frames to MQTT or HTTPS messages), local aggregation (buffering end-node data during upstream connectivity outages), security termination (handling TLS from the internet side, and the constrained protocol from the end-node side), and provisioning (distributing encryption keys, firmware updates, and configuration to end nodes).

Gateway hardware must simultaneously manage two network interfaces: a constrained network radio (LoRa concentrator, Zigbee coordinator, BLE mesh proxy, Z-Wave controller) and an internet-facing interface (Ethernet, cellular modem, or Wi-Fi). This dual connectivity requirement, combined with the need for persistent operation and moderate processing capability for data formatting and TLS, makes Linux-based SBCs (Raspberry Pi, BeagleBone, industrial ARM SBCs) the natural gateway platform.

The LoRaWAN network architecture offers a canonical example

of the gateway role: a LoRaWAN gateway (also called a concentrator) simultaneously listens on eight or more channels using a multi-channel radio frontend (Semtech SX1302 or SX1303), receives packets from hundreds of end nodes, and forwards raw packets as JSON over UDP to a LoRaWAN Network Server. The Network Server handles join procedures, frame counter validation, duplicate rejection (the same packet may arrive at multiple gateways), and downlink scheduling. The gateway itself is thus stateless and replaceable: a clean separation of concerns that simplifies fleet management.

2.5.3 Edge Endpoints: Intelligence at the Network Periphery

Edge endpoints are a distinct role from gateways: where a gateway primarily translates and forwards data, an edge endpoint performs meaningful local computation, running ML inference models, executing control algorithms, maintaining local state, or making autonomous decisions without cloud round-trips. Edge endpoints may also function as gateways (maintaining upstream connectivity) but their defining capability is local intelligence.

The motivation for edge endpoints arises from three constraints. Latency: cloud round-trip times of 50-200 ms are unacceptable for real-time control applications such as industrial machinery safety interlocks, which require sub-10 ms response. Bandwidth: a factory floor with 500 vibration sensors each sampling at 10 kHz generates 50 MB/s of raw data, transmitting this volume to the cloud is economically and technically impractical; local FFT and anomaly detection reduce this to kilobytes of daily summary data. Availability: cloud connectivity cannot be assumed in remote deployments; the local edge endpoint must be capable of autonomous operation during connectivity outages, storing state and continuing control.

Hardware platforms for edge endpoints include the Raspberry Pi 4 (sufficient for TensorFlow Lite inference, Node-RED orchestration, and InfluxDB local storage), NVIDIA Jetson Nano (adding hardware GPU acceleration for computer vision inference), and industrial IoT edge computers from vendors including Advantech, Moxa, and Siemens (hardened for DIN-rail mounting, extended temperature operation, and redundant power input).

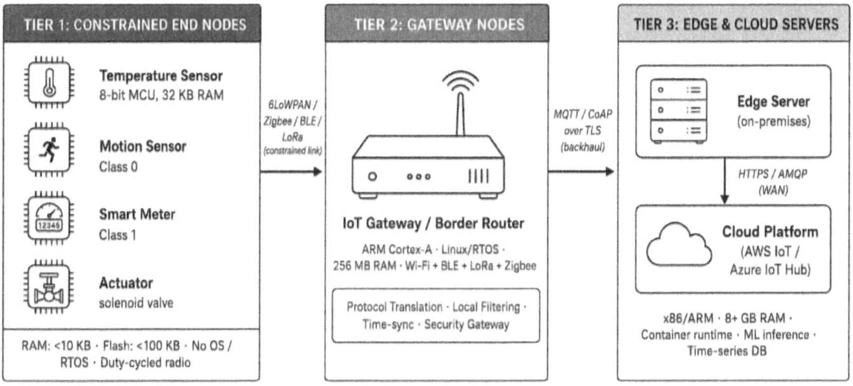

Figure 2.4: Three-Tier IoT Node Role Architecture: End nodes at the sensing/actuation layer, gateways at the aggregation and protocol-translation layer, and edge endpoints at the local intelligence layer.

2.6 Device Addressing and Identity

An IoT device must be uniquely addressable — reachable for command delivery, identifiable in telemetry streams, and distinguishable from all other devices in the same deployment and, for internet-connected devices, globally. Addressing and identity in IoT operate at multiple layers: link-layer addresses, network-layer IP addresses, application-layer identifiers, and cryptographic identities are distinct concepts that must each be managed correctly for a secure and scalable deployment.

2.6.1 Link-Layer Addressing: MAC and EUI-64

At the link layer, every network interface has a hardware address that uniquely identifies it within its local network segment. The IEEE 802 standard defines the Extended Unique Identifier (EUI) format for hardware addresses: EUI-48 (the familiar 48-bit MAC address used in Wi-Fi and Ethernet) and EUI-64 (64-bit, used natively in IEEE 802.15.4 and Bluetooth). EUI addresses are composed of a 24-bit Organisationally Unique Identifier (OUI), assigned by the IEEE Registration Authority to the device manufacturer, and a 24-bit or 40-bit extension identifier assigned by the manufacturer.

In IPv6 networks, EUI-64 addresses serve a dual purpose: as the link-layer address and as the basis for stateless address autoconfiguration (SLAAC). The 6LoWPAN adaptation layer can derive an IPv6 interface identifier directly from a device's EUI-64 address, embedding it as the low 64 bits of the IPv6 address and eliminating the need for DHCPv6 in many constrained deployments. For privacy reasons, RFC 8981 (Temporary Address Extensions for SLAAC) allows devices to periodically rotate their IPv6 interface identifier, though IoT devices typically prefer stable addresses for management purposes.

2.6.2 Application-Layer Identifiers

Above the network layer, IoT platforms assign application-layer identifiers that are independent of network addresses and persist across network changes. AWS IoT Core uses a Thing Name: a string that uniquely identifies a device within an AWS account and serves as the primary key for the Device Shadow, policy attachment, and telemetry routing. Azure IoT Hub uses a Device ID. LoRaWAN uses a 64-bit globally unique DevEUI (derived from or identical to the EUI-64) assigned at manufacture, plus a 32-bit DevAddr dynamically assigned at join.

The IETF CoRE (Constrained RESTful Environments) working group defines a URI-based naming scheme for IoT resources: a device is identified by its IPv6 address and port, and its individual data points (temperature reading, actuator state) are sub-resources identified by path — coap://[2001:db8::1]/sensors/temperature. This RESTful naming aligns IoT resource addressing with the broader internet architecture and enables generic discovery and access without proprietary APIs.

2.6.3 Cryptographic Identity: X.509 Certificates and Pre-Shared Keys

Network addresses identify where a device is; cryptographic identities establish who it is. In TLS-based IoT deployments, each device holds an X.509 certificate: a signed document binding a public key to a device identifier, issued by a certificate authority (CA) in the deployment's public-key infrastructure (PKI). During TLS handshake, the device presents its certificate; the server verifies the certificate chain back to a trusted root CA; both parties derive a shared session key. Mutual TLS (mTLS) extends this by requiring the server to also present a certificate verified by the client, preventing both eavesdropping and connection to rogue servers.

X.509 certificates introduce provisioning and lifecycle management overhead: each device requires a unique certificate generated at manufacture or first activation, and certificates have expiry dates requiring renewal. Constrained devices that cannot afford TLS use DTLS with pre-shared keys (PSK) as a lighter-weight alternative: the device and server share a secret key established during provisioning, used directly as the DTLS session key without certificate exchange. PSK eliminates PKI overhead at the cost of per-device key management and the security risk of key reuse across devices.

The IETF ACE (Authentication and Authorisation for Constrained Environments) framework provides a token-based authorisation model for IoT: a trusted authorisation server issues access tokens encoding what a client is permitted to do, and resource servers (IoT devices) validate tokens without contacting the authorisation server on every request. ACE separates authentication (handled by the AS) from resource-level enforcement (handled by the device), enabling fine-grained, revocable access control even on Class 1 constrained devices.

TECHNOLOGY SPOTLIGHT: *Tech Spotlight: Device Identity Provisioning at Scale*

Large IoT deployments face a practical challenge: provisioning unique cryptographic identities to millions of devices at manufacture time, without those identities being readable by an attacker who intercepts a device in the supply chain. The industry has converged on hardware security modules (HSMs) embedded at the chip level.

The Microchip ATECC608B (also found in Arduino MKR boards) is an ECC508/608-family cryptographic co-processor that generates and stores ECC P-256 private keys in tamper-resistant hardware: the private key never leaves the chip in plaintext. The chip performs ECDH key agreement and ECDSA signing on behalf of the host MCU, enabling TLS and code signature verification on devices too constrained for software cryptography. Amazon's FreeRTOS and AWS IoT Device Defender both have native ATECC608 integration.

For cellular IoT, the GSMA eSIM/eUICC (Embedded SIM, Embedded Universal Integrated Circuit Card) standard allows cellular operator profiles to be provisioned over the air post-manufacture, eliminating the logistics of pre-installing physical SIM cards in devices destined for international markets. eUICC is mandatory for Cat-M and NB-IoT deployments at scale, and the GSMA SGP.02 (M2M) and SGP.22 (consumer) specifications define the remote SIM provisioning protocol stack.

2.7 Energy Management in Constrained IoT Devices

Energy management is the defining engineering discipline of constrained IoT hardware. Unlike smartphones or laptops, where the user can recharge daily, many IoT end nodes are installed in locations where battery replacement is expensive or impractical: inside a wall, on a bridge cable, in an agricultural field, or within a sealed industrial enclosure with a five-year operational requirement. The energy budget of such a device is fixed at deployment;

every design decision (sampling rate, transmission frequency, processor clock speed, peripheral power-down discipline) directly determines whether the device meets its operational lifetime.

This section examines the principal sources of energy consumption in IoT nodes, the sleep-mode architecture of modern microcontrollers, radio power management, energy harvesting as a supplement or alternative to primary batteries, and the Time-Slotted Channel Hopping (TSCH) MAC protocol as a network-level energy management mechanism.

2.7.1 Sources of Energy Consumption

The energy budget of an IoT end node is dominated by three consumers: the radio transceiver, the microcontroller, and the sensors and peripherals. Of these, the radio is typically the largest single consumer by a wide margin, transmitting at maximum power consumes 100-400 mA on a BLE or Wi-Fi radio versus 1-20 mA for an active microcontroller and under 1 mA for most sensors. This asymmetry explains why IoT energy management is primarily radio energy management: minimising transmission frequency, shortening transmission duration, and reducing output power to the minimum required for reliable link margin.

A useful decomposition divides node energy consumption into four operating states: active (processor and radio fully on, sensing and transmitting), processing-only (radio off, processor performing local computation or data pre-processing), sleep (processor in low-power mode, peripherals off, only timer running), and system-off (minimum possible consumption, RAM contents lost, wake only by GPIO or RTC). The fraction of time spent in each state, multiplied by the current draw of that state, yields average current consumption: the key figure for battery life estimation.

As a worked example, consider an nRF52840-based temperature sensor reporting every 10 minutes over BLE. The node wakes every 600 seconds: it acquires a temperature reading over I2C (2 ms at 0.5 mA), formats a BLE advertisement packet (1 ms at 3 mA), transmits (5 ms at 7.7 mA), and returns to deep sleep (consumes 1.5 microamperes). The total charge per cycle is approximately 0.002 s x 0.5 mA + 0.001 s x 3 mA + 0.005 s x 7.7 mA + 599.992 s x 0.0015 mA = 0.001 + 0.003 + 0.039 + 0.900 = 0.943 milliamp-seconds (approximately 0.26 microamp-hours). Average current = total charge per cycle / cycle period = 0.943 mA·s / 600 s = 1.57 microamperes. A 220 mAh coin cell (CR2032) at 70% usable capacity provides 154 mAh. Theoretical battery life = 154,000 μAh / 1.57 μA = 98,089 hours ≈ 11.2 years, in practice limited to 5-10 years by the CR2032's self-discharge rate of approximately 1% per year, confirming that self-discharge, not active current draw, is the life-limiting factor once radio duty cycling is correctly implemented.

Practical Note: *Energy Budget Planning Tools. The Nordic Power Profiler Kit II (PPKII) is the standard tool for measuring real IoT node current consumption at 100 nA resolution — essential for validating energy budget calculations against actual hardware. Nordic's online Energy Estimator (available at infocenter.nordicsemi.com) allows duty cycle and protocol parameter modelling for nRF52 series devices. For ESP32 deployments, the INA219 current sensor module (I2C, 0.8 mA resolution) provides in-circuit current measurement at minimal cost. Energy budget spreadsheets should always validate theoretical calculations against measured hardware values before committing to a battery size or harvesting system design.*

2.7.2 Microcontroller Sleep Modes

Modern microcontrollers implement a hierarchy of power reduction states, trading off recovery latency against current consumption. The ARM Cortex-M architecture defines Sleep (only the CPU is halted; peripherals continue), Deep Sleep (CPU and most peripherals halted; SRAM retained; wake from RTC or GPIO), and implementation-defined vendor states. Nordic's nRF52840 adds System Off (1.5 microamperes; only the RTC and one GPIO retained for wake-up), which is the lowest power state achievable while retaining wake capability. STM32L-series microcontrollers (used in the chapter-opening cold-chain node) are specifically optimised for ultra-low-power operation, offering Stop 2 mode at 1.1 microamperes with full SRAM retention and a 5 microsecond wake-up time.

Effective use of sleep modes requires discipline in peripheral management: floating GPIO inputs draw leakage current; active pull-up resistors on I2C buses waste current continuously; sensors with on-board regulators must be power-gated via a load switch rather than simply de-asserted. A common oversight in IoT hardware design is failing to power-gate high-power peripherals during sleep, leaving a 1 mA sensor supply continuously enabled and consuming more than the MCU itself. Production IoT hardware reviews routinely identify power-gating gaps as the primary cause of battery life underperformance relative to design estimates.

2.7.3 Radio Power Management and Duty Cycling

Radio duty cycling: the practice of keeping the transceiver powered only during scheduled transmission and reception windows is the primary mechanism for achieving multi-year battery life in IoT end nodes. LoRaWAN Class A devices exemplify maximum duty cycling: a node transmits an uplink message, then opens two brief receive windows (1 and 2 seconds later) for any pending downlink, and then the radio is completely powered off until the next scheduled uplink. Between messages, the transceiver draws zero current. The network server must queue any downlink messages and deliver them only during these brief windows.

BLE duty cycling uses a different mechanism: the BLE connection event model allows the central (typically the gateway) and peripheral (the end node) to negotiate a connection interval: the time between successive communication slots. At a 1-second connection interval, the peripheral's radio is active for approximately 2-3 ms per second, consuming approximately 0.004 mAh per hour versus 4-6 mAh for continuous operation. BLE 5.0 introduced extended advertising with configurable interval from 20 ms to 10,485 seconds, enabling ultra-low-duty-cycle beacon applications.

IEEE 802.15.4e Time-Slotted Channel Hopping (TSCH) provides a deterministic MAC layer that schedules all transmissions and receptions in a repeating slot frame. Nodes sleep between their assigned slots; the slot frame is coordinated across the network, so each node knows exactly when to wake, transmit or receive, and return to sleep. TSCH simultaneously achieves very low duty cycle, deterministic latency bounded by the slot frame length, and frequency diversity (each successive slot uses a different channel from a hopping sequence) that provides resilience to narrowband interference. 6TiSCH (IPv6 over TSCH, RFC 9030) layers IPv6 routing over TSCH, enabling scheduled industrial mesh networks that combine 802.15.4e's deterministic radio behaviour with standard IP protocols.

2.7.4 Energy Harvesting

Energy harvesting, generating electrical power from ambient sources in the deployment environment, which can supplement or replace primary batteries in IoT nodes, extending operational lifetime indefinitely in energy-rich environments. The four principal harvesting sources for IoT are solar photovoltaic, thermoelectric (heat flow), piezoelectric (vibration or pressure), and RF energy harvesting.

Solar harvesting is the most energy-dense and widely deployed: a 6 V, 2 W crystalline silicon panel (approximately 10 x 15 cm) can generate 400–800 mWh per day under temperate outdoor conditions, sufficient to sustain an ESP32 node reporting every 5 minutes with substantial margin for cloudy days. Indoor solar cells (amorphous silicon, GaAs) are optimised for the lower illuminance of office lighting (100-1,000 lux versus 50,000-100,000 lux outdoors) and can sustain sub-100-microampere loads from fluorescent or LED lighting indefinitely.

Thermoelectric harvesting uses Peltier devices in reverse: when a temperature gradient exists across the module, the Seebeck effect generates a voltage proportional to the temperature difference. Industrial pipes carrying hot fluids provide gradients of 20-80 degrees Celsius, yielding microwatts to milliwatts per square centimetre, sufficient for autonomous vibration and temperature monitors on pipe infrastructure without any wiring. The EnOcean STM 312 temperature sensor module, for example, harvests thermal energy from HVAC pipes and transmits wirelessly without any battery.

Piezoelectric harvesting converts mechanical vibration (from machinery, vehicle traffic, or human motion) to electricity. Harvesters are typically tuned cantilever beams that resonate at the dominant vibration frequency of their mounting structure. Available power is highly variable (1-1,000 microwatts) and application-specific. Kinetic energy harvesters in wearables (using electromagnetic induction from body motion) can sustain step-counting and health-monitoring functionality without a battery in active users.

RF energy harvesting recovers power from ambient radio-frequency signals (cellular, Wi-Fi, broadcast television). Harvestable power densities are very low (typically 0.1-10 microwatts at 1-10 metres from an 802.11 access point), limiting practical applications to ultra-low-power sensing with infrequent transmission. Ambient Backscatter (Liu et al., 2013, University of Washington) demonstrated communication by modulating reflections of existing Wi-Fi signals, enabling battery-free sensor nodes at extremely low data rates: a research direction commercialised by companies including Wiliot (Bluetooth-backscatter IoT stickers) and Everactive (perpetually powered industrial sensors).

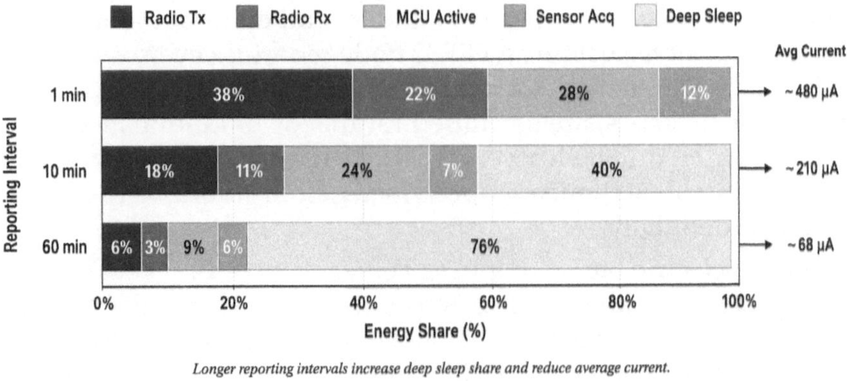

Figure 2.5: IoT Node Energy Budget Breakdown: Relative contribution of radio transmission, microcontroller active state, sensor acquisition, and deep sleep to total node energy consumption over a duty-cycled reporting interval.

2.7.5 Sleep Mode and Energy Comparison Across Platforms

Table 2.3 compares sleep-mode current consumption, active current, and wake-up latency across the five hardware platforms surveyed in Section 2.4. These figures, drawn from vendor datasheets, are the primary inputs to battery-life calculations for constrained IoT node designs.

Platform	Active Current	Sleep Current	Wake Latency	Battery Suitability	Notes
Arduino MKR WAN 1310 (SAMD21)	~3 mA	~100 uA (sleep)	~4 ms	Moderate	Good for LoRaWAN; MCU sleep well managed; radio power-gated separately
ESP32-WROOM-32	~180 mA (Wi-Fi Tx) ~30 mA (idle)	~10 uA (deep sleep)	~1.5 ms	Moderate-High	Deep sleep effective; Wi-Fi startup time adds latency; ULP co-proc available
Raspberry Pi 4	~700 mA (active)	~1.2 W (idle) No true deep sleep	N/A	High	No battery-suitable sleep; designed for mains power; not suitable for constrained nodes
Raspberry Pi Zero 2 W	~130 mA (active)	~80 mA (idle) No deep sleep	N/A	Medium	Lower than Pi 4 but still mains-class; suitable for gateway, not end nodes
BeagleBone Black	~500 mA (active)	~80 mA (standby)	~500 ms	High	Industrial Linux platform; no meaningful sleep for IoT end-node use

Nordic nRF52840	~8 mA (BLE Tx) ~4.5 mA (active)	~1.5 uA (system off)	~0.5 ms	Very Low	Best-in-class ultra-low power; designed for coin-cell / energy harvesting operation

Table 2.3: Sleep Mode and Power Consumption Comparison Across IoT Platforms

Professional Checklist: IoT Hardware Selection

Before selecting IoT hardware, confirm the following:

- *The sensor or actuator matches the required measurement range, accuracy, response time, and environmental conditions.*
- *The microcontroller, single-board computer, or module has sufficient processing, memory, interface, and expansion capability.*
- *The selected communication interface supports the required range, power profile, and deployment environment.*
- *The device can operate reliably under expected temperature, humidity, vibration, dust, and power conditions.*
- *Energy budget, sleep modes, battery capacity, and maintenance interval are suitable for the intended deployment.*
- *Device identity, firmware update, and security support are available from the beginning of the design.*

2.8 Chapter Summary

This chapter has examined the hardware foundations of IoT systems: the physical devices that sense the world, act upon it, process data locally, and communicate across networks. The chapter opened with the Invisible Custodian scenario: a pharmaceutical cold-chain monitoring unit travelling from Hyderabad to Muscat, integrating an RTD temperature sensor, MEMS accelerometer, solenoid valve, Peltier cooler, STM32L microcontroller, and LoRa radio into a closed-loop autonomous system. Every hardware concept developed in the chapter maps directly to a component or design decision in that unit.

Section 2.1 introduced transducers as the conceptual category encompassing both sensors and actuators: devices that convert energy from one form to another at the boundary between the physical and digital worlds. The distinction between active transducers (generating their own output from the measurand) and passive transducers (requiring an external excitation signal) was established, along with the signal-conditioning chain (amplification, filtering, and analogue-to-digital conversion) that transforms a raw transducer output into a digitally processable value.

Section 2.2 surveyed the principal sensor technologies deployed in IoT across six physical measurement domains: temperature (thermocouples, RTDs, thermistors, digital sensors), humidity (capacitive and resistive), motion (PIR and MEMS accelerometers), light (photometric and ranging), gas and air quality (MQ-series electrochemical, NDIR CO2, optical PM2.5), and proximity (ultrasonic, IR, capacitive, Hall effect). Table 2.1 provided a structured comparison of twelve representative sensors across operating principle, accuracy, range, interface, power, and typical IoT use case. The section established the four-criterion sensor selection framework: measurement accuracy, operating range, power consumption, and interface compatibility.

Section 2.3 examined actuator categories and the control strategies that connect microcontrollers to physical effectors. Electromechanical actuators, relays and solenoid valves, provide galvanic isolation and reliable on/off control but are limited by switching speed and mechanical lifetime. Electric motors (DC, servo, stepper) enable rotational motion with PWM-controlled speed and, for servo and stepper types, precise position control. Thermal actuators, resistive heaters and Peltier TECs, provide bidirectional temperature control critical for pharmaceutical cold-chain applications. Piezoelectric and electroacoustic actuators address precision micro-motion and audio output requirements. The section concluded with a treatment of pulse-width modulation as the universal power-delivery mechanism and PID control as the standard feedback-loop algorithm for closed-loop regulation of any continuous physical variable.

Section 2.4 surveyed five representative hardware platforms across the IoT computing spectrum. The Arduino MKR WAN 1310 integrates a SAMD21 Cortex-M0+ processor with LoRaWAN and cryptographic hardware in a production-viable LoRaWAN end-node form factor. The ESP32 delivers dual-core 240 MHz processing with integrated Wi-Fi and BLE at under USD 5, enabling a generation of low-cost connected products. The Raspberry Pi 4 provides full Linux with gigabytes of RAM for IoT gateway and edge-intelligence roles. The BeagleBone Black adds dual PRU real-time co-processors for deterministic industrial control. The Nordic nRF52840 achieves 1.5 microampere system-off current with multi-protocol radio support (BLE 5.3 and IEEE 802.15.4) for ultra-low-power end nodes.

Table 2.2 provided a structured comparison across nine specification dimensions, and Section 2.4.6 articulated the constraint-hierarchy selection logic: power budget first, real-time requirements second, connectivity protocol third, software complexity fourth.

Section 2.5 defined the three IoT node roles in system architecture. End nodes are constrained devices that interface with the physical world; their resource limitations are formalised by RFC 7228's Class 0, Class 1, Class 2 taxonomy. Gateways bridge constrained end nodes to the internet through protocol translation, local aggregation, and security termination. Edge endpoints extend gateway capability with local intelligence, running ML inference, executing control algorithms, and maintaining autonomous operation during cloud connectivity outages. The section illustrated these roles with the LoRaWAN network architecture as a canonical gateway design pattern.

Section 2.6 addressed device addressing and identity across three layers. Link-layer addressing uses IEEE EUI-48 and EUI-64 identifiers, with EUI-64 serving as the basis for IPv6 stateless address autoconfiguration in 6LoWPAN networks. Application-layer identifiers (AWS Thing Names, LoRaWAN DevEUI, CoAP URIs) provide persistent naming independent of network topology. Cryptographic identity uses X.509 certificates in TLS-capable deployments and pre-shared keys for more constrained nodes, with the IETF ACE framework providing token-based authorisation for fine-grained access control on Class 1 devices. The Tech Spotlight examined hardware security modules (ATECC608B) and eUICC as the production mechanisms for tamper-resistant key storage and remote SIM provisioning at scale.

Section 2.7 treated energy management as the defining discipline of constrained IoT hardware. The section established that radio transmission dominates energy consumption and that duty cycling, minimising the fraction of time the radio is powered, is the primary lever for multi-year battery life.

A worked numerical example demonstrated that an nRF52840 temperature sensor reporting every 10 minutes achieves an average current of 1.57 microamperes, confirming that battery self-discharge, not capacity, governs practical lifetime. Sleep mode architectures, peripheral power-gating discipline, BLE connection intervals, LoRaWAN Class A duty cycling, and IEEE 802.15.4e TSCH were examined as the implementation mechanisms of duty cycling at device and network levels. Energy harvesting from solar, thermoelectric, piezoelectric, and RF ambient sources was presented as a route to battery-free or battery-supplemented operation, with the Wiliot and Everactive commercial deployments as contemporary examples.

The cold-chain unit that opened the chapter now reads differently: the RTD is a Class A 4-wire PT100 (Section 2.2, temperature sensors); the solenoid valve is normally closed, failing safe on power loss (Section 2.3, solenoid actuators); the Peltier TEC is driven by a PID controller running on the STM32L main core (Section 2.3, PID control); the STM32L is a Class 2 constrained node using Stop 2 sleep mode at 1.1 microamperes between measurements (Section 2.7, sleep modes); the LoRa radio is duty-cycled to the legally mandated 1% channel occupancy limit (Section 2.7, radio power management). The hardware architecture of a production IoT device is a system of constrained choices, each rooted in the physical principles and engineering trade-offs this chapter has examined.

Part II

Architecture, Protocols, and Design

Chapter 3

IoT Architecture

Evolution, Models, and Reference Frameworks

Chapter 3 presents the architectural foundation of IoT systems by explaining how connected devices, networks, platforms, services, and applications are organised into scalable system structures. It traces the transition from traditional machine-to-machine communication to modern IoT architectures, highlighting the shift from isolated vertical solutions to interoperable, platform-based ecosystems. The chapter explains the core components of an IoT system, including devices, gateways, edge nodes, cloud platforms, data services, applications, and operational stakeholders. It also examines major layered architecture models, functional blocks, communication models, and recognised reference architectures used to design and evaluate IoT deployments. In addition, the chapter discusses the principles required for designing IoT systems at scale, including modularity, interoperability, distributed processing, resilience, security, and lifecycle manageability. Overall, this chapter provides the architectural framework needed to understand how IoT systems are structured, integrated, expanded, and governed across real-world deployment environments.

Architecture is the skeleton upon which every engineering discipline builds its structures. In the context of the Internet of Things, architecture is not merely a blueprint for connecting devices; it is the intellectual framework that determines how billions of physical objects communicate, share data, operate autonomously, and deliver value to people and organisations. This chapter examines the architectural foundations of IoT from first principles, tracing the evolutionary journey from rudimentary machine-to-machine communication systems to the sophisticated, multi-layered platforms that underpin modern smart environments.

The chapter begins by establishing what distinguishes IoT from its predecessor technologies, particularly M2M systems, before introducing the core components found in any IoT deployment. It then explores layered architecture models, the functional block approach, and the four canonical communication paradigms that govern how IoT nodes exchange information. The chapter concludes with an analysis of the major international reference architecture models that standards bodies and industry consortia have produced, providing practitioners and researchers with a structured vocabulary for architectural decision-making.

This chapter provides the structural vocabulary and analytical frameworks for principled IoT system design, examines the trade-offs that architects face at every tier, and situates those design decisions within the context of the international standardisation efforts that are progressively bringing coherence to a historically fragmented landscape.

3.1 From M2M to IoT: The Evolution of Connected Systems

3.1.1 The M2M Era

Long before the term Internet of Things entered the engineering lexicon, industries were deploying networks of communicating machines. Machine-to-machine communication emerged in the 1970s and 1980s through SCADA (Supervisory Control and Data Acquisition) systems, which enabled remote monitoring of industrial equipment over dedicated serial links. By the 1990s, cellular networks offered a new transport channel, allowing vending machines, utility meters, and vehicle fleets to transmit telemetry data to centralised servers without human intervention.

M2M architectures were characterised by a highly vertical orientation. Each application domain deployed its own proprietary sensing hardware, its own network infrastructure, and its own back-end software. A gas utility company, for example, might install dedicated GPRS (General Packet Radio Service) modems in every meter across its network, with those modems reporting exclusively to a billing server operated by the utility. The system worked reliably for its intended purpose, but it was architecturally closed: data could not be shared across applications, hardware could not be repurposed, and scaling required proportionally increasing every element of the stack.

DEFINITION: *Machine-to-Machine (M2M) Communication*

A direct, automated data exchange between two or more devices using wired or wireless communications, typically over a dedicated, proprietary network, without human interaction. M2M systems are characterised by a closed, vertical architecture designed for a single application domain. Each deployment operates as a self-contained silo with no capacity for cross-application data sharing.

Source: ITU-T Y.2060 (2012); ETSI TS 102 690 (2011)

3.1.2 The Transition to IoT

The paradigm shift from M2M to IoT was driven by several converging forces: the commoditisation of microprocessors and sensors, the widespread rollout of broadband and cellular data networks, the maturation of cloud computing platforms, and the emergence of open communication standards such as MQTT (Message Queuing Telemetry Transport), CoAP (Constrained Application Protocol), and RESTful APIs (Application Programming Interfaces). Where M2M systems were engineered for a single, well-defined task, IoT platforms were designed from the outset to be horizontal, enabling the same underlying infrastructure to support dozens of application domains simultaneously.

The shift was not merely technical. IoT introduced an expectation that data generated by physical devices would flow freely across organisational and application boundaries, be processed and enriched in the cloud, and generate actionable intelligence through analytics and machine learning. A temperature sensor in a smart building, for instance, might simultaneously serve an HVAC control system, an energy management application, and a predictive maintenance platform, all without any modification to the sensor hardware or its communication protocol.

This cross-domain data reuse is architecturally impossible in a traditional M2M deployment and represents one of the defining value propositions of the IoT paradigm.

Key Insight: *The Horizontal Platform Advantage. The defining architectural shift from M2M to IoT is from vertical, single-purpose systems to horizontal platforms. A vertical M2M system routes every sensor reading to one dedicated application. A horizontal IoT platform allows the same data stream to simultaneously serve HVAC control, energy management, predictive maintenance, and occupancy analytics — multiplying the return on a single sensing investment across every application that can extract value from it. This cross-domain reuse is architecturally impossible without an open, standards-based platform layer.*

The table below captures the essential differences between M2M and IoT across eight architectural and operational dimensions. These differences should be understood not as an indictment of M2M but as an acknowledgement of the different problems each paradigm was designed to solve.

Table 3.1 Comparative characteristics of M2M and IoT architectures

Characteristic	M2M	IoT
Architecture orientation	Vertical (closed silo)	Horizontal (open platform)
Network type	Proprietary / dedicated	internet-based / heterogeneous
Device addressability	Often not IP-addressed	IP-addressed (IPv6 preferred)
Data sharing	Single application only	Multi-application, cross-domain
Scalability	Limited, cost-proportional	Elastic, cloud-native
Standards	Vendor-specific, proprietary	Open (MQTT, CoAP, HTTP, AMQP)
Intelligence location	Centralised server	Distributed: device, edge, cloud
Typical domain	Utilities, fleet, industrial	Smart cities, health, agriculture, industry

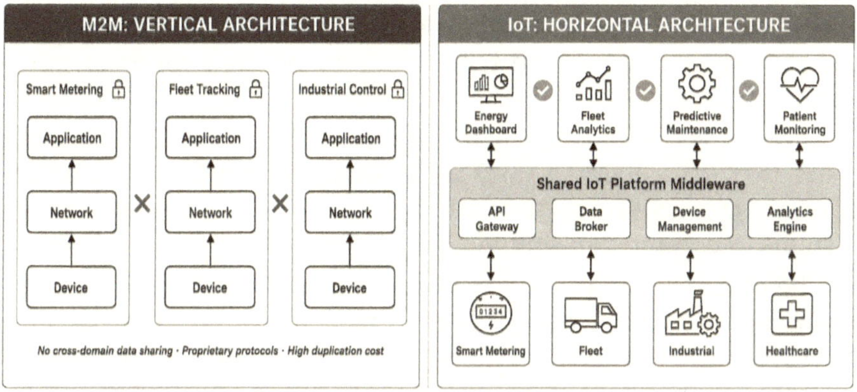

Figure 3.1 Structural comparison of the closed, vertical M2M model and the open, horizontal IoT ecosystem

3.2 Defining the IoT Ecosystem

DEFINITION: *Internet of Things (IoT)*

A global infrastructure for the information society, enabling advanced services by interconnecting physical and virtual things based on existing and evolving interoperable information and communication technologies. Things are objects of the physical world (physical things) or the information world (virtual things), which are capable of being identified and may be integrated into communication networks.

Source: ITU-T Recommendation Y.2060, Overview of the Internet of Things (2012)

The IoT ecosystem is best understood not as a single technology but as an interconnected web of technologies, business actors, and regulatory frameworks. At its most tangible level, the ecosystem encompasses the physical devices that sense or actuate; the network infrastructure that moves data between devices, edge nodes, and cloud platforms; the platform services that store, process, and expose data through APIs; and the application layer where end-user value is created. Each tier of this ecosystem has its own supply chain, its own standards landscape, and its own technical maturity curve.

A useful lens for understanding the IoT ecosystem is the value chain model, which identifies the discrete roles that different actors play in transforming raw sensor data into a service that an end user is willing to pay for. Device manufacturers design and fabricate hardware, embedding firmware that enables communication. Connectivity providers operate the radio access networks and wired backbones over which data travels. Platform operators maintain the cloud services that aggregate and process data. Application developers build the software that presents insights to users. Integrators and system engineers bind these components into coherent, functioning deployments.

Each actor in the value chain captures a portion of the economic value that IoT generates, and understanding this structure is important for practitioners who must procure, design, and govern IoT systems in commercial settings.

The global IoT market illustrates the scale of this ecosystem. Industry analysts consistently project tens of billions of connected devices in active deployment by the late 2020s, with economic value creation spanning manufacturing, agriculture, healthcare, transportation, energy, and public services. The architectural decisions made at the platform and standards level today will shape this ecosystem for decades, which is why reference architecture work by bodies such as oneM2M, ITU-T (ITU Telecommunication Standardization Sector), and the W3C (World Wide Web Consortium) carries implications far beyond the technical community.

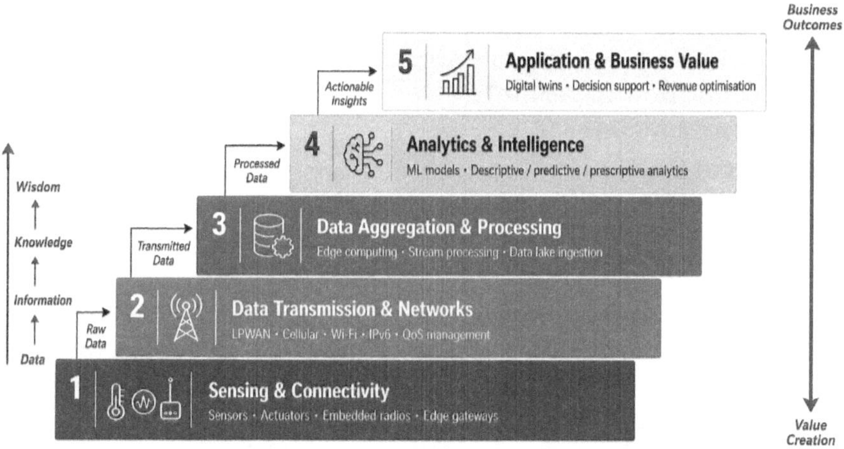

Figure 3.2: The IoT Value Chain: From Physical Sensing to User-Facing Applications

3.3 Core Components of an IoT System

Every IoT deployment, regardless of its application domain or scale, can be decomposed into a standard set of functional components. Understanding these components and the roles they play is a prerequisite for principled architectural design. The four primary tiers are the sensing and actuation layer, the connectivity layer, the processing and analytics layer, and the application layer.

3.3.1 Sensing and Actuation

The sensing and actuation layer is the physical frontier of the IoT system. Sensors convert physical phenomena such as temperature, pressure, light intensity, humidity, sound, or motion into electrical signals, while actuators convert electrical signals back into physical actions, such as opening a valve, rotating a motor, or switching a relay. Sensors are characterised by parameters including measurement range, resolution, accuracy, drift, response time, and power consumption. These parameters directly influence the design of the communication protocol and the cloud processing architecture above them.

Modern IoT nodes increasingly integrate sensing, local processing, and communication into a single hardware unit. Microcontrollers such as the ARM Cortex-M series, combined with radio transceivers and MEMS (Micro-Electro-Mechanical Systems) sensors, enable self-contained IoT devices with power budgets measured in microwatts. This integration has dramatically reduced the cost and size of IoT endpoints, enabling deployment densities that were not economically feasible with earlier M2M hardware. A contemporary commercial temperature and humidity sensor on a coin cell battery can transmit hourly readings over LoRaWAN for more than five years without maintenance.

- Passive sensors (temperature, pressure, light) detect physical phenomena without influencing the environment and generally require very low power, making them ideal for battery-operated IoT nodes.
- Active sensors (radar, ultrasound, active infrared) emit a signal and detect the reflection. They consume more power but are capable of distance measurement, object detection, and motion tracking.
- Actuators include solenoid valves, relay switches, servo motors, heating elements, and LED drivers. In closed-loop IoT systems, actuator commands are generated automatically by the analytics layer in response to sensor readings.

3.3.2 Connectivity

The connectivity layer is responsible for transporting data from IoT devices to the processing infrastructure, and for delivering commands in the reverse direction. No single wireless technology satisfies all IoT use cases. The selection of a connectivity technology is a multi-dimensional optimisation problem involving range, data rate, power consumption, spectral cost, and deployment complexity.

Short-range technologies, including IEEE 802.15.4 (Zigbee, Thread), Bluetooth Low Energy, and Z-Wave, are well suited to building automation and personal area networks where nodes are within tens of metres of a gateway. Wi-Fi (IEEE 802.11) offers high throughput for applications that can tolerate higher power budgets, such as IP cameras and smart appliances.

Long-range, low-power technologies including LoRaWAN, Sigfox, and NB-IoT (Narrowband IoT) serve applications requiring coverage over kilometres with battery lifetimes measured in years, at the expense of very low data rates. The ongoing rollout of 5G networks, particularly the massive machine-type communication (mMTC) mode, promises to enable ultra-dense IoT deployments with per-device connectivity costs that approach those of LPWAN technologies while offering substantially higher data rates.

3.3.3 Processing and Analytics

Raw sensor data seldom delivers direct value. The processing and analytics layer transforms raw measurements into actionable information through a pipeline that typically includes data ingestion, filtering and normalisation, storage, real-time stream processing, batch analytics, and machine learning inference. This processing may occur at the cloud, at intermediate edge nodes, or on the device itself, depending on latency requirements, bandwidth constraints, and the computational complexity of the algorithms involved.

Edge processing has become increasingly important as IoT deployments have scaled. Transmitting raw data from millions of sensors to a central cloud incurs substantial bandwidth costs and introduces latency that is unacceptable for time-critical control applications. Edge nodes, which may be industrial PCs, embedded Linux gateways, or purpose-built edge AI accelerators, perform pre-processing close to the data source, reducing the volume of data transmitted to the cloud while enabling low-latency local decision-making.

NVIDIA Jetson, Intel Neural Compute Stick, and Google Coral are representative commercial edge AI platforms that bring neural network inference to the device tier.

3.3.4 Application Layer

The application layer is where the sensor data, enriched and contextualised by the processing layer, is consumed by human operators or software systems to drive decisions and actions. Applications range from simple dashboards displaying current sensor readings to sophisticated AI-driven optimisation engines that autonomously manage complex physical systems. The application layer also encompasses the APIs and data exchange mechanisms through which IoT platforms expose their data to third-party developers, enabling the construction of ecosystems of complementary applications around a core platform.

Table 3.2 Key characteristics of major IoT connectivity technologies

Technology	Range	Data Rate	Power Profile	Typical Use Case
Zigbee / Thread	10-100 m	250 kbps	Very low	Building automation, smart home mesh
Bluetooth LE 5.x	10-400 m	1-2 Mbps	Very low	Wearables, asset tracking, BLE beacons

Z-Wave	30 m	100 kbps	Low	Home automation, security systems
Wi-Fi 6 (802.11ax)	50-150 m	600 Mbps+	High	IP cameras, smart appliances, gateways
LoRaWAN	2-15 km	0.3-50 kbps	Ultra low	Agriculture, smart metering, tracking
NB-IoT (3GPP)	1-10 km	200 kbps	Low	Smart city sensors, utility meters
5G NR (mMTC)	1-5 km	Variable	Low to medium	Industrial IoT, connected vehicles

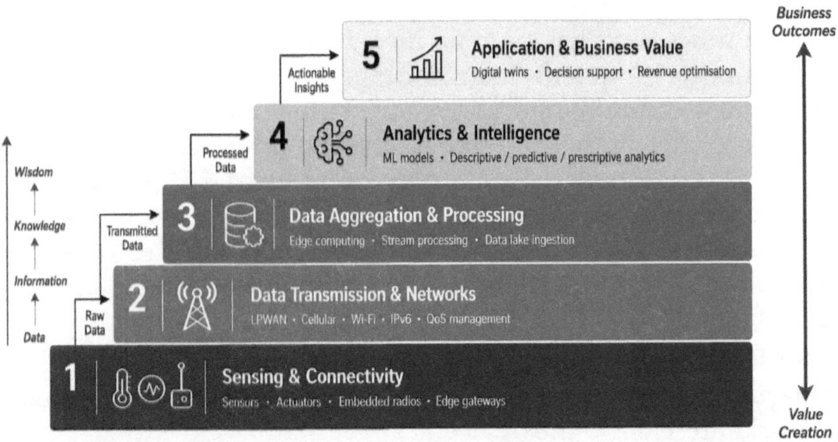

Figure 3.3 The four-tier IoT component architecture from physical sensing through connectivity and processing to end-user application

Regional Example: Smart Metering in Oman. Oman's water and electricity utilities have deployed LoRaWAN-based smart metering networks in Muscat and Sohar, connecting residential and industrial meters to a central data platform. End-node meters report consumption data at 15-minute intervals over LoRaWAN; gateways mounted on utility poles perform protocol translation and local aggregation; the cloud platform stores time-series data and exposes it through REST APIs to billing, demand-forecasting, and leak-detection applications. This deployment illustrates the horizontal IoT architecture in practice: a single sensor investment serves three distinct application domains simultaneously. The oneM2M Common Service Layer provides the standardised abstraction that enables cross-domain data sharing without requiring any modification to the meter firmware, precisely the architectural property that distinguishes the IoT platform model from the closed M2M metering systems it replaced.

3.4 IoT Layered Architecture Models

Standardising the architecture of IoT systems has been a persistent challenge for the research and engineering community. Unlike the OSI model, which achieved broad consensus for computer networking, IoT has given rise to several competing layered architecture models, each reflecting the priorities and perspectives of its authors. Three models have attracted sustained attention in the literature: the three-layer model, the five-layer model, and the seven-layer industrial model.

3.4.1 The Three-Layer Model

The three-layer model is the most widely cited introductory framework for IoT architecture. It organises system functionality into three tiers: the Perception Layer, the Network Layer, and the Application Layer. The Perception Layer encompasses all physical sensing and actuation functionality. The Network Layer handles connectivity, routing, and data transmission between the perception layer and the application infrastructure. The Application Layer delivers domain-specific services to users.

The appeal of the three-layer model lies in its simplicity and its intuitive alignment with the physical structure of IoT deployments. It maps naturally onto the hardware, communication, and software concerns that practitioners encounter, and it provides an accessible entry point for newcomers to the field. However, practitioners have found it insufficient for detailed architectural design work. It provides no guidance on where processing and analytics functionality should reside, nor does it account for the emerging role of edge computing nodes that sit between the device layer and the cloud.

DEFINITION: *Three-Layer IoT Architecture*

A foundational IoT architectural model comprising three tiers: (1) Perception Layer, responsible for sensing physical phenomena and actuating physical processes; (2) Network Layer, responsible for transmitting data between the perception layer and processing infrastructure; and (3) Application Layer, responsible for delivering domain-specific services and user interfaces. This model provides a high-level conceptual overview but does not address middleware, edge computing, or business integration concerns.

Source: Khan et al. (2012); Qin et al. (2016)

3.4.2 The Five-Layer Model

The five-layer model extends the three-layer framework by introducing two additional tiers: the Processing Layer and the Business Layer. The Processing Layer, also called the middleware layer, is responsible for storing, analysing, and processing large volumes of data arriving from the network layer. It encompasses cloud databases, stream processing engines, and middleware services such as message brokers. The Business Layer sits above the application layer and provides enterprise-level governance, business process integration, and service lifecycle management.

The five-layer model is better suited to enterprise IoT deployments where integration with existing IT systems, regulatory compliance, and business process automation are first-class concerns. It explicitly acknowledges that IoT platforms are not standalone systems but components of a broader enterprise architecture that must interoperate with ERP (Enterprise Resource Planning), CRM (Customer Relationship Management), and asset management systems through well-defined integration interfaces.

3.4.3 The Seven-Layer Industrial IoT Model

The Cisco / IoT World Forum Reference Model (2014) provides a seven-layer decomposition of industrial IoT deployments, spanning real-time control, operational technology integration, and enterprise system connectivity requirements. The seven layers are: Physical Devices and Controllers; Connectivity; Edge Computing; Data Accumulation; Data Abstraction; Application; and Collaboration and Processes.

The seven-layer model is particularly well suited to Industry 4.0 scenarios, where IoT infrastructure must bridge the historically separate worlds of operational technology (OT), which manages physical processes, and information technology (IT), which manages business data and enterprise systems. The Data Abstraction layer, which normalises data from diverse source systems into a common representation, is the key architectural innovation of this model and directly addresses the semantic interoperability challenge.

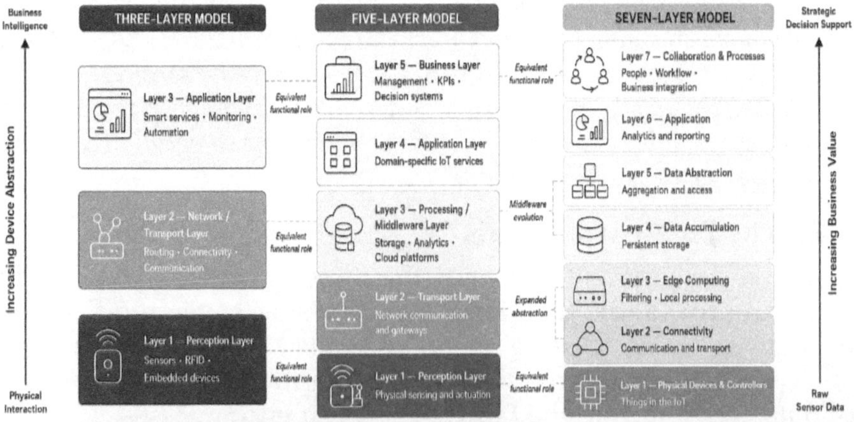

Figure 3.4 Side-by-side alignment of the principal IoT layered architecture models with functional correspondence shown by dashed lines

Table 3.3 *Comparison of IoT layered architecture models across key design dimensions*

Dimension	**Three-Layer**	**Five-Layer**	**Seven-Layer (IIC)**
Number of tiers	3	5	7
Edge computing	Not addressed	Not explicit	Dedicated tier
Middleware / processing	Implicit in App Layer	Explicit Processing Layer	Data Accumulation + Abstraction
Business integration	Absent	Business Layer	Collaboration and Processes
Primary audience	Academic introduction	Enterprise IoT	Industrial IoT (IIoT)

3.5 IoT Functional Blocks

Alongside layered models, a complementary approach to IoT architecture decomposes system functionality into a set of horizontal functional blocks rather than vertical layers. The functional block model, systematised by Srinivasa Rao, Vyas, and colleagues (2018) building on the foundational work of Gubbi et al. (2013), identifies seven canonical blocks that together constitute a complete IoT platform. Each block encapsulates a distinct capability and communicates with the others through well-defined interfaces, making the model particularly useful for platform evaluation and gap analysis.

1. Device: The Device block encompasses all physical hardware: sensors, actuators, embedded controllers, and communication modules. It is the block responsible for interacting with the physical world. Design decisions in this block, particularly regarding power management and communication duty cycling, determine the operational lifetime and maintenance cost of the deployment.
2. Communication: The Communication block manages data transport between devices and the cloud or edge infrastructure, implementing the protocols and network access mechanisms appropriate to each deployment context. It abstracts the diversity of physical connectivity options and presents a uniform interface to the services block above it.
3. Services: The Services block provides middleware capabilities including device management, data management, identity and access management, and protocol adaptation. It is the broker that decouples device capabilities from application requirements. Commercial IoT platforms such as AWS IoT Core and Azure IoT Hub are principally implementations of this block.

4. Management: The Management block handles the operational lifecycle of the IoT system: device provisioning, firmware updates, fault detection, and performance monitoring. In large-scale deployments involving hundreds of thousands of devices, this block is the operational backbone of the platform. Over-the-air firmware update capability is a particularly critical management function, as it enables security patches to be deployed rapidly across an entire device fleet.
5. Security: The Security block implements cross-cutting security controls including device authentication, authorisation, data encryption in transit and at rest, secure boot sequences, and anomaly detection. Rather than being an afterthought, the Security block is designed as an integral component from the outset of platform design. The attack surface of an IoT system spans from physically exposed hardware to cloud-hosted APIs, requiring defence at every tier.
6. Analytics: The Analytics block transforms raw device data into information. It encompasses real-time stream processing, batch analytics, historical trend analysis, and machine learning inference. The outputs of the Analytics block feed the Application block and, in closed-loop systems, may also feed back to the Communication block to trigger device-side actions.
7. Application: The Application block delivers the user-facing functionality of the IoT system. It may take the form of dashboards, control interfaces, notification services, or automated decision systems. The Application block is the layer at which return on investment is realised, and it is the primary point of contact between the IoT platform and the business processes it supports.

The seven-block model has practical value because it provides a vendor-agnostic checklist for IoT platform evaluation. When assessing a commercial IoT platform or designing a custom one, an architect can systematically examine how each functional block is implemented, what its scalability characteristics are, and where the boundaries of vendor responsibility end and customer responsibility begins. This is particularly valuable in hybrid deployments where different blocks are sourced from different vendors.

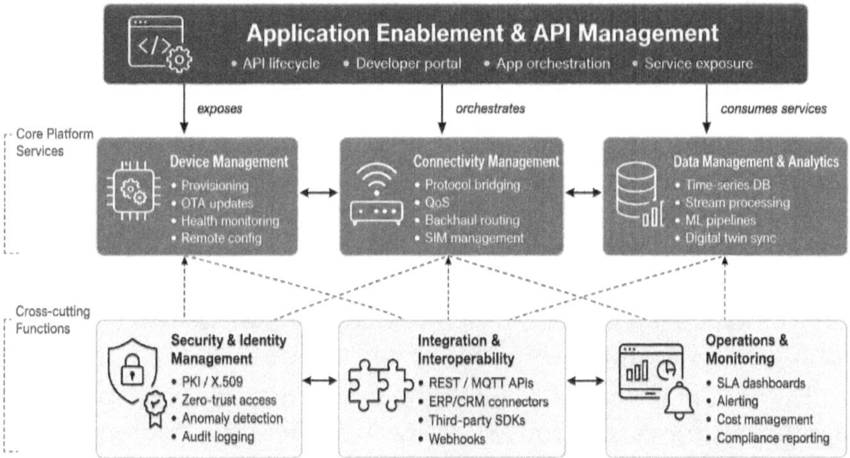

Figure 3.5 Functional block decomposition of an IoT platform showing the seven core capability areas and their interdependencies

Table 3.4 *IoT functional blocks: core capabilities and representative implementation technologies*

Functional Block	Core Capability	Implementation Examples
Device	Sensing, actuation, embedded control	STM32, Arduino, Raspberry Pi, Nordic nRF52
Communication	Protocol management, data transport	MQTT client, CoAP, LoRaWAN stack, LTE-M modem
Services	Middleware, device registry, data APIs	AWS IoT Core, Azure IoT Hub, Google Cloud IoT
Management	Provisioning, OTA updates, health monitoring	Pelion Device Management, Balena, Eclipse Hawkbit
Security	Auth, encryption, anomaly detection	X.509 PKI, TLS 1.3, TPM 2.0, AWS GuardDuty
Analytics	Stream and batch processing, ML inference	Apache Kafka, AWS Kinesis, TensorFlow Lite, Flink
Application	User interfaces, APIs, automated decisions	Grafana, Node-RED, ThingsBoard, custom REST APIs

3.6 IoT Communication Models

How IoT nodes communicate is as architecturally significant as how they are structured. Four canonical communication models have emerged from the literature and from practical IoT platform design. Each model embodies a different set of assumptions about the roles of sender and receiver, the timing of data exchange, and the nature of the communication relationship. Selecting the appropriate model for a given use case has direct implications for system scalability, latency, reliability, and power consumption.

3.6.1 Request-Response Model

The request-response model, also known as the client-server model, is the most familiar communication paradigm in networked computing. A client sends a request to a server and waits for a response. HTTP, the foundation of the World Wide Web, is the canonical implementation. In IoT, this model is widely used in RESTful API interactions between IoT gateways and cloud platforms, and in device management operations where a management server sends configuration commands to individual devices.

The model is simple to implement and reason about, but it has significant drawbacks for IoT at scale. A client must know the address of the server and must actively poll for new data, leading to unnecessary network traffic and energy consumption when data updates are infrequent. HTTP connection overhead also makes it unsuitable for constrained devices operating on duty-cycled radio links. The Constrained Application Protocol (CoAP), standardised in RFC 7252, was designed to bring RESTful interactions to constrained IoT devices by operating over UDP and removing HTTP overhead, while preserving the request-response interaction model.

DEFINITION: *Request-Response (Client-Server) Model*

A synchronous communication pattern in which a client sends a request message to a server and blocks until it receives a corresponding response. The client initiates all interactions; the server is passive until addressed. Applicable protocols: HTTP, CoAP (RFC 7252). Primary IoT use: device management, RESTful data retrieval, configuration delivery.

Source: Fielding and Taylor (2002); Shelby et al., RFC 7252 (2014)

3.6.2 Publish-Subscribe Model

The publish-subscribe model decouples producers of data (publishers) from consumers of data (subscribers) through an intermediary component called a message broker. Publishers send messages to named channels called topics; subscribers register their interest in specific topics with the broker. When a publisher sends a message to a topic, the broker distributes that message to all current subscribers of that topic, without either party being aware of the other identity or location.

MQTT, originally developed by Andy Stanford-Clark at IBM and Arlen Nipper at Arcom in 1999, is the most widely adopted IoT messaging protocol implementing this model. Its lightweight overhead, quality-of-service levels ranging from at-most-once to exactly-once delivery, and support for persistent sessions make it exceptionally well suited to constrained IoT devices operating over unreliable networks.

Commercial brokers including Eclipse Mosquitto, HiveMQ, and AWS IoT Core implement MQTT at scale, supporting millions of concurrent device connections. AMQP (Advanced Message Queuing Protocol) and DDS (Data Distribution Service) are alternative publish-subscribe protocols used in enterprise and real-time industrial contexts respectively.

DEFINITION: *Publish-Subscribe Model*

An asynchronous messaging pattern in which publishers send messages to named topics managed by a broker, and subscribers receive all messages published to their registered topics. Publishers and subscribers have no direct awareness of each other. This loose coupling enables one-to-many and many-to-many communication at scale. Applicable protocols: MQTT (OASIS standard), AMQP, DDS.

Source: OASIS MQTT Version 3.1.1 (2014); OASIS MQTT Version 5.0 (2019)

Key Insight: *Why Publish-Subscribe Dominates IoT. The publish-subscribe model's loose coupling is essential at IoT scale. When a smart city deploys 100,000 environmental sensors, it is architecturally impractical for each sensor to maintain a direct connection to every consuming application. The broker mediates this fan-out: sensors publish to topics, and any number of consumers — dashboards, alert engines, data historians, analytics pipelines — subscribe independently. Adding a new consumer requires no change to sensor firmware or network configuration, enabling the IoT ecosystem to grow without coordinated re-engineering of the device layer.*

3.6.3 Push-Pull Model

The push-pull model, sometimes called the pipeline or task queue model, is well suited to applications that must distribute data processing workloads across multiple consumers. Producers push data items into a queue; consumers pull items from the queue for processing. Unlike publish-subscribe, each data item is typically consumed by exactly one consumer, making the model appropriate for workload distribution rather than event broadcasting.

In IoT, the push-pull model is commonly used in data ingestion pipelines. A gateway collects sensor readings and pushes them to a distributed message queue; multiple cloud processing workers pull from the queue and perform analytics tasks in parallel. Technologies such as Apache Kafka, RabbitMQ, and Amazon SQS implement this model and are widely used in production IoT platforms. Kafka in particular has become a de facto standard for high-throughput IoT data ingestion, capable of handling millions of messages per second across a distributed cluster.

3.6.4 Exclusive Pair Model

The exclusive pair model establishes a persistent, full-duplex communication channel between a specific pair of nodes. Unlike the other three models, which support many-to-many or one-to-many communication, the exclusive pair model is inherently one-to-one. WebSockets, which enable persistent bidirectional channels over a single HTTP connection upgrade, are the most common implementation in web-facing IoT applications.

The exclusive pair model is appropriate when an IoT device requires continuous, bidirectional interaction with a specific back-end service, such as a real-time control application or a live video analytics pipeline. Its limitation is scalability: maintaining millions of persistent connections on the server side requires substantial resources and careful session management. For this reason, the exclusive pair model is typically reserved for applications where the real-time interaction requirement cannot be satisfied by the publish-subscribe model.

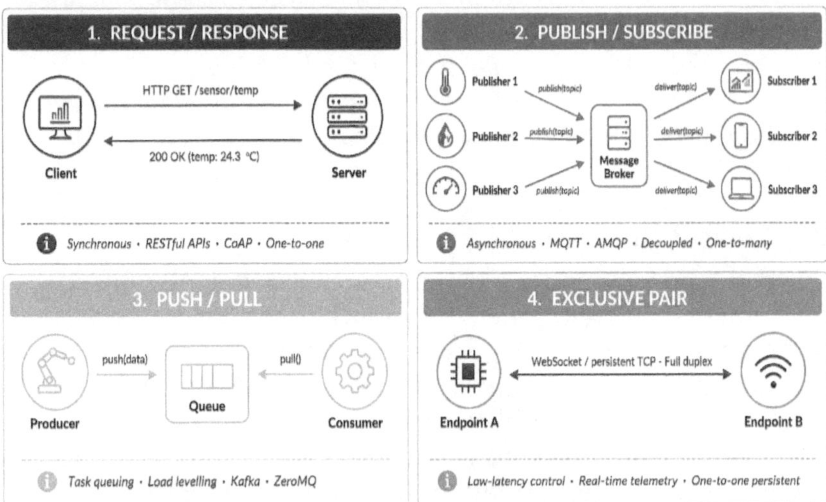

Figure 3.6 Structural comparison of Request-Response, Publish-Subscribe, Push-Pull, and Exclusive Pair IoT communication models

Table 3.5 Comparative analysis of the four IoT communication models

Model	Coupling	Direction	Protocol Example	Typical IoT Application
Request-Response	Tight	Bidirectional, synchronous	HTTP, CoAP	Device management, REST data retrieval
Publish-Subscribe	Loose	Many-to-many, async	MQTT, AMQP, DDS	Sensor telemetry, event alerts, notifications
Push-Pull	Moderate	Unidirectional pipeline	Kafka, RabbitMQ, SQS	Data ingestion, parallel workload distribution
Exclusive Pair	Tight	Full-duplex, persistent	WebSocket, XMPP	Real-time control, live monitoring streams

3.7 IoT Reference Architecture Models

The proliferation of proprietary IoT platforms and the fragmentation of the connectivity standards landscape created a pressing need for reference architecture models that could provide a common vocabulary and structural template for IoT system design. Several international standards bodies, industry consortia, and research projects produced reference architecture models between 2010 and 2022, each approaching the problem from a different vantage point. Six of these models have had the most significant influence on the field and are examined below.

DEFINITION: *Architectural Reference Model (ARM)*

A normative framework that defines the high-level structure of a system, the major functional components it contains, the interfaces between those components, and the design principles that govern their interactions. An ARM does not specify implementation details; it provides a conceptual template that conformant implementations must satisfy. ARMs are typically produced by standards bodies, industry consortia, or publicly funded research projects.

Source: IoT-A Project Deliverable D1.5 (2013); ISO/IEC/IEEE 42010:2022

3.7.1 ETSI M2M

The European Telecommunications Standards Institute published its M2M architecture specification (TS 102 690) in 2011, predating oneM2M and contributing substantially to its design. The ETSI M2M architecture defines three domains: the Device and Gateway Domain, the Network Domain, and the Application Domain. A service capabilities layer abstracts device-specific capabilities and exposes them to applications through standardised reference points labelled mIa, dIa, and mId.

ETSI M2M laid the conceptual foundation for much of what followed in IoT standardisation. Its work on reference points and capability abstraction established a pattern of thinking about IoT platforms as capability providers rather than monolithic application systems, a pattern that directly influenced the oneM2M Common Service Entity architecture.

3.7.2 IoT-A: The European Architectural Reference Model

The IoT Architecture project, funded under the European Union Seventh Framework Programme and completed in 2013, produced one of the most comprehensive Architectural Reference Models in the IoT field. The IoT-A ARM comprises five integrated sub-models.

The Domain Model identifies the key concepts and their relationships within an IoT domain, establishing a shared vocabulary for describing things, services, users, and resources. The Information Model defines how IoT-relevant information is represented and structured, enabling semantic interoperability between systems. The Functional Model specifies the functional components and their interactions. The Communication Model describes how IoT entities communicate, addressing both protocol selection and interaction patterns. The Security Model addresses trust establishment, privacy protection, and access control mechanisms.

The IoT-A project was notable for its breadth and rigour. By producing a reference model spanning from semantic information modelling to communication protocols to security architectures, it provided the research community with a comprehensive scaffold for IoT system analysis and design. The project output has been widely cited in academic literature and has informed several subsequent standardisation efforts, particularly in Europe.

3.7.3 ITU-T Y.2060 and the IoT Reference Model

The International Telecommunication Union Telecommunication Standardization Sector published Recommendation Y.2060 in 2012, providing the first authoritative definition of the Internet of Things and a reference model for IoT systems. The Y.2060 reference model organises IoT functionality into four horizontal layers: the Application Layer, the Service Support and Application Support Layer, the Network Layer, and the Device Layer. Two vertical management and security capability sets span all four horizontal layers.

Y.2060 is significant not only for its technical content but for its status as an official ITU-T Recommendation, carrying the weight of the United Nations specialised telecommunications agency. It has been adopted as a normative reference in national IoT strategies and regulatory frameworks in numerous countries, particularly in the Asia-Pacific region. Y.2060 was followed by a family of related ITU-T Recommendations, including Y.2061 (requirements for support of machine-oriented communication applications) and Y.4000 (IoT and its applications).

3.7.4 oneM2M

oneM2M is a global standards partnership founded in 2012 by seven of the world's leading ICT standards development organisations (SDOs): ARIB, ATIS, CCSA, ETSI, TIA, TTA, and TTC (Telecommunication Technology Committee, Japan). TSDSI (Telecommunications Standards Development Society, India) joined as the eighth partner in 2015. Its mission is to develop technical specifications for a common M2M and IoT service layer that can be embedded within a variety of hardware and software packages. The oneM2M architecture defines a horizontal service layer that sits between applications and diverse network and device implementations, providing standardised services including device registration, data management, subscription and notification, and access control.

The central concept of the oneM2M architecture is the Common Service Entity, a component present in every node type that provides a defined set of Common Service Functions. Three node types are defined: Application Service Nodes residing on IoT devices, Middle Nodes on gateways or edge infrastructure, and Infrastructure Nodes on cloud servers. oneM2M Release 4 and subsequent releases have added support for semantic interoperability, edge computing, and 5G network integration, keeping the standard current with the evolution of the IoT technology landscape.

3.7.5 W3C Web of Things

The World Wide Web Consortium Web of Things Working Group has been developing standards since 2016 that aim to extend the architectural patterns of the World Wide Web to the IoT domain. The central innovation of W3C WoT is the Thing Description, a JSON-LD (JavaScript Object Notation for Linked Data) document providing a machine-readable description of an IoT device properties, actions, events, and communication endpoints. Thing Descriptions enable automated discovery and composition of IoT services in a manner analogous to how WSDL documents enable programmatic web service consumption.

The W3C WoT architecture defines four reference components: the WoT Client, the WoT Intermediary, the WoT Server, and the Digital Twin. By grounding IoT in the well-understood architectural principles of the Web, the WoT architecture uses the existing developer ecosystem, tooling, and security infrastructure of the Web platform. The Thing Description specification reached W3C Recommendation status in 2020, and WoT Discovery reached Recommendation status in 2023.

3.7.6 Matter: Convergence for Consumer IoT

Matter, developed by the Connectivity Standards Alliance with founding contributions from Apple, Google, Amazon, and Samsung, is a relatively recent but highly consequential architectural development in the consumer IoT space. Ratified in 2022 as version 1.0, Matter defines a unified application layer and device model for smart home devices, enabling interoperability across ecosystems that were previously walled gardens with no capacity for cross-platform device control.

Matter operates over Thread, Wi-Fi, and Ethernet networks, using IP as its universal network layer. Its security model mandates certificate-based device attestation, encrypted transport using TLS 1.3, and role-based access control for all certified devices. Matter demonstrates that a cross-industry standards process, when backed by major market actors with aligned commercial interests, can achieve rapid and widespread adoption. Within two years of its ratification, over 3,000 Matter-certified products were available on the consumer market, representing a speed of adoption unprecedented in the IoT standardisation history.

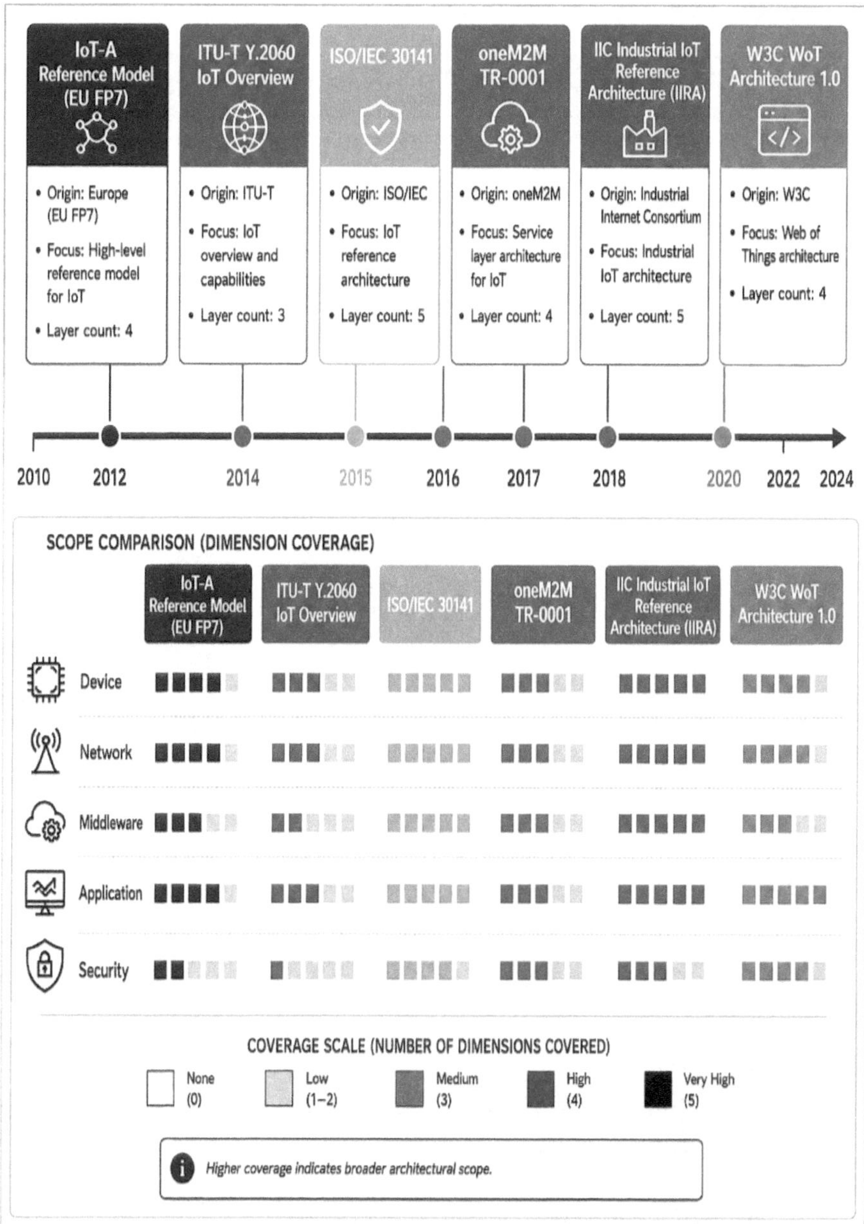

Figure 3.7 Timeline and scope comparison of the six major IoT reference architecture models from 2011 to 2022

Table 3.6 *Comparative overview of major IoT reference architecture models*

Model	Origin	Year	Key Architectural Innovation	Primary Target Domain
ETSI M2M	ETSI, Europe	2011	Service capability abstraction, reference points mIa/dIa/mId	Telecom / M2M
IoT-A ARM	EU FP7 Project	2010-2013	Five integrated sub-models, semantic information modelling	Research / cross-domain
ITU-T Y.2060	ITU-T, UN	2012	First official IoT definition, four-layer reference model	Global policy and regulation
oneM2M	8 SDO Partnership (7 founding, 2012)	2012+	Common Service Entity, horizontal service layer, CSFs	Enterprise and industry
W3C WoT	W3C	2016-2020	Thing Description (JSON-LD), Web-based discovery and composition	Web integration / IoT
Matter (CSA)	CSA (Apple, Google, Amazon)	2022	Unified app layer, cross-ecosystem smart home interoperability	Smart home / consumer

3.8 Designing for Scale: Architectural Principles

Understanding architecture models is necessary but not sufficient for designing production-grade IoT systems. Architects must also contend with non-functional requirements that become dominant concerns as deployments grow in scale and operational maturity. Four dimensions deserve particular attention: scalability, interoperability, security by design, and the distribution of intelligence between edge and cloud.

3.8.1 Scalability

An IoT system that functions reliably at a pilot scale of 100 devices may exhibit severe performance degradation when scaled to 100,000 or one million devices. Scalability must be considered across multiple dimensions: device connectivity scalability (the number of concurrent device connections the platform can maintain), data ingestion scalability (the volume of data the platform can ingest and process per second), storage scalability (the total volume of time-series data the platform can retain), and query scalability (the platform ability to serve analytical queries across large datasets without performance degradation).

Cloud-native architectures, built on horizontally scalable microservices, containerised workloads, and managed database services, have become the de facto approach to IoT platform scalability. Infrastructure-as-code practices enable IoT platforms to scale compute resources automatically in response to load fluctuations, ensuring cost efficiency without manual intervention.

Industrial deployments at the scale of a major smart city or a global industrial enterprise may involve ingesting hundreds of thousands of messages per second, requiring careful architectural design of the data ingestion pathway, the stream processing infrastructure, and the storage tier.

3.8.2 Interoperability

The heterogeneity of the IoT device landscape is a fundamental source of architectural complexity. In a typical smart city deployment, thousands of devices from dozens of manufacturers may communicate over different protocols, represent data in different formats, and expose different management interfaces. Achieving semantic interoperability, meaning the ability of two systems to exchange data and assign the same meaning to it, requires not only syntactic protocol translation but ontological alignment between the data models used by different device types.

Reference architectures address this through semantic layer components: the oneM2M Semantic Support Common Service Function, W3C WoT Thing Descriptions, and the FIWARE NGSI-LD data model are examples of approaches that provide a common vocabulary for describing device capabilities and data semantics. In practice, most production deployments rely on middleware components called protocol adapters or edge connectors that translate between device-native protocols and the canonical data model of the central platform, a necessary but expensive engineering effort that well-designed reference architectures aim to minimise.

3.8.3 Security by Design

Security in IoT cannot be retrofitted after deployment. The attack surface is vast: millions of physically exposed devices, many operating without tamper protection; diverse communication channels with varying levels of cryptographic support; and cloud back-ends that aggregate sensitive operational and personal data from across an entire deployment. Architectural security must be addressed at every tier, from the hardware root of trust embedded in device silicon to the identity and access management policies governing cloud API access.

The principle of security by design requires that security requirements are identified and addressed during the architectural design phase. In practice, this means specifying unique device identities backed by hardware security modules or Trusted Platform Modules, mandating mutual TLS authentication for all device-to-cloud communication, implementing the principle of least privilege in all access control policies, and designing update mechanisms capable of delivering cryptographically signed firmware patches to all devices in a deployment within a defined operational window. ETSI EN 303 645 and NIST IR 8259 provide the most widely referenced normative guidance for IoT security by design.

3.8.4 Edge versus Cloud Intelligence

The appropriate distribution of intelligence between the edge and the cloud is one of the most consequential architectural decisions in IoT system design. A centralised, cloud-first architecture offers simplicity, unlimited computational resources, and the ability to apply complex analytics across the full breadth of the deployment data. However, it introduces latency, increases bandwidth costs, creates a single point of failure, and may conflict with data residency regulations requiring that certain categories of data remain within national borders.

An edge-first architecture pushes intelligence as close to the data source as possible. Local edge nodes perform pre-processing, filtering, and machine learning inference, transmitting only summarised results to the cloud. This reduces latency and bandwidth costs but introduces operational complexity: edge nodes must be managed, updated, and monitored at scale, and the partitioning of analytics between edge and cloud must be carefully designed to avoid inconsistency and data loss.

Most mature IoT deployments adopt a tiered intelligence model, allocating workloads to the tier best suited to their latency, bandwidth, and computational characteristics. Time-critical control loops execute locally on the device or edge node. Aggregate analytics and machine learning model training execute in the cloud. Inference from trained models may then be deployed back to the edge for low-latency application. This pattern, sometimes called the cloud-to-edge ML lifecycle, is supported by an emerging set of tools including TensorFlow Lite, ONNX (Open Neural Network Exchange) Runtime, and AWS IoT Greengrass that facilitate model training in the cloud and deployment to edge hardware.

***Table 3.7** IoT architectural design dimensions: challenges, responses, and reference standards*

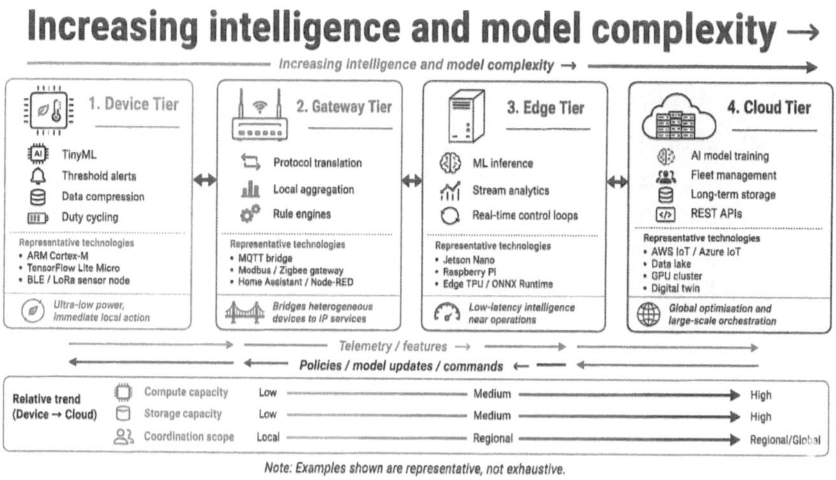

Figure 3.8 IoT intelligence distribution across device, gateway, edge, and cloud tiers, showing example workloads and representative technologies at each tier of the architecture.

Design Dimension	Primary Challenge	Architectural Response	Reference Standard
Scalability	Exponential growth in devices and data	Cloud-native microservices, horizontal auto-scaling, time-series DBs	NIST SP 800-183
Interoperability	Heterogeneous devices, protocols, data models	Semantic layers, protocol adapters, W3C WoT Thing Description	oneM2M TS-0001, W3C WoT
Security by Design	Vast attack surface, constrained devices	Hardware root of trust, mTLS, PKI, RBAC, signed OTA updates	ETSI EN 303 645, NIST IR 8259
Edge vs Cloud	Latency, bandwidth, data residency constraints	Tiered intelligence: device, edge, cloud continuum with ML lifecycle	IEC 62443, IIC IIoT Reference Architecture

3.9 Chapter Summary

This chapter has traced the architectural evolution of IoT from the closed, vertically oriented M2M systems of the 1990s and 2000s to the open, multi-tiered, standards-driven platforms that characterise the contemporary IoT landscape. The fundamental shift was from proprietary, application-specific architectures to horizontal platforms capable of supporting diverse application domains over shared infrastructure, with that shared infrastructure governed by open standards that any implementer can adopt.

The core components of an IoT system, spanning the sensing and actuation, connectivity, processing, and application layers, provide the vocabulary for decomposing any IoT deployment into its constituent parts. Layered architecture models, from the three-layer academic framework to the seven-layer industrial model, offer different levels of abstraction suited to different design contexts, with the choice of model reflecting both the complexity of the deployment and the primary concerns of the architect. The seven-block functional model provides a horizontal, capability-oriented alternative that is particularly useful for platform evaluation and procurement.

The four communication models, request-response, publish-subscribe, push-pull, and exclusive pair, define the fundamental interaction patterns from which IoT system behaviour is constructed. Each carries distinct implications for coupling, scalability, and latency, and the selection of an appropriate communication model is among the most consequential early design decisions in any IoT project. Most production systems employ more than one communication model, selecting the appropriate pattern for each interaction type within the overall architecture.

Six international reference architecture models, from ETSI M2M and ITU-T Y.2060 to the W3C Web of Things and Matter, represent the global effort to bring architectural coherence to a historically fragmented field. Understanding these models equips practitioners to engage with the growing body of IoT standards, to evaluate commercial platforms against principled criteria, and to design systems that are interoperable, secure, and scalable by construction rather than by accident.

The architectural principles addressed in the final section, scalability, interoperability, security by design, and edge-cloud intelligence distribution, are not merely technical concerns. They are the dimensions along which IoT systems succeed or fail in production, and they must be addressed during the architectural design phase if they are to be managed effectively. Subsequent chapters build on these foundations, examining specific protocol families, data management strategies, security frameworks, and domain-specific application architectures in greater depth.

Chapter 4

IoT Communication Protocols

Chapter 4 provides a structured technical foundation for understanding IoT communication protocols across the complete protocol stack. It explains how IoT devices communicate from the physical and link layers through network, transport, application, and management layers, with emphasis on protocol selection under constraints such as power, range, bandwidth, latency, reliability, and device capability. The chapter examines key link-layer technologies including Zigbee, BLE, LoRaWAN, Wi-Fi, and cellular IoT, and then extends the discussion to IPv6, 6LoWPAN, RPL, TCP, UDP, DTLS, MQTT, CoAP, AMQP, and related application protocols. It also highlights protocol-layer security mechanisms and explains how encryption, authentication, secure transport, and constrained-device security influence IoT system design. Overall, this chapter equips readers with the technical framework required to choose, compare, and integrate IoT protocols for reliable, secure, and scalable connected systems.

Opening Scenario: The Smart Building Protocol Audit

A facilities technology consultant is commissioned to integrate the IoT systems of a newly completed 18-floor commercial tower. The building has already been fitted by four separate contractors: a HVAC subcontractor using Zigbee-based wireless sensors, a lighting vendor whose occupancy sensors transmit over Z-Wave, an access-control integrator running a proprietary 900 MHz mesh, and an energy metering company whose smart meters communicate via LoRaWAN to a rooftop gateway.

The consultant's mandate is to deliver a single dashboard that shows live data from all four systems. On day one, she discovers that the four systems share no common protocol layer above the physical. The HVAC data is in Zigbee clusters; the lighting uses Z-Wave command classes; the access control system speaks a vendor binary format; and the energy meters use Low Power Payload (LPP) encoded CBOR (Concise Binary Object Representation) over LoRaWAN. This chapter provides the analytical framework to diagnose precisely why each problem occurred, how a principled protocol selection process would have prevented the integration failure from the outset, and what a standards-aligned multi-layer architecture looks like for this building.

4.1 The IoT Protocol Stack

Communication is the nervous system of every IoT deployment. Sensors generate data that has no value until it reaches an application platform; actuators have no effect until they receive a command. Between device and platform lies a communication chain that spans physical radio transmission, logical addressing, reliable delivery, and application-level semantics. Understanding this chain, and the protocol choices available at each layer, is the prerequisite for designing deployments that are scalable, secure, and maintainable.

The classical OSI seven-layer model and the TCP/IP four-layer model were both designed for full-capability computing hosts connected by wired or high-bandwidth wireless infrastructure. IoT devices are fundamentally different: they are typically battery-powered, operate on microcontrollers with kilobytes of RAM, transmit infrequently, and operate in lossy radio environments.

Applying a conventional TCP/IP stack to a Cortex-M0 microcontroller with 16 KB of RAM and a 250 kbps radio is technically possible but practically wasteful. The IoT community has therefore developed an adapted four-layer stack that preserves IP-based end-to-end addressing while replacing bandwidth-heavy protocols with constrained equivalents at every layer.

4.1.1 The Four-Layer IoT Stack

The IoT protocol stack is most usefully conceived as four functional layers, each addressed by a distinct set of standards.

- Link Layer — responsible for physical radio transmission and local connectivity within a single network segment. Protocols at this layer include IEEE 802.15.4 (the foundation for Zigbee and Thread), Z-Wave, Bluetooth Low Energy (BLE), LoRa/LoRaWAN, and Wi-Fi (IEEE 802.11). The link layer defines modulation, channel access (CSMA/CA or TDMA), addressing within the local segment, and, in many cases, link-level encryption.
- Network/Internet Layer — provides end-to-end addressing and routing across multiple network segments, enabling a sensor in a factory to be directly addressed by a cloud platform on another continent. IPv6 is the mandated addressing protocol; 6LoWPAN (IPv6 over Low-Power Wireless Person-

al Area Networks) provides the adaptation layer that compresses IPv6 headers to fit within the 127-byte IEEE 802.15.4 frame. RPL (Routing Protocol for Low-Power and Lossy Networks) handles routing within constrained mesh networks.

- Transport Layer — manages end-to-end data delivery between processes. TCP provides reliable, ordered delivery but its connection-oriented design is expensive for constrained devices. UDP sacrifices reliability for efficiency and is the preferred transport for constrained IoT protocols. DTLS (Datagram Transport Layer Security) adds encryption and authentication over UDP, providing the security properties of TLS without the overhead of a persistent TCP connection.
- Application Layer — defines the message format, payload encoding, and interaction model between device and platform. The dominant IoT application protocols are MQTT (publish-subscribe, TCP-based), CoAP (RESTful request-response, UDP-based), AMQP (enterprise message queuing), HTTP/REST (for configuration and integration APIs), and DDS (peer-to-peer data-centric middleware for real-time systems).

Two cross-cutting concerns sit outside this four-layer view but interact with every layer. The management plane (addressed by LwM2M, NETCONF/YANG, and TR-069) handles device configuration, firmware updates, and lifecycle operations independently of the telemetry data plane. Security is a vertical hardening discipline that must be applied at every layer: link-layer encryption, DTLS at the transport layer, mutual authentication at the application layer, and certificate lifecycle management spanning all layers. Both concerns are treated in detail in Section 4.6 and Section 4.7 respectively.

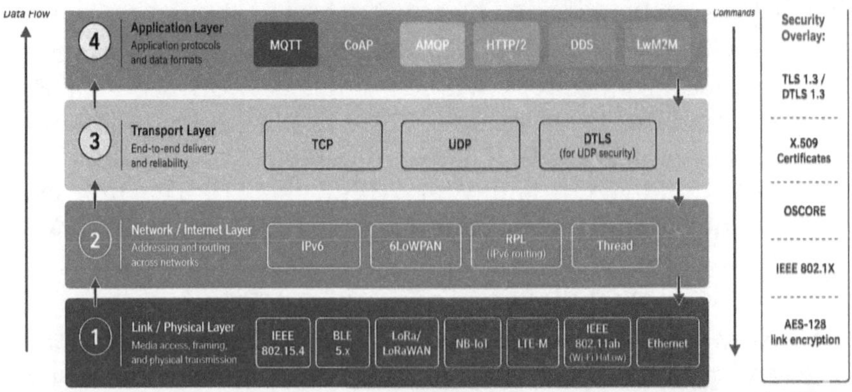

Figure 4.1: The IoT four-layer protocol stack. Each layer box lists representative protocols.

4.1.2 Why IoT Needs Its Own Stack View

RFC 7228 formalises the vocabulary of constrained IoT nodes, defining three device classes based on available RAM and flash storage. A Class 0 device has less than 10 KB of RAM and less than 100 KB of code flash; it cannot run a full IP stack. A Class 1 device (approximately 10 KB RAM, 100 KB flash) can run a constrained IP stack such as uIP or lwIP but not TLS. Only a Class 2 device (approximately 50 KB RAM, 250 KB flash) approaches the resource level at which conventional TCP/IP becomes viable.

The protocols examined in this chapter are precisely calibrated to these constraints: 6LoWPAN compresses IPv6 headers to fit 802.15.4 frames, CoAP replaces HTTP's verbose headers with a four-byte binary header, and DTLS replaces TLS's three-way handshake with a stateless cookie exchange that prevents amplification attacks on constrained networks.

DEFINITION: *Constrained Node (RFC 7228)*

A device in an IoT network characterised by limited processing power, memory, and energy availability that prevents it from running a full IP stack or standard security protocols without modification. RFC 7228 classifies constrained nodes into three classes (C0, C1, C2) based on RAM and flash storage thresholds, providing a common vocabulary for protocol designers and system architects.

Key Insight: The Constraint-Protocol Fit Principle. *RFC 7228 device classes are not merely academic taxonomy — they directly determine which protocols are viable. A Class 0 device with 4 KB RAM cannot run TCP, TLS, or a full IPv6 stack. A Class 1 device can run 6LoWPAN and CoAP but not DTLS. Only a Class 2 device approaches the resource envelope where MQTT over TLS becomes practical. Specifying a protocol stack without first establishing the target device class leads to architectural mismatch that cannot be corrected after hardware procurement. The constraint class is the starting point for every protocol decision in this chapter.*

The sections that follow treat each layer in sequence: Section 4.2 covers link-layer protocols, Section 4.3 the network layer, Section 4.4 the transport layer, and Section 4.5 the application layer. Section 4.6 addresses management protocols and Section 4.7 examines protocol-layer security holistically. Section 4.8 synthesises the preceding content into a practical protocol selection framework, and the chapter closes with the Summary, Key Terms, and References in Section 4.9.

4.2 Link Layer Protocols

The link layer determines how bits move between a device and its immediate neighbours: which radio frequency band is used, how devices share the channel, what addressing scheme identifies each node locally, and whether link-level encryption is applied. The choice of link-layer protocol is often the most consequential decision in IoT system design because it fixes the deployment's power budget, physical range, data throughput ceiling, and network topology.

No single link-layer protocol dominates IoT; instead, a spectrum of standards has evolved, each optimised for a specific combination of range, data rate, power consumption, and cost. This section surveys the six protocols most widely encountered in professional IoT deployments, using a consistent template for each: operating parameters, topology, security, use-case fit, and key limitations.

4.2.1 IEEE 802.15.4: The Foundational Standard

IEEE 802.15.4 is the foundational PHY and MAC standard for low-rate wireless personal area networks (LR-WPANs). First published in 2003 and significantly revised in 2006, 2011, and 2020, it defines the radio characteristics and medium access rules on top of which Zigbee, Thread, 6LoWPAN, and WirelessHART are all built. Understanding 802.15.4 is therefore a prerequisite for understanding most constrained IoT link-layer technology.

At 2.4 GHz (the globally available band), 802.15.4 provides 16 channels each with a 250 kbps raw data rate. The MAC uses CSMA/CA (Carrier Sense Multiple Access with Collision Avoidance) to arbitrate channel access, with optional beacon-enabled superframe structures that allow nodes to sleep between scheduled transmission slots, achieving duty cycles below one percent. The maximum MAC Service Data Unit (MSDU) payload is 102 bytes after header and footer overhead from the 127-byte maximum frame: a constraint that directly motivates the 6LoWPAN header compression standard discussed in Section 4.3.

802.15.4 supports both star and peer-to-peer topologies and defines three device roles: Full Function Device (FFD), Reduced Function Device (RFD), and Coordinator. Link-level security uses AES-128 in CCM* mode, providing confidentiality, integrity, and replay protection at the MAC layer.

DEFINITION: *IEEE 802.15.4*

The IEEE standard defining the PHY and MAC layers for low-rate wireless personal area networks. It operates at 250 kbps on 16 channels in the 2.4 GHz band, supports CSMA/CA medium access, and provides AES-128 CCM link-layer security. It is the foundational standard on which Zigbee, Thread, 6LoWPAN, and WirelessHART are built.*

4.2.2 Zigbee

Zigbee is a complete networking and application protocol stack built on the IEEE 802.15.4 PHY/MAC. Maintained by the Connectivity Standards Alliance (CSA, formerly the Zigbee Alliance), Zigbee adds a mesh network layer with self-healing routing and an application layer that defines standardised device profiles for home automation, building automation, and smart energy metering.

Zigbee operates at 250 kbps in the 2.4 GHz band with a typical indoor range of 10 to 100 metres per hop. Its mesh topology allows messages to be relayed through intermediate router nodes, extending the effective network range far beyond the single-hop radio limit. A Zigbee network supports up to 65,000 nodes, making it well suited to large-scale building automation deployments. Power consumption is extremely low in sleep mode: end devices can operate for years on AA batteries by sleeping between infrequent transmissions and waking only to transmit or receive.

Zigbee's security model uses AES-128 at two levels: link keys shared between neighbouring nodes and network keys shared across the entire mesh. The Trust Centre, typically the network coordinator, manages key distribution. Zigbee 3.0 unified previously fragmented application profiles into a single specification, improving interoperability between vendors. The Zigbee use-case sweet spot is smart home and commercial building automation: smart bulbs, thermostats, occupancy sensors, door and window sensors, and energy monitors all benefit from Zigbee's mesh range extension, ultra-low power, and rich device profile library.

4.2.3 Z-Wave

Z-Wave is a proprietary sub-GHz mesh protocol designed specifically for home automation. Originally developed by Zensys and now controlled by Silicon Labs (which acquired the Z-Wave IP in 2018), Z-Wave operates at 868 MHz in Europe and 908 MHz in North America, deliberately avoiding the crowded 2.4 GHz band shared by Wi-Fi, Bluetooth, and Zigbee.

Z-Wave operates at 100 kbps (Z-Wave Plus, SDK 7.x), supports mesh routing with a maximum of four hops, and achieves indoor range of approximately 30 metres per hop. Classic Z-Wave mesh networks support up to 232 nodes, adequate for residential deployments but insufficient for large commercial buildings, while Z-Wave Long Range extends scalability up to 4000 nodes in a star topology when both the hub and end devices support Z-Wave LR. The sub-GHz operation provides better wall-penetration characteristics than

2.4 GHz alternatives. Z-Wave uses AES-128 encryption with the S2 (Security 2) framework, which introduced mutual authentication and forward secrecy in SDK 6.7, significantly improving on the earlier S0 scheme that was vulnerable to relay attacks.

Z-Wave's primary competitive advantage is interoperability: all Z-Wave certified products must pass mandatory conformance testing, giving installers higher confidence that devices from different manufacturers will work together reliably. Its limitation is the proprietary nature of the specification — Z-Wave Alliance membership is required for full documentation access and chip sourcing is concentrated with Silicon Labs. Z-Wave is predominantly deployed in residential security systems, smart locks, thermostats, and motorised blinds.

4.2.4 Bluetooth Low Energy (BLE)

Bluetooth Low Energy, introduced in Bluetooth 4.0 (2010) and significantly enhanced in Bluetooth 5.x, is a low-power variant of the Bluetooth standard optimised for short-burst, infrequent data transmission from battery-powered devices. Unlike Classic Bluetooth, which was designed for continuous audio streaming, BLE was designed from the ground up for IoT sensor applications where devices transmit small amounts of data infrequently and must survive years on a coin-cell battery.

BLE operates in the 2.4 GHz ISM band across 40 channels (37 data channels and 3 advertising channels). Bluetooth 5.0 introduced three PHY options: LE 1M (1 Mbps, standard range), LE 2M (2 Mbps, higher throughput, reduced range), and LE Coded (125 kbps or 500 kbps with up to 4x range extension via forward error correction). Under ideal line-of-sight conditions, Bluetooth 5.0 with coded PHY achieves ranges exceeding 400 metres; typical indoor range is 10 to 50 metres. Bluetooth Mesh (introduced in 2017) adds a many-to-many publish-subscribe mesh networking capability to BLE, enabling large-scale building lighting and sensor deployments.

BLE's distinctive advantage is ubiquity: every smartphone, tablet, and laptop manufactured since 2012 includes a BLE radio, enabling direct device-to-phone communication without a dedicated gateway. This makes BLE the natural choice for consumer wearables, medical monitoring patches, retail beacons (iBeacon, Eddystone), and asset tracking tags. The advertising mode, where a BLE device broadcasts a short packet periodically without establishing a connection, enables ultra-low-power beacon applications with coin-cell batteries lasting over a year at room temperature.

TECHNOLOGY SPOTLIGHT: Bluetooth Mesh in Commercial Lighting

Bluetooth Mesh has become a leading wireless standard for intelligent commercial building lighting, gaining significant adoption alongside Zigbee-based systems in large new installations. A typical deployment connects hundreds of luminaires, occupancy sensors, daylight sensors, and wall switches into a self-configuring mesh network managed from a smartphone or building management system. The Bluetooth SIG's Mesh Profile specification uses a publish-subscribe model with group addressing: an occupancy sensor publishes a 'room occupied' message to a group address, and all luminaires subscribed to that group respond simultaneously.

Managed flooding with relay nodes ensures message delivery without a single point of failure. The DALI Alliance and Bluetooth SIG have developed a joint standard (DALI-2 + Bluetooth Mesh) that bridges the wired DALI-2 lighting control ecosystem with wireless mesh, enabling gradual migration from legacy wired installations. A 2022 deployment by Signify (Philips Hue Professional) at Amsterdam's Schiphol Airport connected over 2,400 luminaires via Bluetooth Mesh, achieving individualised light scheduling, real-time energy monitoring, and occupancy-driven dimming across all terminal gates.

4.2.5 LoRa and LoRaWAN

LoRa (Long Range) is a proprietary chirp-spread-spectrum (CSS) radio modulation technique developed by Semtech. LoRaWAN is the open network protocol and system architecture standard built on top of LoRa, maintained by the LoRa Alliance. Together they form the dominant Low-Power Wide Area Network (LPWAN) technology for IoT deployments requiring long range with ultra-low power consumption.

LoRaWAN operates in unlicensed sub-GHz ISM bands: 868 MHz in Europe, 915 MHz in North America, and 433/923 MHz in Asia-Pacific regions. Data rates range from 0.3 kbps to 50 kbps, selectable via Spreading Factor (SF7 through SF12). Higher spreading factors increase range at the cost of reduced data rate and increased airtime. A LoRaWAN network uses a star-of-stars topology: end devices transmit to one or more gateways (which are transparent forwarders), and gateways forward packets to a centralised Network Server over standard backhaul (4G, Ethernet, or Wi-Fi). The Network Server's Adaptive Data Rate (ADR) algorithm continuously tunes each device's spreading factor and transmit power to maximise network capacity: a multi-variable optimisation that network operators increasingly address with ML-assisted predictive models that anticipate link quality shifts before they degrade delivery rates. Range achieves 2 to 5 km in dense urban environments and 10 to 15 km in rural line-of-sight conditions.

LoRaWAN defines three device classes. Class A (All) devices initiate all uplink transmissions and open two short downlink receive windows immediately after each uplink: the most energy-efficient mode, suitable for sensors that report infrequently. Class B (Beacon) adds scheduled receive slots synchronised by network beacon, reducing latency for actuator commands at the cost of slightly higher power. Class C (Continuous) devices keep their receiver open at all times except during transmission, enabling near-real-time downlink but requiring mains power.

LoRaWAN v1.1 uses AES-128 encryption at two layers: a Network Session Key (NwkSKey) that encrypts network-level metadata and authenticates the Message Integrity Code (MIC), and an Application Session Key (AppSKey) that end-to-end encrypts the application payload. This dual-key architecture means the network operator can route traffic without decrypting application data: a significant privacy advantage in multi-tenant network deployments.

Join procedures follow either Over-the-Air Activation (OTAA), which derives fresh session keys per join and provides forward secrecy, or Activation By Personalisation (ABP), which hardcodes keys. OTAA is strongly preferred for new deployments.

CASE STUDY: Actility and the Paris Smart City LoRaWAN Network

Paris, France / 2016 — ongoing

In 2016, the City of Paris and Actility (operator of the ThingPark Network Server platform) deployed one of the first large-scale municipal LoRaWAN networks in Europe. The network used fewer than 100 gateways to cover the entire Paris metropolitan area, connecting applications spanning smart street lighting, waste bin fill-level monitoring, noise pollution sensors, and parking space occupancy detectors.

The deployment demonstrated LoRaWAN's economic model: a single gateway serving a 2 km radius can support thousands of Class A sensors simultaneously, enabling city-scale IoT coverage at a fraction of the infrastructure cost of cellular deployments.

Subsequent deployments in Amsterdam, Barcelona, and Antwerp followed the Paris model, and by 2020 the LoRa Alliance reported operational LoRaWAN networks in over 170 countries. The Paris case also con-

firmed the technology's boundaries: LoRaWAN's regulatory duty-cycle restrictions (1 percent in Europe) and low data rate make it unsuitable for high-frequency or large-payload applications, confirming that LPWAN complements rather than replaces cellular and short-range wireless technologies.

Regional Example: LoRaWAN Deployments in the Gulf Region. *The Gulf Cooperation Council region has seen significant LoRaWAN adoption for smart city and utility infrastructure. In the UAE, du (Emirates Integrated Telecommunications) operates a national LoRaWAN network covering all seven emirates, supporting smart metering, parking, and environmental monitoring. Oman's PDO (Petroleum Development Oman) has piloted LoRaWAN-connected well-site sensors across Interior and Dhofar regions, transmitting daily production parameters with 10+ km range over open desert terrain — conditions where cellular coverage is unavailable and cable infrastructure prohibitively expensive. These deployments confirm LoRaWAN's Class A energy model in practice: sensors reporting once per hour on primary lithium cells achieve projected field lifetimes exceeding eight years, matching the utility industry's standard meter maintenance cycle.*

4.2.6 Wi-Fi (IEEE 802.11)

Wi-Fi, governed by the IEEE 802.11 family of standards, is the highest-bandwidth option in the IoT link-layer landscape. Operating at 2.4 GHz (802.11b/g/n), 5 GHz (802.11a/n/ac), and 6 GHz (802.11ax/Wi-Fi 6E), Wi-Fi delivers data rates from 150 Mbps (802.11n single-stream) to multi-gigabit throughput with 802.11ax (Wi-Fi 6). Indoor range is typically 30 to 100 metres, depending on building materials and channel congestion.

Wi-Fi's IoT role is constrained by its power consumption: a Wi-Fi radio requires significantly more energy than BLE, Zigbee, or LoRa to associate, transmit, and maintain connectivity. This makes Wi-Fi unsuitable for battery-operated sensors unless supplemented by aggressive sleep scheduling. It is, however, the natural choice for IoT nodes that are mains-powered and require high data throughput: IP cameras, industrial human-machine interfaces, energy monitoring gateways, smart televisions, and appliances with rich configuration interfaces all benefit from Wi-Fi's ubiquitous infrastructure compatibility and high bandwidth ceiling.

Wi-Fi 6 (802.11ax) introduced Target Wake Time (TWT), which allows IoT devices to negotiate scheduled wake intervals with the access point, dramatically reducing power consumption in environments with many concurrent IoT devices. WPA3 (Wi-Fi Protected

Access 3), mandatory for Wi-Fi 6 certified devices, provides SAE (Simultaneous Authentication of Equals) for stronger handshake protection and forward secrecy, addressing the KRACK vulnerability class that affected WPA2.

4.2.7 Link Layer Protocol Comparison

Table 4.1 summarises the key characteristics of the six link-layer protocols across seven comparison dimensions. No protocol wins on every dimension; selection depends entirely on the deployment's requirements for power, range, data rate, topology, and regulatory environment.

Table 4.1: Link Layer Protocol Comparison

Protocol	Frequency	Data Rate	Range	Topology	Power	Typical IoT Use Cases
IEEE 802.15.4	2.4 GHz / Sub-GHz	250 kbps	10–100 m	Star / P2P	Ultra- low	Foundation layer for Zigbee, Thread, WirelessHART
Zigbee	2.4 GHz	250 kbps	10–100 m/hop	Mesh (65k nodes)	Ultra- low	Smart home, building automation, smart energy
Z-Wave	868/908 MHz	100 kbps	30 m/ hop (max 4)	Classic mesh: 232 nodes; Z-Wave LR: up to 4000 nodes	Ultra- low	Residential security, smart locks, thermostats
BLE	2.4 GHz	125 kbps–2Mbps	(10–400 m BT5 coded)	Star / Mesh	Ultra- low	Wearables, beacons, retail, medical patches
LoRa WAN	Sub-GHz (regional)	0.3–50 kbps	2–15 km	Star-of-stars	Ultra- low	Smart city, agriculture, logistics, metering
Wi-Fi 6	2.4/5/6 GHz	150 Mbps –multi-Gbps	30–100 m	Infrastructure star	High(TWT reduces for IoT)	IP cameras, appliances, industrial HMIs

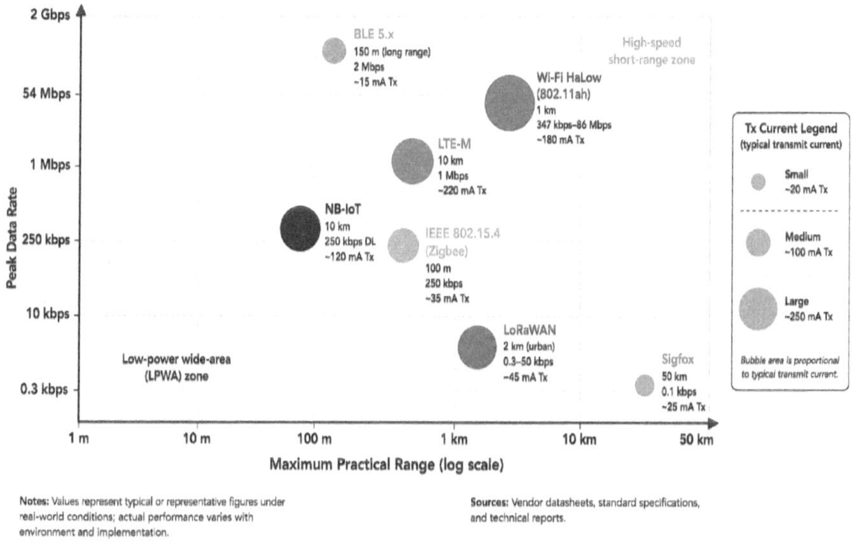

Figure 4.2: Link layer protocol comparison chart.

4.3 The Network/Internet Layer: IPv6, 6LoWPAN, and RPL

The network layer is where IoT devices acquire globally routable addresses and participate in end-to-end IP communication. For the IoT, the network layer presents a fundamental tension: IPv6 was designed for full-capability computing hosts, yet the devices that need IP addresses most urgently, hundreds of billions of constrained sensors, cannot run a standard IPv6 stack. The IETF's response was a suite of adaptations that compress, fragment, and route IPv6 traffic across constrained mesh networks while preserving full end-to-end IP addressability.

4.3.1 IPv6 for IoT

IPv4's 32-bit address space, providing approximately 4.3 billion unique addresses, was exhausted at the IANA level in 2011. IPv6's 128-bit address space provides approximately 3.4 x 10^38 addresses, sufficient to assign unique IP addresses to every sensor on every device on the planet many times over. For IoT, IPv6 is not merely a convenience; it is an architectural necessity. Without IPv6, IoT deployments are forced into NAT (Network Address Translation) hierarchies that break end-to-end connectivity, complicate security, and add latency.

A key IPv6 feature for IoT is Stateless Address AutoConfiguration (SLAAC), defined in RFC 4862. SLAAC allows an IPv6 device to derive its own globally unique interface identifier from its MAC address using the EUI-64 format, without requiring a DHCP server. An IoT device joining a network can construct its link-local address (fe80::/10 prefix) and, once it receives a Router Advertisement with a global prefix, construct a globally routable address entirely autonomously. This eliminates address management overhead that would be prohibitive at the scale of millions of devices.

IPv6 also introduces Neighbour Discovery Protocol (NDP), which replaces ARP for link-layer address resolution and provides router discovery, prefix distribution, and duplicate address detection. In 6LoWPAN networks (described below), NDP is compressed and adapted to reduce its overhead on constrained links. IPv6 multicast addresses enable efficient group communication patterns, for example, all-routers (ff02::2) and all-nodes (ff02::1) multicast groups that are essential for mesh routing protocol operation.

DEFINITION: SLAAC (Stateless Address AutoConfiguration)

An IPv6 mechanism defined in RFC 4862 by which a device autonomously constructs its own globally unique IPv6 address from a network-advertised prefix and its EUI-64 interface identifier derived from the MAC address. SLAAC eliminates the need for a DHCP server in IPv6 networks, which is particularly valuable in large-scale IoT deployments where manual address management would be impractical.

4.3.2 6LoWPAN: Fitting IPv6 into Constrained Frames

IEEE 802.15.4 frames have a maximum size of 127 bytes. After MAC header, footer, and link-layer security overhead, the usable payload is approximately 81 to 102 bytes. A standard IPv6 header alone is 40 bytes, leaving fewer than 42 bytes for transport header and application payload, far too little for useful IoT messages. 6LoWPAN (IPv6 over Low-Power Wireless Personal Area Networks), standardised in RFC 4944 and updated by RFC 6282, solves this through header compression and fragmentation.

RFC 6282 defines IPHC (IP Header Compression), which compresses a standard 40-byte IPv6 header to as few as 2 bytes when contextual information, such as the source and destination prefixes, can be inferred from the link-layer context or stored in a shared compression context. Similarly, UDP headers can be compressed from 8 bytes to 4 bytes using NHC (Next Header Compression). In practice, a 6LoWPAN-compressed IPv6/UDP header requires 7 to 10 bytes, leaving 70 to 90 bytes for application payload within a single 802.15.4 frame.

For messages that cannot fit in a single 802.15.4 frame even after compression, 6LoWPAN defines a fragmentation and reassembly mechanism. Large IPv6 packets are split into multiple 802.15.4 frames, each carrying a fragmentation header with a datagram tag and offset. The receiving node reassembles fragments before passing the reconstructed IPv6 packet to higher layers. This fragmentation introduces latency and increases the probability of packet loss if any fragment is dropped; application designers should therefore prefer payloads that fit within a single frame wherever possible.

Figure 4.3: 6LoWPAN Compression Overview

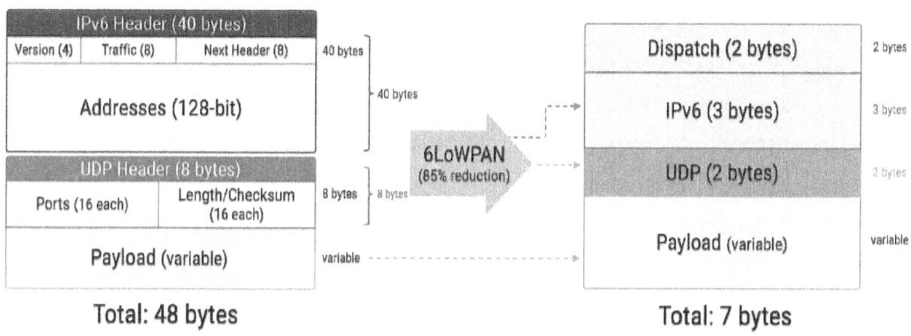

Figure 4.3: 6LoWPAN header compression diagram.

4.3.3 RPL: Routing in Low-Power Lossy Networks

Once devices have IPv6 addresses, they need a routing protocol to forward packets across a multi-hop mesh network. Standard IP routing protocols such as OSPF and BGP are designed for stable, high-bandwidth links; they are wholly unsuitable for constrained mesh networks where links are intermittent, asymmetric, and battery-powered nodes must minimise transmission. RPL (Routing Protocol for Low-Power and Lossy Networks), standardised in RFC 6550, was designed specifically for this environment.

RPL builds a Destination-Oriented Directed Acyclic Graph (DODAG): a tree-shaped routing structure rooted at a border router, with all nodes oriented toward the root. Each node computes a rank value using an Objective Function (OF) that typically minimises the Expected Transmission Count (ETX): a metric that reflects link quality by estimating how many transmissions are needed to deliver a packet successfully. Nodes select a preferred parent (the neighbour with the best rank toward the root) and build their upward route through successive preferred parents to the DODAG root.

RPL supports three traffic patterns: upward traffic (node to root, the dominant pattern for sensor telemetry), downward traffic (root to node, for actuator commands), and peer-to-peer traffic (node to node, which must traverse up to a common ancestor and then down). RPL's control message overhead is deliberately minimal: DODAG Information Objects (DIOs) are sent periodically to advertise routing information downward, and DODAG Information Solicitations (DIS) allow new nodes to request a DIO upon joining. The Trickle algorithm (RFC 6206) controls DIO transmission frequency, reducing overhead when the network is stable and increasing it after topology changes.

The 6LoWPAN Border Router (6LBR) serves as the DODAG root and the translation point between the constrained 802.15.4 mesh and the standard IPv6/internet infrastructure. The border router performs 6LoWPAN header decompression, reassembles fragmented packets, and routes them to the upstream IP network. In the reverse direction, it compresses standard IPv6 headers and routes downward traffic into the constrained mesh. In practice, the 6LBR function is implemented in gateway devices such as the Raspberry Pi running Contiki-NG, Silicon Labs' OTBR (OpenThread Border Router), or dedicated industrial gateway hardware.

DEFINITION: RPL DODAG (Destination-Oriented Directed Acyclic Graph)

A tree-shaped routing topology constructed by RPL in which all nodes are oriented toward a single root (the 6LoWPAN border router). Each node selects a preferred parent based on an Objective Function that minimises routing cost (typically Expected Transmission Count). The DODAG structure efficiently supports the dominant IoT traffic pattern of many sensors reporting to a single collection point.

4.4 The Transport Layer: TCP, UDP, and DTLS

The transport layer arbitrates the fundamental trade-off between reliability and efficiency. TCP provides ordered, reliable byte-stream delivery at the cost of connection establishment overhead, acknowledgement traffic, and congestion control mechanisms that penalise lossy links. UDP provides lightweight, connectionless datagram delivery with no guarantees, transferring the reliability responsibility to higher layers. IoT deployments must choose their transport protocol with an explicit understanding of this trade-off and its energy, latency, and correctness implications.

4.4.1 TCP in IoT: When It Is and Is Not Justified

TCP's three-way handshake (SYN, SYN-ACK, ACK) requires three round trips before any application data can be exchanged.

For a Class 1 IoT device transmitting a 50-byte temperature reading every 15 minutes, the connection establishment overhead can easily exceed the payload itself. TCP's congestion control algorithms (Slow Start, Congestion Avoidance, Fast Retransmit) were designed for stable wired networks; on lossy wireless links, packet loss that is due to radio interference is misinterpreted as congestion, triggering unnecessary window reductions that reduce throughput and waste retransmission energy.

TCP is nonetheless justified in specific IoT scenarios. Cloud-connected gateway nodes that are mains-powered, maintain persistent MQTT broker connections, and transmit large volumes of aggregated telemetry benefit from TCP's flow control and ordering guarantees. Firmware update downloads, which must be byte-perfectly received and cannot tolerate gaps are appropriately served over TCP. HTTP/REST APIs for device configuration, provisioning, and dashboard integration use TCP as their natural transport. The guideline is: use TCP when the node has stable power, maintains a persistent connection rather than waking to transmit, and requires in-order reliable delivery that would be complex to implement at the application layer.

4.4.2 UDP in IoT: Lightweight Datagram Transport

UDP eliminates connection establishment entirely: a sender simply transmits a datagram without prior negotiation. There are no acknowledgements, no retransmissions, no congestion window, and no ordered delivery. The entire UDP header is 8 bytes (source port, destination port, length, checksum), compared to TCP's minimum 20 bytes. For constrained IoT devices that transmit infrequent small readings and can tolerate occasional loss, UDP is the natural transport choice.

UDP is used by CoAP, DNS, DTLS, and NTP: the four protocols most commonly needed by constrained IoT devices. When reliability is required over UDP, the application or protocol layer must provide it explicitly: CoAP's Confirmable (CON) message type implements a simple stop-and-wait acknowledgement scheme, while application-layer sequence numbering can detect gaps in telemetry streams. The engineering choice is deliberate: rather than imposing TCP's full reliability machinery on all traffic, IoT protocols implement lightweight reliability only where it is needed.

4.4.3 DTLS: Security for Datagram Transports

TLS (Transport Layer Security), the standard encryption and

authentication protocol for TCP-based communication, cannot operate directly over UDP because it assumes ordered, reliable delivery for its record layer. DTLS (Datagram TLS), standardised as RFC 6347 (DTLS 1.2) and RFC 9147 (DTLS 1.3), adapts TLS for datagram transports by adding the mechanisms needed to handle loss and reordering.

DTLS modifies TLS in three important ways. First, it adds explicit sequence numbers to records so that the receiver can detect reordering and retransmit lost handshake messages. Second, it introduces a cookie exchange at the start of the handshake: before committing state, the server sends a HelloVerifyRequest containing a cryptographic cookie derived from the client's IP address and a server secret. The client must echo this cookie in its ClientHello before the server allocates handshake state, preventing amplification attacks in which an attacker spoofs source addresses to cause the server to send large responses to innocent victims.

Third, it adds message fragmentation and reassembly for handshake messages that exceed the PMTU (Path Maximum Transmission Unit).

DTLS 1.3 (RFC 9147) inherits TLS 1.3's significant improvements: removal of the RSA key exchange (replaced by ephemeral Diffie-Hellman only), elimination of legacy cipher suites, and a reduced handshake to 1 round-trip for new connections and 0 round-trips for session resumption. For constrained IoT devices, DTLS 1.3 with ChaCha20-Poly1305 (a cipher suite designed for software efficiency on processors without hardware AES acceleration) or AES-128-CCM-8 (optimised for constrained nodes, offering a truncated 8-byte authentication tag) is the recommended secure transport for CoAP and other UDP-based IoT protocols.

TECHNOLOGY SPOTLIGHT: OSCORE: End-to-End Security Beyond DTLS

DTLS provides hop-by-hop security: the channel between each pair of communicating peers is encrypted, but an intermediate CoAP proxy must decrypt and re-encrypt the message to perform its forwarding function. In deployments where proxies are operated by third parties, such as cloud gateways managed by connectivity operators, this represents a genuine confidentiality boundary.

OSCORE (Object Security for Constrained RESTful Environments, RFC 8613) addresses this by encrypting the CoAP payload and selected header fields at the application layer, independently of the transport. An OSCORE-protected message travels end-to-end from the originating device to the final recipient with its payload encrypted throughout, even as it passes through intermediate proxies that can still perform routing functions on the unencrypted outer headers.

OSCORE uses AEAD (Authenticated Encryption with Associated Data) encryption with AES-CCM and derives session keys from a shared master secret using HKDF (HMAC-based Key Derivation Function). Because OSCORE operates at the application layer, it can be used over any transport (UDP, TCP, WebSockets, or SMS) without modification, making it particularly valuable in multi-hop or proxied IoT architectures.

4.5 Application Layer Protocols

The application layer is where IoT protocols carry the most visible architectural significance. It defines not just message format but the interaction pattern: the fundamental model by which devices and platforms exchange information. Two paradigms dominate IoT application-layer design, and the choice between them shapes every subsequent decision about broker infrastructure, security model, and platform integration.

Publish-Subscribe (Pub-Sub) decouples producers from consumers via an intermediary broker or message bus. A sensor publishes a message to a named topic; any number of subscribers that have expressed interest in that topic receive the message. Neither publisher nor subscriber needs to know about each other's existence, enabling flexible, scalable architectures where new consumers can be added without modifying device firmware. MQTT, AMQP, and DDS use this pattern.

Request-Response follows the familiar web model: a client sends a request to a known server endpoint and waits for a response. The interaction is synchronous (from the client's perspective) and point-to-point. This pattern is natural for command-and-control interactions (send an actuation command, confirm the result) and for configuration APIs. CoAP and HTTP/REST use this pattern. The sections below examine each major protocol using a consistent template.

4.5.1 MQTT (Message Queuing Telemetry Transport)

MQTT was originally developed by Andy Stanford-Clark (IBM) and Arlen Nipper (Arcom) in 1999 for monitoring oil pipelines over satellite links: a use case that demanded the smallest possible protocol overhead and tolerance for unreliable connections. It was open-sourced in 2010, standardised by OASIS in 2014 (MQTT v3.1.1), and significantly extended in 2019 (MQTT v5.0). It is now the de facto standard application protocol for cloud-connected IoT telemetry.

MQTT operates over TCP. The protocol is broker-centric: all messages flow through a central broker (such as Eclipse Mosquitto, HiveMQ, or AWS IoT Core), which receives published messages and distributes them to matching subscribers. Publishers identify their messages by topic strings (hierarchical, slash-separated paths such as 'factory/line3/sensor/temperature'). Subscribers specify topic filters using wildcards: '+' matches a single level, '#' matches multiple levels.

MQTT defines three Quality of Service (QoS) levels that control delivery guarantees. QoS 0 (At-most-once) fires and forgets: the message is delivered at best effort with no acknowledgement, suitable for high-frequency telemetry where occasional loss is acceptable. QoS 1 (At-least-once) requires an acknowledgement (PUBACK) from the broker; if the acknowledgement is not received, the publisher retransmits. The message may be delivered multiple times.

QoS 2 (Exactly-once) uses a four-message handshake (PUBLISH, PUBREC, PUBREL, PUBCOMP) to guarantee delivery exactly once, at significantly higher overhead, appropriate only for financial transactions or control commands where duplicate delivery would have consequences.

MQTT v5.0 introduced request-response correlation (via Correlation Data and Response Topic properties), message expiry intervals (preventing stale readings from being delivered after a device reconnects), shared subscriptions for load-balanced consumer groups, and reason codes for all acknowledgement packets. Security in MQTT v3.1.1 is provided by username/password authentication in the CONNECT packet (transmitted in the clear unless TLS is used). MQTT over TLS on port 8883 is mandatory for any internet-accessible broker; MQTT over TCP on port 1883 is acceptable only on isolated private networks.

CASE STUDY: AWS IoT Core and MQTT at Scale: Connected Vehicles

Amazon Web Services / Global / 2018 -- ongoing

AWS IoT Core is a managed MQTT broker service that serves as the backbone for many of the world's largest IoT deployments. In the connected vehicles domain, automotive OEMs including BMW, Volkswagen, and Stellantis route telematics data from millions of vehicles through AWS IoT Core using MQTT over TLS. Each vehicle establishes an MQTT connection authenticated by an X.509 device certificate, publishes telemetry on vehicle-specific topics (vehicle/{VIN (Vehicle Identification Number)}/telemetry), and subscribes to a command topic for OTA update notifications and remote configuration.

AWS IoT Core handles connection management, topic routing, rule engine processing (which transforms incoming MQTT messages and routes them to DynamoDB, Lambda, Kinesis, or S3), and device shadow synchronisation (a JSON document representing each device's desired and reported state). At peak load, AWS IoT Core processes hundreds of billions of messages per month. The deployment demonstrates MQTT's architectural scalability: the protocol's lightweight 2-byte fixed header, QoS flexibility, and persistent session support make it the only practical choice for maintaining persistent connections from battery-constrained or intermittently connected mobile devices at this scale. Beyond raw telemetry, MQTT's bi-directional broker model increasingly carries a second class of payload: ML inference results generated at the edge (anomaly scores, predictive maintenance alerts, and classification outputs) flowing back through the same broker infrastructure that carries sensor readings, closing the loop between physical sensing and intelligent response without a separate messaging layer.

4.5.2 CoAP (Constrained Application Protocol)

CoAP is the IETF's RESTful application protocol for constrained nodes, standardised in RFC 7252. It mirrors the HTTP request-response model (using GET, POST, PUT, and DELETE methods on URI-identified resources) but replaces HTTP's verbose text headers with a compact binary encoding that fits in a single UDP datagram. The CoAP fixed header is only 4 bytes, compared to HTTP's minimum of several hundred bytes of ASCII headers.

CoAP defines four message types. Confirmable (CON) messages require an acknowledgement (ACK) and are retransmitted if not acknowledged within a timeout, providing reliable delivery over UDP for messages that must be received. Non-confirmable (NON) messages are delivered best-effort with no retransmission, suitable for high-frequency sensor readings. ACK messages confirm receipt of a CON message. RST (Reset) messages indicate that a message was received but could not be processed (for example, because the receiver has no context for the token).

CoAP's Observe extension (RFC 7641) enables a server-push model for continuous sensor monitoring. A client sends a GET request with the Observe option set; the server registers the client as an observer and sends notifications whenever the resource changes. This transforms CoAP from a pure polling protocol into an event-driven streaming protocol without requiring a persistent TCP connection. OSCORE (RFC 8613) provides end-to-end application-layer security for CoAP, encrypting payload and sensitive options independently of the underlying transport. CoAP over DTLS

(RFC 7252 Section 9) is the IETF-recommended secure transport when hop-by-hop rather than end-to-end security is sufficient.

DEFINITION: *CoAP Observe (RFC 7641)*

A CoAP extension that allows a client to register with a server to receive automatic notifications whenever a resource changes, without polling. The client sends a GET with the Observe option; the server maintains an observer list and sends unsolicited responses when the resource value updates. This transforms CoAP into an event-driven protocol suitable for continuous sensor monitoring without a persistent TCP connection.

4.5.3 AMQP (Advanced Message Queuing Protocol)

AMQP (Advanced Message Queuing Protocol), standardised as OASIS AMQP v1.0, is an enterprise-grade, broker-mediated, TCP-based messaging protocol designed for reliable business messaging. It supports transactions, message routing rules, dead-letter queues, delivery guarantees, and rich message metadata, capabilities that exceed MQTT's scope but come with correspondingly higher overhead.

AMQP's IoT role is not at the device level but at the platform and gateway tiers. Industrial IoT gateways that aggregate telemetry from hundreds of constrained devices and forward processed data to enterprise systems use AMQP for gateway-to-platform or platform-to-platform message exchange. Apache ActiveMQ, RabbitMQ, and Azure Service Bus all support AMQP v1.0. Azure IoT Hub supports AMQP as a first-class protocol alongside MQTT and HTTPS, and industrial IoT reference architectures (such as the Industrial internet Reference Architecture from the IIC) frequently specify AMQP for the enterprise integration tier.

4.5.4 HTTP/REST

HTTP/REST is the ubiquitous web protocol, and its presence in IoT is a reflection of its ecosystem advantages: every programming language has HTTP client libraries, every developer knows REST, and every platform exposes HTTP endpoints. Its IoT role, however, is necessarily limited to nodes that are mains-powered and have sufficient processing resources to handle HTTP's verbose ASCII header format and TCP connection overhead.

HTTP is appropriate for IoT configuration APIs (REST endpoints for device provisioning, certificate management, and firmware update orchestration), dashboard integration (pulling aggregated metrics from a time-series database), and webhook-based event delivery (platform POST to a customer endpoint on alert trigger). HTTPS

(HTTP over TLS) is mandatory for any internet-exposed endpoint without exception. HTTP/1.1 keep-alive connections and HTTP/2 multiplexing reduce connection overhead for high-frequency request scenarios, and HTTP/3 (QUIC-based) eliminates TCP head-of-line blocking for environments with packet loss.

4.5.5 DDS (Data Distribution Service)

DDS (Data Distribution Service), standardised by the Object Management Group (OMG) as DDS v1.4, is a peer-to-peer, broker-free publish-subscribe middleware standard designed for real-time, safety-critical systems. Unlike MQTT and AMQP, DDS does not use a central broker; instead, it implements a data-centric bus in which participants discover each other through a built-in discovery protocol (RTPS, Real-Time Publish Subscribe Protocol) and exchange data directly.

DDS's defining characteristic is its rich Quality of Service (QoS) policy system. Over 20 QoS policies govern different aspects of data exchange: Reliability (best effort or reliable), Deadline (maximum time between data updates), Liveliness (maximum time before a participant is considered dead), Ownership (which publisher has priority if multiple publish to the same topic), and History (how many past samples are retained for late-joining subscribers).

This QoS richness makes DDS the appropriate choice for safety-critical industrial IoT: robotic control systems, autonomous vehicles, avionics, and surgical robots where end-to-end latency, reliability, and determinism must be contractually guaranteed rather than probabilistically expected.

DDS is the underlying middleware for ROS 2 (Robot Operating System 2), the de facto framework for autonomous robotics research and industrial deployment. ROS 2 replaced ROS 1's custom transport with DDS specifically to gain the QoS guarantees and real-time determinism required for safety-certified robotic systems. DDS is not appropriate for battery-powered constrained sensors (its discovery overhead and memory footprint are too large for Class 0/1 devices) but is the correct choice when sub-millisecond latency and hard reliability guarantees matter more than power efficiency.

4.5.6 Application Layer Protocol Comparison

Table 4.2 provides a consolidated comparison of the five major IoT application layer protocols across seven dimensions. The table is intended as a quick-reference decision aid; the sections above provide the analytical depth behind each entry.

Table 4.2: IoT Application Layer Protocol Comparison

Protocol	Transport	Pattern	Reliability	Security	Overhead	Typical Use Case
MQTT v5	TCP	Pub-Sub	QoS 0/1/2	TLS (port 8883)	Low (2B header)	Cloud telemetry, connected vehicles, consumer IoT
CoAP	UDP	Request-Response + Observe	CON/ NON	DTLS / OSCORE	Very low (4B header)	Constrained sensors, actuator control, smart building
AMQP v1.0	TCP	Pub-Sub / Queue	Transactions, routing	TLS	High	Gateway-to-platform, enterprise IoT integration
HTTP/ REST	TCP	Request-Response	App-layer	TLS (HTTPS)	High (verbose headers)	Config APIs, dashboards, webhooks, firmware updates
DDS v1.4	UDP/ TCP	Peer-to-peer Pub-Sub	20+ QoS policies	DDS Security plugin	Medium	Robotics, autonomous vehicles, industrial real-time

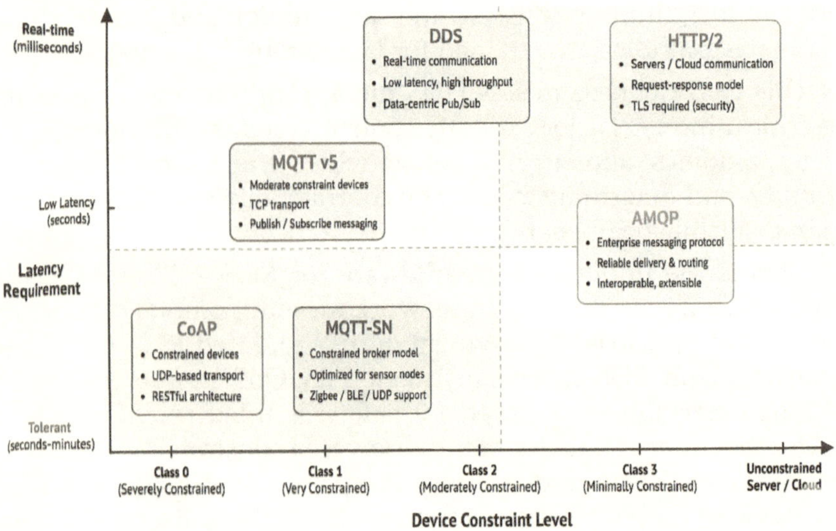

Figure 4.4: IoT application protocol selection map.

4.6 Management Protocols: The Management Plane

Many IoT deployments fail in production not because of telemetry protocol choice but because of inadequate device management infrastructure. The management plane is distinct from both the data plane (sensor telemetry) and the control plane (actuator commands):

it handles device configuration, firmware updates, diagnostics, and lifecycle operations. Without a standardised management protocol, operators are forced into vendor-proprietary management tools that cannot scale, cannot be audited, and cannot be integrated with enterprise asset management systems.

4.6.1 OMA LwM2M (Lightweight Machine-to-Machine)

OMA LwM2M v1.2 is the primary IoT device management standard for constrained devices. It is built on CoAP over DTLS and defines a hierarchical resource model and four standardised interfaces that together provide complete device lifecycle management.

LwM2M's resource model organises device data and operations into Objects, Instances, and Resources. An Object represents a category of functionality (for example, Object 1 is Server, Object 3 is Device, Object 5 is Firmware Update, Object 3303 is Temperature Sensor). An Instance is a specific instance of an object (for example, Instance 0 of Object 3303 is the first temperature sensor). A Resource is an individual data item or operation within an instance (for example, Resource 5700 is Sensor Value, Resource 5701 is Sensor Units). This three-level hierarchy provides a standardised, self-describing data model that any LwM2M server can interrogate without prior knowledge of the device.

LwM2M defines four management interfaces. The Bootstrap Interface establishes the initial trust relationship between a factory-fresh device and its management server by provisioning the server URI, security credentials, and initial configuration. The Registration Interface allows the device to announce its presence and its supported object list to the management server. The Device Management and Service Enablement Interface provides read, write, execute, and observe operations on device resources. The Information Reporting Interface handles observe and notify operations for continuous telemetry.

LwM2M v1.2 added support for MQTT and HTTP as alternative transports alongside CoAP/DTLS, improving interoperability with cloud IoT platforms.

DEFINITION: OMA LwM2M Object/Instance/Resource Model

The hierarchical data model used by OMA LwM2M to represent device state and capabilities. An Object (identified by a numeric ID) represents a category of functionality; an Instance is a specific occurrence of that object; a Resource is an individual data item or operation within the instance. The model is self-describing: a management server can discover and interrogate any resource without device-specific knowledge, enabling interoperable device management across vendors and platforms.

4.6.2 NETCONF and YANG

NETCONF (Network Configuration Protocol, RFC 6241) is the IETF's standard for programmatic network device configuration. It operates over SSH or TLS and uses XML-encoded Remote Procedure Calls (RPCs) to get, edit, copy, delete, and validate configuration datastores on managed devices. YANG (Yet Another Next Generation, RFC 7950) is the data modelling language used with NETCONF: YANG models define the structure and semantics of configuration and operational data in a tree-based schema that can be compiled into code stubs, validated automatically, and exchanged between management systems.

In the IoT context, NETCONF/YANG is primarily relevant to industrial IoT and network infrastructure management rather than to constrained sensor deployments. Industrial IoT gateways, industrial Ethernet switches, and programmable logic controllers (PLCs) with network interfaces increasingly support NETCONF for integration with network management systems (NMS) and orchestration platforms. YANG models for industrial devices are being developed by the IETF ANIMA and OPSAWG working groups, enabling automated network configuration in IIoT environments. RESTCONF (RFC 8040), a RESTful variant of NETCONF over HTTPS, reduces the barrier to adoption by allowing standard HTTP tooling to manage YANG-modelled device configuration.

4.6.3 TR-069 (CPE WAN Management Protocol)

TR-069 (Technical Report 069, published by the Broadband Forum as CPE WAN Management Protocol, CWMP) was originally designed in 2004 for managing broadband Customer Premises Equipment (CPE) (home gateways, modems, and set-top boxes) remotely from an ISP (internet Service Provider) Auto Configuration Server (ACS). It uses HTTPS/SOAP over TCP and defines a session-based model in which the device (CPE) initiates a management session with the ACS, exchanges configuration and diagnostic information, and terminates the session.

TR-069 is legacy but remains heavily deployed in consumer IoT and ISP-managed devices. Hundreds of millions of home routers and smart home gateways worldwide are managed via TR-069 by their ISPs. The Broadband Forum's TR-369 (User Services Platform, USP) is TR-069's successor, replacing SOAP with a more modern protocol stack (WebSockets, MQTT, STOMP, or CoAP) and adding support for disaggregated device management architectures. USP adoption is growing in new deployments as ISPs migrate their management infrastructure.

4.6.4 SNMP in IoT

SNMPv3 (Simple Network Management Protocol version 3) is used in some legacy industrial IoT monitoring systems and network infrastructure management contexts. SNMPv3 added user-based security (USM) with authentication (HMAC (Hash-based Message Authentication Code) with MD5 or SHA variants) and privacy (DES or AES-128) to address the serious security weaknesses of SNMPv1 and v2c.

However, SNMP is not recommended for new IoT device management deployments: its polling-based architecture is inefficient for large fleets, its data model is less expressive than YANG, and its performance on constrained devices is poor. Existing SNMPv3 deployments in industrial environments should be retained where replacement costs are prohibitive, but new architectures should use LwM2M or NETCONF/YANG as appropriate for the device class.

4.7 Protocol-Layer Security

Chapter 8 addresses IoT security comprehensively at the system level. This section focuses specifically on the protocol-layer security mechanisms — the authentication, encryption, and integrity provisions built into or layered over each protocol examined in this chapter. Protocol-layer security is the first line of defence: vulnerabilities introduced by poor protocol security choices cannot be remediated at higher levels of the architecture.

4.7.1 Link Layer Security

IEEE 802.15.4 provides AES-128 security at the MAC layer in CCM* mode (Counter with CBC-MAC), which combines counter-mode encryption (CTR) for confidentiality with CBC-MAC for integrity and authentication. The security suite is configurable: operators can choose encryption only, authentication only, or both. Key management at the 802.15.4 MAC layer is not standardised by IEEE and is delegated to higher-layer protocols (Zigbee Trust Centre, Thread Commissioner).

Zigbee uses two independent AES-128 keys. The network key is shared across all devices in the network and encrypts inter-device traffic at the network layer. Link keys are pairwise keys shared between adjacent nodes, providing an additional encryption layer for sensitive unicast traffic. The Trust Centre manages network key distribution and rotation. A well-known historical vulnerability in Zigbee deployments was the transmission of the network key in plaintext during the join process in early implementations; Zigbee 3.0 mandated Install Codes to ensure encrypted key distribution during join.

BLE uses LE Secure Connections, introduced in Bluetooth 4.2, which implements Elliptic Curve Diffie-Hellman (ECDH) key exchange using the P-256 curve to establish a shared secret during pairing. Long-term keys (LTKs) are derived from the shared secret and stored for reconnection. BLE advertising PDUs can be passively observed; Bluetooth 5.1 introduced Advertising Address Resolution to prevent tracking by rotating the Resolvable Private Address (RPA) used in advertising packets.

LoRaWAN uses AES-128 at two independent layers. The Network Session Key (NwkSKey) authenticates the Message Integrity Code (MIC) over the entire frame and encrypts MAC commands in the FOpts field. The Application Session Key (AppSKey) encrypts the FRMPayload (the application data). This architecture allows the network server to verify frame integrity without decrypting application data: a significant privacy design advantage. Devices should use OTAA with fresh session keys per join to ensure forward secrecy; ABP with static keys is strongly discouraged in production deployments.

4.7.2 DTLS for UDP-Based Protocols

CoAP over DTLS is the IETF-recommended secure transport for constrained IoT communication. For devices that cannot afford the memory and processing cost of a full DTLS implementation, OSCORE (RFC 8613) provides application-layer end-to-end security that survives hop-by-hop proxying. The IETF ACE (Authentication and Authorization for Constrained Environments, RFC 9200) framework provides token-based authorisation for CoAP resources, using OAuth 2.0 concepts adapted for constrained nodes.

Cipher suite selection for constrained DTLS implementations should favour AES-128-CCM-8 (the truncated 8-byte authentication tag variant defined in RFC 6655) or ChaCha20-Poly1305 (for processors without hardware AES acceleration). Elliptic curve key exchange (ECDHE with secp256r1 or Curve25519) is substantially more efficient than RSA-based key exchange on constrained processors: a 256-bit ECDH operation is computationally equivalent to a 3072-bit RSA operation in security level but requires far less CPU time and memory.

4.7.3 MQTT Security

MQTT v3.1.1 provides username/password authentication in the CONNECT packet, but these credentials are transmitted in the clear if TLS is not used. Any MQTT broker accessible from the internet without TLS is trivially compromised. MQTT over TLS 1.3 on port 8883 is mandatory for all internet-accessible deployments. Broker-level Access Control Lists (ACLs) restrict which clients can publish and subscribe to which topics; a device should be permitted to publish only to its own device-specific topic path and subscribe only to its own command topic.

A pervasive vulnerability in early IoT MQTT deployments was the use of a single shared credential across all devices in a fleet. If any device is compromised, the shared credential allows the attacker to impersonate any device, inject false telemetry, or issue commands to the entire fleet. The correct architecture uses per-device X.509 certificates (mutual TLS, mTLS) for device authentication, with each certificate scoped to the device's own topic namespace in the broker ACL. AWS IoT Core, Azure IoT Hub, and Google Cloud IoT Core all enforce mTLS by default.

4.7.4 CoAP Security Vulnerabilities

CoAP's use of UDP multicast introduces a specific amplification attack vector. A small CoAP request (as few as 10 bytes) sent to a multicast address (such as ff02::fd, the All CoAP Nodes address) can elicit large responses from many devices simultaneously, enabling a distributed denial-of-service amplification attack. RFC 7967 (No-Response option) allows servers to suppress responses to multicast requests, and network-level rate limiting on multicast-capable interfaces mitigates this risk. OSCORE eliminates most CoAP-specific attack surfaces by encrypting options that would otherwise be visible to intermediate proxies, including the Uri-Path that could leak information about device resource structure.

Table 4.3 summarises the authentication mechanism, encryption, integrity protection, and replay protection provided by each protocol and its recommended security configuration.

Table 4.3: Protocol-Layer Security Summary

Protocol	Authentication	Encryption	Integrity	Replay Protection	Key Recommendation
IEEE 802.15.4	Per-frame key identifier	AES-128 CCM*	CBC-MAC MIC	Frame counter	Mandatory for production; key rotation via higher layer
Zigbee	Network Key / Link Key	AES-128	MIC-32/64/128	Frame counter	Use Install Codes; rotate network key annually
BLE	LE Secure Connections (ECDH P-256)	AES-128 CCM	Packet MIC	Packet counter	Use RPA; mandatory SC for IoT medical
LoRa WAN	DevEUI + AppKey (OTAA)	AES-128 (AppSKey)	MIC via NwkSKey	FCnt (32-bit)	Always use OTAA; never reuse AppSKey
DTLS 1.3	Certificate / PSK (Pre-Shared Key)	AES-128-CCM-8 / ChaCha20	AEAD tag	Sequence number	Prefer ECDHE; avoid RSA; use cert per device
MQTT +TLS	Username/ Password + mTLS cert	TLS 1.3 cipher	HMAC / AEAD	TLS record seq	Per-device cert; restrict topic ACLs
CoAP +OS-CORE	OSCORE Master Secret (HKDF)	AES-128-CCM	AEAD tag	Sender sequence ID	Preferred for proxied multi-hop deployments

4.8 Protocol Selection Framework

The preceding sections have established a comprehensive reference library of IoT protocols. This section transforms that reference knowledge into actionable guidance for system designers. Protocol selection is not a single decision but a stack of decisions, one per layer, and the decisions at each layer constrain the options available at the layer above. A LoRaWAN link layer, for example, precludes MQTT over TCP (because LoRaWAN's low data rate and duty-cycle restrictions are incompatible with TCP's connection maintenance overhead) and steers the application layer toward CBOR-encoded payloads with minimal headers.

4.8.1 Selection Criteria

Seven criteria determine the optimal protocol stack for a given deployment. Each criterion must be evaluated for the device, not for the gateway or cloud platform; gateways typically support all protocols and the selection constraint lies in the most resource-constrained element of the deployment.

- Power budget is the device battery-powered or mains-powered? Battery-powered devices require ultra-low power link layers (Zigbee, Z-Wave, BLE, LoRaWAN) and connectionless transport (UDP). Mains-powered devices can afford Wi-Fi and TCP.

- Range requirement — what is the maximum distance between device and gateway? Local area (under 10 m): BLE or Zigbee. Building-scale (10 to 100 m): Zigbee, Z-Wave, or BLE Mesh. Campus (100 m to 1 km): LoRaWAN or private cellular. Wide area (over 1 km): LoRaWAN or NB-IoT/LTE-M.
- Data rate requirement — what volume of data must be transmitted, and how frequently? Infrequent small readings (under 100 bytes, every 15 minutes): LoRaWAN or Zigbee. Moderate telemetry (1 KB/s): BLE or Wi-Fi. High bandwidth (video, waveform): Wi-Fi only.
- Latency requirement — how quickly must a command reach the device? Sub-100 ms: BLE, Zigbee, or Wi-Fi with DDS. Up to 1 second: MQTT with QoS 1. Tens of seconds: LoRaWAN Class B/C. Minutes: LoRaWAN Class A.
- Network topology — how many devices are deployed in what spatial arrangement? Point-to-point: BLE or Wi-Fi. Small star (under 50 devices, one gateway): Zigbee, Z-Wave, or BLE. Large mesh (50 to 65,000 devices): Zigbee Mesh or BLE Mesh. Wide-area star-of-stars: LoRaWAN.
- Regulatory environment — which frequency bands are approved in the deployment region? 2.4 GHz is globally available. Sub-GHz bands (Z-Wave, LoRaWAN) vary by region. Duty-cycle restrictions in Europe (1 percent for LoRaWAN) limit uplink frequency.
- Security requirements — what level of authentication and encryption is mandated by regulation or customer contract? Healthcare and critical infrastructure deployments require mTLS (per-device certificates), end-to-end encryption (OSCORE or DTLS), and key rotation. Consumer deployments at minimum require TLS transport security and per-device credentials.

Key Insight: Protocol Diversity Reflects Physical Reality. The range of IoT protocols is not market fragmentation — it is a direct consequence of physics. LoRaWAN achieves 15 km range by using very narrow bandwidth and very slow data rates; the physics that gives it range makes high data rates impossible. Wi-Fi achieves gigabit throughput by consuming orders of magnitude more power; the same physics that gives it bandwidth prevents battery operation. There is no universal IoT protocol because there is no universal IoT deployment. Understanding each protocol as occupying a specific region of the power-range-data-rate design space — rather than competing on the same dimensions — is the foundation of sound protocol selection.

4.8.2 Protocol Selection Decision Matrix

Table 4.4 applies the seven selection criteria to six representative IoT deployment scenarios, recommending a complete communication stack for each. The recommendations follow from the analytical framework above and should be treated as informed starting points rather than absolute prescriptions — site-specific constraints, existing infrastructure, and team expertise may justify departures from the matrix.

Table 4.4: Protocol Selection Decision Matrix

Deployment Scenario	Link Layer	Network Layer	Transport	Application Protocol	Management Protocol
Smart home sensor (temp/humidity, battery, 10 m indoor)	Zigbee or Z-Wave	6LoWPAN / IPv6	UDP	CoAP + DTLS	LwM2M
Industrial motor monitor (mains-powered, 50 m, sub-100 ms latency)	IEEE 802.15.4 / Wi-Fi	IPv6	UDP / TCP	DDS or MQTT	NETCONF/ YANG
Agricultural soil probe (battery, 3 km field, 15-min readings)	LoRaWAN Class A	LoRa WAN Network Server	N/A (LoRa WAN native)	Custom CBOR payload	LwM2M over LoRaWAN
Retail beacon (battery, 5 m, asset tracking)	BLE (advertising mode)	BLE scan -> gateway	N/A (gateway handles IP)	Custom advert payload	Via gateway API
Smart city parking sensor (battery, 500 m urban, hourly)	LoRaWAN Class A	LoRa WAN Network Server	N/A	CBOR / LPP	LwM2M
IP camera (mains, 50 m, HD video stream)	Wi-Fi 6 (802.11ax)	IPv6	TCP	HTTP/ RTSP over TLS	TR-069 / USP

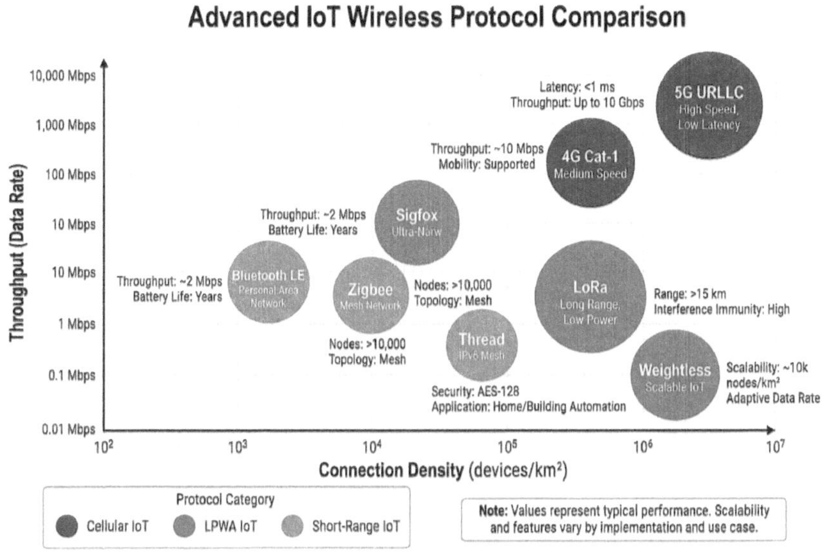

Figure 4.5: IoT Wireless Protocol Design Space: each protocol occupies a distinct region of the range-data-rate-power trade-off envelope, illustrating why no single protocol serves all deployment scenarios.

4.8.3 Worked Example: The Smart Building Protocol Audit

Returning to the chapter's opening scenario: the 18-floor commercial tower with four incompatible IoT subsystems. Applying the selection matrix to each subsystem in turn reveals both why the problems occurred and what a properly engineered architecture would look like.

The HVAC system's Zigbee sensors are the most defensible technology choice: Zigbee's mesh range, ultra-low power, and building-automation device profiles (HVAC clusters are defined in the Zigbee Building Automation profile) make it a natural fit. The problem was not the link-layer choice but the absence of a 6LoWPAN border router and LwM2M management server: the installer used a proprietary Zigbee coordinator that exposed no standard API. The remediation is to replace the coordinator with an open-standard Zigbee border router (running OpenThread or Silicon Labs Multiprotocol) that bridges the Zigbee mesh to IPv6 and exposes LwM2M endpoints.

The lighting system's Z-Wave sensors were installed by a lighting vendor who chose Z-Wave for its certified interoperability with the lighting controller ecosystem. Classic Z-Wave's 232-node mesh limit is sufficient for a single floor but will constrain future expansion. The integration problem arises because Z-Wave has no native IP stack: a Z-Wave USB controller or IP gateway is required to translate Z-Wave commands into REST/MQTT calls. The recommended architecture is a floor-level Z-Wave gateway per two floors, publishing occupancy events to a centralised MQTT broker over TLS.

The access control system's proprietary 900 MHz mesh is the most problematic component: its binary protocol has no published specification, making third-party integration impossible without a vendor API. The lesson for future procurements is clear: any IoT subsystem installed in a multi-vendor building should be required to expose a standard API (MQTT, CoAP, or REST/JSON over HTTPS) as a contract condition. Sub-GHz proprietary meshes should be specified only when regulatory or security requirements mandate it and a standard API is contractually guaranteed.

The LoRaWAN energy meters are the most clear to integrate: LoRaWAN network servers (TTN, ChirpStack, Actility ThingPark) expose standard MQTT or REST APIs for downstream application consumption. The meter vendor's LPP-encoded CBOR payload is decodable using the LPP codec library and can be normalised to the building management platform's data model at the integration layer. A ChirpStack instance deployed on the building network server can forward decoded meter readings to the centralised MQTT broker in normalised JSON within hours of configuration.

The unified dashboard architecture would consist of a centralised MQTT broker (Eclipse Mosquitto or HiveMQ) receiving normalised JSON from four integration adapters: a Zigbee border router with LwM2M-to-MQTT bridge for HVAC, floor-level Z-Wave gateways for lighting, an access control vendor REST API poller for the proprietary system (pending vendor API delivery), and a ChirpStack LoRaWAN network server for energy metering. All device-to-platform connections use MQTT over TLS 1.3 with per-subsystem certificates and topic-level ACLs. This architecture transforms the four isolated subsystems into a unified, auditable, and extensible building management platform.

The final caution for protocol selection: the decision matrix provides a structured starting framework, not a final answer. Network planning tools are beginning to apply ML models to predict coverage, interference, and gateway capacity from site-survey data and historical deployment statistics, useful as a pre-deployment sanity check, but not a substitute for the engineering judgement that the constraint analysis above requires. Regulatory requirements, vendor ecosystem maturity, team expertise, existing infrastructure, and total cost of ownership may all justify departures from theoretical optimality. Real protocol selection is iterative: the first architecture will evolve, and designing for extensibility and standard interfaces is more durable than optimising for any single protocol choice made at inception.

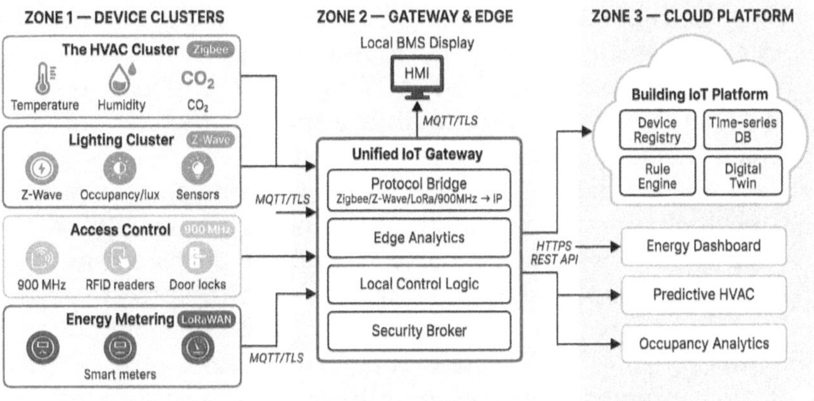

Figure 4.6: The Unified Smart Building Architecture.

Professional Checklist: IoT Protocol Selection

Before choosing an IoT protocol stack, confirm the following:

- *The protocol matches the required range, bandwidth, latency, mobility, and power consumption.*
- *The network topology supports the expected device density, gateway availability, and coverage area.*
- *Security mechanisms such as authentication, encryption, key management, and secure onboarding are supported.*
- *The protocol can scale from pilot deployment to production deployment without major redesign.*
- *Interoperability with cloud platforms, gateways, and enterprise systems is practical.*
- *Operational cost, spectrum availability, regional regulation, and long-term support are acceptable.*

4.9 Chapter Summary

This chapter has provided a systematic examination of the IoT communication protocol landscape, organised around the four-layer stack that has emerged as the standard architectural framework for IoT networking: Link, Network/Internet, Transport, and Application layers, with Management and Security as cross-cutting disciplines. The chapter opened by establishing why IoT requires a tailored protocol stack view: the constrained-node classes defined by RFC 7228 impose hard limits on RAM, flash, and energy that preclude direct adoption of conventional TCP/IP protocols.

Section 4.2 surveyed six link-layer technologies that together cover the full spectrum of IoT deployment requirements. IEEE 802.15.4 was established as the foundational standard on which Zigbee, Thread, and WirelessHART are built. Zigbee's mesh topology and rich device profile library make it the natural choice for smart home and building automation. Z-Wave's sub-GHz operation and mandatory certification programme serve residential security deployments. Bluetooth Low Energy's smartphone ubiquity and advertising mode enable wearables, beacons, and short-range consumer applications. LoRaWAN's chirp-spread-spectrum modulation achieves multi-kilometre range at ultra-low power for wide-area sensing. Wi-Fi 6 with TWT and WPA3 extends Wi-Fi's role to IoT in environments where bandwidth and existing infrastructure justify its higher power cost.

Section 4.3 addressed the network layer challenge of fitting IPv6, designed for full-capability hosts, onto constrained 802.15.4 devices with 127-byte frame limits. 6LoWPAN's IPHC compression reduces the 40-byte IPv6 header to as few as 2 bytes, while RPL's DODAG topology provides efficient routing in low-power lossy mesh networks. The 6LoWPAN Border Router was identified as the critical translation point between constrained mesh and standard IPv6 infrastructure.

Section 4.4 analysed the transport-layer trade-off between TCP's reliability and UDP's efficiency. TCP is justified for persistent cloud connections, firmware downloads, and configuration APIs; UDP is the correct choice for constrained devices transmitting infrequent readings. DTLS 1.3 was shown to provide the security properties of TLS over UDP, with its cookie exchange mechanism preventing amplification attacks, and OSCORE was introduced as the superior choice when end-to-end security must survive hop-by-hop proxying.

Section 4.5 examined five application-layer protocols across the two dominant paradigms. MQTT's broker-centric publish-subscribe model with three QoS levels makes it the de facto standard for cloud-connected telemetry. CoAP's binary REST model over UDP, enhanced by the Observe extension and OSCORE, serves constrained devices requiring resource-efficient interaction. AMQP provides enterprise-grade message queuing at the gateway-to-platform tier. HTTP/REST remains appropriate for configuration APIs and dashboard integration. DDS delivers the deterministic QoS guarantees required by safety-critical industrial and robotic systems.

Section 4.6 examined the management plane protocols that determine whether a deployment remains maintainable in production. OMA LwM2M v1.2 was shown to be the primary standard for constrained device management, providing Bootstrap, Registration, Device Management, and Information Reporting interfaces over CoAP/DTLS. NETCONF/YANG serves industrial IoT and network infrastructure. TR-069 (CWMP) and its successor USP remain widely deployed for ISP-managed consumer IoT devices.

Section 4.7 mapped the security provisions at each protocol layer, establishing the principle that security must be applied at every layer rather than compensated at a higher layer. Key findings included the requirement for per-device X.509 certificates in MQTT deployments, the superiority of OSCORE over hop-by-hop DTLS in proxied CoAP architectures, and the importance of OTAA over ABP in LoRaWAN deployments.

Section 4.8 synthesised the preceding content into a seven-criterion selection framework (power, range, data rate, latency, topology, regulatory environment, and security requirements) and applied it both to a decision matrix covering six canonical deployment scenarios and to the chapter's smart building opening scenario. The worked example demonstrated that protocol integration failures are primarily caused not by poor link-layer choices but by the absence of standard management interfaces and IP-layer interoperability, lessons that apply directly to any multi-vendor IoT deployment.

Chapter 5

IoT System Design: Methodology, Prototyping, and Deployment

Chapter 5 presents a systematic methodology for designing, prototyping, and deploying IoT systems from concept to implementation. It introduces a ten-step design process that guides the development of IoT solutions through conceptual, logical, physical, and application-level decisions. The chapter explains how purpose specification, process modelling, domain modelling, information modelling, service design, IoT level selection, functional architecture, protocol selection, hardware selection, implementation, and testing contribute to a complete IoT system design. It also discusses communication APIs, cloud backend choices, and practical deployment considerations that connect devices, gateways, platforms, data services, and user applications. Through the AgroSense smart agriculture case study, the chapter demonstrates how the design methodology can be applied to a real-world IoT solution. Overall, this chapter provides a structured engineering framework for transforming an IoT idea into a technically sound, scalable, secure, and deployable system.

Opening Scenario: The Farm That Could Not Afford to Guess

The Rajasthan summer had come early, and Aisha Desai was staring at a blank engineering notebook. Twenty-three kilometres from the nearest town, the cooperative of fourteen smallholder farmers she had been sent to help had just finished counting the cost of last season's failures. Three hundred and forty hectares of mixed cereal and vegetable production. An estimated 23% harvest loss. Some plots over-irrigated, roots waterlogged and rotting while the farmer waited for visual signs that came too late. Others under-irrigated, soil moisture that had fallen below the wilting threshold days before the leaves began to curl, by which time the cellular structure of the crop had already been damaged.

The cooperative had secured a grant for an IoT-based precision agriculture pilot. The budget was modest. The technology requirement was not: sensors at forty locations across three distinct field types, wireless connectivity across a three-kilometre perimeter with no cellular signal, a platform to collect and visualise eighteen months of data, automated irrigation valve control, and a mobile application that the farmers could use without any technical training. The farmers spoke Marwari and Hindi. They trusted the soil under their fingers more than any screen.

Aisha had read about IoT. She had assembled Arduino kits in her undergraduate laboratory and had connected a Raspberry Pi to a temperature sensor for a course project. She knew, roughly, what the components were. What she did not know was how to design a system; how to move from 'we need to know when to irrigate' to a deployable architecture with forty sensor nodes, two gateways, twelve solenoid valves, and a farmer-facing mobile application, all working together reliably in a semi-arid field environment where the nearest repair technician was three hours away by road.

She had been given one piece of advice by her professor before she left: 'Start with the purpose. Not the hardware.' She had written the phrase at the top of the blank page and then stared at it for fifteen minutes, uncertain what it meant in practice.

This chapter gives Aisha, and every engineer facing the same blank page, the answer. The ten-step IoT Design Methodology provides a structured path from a single sentence ('we need to know when to irrigate') to a complete, deployable system specification. Each section of this chapter teaches one or more steps of the methodology, and then applies those steps directly to the AgroSense smart agriculture deployment. By Section 5.8, Aisha's blank page has become a design document. By then, every decision, made in the order it was made, is fully visible and traceable.

5.1 Introduction to the Ten-Step IoT Design Methodology

Most IoT project failures are not hardware failures. They are not software bugs or radio connectivity problems. They are design failures: the wrong sensors chosen because requirements were never written down; the wrong platform selected because scalability was not considered until ten thousand devices had already been deployed; the wrong communication protocol built in because the network topology was not analysed before firmware was written. These failures are expensive (hardware already purchased, firmware already written, infrastructure already installed) and they are avoidable.

A structured design methodology exists precisely to prevent them by ensuring that every design decision that must be made gets made, in the right order, with the right information.

The ten-step IoT Design Methodology, formalised by Srinivasa, Siddesh, and Hanumantha Raju (2018) and aligned with the broader systems engineering literature, provides that structure. It is not a rigid checklist but a layered thinking framework: each step builds on the one before it, and each layer of the design depends on the layer above it being correct. Errors at the purpose specification layer propagate through every subsequent layer: a vague purpose statement produces incomplete requirements, which produce a flawed domain model, which produces an information model that does not capture the data the system actually needs. The methodology front-loads thinking precisely to reduce downstream cost.

5.1.1 Design Philosophy: From Abstract to Concrete

IoT design is iterative and directional. It proceeds from abstract to concrete and from requirement to specification. In the abstract-to-concrete direction, the designer begins with a statement of purpose: a sentence describing what the system must achieve and for whom, and progressively refines this into models (domain model, information model), then into logical specifications (services, functional architecture), and finally into physical choices (hardware platform, protocol, deployment topology). Only at the final stages are specific products named and purchased.

In the requirement-to-specification direction, the designer works from what the system must do (requirements) to how it will do it (specifications). A requirement states an observable behaviour: 'Soil moisture shall be measured at each node with an accuracy of plus or minus 3% volumetric water content.' A specification names the mechanism: 'The Vegetronix VH400 capacitive soil moisture sensor shall be used, with factory calibration verified against gravimetric measurement at installation.' Requirements are technology-agnostic; specifications are technology-specific. Mixing the two, writing requirements that already specify the implementation, is a common error that forecloses better solutions before the design space has been explored.

5.1.2 Why a Ten-Step Process?

Simpler approaches to IoT design ('choose a sensor, connect it to a cloud platform, and iterate') consistently fail at scale because they bypass the modelling steps that ensure system coherence before hardware is purchased. The most common failure mode is the integration crisis: device firmware and cloud ingestion code are developed in parallel by different team members using different assumptions about data formats, topic structures, and timing, and the mismatch is discovered only at integration testing; when rework costs are at their highest. The ten-step methodology prevents this by making the information model (what data flows where, in what format) a completed, agreed artefact before any firmware or cloud code is written.

A second failure mode is scope creep at the wrong layer: a requirement surfaces during hardware integration ('the farmers want to see rain forecasts alongside soil moisture') that would have been trivial to accommodate in the service specification but now requires redesigning both the data pipeline and the user interface. Front-loading requirement elicitation (Step 1) and service specification (Step 5) captures this requirement at the appropriate point in the design, when accommodating it costs nothing.

5.1.3 The Three Design Phases and Ten Steps

The ten steps naturally group into three design phases that correspond to the classic systems engineering progression from concept to implementation:

The Conceptual Design phase (Steps 1 to 3) answers the question: what is this system for, and what does it need to do? It produces a purpose statement, a requirements document, a process flow diagram, and a domain model. No technology choices are made. No hardware is named. The conceptual design is entirely technology-agnostic; it could, in principle, describe a manual process or a paper-based system. Its value lies in forcing clarity about the problem before any solution is proposed.

The Logical Design phase (Steps 4 to 6) answers the question: what data does the system handle, what services does it provide, and how are its components logically connected? It produces an information model, a service specification with API contracts, and a functional architecture diagram. Technology categories may appear (a time-series database, a publish-subscribe broker, a rule engine) but specific products are not yet committed to. The logical design is the bridge between what the system does and how it will be built.

The Physical Design phase (Steps 7 to 10) answers the question: how is the system physically built, deployed, and operated? It produces a network deployment diagram, a bill of materials, application specifications, a test plan, and a deployment and iteration framework. Specific hardware products are named, firmware is written, and the system is tested and deployed. Every physical choice at this stage should be traceable, directly and explicitly, to a requirement in Step 1.

Throughout this chapter, each methodology step will be applied to a single running case study: the AgroSense smart agriculture monitoring and irrigation control system for the cooperative farm introduced in the opening scenario. By Section 5.8, the complete AgroSense design, purpose statement through to bill of materials and deployment plan, will be visible as a unified design document that practitioners can draw upon as a template for their own design engagements.

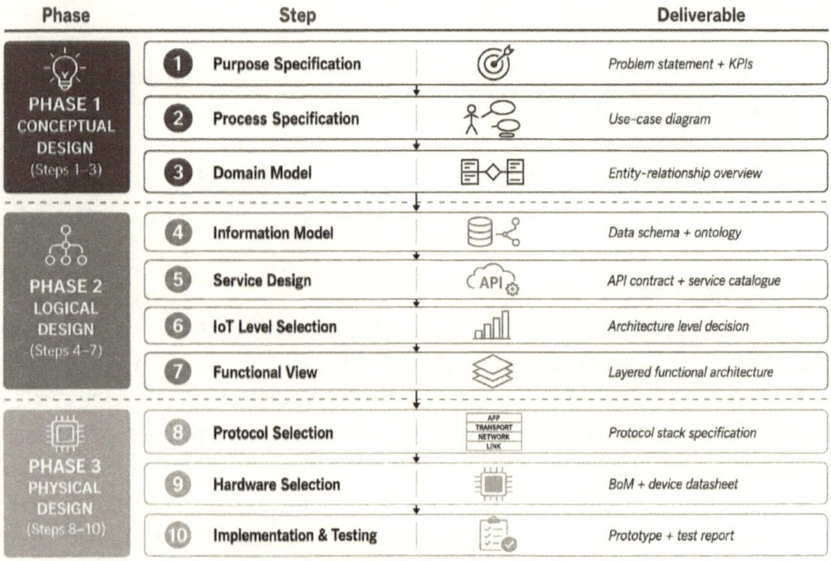

Figure 5.1: The Ten-Step IoT Design Methodology

5.2 The Ten Steps: Reference Definitions

This section provides the reference definitions for all ten design steps. The four subsequent sections (5.3 to 5.6) work through the steps in their three natural groups, applying each step to the Agro-Sense case study. Practitioners applying the methodology to a new project are encouraged to return to this section as a reference at the start of each design phase.

Step 1: Purpose and Requirement Specification

Purpose: To define why the system exists: the problem it solves, the stakeholders it serves, and the value it creates. Requirements translate the purpose into specific, testable statements of what the system must do.

Inputs: Stakeholder interviews, domain expertise, problem context documentation.

Outputs: A purpose statement (one paragraph), a structured requirements document with functional requirements (what the system does), non-functional requirements (how well it does it: accuracy, availability, latency, battery life), and constraints (what limits the design — budget, physical environment, regulatory requirements).

Key questions: Why does this system need to exist? Who benefits and how? What does it need to measure or control? How accurately and how frequently? What are the environmental, power, connectivity, and cost constraints?

Step 2: Process Specification

Purpose: To define the processes the system executes: the sequence of operations from sensor measurement through to user output or physical actuation. Process specification transforms the purpose statement into a concrete description of system behaviour.

Inputs: Purpose statement and requirements from Step 1.

Outputs: A process flow diagram showing data flows, decision points, triggers, actors, and actions on both the device side (sense, filter, transmit) and the platform side (receive, store, analyse, alert, control).

Key questions: What events trigger the system? What sequence of operations follows each trigger? Where are decisions made — on the device, at the gateway, or in the cloud? What actions result from each decision?

Step 3: Domain Model

Purpose: To identify the real-world entities in the system's operational domain and model their relationships. The domain model is the conceptual map of the problem space, independent of implementation technology.

Inputs: Purpose statement, requirements, and process flow diagram.

Outputs: A Unified Modelling Language (UML)-style domain model diagram showing entity classes (physical entities such as sensors and valves, digital entities such as records and alerts, and actor entities such as farmers and technicians) and the relationships between them (multiplicities, associations, composition).

Key questions: What are the distinct things in this domain? What data does each thing have? How do things relate to each other? What actors interact with the system and how?

Step 4: Information Model

Purpose: To define precisely what data the system collects, stores, processes, and transmits: the system's data vocabulary. The information model is the foundation for all downstream data pipeline design.

Inputs: Domain model from Step 3.

Outputs: An entity-attribute table or structured data schema defining each IoT resource, its attributes (name, data type, unit, range, accuracy, update frequency), and its relationships to other resources. Also specifies retention policies and data quality requirements.

Key questions: What data does each sensor produce? In what format, at what rate, with what accuracy? What data must be stored, and for how long? What derived data (aggregates, alerts, predictions) must the system produce?

Step 5: Service Specification

Purpose: To define the services the system provides: the functional capabilities that components must deliver and the APIs through which they communicate. Service specification translates the information model into an architecture of interacting services.

Inputs: Information model from Step 4.

Outputs: A service catalogue listing each service (data collection, storage, analytics, control, notification, management) with its interface definition: protocol, endpoint or topic structure, payload format, and quality-of-service requirements. This is the API contract that governs all subsequent development.

Key questions: What services must the system provide? How do components communicate; what protocols, what message formats, what topic structures? What are the latency and reliability requirements for each service?

Step 6: IoT Functional View

Purpose: To produce a technology-agnostic logical architecture showing what functional components the system requires and how they connect. The functional view organises the services from Step 5 into a coherent architectural model.

Inputs: Service specification from Step 5.

Outputs: A functional architecture diagram organised around

the standard IoT functional layers: Sensing and Actuation, Connectivity, Processing, Application, and User Interface. Components are shown as logical functions (not yet as specific hardware or software products).

Key questions: What functional layers does the system require? What components exist at each layer? How do they interact? What is the data flow path from physical measurement to user decision?

Step 7: Operational View

Purpose: To specify the physical deployment environment: where devices are located, how they are connected, what environmental and operational constraints they face, and what the end-to-end signal path looks like in a real installation.

Inputs: Functional view from Step 6, site survey data, environmental specification from requirements.

Outputs: A network deployment diagram showing physical device locations and wireless links, an operational specification covering environmental ratings (IP code, temperature range), power sources, maintenance access requirements, and contingency provisions.

Key questions: Where will each device be physically installed? What are the radio coverage requirements? What environmental conditions (temperature, humidity, dust, vibration) must devices tolerate? How will devices be powered, maintained, and replaced?

Step 8: Device and Component Integration

Purpose: To map the functional view and information model to specific hardware components, software platforms, and integration specifications. Step 8 is the first step at which specific products are named and committed to.

Inputs: Operational view from Step 7, information model (Step 4), service specification (Step 5), requirements (Step 1) for traceability verification.

Outputs: A bill of materials (BoM) listing specific hardware components and quantities, a device integration specification documenting interfaces and protocols, and a prototype-to-production checklist for design verification.

Key questions: Which hardware platform best satisfies the power, connectivity, processing, and cost requirements? Which sensors meet the accuracy and interface specifications in the information model? Which gateway platform supports the required protocol translation? Is every component choice traceable to a specific requirement?

Step 9: Application Development

Purpose: To specify and build the software applications that implement the services defined in Step 5: device firmware, cloud data pipelines, and user-facing applications.

Inputs: Service specification (Step 5), information model (Step 4), device integration specification (Step 8).

Outputs: Device firmware implementing the sensor read loop, duty cycling, and message formatting and transmission; cloud pipeline implementing data ingestion, storage, analytics, and control automation; user-facing application implementing dashboards and mobile interfaces; API documentation.

Key questions: What firmware architecture supports the required duty cycle and sensor management? What cloud services implement each specified service? What does the user need to see and do in the application interface?

Step 10: Testing, Deployment, and Iteration

Purpose: To validate the system against requirements at three levels (unit, integration, acceptance), execute a controlled deployment, and establish the monitoring and iteration framework for ongoing operation.

Inputs: Requirements from Step 1 (as the basis for acceptance criteria), system components from Steps 8 and 9.

Outputs: A test plan with pass/fail criteria at each testing level, a deployment checklist for staged rollout, and an iteration framework defining metrics review periods and design change procedures.

Key questions: Has every functional requirement been tested and verified? Has the system been tested under realistic field conditions? What is the staged deployment sequence? How will performance data trigger design improvements?

Table 5.1 provides the complete ten-step reference summary. Designers should consult this table at the start of any design engagement to confirm the sequence, phase assignment, and artefact output for each step.

Step	Name	Phase	Primary Input	Primary Output	Key Question
1	Purpose and Requirement Specification	Conceptual	Stakeholder needs, problem context	Purpose statement, requirements document	Why does this system exist?
2	Process Specification	Conceptual	Purpose statement, requirements	Process flow diagram	What sequence of operations does it execute?
3	Domain Model	Conceptual	Purpose, requirements, process flow	Entity-relationship / UML domain model	What are the real-world entities and their relationships?
4	Information Model	Logical	Domain model	Resource-attribute table, data schema	What data does the system collect, store, and transmit?
5	Service Specification	Logical	Information model	Service catalogue, API contracts	What services does the system provide and how are they accessed?
6	IoT Functional View	Logical	Service specification	Functional architecture diagram	What logical components exist and how do they connect?
7	Operational View	Physical	Functional view, site survey	Deployment diagram, operational spec	Where are devices installed and how are they connected?
8	Device and Component Integration	Physical	Operational view, information model	Bill of materials, integration spec	Which specific hardware and software implements the design?
9	Application Development	Physical	Service spec, information model, BoM	Firmware, pipeline, user application	What software implements the specified services?
10	Testing, Deployment, and Iteration	Physical	Requirements, system components	Test plan, deployment checklist, iteration framework	How is the system validated, deployed, and improved?

Table 5.1: Ten-Step IoT Design Methodology Summary

5.3 Conceptual Design: Purpose, Process, and Domain Model (Steps 1-3)

The conceptual design phase is the most important and most frequently shortcut phase of the entire methodology. Engineers who are comfortable with hardware find it uncomfortable to spend time on documents that contain no component names, no wiring diagrams, and no code. Yet the evidence from IoT project post-mortems is consistent: the projects that fail most expensively are those that shortcut Steps 1 through 3 and went directly to hardware selection. The conceptual design phase costs nothing; it requires only time, clear thinking, and honest stakeholder engagement. The cost of skipping it is paid in rework, at the worst possible moment: when hardware has been purchased, firmware has been written, and the system is being tested against requirements that were never properly specified.

Key Insight: *Front-Loading Design Thinking. The cost-of-change curve in IoT projects rises steeply once hardware is ordered and firmware is written. A requirement ambiguity that takes ten minutes to resolve in a specification workshop can require coordinated firmware updates, gateway reconfigurations, and database schema migrations after deployment. The ten-step methodology concentrates design effort in the phases where change is cheapest — documents, diagrams, and specifications — precisely to reduce the cost of change at the phases where it is most expensive.*

5.3.1 Step 1: Purpose and Requirement Specification

The **purpose statement** is the foundation of the entire design. It answers three questions in one paragraph: what does the system do, for whom does it do it, and what value does it create? A well-formed purpose statement is concrete enough to be testable (a proposed design can be evaluated against it) and abstract enough to remain valid as implementation details change. It names the problem, not the solution.

Requirements operationalise the purpose statement. A requirement is a statement of what the system must do or how well it must do it, written in a form that can be verified, either by measurement, by inspection, or by test. Three categories of requirement are essential in IoT design:

Functional requirements state what the system must do: observable behaviours, data it must collect, actions it must take, outputs it must produce. A functional requirement example: 'The system shall measure volumetric soil water content at each sensor node with a frequency of not less than once every fifteen minutes.' This can be verified by timing measurement intervals against a reference clock.

Non-functional requirements state how well the system must do it: performance parameters, reliability targets, safety bounds, and quality attributes. A non-functional requirement example: 'The system shall maintain availability of not less than 99.5% over any thirty-day measurement period.' Availability is measured and verified from operational logs.

Constraints state the boundaries within which the design must operate: budget, physical environment, regulatory limits, technology restrictions, and skill constraints on the operating team. Constraints are not negotiable and are not subject to trade-off analysis; they are fixed. A constraint example: 'Cellular connectivity is not available at the deployment site. All wireless communication must use unlicensed spectrum.'

DEFINITION: *Requirement (Systems Engineering)*

A statement of a condition or capability that a system must possess to satisfy a standard, specification, contract, or other formally imposed document. Requirements must be necessary, unambiguous, consistent, verifiable, and traceable to a higher-level need or objective.

Source: ISO/IEC/IEEE 29148:2018, Systems and Software Engineering — Requirements Engineering

The requirements document structure recommended for IoT projects uses four columns: Requirement ID (a unique alphanumeric identifier for traceability), Requirement Statement (the complete, precise statement), Requirement Type (Functional / Non-functional / Constraint), Priority (Must Have / Should Have / Nice to Have, using the MoSCoW prioritisation framework (Must Have / Should Have / Could Have / Won't Have)), and Verification Method (Test / Demonstration / Inspection / Analysis). Table 5.2 shows this structure applied to the AgroSense case study.

Req. ID	Requirement Statement	Type	Priority	Verification Method
AS-FR-01	The system shall measure volumetric water content (VWC) at each of 40 sensor nodes at intervals not exceeding 15 minutes.	Functional	Must Have	Test: log review over 48 hours
AS-FR-02	The system shall measure soil temperature at each sensor node at intervals not exceeding 15 minutes.	Functional	Must Have	Test: log review
AS-FR-03	The system shall issue an irrigation valve open command when VWC in a zone falls below the configured threshold.	Functional	Must Have	Test: threshold simulation
AS-FR-04	The system shall issue a valve close command 30 minutes after opening if VWC has reached the upper threshold.	Functional	Must Have	Test: timed valve sequence
AS-FR-05	The farmer mobile application shall display current VWC and temperature for each zone and shall send a push notification on each valve event.	Functional	Must Have	Demonstration: acceptance test

AS-NF-01	VWC measurement accuracy shall be plus or minus 3% VWC or better.	Non-functional	Must Have	Test: calibration against gravimetric reference
AS-NF-02	Sensor node battery life shall exceed 12 months under normal operation.	Non-functional	Must Have	Analysis: power budget model + 30-day pilot measurement
AS-NF-03	The system shall maintain data collection availability of not less than 99.5% over any 30-day period.	Non-functional	Must Have	Analysis: uptime logs
AS-C-01	Cellular connectivity is not available. All wireless communication must use unlicensed spectrum.	Constraint	Must Have	Inspection: network plan review
AS-C-02	Unit cost per sensor node (hardware and enclosure) shall not exceed USD 50.	Constraint	Must Have	Inspection: bill of materials

Table 5.2: AgroSense Requirements Specification (Selected Requirements)

5.3.2 Step 2: Process Specification

The process specification transforms the requirements into a description of the system's operational behaviour: the sequence of events, data flows, decisions, and actions that the system executes during normal operation. Where the requirements document describes what the system must do in static terms, the process flow describes how it does it in dynamic terms.

An IoT process flow has two distinct sides that must be specified separately before being integrated. The device-side process covers everything that happens on and between the sensor node and the gateway: power-on initialisation, sensor acquisition, signal conditioning and validation, data encoding, transmission, acknowledgement handling, sleep, and wake scheduling. The platform-side process covers everything from the gateway upward: message reception, protocol translation, ingestion, storage, rule evaluation, actuation command generation, user notification, and data retention.

A common design error is to sketch only the happy path: the sequence when everything works. A complete process specification includes the exception paths: what happens when the radio link is lost and a measurement cannot be transmitted? What happens when the database is temporarily unavailable and an alert cannot be logged? What happens when a valve actuation command is not acknowledged? The answers to these questions surface requirements that are routinely missed in informal design approaches (local buffering, retry logic, fail-safe states) which must be designed into the system from the beginning, not retrofitted after a field failure.

For the AgroSense system, the device-side process is: wake from deep sleep on real-time clock (RTC) alarm; power on sensors; wait for sensor stabilisation (SHT31: 8 ms, VH400: 10 ms warm-up); acquire VWC reading (three samples, averaged), soil temperature (DS18B20 conversion: 750 ms at 12-bit), and ambient temperature and humidity (SHT31 single-shot); encode as JSON payload with node ID, zone ID, timestamp, and four measurement values; transmit LoRa uplink; wait for LoRaWAN receive window 1 (1 second) and window 2 (2 seconds); if a downlink command is received (valve instruction), record locally and forward to valve controller via wired RS-485 link; return to deep sleep until next 15-minute RTC alarm.

The platform-side process is: LoRaWAN Network Server receives uplink via gateway; validates frame counter and MIC (message integrity code); forwards decrypted payload to AWS IoT Core via MQTT; IoT Core Rule evaluates: if VWC below zone threshold AND valve not already open, publish valve_open command to valve controller topic; Lambda function writes telemetry record to InfluxDB; Node-RED subscription receives VWC data, applies rolling-average smoothing, re-evaluates threshold, schedules valve close check at T+30 minutes; farmer notification published to FCM (Firebase Cloud Messaging) push service at each valve event.

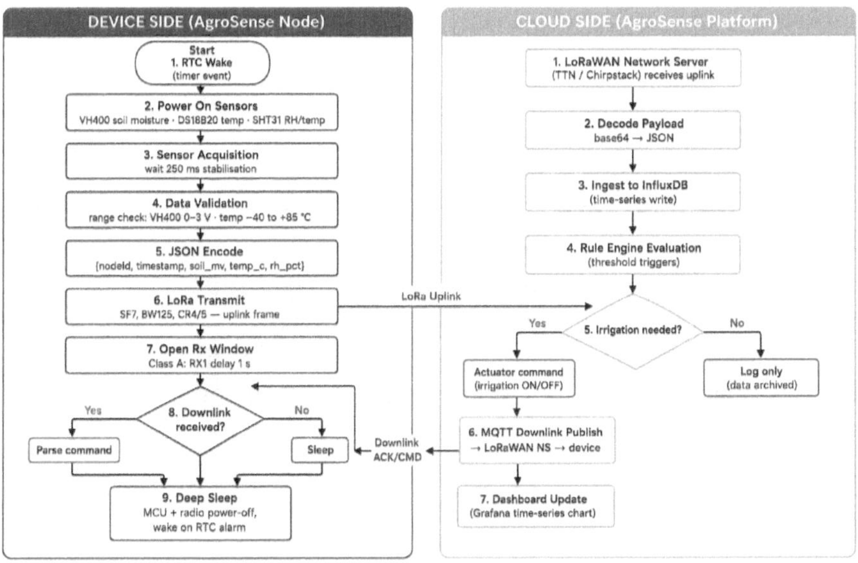

Figure 5.2: AgroSense Process Flow Diagram

5.3.3 Step 3: Domain Model

The domain model identifies the entities, the things, that exist in the system's operational domain, and maps the relationships between them. It is not a database schema (which is a physical storage structure) and not a system architecture (which shows components and their interactions). It is a conceptual map of the problem space: what things exist, what do they know about themselves, and how do they relate to each other?

An IoT domain model contains three categories of entity. Physical entities are real-world objects that the system senses, controls, or manages: in AgroSense, these are the Farm, the Field Zone, the Sensor Node, the Irrigation Valve, and the Gateway. Digital entities are information objects that the system creates, stores, and processes: Telemetry Record, Alert, Valve Event, and Firmware Version. Actor entities are the people and external systems that interact with the IoT system: Farmer, Agronomist, Field Technician, and the AWS IoT platform as an external actor.

Relationships in the domain model carry multiplicity: a Farm contains one or more Field Zones (1 to many); a Field Zone contains one or more Sensor Nodes and one or more Irrigation Valves (1 to many in each case); a Sensor Node generates many Telemetry Records over its operational lifetime (1 to many); an Alert is associated with one Sensor Node and one or more Farmers who receive it (many to many through a notification relationship). These multiplicities are not incidental; they determine the data model's key structure, the query patterns the analytics platform must support, and the provisioning hierarchy for device management.

The domain model also exposes entities that were not explicitly mentioned in the requirements but are implied by the design context. The AgroSense domain model reveals the need for a Zone Configuration entity: a persistent record of the VWC threshold for each zone, maintained by the agronomist and referenced by the rule engine. This entity was not mentioned in the requirements interview but is clearly necessary for the system to function correctly. Discovering it at the domain modelling stage, before any firmware is written, costs nothing. Discovering it during system integration, when the Node-RED rule engine has no threshold to compare against, costs a redesign of the data pipeline and the device management interface.

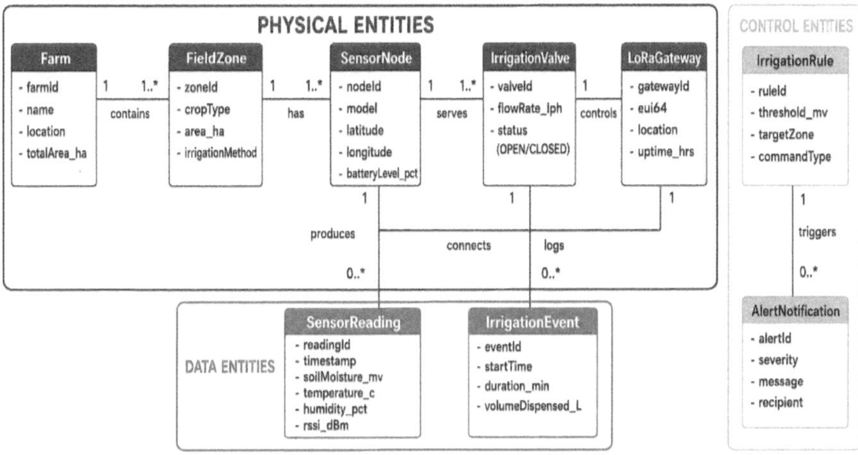

Structural relationships among physical, data, and control entities in the AgroSense smart agriculture system.

Figure 5.3: AgroSense Domain Model

5.4 Logical Design: Information Model, Services, and Functional View (Steps 4-6)

The logical design phase is where the conceptual design's models are translated into precise specifications that will govern every subsequent development and integration decision. Engineers who have worked through the conceptual phase sometimes expect the logical design to feel more concrete, to involve hardware names and code. It does not, and deliberately so. The value of the logical design is its technology-agnosticism: a well-formed information model and service specification can be implemented on any technology stack that satisfies the requirements. When the technology landscape changes (a new database engine, a better protocol, a lower-cost sensor) the logical design remains valid, and only the physical implementation choices need to be updated.

5.4.1 Step 4: Information Model

The information model is the system's data vocabulary: a precise, unambiguous specification of every data item the system collects, stores, transmits, or derives. It is the single source of truth for data format agreements between all components of the system: device firmware developers, cloud pipeline engineers, database administrators, and application developers all use the information model as their shared reference. When it is absent, each team makes its own assumptions, and the integration crisis that results when those assumptions conflict is virtually guaranteed.

The information model is built by working through the domain model's entities and specifying, for each IoT resource, the attributes it carries. Four specification elements are required for each attribute: data type and format (integer, float, string, boolean, ISO 8601 timestamp); unit and scale (degrees Celsius, percent VWC, milliseconds); valid range and accuracy (minimum value, maximum value, measurement uncertainty); and update frequency and retention policy (how often the attribute changes, how long historical values must be stored).

For the AgroSense SoilMoistureNode resource, the primary IoT data source, the information model specifies the following attributes: node_id (string, universally unique identifier (UUID) format, immutable device identifier); zone_id (string, foreign key to Zone entity, assigned at provisioning); VWC_percent (float, unit: % VWC, range 0.0 to 100.0, accuracy plus or minus 3.0% VWC, update frequency: 900 seconds, retention: 18 months); soil_temperature_C (float, unit: degrees Celsius, range minus 10.0 to 70.0, accuracy plus or minus 0.5 degrees Celsius, update frequency: 900 seconds, retention: 18 months); ambient_temperature_C (float, unit: degrees Celsius, range minus 10.0 to 60.0, accuracy plus or minus 0.3 degrees Celsius, retention: 18 months); ambient_humidity_RH (float, unit: % RH, range 0.0 to 100.0, accuracy plus or minus 2.0% RH, retention: 18 months); timestamp (string, ISO 8601 UTC, generated at device measurement time); battery_voltage_V (float, unit: V, range 3.0 to 4.2, update frequency: same as telemetry, retention: 18 months); LoRa_RSSI_dBm (integer, unit: dBm, range minus 140 to 0, measured at gateway, appended by network server, retention: 90 days for link quality monitoring).

The information model also specifies derived data — data calculated from raw sensor readings rather than measured directly. For AgroSense, derived data includes: zone_avg_VWC (float, rolling 15-minute average across all nodes in a zone, computed by Node-RED, used for threshold evaluation to eliminate single-node spike-triggered irrigation); daily_min_VWC, daily_max_VWC, daily_avg_VWC (daily statistics per node, computed by InfluxDB continuous queries, retained for trend analysis); irrigation_volume_estimate_L (float, estimated water volume delivered per valve open event, computed from valve open duration and known flow rate, used for water consumption reporting).

The information model's data types and formats directly determine the payload schema for MQTT messages, the database table structure for InfluxDB, and the API response format for the mobile application. Where predictive analytics or machine learning models are later introduced, for example, an evapotranspiration forecast model or an anomaly detector for sensor drift: the information model's attribute definitions also serve as the feature schema: model inputs are drawn directly from the typed, documented attributes defined here. Deeper treatment of AI and ML integration in IoT systems is provided in Chapter 11. Writing the information model before any of these implementations is the API-first principle applied to data; it prevents the format inconsistencies that cause the integration failures described in Section 5.3.

5.4.2 Step 5: Service Specification

The service specification defines what the system does in terms of discrete, named services, functional capabilities that components provide to each other or to external actors. The service specification bridges the information model (what data exists) and the functional view (what components exist): it says which component provides which service and how that service is accessed through a defined interface.

IoT systems typically require services in six categories. Data Collection Services handle the ingestion of telemetry from end nodes to the platform: in AgroSense, this is the MQTT publish service through which sensor nodes deliver telemetry to AWS IoT Core. Data Storage Services persist raw and derived telemetry for historical query: InfluxDB provides this for time-series data, with S3 as the long-term archive for raw message logs. Analytics Services compute derived metrics and evaluate rules: the Node-RED flow provides real-time threshold evaluation; InfluxDB continuous queries provide daily aggregation.

Control Services issue actuation commands to physical devices: in AgroSense, these are the MQTT-published valve open and close commands forwarded to the Arduino valve controller. Notification Services deliver alerts and status updates to human actors: Firebase Cloud Messaging delivers push notifications to the farmer mobile application. Management Services handle device provisioning, key management, over-the-air (OTA) firmware update, and device health monitoring: LwM2M over the Constrained Application Protocol (CoAP), hosted on the LoRaWAN Application Server.

For each service, the specification must define the interface contract: the communication protocol, the endpoint or topic address, the message payload format, and the quality-of-service requirement. For the AgroSense Data Collection Service, the contract is: protocol MQTT over Transport Layer Security (TLS) 1.3; topic agrosense/{farm_id}/{zone_id}/{node_id}/telemetry; payload: JSON object containing the nine attributes defined in the information model; quality-of-service (QoS) level 1 (at-least-once delivery, acknowledged); maximum message size 512 bytes; expected message frequency one per node per 15 minutes. This contract is sufficient for both the device firmware developer (who writes the MQTT publish function) and the cloud platform engineer (who configures the AWS IoT Rule) to implement their respective sides of the interface independently and correctly.

The API-first principle governs Step 5: service contracts must be agreed and documented before any implementation begins. The contract is the commitment; the implementation fulfils it. If the contract changes after implementation has started, all implementations on both sides of the interface must be reviewed and potentially rewritten. Changing a JSON field name in the information model after firmware has been written, the IoT Rule has been configured, and the database schema has been created requires coordinated changes in at least three separate systems: a disproportionately expensive consequence of a one-word change. The information model and service specification must therefore be treated as formally approved documents before implementation begins, with a change control procedure for any subsequent modifications.

5.4.3 Step 6: IoT Functional View

The functional view organises the system's services into a coherent logical architecture showing what functional components exist, which layer of the IoT stack each occupies, and how data flows between them. The functional view is still technology-agnostic: it names functional roles (rule engine, time-series database, MQTT broker) not specific products (Node-RED, InfluxDB, Mosquitto). This distinction matters because the functional view will be consulted across the entire project lifecycle; it guides technology selection in Step 8, onboarding of new team members, and system documentation for operators and maintainers.

The standard IoT functional layer model provides the structure for the functional view. The Sensing and Actuation Layer contains the physical IoT hardware: sensors, actuators, and the microcontrollers that drive them. In AgroSense, this layer contains the forty sensor nodes and twelve solenoid valves. The Connectivity Layer contains the communication protocols and network infrastructure that links the sensing and actuation layer to the processing layer: LoRaWAN (uplink telemetry and downlink commands), the LoRaWAN Network Server (packet routing and session management), and the MQTT broker (message distribution).

The Processing Layer contains the components that receive, store, and compute upon sensor data: the IoT platform ingestion service, the time-series database, and the rule engine and analytics services. The Application Layer contains the services that interpret processed data and generate user-facing outputs and control actions: the automation and alerting logic, the data visualisation service, and the API gateway for mobile access. The User Interface Layer contains the interfaces through which human actors interact with the system: the agronomist's web dashboard and the farmer's mobile application.

A functional view diagram makes explicit the data flow paths that the service specification implies. In AgroSense, two paths are visible: the telemetry path (sensor node to LoRa uplink to gateway to Network Server to MQTT to ingestion service to InfluxDB to dashboard and mobile app) and the control path (rule engine threshold evaluation to MQTT command publish to gateway to LoRa downlink to sensor node to valve controller to solenoid valve). The functional view makes these two paths visible simultaneously, revealing their intersection at the gateway and the rule engine, and confirming that the design correctly handles both directions of data flow.

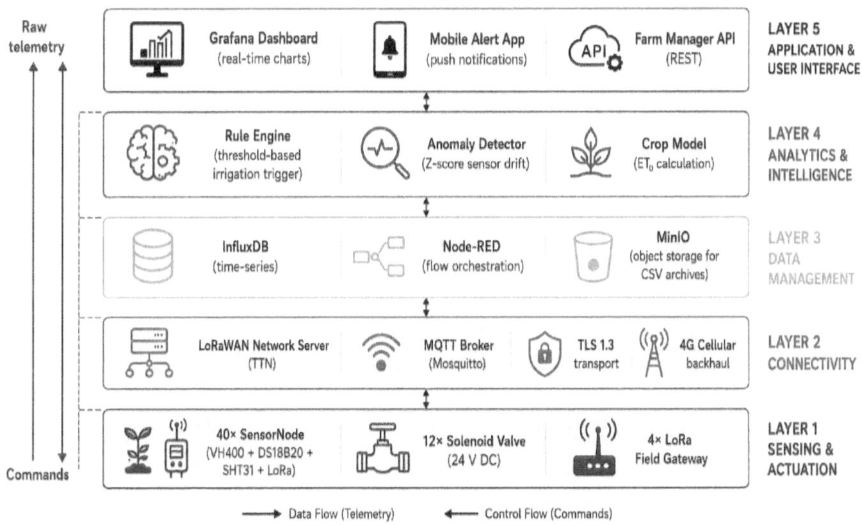

Figure 5.4: AgroSense IoT Functional View

CASE STUDY: *Case Study Application: AgroSense Logical Design (Steps 4-6)*

Rajasthan, India — Design Phase

Step 4: Information Model: The AgroSense information model defines two primary IoT resources. The SoilMoistureNode resource carries nine attributes: node_id, zone_id, VWC_percent (float, 0-100, plus or minus 3% VWC, 15-min interval), soil_temperature_C (float, -10 to 70, plus or minus 0.5 degrees Celsius), ambient_temperature_C, ambient_humidity_RH, timestamp (ISO 8601 UTC), battery_voltage_V, and LoRa_RSSI_dBm. The IrrigationValve resource carries: valve_id, zone_id, state (OPEN/CLOSED), last_command_timestamp, and cumulative_open_duration_minutes. Three derived attributes are specified for zone-level analytics: zone_avg_VWC, daily_min_VWC, and irrigation_volume_estimate_L. The information model is frozen as a shared reference before firmware or pipeline development begins.

Step 5: Service Specification: Six services are specified with interface contracts. Data Collection: MQTT QoS 1 over TLS, topic agrosense/{farm_id}/{zone_id}/{node_id}/telemetry, JSON payload, one message per 15 minutes. Data Storage: InfluxDB write API, bucket 'agrosense_telemetry', measurement name 'soil_node', tag keys: node_id, zone_id, field keys: all numeric attributes. Control: MQTT QoS 1, topic agrosense/{farm_id}/{zone_id}/valve/{valve_id}/command, JSON payload {action: OPEN|CLOSE, duration_minutes: integer}. Notification: FCM HTTP v1 API, triggered by Node-RED on valve event and low-VWC alert. Analytics: Node-RED HTTP GET /api/zone/{zone_id}/threshold for threshold retrieval; InfluxDB Flux continuous queries for daily aggregation. Management: LwM2M v1.2 over CoAP for OTA firmware update and device registration.

Step 6: IoT Functional View: The AgroSense functional architecture maps services to five layers. Sensing and Actuation: 40 sensor nodes (ESP32 + LoRa) and 12 solenoid valves (Arduino-controlled). Connectivity: LoRaWAN radio uplink and downlink; Raspberry Pi LoRaWAN gateway with Ethernet uplink. Processing: AWS IoT Core ingestion and rule engine; InfluxDB Cloud time-series storage; Node-RED analytics and automation. Application: Grafana visualisation; FCM notification service; REST API gateway for mobile. User Interface: Agronomist Grafana web dashboard; React Native farmer mobile application. Two data flow paths are visible: the telemetry path (upward from sensor node to dashboard) and the control path (downward from rule engine to solenoid valve).

5.5 Physical Design: Operational View and Device Integration (Steps 7-8)

The physical design phase is where the design becomes tangible. Steps 7 and 8 mark the transition from logical specifications to physical commitments: specific hardware is selected and named, specific deployment locations are identified, and a bill of materials is produced. This transition is one-directional in terms of cost: the logical design phase was essentially free; the physical design phase ends with purchase orders, and changes after that point carry real financial and schedule consequences.

The discipline that makes this transition manageable is traceability. Every hardware choice made in Step 8 must trace back to a requirement in Step 1, through the chain of models and specifications produced in Steps 2 through 7. If a component cannot be traced to a requirement, one of two things is true: either the component is unnecessary and should be removed, or there is a requirement that was missed and must be added to the specification. Traceability is not bureaucratic overhead; it is the mechanism that keeps the physical design honest.

5.5.1 Step 7: Operational View

The operational view specifies how the system will be deployed in its physical environment. Where the functional view described logical components and their connections, the operational view describes physical devices and their locations, the wireless and wired links between them, the environmental conditions they must withstand, the power sources available, and the maintenance access constraints that govern serviceability over the system's operational lifetime.

The network deployment diagram is the operational view's primary artefact. For a distributed IoT deployment like AgroSense, it shows each sensor node as a point on a map or schematic of the deployment site, with its zone assignment, approximate GPS coordinates, link distance to the gateway, and antenna orientation. The gateway location is shown with its backhaul link — in AgroSense, an Ethernet cable to a router at the farm office with a cellular modem as backup. The valve controller location is shown with its wired connection to the twelve solenoid valves distributed along the irrigation main.

A critical element of the operational view that is frequently underestimated is the radio link budget analysis. A LoRa link that performs reliably in bench testing at three metres may fail in field deployment at three kilometres across terrain with vegetation, ground clutter, and seasonal foliage variation.

The link budget calculation estimates the received signal power at the gateway given the transmit power, antenna gains, spreading factor, free-space path loss at the deployment distance, and a margin for obstructions. For AgroSense's three-kilometre maximum range with SF10 spreading factor at 125 kHz bandwidth, the expected received power is approximately minus 120 dBm, comfortably above the SX1276 receiver sensitivity of minus 129 dBm at SF10, giving a 9 dB link margin before any obstructions. Field trials with two sensor nodes at maximum range with representative vegetation between them are conducted during Step 7 to validate this calculation before the full 40-node deployment.

Environmental specification is the second major output of Step 7. IoT devices in outdoor agricultural deployments face temperature extremes (Rajasthan field temperatures exceed 45 degrees Celsius in summer; night-time temperatures drop to near zero in winter), humidity (monsoon season brings sustained 90%+ relative humidity), dust (a particular concern for any enclosure with ventilation holes), and insects (which can penetrate surprisingly small gaps). The AgroSense sensor node enclosure must meet IP67 rating (dust-tight, submersion to 1 metre for 30 minutes) and operate across minus 10 to plus 60 degrees Celsius. The gateway enclosure at the farm office is indoor and requires only IP20, but the outdoor LoRa antenna and its coaxial feeder must be UV-rated and weatherproofed at all connections.

Power planning is the third element of the operational view. Sensor nodes at AgroSense are battery-powered with solar supplementation (per requirement AS-NF-02: battery life exceeding 12 months). The operational view confirms that the 2W solar panel and 3,000 mAh LiPo combination are adequate by using the power budget model from Chapter 2: average node current at 15-minute LoRaWAN reporting interval with ESP32 deep sleep is approximately 65 microamperes in deep sleep, with a system average of approximately 170 microamperes at the 15-minute LoRaWAN duty cycle; the 3,000 mAh battery provides approximately 24 months of operation without solar; the 2W panel in Rajasthan generates approximately 400 mAh per day at minimum winter insolation, giving indefinite autonomous operation with substantial margin. The gateway is mains-powered with an uninterruptible power supply providing 4 hours of autonomy during grid outages.

Regional Example: Smart Agriculture in Oman and the Gulf. *Oman's Vision 2040 agricultural programme includes precision irrigation deployments across the Al Batinah coastal plain and the Nejd plateau, where rapid groundwater depletion has driven adoption of soil-moisture-guided drip irrigation systems. IoT deployments in this environment share the AgroSense design challenges — distributed sensor networks, no cellular coverage, battery-powered nodes — but with additional environmental constraints: ambient temperatures exceeding 48 °C in summer require extended IP67 enclosure testing and derating of battery capacity models. Solar panel sizing must account for dust and sand accumulation on panel surfaces during the khareef season, requiring effective area corrections of 15–20% above the theoretical minimum. UAE and Saudi Arabian agricultural IoT deployments face structurally similar challenges, making the operational view's environmental specification step particularly critical across the region.*

5.5.2 Step 8: Device and Component Integration

Step 8 maps every element of the functional view and information model to specific hardware components and software platforms, producing a bill of materials and an integration specification. It is the culmination of the design process: a complete description of what will be purchased, assembled, configured, and deployed.

Hardware selection for each platform tier should be justified against the requirements using the selection logic established in Chapter 2. For AgroSense sensor nodes, the constraints are: power (battery life exceeding 12 months, favours deep sleep current below 100 microamperes), connectivity (LoRa radio required, no cellular), processing (ESP32 is Class 2 with adequate RAM for LoRaWAN stack and JSON encoding), cost (ESP32-WROVER-B at approximately USD 4 in module form, satisfying the USD 50 node constraint). The Raspberry Pi 4 as gateway is justified by its Linux environment (required to run ChirpStack LoRaWAN Network Server and Node-RED), Ethernet interface (required for reliable cloud connectivity), and USB host (for cellular modem backup dongle).

Sensor selection is governed directly by the information model's accuracy and interface specifications. The Vegetronix VH400 capacitive soil moisture sensor meets the plus or minus 3% VWC accuracy requirement and outputs an analogue voltage (0-3V) readable by the ESP32's analogue-to-digital converter (ADC). The DS18B20 digital temperature sensor meets the plus or minus 0.5 degree Celsius soil temperature requirement and uses the 1-Wire protocol, requiring only a single GPIO and a 4.7 kOhm pull-up resistor. The SHT31 meets the ambient temperature and humidity specifications and communicates over I2C, sharing the bus with no other device. These are not arbitrary choices, each maps directly to a row in the information model and is traceable to a requirement in Table 5.2.

The integration specification documents how components connect: which GPIO pin connects to which sensor, what pull-up resistors are required, what the I2C address of each device is, how power is sequenced at startup, and how the LoRa module SPI clock polarity is configured. This level of detail is not superfluous precision; it is the document that a field technician uses to assemble 40 identical sensor nodes reproducibly, and that a replacement technician three years into deployment uses to diagnose and repair a failed node.

The prototype-to-production pathway is the final element of Step 8. Before 40 nodes are assembled and deployed, a prototype (one sensor node, one gateway, and one valve controller, assembled on a breadboard or test PCB) validates the integration specification against real hardware. The prototype validation is governed by a Design Verification Test (DVT) checklist: a set of acceptance criteria that the prototype must satisfy before volume assembly begins. Table 5.3 shows the AgroSense DVT checklist.

Verification Item	Method	Acceptance Criterion	Status
Power budget verification	Measure average node current over 24-hour period with oscilloscope/ current logger	Less than 100 microamperes average	
LoRa range test	Deploy single node at 3 km maximum range across representative terrain; transmit 100 packets	Less than 5% packet loss rate; RSSI above minus 125 dBm	
MQTT connectivity	Confirm TLS handshake to AWS IoT Core; publish 100 messages; verify receipt in InfluxDB	100% delivery at QoS 1; all messages appear in DB within 30 seconds	
Sensor accuracy	Calibrate VH400 against gravimetric reference at 5 known VWC values; validate DS18B20 against National Institute of Standards and Technology (NIST)-traceable thermometer at 3 temperatures	VWC: within +/-3% at all points; temperature: within +/-0.5 degC	
Valve actuation	Issue valve open command via MQTT from cloud; measure valve open latency; confirm valve close at T+30 min	Open latency less than 5 seconds; close executed within 60 seconds of schedule	
Battery life projection	Measure deep sleep current, active Tx current, sensor acquisition current; compute daily charge consumption vs. solar harvest	Battery life model shows greater than 12 months at minimum winter insolation	

Data format validation	Capture 50 MQTT messages; parse JSON against information model schema	100% of messages conform to schema; no null values; timestamps within 1 second of Network Time Protocol (NTP)	
IP67 enclosure test	Submerge populated enclosure in 1 m water for 30 minutes; inspect for ingress	No water ingress; electronics functional after drying	

Table 5.3: AgroSense Design Verification Test (DVT) Checklist

5.6 Application Development and Testing (Steps 9-10)

Steps 9 and 10 close the design loop from specification to working system. Step 9 builds the software that implements the services defined in Step 5. Step 10 validates that what was built matches what was specified in Step 1, deploys it under controlled conditions, and establishes the framework for ongoing improvement. Together, they represent the transition from design to engineering, and the final evidence that the methodology produced a real, deployable system rather than a paper specification.

5.6.1 Step 9: Application Development

The AgroSense software stack has three tiers that must be developed and validated independently before integration: device firmware, the cloud data pipeline, and the user-facing application.

The device firmware runs on the ESP32-WROVER-B and is developed using the Arduino framework for ESP32 (or alternatively ESP-IDF with FreeRTOS). The firmware architecture has four modules: the sensor management module (drives VH400 ADC, DS18B20 1-Wire, and SHT31 I2C; applies factory calibration coefficients; validates readings against plausible range bounds; returns a populated measurement struct); the power management module (configures wake sources — RTC alarm for scheduled measurement, general-purpose input/output (GPIO) interrupt for downlink command reception, and calls esp_deep_sleep_start()); the LoRaWAN communications module (wraps the LMIC Arduino library for LoRaWAN Class A operation; handles over-the-air activation (OTAA) join; serialises the measurement struct to a compact binary payload for air transmission, expanded to JSON by the Application Server); and the local command handler (receives downlink valve commands via LoRaWAN port 2; forwards over RS-485 UART to the Arduino valve controller using a simple three-byte command frame).

The cloud data pipeline implements the services specified in Step 5. AWS IoT Core receives MQTT telemetry, decrypts and validates device certificates (X.509 mutual TLS), and applies a Rule that: (a) writes raw JSON to an S3 bucket for archival; (b) invokes a Lambda function that parses the payload and writes a line protocol record to InfluxDB Cloud using the InfluxDB Python client; (c) publishes to an SNS topic that triggers a Node-RED webhook for real-time processing. The Node-RED flow subscribes to the MQTT telemetry topic, retrieves the zone threshold configuration from a local configuration store, computes a rolling five-sample average of zone VWC, and evaluates the threshold condition. When triggered, it publishes a valve command to the appropriate MQTT control topic and calls the Firebase Cloud Messaging API to send a push notification to registered farmer devices.

The user-facing application has two components. The agronomist web dashboard is built in Grafana with InfluxDB as its data source. Panels display: a farm map with colour-coded zone VWC (blue for well-watered, yellow for approaching threshold, red for below threshold); time-series graphs of VWC and soil temperature per node over configurable windows (last 24 hours, last 7 days, last season); valve event log with duration and estimated water volume; and battery voltage monitoring with alerts when any node drops below 3.5 V.

The farmer mobile application is built in React Native for cross-platform Android and iOS deployment. It provides a simplified single-screen view: current zone status (green / yellow / red), last measurement time, and a manual valve override button for each zone. Push notifications (delivered via FCM) alert the farmer when a valve opens or closes, including the zone name in the farmer's preferred language.

TECHNOLOGY SPOTLIGHT: *Tech Spotlight: Node-RED as an IoT Automation Engine*

Node-RED is a flow-based programming tool originally developed by IBM and now a project of the OpenJS Foundation. It provides a browser-based editor in which processing logic is built by connecting nodes (each representing an input, a transformation, or an output) with wires. Flows are deployed to a Node.js runtime, typically on a Raspberry Pi gateway or a cloud VM.

In the AgroSense architecture, a Node-RED flow implements the entire real-time threshold evaluation and valve control logic: an MQTT input node subscribes to the telemetry topic; a function node computes the rolling zone average and evaluates the threshold; a switch node routes the message to either a valve-open or no-action path; an MQTT output node publishes the valve command; an HTTP request node calls the FCM API. This complete automation logic is implemented visually in approximately fifteen nodes, with no traditional application code is required.

Node-RED's value in IoT design extends beyond its simplicity: its flows can be exported as JSON and version-controlled in Git, deployed to remote instances via the Node-RED admin API, and monitored in production using the Node-RED Dashboard and built-in debug nodes. AWS IoT Core, Azure IoT Hub, InfluxDB, Grafana, Telegram, and hundreds of other platforms have official or community-contributed Node-RED connector nodes, making it a practical integration hub for most small-to-medium IoT deployments.

5.6.2 Step 10: Testing, Deployment, and Iteration

IoT system testing operates at three levels, each building on the results of the level below it. Skipping directly to integration testing, which is tempting when prototype hardware is assembled and the impulse to 'see if it works' is strong, consistently produces misleading results because defects at the unit level manifest as mysterious integration failures that are hard to attribute and expensive to diagnose.

Unit testing validates individual software modules in isolation. For AgroSense firmware, unit tests verify: the sensor management module returns correctly formatted output for known simulated inputs (including error conditions such as sensor not present and out-of-range reading); the MQTT publish function handles a network timeout correctly (queues the message locally and retries on next wake cycle without data loss); and the JSON payload parser in the Lambda function correctly handles all message variants defined in the information model, including edge cases at attribute range boundaries.

Integration testing validates the end-to-end data flow with real components. A single sensor node is deployed in a controlled environment and operated for 72 hours. Tests verify: sensor data appears in InfluxDB within 90 seconds of each measurement cycle; packet loss rate at representative field distances is below the 5% acceptance criterion; valve open and close commands are received and executed within the specified latency; Grafana dashboard updates within 120 seconds of each measurement cycle; and farmer push notification is received on a test device within 30 seconds of each valve event.

Acceptance testing validates the complete system against the requirements in Table 5.2, with the actual end users as the test audience. For AgroSense, acceptance testing is conducted with five sensor nodes in one pilot field zone, with the cooperating agronomist monitoring the Grafana dashboard and two participating farmers using the mobile application. Test scenarios include: normal 15-minute reporting cycle sustained for 24 hours; manual threshold adjustment by the agronomist triggering an irrigation event; farmer acknowledgement of the push notification and confirmation that the valve status on the mobile app updates correctly; and deliberate gateway disconnection (simulating internet outage) with confirmation that local Node-RED continues threshold evaluation and valve control using buffered data.

Deployment follows a staged rollout plan: five nodes in pilot Zone 1 for a two-week validation period; if all DVT criteria are sustained, expand to full Zone 1 (twelve nodes); after one month of stable Zone 1 operation, deploy Zones 2 and 3 (fourteen and fourteen nodes respectively). OTA firmware update capability, implemented via LoRaWAN port 3 and a custom bootloader, is validated during the Zone 1 expansion phase by pushing a firmware update to all twelve Zone 1 nodes and confirming successful update and automatic restart.

Iteration is the final, ongoing element of Step 10, and the step that most resembles engineering practice rather than a design exercise. After the first complete growing season, the AgroSense design team reviews three categories of performance data: data quality (are there nodes with persistently high VWC variance that suggest sensor positioning problems?), model accuracy (did the threshold values set in Step 5 actually correlate with crop health outcomes, or should they be recalibrated?), and system reliability (which failure modes were observed in the field, and what design changes would prevent them?).

In the AgroSense pilot, three iteration improvements were identified after the first kharif season: three nodes required repositioning after crop root development altered local soil drainage; the VWC threshold for the drip-irrigated vegetable zone required calibration downward by 8% VWC after the agronomist analysed yield data; and a firmware update was issued to add an exponential moving average filter to reduce false valve-open triggers from single-measurement VWC spikes caused by rain splatter on the sensor.

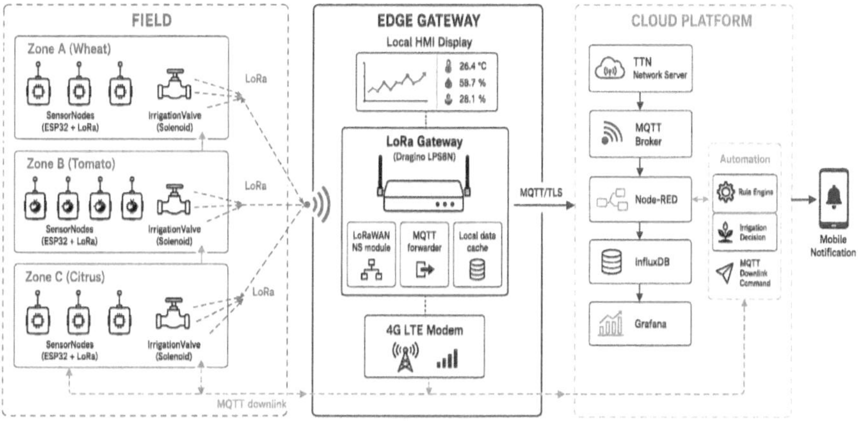

Figure 5.5: AgroSense end-to-end system architecture

5.7 Communication APIs and Cloud Backend Design

The service specification produced in Step 5 names services and defines their interface contracts at a conceptual level. This section provides the practical depth that a designer needs to implement those contracts: the API taxonomy relevant to IoT systems, the principal cloud backend architecture options, and the API-first design discipline that prevents the most common and costly IoT integration failures.

5.7.1 IoT API Taxonomy

Three distinct categories of API must be specified in an IoT system design, each operating at a different architectural boundary and requiring different specification detail.

Device-to-Cloud APIs govern how IoT end nodes and gateways communicate with the cloud platform. In MQTT-based systems, the API specification defines the topic hierarchy, payload format, QoS level, and TLS requirements. The topic hierarchy is the most consequential design decision in an MQTT deployment: it determines how messages are filtered and routed, what wildcard subscriptions are possible, and whether the structure can accommodate future extensions without breaking existing consumers.

The recommended IoT MQTT topic hierarchy pattern is hierarchical-entity-based: {organisation}/{project}/{entity-type}/{entity-id}/{message-type}. For AgroSense: agrosense/{farm_id}/{zone_id}/{node_id}/telemetry for uplink sensor data; agrosense/{farm_id}/{zone_id}/valve/{valve_id}/command for downlink control; agrosense/{farm_id}/{zone_id}/{node_id}/status for device health; and agrosense/{farm_id}/{zone_id}/{node_id}/ota for firmware update. This structure allows the cloud backend to subscribe to agrosense/{farm_id}/# to receive all messages for a farm, or to agrosense/{farm_id}/{zone_id}/+/telemetry to receive telemetry for all nodes in a specific zone.

In CoAP REST-based systems (more common in constrained 6LoWPAN deployments), the API specification defines resource paths, HTTP method mappings (GET for retrieve, PUT for update, POST for create), and CoAP observe subscriptions for push-based data delivery. A CoAP resource URI for an AgroSense equivalent would be: coap://[node-ipv6-address]/sensors/soil for the soil measurement resource, with a GET response returning the current measurement struct and an OBSERVE subscription enabling server-push delivery on each new measurement.

Service-to-Service APIs govern the integrations between cloud platform components. In AgroSense, these include: the AWS IoT Rule Action that invokes the Lambda function (governed by the AWS IoT Core Rule engine API); the Lambda function's call to the InfluxDB write API (governed by the InfluxDB Cloud Data API specification: a line protocol HTTP POST to the /api/v2/write endpoint with org, bucket, and precision parameters); the Node-RED HTTP node that calls the FCM HTTP v1 API for push notifications (governed by the Firebase documentation, requiring an OAuth 2.0 access token and a JSON notification payload).

User-Facing APIs govern how client applications, web dashboards and mobile apps, access system data and issue commands. For AgroSense, the Grafana dashboard accesses InfluxDB directly through the Grafana InfluxDB data source plugin (no custom API required). The React Native mobile application accesses a thin REST API layer, implemented as AWS API Gateway + Lambda, that provides: GET /api/v1/farms/{farm_id}/zones for zone list and current status; GET /api/v1/zones/{zone_id}/telemetry?from={iso_date}&to={iso_date} for historical data; POST /api/v1/zones/{zone_id}/valve/{valve_id}/command for manual valve override (requires farmer authentication via AWS Cognito JWT token).

5.7.2 Cloud Backend Architecture Options

Three cloud backend patterns are commonly encountered in IoT deployments, each with distinct cost, operational, and capability trade-offs. The appropriate choice depends on the deployment scale, the team's operational maturity, the regulatory data residency requirements, and the connectivity environment.

Managed IoT Platform (using AWS IoT Core, Azure IoT Hub, or Google Cloud IoT Core) is the recommended choice for most new IoT deployments. The platform provides device authentication and certificate management, a scalable MQTT broker, a rule engine for message routing and processing triggers, device shadow (a cloud-side replica of device state that allows the application to read last-known state even when the device is offline), and OTA update management. The cost model is consumption-based, charging per message and per connected device, which is economically attractive for small deployments but can become significant at scale. The operational burden on the deploying team is low: the platform is fully managed, with no MQTT broker or certificate infrastructure to maintain.

Self-hosted broker and database (Mosquitto MQTT broker, InfluxDB time-series database, and Grafana visualisation, running on a cloud VM or on-premises server) offers lower recurring cost and complete data sovereignty, at the price of higher operational overhead (the team must manage broker security configuration, database backups, SSL certificate renewal, and broker scaling). This pattern is appropriate for teams with Linux server administration experience, for air-gapped industrial deployments that cannot send data to a public cloud, and for high-volume deployments where per-message cloud platform costs become prohibitive. The AgroSense design uses a hybrid of this pattern and the managed platform pattern: AWS IoT Core handles security-sensitive internet-facing ingestion, while InfluxDB and Grafana (cloud-hosted versions) handle storage and visualisation.

Hybrid edge-cloud architecture places significant processing capability at the IoT gateway, running local instances of Node-RED, InfluxDB, and a local MQTT broker, with cloud synchronisation for long-term archival and remote access. This pattern provides autonomous operation during internet outages (critical for remote agricultural deployments where connectivity may be intermittent), real-time local control without cloud round-trip latency, and reduced cloud bandwidth and cost by performing local aggregation and sending only summaries to the cloud. AgroSense uses this pattern for the control path: the Node-RED threshold evaluation and valve command generation run on the Raspberry Pi gateway, ensuring that irrigation control continues during internet outages. Cloud InfluxDB receives only the aggregated daily statistics and the raw telemetry stream for historical analysis.

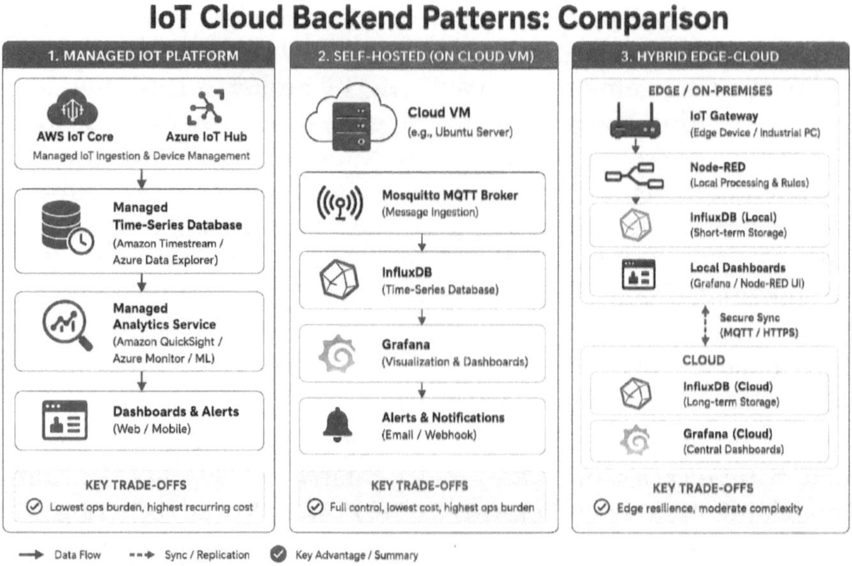

Figure 5.6: IoT Cloud Backend Architecture Patterns: Managed vs. Self-Hosted vs. Hybrid

5.7.3 The API-First Design Principle

The API-first principle states that API contracts: the complete interface specifications for every service boundary in the system, which must be defined, reviewed, and formally agreed before any implementation begins. This is the application of Step 5's service specification to engineering practice: the contract is the commitment; the implementation fulfils it.

Key Insight: *The API-First Principle in IoT Systems. An agreed interface contract — specifying protocol, topic structure, payload schema, quality-of-service level, and a fully worked example message — is the single most effective tool for preventing integration failures in distributed IoT systems. A format mismatch discovered at acceptance testing on deployed hardware can require a field firmware update campaign. The same mismatch, caught in a ten-minute specification review before implementation begins, costs a sentence change. Machine learning pipelines, which depend on consistent, well-typed telemetry fields as model input features, are especially sensitive to undocumented schema drift — a further reason to treat the API contract as a formally approved document.*

The failure mode that API-first design prevents is the integration crisis: two teams develop their respective sides of an interface in parallel, each making reasonable assumptions about the format and behaviour of the other side, and discover their assumptions are incompatible at integration testing. A concrete IoT example: the firmware team encodes the timestamp as a Unix epoch integer (seconds since 1 January 1970) to minimise payload size; the pipeline team writes the InfluxDB Lambda function expecting an ISO 8601 string because the information model used the phrase 'ISO 8601 UTC'. Both teams were following their understanding of the specification. The result is that every message arrives at InfluxDB with an invalid timestamp field, silently storing all records at the Unix epoch (1 January 1970) until someone notices that the Grafana time-series graph is displaying no recent data.

Fixing this requires a firmware update to all deployed nodes: a field operation in a remote agricultural deployment. The API-first principle, and specifically, an agreed example payload in the service specification with a worked timestamp value, which would have caught this discrepancy in a ten-minute specification review.

Implementing API-first in practice requires three artefacts in addition to the Step 5 service specification: an example message for each API endpoint (a complete worked instance of the payload with realistic values for every field); a schema document (JSON Schema or Avro schema for JSON payloads; Protobuf for binary payloads) that can be used to automatically validate messages at every system boundary; and a versioning policy (semantic versioning for API contracts, with a defined compatibility guarantee and deprecation procedure) so that firmware updates, pipeline changes, and application updates can be deployed independently without breaking existing consumers.

CASE STUDY: *Case Study Application: AgroSense API Specification (Step 5 Detail) Rajasthan, India — API Design*

MQTT Topic Structure: The AgroSense topic hierarchy follows the agrosense/{farm_id}/{zone_id}/{node_id}/{message_type} pattern. Farm IDs are four-character alphanumeric codes assigned at registration (e.g., RS01 for the Rajasthan pilot). Zone IDs are two-character codes (Z1, Z2, Z3). Node IDs are the EUI-64 of the ESP32's built-in MAC address, formatted as eight colon-separated hex bytes. Example telemetry topic: agrosense/RS01/Z1/70:B3:D5:7E:D0:06:A2:1F/telemetry.

Telemetry Payload: JSON object, maximum 256 bytes (within LoRaWAN payload constraints after base64 encoding). Fields: {"node_id": "70:B3:D5:7E:D0:06:A2:1F", "zone_id": "Z1", "ts": "2024-06-15T08:30:00Z", "vwc": 28.4, "soil_t": 31.2, "amb_t": 38.6, "amb_rh": 42.1, "batt_v": 3.82}. Note: timestamp is ISO 8601 UTC string. RSSI is appended by the LoRaWAN Network Server as metadata and is not included in the device payload.

Valve Command API: REST POST to the AWS API Gateway end-

point /api/v1/zones/{zone_id}/valve/{valve_id}/command. Request body: {"action": "OPEN", "duration_minutes": 30, "issued_by": "auto_rule"}. Response: {"command_id": "uuid", "status": "queued", "estimated_delivery_window": "60s"}. Commands are queued for delivery in the next LoRaWAN downlink receive window. Authentication: Bearer token from AWS Cognito (farmers) or service account key (Node-RED automation). Manual farmer overrides require farmer JWT; automated rule commands use a Node-RED service account with restricted scope (valve:write only).

Professional Checklist: IoT Project Design

Before moving from concept to deployment, confirm the following:

- *The problem statement, users, stakeholders, and success criteria are clearly defined.*
- *Device, gateway, edge, cloud, application, and integration responsibilities are separated clearly.*
- *Data flow from sensing to storage, analytics, decision-making, and actuation is documented.*
- *Security, privacy, governance, and maintenance requirements are included from the design stage.*
- *Prototype testing covers connectivity, reliability, latency, power consumption, and failure conditions.*
- *Deployment planning includes monitoring, updates, support responsibility, and lifecycle management.*

5.8 AgroSense: A Complete IoT Design Document

This section presents the AgroSense smart agriculture monitoring and irrigation control system as a unified design document: the accumulated output of all ten methodology steps applied to a single deployment. Each step is presented as a structured sub-section of approximately 100 words: concise enough to demonstrate that every step was executed, detailed enough to show exactly what it produced. This format is intended as a template: a practitioner who has worked through this chapter can use the AgroSense design document as the structural model for their own IoT design project, substituting the AgroSense content with content specific to their own deployment.

The design document is also the narrative resolution of the chapter's opening scenario. Aisha's blank page: the engineering notebook she was staring at in the opening paragraphs is now fully populated. Every element of the complete design below traces back to the single sentence she wrote at the top of that page: 'Start with the purpose, not the technology.'

AgroSense Design — Step 1: Purpose and Requirement Specification

Purpose Statement: AgroSense provides smallholder farmers in water-constrained agricultural environments with real-time soil moisture, soil temperature, and ambient climate data, enabling data-driven irrigation scheduling decisions that reduce water consumption, prevent crop loss from over- and under-irrigation, and improve harvest yield predictability. The system supplements human agronomic judgement with continuous, spatially distributed measurement, replacing irregular visual inspection with an always-on digital sensing network.

The requirements document (Table 5.2) specifies ten requirements across three categories. Must-Have Functional: VWC measurement at 40 nodes every 15 minutes; soil temperature measurement at the same interval; automated valve open on VWC below zone threshold; automated valve close 30 minutes after opening if threshold is met; farmer mobile push notification on each valve event. Must-Have Non-functional: VWC accuracy plus or minus 3% VWC; node battery life exceeding 12 months; data availability not less than 99.5% over any 30-day period. Must-Have Constraints: no cellular connectivity (unlicensed spectrum only); node hardware cost not exceeding USD 50.

AgroSense Design — Step 2: Process Specification

Device-side process: RTC alarm wakes the ESP32 from deep sleep every 900 seconds. The sensor management module powers on the VH400, DS18B20, and SHT31; waits for stabilisation; acquires and validates four measurements; encodes as a compact binary payload. The LoRaWAN module transmits the uplink and opens two receive windows for any pending downlink command. If a valve command is received on port 2, it is forwarded to the Arduino valve controller via RS-485. The ESP32 returns to deep sleep.

Platform-side process: The Raspberry Pi LoRaWAN gateway receives the uplink and forwards it to the ChirpStack Network Server. ChirpStack validates the device session and forwards the decrypted payload to AWS IoT Core via MQTT. An IoT Core Rule writes to S3 (archival), invokes Lambda (InfluxDB write), and publishes to Node-RED via webhook. Node-RED evaluates the zone rolling-average VWC against the zone threshold. If below threshold and valve not already open: publish valve open command to MQTT, send FCM push notification, start 30-minute timer. At T+30 minutes, re-evaluate: if VWC above upper threshold, publish valve close command and notify farmer.

AgroSense Design — Step 3: Domain Model

The AgroSense domain model contains eleven entity classes in three categories. Physical entities: Farm (one instance, RS01), Field Zone (three instances Z1/Z2/Z3), Sensor Node (forty instances), Irrigation Valve (twelve instances), LoRa Gateway (two instances). Digital entities: Telemetry Record (continuous time-series, retained 18 months), Zone Configuration (one per zone, containing VWC lower and upper thresholds), Alert (generated on threshold breach), Valve Event (logged on every open/close). Actor entities: Farmer (fourteen individuals, mobile app access), Agronomist (one, Grafana dashboard and threshold management), Field Technician (one, device provisioning and maintenance).

Key relationships and multiplicities: Farm 1 to 3 Field Zone; Field Zone 1 to N Sensor Node (twelve to sixteen nodes per zone); Field Zone 1 to N Irrigation Valve (three to five valves per zone); Sensor Node 1 to many Telemetry Record; Zone Configuration 1 per Field Zone; Alert associated with Sensor Node (N to 1); Farmer receives Alert (M to N through subscription relationship). The Zone Configuration entity was identified during domain modelling as a necessary digital entity not mentioned in the initial requirements interview, demonstrating the domain model's value in surfacing implicit design requirements.

AgroSense Design — Step 4: Information Model

Primary IoT resource: SoilMoistureNode. Attributes: node_id (string, EUI-64 format, immutable); zone_id (string, Z1/Z2/Z3, assigned at provisioning); vwc (float, percent VWC, range 0.0-100.0, accuracy plus or minus 3.0, interval 900 s, retained 18 months); soil_t (float, degrees Celsius, range -10 to 70, accuracy plus or minus 0.5, interval 900 s, retained 18 months); amb_t (float, degrees Celsius, range -10 to 60, accuracy plus or minus 0.3, retained 18 months); amb_rh (float, percent RH, range 0-100, accuracy plus or minus 2.0, retained 18 months); ts (ISO 8601 UTC string, device clock, NTP-synchronised at gateway); batt_v (float, V, range 3.0-4.2, retained 6 months); rssi (integer, dBm, appended by network server, retained 90 days).

Secondary resource: IrrigationValve. Attributes: valve_id (string); zone_id (string); state (enum: OPEN/CLOSED); last_command_ts (ISO 8601); cumulative_open_min (integer, running total). Derived attributes: zone_avg_vwc (float, 5-sample rolling average, computed by Node-RED, used for threshold evaluation); daily_min_vwc, daily_max_vwc, daily_avg_vwc (InfluxDB daily rollup, retained

18 months); irrigation_vol_L (float, open duration multiplied by measured flow rate 8 L/min, retained 18 months for water budget reporting).

AgroSense Design — Step 5: Service Specification

Six services are specified with interface contracts. (1) Data Collection: MQTT QoS 1 over TLS 1.3; topic agrosense/RS01/{zone_id}/{node_id}/telemetry; JSON payload 9 fields, max 256 bytes; frequency 1 per 900 s per node. (2) Data Storage: InfluxDB Cloud Write API; bucket agrosense_telemetry; measurement soil_node; tags node_id, zone_id; fields vwc, soil_t, amb_t, amb_rh, batt_v, rssi; precision seconds. (3) Analytics: Node-RED HTTP webhook; 5-sample zone VWC rolling average; threshold evaluation at each message receipt; InfluxDB Flux task for daily rollup at 00:00 UTC. (4) Control: MQTT QoS 1; topic agrosense/RS01/{zone_id}/valve/{valve_id}/command; JSON {action, duration_minutes, issued_by}; LoRaWAN downlink port 2; delivery in next receive window. (5) Notification: FCM HTTP v1 API; triggered by Node-RED; payload includes zone name, action, and current VWC; supported languages: Hindi and English. (6) Management: LwM2M v1.2 over CoAP; device registration, OTA firmware update via LoRaWAN port 3, battery voltage monitoring with configurable low-battery alert threshold.

AgroSense Design — Step 6: IoT Functional View

Five functional layers are defined. Sensing and Actuation: forty ESP32-based sensor nodes (VWC, soil temperature, ambient temperature and humidity measurement; deep-sleep duty cycling; LoRaWAN uplink) and twelve solenoid valves (Arduino-controlled, 24V AC). Connectivity: LoRaWAN Class A radio (SF10, 125 kHz, OTAA join); two Raspberry Pi LoRaWAN gateways (RAK2287 concentrator, 8 channels); ChirpStack Network Server (local, on Raspberry Pi); Ethernet backhaul with 4G LTE backup. Processing: AWS IoT Core (MQTT broker, TLS mutual authentication, rule engine); AWS Lambda (InfluxDB write, FCM trigger); InfluxDB Cloud (time-series storage and daily rollup); Node-RED (real-time threshold evaluation and valve command automation, running locally on gateway for offline resilience). Application: Grafana (agronomist dashboard, InfluxDB data source); AWS API Gateway and Lambda (REST API for mobile app). User Interface: Grafana web dashboard (agronomist); React Native mobile app (farmers).

AgroSense Design — Step 7: Operational View

Network deployment: forty sensor nodes distributed across

three field zones (Zone 1: twelve nodes, 85 ha; Zone 2: fourteen nodes, 130 ha; Zone 3: fourteen nodes, 125 ha). Maximum node-to-gateway distance: 3.1 km (Zone 3 NW corner to gateway at farm office). LoRa link budget at 3.1 km with SF10: margin of 9 dB before obstruction allowance; validated in pre-deployment range trial. Two gateways deployed (primary at farm office, secondary at Zone 2 irrigation shed) for redundancy; both connect to ChirpStack NS; duplicate packets deduplicated by NS. Valve controller: Arduino Mega at each of three pump houses, connected to gateway via RS-485 over 200 m shielded cable.

Environmental specification: sensor node enclosures IP67, operating temperature -10 to +60 degrees Celsius, UV-stable polycarbonate. Antenna: quarter-wave whip, externally mounted on enclosure lid, sealed N-connector. Power: ESP32 deep sleep 65 microamperes average; 3,000 mAh LiPo with 2W solar; modelled battery life 24 months without solar at minimum insolation, indefinite with solar. Gateway power: mains with 4-hour UPS; cellular 4G LTE modem as internet backup on SIM from regional BSNL operator. Maintenance: sensor node replacement by field technician using integration specification (pin-out, calibration procedure, LoRaWAN OTAA join via zero-touch provisioning from DevEUI list).

AgroSense Design — Step 8: Bill of Materials

Table 5.4 presents the AgroSense production Bill of Materials. Every line item is traceable to a requirement: platform selection to AS-C-02 (USD 50 node cost) and AS-C-01 (LoRaWAN radio); VH400 sensor to AS-NF-01 (plus or minus 3% VWC accuracy); 3,000 mAh LiPo and solar panel to AS-NF-02 (12-month battery life); IP67 enclosure to the operational specification (Rajasthan field environment); dual gateways to AS-NF-03 (99.5% availability).

Component	Qty	Unit Cost	Total	Notes / Traceability
ESP32-WROVER-B (16MB) module	40	USD 4.20	USD 168	Sensor node MCU; Wi-Fi/BLE disabled in firmware; deep sleep 65 uA
Semtech SX1276 LoRa module (868 MHz)	40	USD 3.50	USD 140	LoRaWAN Class A radio; OTAA join; SF10/125 kHz
Vegetronix VH400 soil moisture sensor	40	USD 18.00	USD 720	Capacitive; 0-3V analogue output; +/-3% VWC; req. AS-NF-01
DS18B20 waterproof temperature probe (1m)	40	USD 3.20	USD 128	1-Wire; +/-0.5 degC; soil temperature measurement
SHT31 temp/humidity sensor (I2C)	40	USD 4.10	USD 164	Ambient temperature +/-0.3 degC; humidity +/-2% RH

3.7V 3000 mAh LiPo battery	40	USD 5.50	USD 220	Primary node power; 24+ months modelled life with solar
6V 2W solar panel	40	USD 3.80	USD 152	Solar supplementation; ensures indefinite operation outdoors
IP67 polycarbonate enclosure (120x80x-55mm)	40	USD 4.50	USD 180	Field environment protection; UV-stable; AS operational spec
Raspberry Pi 4 Model B (4GB)	2	USD 65.00	USD 130	LoRaWAN gateway; ChirpStack NS; Node-RED; IP20 indoor install
RAK2287 LoRa concentrator HAT (868 MHz, 8ch)	2	USD 110.00	USD 220	Multi-channel LoRa frontend for gateway; mounts on Pi 4
Arduino Mega 2560	3	USD 14.00	USD 42	Valve controller (one per pump house); 12-channel relay drive
24V AC solenoid valve (normally closed)	12	USD 22.00	USD 264	Irrigation flow control; NC fail-safe on power loss
12-channel relay module (5V coil, 250VAC/10A contact)	3	USD 12.00	USD 36	Arduino-driven relay array for solenoid valve switching

Table 5.4: AgroSense Bill of Materials (Key Components)

AgroSense Design — Step 9: Application Development

Device firmware (ESP32 Arduino): The sensor management module drives VH400 ADC (12-bit, 11 dB attenuation, calibrated against two-point reference), DS18B20 (DallasTemperature library, 12-bit resolution, 750 ms conversion), and SHT31 (Adafruit SHT31 library, single-shot mode). After acquisition, the power management module configures RTC timer wake (900 s) as the primary wake source and calls esp_deep_sleep_start(). The LMIC LoRaWAN library handles OTAA join (DevEUI from ESP32 MAC, AppKey from ATECC608A secure storage), SF10 data rate, and ADR disabled (fixed data rate for predictable battery consumption). Binary payload encodes six values as four-byte IEEE 754 floats plus a one-byte flags field: 25 bytes total, well within the 51-byte SF10 maximum payload.

Cloud pipeline: AWS Lambda (Python 3.12) parses the ChirpStack application payload, validates against JSON Schema, and writes to InfluxDB Cloud using the influxdb-client-python library. A Node-RED flow on the Raspberry Pi gateway subscribes to the MQTT telemetry topic, maintains a per-zone deque of five measurements for rolling average computation, queries the local Zone Configuration Redis store for thresholds, and publishes valve commands and FCM notifications on threshold breach. The Node-RED flow runs locally, providing autonomous irrigation control during internet outages: a critical requirement for the remote Rajasthan deployment.

User applications: Grafana dashboard (Cloud free tier) with four panels: farm map heatmap (InfluxDB Flux query, zone VWC as colour), per-node time-series (last 7 days, configurable), valve event log (table panel, InfluxDB annotation query), and battery voltage trend (threshold alert at 3.5 V). React Native mobile app: single-screen zone status view with green/yellow/red VWC indicators, last reading timestamp, and a manual valve override button per zone. Localisation: Hindi and English string tables. Push notifications via FCM include zone name, valve action, and current VWC in the farmer's language. App distributed via APK sideload (no Google Play account required for the cooperative's Android feature phones).

AgroSense Design — Step 10: Testing, Deployment, and Iteration

Unit testing: sensor management module validated against hardware in the loop with reference instruments (VWC: 5-point calibration curve against gravimetric reference; temperature: two-point calibration against NIST-traceable thermometer). Firmware MQTT publish tested with Wireshark packet capture confirming TLS 1.3 handshake and QoS 1 acknowledgement. Lambda function unit-tested with 200 synthetic payloads covering all attribute range boundaries and three malformed-message error cases.

Integration testing (single Zone 1 pilot, 5 nodes, 2 weeks): end-to-end latency from sensor measurement to Grafana display measured at 47 seconds average (requirement: under 90 seconds); packet loss rate at maximum range: 1.8% (requirement: under 5%); valve open-command latency: 3.2 seconds average; Grafana update latency: 52 seconds average. All DVT criteria in Table 5.3 passed.

Acceptance testing: agronomist reviewed dashboard with full 5-node Zone 1 data; confirmed zone heatmap accurately reflected known irrigation schedule; two farmers demonstrated push notification receipt and manual valve override on mobile app. Gateway internet disconnection test confirmed Node-RED continued autonomous valve control for 4-hour simulated outage with 17 automatic measurements and one threshold-triggered irrigation event completed without cloud connectivity.

Deployment: staged rollout — Zone 1 full (12 nodes, kharif pilot); Zones 2 and 3 added at start of rabi season after Zone 1 validation. OTA firmware update validated during Zone 1 expansion: firmware v1.1 pushed to all 12 Zone 1 nodes via LoRaWAN; all nodes updated and restarted within 45 minutes; no data loss. Iteration improvements after first kharif season: three Zone 3 nodes repositioned after root zone development altered drainage; Zone 2 vegetable VWC threshold recalibrated from 35% to 27% VWC based on yield analysis; firmware v1.2 issued adding exponential moving average VWC filter (alpha = 0.3) to reduce rain-splatter false triggers from 4 per week to zero.

Aisha's blank page is now a complete design. She has a purpose statement, a requirements document with ten verifiable requirements, a process flow diagram, a domain model with eleven entity classes, an information model specifying every data attribute in the system, a service catalogue with six interface contracts, a functional architecture diagram, a network deployment plan with link budget validation, a bill of materials for forty sensor nodes and twelve valves, firmware and pipeline specifications, a test plan with three testing levels, and an iteration framework validated by one growing season of pilot data.

None of these required a single line of code. The firmware was not written until Step 9, and when it was written, the developer had a complete, unambiguous specification: which sensors, which GPIO pins, which data types, which MQTT topic, which JSON schema, which QoS level. There were no integration surprises because the API contracts were agreed before development began. There were no hardware surprises because the link budget and power budget were calculated before components were ordered. There were no user interface surprises because the farmers were consulted in Step 1 and the application was designed to their literacy and language constraints from the beginning.

The IoT design methodology does not make engineering decisions for the engineer. It ensures that every decision that must be made gets made, in the right order, with the right information. A purpose statement before requirements. Requirements before hardware selection. An information model before firmware. A service specification before a single API call is written. A prototype test before volume assembly. A staged deployment before full commitment. An iteration review after real-world data arrives. That sequence, and the discipline of completing each step before the next begins is what transforms a good idea into a deployable system.

5.9 Chapter Summary

This chapter has answered the IoT engineer's most fundamental practical question: given a knowledge of IoT concepts, hardware, architecture, and protocols, how does one actually design a complete system from scratch? The answer is the ten-step IoT Design Methodology: a structured, layered framework that guides the designer from a statement of purpose, through models and specifications, to a deployable physical system. The chapter followed a single running case study: the AgroSense smart agriculture deployment for a fourteen-farmer cooperative in Rajasthan: from the opening scenario's blank page to the complete design document in Section 5.8.

Section 5.1 introduced the methodology's philosophy: IoT design proceeds from abstract to concrete and from requirement to specification. The front-loading of thinking in the conceptual and logical design phases reduces downstream cost by preventing the integration crises and requirement gaps that cause the majority of IoT project failures. The ten steps were introduced in three natural phases: Conceptual Design (Steps 1-3), Logical Design (Steps 4-6), and Physical Design (Steps 7-10). Section 5.2 provided the reference definitions for all ten steps, establishing the input, output, and key questions for each, and summarised them in Table 5.1.

Section 5.3 worked through the Conceptual Design phase. Step 1 (Purpose and Requirement Specification) established the distinction between purpose (why the system exists), functional requirements (what it must do), non-functional requirements (how well it must do it), and constraints (the non-negotiable boundaries within which the design must operate). The MoSCoW prioritisation framework and the five-column requirements table structure were presented as practical tools.

Step 2 (Process Specification) produced the AgroSense process flow — distinguishing device-side processes (sensor acquisition through LoRaWAN transmission and deep sleep return) from platform-side processes (gateway receive through AWS IoT Core, InfluxDB write, Node-RED threshold evaluation, and valve command and FCM notification). Step 3 (Domain Model) identified eleven entity classes in the AgroSense domain, revealing the Zone Configuration entity as a necessary design artefact that the initial requirements interview had not surfaced.

Section 5.4 worked through the Logical Design phase. Step 4 (Information Model) specified every data attribute of the SoilMoistureNode and IrrigationValve resources (data type, unit, range, accuracy, update frequency, and retention policy) establishing the shared data vocabulary that governs all subsequent firmware and pipeline development. The critical role of the information model in preventing integration failures through the API-first principle was demonstrated with a concrete timestamp format incompatibility example. Step 5 (Service Specification) produced six interface contracts for the AgroSense services: data collection, storage, analytics, control, notification, and management. Step 6 (IoT Functional View) organised these services into a five-layer technology-agnostic architecture diagram, making visible both the telemetry path (upward from sensor to dashboard) and the control path (downward from rule engine to valve).

Section 5.5 worked through the first two steps of the Physical Design phase. Step 7 (Operational View) produced the network deployment plan with LoRa link budget analysis validating the 3.1 km maximum range, environmental specification (IP67, -10 to +60 degrees Celsius), and power plan confirming indefinite solar-supplemented operation. The Design Verification Test checklist (Table 5.3) was introduced as the gate between prototype validation and volume production. Step 8 (Device and Component Integration) produced the AgroSense bill of materials (Table 5.4), with every component traceable to a specific requirement, and the integration specification documenting all hardware interfaces.

Section 5.6 completed the Physical Design phase. Step 9 (Application Development) specified the three-tier AgroSense software stack: ESP32 firmware (LMIC LoRaWAN, sensor management, deep-sleep duty cycling, binary payload encoding); cloud pipeline (AWS IoT Core, Lambda, InfluxDB, Node-RED); and user applications (Grafana agronomist dashboard, React Native farmer mobile app). The Tech Spotlight on Node-RED demonstrated how visual flow programming can implement complete IoT automation logic. Step 10 (Testing, Deployment, and Iteration) defined three testing levels (unit, integration, acceptance), a staged deployment sequence, and the iteration framework that produced three concrete design improvements after the first growing season.

Section 5.7 provided depth on the Communication APIs and Cloud Backend Design decisions that bridge the logical and physical layers. The three API categories — device-to-cloud (MQTT topic hierarchy, CoAP resources), service-to-service (AWS IoT Rule, Lambda, InfluxDB write), and user-facing (REST API, Grafana data source) were defined with the AgroSense specifications as worked examples. Three cloud backend patterns were compared: managed IoT platform, self-hosted broker and database, and hybrid edge-cloud. The API-first design principle was articulated as the practice discipline that prevents integration crises by requiring interface contracts to be agreed before implementation begins.

Section 5.8 presented the complete AgroSense design as a unified ten-step document: a reusable template for any IoT design engagement. The closing narrative returned to Aisha and her blank page: the methodology did not make her design decisions for her; it ensured that every decision that had to be made was made in the right order, with the right information, and was traceable to the requirements that justified it. Traceability: the thread connecting every physical component back through integration specification, functional view, service contract, information model, domain model, process flow, and requirements to the purpose statement is the methodology's ultimate value. It makes the design auditable, maintainable, and improvable throughout the system's operational life.

Chapter 6 examines the data and platform layer that the AgroSense design depends on: the InfluxDB time-series database, the AWS IoT Core ingestion pipeline, the analytics that transform raw soil moisture readings into irrigation decisions, and the broader landscape of IoT data management — from edge processing to cloud storage to machine learning inference. The AgroSense design choices encountered in this chapter will reappear in Chapter 6 as concrete examples of the data management principles it teaches.

Part III

Data, Platforms, and Applications

Chapter 6

Data Management, Analytics, and Cloud/Edge Platforms

From Raw Sensor Readings to Operational Intelligence

Chapter 6 examines how IoT data is collected, structured, transmitted, processed, stored, analysed, and governed across cloud, edge, and fog environments. It explains the distinctive characteristics of IoT data, including volume, velocity, variety, veracity, and value, and discusses suitable data serialisation formats, processing models, storage architectures, and communication APIs. The chapter presents key data processing approaches such as batch processing, stream processing, Lambda architecture, and Kappa architecture, while also explaining how edge and fog computing reduce latency, bandwidth usage, and cloud dependency. It further explores cloud IoT platforms, time-series databases, data lakes, analytics pipelines, machine learning workflows, and data quality frameworks that transform raw sensor signals into operational intelligence. In addition, the chapter highlights data governance, privacy, ownership, retention, and compliance considerations that are essential for responsible IoT data management. Overall, this chapter provides the data-centric foundation required to design IoT systems that can convert continuous device telemetry into reliable insight, automated decisions, and measurable business value.

Data is the lifeblood of every IoT system, yet raw sensor data in isolation has no value. A temperature reading of 87.3 degrees Celsius from a bearing sensor on an industrial compressor means nothing by itself. It acquires meaning only when it is compared against a historical baseline, correlated with vibration data from the same bearing, analysed in the context of the machine's current operating load, and delivered to a maintenance engineer alongside a recommended action. The journey from raw sensor reading to actionable intelligence is the subject of this chapter, and it is a journey that spans multiple computing tiers, multiple storage technologies, multiple analytics paradigms, and an increasingly complex landscape of governance and regulatory obligations.

The scale of the challenge is formidable. A single modern IoT deployment may involve tens of thousands of devices, each generating hundreds of readings per second. A smart city of one million residents may have 500,000 sensors generating 50 terabytes of data per day. An industrial plant with 10,000 instrumented machines may produce more data in a week than the entire internet carried in a day in the mid-1990s. Deciding what to collect, how to transmit it efficiently, where to process it, how to store it, and what to extract from it are the defining engineering challenges of IoT data management, and getting these decisions wrong is one of the most common causes of IoT deployment failure.

This chapter examines eight interconnected dimensions of IoT data management. It begins with the characteristics of IoT data and the serialisation formats that govern how it is encoded for transmission. It then examines data processing architectures, the edge-fog-cloud computing continuum, commercial cloud IoT platforms, storage models, the four-level analytics hierarchy, and the governance and privacy frameworks that must govern the entire pipeline. Case studies from commercial deployments at Amazon Web Services, Microsoft Azure, Apache Kafka deployments at LinkedIn and Uber, and the InfluxDB time-series platform illustrate how these concepts are implemented in production systems at scale.

6.1 IoT Data Characteristics: The Five Vs

Before designing a data pipeline, the engineer must understand the nature of the data that will flow through it. IoT data has a distinctive profile that differentiates it from conventional enterprise data and from most other categories of big data. This profile is captured in the five Vs framework, which provides a vocabulary for analysing the demands that IoT data places on infrastructure, storage, and analytics systems.

DEFINITION: *IoT Data Pipeline*

The end-to-end sequence of stages through which IoT sensor data flows, from raw device reading through transmission, ingestion, storage, processing, and analytics to actionable output at the application layer. The pipeline design determines the latency, cost, reliability, and analytical capability of the IoT system.

Source: Adapted from Gubbi et al. (2013); Al-Fuqaha et al. (2015)

6.1.1 Volume

Volume refers to the sheer quantity of data generated by IoT systems. IDC's Global DataSphere report estimated that IoT devices would generate approximately 73 zettabytes of data annually by 2025, representing over 30 percent of the total global data created. A single industrial gas turbine equipped with 5,000 sensors generates approximately 500 gigabytes of operating data per day. A fleet of 100 such turbines generates 50 terabytes per day.

Transmitting all of this data to the cloud in raw form is neither technically feasible at scale nor economically viable: at typical cloud data ingestion pricing of USD 0.08 per gigabyte, ingesting 50 terabytes per day would cost USD 4,000 per day or approximately USD 1.5 million per year, before any storage or processing costs. Volume therefore drives the most fundamental architectural decision in IoT data management: how much data to filter at the edge before cloud transmission.

6.1.2 Velocity

Velocity refers to the speed at which IoT data is generated and must be processed. IoT systems generate continuous data streams where the analytical value of a reading may be time-limited: a temperature anomaly detected two minutes after it occurs may have already allowed equipment to overheat and fail. Different IoT use cases have very different velocity requirements. A soil moisture sensor reporting once per hour imposes minimal velocity demands on the data pipeline. A vibration sensor on a high-speed turbine sampling at 20,000 Hz and streaming data to an edge processor for real-time fault detection imposes extreme velocity demands. Industrial control loops in real-time systems may require end-to-end processing latencies below 10 milliseconds. The velocity requirement of the most latency-sensitive use case in a deployment sets the floor for the entire pipeline design.

6.1.3 Variety

Variety reflects the diversity of data types generated by IoT systems. Numeric time-series telemetry from temperature and pressure sensors represents only one category. IoT systems also generate event data recording discrete state changes (valve opened, alarm triggered, motor started); image and video streams from cameras and thermal imagers; audio streams from acoustic sensors and microphones; location data from GPS and indoor positioning systems; and rich metadata including device identity, firmware version, configuration parameters, and communication quality indicators. Each data type has different schema requirements, storage characteristics, and analytics tooling, demanding a data architecture flexible enough to accommodate structured, semi-structured, and unstructured data within a single cohesive pipeline.

6.1.4 Veracity

Veracity refers to the accuracy, reliability, and trustworthiness of IoT data. IoT data quality is inherently imperfect. Sensors drift over time: a temperature sensor that was accurate to plus or minus 0.5 degrees at installation may have drifted to plus or minus 2 degrees after 18 months of operation in an industrial environment without recalibration. Communication errors produce corrupted readings or missing data packets. Sensors fail entirely, producing flat-line readings or returning maximum-scale values.

Environmental interference causes false readings: an outdoor humidity sensor affected by rain splash may report 100 percent relative humidity when ambient humidity is 65 percent. IoT data pipelines must therefore incorporate data quality validation at ingestion, with range checks, cross-sensor consistency validation, and temporal gap detection identifying suspect readings before they propagate into analytics and corrupt model outputs.

DEFINITION: *Veracity (IoT Data Quality)*

The degree of accuracy, reliability, and trustworthiness of data collected by IoT sensors. Veracity is degraded by sensor drift over time, calibration errors, communication packet loss, physical sensor damage, and electromagnetic interference. IoT data pipelines must implement automated data quality checks at ingestion to prevent low-veracity data from producing incorrect analytical outputs.

Source: Al-Fuqaha et al. (2015); Ziegler et al. (2019)

6.1.5 Value

Value is the fifth V and arguably the most important: the degree to which IoT data, once collected, processed, and analysed, generates outcomes worth more than the cost of the infrastructure required to produce them. The value dimension highlights a phenomenon sometimes called data dark matter: the observation that the vast majority of IoT sensor data that is captured is never processed, analysed, or acted upon. A 2018 report by McKinsey Global Institute estimated that in industrial deployments, less than 1 percent of the data generated by industrial equipment was ever used for decision-making.

Data dark matter represents simultaneously a failure of pipeline design (data is not routed to analytics that could use it) and a failure of the analytics capability (the organisation lacks the models and processes needed to extract value from available data). Addressing the value dimension requires not just technical investment but organisational investment in analytics capabilities and data-driven decision processes.

DEFINITION: ***Data Dark Matter***

The majority of IoT sensor data that is captured by devices and transmitted to storage but is never processed, analysed, or acted upon, generating cost without generating value. Data dark matter results from misalignment between data collection scope and analytics capability, and from the absence of defined processes for acting on available insights.

Source: McKinsey Global Institute (2018)

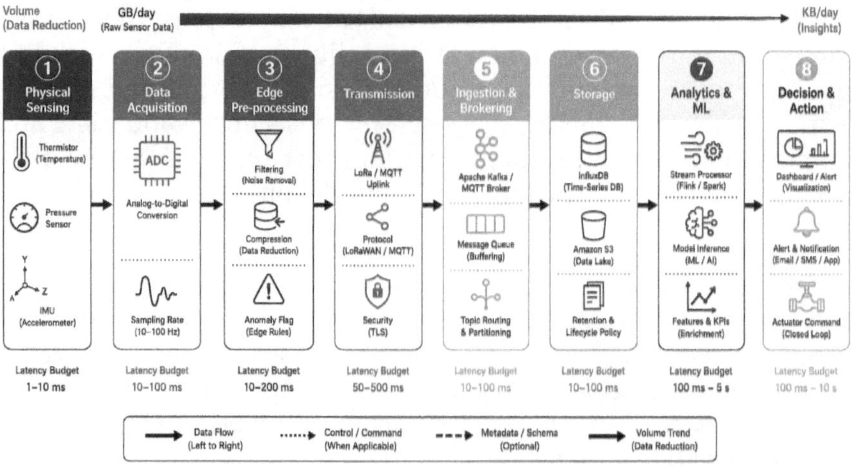

Figure 6.1: The IoT Data Pipeline: End-to-End Flow from Device to Decision

The five Vs provide a diagnostic framework for IoT data pipeline design. A deployment characterised by extreme volume but low velocity, such as a nationwide smart metering network, favours batch processing architectures with aggressive edge filtering. A deployment with moderate volume but extreme velocity, such as an industrial control system, favours stream processing with edge computing for real-time inference. A deployment with high variety, such as a smart city platform aggregating transport, environmental, and utilities data, requires a data architecture that handles multiple schema types and storage models within a unified governance framework. The remainder of this chapter addresses each dimension of the pipeline in turn.

Key Insight: The Value Imperative in IoT Data Design. The most common failure mode in IoT data programmes is not technical — it is strategic: data is collected and stored without a defined consumer or a specified decision it will inform. Before selecting a processing architecture, agree on the specific question the data will answer, who will act on the answer, and at what frequency. An IoT system that reliably answers one well-specified question is worth more than a data lake filled with unqueried telemetry. The 'data dark matter' problem — less than 1% of industrial IoT data ever used for decision-making — is a design failure, not a technology failure.

6.2 IoT Data Serialisation Formats

Before IoT data can be transmitted from a sensor to a gateway or from a gateway to the cloud, it must be serialised: converted from an in-memory data structure into a byte sequence that can be written to a communication channel. The choice of serialisation format has direct consequences for transmission bandwidth consumption, device processor load, cloud ingestion cost, and human debuggability. In deployments where millions of devices each send hundreds of readings per day, even a 30 percent reduction in serialised payload size can reduce annual data transmission costs by tens of thousands of dollars and extend battery life on constrained devices by a meaningful margin.

DEFINITION: Data Serialisation

The process of converting a data structure or object state into a format suitable for storage or transmission, from which it can later be reconstructed. In IoT contexts, serialisation formats determine the compactness and parsing efficiency of messages transmitted between devices, gateways, and cloud platforms. The choice of format involves trade-offs between payload size, parsing CPU overhead, human readability, and tooling ecosystem.

Source: Bormann et al., RFC 7049 (2013)

6.2.1 JSON: The Dominant Web-Facing Format

JSON (JavaScript Object Notation), standardised in ECMA-404 and RFC 8259, is the most widely used serialisation format in IoT systems that interface with web applications and REST APIs. Its text-based, human-readable structure makes it clear to debug and inspect, and every major programming language provides native JSON parsing libraries. A typical JSON IoT message encoding a temperature and humidity reading with device metadata and timestamp occupies approximately 150 to 250 bytes.

The verbosity of JSON is its primary drawback in constrained IoT environments. Field names are repeated in every message: a device transmitting 1,000 readings per day at 200 bytes per reading generates 200 kilobytes of data per day per device, 95 percent of which is structural overhead rather than sensor values. For a 10,000-device deployment, this totals 2 gigabytes of structural overhead per day.

Despite this inefficiency, JSON remains the dominant format for cloud-tier IoT APIs because of its universal tooling support and the relatively low cost of storage and processing at the cloud tier compared to constrained device and network tiers.

6.2.2 CBOR: Binary Efficiency for Constrained Devices

CBOR (Concise Binary Object Representation), standardised in RFC 7049 and updated in RFC 8949, was designed specifically to address the verbosity of JSON in constrained IoT environments. CBOR encodes the same data types as JSON (strings, numbers, arrays, maps, booleans, null) but uses a compact binary encoding that eliminates the overhead of repeated field name strings and replaces text-encoded numbers with fixed-width binary integers and IEEE 754 floating-point values. A JSON message of 200 bytes typically compresses to approximately 60 to 80 bytes in CBOR, a reduction of 60 to 70 percent.

CBOR is natively supported in CoAP (RFC 7252), the lightweight protocol designed for constrained IoT devices, and is recommended for use with MQTT in environments where payload minimisation is critical. The IETF's CBOR Object Signing and Encryption (COSE) framework provides lightweight cryptographic services for CBOR-encoded messages, enabling authenticated and encrypted IoT messages with minimal overhead. CBOR is used in the Matter smart home standard and in several IETF IoT security protocols including EDHOC, the Ephemeral Diffie-Hellman Over COSE key exchange protocol designed for constrained devices.

DEFINITION: CBOR (Concise Binary Object Representation)

A binary data serialisation format standardised in RFC 8949, designed to encode JSON-equivalent data structures in significantly fewer bytes. CBOR achieves compactness through binary type encoding, numeric field keys, and fixed-width binary number representations. Widely used in constrained IoT devices to reduce transmission bandwidth and processing overhead compared to text-based JSON.

Source: Bormann and Hoffman, RFC 8949 (2020)

6.2.3 Protocol Buffers and MessagePack

Protocol Buffers (Protobuf), developed by Google and open-sourced in 2008, offer the highest level of compactness and parsing performance among commonly used IoT serialisation formats. Protobuf uses a schema definition language to define message structures at design time; the schema compiler generates serialisation and deserialisation code in multiple target languages. Because field names are replaced by field number identifiers in the binary encoding, Protobuf messages can be 3 to 10 times smaller than equivalent JSON messages. Protobuf is widely used in high-throughput Industrial Internet of Things (IIoT) and telemetry systems where both bandwidth and parsing CPU overhead are critical constraints, including the gRPC remote procedure call framework that is increasingly used for IoT-to-cloud streaming in high-performance deployments.

MessagePack is a binary serialisation format that preserves the self-describing nature of JSON (no separate schema required) while achieving binary compactness comparable to CBOR. It is simpler to adopt than Protobuf because no schema compilation step is required, making it appropriate for deployments where schema flexibility is valued over maximum compression. XML, while mentioned here for completeness, is generally unsuitable for constrained IoT devices because of its extreme verbosity and high parsing cost; it remains in use in legacy industrial and healthcare systems where data exchange formats are mandated by established standards such as HL7 and IEC 61968.

Table 6.1: Comparison of IoT Data Serialisation Formats

Format	Encoding	Relative Size	Human Readable	Primary IoT Use
JSON	Text (UTF-8)	100% (baseline)	Yes (fully)	Web APIs, cloud-tier messaging, debugging
CBOR	Binary	35-50% of JSON	No	Constrained devices, CoAP payloads, Matter
Protocol Buffers	Binary (schema)	10-30% of JSON	No	High-throughput IIoT, gRPC streaming
Message-Pack	Binary	40-60% of JSON	No	Mid-tier IoT, schema-flexible binary transport
XML	Text	150-300% of JSON	Yes (verbose)	Legacy industrial/healthcare (HL7, IEC 61968)

TECHNOLOGY SPOTLIGHT: *Calculating the Value of Serialisation Format Choice*

Consider a deployment of 5,000 IoT sensors, each transmitting one reading every 30 seconds. Each reading contains four fields: device ID (string), timestamp (integer), sensor value (float), and battery level (integer). As a JSON message this payload occupies approximately 120 bytes. As CBOR it occupies approximately 45 bytes. As Protobuf with a compiled schema it occupies approximately 18 bytes.

Daily data volume in JSON: 5,000 devices × (86,400 / 30) readings × 120 bytes = 1.73 GB/day.

Daily data volume in Protobuf: 5,000 × 2,880 × 18 bytes = 0.26 GB/day. Annual saving: (1.73 - 0.26) × 365 = 537 GB/year.

At a cloud data ingestion cost of USD 0.08/GB, the annual saving from switching to Protobuf is approximately USD 43 per year for this deployment. At 500,000 devices (a national smart metering scale), the saving exceeds USD 4,300 per year from serialisation format choice alone. This calculation illustrates why serialisation format decisions deserve careful analysis at the architecture stage, not as an afterthought.

6.3 Data Processing Architectures: Batch, Stream, Lambda, and Kappa

The processing architecture of an IoT data pipeline determines how quickly sensor data is converted into analytical outputs and what trade-offs are accepted between processing latency, computational cost, and analytical accuracy. Three fundamental processing architectures have emerged as the dominant patterns in production IoT systems: batch processing, stream processing, and the Lambda architecture that combines elements of both. A fourth pattern, the Kappa architecture, has gained traction as stream processing technology has matured to the point where it can serve both real-time and historical analytical workloads from a single processing stack.

6.3.1 Batch Processing

DEFINITION: Batch Processing

A data processing paradigm in which a large accumulated volume of data is processed as a single unit at scheduled intervals, rather than record by record as data arrives. Batch processing is characterised by high throughput and high latency, typically measured in minutes to hours. It is well suited to IoT workloads where analytical outputs are not time-sensitive, such as daily energy consumption reports, weekly predictive maintenance model retraining, or monthly fleet performance summaries.

Source: Marz and Warren (2015)

Apache Hadoop, built around the MapReduce programming model and the Hadoop Distributed File System (HDFS), was the foundational batch processing framework for big data workloads. A Hadoop job reads a large dataset from HDFS, applies a map function to each record to produce intermediate key-value pairs, shuffles and sorts the pairs by key, and applies a reduce function to each group to produce the final output. The MapReduce model is highly parallelisable across large clusters but has substantial overhead per job, making it economically unsuitable for workloads that require frequent small batches.

Apache Spark, introduced in 2010 and donated to the Apache Software Foundation in 2013, dramatically improved on Hadoop's performance for iterative and interactive workloads by caching intermediate results in distributed memory rather than writing them to disk between computation stages. Spark's in-memory execution engine can process IoT datasets 10 to 100 times faster than Hadoop MapReduce for workloads involving multiple passes over the same data, such as machine learning model training. Spark provides APIs for SQL queries (Spark SQL), streaming (Spark Structured Streaming), machine learning (MLlib), and graph analytics (GraphX), making it the most versatile processing framework in the Hadoop ecosystem.

In IoT contexts, batch processing is appropriate for workloads where the analytical output has low time sensitivity. End-of-day energy consumption summaries for a smart metering network, weekly retraining of predictive maintenance models on accumulated sensor data, and monthly fleet utilisation reports for a connected vehicle programme are all well-served by nightly or weekly batch jobs. The data accumulates in cloud storage during the day and is processed overnight when compute resources are cheapest.

6.3.2 Stream Processing

DEFINITION: Stream Processing

A data processing paradigm in which data is processed continuously as it arrives, record by record or in micro-batches, with latency typically measured in milliseconds to seconds. Stream processing maintains stateful context across events, enabling pattern detection, aggregation over sliding time windows, and real-time anomaly detection that would be impossible with batch processing latency.

Source: Kleppmann (2017)

Apache Kafka, developed at LinkedIn and open-sourced in 2011, has become the de facto standard infrastructure layer for IoT event streaming. Kafka functions as a distributed, durable, high-throughput message log: IoT device data is written by producers to named topics, persisted on disk with configurable retention, and consumed by one or more consumer applications at their own pace. Kafka's log-based architecture decouples IoT data producers from consumers, meaning that a cloud processing application can be temporarily unavailable without losing any data, which resumes from its last committed offset when it recovers. LinkedIn processes over 7 trillion messages per day through Kafka infrastructure, and the platform has demonstrated sustained throughput exceeding 2 million messages per second on a single cluster.

Apache Flink is the leading stateful stream processing framework for production IoT deployments. Unlike Spark Streaming, which processes data in micro-batches, Flink processes each event as it arrives and maintains exactly-once processing semantics through a checkpoint mechanism that periodically persists the state of all running operators. Flink's support for event-time processing, where computations are based on the time at which events occurred at the sensor rather than the time they arrived at the processor, is critical in IoT systems where network latency and device clock drift cause events to arrive out of sequence.

Flink's windowing operators, including tumbling windows (fixed non-overlapping time intervals), sliding windows (overlapping intervals that advance at a defined step), and session windows (dynamic intervals bounded by inactivity gaps), provide the temporal aggregation primitives needed for IoT anomaly detection and KPI computation.

TECHNOLOGY SPOTLIGHT: Apache Kafka in Production IoT: The Architecture Explained

Kafka organises messages into topics, each partitioned across multiple broker nodes for parallel consumption. Within each partition, messages are written to an append-only log and retained for a configurable period (hours to weeks). Consumer groups enable multiple independent processing applications to read the same topic simultaneously at different offsets, so a real-time alerting application and a batch analytics application can both consume the same sensor data stream without interfering with each other.

For IoT deployments, Kafka Connect provides ready-made connectors that ingest data from MQTT brokers, databases, and cloud storage systems without custom code. The Kafka MQTT Connector can bridge an existing MQTT-based IoT infrastructure to Kafka, making Kafka's durable streaming capabilities available to deployments that use MQTT for device-to-cloud communication. Major industrial IoT platform vendors including PTC ThingWorx, Siemens MindSphere, and GE Predix use Kafka as their internal event streaming backbone.

Confluent, the commercial company founded by Kafka's original LinkedIn developers, offers a managed Confluent Cloud platform that reduces Kafka operational overhead for IoT deployments. As of 2024, Confluent Cloud processes over 10 trillion events per day across thousands of enterprise customers, including several of the world's largest IoT deployments.

Managed cloud stream processing services from AWS (Kinesis Data Streams and Kinesis Data Analytics), Azure (Event Hubs and Azure Stream Analytics), and Google Cloud (Pub/Sub and Dataflow) provide Kafka-compatible or equivalent streaming capabilities as fully managed services, eliminating the operational overhead of running and scaling Kafka clusters. For IoT deployments that already use a primary cloud vendor for other services, these managed services offer faster time-to-production and lower operational complexity than self-managed Kafka, at the cost of higher per-event pricing at very large scale.

6.3.3 Lambda and Kappa Architectures

The Lambda architecture, proposed by Nathan Marz in 2011, was designed to address a fundamental tension in large-scale data systems: the trade-off between processing latency and analytical accuracy. Batch processing can produce highly accurate results by reprocessing complete historical datasets to correct errors and incorporate late-arriving data, but it does so at the cost of high latency (hours). Stream processing delivers low-latency results but may be less accurate because it cannot retroactively correct for late-arriving data or apply reprocessed corrections to previously issued outputs.

The Lambda architecture resolves this tension by maintaining two parallel processing layers. The batch layer processes complete historical datasets at regular intervals (typically daily or hourly) to produce highly accurate, complete views of the data. The speed layer processes the same data in real time using stream processing, producing approximate but low-latency results. The serving layer merges the outputs of both layers to answer queries, using the batch layer results for historical data and the speed layer results for recent data that the batch layer has not yet processed. When the batch layer catches up, it overwrites the speed layer's approximate results with its more accurate batch-computed values.

In IoT contexts, the Lambda architecture is commonly applied to predictive maintenance systems. The batch layer retrains machine learning models nightly on accumulated sensor history, producing high-accuracy failure prediction models. The speed layer applies the current model in real time to live sensor streams, generating anomaly scores and alerts with sub-second latency. The serving layer exposes both the real-time alert feed and the historical trending dashboard, with the batch layer's nightly reprocessing correcting any sensor calibration errors or late-arriving readings from intermittently connected devices.

The Kappa architecture, proposed by Jay Kreps (Kafka co-author) in 2014, simplifies the Lambda architecture by eliminating the batch layer entirely. In the Kappa architecture, all data, including historical data, is stored in a replayable event log (typically Kafka with long retention). The stream processing layer handles both real-time processing and historical reprocessing by replaying the log from the beginning. When a new model or algorithm is deployed that requires reprocessing historical data, a new consumer is started at the beginning of the Kafka log; it processes all historical data through the new algorithm and catches up to real time, at which point it replaces the previous consumer.

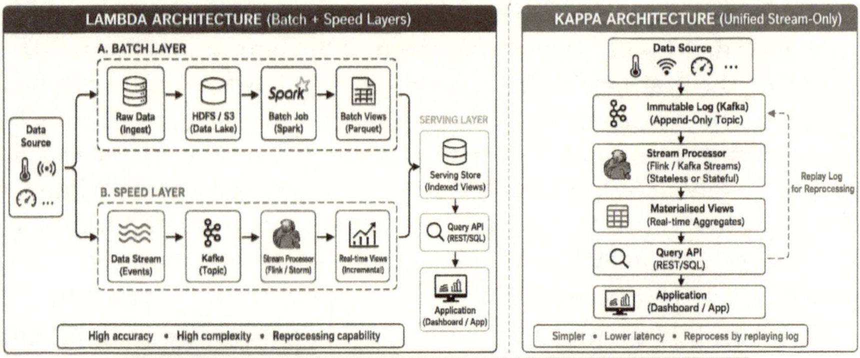

Dimension	Lambda	Kappa
Complexity	High (Two processing layers + merge logic)	Low (Single stream pipeline)
Latency	Medium (Batch + real-time merge)	Low (Single stream path)
Reprocessing	Full replay (Batch layer reprocess from data lake)	Log replay (Replay immutable log)

Figure 6.2: Lambda Architecture versus Kappa Architecture for IoT Data Processing

Table 6.2: Comparison of IoT Data Processing Architecture Patterns

Dimension	Batch	Stream	Lambda / Kappa
Processing latency	Minutes to hours	Milliseconds to seconds	Both: ms (speed) + hours (batch)
Accuracy	High (complete data)	Approximate (real-time)	High (Lambda merges both)
Operational complexity	Low (scheduled jobs)	Medium (stateful operators)	High (Lambda) / Medium (Kappa)
Typical IoT workload	Model retraining, reporting	Anomaly detection, alerting	Production ML inference + analytics

6.4 Edge and Fog Computing: The Distributed Processing Continuum

For much of IoT's early history, the dominant architectural assumption was that devices would collect data and transmit it to the cloud, where all meaningful processing would occur. This cloud-centric model was reasonable when IoT deployments were small, connectivity was abundant, and the cloud processing costs were justified by the analytical value generated.

As deployments scaled to millions of devices and the volume, velocity, and variety of IoT data grew correspondingly, the limitations of the cloud-centric model became progressively more apparent. Transmitting all data to the cloud consumed excessive bandwidth. Round-trip latency to remote cloud data centres made real-time control impossible. Data sovereignty regulations prevented certain categories of data from leaving national borders. And the economics of transmitting, storing, and processing raw sensor data at cloud scale became prohibitive.

The response to these limitations was a fundamental architectural shift: moving computation toward the data source. This shift gave rise to the concepts of edge computing and fog computing, and to the notion of a distributed processing continuum in which computation is allocated to the tier best suited to each workload's latency, bandwidth, and computational requirements.

DEFINITION: Edge Computing

A distributed computing paradigm in which data processing occurs at or near the source of data generation, on the IoT device itself or on a local gateway, rather than in a centralised remote cloud data centre. Edge computing reduces transmission latency, decreases bandwidth consumption, enables real-time local decision-making, and addresses data sovereignty requirements by processing sensitive data without transmitting it to the cloud.

Source: Shi et al. (2016)

DEFINITION: Fog Computing

A distributed computing paradigm that extends cloud computing capabilities to intermediate network tiers between IoT devices and the cloud, including network switches, routers, cellular base stations, and regional data centres. Fog computing enables aggregation, analytics, and low-latency services across wider geographic areas than edge computing, while maintaining lower latency than centralised cloud processing.

Source: Bonomi et al. (2012); IEEE 1934-2018

6.4.1 The Edge-Fog-Cloud Continuum

The edge-fog-cloud continuum is best understood as a three-tier computational hierarchy aligned with the physical topology of

IoT deployments. At the device tier, sensors and actuators perform minimal local processing, typically limited to signal conditioning, threshold comparison, and data buffering. Some modern IoT microcontrollers, including the STM32 series with its DSP and floating-point units, can execute lightweight machine learning inference (TinyML) directly on the device, enabling the most latency-critical decisions to be made in microseconds without any network communication.

At the edge tier, local gateways and edge servers perform the bulk of time-sensitive processing for their attached device populations. An industrial edge server on a factory floor processes sensor data from hundreds of machines, running real-time vibration analysis algorithms, applying pre-trained fault detection models, and managing local Supervisory Control and Data Acquisition (SCADA) integration, all within a few milliseconds of data generation.

An edge gateway in a connected vehicle processes camera feeds and LiDAR point clouds from multiple sensors to make real-time driving decisions that cannot tolerate the 50 to 200 milliseconds of round-trip latency to a cloud server. A building automation edge controller responds to occupancy sensor changes by adjusting HVAC setpoints in under one second, maintaining thermal comfort without cloud dependency.

At the fog tier, regional aggregation nodes serve multiple edge gateways across a wider geographic area. A city-level fog node might aggregate traffic data from hundreds of roadside edge gateways, running medium-latency analytics that require cross-site context, such as detecting congestion patterns that span multiple intersections. A regional fog server for a wind farm might aggregate performance data from dozens of turbines, identifying farm-level production optimisation opportunities that individual turbine edge controllers cannot detect in isolation. The fog tier typically has latency in the range of 1 to 50 milliseconds for devices in its service area, compared to device-tier latency below 1 millisecond and cloud latency of 50 to 200 milliseconds or more for geographically distant deployments.

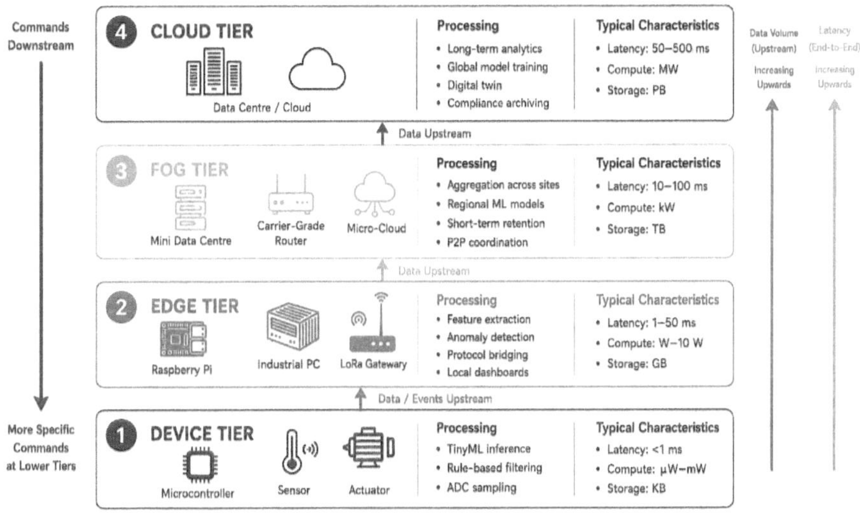

Figure 6.3: The Edge-Fog-Cloud Computing Continuum for IoT

6.4.2 Edge Computing Hardware for IoT

The hardware landscape for IoT edge computing spans a wide range from ultra-low-power microcontrollers running TinyML models to full-featured industrial edge servers capable of running containerised cloud workloads locally. At the microcontroller end, ARM Cortex-M series processors (STM32, Nordic nRF52, NXP LPC series) with dedicated DSP extensions and hardware floating-point units can execute compact neural network models with power consumption in the range of 0.5 to 5 milliwatts, enabling on-device inference on battery-powered sensors. The TensorFlow Lite Micro framework and the Edge Impulse platform have made TinyML model deployment to constrained microcontrollers accessible to engineers without deep ML expertise.

Single-board computers and embedded Linux gateways, including Raspberry Pi 4 (Broadcom Cortex-A72, 4GB RAM), NVIDIA Jetson Nano (128 CUDA cores, 4GB RAM), and Intel NUC with integrated Neural Compute Stick 2, provide gateway-tier edge computing with significantly greater processing power. The NVIDIA Jetson Nano is widely used in computer vision applications at the edge, including smart camera systems that perform pedestrian detection, licence plate recognition, and defect inspection locally, generating only metadata and alert events rather than raw video streams for cloud transmission. NVIDIA's Jetson Orin series, introduced in 2023, provides up to 275 TOPS (tera-operations per second) of AI inference capability in a power envelope of 15 to 60 watts, enabling factory-floor deployment of models that previously required cloud GPU servers.

Industrial edge servers from vendors including Siemens (SIMATIC IPC), Advantech, and Kontron are purpose-built for harsh industrial environments. They meet IP65 or IP67 ingress protection ratings, operate reliably across temperature ranges of -20 to +60 degrees Celsius, support MTBF ratings above 50,000 hours, and use conformal-coated PCBs resistant to dust, humidity, and vibrating environments. These characteristics are essential in factory floors, substations, and outdoor infrastructure deployments where consumer-grade computing hardware would fail rapidly.

6.4.3 Edge AI: Machine Learning at the Network Edge

Edge AI, the deployment of trained machine learning models on edge hardware for local inference, represents one of the most significant developments in IoT architecture of the past five years. The traditional ML workflow requires large volumes of training data to be centralised in a cloud data warehouse, model training to run on powerful cloud GPU servers, and the resulting model to be deployed back to edge devices for inference. This workflow is well-established for cloud-native applications but creates challenges for IoT: raw training data may be too voluminous to transmit to the cloud economically, data privacy regulations may prohibit raw sensor data from leaving the facility, and inference latency via cloud round-trip may be too high for real-time control applications.

Key Insight: *Edge AI Design Constraints. Deploying machine learning models on edge hardware introduces two constraints absent from cloud inference: model size (constrained by device RAM — typically 100 KB to 2 MB for microcontroller targets) and update management (over-the-air model updates require bandwidth budget, version control, and a rollback procedure in case the updated model degrades accuracy on production data). TinyML frameworks such as TensorFlow Lite Micro address size constraints through model quantisation and operator pruning. MLOps pipelines address update management through staged rollout and continuous performance monitoring. Both must be designed before first deployment, not added afterwards.*

TensorFlow Lite, ONNX Runtime, and PyTorch Mobile are the three dominant frameworks for deploying trained neural network models on constrained edge hardware. TensorFlow Lite provides quantisation-aware training that compresses model weights from 32-bit floats to 8-bit integers, reducing model size by 4x and inference latency by 2 to 4x with minimal accuracy loss, enabling neural networks to run on microcontrollers with as little as 256 kilobytes of RAM. ONNX (Open Neural Network Exchange) Runtime provides a hardware-agnostic inference engine that optimises model execution for specific hardware targets including ARM CPUs, Intel neural compute accelerators, and NVIDIA CUDA GPUs, making it the standard deployment framework for industrial edge AI applications where hardware heterogeneity is a practical reality.

CASE STUDY: NVIDIA Jetson and Edge AI in Smart Manufacturing: Cognex and Siemens

Global Manufacturing Deployments, 2020-2024

Cognex Corporation, the world's largest machine vision company, deploys NVIDIA Jetson-based edge AI systems in manufacturing quality control applications across automotive, electronics, and pharmaceutical production lines. A typical deployment processes high-resolution camera images from production lines at 30 to 120 frames per second, applying trained convolutional neural network models to detect surface defects, assembly errors, and dimensional deviations in real time at the point of production.

The edge AI approach provides inspection latency below 50 milliseconds, enabling reject decisions to be made before defective components leave the production station. Transmitting raw 5-megapixel images at 60 fps to a cloud server would require 1.8 gigabits per second of bandwidth per camera and introduce 100 to 200 milliseconds of additional processing latency. By running inference locally on a Jetson Orin module, Cognex reduces bandwidth requirements by 99.9 percent (transmitting only metadata: pass/fail verdict, defect classification, coordinates) while achieving latency 4 to 8 times lower than cloud inference.

Siemens has integrated similar edge AI capabilities into its Industrial Edge platform, which enables containerised ML inference applications to be deployed, updated, and monitored across thousands of factory-floor edge devices through a central management console. The platform supports OTA (over-the-air) model updates that can push an improved defect detection model to 500 factory cameras worldwide within a scheduled maintenance window, ensuring all production lines are running the latest model version simultaneously.

6.4.4 Fog Computing and the OpenFog/IEEE Standard

Fog computing, a term introduced by Cisco in 2012, describes a distributed computing paradigm that places intelligence, processing, and storage at network aggregation points between IoT devices and the cloud. Where edge computing is physically co-located with the data source (on the device or in the immediate local network), fog computing is positioned in the network infrastructure: at cellular base stations, enterprise network aggregation switches, regional ISP points of presence, and district-level data centres.

The OpenFog Consortium, founded in 2015 by ARM, Cisco, Dell, Intel, Microsoft, and Princeton University, and subsequently merged into the IEEE Standards Association, produced the IEEE 1934-2018 standard for fog computing and networking. The standard defines eight pillars of fog architecture: Security, Scalability, Openness, Autonomy, RAS (Reliability, Availability, Serviceability), Agility, Hierarchy, and Programmability (summarised as SCALE + RAH + P). The hierarchy pillar is particularly important for IoT: IEEE 1934 explicitly models fog as a multi-tier hierarchy in which fog nodes at different levels of the network topology collaborate to process data at the most appropriate tier.

In practice, the distinction between edge and fog computing is often collapsed by practitioners. Many commercial IoT platforms use the term edge to refer to all processing that occurs outside the primary cloud data centre, regardless of whether it occurs on a device gateway or on a regional aggregation node. AWS IoT Greengrass, Azure IoT Edge, and Google Distributed Cloud Edge all use the marketing term edge to describe fog-tier computing nodes deployed in customer facilities or at network edges. The IEEE distinction between edge (device-proximate) and fog (network infrastructure-hosted) is conceptually useful for architects but should not be treated as a rigid operational boundary in commercial deployments.

6.4.5 Decision Framework: Allocating Workloads Across the Continuum

Allocating IoT processing workloads to the appropriate tier of the edge-fog-cloud continuum is among the most consequential architectural decisions in IoT system design. The following principles provide a practical decision framework. Workloads that require response latency below 10 milliseconds must be placed at the device or edge tier: no cloud service can reliably meet this latency requirement.

Workloads involving sensitive personal data that must not leave a facility or national jurisdiction must be processed at the edge or fog tier, with only anonymised or aggregated results transmitted to the cloud. Workloads requiring access to large historical datasets for model training or retrospective analytics must be placed in the cloud, which provides the storage capacity and compute elasticity that edge hardware cannot match. Workloads that require correlation of data from multiple geographically dispersed edge sites, such as regional traffic optimisation, are natural candidates for the fog tier.

Table 6.3: Edge, Fog, and Cloud Computing: Characteristics and IoT Workload Allocation

Characteristic	Device / Edge Tier	Fog Tier	Cloud Tier
Processing latency	<1 ms to 10 ms	10-50 ms	50-500 ms
Computational power	Milliwatts to tens of watts	Kilowatts	Effectively unlimited
Storage capacity	Kilobytes to gigabytes	Gigabytes to terabytes	Petabytes to exabytes
Data volume handled	Filtered subset (1-5% of raw)	Regional aggregation	Full historical archive
Cost profile	High capex, low opex	Medium capex and opex	Low capex, variable opex
Primary IoT workloads	Real-time control, local ML inference	Regional aggregation, medium analytics	Model training, global analytics, long-term storage

6.5 Cloud IoT Platforms

A cloud IoT platform is a managed service that provides the full software stack for connecting, managing, and processing data from IoT device fleets. It abstracts the complexity of building individual components of the IoT data pipeline, including MQTT broker infrastructure, device registry, message routing, protocol translation, data storage integration, and security, into a unified service with a pay-per-use billing model. The major cloud vendors offer mature IoT platform products; open-source alternatives provide vendor-independent options for deployments where commercial platform costs or lock-in risks are primary concerns.

DEFINITION: Cloud IoT Platform

A managed cloud service providing the full software stack for IoT device connectivity, management, data ingestion, message routing, and analytics integration. Cloud IoT platforms abstract the complexity of operating MQTT brokers, device registries, certificate management, and data pipeline infrastructure at scale, typically billing on a per-message or per-device-per-month basis.

Source: AWS (2024); Microsoft (2024)

6.5.1 AWS IoT Core

AWS IoT Core is Amazon Web Services' flagship IoT connectivity and management service. It provides a fully managed MQTT broker capable of handling billions of device messages per day and millions of concurrent device connections. Devices connect to IoT Core using MQTT, HTTPS, or WebSockets, authenticating via X.509 certificates managed by AWS IoT Core's built-in certificate authority or an external PKI. The Device Registry stores metadata for each registered device, and Device Shadows (called Thing Shadows) provide a persistent virtual representation of each device's last known state and desired state, enabling cloud-side control even when devices are intermittently connected.

The IoT Core Rules Engine evaluates every incoming message against a configurable set of SQL-based rules and routes matching messages to downstream AWS services. A rule might route temperature readings above a threshold to an AWS Lambda function that sends an SMS alert, store all readings from a specific device type to an Amazon DynamoDB NoSQL database, and write all messages to an Amazon Kinesis data stream for real-time analytics, all simultaneously. This rules engine eliminates the need for custom message routing middleware code in most IoT applications, significantly reducing development time and operational complexity.

6.5.2 Azure IoT Hub and Azure IoT Edge

Microsoft Azure IoT Hub provides device-to-cloud and cloud-to-device bidirectional messaging with MQTT, Advanced Message Queuing Protocol (AMQP), and HTTPS protocol support. Device Twins, Azure's equivalent of AWS Device Shadows, store the desired and reported state of each device in a JSON document, enabling configuration management and state synchronisation for fleets of millions of devices. Azure IoT Hub's per-tier pricing (Basic, Standard) provides an economical entry point for small deployments and scales to hundreds of millions of messages per day at the Standard tier.

Azure IoT Edge, Microsoft's edge computing runtime, enables containerised workloads to be deployed from the Azure cloud to edge gateway devices running Linux or Windows, managing the device's connection to IoT Hub, local message routing, and module lifecycle. IoT Edge modules are Docker-compatible containers, enabling any cloud workload that runs in Azure to be deployed and managed at the edge using the same development tools and CI/CD pipelines. Azure Digital Twins, launched in 2020, extends IoT Hub with a graph-based environment modelling service that enables digital twin representations of physical environments including buildings, factories, and cities, with live data from IoT devices updating the twin state in real time.

6.5.3 Google Cloud IoT: Evolution and Migration

Google Cloud IoT Core, Google's managed IoT connectivity service, was deprecated in August 2022, with official end-of-life in August 2023. Google's decision reflected the competitive dynamics of the cloud IoT platform market, where AWS IoT Core and Azure IoT Hub had established dominant market positions. Organisations that had built IoT deployments on Google Cloud IoT Core were directed to migrate to a combination of Google Cloud Pub/Sub for device messaging, BigQuery for time-series analytics, and Cloud Functions for event-driven processing. Several third-party migration paths were also certified, including migration to HiveMQ Cloud and Solace PubSub+ Event Broker for MQTT connectivity.

The deprecation of Google Cloud IoT Core is a significant case study in the vendor lock-in risk of proprietary cloud IoT platforms. Organisations that had standardised on Google's device shadow API and provisioning service were required to invest in migration engineering within a 12-month window. The episode reinforces the architectural principle of using open protocols (MQTT with standard certificate-based authentication) and avoiding proprietary platform-specific device firmware APIs where possible, to preserve the option of migrating to an alternative platform without device-side firmware changes.

6.5.4 Open-Source Platforms: ThingsBoard and Eclipse IoT

ThingsBoard is an open-source IoT platform that provides device management, data collection via MQTT/CoAP/HTTP, a rule engine for event processing, and a dashboard builder for visualisation, deployable on-premises or as a cloud-managed service. ThingsBoard Community Edition is freely available under the Apache 2.0 licence; the Professional and Cloud editions provide additional features including white-labelling, advanced analytics, and commercial support. ThingsBoard is widely used in resource-constrained academic and startup deployments and in commercial projects where data sovereignty requirements prohibit use of public cloud platforms.

The Eclipse IoT open-source ecosystem, maintained by the Eclipse Foundation, provides a comprehensive suite of open-source IoT components including Eclipse Mosquitto (MQTT broker), Eclipse Paho (MQTT client libraries), Eclipse Hono (IoT connectivity and protocol abstraction), Eclipse Ditto (digital twin service), and Eclipse Kura (IoT gateway framework). Together, these components provide a vendor-independent alternative to proprietary cloud IoT platforms, at the cost of higher integration and operational engineering effort. Eclipse IoT components are used as the foundation of commercial IoT platforms by Red Hat (AMQ), Bosch (IoT Suite), and other enterprise vendors.

CASE STUDY: *AWS IoT at Scale: Volkswagen Industrial Cloud and CARIAD*

Wolfsburg, Germany, and Global, 2019-Present

In 2019, Volkswagen Group announced a partnership with Amazon Web Services to build the Volkswagen Industrial Cloud, a unified IoT data platform connecting over 120 Volkswagen manufacturing plants worldwide with their machine data, production KPIs, and logistics information. The platform, built on AWS IoT Core, AWS Kinesis, and AWS S3, processes data from over 1,500 production lines and thousands of manufacturing robots, conveyor systems, and quality inspection stations.

The Volkswagen Industrial Cloud uses AWS IoT Greengrass for edge processing at individual plant level, enabling local real-time anomaly detection and SCADA data collection without raw data leaving the plant network. Aggregated, anonymised production metrics are transmitted to the central AWS cloud infrastructure for cross-plant benchmarking, predictive maintenance model training, and supply chain coordination.

The business case for the platform is based on production efficiency improvements achievable when best practices identified at one plant can be rapidly replicated across the global fleet. Volkswagen reported that identifying and replicating a process improvement that eliminates a 2-minute changeover delay from one production line to all 120 plants could generate annual savings exceeding EUR 100 million. The platform enables these cross-plant comparisons with granularity and speed that manual benchmarking processes cannot match.

Table 6.4: Cloud IoT Platform Comparison: Key Capabilities and Selection Criteria

Capability	AWS IoT Core	Azure IoT Hub	ThingsBoard (OSS)
Device connectivity	MQTT, HTTPS, WebSocket	MQTT, AMQP, HTTPS	MQTT, CoAP, HTTP
Max concurrent devices	Billions (managed)	Millions per hub	Unlimited (self-hosted)
Device shadow / twin	Thing Shadow (JSON)	Device Twin (JSON)	Device attributes (JSON)
Rule / event engine	IoT Core Rules Engine (SQL)	IoT Hub message routing	Rule engine (visual + DSL)
Edge computing	AWS IoT Greengrass	Azure IoT Edge (Docker)	ThingsBoard Edge
Digital twin	AWS IoT TwinMaker	Azure Digital Twins	ThingsBoard (basic)

Pricing model	Per message + per device	Per tier, per message	Free (OSS) / per device (SaaS)
Vendor lock-in risk	High (proprietary APIs)	High (proprietary APIs)	Low (open source)

6.6 IoT Data Storage Models and Communication APIs

IoT data exhibits extreme diversity across multiple dimensions that no single storage technology can efficiently serve. High-frequency numeric sensor telemetry demands write throughput that relational databases cannot sustain. Large video and image files require the cost-effective, infinitely scalable object storage that traditional databases cannot economically provide. Device configuration documents with evolving schemas require the flexibility of document stores. Regulatory audit trails and user consent records require the transactional guarantees of relational databases.

A mature IoT data architecture therefore typically employs multiple specialised storage systems, each selected for the specific data type and access pattern it serves, federated through a data governance layer that enforces consistent access control and lineage tracking.

6.6.1 Time-Series Databases

DEFINITION: Time-Series Database (TSDB)

A database management system specialised for storing and querying timestamped data, providing built-in functions for time-based aggregation, downsampling, data retention management, and high-throughput append-only writes. TSDBs store each data point as a (timestamp, value, tags) tuple, with tags providing the dimensions for filtering and grouping. They are the standard storage technology for IoT sensor telemetry.

Source: InfluxData (2024)

InfluxDB, developed by InfluxData and first released in 2013, is the most widely deployed open-source time-series database and the de facto standard for IoT sensor telemetry storage. InfluxDB's data model organises measurements into time series identified by a measurement name and a set of tag key-value pairs. The 3.x architecture (InfluxDB Cloud Serverless), built on Apache Parquet columnar storage and the Apache Arrow in-memory format, provides query performance and storage efficiency improvements of 2 to 3 orders of magnitude over earlier InfluxDB versions for analytical workloads.

InfluxDB's Flux query language provides time-series-native operations including windowed aggregation (mean temperature per

5-minute window), moving averages, rate-of-change calculations, and join operations between multiple sensor streams, all expressed in a functional data pipeline syntax.

TimescaleDB extends PostgreSQL with time-series optimisation through automatic partitioning of time-series data into chunks (hypertables) that are compressed and archived according to configurable retention policies. TimescaleDB is preferred when IoT applications need both time-series performance for sensor data and relational capability for joins with device metadata, user records, and configuration data stored in the same PostgreSQL instance. OpenTSDB (Open Time Series Database), built on Apache HBase, scales to trillions of data points for large-scale IoT deployments and has been deployed at Tumblr, Arista Networks, and StumbleUpon for metrics and monitoring at hyperscale.

6.6.2 Object Storage for Unstructured IoT Data

IoT systems that collect image, video, or audio data require object storage rather than database-style row storage. Object storage systems such as Amazon S3, Azure Blob Storage, and Google Cloud Storage provide infinitely scalable, content-addressed storage where each object is identified by a unique key within a named bucket. At costs typically below USD 0.025 per gigabyte per month, object storage makes it economically feasible to retain the full raw image or video archive from a production quality inspection system or a smart city camera network for months or years, enabling retrospective analysis, model retraining, and compliance auditing.

IoT pipelines typically write raw sensor images or video frames directly to object storage from the edge gateway, with structured metadata (device ID, timestamp, location, processing results) written to a time-series or relational database. Cloud analytics and machine learning services access both the objects and their metadata for model training. Amazon Rekognition, Google Cloud Vision AI, and Azure Computer Vision provide managed ML inference services that can process images stored in their respective cloud object stores without the IoT application managing model infrastructure.

6.6.3 Data Lakes and Data Lakehouses

A data lake is a centralised repository that stores large volumes of raw IoT data in its native format at low cost, intended for future processing and analytics. The data lake pattern acknowledges that the analytical value of IoT data may not be known at the time of collection: a vibration signature that appears unremarkable today may become highly valuable three years later when a new machine learning model identifies it as a precursor to a failure mode not previously understood. Retaining raw data in object storage (typically at USD 0.01 to 0.025 per GB per month) provides the option to reprocess historical data with future algorithms without incurring the cost of retransmitting it from devices.

The data lakehouse pattern, pioneered by Databricks with Delta Lake and adopted by Apache Iceberg and Apache Hudi, adds a transactional metadata layer over object-stored raw data, enabling SQL queries, ACID transactions, and schema evolution without migrating data out of the data lake into a traditional data warehouse. For IoT, the lakehouse pattern enables analysts to run ad hoc SQL queries over terabytes of historical sensor data stored in Parquet format on S3 or Azure Data Lake Storage, while the same data can also be consumed by Spark streaming jobs for real-time processing. This convergence of streaming and batch access on a single storage layer is the practical realisation of the Kappa architecture for large-scale IoT deployments.

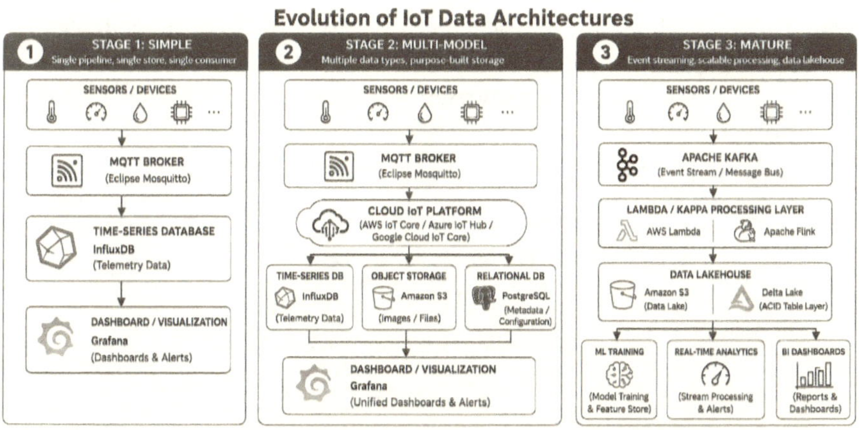

Figure 6.4: IoT Data Architecture Evolution: From Simple TSDB to Data Lakehouse

6.6.4 Communication APIs for IoT Data Access

The communication APIs through which IoT applications access stored data represent the interface between the data management infrastructure and the applications that consume it. RESTful APIs over HTTP/HTTPS are the dominant mechanism for IoT application integration. A REST API exposes IoT data resources, including device readings, event histories, device configurations, and analytics outputs, as URL-addressed endpoints that applications can query using standard HTTP methods. AWS IoT SiteWise, Azure Digital

Twins, and ThingsBoard all expose their data through REST APIs, enabling third-party dashboards, mobile applications, and business systems to consume IoT data without knowledge of the underlying storage implementation.

WebSocket connections provide persistent, low-latency push of IoT data to browser-based dashboards and real-time monitoring applications. Where a REST polling approach requires the dashboard to send an HTTP request every few seconds to check for new readings, a WebSocket connection allows the server to push each new reading to the dashboard immediately upon arrival, reducing both latency and server load. Grafana, the most widely used open-source IoT and metrics dashboard platform, supports WebSocket data sources for real-time panel updates.

gRPC (Google Remote Procedure Call), built on Protocol Buffers and HTTP/2, provides high-performance, schema-defined API communication suited to high-throughput IoT data access. Its bidirectional streaming capability enables a single gRPC channel to carry thousands of readings per second between an edge server and a cloud ingestion service, with significantly lower per-message overhead than REST. gRPC is increasingly used in the server-to-server tier of IoT pipelines, particularly between edge gateways and cloud ingestion endpoints in deployments where bandwidth efficiency is paramount.

Table 6.5: IoT Data Storage Model Selection Guide

Data Type	Recommended Storage	Example Technology	Key Access Pattern
Numeric sensor telemetry (high-frequency)	Time-series database	InfluxDB, TimescaleDB, OpenTSDB	Windowed aggregation, anomaly detection
Images and video frames	Object storage	Amazon S3, Azure Blob, MinIO	Batch retrieval for ML training
Device configuration and metadata	Relational database	PostgreSQL, MySQL, AWS Aurora	Transactional reads/writes, joins
Semi-structured event logs	NoSQL document store	MongoDB, Couchbase, DynamoDB	Schema-flexible document queries
Large raw data archive	Data lake (object store)	AWS S3 + Delta Lake, ADLS + Iceberg	Batch analytics, model retraining
Real-time push to dashboards	Time-series DB + WebSocket	InfluxDB + Grafana Live	Sub-second refresh, live monitoring

6.7 IoT Data Analytics: From Raw Signals to Operational Intelligence

The word "analytics" appears frequently in IoT marketing material but is rarely unpacked with precision. In practice, analytics spans a spectrum from counting yesterday's sensor readings to autonomously adjusting a production line without human involvement. Understanding where a given analytical capability sits on that spectrum matters enormously for architecture design, compute budgeting, and organisational readiness. This section maps the IoT analytics landscape systematically, from the descriptive tier through diagnostic and predictive work to prescriptive and autonomous action, and connects each tier to the real computational infrastructure that supports it.

6.7.1 The Four-Tier Analytics Hierarchy

The analytics hierarchy is best understood not as a ladder of sophistication but as a stack of capabilities, each built on the one below it. An organisation cannot reliably perform predictive analytics on data it has not yet learned to describe accurately. Equally, prescriptive analytics that recommends optimal actions is only as trustworthy as the predictive models it draws upon. Most mature IoT deployments work across all four tiers simultaneously, applying descriptive analytics broadly, diagnostic analytics to significant events, predictive analytics to high-value assets, and prescriptive analytics only where the data and model quality justify autonomous action.

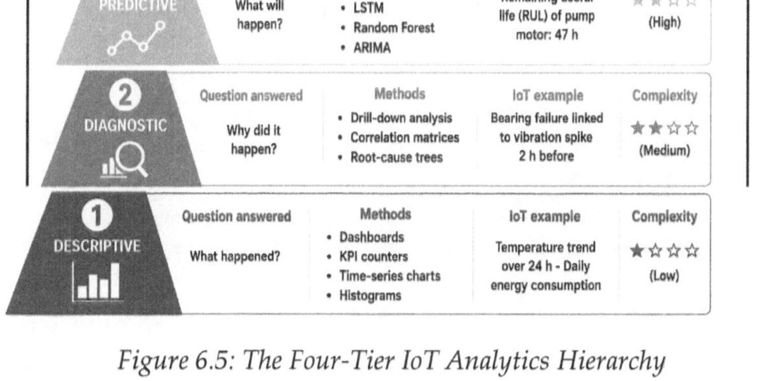

Figure 6.5: The Four-Tier IoT Analytics Hierarchy

DEFINITION: Descriptive Analytics

The application of statistical summaries, aggregations, and visualisations to historical IoT data to characterise what has occurred. Descriptive analytics answers the question "What happened?" and forms the universal foundation of every IoT deployment. Examples include daily energy consumption totals, weekly equipment uptime percentages, and monthly throughput trends.

Descriptive analytics is the starting point for every IoT data programme, and it should not be underestimated. Organisations that invest in clean, reliable descriptive reporting (with consistent metric definitions, timely data pipelines, and accessible dashboards) create the shared factual foundation that makes every higher-order analytical capability possible. Without it, diagnostic and predictive work is built on sand.

The primary tools for descriptive IoT analytics are time-series databases and dashboard platforms. Grafana, connected to InfluxDB or TimescaleDB, is the most widely deployed open-source combination for operational IoT dashboards. Kibana, part of the Elastic Stack, is preferred in environments already using Elasticsearch for log aggregation. Commercial alternatives include Microsoft Power BI (heavily integrated with Azure IoT Hub), Tableau (common in enterprise environments where IoT data is one input among many), and ThingsBoard's built-in dashboard builder, which is purpose-designed for device-level telemetry visualisation.

DEFINITION: Diagnostic Analytics

Analytical methods that investigate the causal or contributing factors behind an observed event or trend in IoT data. Diagnostic analytics answers the question "Why did it happen?" Common techniques include correlation analysis, drill-down filtering, root cause analysis trees, and statistical comparison of operating conditions before and after an event.

Diagnostic analytics in IoT is particularly powerful when event context is preserved alongside raw telemetry. A temperature spike in a server rack is a descriptive fact. A temperature spike that correlates with a specific workload pattern, occurring on hardware of a particular age, in a specific rack position, on a hot day: that is diagnostic insight. This context-preservation requires that IoT platforms capture not just the sensor reading but the full operational state at the time of the event, a requirement that shapes both data schema design and platform selection.

Root cause analysis in industrial IoT frequently employs fishbone (Ishikawa) diagrams translated into data queries: for each potential cause category (machine, method, material, measurement, environment, people), a systematic query tests whether data from that category correlates with the event of interest. Modern IoT analytics platforms implement this as a guided drill-down workflow, with Seeq (focused on process data) and AVEVA PI System (formerly OSIsoft PI) representing purpose-built tools for this type of industrial diagnostic work.

DEFINITION: Predictive Analytics

The use of statistical models and machine learning algorithms trained on historical IoT data to generate probabilistic forecasts of future states, events, or conditions. Predictive analytics answers the question "What will happen?" and enables proactive rather than reactive operational responses. Common IoT applications include remaining useful life estimation, demand forecasting, and anomaly detection.

Predictive maintenance is the most commercially significant application of predictive analytics in IoT. A predictive maintenance model for rotating machinery might be trained on vibration, temperature, current draw, and acoustic emission data from hundreds of similar machines over thousands of operating hours, learning the patterns that precede bearing failure weeks before it becomes detectable by human inspection. The model's value is entirely contingent on the quality of historical data, the accuracy of failure event labelling, and the consistency of sensor calibration, all operational prerequisites that take years to establish in brownfield deployments.

Time-series machine learning has matured significantly since 2020. Facebook Prophet (now Meta Prophet) popularised decomposable forecasting models for business time series. LSTM (Long Short-Term Memory) neural networks have shown strong results in multi-step ahead forecasting for complex time-series patterns. More recently, Temporal Fusion Transformers and PatchTST (a transformer architecture designed specifically for time-series patch embeddings) have achieved state-of-the-art results on benchmark forecasting datasets. Scikit-learn, combined with time-series libraries such as sktime, remains the most accessible starting point for organisations building their first predictive IoT models.

DEFINITION: Prescriptive Analytics

The highest tier of the analytics hierarchy, combining predictive models with optimisation logic to recommend or automatically execute optimal actions in response to predicted future states. Prescriptive analytics answers the question "What should we do?" and closes the loop between IoT data and physical-world actuation. It requires high model confidence, reliable actuation infrastructure, and carefully designed human-in-the-loop or fully autonomous governance frameworks.

Prescriptive analytics is where IoT analytics becomes a control system. In smart building energy management, a prescriptive system does not just predict that the building will be over-temperature at 14:00; it pre-emptively adjusts HVAC setpoints at 12:30 to prevent the condition, accounting for weather forecasts, occupancy predictions, and time-of-use electricity pricing. In autonomous manufacturing, a prescriptive quality control system detects a drift in dimensional measurements during machining and automatically adjusts cutting tool offsets without waiting for an engineer to review the trend. The governance requirements for prescriptive analytics are correspondingly more stringent: every autonomous action must have a defined envelope of authority and a documented fallback behaviour.

6.7.2 Machine Learning Pipelines for IoT

Building machine learning models for IoT data differs in important practical ways from typical enterprise data science applications. IoT data is high-frequency, high-volume, and often multivariate, with complex temporal dependencies and frequent missing or corrupted readings caused by sensor dropouts, network interruptions, and calibration drift. The ML pipeline must be designed with these characteristics in mind from the outset.

Feature engineering for time-series IoT data typically involves transforming raw sensor readings into a richer representation that exposes the temporal structure the model needs to learn. Common transformations include rolling statistics (mean, standard deviation, minimum, maximum over windows of 1 minute, 5 minutes, 1 hour), Fourier features that encode periodicity, lag features that make historical values explicit inputs, and domain-specific engineered features such as harmonic distortion indices for electrical equipment monitoring or spectral kurtosis for bearing fault detection in rotating machinery.

Data labelling is one of the most time-consuming and costly steps in supervised IoT machine learning. For predictive maintenance applications, labelling requires correlating historical sensor data with maintenance records, and those records in operational technology environments are frequently incomplete, inconsistently timestamped, and stored in paper-based systems. Organisations that invest in structured maintenance data capture from the outset of their IoT deployment dramatically accelerate the timeline to viable predictive models.

TECHNOLOGY SPOTLIGHT: *MLOps for IoT: Keeping Models Accurate Over Time*

A machine learning model that was accurate when first deployed will gradually become less accurate as the physical world it monitors changes. Equipment ages, operating profiles shift, new machine variants are introduced, and sensor calibrations drift. This phenomenon, known as model drift or concept drift, is one of the most commonly underestimated challenges in production IoT ML deployments.

MLOps (Machine Learning Operations) is the discipline of managing this lifecycle: monitoring model performance in production, detecting when drift is occurring, triggering retraining on fresh data, validating the retrained model against a holdout set, and deploying the updated model with minimum operational disruption. For IoT systems, these tasks require both a software pipeline (typically built with MLflow, Kubeflow, or AWS SageMaker Pipelines) and an operational process for collecting correctly labelled new examples from the field.

A practical MLOps approach for IoT predictive maintenance includes three monitoring streams: data drift monitoring (checking whether the statistical distribution of incoming sensor data has changed), model performance monitoring (tracking precision and recall on newly labelled events), and infrastructure monitoring (verifying that the inference service is operating within latency and throughput bounds). When any monitor crosses a threshold, the pipeline triggers retraining automatically, with human review of the retrained model before production deployment.

AWS SageMaker Model Monitor, Azure ML Dataset Monitor, and the open-source Evidently AI library are commonly used tools for implementing data and model drift detection in production IoT deployments. The Volkswagen Industrial Cloud uses SageMaker Pipelines for automated retraining of quality prediction models across its global manufacturing network, retraining weekly on the previous month's production data.

Federated learning is an increasingly relevant ML paradigm for IoT deployments where training data cannot or should not be centralised. In federated learning, each edge device or local server trains a local model on its own data and contributes only gradient updates, not raw data, to a central aggregation server. The aggregated updates improve the global model without any individual device's raw data leaving its local environment. Google pioneered federated learning for keyboard prediction on Android devices, and the technique is now being applied to healthcare IoT (where patient data must not leave the hospital), industrial IoT (where process data is commercially sensitive), and automotive IoT. PySyft and TensorFlow Federated provide Python-based implementations for practitioners.

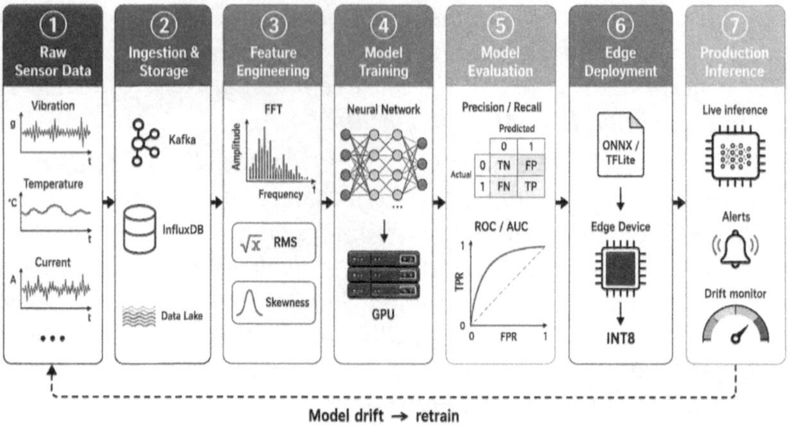

Figure 6.6: IoT Machine Learning Pipeline: From Raw Sensor Data to Production Inference

6.7.3 Real-Time Analytics at the Edge

Not all IoT analytics can wait for data to reach the cloud. Applications with millisecond response requirements (autonomous machinery, real-time quality inspection, safety interlocks) must perform analytical computations close to the data source. Even applications with looser latency requirements may benefit from edge analytics when connectivity is intermittent, when data volumes make cloud transmission uneconomic, or when data sovereignty regulations prohibit off-site processing of certain data categories.

Edge inference is the deployment of trained machine learning models on edge hardware for real-time prediction without cloud connectivity. The model is trained in the cloud on historical data from many devices, then compressed and optimised for edge deployment using model quantisation (converting 32-bit floating point weights to 8-bit integers with typically less than 1% accuracy loss) and pruning (removing weights below a significance threshold). TensorFlow Lite, ONNX Runtime, and Intel's OpenVINO are the principal frameworks for this workflow, each targeting different hardware profiles from microcontrollers to industrial edge servers.

Anomaly detection is the most widely deployed edge analytics use case. Statistical process control methods (Shewhart control charts, CUSUM (Cumulative Sum) charts, EWMA (Exponentially Weighted Moving Average)) have been used in manufacturing quality control for decades and translate naturally to real-time edge computation. More sophisticated edge anomaly detection uses autoencoder neural networks trained to reconstruct normal operating patterns; an anomaly is flagged when reconstruction error exceeds a threshold, indicating that the input pattern falls outside the distribution of normal behaviour the model learned during training.

CASE STUDY: Real-Time Quality Inspection at Bosch Rexroth

Homburg, Germany | 2022–Present

Bosch Rexroth manufactures hydraulic components used in industrial machinery, construction equipment, and aerospace applications. Each component undergoes end-of-line quality testing involving dozens of measurements, and historically a trained engineer reviewed marginal test results to decide whether to pass, rework, or scrap each component. As production volumes increased, this manual review became a bottleneck.

Starting in 2022, Bosch Rexroth deployed edge inference servers at each production line test station, running a gradient boosted tree model (XGBoost) trained on three years of test data and corresponding quality outcomes. The model generates a pass, rework, or scrap recommendation in under 200 milliseconds of test completion, faster than the test fixture can transfer the component to the next station. The model runs entirely on-premises with no cloud connectivity required during production, ensuring continuity even during network outages.

The deployed model achieved 97.3% agreement with expert engineer decisions on the validation dataset. More importantly, by routing borderline components to a targeted rework process rather than general scrap, the system reduced material waste by 23% in the first year of operation. A continuous retraining pipeline running nightly on accumulated production data ensures the model adapts as component variants and production conditions evolve over time.

This case illustrates the edge analytics pattern at its most commercially compelling: a model that runs faster than the physical process it monitors, operates independently of cloud connectivity, and delivers measurable financial return through waste reduction rather than merely operational visibility.

6.7.4 Streaming Analytics Platforms

For IoT deployments where analytics must operate on data in motion, processing each event or micro-batch as it arrives rather than querying stored historical data, streaming analytics platforms provide the necessary infrastructure. Section 6.3 introduced the Lambda and Kappa architectural patterns; this section examines the platform implementations in production use today.

Apache Flink has emerged as the preferred open-source streaming engine for complex IoT analytics workloads, displacing Apache

Storm for most new deployments. Flink's key differentiators for IoT use are: exactly-once state consistency guarantees (critical for financial-grade telemetry like energy metering); native event-time processing that correctly handles out-of-order events common in cellular-connected IoT; stateful windowed aggregations for computing rolling averages over sensor streams without materialising intermediate data to storage; and a unified batch and streaming execution model enabling the same business logic to run on both historical and real-time data. Alibaba deploys Flink at scale for real-time anomaly detection across its Alibaba Cloud IoT platform serving tens of millions of connected devices.

Amazon Managed Service for Apache Flink (formerly Amazon Kinesis Data Analytics) and Google Dataflow (based on Apache Beam) are the principal managed cloud services for streaming IoT analytics. Both abstract cluster provisioning and scaling, allowing data engineering teams to focus on business logic rather than infrastructure operations. For simpler streaming analytics requirements (threshold alerting, basic aggregations, event routing) many IoT platforms provide built-in rule engines that operate on the stream without requiring a separate streaming analytics cluster. AWS IoT Core Rules Engine, Azure IoT Hub message routing, and ThingsBoard's rule chain editor handle a large proportion of common IoT analytics requirements without the operational complexity of Apache Flink.

6.8 Data Governance and Privacy in IoT Systems

The technical capabilities described in the preceding sections (telemetry pipelines, cloud platforms, edge inference, streaming analytics) are necessary but not sufficient for a defensible IoT deployment. Without deliberate governance, those capabilities generate legal liability, erode user trust, and create systemic risks that may be far costlier than the operational value they create. This section addresses the governance and privacy framework that every IoT system must have, explaining why the law requires it, how privacy-by-design translates into engineering practice, and what data lineage and quality management mean in operational terms.

6.8.1 The Regulatory Landscape

IoT systems are subject to a complex and evolving patchwork of data protection regulations across jurisdictions. The EU General Data Protection Regulation (GDPR), which entered force in May 2018, is the most globally consequential because many IoT deployments either process data of EU residents or are operated by organisations subject to EU law. GDPR imposes six data processing principles directly relevant to IoT system design.

GDPR Principle	Article Reference	IoT Engineering Implication
Lawfulness, Fairness, Transparency	Art. 5(1)(a)	Every data processing activity must have a lawful basis (consent, legitimate interest, contractual necessity). Consent mechanisms must be explicit and granular, not bundled with device activation. Processing purposes must be communicated to data subjects in accessible language.
Purpose Limitation	Art. 5(1)(b)	Data collected for one purpose (e.g., equipment monitoring) may not be repurposed for a different use (e.g., employee performance monitoring) without separate lawful basis. Data schemas and pipeline configurations must document collection purposes explicitly.
Data Minimisation	Art. 5(1)(c)	Only the minimum data necessary for the stated purpose should be collected. In IoT terms: sample at the minimum required frequency, collect only the sensor channels needed, and discard raw readings once derived metrics are computed if the raw data is not independently needed.
Accuracy	Art. 5(1)(d)	Personal data must be accurate and kept up to date. Sensor calibration records, drift correction procedures, and data quality monitoring are not just good engineering practice; they are legal requirements for data about individuals.
Storage Limitation	Art. 5(1)(e)	Data must not be retained longer than necessary. IoT platforms must implement automated retention policies with configurable expiry for each data category, including deletion from cold storage and backup systems.
Integrity and Confidentiality	Art. 5(1)(f)	Appropriate security measures must be implemented. For IoT: TLS for all data in transit, AES-256 for data at rest, key rotation policies, access logging, and anomaly detection on data access patterns.

Table 6.6: GDPR Data Processing Principles and Their IoT Engineering Implications

The GDPR's special categories of personal data (Article 9) are directly relevant to healthcare IoT, wearables, and any system that can infer sensitive attributes from sensor data. Health data, biometric data, and data revealing racial or ethnic origin require explicit consent and are subject to additional restrictions on processing and transfer. An activity tracker that infers health conditions from movement patterns is processing health data under GDPR, regardless of whether it is marketed as a fitness device.

The California Consumer Privacy Act (CCPA, 2018) and its successor the California Privacy Rights Act (CPRA, 2020) establish a parallel framework for US-based consumers. While CCPA/CPRA is less stringent than GDPR in several respects, it covers a significant proportion of global IoT device users. The CPRA introduced the concept of "sensitive personal information" and extended rights to data correction and limitation of use, bringing it closer in scope to the GDPR framework.

The EU Cyber Resilience Act (CRA), adopted in 2024, adds a product security dimension to IoT governance. The CRA requires manufacturers of connected products to implement security by design, provide security updates for the expected product lifetime, and report actively exploited vulnerabilities to ENISA within 24 hours. For IoT device manufacturers selling into the EU market, the CRA creates both engineering requirements (secure boot, cryptographic identity, OTA update capability) and operational requirements (vulnerability disclosure programme, incident reporting procedures). The CRA will be discussed further in Chapter 8.

The EU Data Act (2023) addresses a different governance dimension: the right to access data generated by connected products. Under the Data Act, users of IoT products have the right to access the data their devices generate, to share that data with third parties of their choosing, and to have that data ported to alternative service providers. For IoT platform providers, the Data Act creates an obligation to expose standardised data access APIs and to design data portability into platform architectures from the outset, not as an afterthought.

6.8.2 Privacy by Design in IoT Architecture

DEFINITION: Privacy by Design (PbD)

An approach to system engineering, developed by Ann Cavoukian, former Information and Privacy Commissioner of Ontario, in which privacy protection is built into system architecture as a default property rather than added as a compliance overlay after design is complete. The GDPR codifies PbD as a legal requirement under Article 25 ("Data protection by design and by default"). The seven foundational principles of PbD include proactive protection, privacy as default setting, privacy embedded into design, full functionality (positive-sum not zero-sum), end-to-end security, visibility and transparency, and respect for user privacy.

Translating Privacy by Design principles into concrete IoT engineering practices requires architectural decisions at every layer of the system stack. Data anonymisation and pseudonymisation at the edge reduce the privacy risk of telemetry pipelines by ensuring that personal identifiers are stripped or replaced before data leaves the device environment. For a smart meter, this means aggregating consumption data into 30-minute blocks rather than transmitting second-by-second readings that can reveal detailed occupancy patterns, and hashing household identifiers before transmission to the cloud analytics platform.

Differential privacy adds calibrated statistical noise to aggregated query results, providing mathematical privacy guarantees even when data is used for analytics. Apple uses differential privacy in its iOS telemetry collection to gather population-level usage statistics from hundreds of millions of devices without learning anything about individual device usage patterns. Google applied differential privacy to the aggregated mobility data published in its COVID-19 Community Mobility Reports, which were generated partly from smartphone location signals. For IoT deployments where aggregate trends matter but individual-level data should not be identifiable, differential privacy provides a rigorous technical guarantee rather than a policy promise.

Consent management for IoT presents challenges not faced by web or mobile applications. A connected smoke detector cannot display a consent form. A factory sensor cannot ask the maintenance engineer for permission to send data to the cloud. Effective IoT consent management requires clear disclosure at the point of product purchase or deployment; granular consent mechanisms that allow users to opt in or out of specific data processing purposes rather than all-or-nothing choices; persistent consent records linked to device identifiers; and practical revocation mechanisms that actually stop processing rather than merely record the preference.

TECHNOLOGY SPOTLIGHT: Homomorphic Encryption: Analytics on Encrypted IoT Data

One of the most significant emerging privacy-preserving technologies for IoT is homomorphic encryption (HE), which allows computations to be performed directly on encrypted data without ever decrypting it. The result of the computation, when decrypted, is identical to what would have been obtained by computing on the plaintext data. This remarkable property means a cloud analytics platform can compute statistics on a user's health sensor data without ever having access to the raw readings.

Fully Homomorphic Encryption (FHE), theoretically described by Craig Gentry in 2009, was long considered too computationally expensive for practical use. Recent hardware acceleration and algorithmic improvements have begun to change this picture. Microsoft SEAL, IBM HElib, and the TFHE library provide open-source FHE implementations. In 2023, DARPA's DPRIVE programme produced ASIC prototypes that accelerate FHE computation by three to four orders of magnitude over software-only implementations, bringing FHE inference latency into the range of seconds rather than hours for typical ML models.

For healthcare IoT, where patient data sovereignty is paramount but aggregate population analytics have significant medical value, HE offers a technically rigorous path to enabling analytics without privacy compromise. Medical IoT startup Enveil has demonstrated encrypted federated analytics across hospital networks, enabling multi-site clinical trials to extract aggregate insights from IoT patient monitoring data without any hospital sharing raw patient readings with another institution or with the central analysis platform.

HE is not yet practical for high-throughput, latency-sensitive IoT analytics pipelines, but its trajectory suggests it will become a standard privacy-preserving tool for batch analytics on sensitive IoT data within the next five to seven years.

6.8.3 Data Quality Management

Poor data quality is the most common cause of failed IoT analytics projects. A predictive maintenance model trained on data that contains sensor dropout artefacts, uncorrected calibration drift, and misaligned timestamps will produce unreliable predictions regardless of how sophisticated its machine learning algorithm is. The principle is reliable in data science: model quality is bounded by data quality, and no algorithmic sophistication can compensate for systematically bad inputs.

IoT data quality problems fall into several recurring categories. Missing data arises from sensor failures, network outages, and buffer overflows. Duplicate data arises from retry logic in unreliable networks: a device retransmits a reading after a timeout, and both the original and the retransmit are stored. Out-of-range readings arise from sensor saturation, wiring faults, and calibration errors. Timestamp misalignment arises from unsynchronised device clocks and inconsistent time-zone handling at ingestion. Schema violations arise when firmware updates change measurement units, variable names, or data types without coordinated pipeline updates.

A data quality framework for IoT specifies the acceptable quality bounds for each data stream, monitors incoming data against those bounds in real time, and triggers alerts when quality degrades. The Deequ library (open-sourced by Amazon) and Great Expectations (widely used in data engineering) implement data unit testing, automated assertions about data properties such as completeness, uniqueness, value range, and referential integrity that run on each batch or micro-batch of incoming data. Failures generate quality reports that feed into operational monitoring (alerting the device team that sensor X is producing out-of-range readings) and analytical governance (flagging the time window during which bad data was ingested so analytics results from that window are tagged as unreliable).

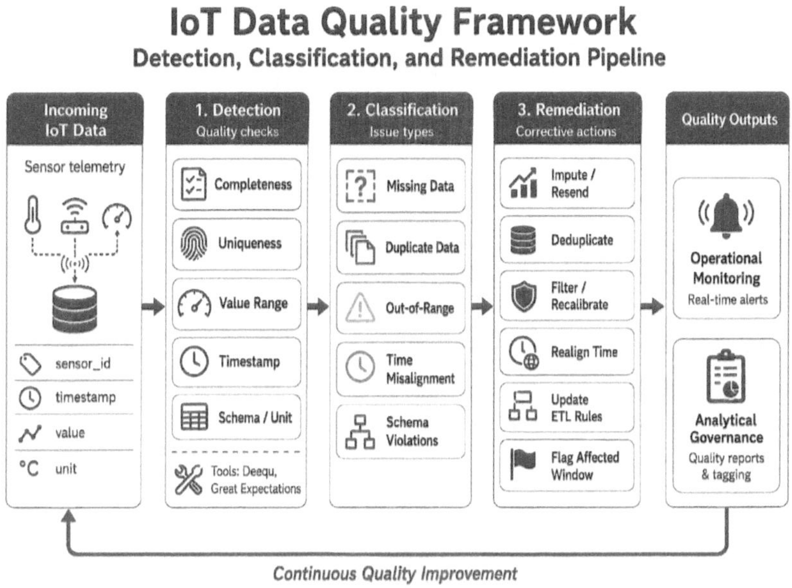

Figure 6.7: IoT Data Quality Framework: Detection, Classification, and Remediation Pipeline

6.8.4 Data Lineage and Audit Trails

DEFINITION: Data Lineage

The documented record of the origin, movement, transformation, and consumption of data through a system. In IoT analytics, data lineage enables engineers to answer questions such as: which physical sensor produced this data point, what transformations were applied between raw measurement and derived metric, and which analytical outputs would be affected if a sensor was found to be miscalibrated. Data lineage is both a governance requirement under GDPR's accountability principle and an operational diagnostic tool that dramatically reduces the time needed to assess the impact of discovered data quality failures.

Implementing data lineage in IoT pipelines requires instrumentation at every stage of data processing. Each transformation (unit conversion at ingestion, rolling average computation in the stream processor, feature extraction in the ML pipeline, aggregation in the analytics query) must be logged with a reference to the input data version and the transformation logic applied. Apache Atlas, a metadata governance framework for Hadoop-ecosystem data platforms, provides a graph-based lineage model. OpenLineage is a newer open standard supported by Airflow, Spark, dbt, and other tools, that enables lineage capture across heterogeneous pipeline components through a common event specification.

Audit trails track data access rather than data transformation, who or what system read, exported, or deleted a piece of data, and when. GDPR's accountability principle requires that controllers be able to demonstrate compliance, which in practice means producing an audit trail showing that personal data was only processed for its stated purpose, only accessed by authorised parties, and deleted at the end of its retention period. AWS CloudTrail, Azure Monitor, and Google Cloud Audit Logs provide native audit logging for data accessed through those platforms' APIs. For on-premises or hybrid IoT deployments, PostgreSQL's pgaudit extension and Apache Ranger provide database-level access auditing.

CASE STUDY: Data Governance at Scale: NHS England's IoT Patient Monitoring Programme

United Kingdom | 2021–2022

The NHS COVID-19 virtual ward programme deployed over 50,000 pulse oximeters and blood pressure monitors connected through a cloud platform to monitor high-risk COVID-19 patients at home. By its conclusion in 2022, the programme had generated over 200 million data points from patients across England, making it one of the largest healthcare IoT deployments in the world at that time.

The data governance architecture had to satisfy simultaneously demanding requirements: NHS Data Security and Protection Toolkit compliance (incorporating Cyber Essentials Plus certification), GDPR Article 9 requirements for health data processing, NHS Digital's Data Security Standards, and clinical governance requirements of individual NHS Trusts who remained the data controllers for their patients' information.

The technical implementation used patient pseudonymisation at the device gateway level, with pseudonymisation keys held by each NHS Trust independently of the central analytics platform. The central platform could compute population-level statistics and generate national clinical insights without ever holding identifiable patient data. Data retention was enforced by automated pipeline rules: raw readings were deleted 90 days after episode completion, derived clinical metrics were retained for 7 years (consistent with NHS clinical record retention standards), and audit logs were retained for 10 years.

Data lineage was implemented using Apache Atlas, tagging every derived metric with references to the source device identifiers, calibration records, and transformation logic applied. When a firmware bug in one oximeter model was discovered to introduce a systematic offset in SpO2 readings under certain conditions, the lineage system enabled NHS Dig-

ital to identify within hours every patient record, every clinical alert, and every population statistic derived from that device model, and to quantify the magnitude of the potential clinical impact. Without lineage, the same discovery would have triggered a weeks-long manual investigation.

6.8.5 Cross-Border Data Transfers and Data Sovereignty

IoT deployments that span multiple countries face the additional complexity of cross-border data transfer regulations. GDPR restricts the transfer of EU personal data to countries outside the European Economic Area unless an adequacy decision exists (the EU has found that the UK, Japan, South Korea, Canada, and approximately 15 other countries provide adequate protection) or unless specific transfer mechanisms are in place, such as Standard Contractual Clauses (SCCs), Binding Corporate Rules (BCRs) for intra-group transfers, or participation in the EU-US Data Privacy Framework established in 2023.

For IoT system architects, cross-border data transfer restrictions translate into concrete infrastructure decisions. If EU personal data may not be transferred to a US-based cloud region without adequate safeguards, then either the data must be processed in an EU cloud region (AWS eu-west, Azure West Europe, GCP europe-west), or the architecture must ensure that personal data is stripped or anonymised before any cross-region transfer occurs. Many IoT platforms now provide data residency configuration options that pin specific data categories to specific geographic regions, with internal routing rules ensuring that EU-origin telemetry is processed and stored only within EU infrastructure.

Data sovereignty: the principle that data is subject to the laws of the country where it resides is increasingly shaping national IoT infrastructure policy as well as commercial system design. China's Data Security Law (2021) and Personal Information Protection Law (2021) require that certain categories of data generated within China be stored on servers located within China, with security assessments required before data can be transferred abroad. India's Digital Personal Data Protection Act (2023) similarly restricts cross-border transfer of personal data of Indian residents. IoT deployments with global footprints must architect for multi-region data residency from the outset, rather than treating regional compliance as a localisation task to be addressed after core architecture is defined.

Regional Example: Data Sovereignty and Cloud Architecture in the GCC. *Gulf Cooperation Council member states have enacted data localisation frameworks that directly constrain IoT cloud architecture de-*

cisions. Saudi Arabia's Personal Data Protection Law (PDPL, 2021) requires that sensitive personal data of Saudi nationals be processed within the Kingdom — a requirement met by AWS, Azure, and Google Cloud through dedicated local regions in Riyadh. The UAE's Federal Decree-Law No. 45 of 2021 on Personal Data Protection similarly establishes localisation requirements for specific data categories. For IoT architects designing connected systems across the GCC, these regulations translate into concrete decisions: cloud platform region selection, edge processing placement to prevent regulated data from crossing national borders, and contractual data processing agreements aligned with each jurisdiction. Oman's data protection framework, evolving under the Ministry of Transport, Communications and Information Technology's Digital Economy strategy, is expected to align with international standards — making early architectural alignment with GDPR-equivalent principles a prudent design choice for any regional deployment.

Professional Checklist: IoT Data Architecture

Before finalising the IoT data architecture, confirm the following:

- *Data sources, formats, frequency, volume, retention period, and ownership are clearly identified.*
- *Edge, fog, and cloud processing responsibilities are assigned according to latency, cost, and privacy requirements.*
- *Storage choices match the nature of the data, including time-series data, event logs, metadata, and historical archives.*
- *Data quality checks are defined for missing values, outliers, duplication, device drift, and inconsistent timestamps.*
- *Access control, encryption, anonymisation, retention, and deletion policies are documented.*
- *Analytics and machine-learning pipelines can be audited, monitored, and updated over time.*

6.9 Chapter Summary

This chapter has mapped the complete journey that IoT data takes from physical sensor reading to operational decision, examining each stage in sufficient technical depth to equip the practising engineer with both the conceptual framework and the implementation vocabulary needed to design production-grade IoT data systems.

The Five Vs framework (Volume, Velocity, Variety, Veracity, and Value) provides the diagnostic lens through which any IoT data management challenge should first be assessed. Volume drives the architectural decision of how aggressively to filter and aggregate at the edge before cloud transmission.

Velocity determines the latency budget for every stage of the pipeline and selects which processing architecture is viable. Variety demands schema flexibility and multi-model storage strategies. Veracity governs the investment required in data quality management, sensor calibration, and ingestion validation. Value is the ultimate criterion against which every architectural decision should be measured: if the pipeline does not produce analytical outputs that are acted upon, no amount of technical sophistication in its construction justifies the investment required to build it.

Serialisation format selection is among the least glamorous and most consequential decisions in IoT data engineering. JSON's human readability makes it the natural choice for development and debugging environments and for low-volume deployments where operational simplicity matters more than bandwidth efficiency. For high-volume deployments where every kilobyte of transmitted telemetry has a direct network cost, Protocol Buffers and CBOR provide binary encoding that reduces message sizes by 60 to 85 percent relative to equivalent JSON representations. The serialisation decision should be revisited at each scale inflection point in a deployment's growth, as the cost calculus changes materially between a 100-device pilot and a 100,000-device production deployment.

The edge-fog-cloud computing continuum is the architectural response to the tension between data proximity (processing where data is generated, to achieve low latency and reduce transmission costs) and data aggregation (consolidating data from many sources to enable population-level analytics that no individual edge node can perform alone). The optimal point on this continuum differs by use case, and the best IoT architectures use all three tiers simultaneously: the device tier for immediate safety interlocks and data compression, the edge tier for local anomaly detection and gateway protocol bridging, the fog tier for multi-device correlation and site-level dashboards, and the cloud tier for historical analysis, model training, and enterprise integration.

Commercial cloud IoT platforms (AWS IoT Core, Azure IoT Hub, Google Cloud IoT (and its deprecation as a cautionary tale about vendor dependency), and open-source alternatives including ThingsBoard and Eclipse IoT) provide managed infrastructure that dramatically accelerates the time to first production for organisations without large in-house IoT platform engineering teams. Platform selection should be driven by the organisation's existing cloud footprint, its data residency and sovereignty requirements, its tolerance for vendor lock-in, and the specific integration capabilities required to connect the IoT data pipeline to existing enterprise systems.

Storage architecture for IoT data requires matching the data type, access pattern, and retention requirement of each data category to the appropriate storage model. Time-series databases such as InfluxDB and TimescaleDB are purpose-optimised for the append-dominant, time-indexed write patterns and range-query access patterns of IoT telemetry. Object storage provides cost-effective persistence for unstructured IoT data types including images, audio, and video. Data lakes built on object storage provide the schema-on-read flexibility required when data consumers are not known at ingestion time. Data lakehouses, combining the cost and scale of object storage with the transactional reliability and query performance of traditional databases through table formats such as Apache Iceberg and Delta Lake, represent the current leading edge of IoT data architecture at enterprise scale.

The four-tier analytics hierarchy (descriptive, diagnostic, predictive, and prescriptive) maps the progressive transformation of raw data into operational intelligence. Most organisations that believe they are doing predictive analytics are actually doing sophisticated descriptive analytics, and the gap between the two is primarily an organisational capability gap (in data labelling, feature engineering, and model operations) rather than a technology gap. Prescriptive analytics, which closes the loop from data to automated action, requires not just technical capability but organisational governance: defined envelopes of autonomous authority, fallback behaviours, and accountability structures for decisions made by algorithms rather than humans. The next frontier, applying large language models and generative AI to IoT time-series interpretation, and extending federated learning to heterogeneous device fleets at scale is addressed in Chapter 11.

Data governance and privacy are not bolt-on compliance requirements but engineering disciplines that must be designed into IoT systems from the first architectural decision. The GDPR's six processing principles, the EU Cyber Resilience Act's security requirements, the EU Data Act's portability obligations, and the data sovereignty restrictions of China, India, and other major IoT markets collectively define the operating envelope within which every commercial IoT deployment must function.

Engineers who understand these requirements early can design systems that are compliant by construction; engineers who discover them late face expensive remediation, potential regulatory action, and reputational damage. Privacy by Design, data minimisation, pseudonymisation at the edge, differential privacy, and data lineage are the engineering practices through which governance principles are translated into architectural reality.

The NHS virtual ward programme, the Volkswagen Industrial Cloud, the Bosch Rexroth edge inference deployment, and the examples drawn from AWS, Azure, and Apache Kafka throughout this chapter collectively illustrate that the technical concepts presented here are not theoretical constructs but engineering patterns in active production use at scale. The organisations that have mastered these patterns (that can reliably ingest, store, analyse, and govern IoT data at the scale their deployments demand) have created a data infrastructure capability that is a genuine source of competitive advantage, not merely an operational necessity.

Chapter 7

IoT Applications

Smart Systems and Sectoral Use Cases

Chapter 7 examines the major application domains in which IoT creates practical, operational, and strategic value. It explains how IoT solutions are designed around real-world needs by connecting sensors, devices, networks, platforms, analytics, and user-facing services within specific domain contexts. The chapter presents a structured taxonomy of IoT applications and explores key sectors such as smart homes, smart buildings, smart cities, industrial IoT, connected healthcare, agriculture, environment, energy management, retail, logistics, and supply chain systems. It highlights how each domain differs in scale, architecture, communication requirements, data characteristics, regulatory concerns, and value creation models. The chapter also discusses brownfield and greenfield deployment approaches, showing how IoT can be introduced into both existing infrastructure and newly designed digital environments. Overall, this chapter demonstrates that IoT is not a single application category, but a versatile technology foundation that enables automation, visibility, optimisation, risk reduction, and new business value across diverse sectors.

Technological frameworks acquire meaning only when applied to the problems that society asks them to solve. The Internet of Things, for all its architectural elegance and protocol sophistication, ultimately earns its relevance at the point where a sensor reading changes a decision, where a data stream prevents a machine failure, where a wearable device alerts a physician before a patient deteriorates. This chapter moves from the structural foundations examined in earlier chapters to the application layer: the domains, sectors, and real-world systems in which IoT technology generates tangible value.

Nine application domains are examined in depth: smart home and building automation, smart cities and urban infrastructure, industrial IoT and Industry 4.0, connected healthcare and remote patient monitoring, precision agriculture and environmental monitoring, smart grid and energy management, retail and supply chain logistics, and the cross-cutting deployment considerations of brownfield versus greenfield integration. Each domain is treated as a complete system, from the sensors at the physical edge to the analytical engines and user-facing applications at the top of the stack. Real deployments, named commercial platforms, and published case studies ground every section in operational reality rather than speculative promise.

The chapter closes with the Four Business Dimensions framework, a structured lens for evaluating IoT initiatives not only on technical merit but on the organisational, process, and data dimensions that determine whether a technically sound deployment delivers its intended business outcomes. This framework recurs in later chapters on governance and emerging trends, making Chapter 7 a conceptual bridge between the technical foundations of the book and its strategic and policy dimensions.

7.1 IoT Application Design: Value Creation and Domain Taxonomy

The term IoT application is used loosely in both industry and academic literature, often applied equally to a simple temperature dashboard and to a fully autonomous industrial control system. For the purposes of this chapter, an IoT application is defined as a software system that consumes data from one or more physical IoT devices, applies domain-specific logic, and delivers an output that changes the state of the physical or informational world. This definition excludes systems that merely log sensor data without acting on it, and it encompasses both human-in-the-loop applications, where a person receives a notification and takes action, and fully automated closed-loop systems that sense, decide, and actuate without human intervention.

DEFINITION: IoT Application

A software system that consumes data streams from one or more IoT devices, applies domain-specific processing and decision logic, and delivers an output that modifies either the physical environment through actuation or the informational environment through alerts, dashboards, or downstream system updates. IoT applications may be human-in-the-loop or fully automated closed-loop systems.

Source: Whitmore, Agarwal, and Da Xu (2015); Atzori, Iera, and Morabito (2010)

IoT applications generate value through three mechanisms that operate at different levels of organisational impact. The first and most immediate is operational efficiency: the same physical process consumes fewer resources, takes less time, or produces fewer errors when guided by IoT data. A building Heating, Ventilation, and Air Conditioning (HVAC) system that adjusts based on occupancy sensors rather than a fixed schedule typically reduces energy consumption by 20 to 30 percent without any change to the building structure or occupant behaviour.

The second mechanism is the creation of new business models that were not economically viable before IoT-scale data collection became possible. Rolls-Royce charges airlines for engine thrust-hours rather than selling engines outright, because IoT sensors on its Trent series engines provide the real-time performance and health data needed to make power-by-the-hour guarantees commercially viable. The third mechanism is societal outcomes: IoT enables services that benefit communities and populations rather than individual commercial actors, from flood early-warning systems to air quality monitoring networks that inform public health policy.

DEFINITION: Value Chain for IoT Applications

The four-stage process through which IoT systems transform physical phenomena into actionable value: (1) Sense: physical sensors detect a condition or event and convert it to a digital signal; (2) Connect: the signal is transmitted through a network to a processing destination; (3) Process: data is cleaned, fused, analysed, and interpreted; (4) Act: an automated actuator command, alert, or decision output is generated. Value is created at the Act stage; all preceding stages are enabling infrastructure.

Source: Adapted from Gubbi et al. (2013)

A useful taxonomy organises IoT applications along two dimensions: the degree of automation and the breadth of the application domain. On the automation axis, applications range from pure monitoring systems, which display sensor data to human operators who make all decisions, through alerting and advisory systems, which flag anomalous conditions for human action, to optimisation systems, which continuously adjust system parameters within defined bounds, to fully autonomous systems that sense, decide, and act without human involvement.

On the domain axis, applications span from narrowly specialised single-asset systems such as a condition monitoring sensor on a single pump, to multi-domain integrated platforms such as a smart city operating system managing transport, utilities, and emergency services from a unified data fabric.

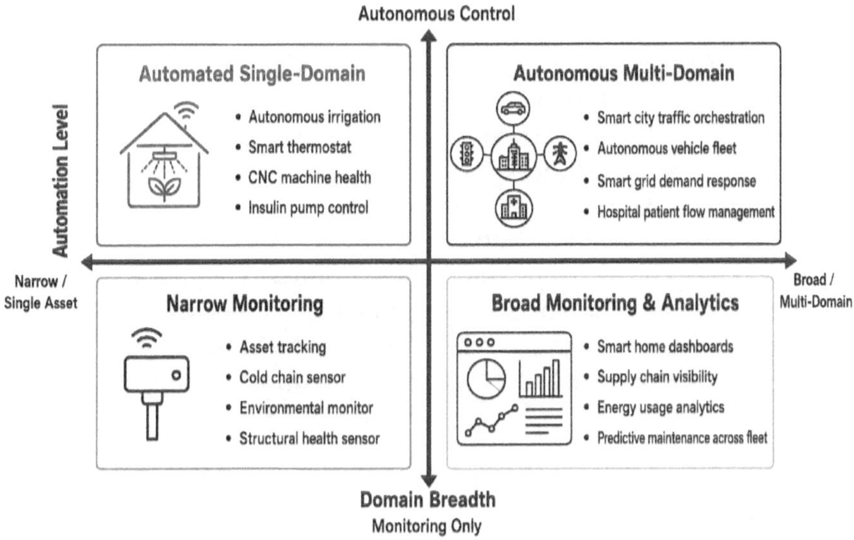

Figure 7.1: IoT Application Domain Taxonomy: Automation Level versus Domain Breadth

The nine sectoral domains explored in the sections that follow span all four quadrants of this taxonomy. Smart home systems today occupy primarily the monitoring and control quadrants, offering rich functionality while retaining human decision-making at the centre. Industrial IoT deployments are migrating steadily toward fully autonomous operation, as machine learning and edge computing bring closed-loop control within operational reach. Understanding where a domain currently sits on this taxonomy, and where it is headed over the next five to ten years, helps practitioners set realistic expectations for what an IoT deployment can deliver today and what requires further technical or organisational maturation.

Key Insight: *How IoT Applications Generate Value. Three distinct mechanisms explain why organisations invest in IoT: operational efficiency (achieving the same physical process with fewer resources, less time, or fewer errors); new business model creation (monetising data-driven outcomes rather than hardware sales); and quality-of-life improvement (ambient healthcare, adaptive living environments, safer transportation).*

These mechanisms are not interchangeable. A deployment justified on efficiency grounds cannot be redesigned mid-project to generate new revenue without fundamentally reconsidering architecture, commercial agreements, and data governance. Identifying the primary value mechanism before selecting any sensor, protocol, or platform is the single most consequential early decision in any IoT programme.

7.2 Smart Home and Smart Building Automation

The smart home is the application domain that has brought IoT into the daily lives of the largest number of people worldwide. By 2024, analysts at Strategy Analytics and IDC estimated that over 1.4 billion smart home devices were in active use globally, with smart speakers, smart thermostats, connected security cameras, and smart lighting representing the four largest product categories by installed base. The smart home domain is simultaneously the most commercially competitive, the most standards-fragmented, and the most privacy-sensitive of all IoT application areas, making it an instructive case study in how market forces, technical standards, and regulatory frameworks interact to shape an emerging technology landscape.

7.2.1 Architecture of a Smart Home System

A smart home system can be decomposed into five functional layers that map directly onto the IoT component model introduced in Chapter 3. At the physical layer, sensors and actuators are distributed throughout the residential space: passive infrared motion detectors, door and window contact sensors, smart plugs and dimmer switches, thermostats with built-in occupancy sensing, water leak detectors beneath sinks and appliances, smart door locks at entry points, and multi-sensor environmental monitors measuring temperature, humidity, and air quality. These devices communicate through short-range wireless protocols to a central hub or directly to a cloud gateway, depending on the platform architecture.

The local network layer connects devices using one or more short-range protocols. Zigbee (IEEE 802.15.4-based) and Z-Wave are the dominant mesh networking protocols for smart home sensors and actuators because of their very low power consumption and their self-healing mesh topology, which provides path redundancy without requiring each device to maintain a direct link to the gateway.

Bluetooth Low Energy is widely used for proximity-sensitive applications including smart locks, presence detection, and wearable sensors. Wi-Fi (IEEE 802.11) provides the backbone for high-bandwidth devices such as IP cameras and video doorbells. Thread, the IPv6-based mesh protocol that forms the network foundation of the Matter standard, is increasingly displacing earlier mesh protocols in interoperability-focused deployments because of its direct IP addressability.

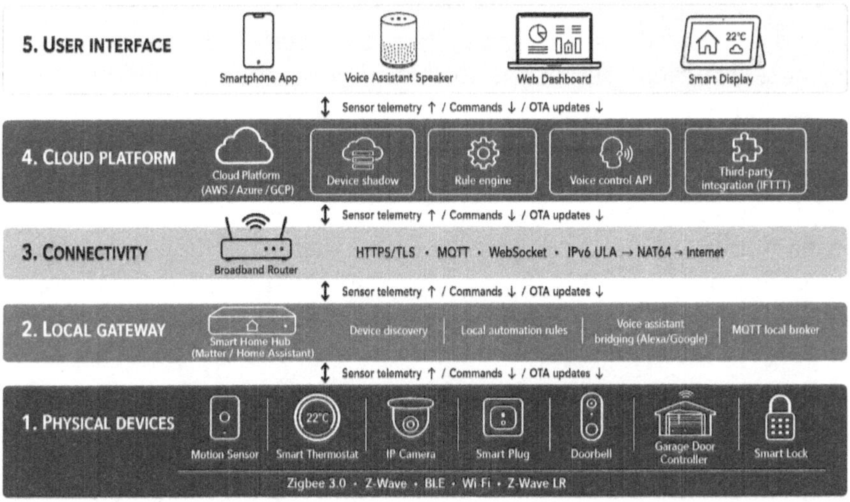

Figure 7.2: Smart Home System Architecture: Five-Layer Data and Control Flow

The gateway or hub aggregates device communications, performs local processing including device state management and automation rule execution, and maintains connectivity to the cloud platform. Commercial smart home hubs such as the Samsung SmartThings Hub, the Amazon Echo (functioning as a Zigbee and Matter controller), and the Apple HomePod mini serve this function.

The hub is the critical dependency in most smart home architectures: when the hub loses cloud connectivity, whether local automation continues to function depends entirely on the platform design. Platforms that retain automation logic on the hub continue to execute rules and respond to device commands without internet access; cloud-dependent platforms lose functionality entirely. This distinction has significant implications for reliability in regions with intermittent internet connectivity.

The cloud platform layer provides storage, analytics, and remote access capabilities that extend smart home functionality beyond the home network perimeter. Cloud platforms process voice commands from smart speakers, maintain historical sensor records, execute automations requiring external data inputs such as weather forecasts and time-of-use electricity pricing, and expose APIs that allow third-party developers to integrate with the platform. The user interface layer, primarily smartphone applications and voice assistants, is the point at which residents interact with the system, whether by issuing commands, reviewing energy consumption dashboards, or receiving security alerts when away from home.

7.2.2 The Matter Standard: Solving Interoperability

For the first decade of consumer IoT, smart home interoperability was the most persistent source of consumer dissatisfaction. A home equipped with Philips Hue lighting (Zigbee), a Nest thermostat (proprietary Wi-Fi), a Ring video doorbell (Wi-Fi, cloud-dependent), and a Yale smart lock (Z-Wave) required at least four separate applications to control and could not execute cross-device automations without a third-party hub. Every major technology company operated a proprietary ecosystem with minimal interoperability, and device certification processes from the Zigbee Alliance, Z-Wave Alliance, and Apple HomeKit were mutually incompatible.

The Matter standard, launched by the Connectivity Standards Alliance in November 2022 with founding support from Apple, Google, Amazon, and Samsung, represents the most significant structural response to this fragmentation. Matter defines a unified application layer protocol operating over Thread for battery-powered devices, Wi-Fi for mains-powered devices, and Ethernet. A Matter-certified device can be controlled natively by any Matter-compatible controller regardless of manufacturer or ecosystem affiliation. By early 2024, over 3,500 Matter-certified products had been released, and all major platform vendors had shipped controller updates supporting Matter commissioning.

The multi-admin capability introduced in Matter 1.0 is the most commercially significant feature: a single device can be registered simultaneously with multiple ecosystem controllers, allowing a homeowner to control their smart home through Apple Home, Google Home, and Amazon Alexa simultaneously without factory resetting or re-pairing devices. This is qualitatively different from the pre-Matter experience, where adding a device to a second ecosystem required a cloud-to-cloud integration agreement between platform vendors and often provided a degraded feature set relative to the primary ecosystem.

CASE STUDY: Matter Adoption and the Samsung SmartThings Platform

South Korea and Global Markets, 2022-2024

Samsung SmartThings was among the earliest platforms to ship full Matter controller support, updating its app and hub firmware in November 2022 to commission Matter devices over Wi-Fi and Thread. By mid-2023, SmartThings supported over 100 Matter-certified devices from third-party manufacturers, including Eve Energy smart plugs previously exclusive to Apple HomeKit and Nanoleaf lighting panels.

The practical implication was commercially significant: Matter allowed SmartThings to expand its compatible device ecosystem without bilateral integration agreements with each manufacturer. A SmartThings user could purchase any Matter-certified device, scan its QR code in the SmartThings app, and have it operational within minutes, regardless of which company made it. This contrasts sharply with the pre-Matter model, where SmartThings compatibility required explicit certification and dedicated driver development by the SmartThings engineering team.

The case also illustrates the early limits of Matter. Camera integration was not included in Matter 1.0, meaning third-party IP cameras still required manufacturer-specific applications. Samsung addressed this by maintaining its parallel Works with SmartThings certification programme for categories not yet covered by Matter, demonstrating that the two approaches will coexist for several years during the transition.

7.2.3 Smart Building Automation

Smart building automation extends the concepts of smart home to commercial, industrial, and institutional buildings, where the scale of infrastructure, complexity of stakeholder relationships, and stringency of regulatory requirements demand more rigorous architectural and governance approaches. A commercial office building of 50,000 square metres may contain thousands of IoT-enabled endpoints: VAV (Variable Air Volume) controllers, chiller plant sensors, lighting control modules, elevator condition monitors, access control readers, and occupancy sensors, all integrated through a Building Management System (BMS) or Building Automation System (BAS).

The predominant communication protocols in building automation are KNX, BACnet, and LonWorks, all of which predate the IoT era but have been progressively extended to support IP connectivity and cloud platform integration. KNX, the dominant protocol in European commercial buildings, is supported by over 500 certified manufacturers and is installed in approximately 700,000 buildings worldwide.

BACnet (Building Automation and Control Networks, ANSI/ASHRAE Standard 135) is the dominant standard in North American commercial HVAC and energy management applications. Modern IoT gateways from Tridium, Beckhoff, and Siemens provide protocol translation between these legacy building protocols and MQTT or REST APIs, enabling existing BAS infrastructure to feed cloud-based energy management and analytics platforms without replacing installed hardware.

The business case for smart building IoT is driven primarily by energy cost reduction and sustainability compliance. A 2023 analysis by the International Energy Agency estimated that commercial buildings account for approximately 28 percent of global final energy consumption and that smart building technologies including automated HVAC, occupancy-based lighting control, and real-time energy monitoring could reduce this consumption by 25 to 40 percent. For large commercial real estate portfolios, this represents tens of millions of dollars in annual energy savings and a meaningful contribution to Scope 1 and Scope 2 greenhouse gas emission reduction commitments under corporate sustainability frameworks.

CASE STUDY: The Edge Building, Amsterdam: A Benchmark for Smart Building IoT

Amsterdam, Netherlands, 2014-Present

Completed in 2014 for Deloitte Netherlands, The Edge in Amsterdam's Zuidas business district was designated by Bloomberg as the world's smartest building at the time of its opening. The building integrates approximately 28,000 sensors monitoring temperature, light levels, humidity, occupancy, and power consumption across 40,000 square metres of office space on 15 floors.

Ethernet-connected LED ceiling panels serve a dual function: each panel contains integrated sensors for measuring light intensity and occupancy, and communicates both lighting control signals and sensor telemetry over a single Ethernet connection. This design eliminates the need for separate sensor cabling and dramatically reduces installation complexity. The BMS uses occupancy data from ceiling sensors and smartphone check-in data to allocate desk space dynamically, reducing the number of physical desks required by approximately 30 percent compared to a conventional fixed-desk layout.

The energy performance of The Edge has been independently certified at an energy performance coefficient of 0.18, against a Dutch regulatory requirement of 1.0, representing an 82 percent improvement over the regulatory minimum. This performance is achieved through a combination of 4,000 square metres of rooftop solar panels providing approximately 50 percent of the building's electrical demand, aquifer thermal energy storage for seasonal heating and cooling, and continuous IoT-driven optimisation of HVAC, lighting, and plug load management based on real-time occupancy and weather data.

Table 7.1: Comparison of Smart Home Short-Range Wireless Protocols

Protocol	Frequency	Range	Topology	Key IoT Application
Zigbee (IEEE 802.15.4)	2.4 GHz	10-100 m	Mesh	Smart home sensors, lighting control
Z-Wave	868/908 MHz	30 m	Mesh	Home automation, smart locks, security
Bluetooth LE 5.x	2.4 GHz	10-400 m	Star/ Mesh	Smart locks, wearables, BLE beacons
Wi-Fi 6 (802.11ax)	2.4/5 GHz	50-150 m	Star (AP)	IP cameras, smart appliances, gateways
Thread (IPv6 mesh)	2.4 GHz	10-100 m	Mesh	Matter-certified battery devices

7.3 Smart Cities: Infrastructure, Services, and Urban Intelligence

The smart city concept represents the most ambitious application of IoT at scale: the instrumentation of an entire urban environment to improve the efficiency, sustainability, and quality of life of its residents. A mature smart city is not a single system but a federation of interconnected IoT subsystems spanning transport, utilities, environment, public safety, health services, and governance, all sharing data through a common urban data platform and generating collective intelligence that no single subsystem could produce in isolation.

DEFINITION: Smart City

An urban environment that uses digital and information communication technologies, including IoT sensor networks, data analytics, and connected infrastructure, to improve the quality and performance of urban services, reduce resource consumption and costs, and enhance the engagement and wellbeing of its citizens. Smart city implementations vary widely in scope, with deployments ranging from targeted single-domain projects to comprehensive city-wide digital transformation programmes.

Source: Zanella et al. (2014); ITU-T Focus Group on Smart Sustainable Cities (2015)

7.3.1 Smart City IoT Architecture

The architecture of a smart city IoT platform follows the same layered model described in Chapter 3 but at a scale and complexity that introduces additional architectural concerns. At the perception layer, thousands to millions of sensors are deployed across the urban fabric: inductive loop detectors and radar sensors in road surfaces measuring vehicle flows; environmental monitoring stations measuring air quality parameters including PM2.5, NO2, and ozone; water level sensors in storm drains and rivers providing flood early-warning data; smart lighting poles equipped with motion sensors, noise monitors, and environmental sensors; and utility meters for electricity, gas, and water providing real-time consumption data.

The network layer of a smart city is inherently heterogeneous. Fixed fibre and Ethernet connections serve sensing infrastructure at fixed locations such as traffic signals and utility substations. Public Wi-Fi networks serve dual purpose as both citizen connectivity and sensor backhaul. LPWAN technologies, particularly LoRaWAN and NB-IoT, serve the vast majority of low-bandwidth sensor deployments including parking sensors, waste bin fill-level monitors, and environmental stations because of their low per-device cost and multi-year battery life. 5G NR serves high-bandwidth and low-latency applications including connected vehicles, real-time video analytics, and augmented reality civic services.

The platform layer of a smart city is commonly called an Urban Data Platform (UDP) or City Data Fabric. The UDP aggregates data streams from all city subsystems, normalises data into a common representation, applies access control policies governing which applications and organisations can access which data streams, and exposes the aggregated data through standardised APIs. The FIWARE open source platform, developed with European Commission funding, and its NGSI-LD data model have been adopted in dozens of European smart city deployments as the basis for interoperable urban data platforms.

DEFINITION: Urban Data Platform (UDP)

A shared data infrastructure that aggregates IoT sensor streams from multiple city subsystems, normalises them into a common data model, enforces data governance policies, and exposes the aggregated data through standardised APIs to authorised applications and third-party developers. The UDP enables cross-domain analytics and coordinated city-wide response that isolated single-domain systems cannot achieve.

Source: European Commission Horizon 2020, FIWARE Programme (2014)

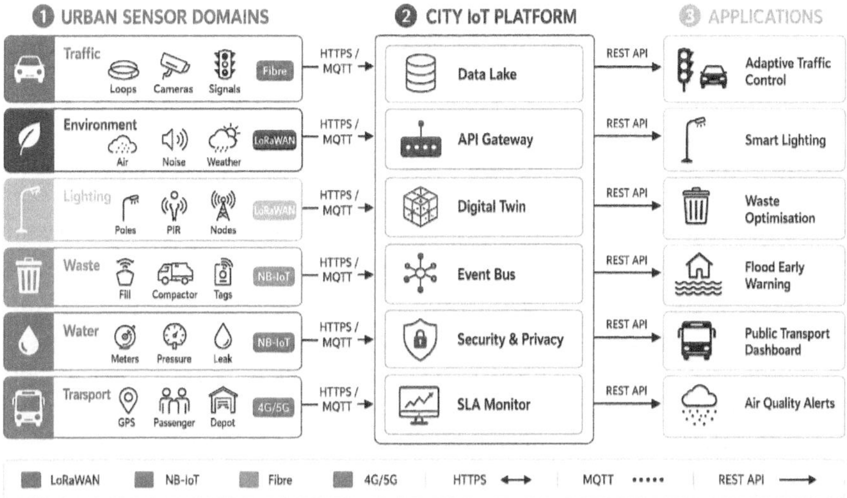

Figure 7.3: Smart City IoT Architecture: From Urban Sensors to Citizen Services

7.3.2 Smart City Application Domains

Smart transportation is typically the highest-priority and highest-visibility component of any smart city programme because of its direct impact on the daily experience of commuters and the economic cost of traffic congestion. IoT-enabled smart traffic management systems use real-time data from road sensors, cameras, and connected vehicles to dynamically adjust signal timings, reroute vehicles around incidents, and provide journey time information through variable message signs and navigation applications. Cities including Barcelona, Singapore, and Amsterdam have demonstrated congestion reductions of 15 to 25 percent through adaptive traffic control systems underpinned by IoT sensor networks.

Smart utilities and metering represent the largest IoT deployment in most cities by device count. Advanced Metering Infrastructure (AMI) programmes, which replace traditional utility meters with smart meters capable of two-way communication, have been rolled out at national scale in several countries. In the United Kingdom, the UK Smart Metering Implementation Programme had installed over 32 million smart electricity and gas meters by 2024, enabling half-hourly consumption data to inform energy demand management, time-of-use tariff pricing, and the integration of distributed renewable energy resources. Similar programmes are underway across the EU, the United States, Australia, and major Asian markets.

Smart environmental monitoring addresses one of the most pressing urban challenges: air quality. WHO estimates that approximately 99 percent of the global urban population breathes air that exceeds WHO air quality guidelines, contributing to 7 million premature deaths annually.

Low-cost IoT air quality sensor networks, deployed on street furniture and building facades, complement expensive regulatory reference stations by providing dense spatial coverage that reveals localised pollution hotspots invisible to sparsely distributed official monitoring networks. Projects including OpenAQ, AirQo in Uganda, and the Netherlands National Air Quality Monitoring Network demonstrate the data quality improvements achievable when citizen-deployed and officially-managed sensor networks are combined through careful calibration protocols.

CASE STUDY: Singapore Smart Nation: Comprehensive Urban IoT at National Scale

Singapore, 2014-Present

Singapore's Smart Nation initiative, launched by Prime Minister Lee Hsien Loong in 2014, is among the most comprehensive national-scale IoT and digital infrastructure programmes in the world. The programme spans transport, healthcare, housing, public safety, and government services, with the Physical Address Management System, National Digital Identity framework, and Smart Nation Sensor Platform constituting its three core infrastructure pillars.

The Smart Nation Sensor Platform (SNSP) provides shared sensing infrastructure deployed on government buildings, public housing estates, and street infrastructure nationwide. Sensors on the SNSP network monitor footfall in public spaces, ambient environmental conditions, and the condition of civic infrastructure such as lifts in public housing blocks. Over 110,000 public housing lift trips are monitored daily for anomalies, with predictive maintenance algorithms generating service alerts before failures occur. This has reduced lift breakdown frequency by over 30 percent in instrumented buildings.

The Virtual Singapore programme created a 3D semantic city model incorporating building information, infrastructure data, environmental sensor readings, and population density estimates. Planning agencies use the model to simulate pedestrian flows, assess solar panel placement on rooftops, model emergency evacuation routes, and evaluate the urban heat island effects of proposed development projects. This digital twin of the city represents one of the most mature municipal applications of IoT-fed spatial analytics in production use anywhere in the world.

CASE STUDY: Barcelona Superblocks: IoT-Enabled Urban Redesign

Barcelona, Spain, 2016-Present

The Superblocks programme in Barcelona transforms 9-block urban grids into pedestrianised, green public spaces by rerouting through traffic to the perimeter of each superblock. IoT sensor networks play a dual role in the programme: they provided the data evidence base that justified the political decision to implement the superblocks, and they now monitor the outcomes of each implementation to inform the rolling programme of further deployments.

Environmental sensors deployed within completed superblocks measure NO2, particulate matter, noise levels, and pedestrian footfall. Data from the first completed superblocks demonstrated NO2 reductions of 25 percent, noise level reductions of 3 dB, and a 34 percent increase in pedestrian activity within the redesigned spaces. These results were published in peer-reviewed journals and used in the city council's successful application for European Commission funding to scale the programme to 503 superblocks across the city.

The Barcelona Urban Mobility Plan uses traffic sensor data from the city's 6,500 sensor loops and 1,200 connected traffic signals to model the impact of each new superblock on surrounding traffic patterns before implementation. This predictive modelling capability, enabled by the city's decade-long investment in traffic IoT infrastructure, has been central to the political viability of the programme by allowing the city to demonstrate that traffic displaced from superblock interiors distributes efficiently rather than creating congestion on perimeter routes.

Table 7.2: Smart City IoT Subsystems: Sensing Technologies, Connectivity, and Primary Outcomes

Subsystem	Primary Sensors	Connectivity	Primary Outcome
Smart transport	Inductive loops, radar, cameras, GNSS	LoRaWAN, 4G/5G, Ethernet	Congestion reduction, transit optimisation
Smart utilities / AMI	Smart meters, pressure sensors, flow meters	NB-IoT, GPRS, Mesh RF	Demand management, leak detection, billing
Environmental quality	PM2.5, NO2, ozone, noise, temperature	LoRaWAN, NB-IoT, Wi-Fi	Public health advisory, regulatory compliance
Smart lighting	Motion sensors, ambient light, energy meters	Powerline, LoRaWAN, Zigbee	40-60% energy saving, adaptive illumination
Waste management	Ultrasonic fill-level sensors, Global Positioning System (GPS) trackers	NB-IoT, Sigfox, cellular	Optimised collection routing, cost reduction
Public safety	CCTV analytics, gunshot detection, crowd sensors	4G/5G, Ethernet fibre	Incident detection, emergency response time

7.4 Industrial IoT and Industry 4.0

Industrial IoT represents the application of connected sensing, edge computing, and cloud analytics to manufacturing, process industry, energy production, and critical infrastructure. Where consumer IoT tolerates intermittent connectivity, moderate data latency, and graceful degradation of functionality, industrial IoT operates in environments where connectivity loss may halt production lines, latency in control signals may damage equipment or endanger workers, and data integrity failures may have regulatory and safety consequences.

These requirements place the Industrial Internet of Things (IIoT) in a qualitatively different design space from consumer and smart city IoT, demanding higher standards of reliability, security, and integration with operational technology.

DEFINITION: Industrial Internet of Things (IIoT)

The application of IoT technologies to industrial and manufacturing environments, characterised by extreme reliability and uptime requirements, real-time control integration, industrial-grade hardware operating in harsh physical environments, and tight integration with operational technology (OT) systems including Supervisory Control and Data Acquisition (SCADA), Programmable Logic Controller (PLC) networks, Manufacturing Execution System (MES), and Enterprise Resource Planning (ERP). IIoT is distinguished from consumer IoT by the safety-critical and mission-critical nature of the systems it monitors and controls.

Source: Industrial Internet Consortium (2019); Lu (2017)

7.4.1 Industry 4.0 and the Digital Factory

Industry 4.0, a term coined in Germany in 2011 as part of a national industrial strategy, describes the fourth industrial revolution characterised by the integration of cyber-physical systems, IoT, cloud computing, and artificial intelligence into manufacturing processes. The preceding three industrial revolutions were defined by steam power and mechanisation in the late 18th century, electrification and mass production in the late 19th century, and automation and electronics in the mid-20th century.

The fourth revolution is distinguished from its predecessors not merely by the introduction of new technologies but by the real-time integration of the physical and digital worlds through IoT sensor networks and digital twin models that allow physical processes to be monitored, simulated, and optimised at every level of granularity.

The digital factory is the most complete expression of the Industry 4.0 vision: a manufacturing environment in which every machine, conveyor, product, and worker is a data-generating node in an interconnected system. In a digital factory, a turbine blade being machined on a five-axis Computer Numerical Control (CNC) machine continuously reports its spindle load, tool wear indicators, and dimensional measurements to an edge analytics system that adjusts cutting parameters in real time to compensate for tool degradation.

The finished component carries a digital thread, a data record linking every manufacturing operation performed on it from raw material receipt to final inspection, enabling traceability, quality analysis, and warranty management that would be impossible with paper-based records.

DEFINITION: Cyber-Physical System (CPS)

A system in which computational processes and physical processes are tightly integrated through sensors, actuators, and communication networks. In a CPS, physical behaviour is continuously monitored and governed by computational algorithms, and computational decisions result directly in physical actions. Examples include robotic manufacturing cells, autonomous vehicles, and smart power grids. IIoT sensor networks are the sensing and communication infrastructure of cyber-physical systems.

Source: Lee, Bagheri, and Kao (2015); National Science Foundation

7.4.2 IT/OT Convergence and the Purdue Model

The most significant architectural challenge in IIoT deployment is the convergence of information technology, the networked computing systems used for business data processing, with operational technology, the hardware and software used to monitor and control physical industrial processes.

These two technology domains have historically been managed by separate organisational teams, used incompatible protocols and data formats, operated on different security postures, and had vastly different expectations regarding acceptable downtime. IT systems can typically tolerate brief maintenance windows for patching and updates; OT systems often run continuously for years without interruption because any downtime represents lost production or, in safety-critical applications, a risk to worker safety.

The Purdue Reference Model for Control Hierarchy, developed in the 1990s at Purdue University and subsequently adopted by ISA-

95 as the standard for industrial automation, organises industrial control systems into five hierarchical levels: Level 0 (field devices: sensors and actuators), Level 1 (basic control: PLCs and RTUs), Level 2 (supervisory control: SCADA and DCS), Level 3 (manufacturing operations: MES), and Level 4 (business planning: ERP). The traditional model maintained strict isolation between OT levels 0 through 3 and IT levels 3 through 5, with security enforced through an air gap or a demilitarised zone between the two domains.

IIoT is fundamentally disrupting this architecture. The business value of IIoT, particularly predictive maintenance, production optimisation, and digital twin synchronisation, requires data to flow from OT devices at Level 0 and 1 directly to cloud analytics platforms at and beyond Level 4. This creates connectivity paths that bypass the traditional air gap, dramatically expanding the attack surface of OT systems. Industrial cybersecurity standards including IEC 62443, NIST SP 800-82, and NERC CIP have been updated to address this expanded threat model, but the organisational and technical challenges of IT/OT convergence remain among the most difficult problems in industrial engineering.

Key Insight: *Why IT/OT Convergence Is the Central IIoT Challenge. Industrial control networks were engineered for deterministic, isolated, safety-critical operations with multi-decade lifecycles. Enterprise IT networks were engineered for flexible, internet-connected, productivity-oriented tasks with update cycles measured in months.*

These two design philosophies produce fundamentally incompatible assumptions about system availability (five-nines versus best-effort), security architecture (air-gapped versus internet-facing), and change management (qualified validation procedures versus agile continuous delivery). IIoT programmes that treat convergence as a purely technical protocol-bridging exercise consistently encounter unexpected costs and timelines. Successful deployments assign dedicated IT/OT integration ownership, establish joint governance committees, and plan for multi-year programmes rather than point-to-point connections.

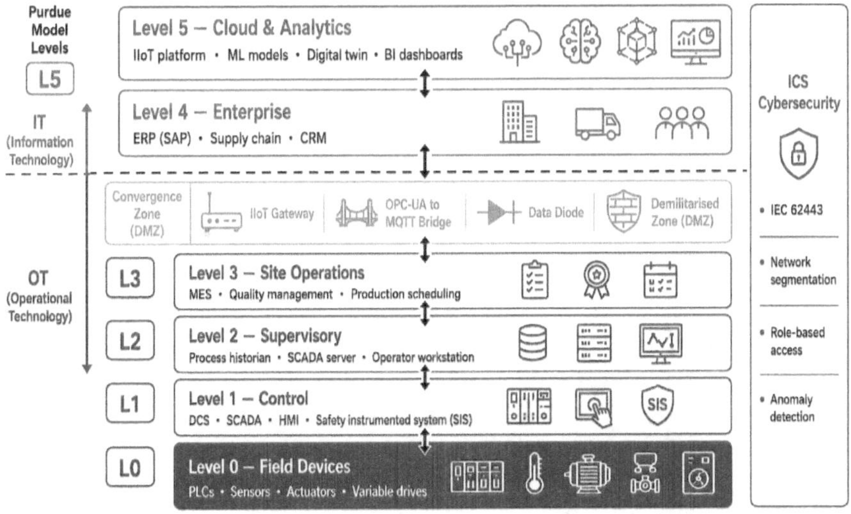

Figure 7.4: IIoT Reference Architecture: IT/OT Convergence Stack

7.4.3 Key IIoT Use Cases

Predictive maintenance is the IIoT use case with the most clearly documented return on investment and the broadest applicability across industrial sectors. Traditional maintenance strategies are either reactive, where equipment is repaired after failure, or preventive, where maintenance is scheduled at fixed time intervals regardless of actual equipment condition. Both strategies are economically inefficient: reactive maintenance incurs unplanned downtime costs that are typically three to ten times higher than planned maintenance costs, while preventive maintenance replaces components that may have significant remaining useful life.

Predictive maintenance uses continuous sensor monitoring of equipment parameters including vibration frequency spectra, bearing temperature, motor current signature, oil particle count, and acoustic emissions to detect the early signatures of degradation modes before they progress to failure.

Machine learning models trained on historical failure data identify the characteristic patterns that precede specific failure modes, enabling maintenance to be scheduled in the window between first detection and projected failure. A 2020 McKinsey analysis estimated that predictive maintenance IoT applications could reduce machine downtime by 30 to 50 percent, extend equipment life by 20 to 40 percent, and reduce maintenance costs by 10 to 25 percent across the manufacturing sector.

TECHNOLOGY SPOTLIGHT: OPC-UA: The Protocol Bridge of Industrial IoT

OPC-UA (Open Platform Communications Unified Architecture), standardised as IEC 62541, is the protocol that makes IT/OT convergence practically achievable. It defines a vendor-neutral, platform-independent data model for industrial equipment that abstracts the diversity of field-level OT protocols (Modbus, PROFINET, EtherNet/IP, HART) into a unified information model accessible via standard IT protocols (TCP/IP, HTTPS, WebSockets).

An OPC-UA server running on an industrial gateway reads data from PLCs and SCADA systems using native OT protocols and exposes it to cloud analytics platforms through OPC-UA over HTTPS or MQTT. Major industrial equipment manufacturers including Siemens, Rockwell Automation, and ABB have embedded OPC-UA servers directly into their PLCs and drives, eliminating the need for intermediate gateways in greenfield deployments. Microsoft Azure IoT Edge, AWS IoT Greengrass, and industrial IoT platforms from PTC ThingWorx and GE Predix all include native OPC-UA client capabilities.

As of 2024, OPC-UA is supported by over 1,000 products from more than 600 manufacturers, making it the de facto standard for industrial IoT data exchange above the field bus level. Its companion specifications for specific industries, including robotics, machine tools, and plastics, define standardised information models for equipment types that enable plug-and-play data integration without custom integration engineering.

CASE STUDY: Siemens Amberg Electronics Plant: The Digital Factory in Practice

Amberg, Bavaria, Germany, 1989-Present

The Siemens Electronics Works in Amberg, Bavaria, is one of the most extensively documented examples of a fully instrumented digital factory. The 108,000 square metre facility manufactures SIMATIC programmable logic controllers, producing approximately 15 million units annually with a defect rate of less than 12 parts per million, achieved in large part through the integration of IoT sensor data into every stage of the manufacturing process.

Every component, circuit board, and finished product carries a unique identifier that is linked to a digital manufacturing record. As each product passes through the 1,200 automated production steps, readings from in-process sensors are recorded against its digital record in real time. Statistical process control algorithms monitor process parameters continuously and trigger automatic adjustments when measurements approach control limits, preventing defects before they occur rather than detecting them after the fact. The factory generates approximately 50 million data points per day, all of which are analysed to identify root causes of quality deviations and opportunities for process optimisation.

Siemens has used the Amberg facility as a proving ground for its Xcelerator digital manufacturing portfolio, including the SINUMERIK CNC platform with integrated IoT data export and the MindSphere industrial IoT cloud platform. The lessons learned at Amberg have been distilled into reference architectures and best practice guides that Siemens offers to industrial customers undertaking digital factory transformations globally.

CASE STUDY: Rolls-Royce TotalCare: Power-by-the-Hour through Engine IoT

United Kingdom and Global, 2000-Present

Rolls-Royce's TotalCare service programme, in which airlines pay for engine thrust-hours rather than purchasing jet engines outright, is one of the most commercially successful examples of IoT enabling a new business model in any industry. The programme depends entirely on the continuous IoT monitoring of the approximately 13,000 gas turbine engines that Rolls-Royce has in service with over 500 airline customers worldwide.

Each Rolls-Royce Trent engine transmits Engine Health Management data to Rolls-Royce's Operations Centres in Derby, UK, and Singapore every 30 seconds during flight. Approximately 20,000 data parameters are monitored per engine per flight, including exhaust gas temperatures, vibration signatures, oil system parameters, and fuel flow rates. Analytics algorithms developed over decades of fleet experience identify the early indicators of component degradation modes including blade erosion, bearing wear, and combustor distress, enabling scheduled maintenance before failures occur.

The financial logic of TotalCare is compelling for both parties: Rolls-Royce earns recurring revenue over the 20 to 30-year service life of each engine rather than a one-time capital sale, and airlines replace capital expenditure with predictable operational expenditure while benefiting from Rolls-Royce's fleet-wide analytics expertise. By 2022, approximately 70 percent of Rolls-Royce civil large engine thrust was covered by long-term service agreements, compared to less than 30 percent in 2000, demonstrating the commercial scale achievable when IoT data enables a genuinely differentiated service business model.

Table 7.3: Consumer IoT Versus Industrial IoT: A Comparative Design Perspective

Design Dimension	Consumer IoT	Industrial IoT (IIoT)
Reliability requirement	Best-effort; graceful degradation acceptable	99.9999% uptime; unplanned downtime unacceptable
Latency tolerance	Seconds to minutes acceptable	Milliseconds for control loops
Hardware environment	Benign (indoor, domestic temperature)	Harsh (vibration, dust, heat, chemicals)
Security posture	Convenience often prioritised	Safety-critical; IEC 62443 compliance required
Maintenance model	Consumer self-service; OTA updates	Planned windows; change management required
Data volume	Moderate (megabytes per day)	Very high (gigabytes per hour per machine)
Lifecycle	3-5 years	20-40 years

7.5 Connected Healthcare and Remote Patient Monitoring

Healthcare is among the application domains where IoT carries the most profound human consequences. A sensor that identifies a patient's atrial fibrillation before it causes a stroke, a remote monitoring system that detects a diabetic patient's hypoglycaemic episode in the night, or an IoT-enabled medication dispenser that alerts a caregiver when a dose is missed: these are not incremental efficiency improvements but potentially life-changing interventions that become possible only when continuous physiological sensing is combined with intelligent analytics and responsive clinical workflows.

The transition from episodic, clinic-based care to continuous, data-rich remote monitoring represents one of the most structurally significant shifts in healthcare delivery of the past two decades, and IoT is the enabling technology at its core.

DEFINITION: Remote Patient Monitoring (RPM)

The use of IoT devices to collect and transmit patient health data from outside a traditional clinical setting, enabling clinicians to monitor patient health status continuously rather than during scheduled appointments. RPM systems typically consist of wearable or home-based sensors, a patient gateway (smartphone or dedicated hub), a cloud health platform, and a clinician-facing monitoring dashboard or alert system.

Source: Islam et al. (2015); Dimitrov (2016)

7.5.1 Healthcare IoT Device Categories

Healthcare IoT devices span a wide range of sensing modalities, regulatory classifications, and deployment contexts. Wearable biometric sensors worn on the body continuously measure physiological parameters and transmit data wirelessly to a gateway device.

Commercial examples include the Apple Watch Series 9, which provides continuous heart rate monitoring, blood oxygen saturation (SpO2) measurement, Electrocardiogram (ECG) waveform capture, and fall detection; the Fitbit Sense 2, which adds electrodermal activity sensing for stress monitoring; and the Garmin Forerunner series, widely used in clinical research studies of exercise physiology. These consumer-grade wearables occupy the lower end of the regulatory spectrum; they are generally classified as wellness devices rather than medical devices and are not subject to the full burden of medical device regulation in most jurisdictions.

At the higher end of the regulatory spectrum sit Food and Drug Administration (FDA)-cleared and CE-marked medical devices that use IoT connectivity for clinical monitoring. The Abbott FreeStyle Libre continuous glucose monitoring system, which uses a small disposable sensor worn on the upper arm to measure interstitial glucose every minute, transmitting readings to a smartphone application, has transformed diabetes management for over 5 million patients in more than 50 countries.

The sensor's 14-day wear period, factory calibration, and smartphone-based data review eliminate the need for the finger-prick blood glucose tests that characterised diabetes self-management for four decades. Clinical studies published in The Lancet have demonstrated that CGM systems including the FreeStyle Libre significantly reduce time spent in hypoglycaemia and improve glycaemic control as measured by HbA1c, the primary clinical outcome metric in diabetes management.

Implantable medical devices with wireless telemetry capabilities represent the most safety-critical category of healthcare IoT. Cardiac rhythm devices, including pacemakers and implantable cardioverter-defibrillators (ICDs), have incorporated remote monitoring capability since the early 2000s. Medtronic's CareLink network and Abbott's Merlin.net platform transmit daily device diagnostics and arrhythmia alerts to clinical monitoring centres. A landmark 2016 study published in the New England Journal of Medicine (the BETTER study) demonstrated that remote monitoring of ICDs reduced the time from arrhythmia detection to clinical evaluation from 21 days under standard in-clinic follow-up to 2 days under remote monitoring, a 90 percent reduction with direct implications for patient safety outcomes.

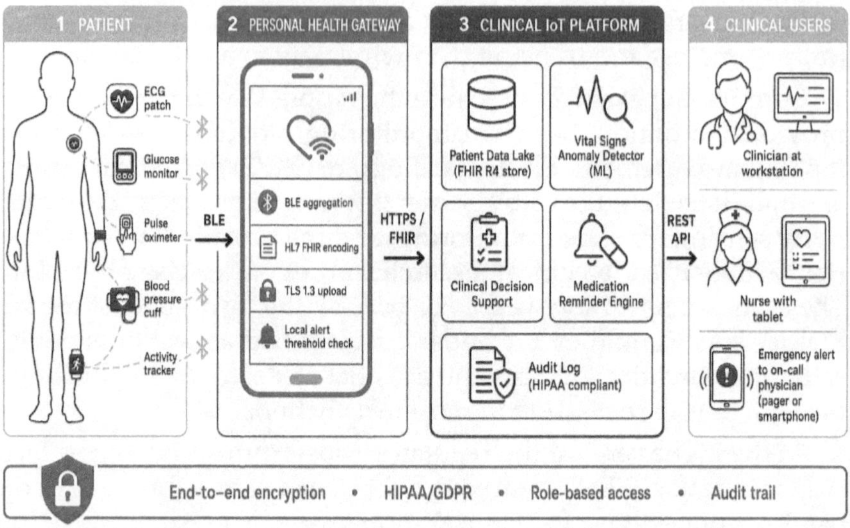

Figure 7.5: Healthcare IoT Architecture: From Wearable Sensor to Clinical Alert

7.5.2 Body Area Networks and IoT Connectivity in Healthcare

The connectivity architecture of healthcare IoT deployments differs from most other IoT domains because the primary sensing substrate is the human body itself. A Body Area Network (BAN), defined in IEEE 802.15.6, is a network of wearable or implantable sensors on or near the human body, typically using Bluetooth Low Energy or proprietary ultra-low-power RF protocols for short-range communication to a smartphone or dedicated hub. The smartphone then serves as the IoT gateway, aggregating data from multiple BAN sensors and forwarding it to a cloud health platform over cellular or Wi-Fi.

DEFINITION: Body Area Network (BAN)

A network of wearable, on-body, or implantable sensors communicating over short-range wireless links, typically Bluetooth Low Energy or IEEE 802.15.6, to aggregate physiological measurements from multiple sensing points on or near the human body. The BAN gateway, usually a smartphone, collects BAN data and forwards it to a cloud health platform for clinical analysis.

Source: IEEE Standard 802.15.6-2012; Islam et al. (2015)

The connectivity requirements of implantable devices are particularly constrained. Cardiac implants must achieve long battery lives (10 to 15 years for pacemakers, 5 to 7 years for ICDs) while maintaining reliable telemetry links that can be activated during clinical interrogation or for daily remote monitoring transmissions.

Proprietary low-power RF protocols operating in the MICS (Medical Implant Communication Service) band at 402-405 MHz, which penetrates human tissue more effectively than 2.4 GHz frequencies, are standard for implant telemetry. The FDA's Cybersecurity guidance for networked medical devices, updated in 2023, requires manufacturers to implement cryptographic authentication and encrypted communication for all implantable and wireless medical devices, addressing a well-documented history of security vulnerabilities in older-generation devices.

7.5.3 Data Governance and Regulatory Compliance

Healthcare data generated by IoT devices carries the highest level of sensitivity and regulatory protection of any IoT data category. In the European Union, GDPR Article 9 classifies health data as a special category of personal data subject to additional processing restrictions and mandatory data protection impact assessments. In the United States, HIPAA (Health Insurance Portability and Accountability Act) governs the processing of protected health information by covered entities and their business associates, with breach notification requirements and civil penalties up to USD 1.9 million per violation category per year.

The regulatory classification of healthcare IoT software is a critical design consideration. The FDA's Software as a Medical Device (SaMD) guidance, aligned with the IMDRF framework, classifies software according to the severity of patient harm that could result from incorrect output. A wellness application that tracks step count is not a medical device; an application that analyses ECG waveforms to detect atrial fibrillation and recommends clinical action is classified as a Class II medical device in the United States and requires FDA 510(k) clearance before commercialisation. Kardia Mobile by AliveCor, the first consumer ECG device to receive FDA clearance for AFib detection, navigated this regulatory pathway and established the template for subsequent direct-to-consumer medical IoT device approvals.

CASE STUDY: NHS Remote Patient Monitoring Programme: IoT in National Healthcare

United Kingdom, 2020-Present

The COVID-19 pandemic catalysed the largest deployment of remote patient monitoring IoT in the history of the National Health Service. The NHS Oximetry at Home and COVID Virtual Wards programmes distributed over 500,000 pulse oximeter devices to COVID-positive patients at high risk of deterioration, enabling nursing teams to monitor blood oxygen saturation remotely and intervene before patients developed the silent hypoxia characteristic of severe COVID-19 pneumonia.

The programme's IoT infrastructure varied by trust and region, with some deployments using simple patient-reported oximetry readings via telephone, and more advanced implementations using Bluetooth-connected oximeters that transmitted readings automatically to nurse monitoring dashboards through NHS-approved clinical remote monitoring platforms from vendors including Doccla, Docotel, and Huma Therapeutics. A controlled evaluation published in the British Medical Journal in 2021 demonstrated that patients monitored through virtual wards had significantly lower rates of emergency admission and 30-day mortality compared to standard discharge with safety-netting advice.

Following the pandemic, NHS England committed to scaling remote patient monitoring beyond COVID to chronic disease management, with programmes targeting heart failure, COPD, and hypertension. The 2022 NHS Long Term Plan included a commitment to enrol 280,000 patients in remote monitoring programmes by 2024, representing a structural shift in how the NHS manages high-risk patients with multiple long-term conditions. Healthcare IoT is thus transitioning from pandemic response to routine clinical infrastructure within one of the world's largest public health systems.

Table 7.4: Healthcare IoT Device Categories: Regulatory Classification and Clinical Application

Device Category	Example Products	Regulatory Class	Primary Clinical Application
Consumer wearable	Apple Watch S9, Fitbit Sense 2	Wellness / Class I	Activity, HR, SpO2, fall detection
Medical-grade wearable	Holter monitor, Zio Patch (iRhythm)	Class II (FDA 510k)	Arrhythmia detection, cardiac monitoring
Continuous glucose monitor	Abbott FreeStyle Libre, Dexcom G7	Class II (FDA / CE)	Diabetes glucose management
Smart insulin pen / pump	Novo NovoPen 6, Medtronic MiniMed	Class II-III	Insulin dose tracking and optimisation
Cardiac implant telemetry	Medtronic CareLink, Abbott Merlin.net	Class III (PMA)	ICD/pacemaker remote follow-up
RPM hub / platform	Doccla, Huma Therapeutics, Current Health	Class II SaMD	Multi-parameter virtual ward monitoring

7.6 Agriculture, Environment, and Energy Management

Three application domains share an important structural characteristic: they involve IoT sensor networks deployed across geographically dispersed physical environments at scales ranging from individual farms to national infrastructure grids. Precision agriculture, environmental monitoring, and smart energy management each demand connectivity solutions capable of covering vast areas at low cost, with hardware designed for outdoor exposure, extreme temperatures, and multi-year battery operation. LoRaWAN and NB-IoT have become the dominant connectivity technologies in all three domains for exactly these reasons, supplemented by satellite IoT (Iridium, Starlink IoT, and Orbcomm) for deployments in locations with no terrestrial network coverage.

7.6.1 Precision Agriculture

Agriculture accounts for approximately 70 percent of global freshwater consumption and 30 percent of global greenhouse gas emissions, making it one of the sectors where IoT-driven efficiency improvements carry the greatest environmental and food security significance. Precision agriculture replaces the traditional practice of managing entire fields uniformly, applying the same amount of water, fertiliser, and pesticide across all areas regardless of local variation in soil condition, crop health, or pest pressure, with a data-driven approach that manages each area of a field according to its specific, measured conditions.

DEFINITION: Precision Agriculture

The use of IoT sensors, satellite remote sensing, data analytics, and variable-rate application technology to manage spatial and temporal variability in field conditions, with the goal of applying the right input (water, fertiliser, pesticide) at the right rate, to the right location, at the right time. Precision agriculture reduces input costs and environmental impact while maintaining or improving crop yields.

Source: Ferrandez-Pastor et al. (2016); FAO (2022)

Soil sensing is the foundation of precision agriculture IoT. Capacitance-based soil moisture sensors buried at multiple depths provide continuous data on the water content profile of the root zone. Electrochemical sensors measure soil electrical conductivity, which correlates with clay content, organic matter, and nutrient availability. Multi-depth temperature sensors monitor soil thermal conditions that influence seed germination timing and root development. Data from these sensors is transmitted to a farm management platform via LoRaWAN or cellular, where it feeds irrigation scheduling algorithms that control variable-rate irrigation systems delivering water only where and when the soil moisture deficit requires it.

Crop monitoring using unmanned aerial vehicles (UAVs) equipped with multispectral and thermal cameras has transformed the spatial resolution at which agronomists can assess crop health. The Normalised Difference Vegetation Index (NDVI), calculated from the ratio of near-infrared to red light reflectance, provides a quantitative measure of photosynthetic activity that correlates with crop biomass and stress status. A single UAV flight over a 100-hectare field generates georeferenced NDVI maps with centimetre-scale resolution in under an hour, enabling early identification of localised crop stress caused by irrigation failures, pest infestations, or nutrient deficiencies that would be invisible in field-averaged satellite imagery.

DEFINITION: *NDVI (Normalised Difference Vegetation Index)*

A spectral index calculated as (NIR - Red) / (NIR + Red), where NIR is near-infrared reflectance and Red is red-band reflectance. NDVI values range from -1 to +1; values above 0.2 indicate vegetation, with healthy dense vegetation typically scoring 0.6 to 0.9. NDVI is widely used in drone-based and satellite-based crop health monitoring to detect stress, disease, and yield potential.

Source: Tucker (1979); Rouse et al. (1974)

Livestock management IoT has progressed beyond simple GPS tracking to comprehensive animal health monitoring. Companies including Allflex, CowManager, and Moocall have deployed ear-tag and collar-mounted sensors that continuously monitor cattle rumination patterns, activity levels, body temperature, and reproductive behaviour. Machine learning algorithms trained on historical data from thousands of animals can detect the onset of lameness, mastitis, and oestrus cycles with accuracy exceeding that of visual inspection by experienced farm workers. Early disease detection reduces veterinary treatment costs and prevents production losses; automated oestrus detection enables precision breeding at the optimal time, improving conception rates by 10 to 20 percent.

CASE STUDY: John Deere Operations Center: Digital Agriculture at Commercial Scale

Moline, Illinois, United States, 2013-Present

John Deere's Operations Center is the world's most widely used farm management platform, with over 350 million acres of agricultural land connected to the system by 2023. The platform aggregates data from John Deere's connected machinery fleet, including telematics from over 500,000 connected machines, field mapping data, soil sampling records, and weather data, to provide farmers and agronomists with a unified view of farm operations. Every John Deere tractor, combine harvester, and sprayer sold since 2014 is equipped with JDLink telematics that transmits machine location, operating parameters, fuel consumption, and diagnostic fault codes to the Operations Center over cellular. Combine harvesters equipped with yield monitors record grain yield at every square metre of a field during harvest, generating georeferenced yield maps that reveal the spatial variability in productivity across the field. These yield maps, combined with soil sensor data and satellite NDVI imagery, form the evidence base for variable-rate application prescriptions that direct next season's fertiliser and seed placement.

The platform's See and Spray technology, deployed in John Deere's ExactApply sprayer systems, uses machine vision and individual nozzle control to apply herbicide only to detected weeds rather than the entire field, reducing herbicide use by up to 77 percent in demonstration trials. This represents a convergence of IoT sensing, edge AI inference, and precision actuation that exemplifies the fully autonomous, multi-sensor closed-loop systems at the top-right of the IoT application taxonomy.

7.6.2 Environmental Monitoring

Environmental monitoring IoT networks serve a dual function: they provide the scientific data required to understand environmental trends and assess regulatory compliance, and they generate the real-time situational awareness needed to protect public health and safety from environmental hazards. The two most significant application areas are air quality monitoring and water quality monitoring, both of which have undergone structural transformation as the cost of IoT sensors has fallen to the point where dense community-scale networks are economically feasible alongside traditional sparse regulatory monitoring stations. Air quality monitoring illustrates the complementarity of IoT sensor networks and traditional reference instruments. Regulatory reference stations use laboratory-grade instruments costing USD 30,000 to 150,000 per parameter to measure pollutant concentrations with measurement uncertainty below 5 percent, meeting the requirements of environmental regulation. These stations are spaced kilometres apart, providing city-scale averages that conceal street-level and neighbourhood-level variation.

Low-cost IoT sensors based on electrochemical cells and optical particle counters, costing USD 200 to 2,000 per unit, can be deployed at densities of one per city block, revealing the spatial distribution of pollution at the scale relevant to individual health decisions. The challenge is data quality: low-cost sensors drift over time, cross-respond to interfering gases, and are sensitive to temperature and humidity. Calibration transfer methods that use co-located reference data to correct low-cost sensor readings have been shown to reduce measurement uncertainty to below 15 percent in field conditions, making co-located networks a scientifically valid complement to sparse reference networks.

Flood early-warning systems represent one of the most safety-critical environmental IoT applications. The 2021 flooding in Ahr Valley, Germany, which killed 184 people, and the 2023 Derna dam collapse in Libya, which caused more than 10,000 deaths, demonstrated the catastrophic consequences of inadequate early-warning infrastructure. IoT-based flood warning networks use ultrasonic water level sensors in rivers, storm drains, and reservoirs, transmitting readings every 5 to 15 minutes over LoRaWAN or NB-IoT to hydrological models that generate inundation forecasts and trigger alerts to emergency services and residents. The UK Environment Agency's flood warning network covers over 50,000 kilometres of rivers and coastline with approximately 3,000 automatic water level and flow gauges, sending automated voice, text, and email alerts to over 1.3 million registered recipients.

CASE STUDY: AirQo: Low-Cost IoT Air Quality Monitoring in Sub-Saharan Africa

Kampala, Uganda, and Pan-African, 2017-Present

AirQo is an air quality monitoring network developed at Makerere University in Uganda, deploying low-cost IoT air quality sensors across African cities to address the near-total absence of air quality data on the continent. Of the 10 most polluted cities in the world by PM2.5, seven are in sub-Saharan Africa or South Asia, yet regulatory monitoring infrastructure in these regions is extremely sparse, with some major African capitals having no operational air quality monitoring station.

AirQo sensors measure PM2.5, PM10, NO2, and CO using a combination of optical particle counters and electrochemical cells. The sensors transmit readings every five minutes over GSM cellular to the AirQo cloud platform. A machine learning calibration pipeline cross-references co-located sensor data with portable reference instruments to apply correction factors that account for local humidity and temperature effects on sensor response, achieving measurement uncertainties below 20 percent for PM2.5 under Kampala ambient conditions. By 2023, AirQo had deployed over 120 sensors across 13 African cities including Kampala, Nairobi, Accra, Lagos, and Bujumbura, generating the first publicly available continuous air quality datasets for many of these cities. The data has been used to quantify the contribution of biomass burning and vehicle exhaust to urban pollution loads, to inform World Bank environmental impact assessments for urban infrastructure projects, and to support health research quantifying the burden of air pollution on respiratory disease in East African populations.

7.6.3 Smart Grid and Energy Management

The electricity grid is undergoing the most fundamental structural transformation in its 140-year history, driven by the integration of variable renewable generation, distributed energy resources, and flexible demand. IoT sensing and communication infrastructure is the enabling technology for this transformation: without real-time visibility into the state of millions of distributed generation and consumption points, grid operators cannot maintain the frequency and voltage stability that modern electrical infrastructure requires.

DEFINITION: Advanced Metering Infrastructure (AMI)

A system comprising smart electricity and gas meters capable of two-way communication, a telecommunications network connecting meters to a data management system, and software platforms for meter data management and analytics. AMI enables half-hourly or sub-hourly consumption data, remote meter reading, tamper detection, outage notification, and the dynamic tariff structures required for demand response programmes.

Source: Tuballa and Abundo (2016); IEA (2023)

Smart metering is the foundational IoT layer of smart grid infrastructure. A smart meter equipped with a Home Area Network (HAN) radio (typically Zigbee or Wi-Fi) communicates consumption data to an in-home display, allowing residents to see the cost of their current electricity consumption in real time. Studies by the UK's Department for Energy Security and Net Zero have demonstrated that in-home display use reduces household electricity consumption by 2 to 5 percent through behaviour change alone, and that the combination of real-time display and time-of-use tariffs (where electricity is cheaper off-peak) can shift 15 to 20 percent of flexible consumption to lower-demand periods, reducing the peak-to-trough ratio on the distribution network.

Demand response represents the most economically valuable grid-scale IoT application. By equipping thermostats, water heaters, Electric Vehicle (EV) chargers, and industrial loads with IoT connectivity and two-way communication with the utility, grid operators can coordinate simultaneous consumption reductions across millions of devices during periods of high demand or constrained supply.

The Nest Rush Hour Rewards programme, operated through Google Nest thermostats, uses machine learning to pre-cool homes before demand response events, reducing participant discomfort while delivering demand reductions of 0.3 to 0.5 kilowatts per participating household. At scale, with millions of participating thermostats, this provides grid operators with a demand flexibility resource equivalent in effect to a peaking power plant, at a fraction of the capital cost.

The integration of distributed energy resources including rooftop solar panels, home battery storage (Tesla Powerwall, Sonnen, Enphase IQ Battery), and electric vehicle chargers creates additional IoT requirements. Each DER must be monitored and, in virtual power plant configurations, controllable by a grid aggregator that can coordinate the collective export or import of energy from thousands of distributed assets. Platforms including Tesla Autobidder, SunPower SunVault, and Centrica Distributed Energy Resources Management System enable aggregators to bid DER flexibility into wholesale electricity markets, providing asset owners with revenue streams from their battery systems and EV chargers while delivering grid stabilisation services to network operators.

Regional Example: *Smart Grid and Smart Metering Across the Gulf Cooperation Council.*

The Gulf Cooperation Council states have become a leading region for Advanced Metering Infrastructure deployment, driven by energy subsidy reform and sustainability commitments embedded in national Vision programmes. Dubai Electricity and Water Authority (DEWA) reported the installation of over 2 million electricity and water smart meters, with meters monitored remotely at 15-minute intervals through DEWA's smart metering infrastructure. The programme supports remote monitoring, consumption visibility, leak detection, operational efficiency, and smarter utility management, and has enabled dynamic tariff structures that incentivise off-peak consumption. Saudi Electricity Company (SEC) launched the National Smart Meter Programme targeting 10 million smart meters by 2025, underpinned by the Vision 2030 National Energy Services Company (TARSHID) efficiency mandate. In Oman, the Authority for Public Services Regulation (APSR) has integrated smart metering data into medium-term demand forecasting for Oman Power and Water Procurement Company (OPWP), improving load-profile granularity across the sultanate's interconnected grid. A cross-GCC challenge has emerged around metering data sovereignty: residential consumption profiles are classified as personal data under Saudi Arabia's Personal Data Protection Law (PDPL 2021) and UAE Federal Decree-Law No. 45/2021, requiring that smart metering data be processed and stored within national cloud infrastructure.

CASE STUDY: Tesla Virtual Power Plant: Aggregating Distributed IoT for Grid Services

South Australia, 2018-Present

The South Australia Virtual Power Plant (VPP), developed by Tesla in partnership with the South Australian Government and energy retailer

Energy Locals, is the largest operational virtual power plant deploying residential IoT at grid scale. The programme installs Tesla Powerwall batteries in up to 50,000 public housing dwellings, each equipped with rooftop solar panels, and connects them to Tesla's Autobidder platform via residential Wi-Fi gateways.

The Autobidder platform continuously monitors the state of charge of each participating Powerwall, the solar generation forecast for each site based on weather predictions, and the real-time electricity wholesale price in the South Australian market. When market conditions favour energy export, Autobidder discharges selected Powerwalls to the grid; when market conditions favour charging, it uses cheap off-peak grid electricity to charge batteries. Participating households receive a bill credit for each charge and discharge cycle, with the programme designed to reduce annual electricity bills by approximately AUD 600 per household.

By 2022, the SA VPP had connected approximately 4,000 households and demonstrated a combined dispatchable capacity of approximately 15 megawatts, with response times of under 100 milliseconds for grid frequency regulation services. A peer-reviewed technical evaluation published in the journal Energies confirmed that the VPP delivered frequency regulation performance comparable to conventional synchronous generators, validating the technical case for IoT-aggregated residential distributed energy resources as grid infrastructure assets.

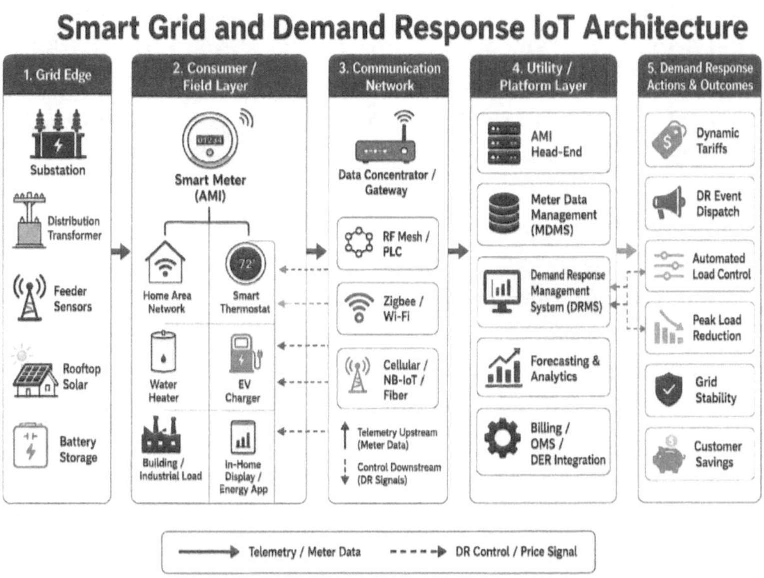

Figure 7.6: Smart Grid and Demand Response IoT Architecture

Table 7.5: Precision Agriculture IoT: Sensor Types, Parameters, and Connectivity Technologies

Sensor Type	Parameter Measured	Connectivity	Application
Soil moisture sensor	Volumetric water content (%)	LoRaWAN, Sigfox	Precision irrigation scheduling
Soil NPK sensor	Nitrogen, phosphorus, potassium	LoRaWAN, cellular	Variable-rate fertiliser application
Weather station	Temperature, humidity, wind, rain	Wi-Fi, cellular	Micro-climate modelling, spray planning
Multispectral UAV camera	NDVI, chlorophyll index, LAI	Wi-Fi (data offload)	Crop health mapping, yield estimation
Livestock ear tag	Activity, rumination, temperature	LoRaWAN, BLE to hub	Health monitoring, oestrus detection
Water flow meter	Irrigation volume (m3)	LoRaWAN, NB-IoT	Water use auditing, leak detection
Grain bin sensor	Temperature, humidity, CO2	LoRaWAN, cellular	Post-harvest storage quality monitoring

7.7 Retail, Logistics, and Supply Chain IoT

The retail and logistics sectors collectively constitute one of the largest IoT application domains by device count and economic value. The global supply chain, which moves trillions of dollars of goods annually from producers through distribution networks to consumers, depends on visibility: knowing where inventory is, what condition it is in, and when it will arrive. IoT provides this visibility through a combination of Radio-Frequency Identification (RFID), Global Positioning System (GPS), sensor networks, and cloud analytics that transform opaque, document-driven supply chains into transparent, data-rich networks where the status of every pallet, container, and vehicle is known in real time.

7.7.1 Retail IoT: Smart Stores and Customer Experience

The Amazon Go concept, introduced in Seattle in 2018 and subsequently expanded across the United States, United Kingdom, and other markets, represents the most complete expression of a fully autonomous retail IoT system. Amazon Go stores use a combination of overhead computer vision cameras, shelf weight sensors, and deep learning algorithms to identify which products customers take from shelves and charge their Amazon account automatically when they leave. There is no checkout process: the system identifies customers through their Amazon app at the entrance, tracks their movement and item selections throughout the store, and processes payment without any human interaction.

The technical infrastructure of Amazon Go is an extreme example, but the underlying IoT capabilities it employs are being adopted in more incremental forms across mainstream retail. Smart shelving, which uses weight sensors or capacitive sensors to detect inventory levels on individual shelf facings, enables continuous inventory visibility that eliminates out-of-stock events. A study by IHL Group estimated that out-of-stocks cost global retailers approximately USD 1 trillion annually in lost sales. IoT-based shelf monitoring systems from vendors including Trigo, Focal Systems, and Invisionbi are being piloted by major grocery chains to provide real-time inventory alerts that trigger restocking tasks before shelves empty.

Customer footfall and flow analytics using Bluetooth Low Energy beacons, Wi-Fi probe tracking, and computer vision provides retailers with detailed understanding of how shoppers navigate stores, which display fixtures attract attention, and which areas are chronically under-visited. This data drives store layout optimisation decisions that would previously have required expensive physical customer observation studies. Privacy regulations in the EU and California restrict the collection of location data without explicit consent, and responsible implementations use anonymised aggregate flow data rather than tracking identified individuals.

CASE STUDY: Amazon Go: Autonomous Checkout Using Computer Vision and IoT

Seattle, USA, and Multiple Markets, 2018-Present

Amazon Go stores deploy ceiling-mounted camera arrays at a density of approximately one camera per 1.5 square metres, combined with weight sensors on every shelf facing and a deep learning computer vision pipeline running on edge computing hardware embedded in the store ceiling. The system tracks approximately 100 million events per day in a single 185 square metre store, including customer entry, product selection, item replacement, and customer exit.

The computer vision pipeline uses multi-view 3D reconstruction to determine which of up to 3,000 SKUs a customer has taken from or returned to the shelf. The system must handle edge cases including two customers reaching for the same product simultaneously, products placed in incorrect locations, and customers who obscure their shopping basket contents. Amazon has not published its overall accuracy figures, but operational reports indicate a small number of post-transaction corrections are applied through the Just Walk Out support process.

The commercial model has proved challenging to scale beyond small convenience store formats. Amazon closed a number of Amazon Go Grocery locations in 2023, citing operational complexity at larger store sizes, and pivoted to licensing the Just Walk Out technology to third-party retailers including airport concessions operators and sports stadium vendors.

As of 2024, Just Walk Out technology is deployed in over 70 third-party locations globally, demonstrating that the technology has commercial value beyond Amazon's own retail operations.

7.7.2 RFID and Inventory Intelligence

Radio Frequency Identification technology is the foundational sensor technology of modern supply chain and retail IoT. An RFID system consists of tags, readers, and a middleware platform. RFID tags are passive (battery-free, powered by the reader's electromagnetic field) or active (battery-powered for longer read ranges and real-time location tracking). Passive UHF RFID tags operating at 860-960 MHz (Electronic Product Code (EPC) Gen2, ISO 18000-63) are the standard for supply chain applications, offering read ranges of 3 to 12 metres at unit costs below USD 0.10 for high-volume applications. This price point makes item-level tagging economically viable for high-velocity consumer goods.

DEFINITION: RFID (Radio Frequency Identification)

A technology that uses electromagnetic fields to automatically identify and track tags attached to objects. An RFID reader emits RF energy that powers passive tags in its field; the tags respond with their unique identifier and any stored data. RFID enables non-line-of-sight reading of multiple tags simultaneously, making it the standard technology for automated inventory counting and supply chain tracking at item, case, and pallet level.

Source: EPCglobal / GS1 EPC Gen2 Standard; ISO 18000-63

Walmart's mandate to its top suppliers to implement RFID item-level tagging across apparel categories, announced in 2020 and progressively expanded, is the most significant deployment of item-level RFID in retail history. By 2023, Walmart required RFID tags on more than 30 apparel and accessories categories in its US stores, enabling automated cycle counting using handheld RFID readers that can count an entire store's apparel inventory in hours rather than the days required for manual barcode scanning. The programme has delivered inventory accuracy improvements from approximately 65 percent under manual counting to over 95 percent under RFID counting, directly translating to reduced out-of-stock rates and improved sales.

7.7.3 Cold Chain Monitoring and Logistics IoT

The cold chain, the temperature-controlled supply chain required for fresh food, vaccines, pharmaceuticals, and biological materials, represents one of the most safety-critical applications of logistics IoT. Temperature excursions during transit or storage that raise product above its maximum recommended temperature, even briefly, can render vaccines ineffective, accelerate food spoilage, or compromise the efficacy of biological medicines. WHO estimates that 25 percent of vaccines arrive at health facilities in developing countries having experienced at least one temperature excursion during distribution, contributing to millions of preventable disease cases annually.

DEFINITION: Cold Chain

The temperature-controlled supply chain required for perishable goods, vaccines, pharmaceuticals, and biological materials. An intact cold chain maintains specified temperature ranges from production through storage and distribution to the point of use. IoT enables continuous real-time temperature monitoring at every stage, replacing periodic manual checks that may miss brief but damaging temperature excursions.

Source: WHO / UNICEF Cold Chain Equipment Optimisation Platform; IATA CEIV Pharma

IoT cold chain monitoring systems use Bluetooth Low Energy data loggers placed inside refrigerated containers, pallet-level cellular loggers for road transport, and cloud platforms that aggregate data from all monitoring points and generate alerts when temperature thresholds are exceeded. Sensitech, Emerson Cargo Track, and Roambee are leading commercial providers. The most sophisticated systems use machine learning to predict temperature excursion risk based on current ambient conditions, transit history, and door-opening frequency, enabling proactive interventions before thresholds are breached rather than reactive responses after the fact.

The COVID-19 vaccine distribution programme created the most challenging cold chain IoT problem in history. Pfizer-BioNTech's mRNA vaccine required storage at -70 degrees Celsius, while Moderna's vaccine required -20 degrees Celsius, temperatures that exceeded the specifications of most existing pharmaceutical cold chain infrastructure.

The global vaccine rollout in 2021 deployed purpose-built IoT temperature monitoring systems at hundreds of thousands of vaccination centres, warehouses, and distribution hubs, many of them using satellite connectivity to provide monitoring visibility in locations without reliable cellular coverage. The success of the mRNA vaccine distribution, which vaccinated over 5 billion people by end of 2022, demonstrated the operational resilience of large-scale cold chain IoT infrastructure under unprecedented pressure.

CASE STUDY: Maersk Remote Container Management: IoT on the High Seas

Copenhagen, Denmark, and Global, 2017-Present

Maersk's Remote Container Management (RCM) platform provides real-time IoT monitoring of over 380,000 refrigerated shipping containers (reefers) across its global fleet. Each reefer is equipped with sensors monitoring internal air temperature at multiple points, compressor operating parameters, door seal integrity, humidity, and cargo atmosphere composition (CO2 and O2 levels for modified atmosphere shipments of fresh produce).

Readings are transmitted every 15 minutes via the ship's satellite communication system when containers are aboard Maersk vessels, and via cellular networks when containers are in port or inland. The RCM platform's cloud analytics engine processes approximately 2 million sensor readings per day, applying anomaly detection algorithms to identify containers showing early signs of refrigeration system degradation before cargo temperatures are affected. Predictive maintenance alerts dispatched to port engineers when containers arrive have reduced emergency refrigeration repairs by over 15 percent.

The commercial value of the system extends beyond equipment maintenance. Cargo owners can access real-time temperature data for their shipments through the Maersk Captain Peter API, providing the chain-of-custody temperature records required for pharmaceutical and premium food exporters to demonstrate regulatory compliance and product provenance. For high-value pharmaceutical shipments where a single container load may be worth millions of dollars, the ability to demonstrate unbroken cold chain from factory to destination represents a significant commercial differentiator.

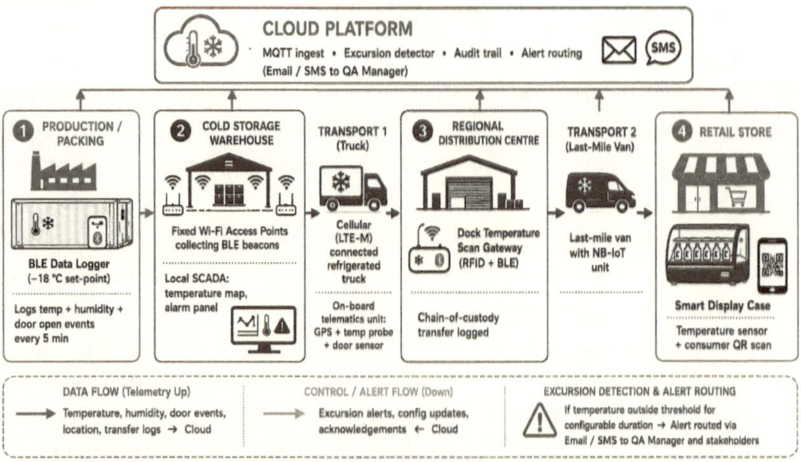

Figure 7.7: Cold Chain IoT Architecture: From Refrigerated Container to Compliance Dashboard

Table 7.6: Logistics and Retail IoT Applications: Technologies and Key Performance Metrics

Application	IoT Technology	Key Metric	Documented Benefit
Item-level inventory management	UHF RFID (EPC Gen2)	Inventory accuracy	65% to 95% accuracy (Walmart apparel)
Cold chain monitoring	BLE loggers, cellular, satellite	Temperature excursion rate	25% reduction in excursion events
Vehicle fleet tracking	GNSS / GPS, 4G cellular	On-time delivery rate	15-25% fuel cost reduction
Smart shelving / out-of-stock	Shelf weight sensors, cameras	Out-of-stock frequency	40-60% reduction in OOS events
Warehouse automation	RFID, Ultra-Wideband (UWB) Real-Time Location System (RTLS), Autonomous Mobile Robot (AMR) robots	Pick rate	3-5x throughput vs manual picking
Last-mile IoT parcel lockers	BLE, cellular, QR code	Failed delivery rate	Near zero (customer self-collection)

7.8 Brownfield versus Greenfield IoT Deployments

One of the most consequential early decisions in any IoT implementation project is whether the deployment context is greenfield, where IoT connectivity is being designed into new-build infrastructure from the outset, or brownfield, where IoT must be integrated into existing infrastructure that was built before IoT considerations existed. This distinction shapes almost every subsequent technical and commercial decision: protocol selection, hardware choices, integration architecture, project timeline, and budget all differ fundamentally between the two contexts. Many real-world deployments are neither purely greenfield nor purely brownfield but hybrid, involving a greenfield IoT data platform receiving data from brownfield-retrofitted legacy systems.

DEFINITION: Greenfield IoT Deployment

The design and construction of an IoT-enabled system from the ground up, where IoT connectivity, data architecture, and security requirements are first-class design constraints from the start. Greenfield deployments benefit from optimal hardware selection, end-to-end protocol standardisation, and security by design, at the cost of higher upfront capital expenditure and a longer period before the first operational data is available.

Source: Guth et al. (2016)

DEFINITION: Brownfield IoT Deployment

The integration of IoT capabilities into existing physical infrastructure

that was not designed with IoT connectivity in mind. Brownfield deployments typically require protocol bridging gateways, retrofit sensor attachments that extract data from legacy equipment without modifying it, and data normalisation middleware that translates proprietary data formats into IoT platform-compatible representations.

Source: Guth et al. (2016)

Brownfield IoT integration in industrial settings confronts a particularly complex technical landscape. A manufacturing facility built in the 1990s may contain CNC machines communicating over RS-232 serial, PLCs using Modbus RTU over RS-485, a SCADA system receiving data over proprietary vendor protocols, and older equipment with no digital output at all. Each layer of this legacy stack requires a different integration approach.

For equipment with digital outputs but proprietary protocols, an industrial IoT gateway running protocol translation software can bridge the existing interface to MQTT or OPC-UA. For equipment with only analogue outputs such as 4-20mA current loops, signal conditioners convert the analogue signal to digital. For completely analogue or mechanical equipment, non-invasive sensing methods such as clamp-on current transformers, vibration sensors attached to motor housings, and acoustic emission sensors mounted on pipe flanges can extract operational data without any modification to the original equipment.

The commercial case for brownfield IoT integration is often stronger in the short term than for greenfield, because brownfield projects can generate immediate returns by instrumenting existing revenue-generating assets rather than waiting for new infrastructure to be built and commissioned. A chemical plant that retrofits vibration and temperature sensors on its existing pump fleet can begin generating predictive maintenance value within weeks of sensor installation. A retail chain that deploys RFID readers at its existing store entry and exit points can immediately improve inventory accuracy on its existing product range. The technical complexity and integration cost are higher than for greenfield, but the time-to-value can be substantially shorter.

CASE STUDY: Retrofitting a Legacy Oil Refinery with Predictive Maintenance IoT

Gulf Region, 2020-2022 (Composite Case)

A major Middle Eastern oil refinery operating since the 1980s undertook a brownfield IoT retrofit programme to implement predictive maintenance on its rotating equipment fleet of 4,800 pumps, compressors, and motors. The facility's existing instrumentation included process control sensors feeding a legacy DCS system, but the rotating equipment had no condition monitoring instrumentation beyond periodic manual vibration readings taken by maintenance technicians on monthly rounds.

The integration approach deployed wireless vibration and temperature transmitters from Emerson AMS Wireless SNAP-ON devices, mounted on motor housings and bearing housings without modifying the underlying equipment. These transmitters communicated over WirelessHART to gateway devices installed on pipe racks throughout the facility, which forwarded data to an on-premises OSIsoft PI historian and then to an Azure-hosted cloud analytics platform. The entire instrumentation and gateway installation was completed in eight months without any process shutdown, as all work was performed on operating equipment.

Within 18 months of commissioning, the predictive maintenance system had identified and facilitated the repair of 23 pump and compressor bearing defects before failure, with an estimated avoided production loss value of USD 7.2 million. The programme paid back its USD 2.1 million installation cost within the first year of operation and demonstrated a benefit-cost ratio of 3.4:1 over the three-year evaluation period, providing a compelling Return on Investment (ROI) case for extension across the remainder of the facility's rotating equipment population.

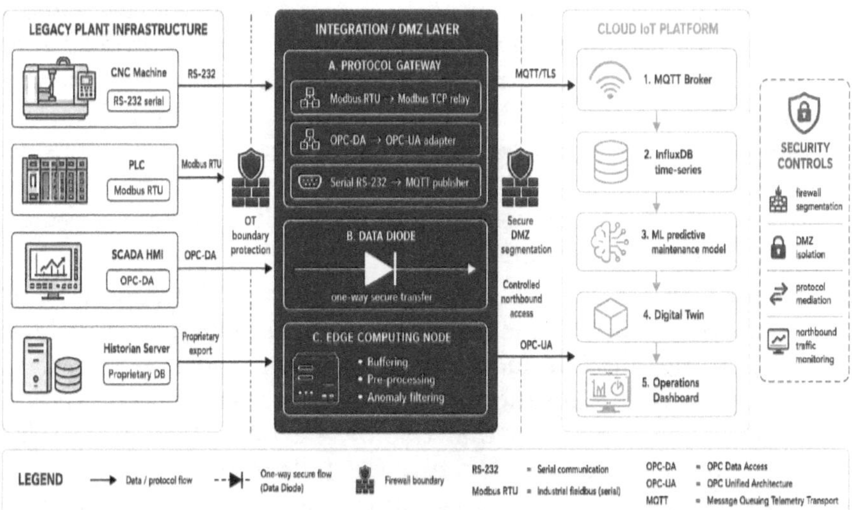

Figure 7.8: Brownfield IoT Integration Architecture for Legacy Industrial Equipment

Table 7.7: Brownfield Versus Greenfield IoT Deployment: Comparative Analysis Across Seven Dimensions

Dimension	Brownfield Deployment	Greenfield Deployment
Infrastructure baseline	Existing legacy systems with proprietary protocols	New build; no legacy constraints
Integration complexity	High; protocol bridging, data normalisation required	Low; standardised protocols from design
Time to first data	Short (weeks to months; retrofit sensors)	Long (months to years; full construction)
Capital cost profile	Lower upfront; phased investment possible	Higher upfront; full system investment
Security posture	Often weak in legacy OT; difficult to patch	Security by design from the outset
Scalability	Limited by legacy system constraints	Unlimited if designed for scale
Typical sector	Oil and gas, manufacturing, older buildings	New smart buildings, digital-native factories

7.9 The Four Business Dimensions Framework

A recurring finding in IoT deployment literature and practitioner reports is that the majority of IoT initiatives that fail to deliver their projected return on investment do so not because of technical failure but because of inadequate attention to the non-technical dimensions of the deployment: the process changes required to act on IoT data, the organisational capabilities needed to sustain the system, and the data governance arrangements that determine whether the right people have access to the right data at the right time. The Four Business Dimensions framework, synthesised from the literature on IoT value creation and digital transformation, provides a structured vocabulary for analysing these non-technical success factors alongside the technical dimension.

The four dimensions are Technology, Data and Analytics, Process, and Organisation. Each dimension represents a distinct layer of the IoT value creation stack, and deficiency in any one dimension can prevent value realisation even when the other three are well executed. An organisation that deploys technically excellent IoT sensors and analytics infrastructure but fails to redesign the maintenance processes that should act on predictive maintenance alerts will not reduce machine downtime. An organisation that successfully redesigns processes but lacks the workforce skills to interpret analytics outputs will not sustain the improvement. The framework is not a sequential checklist but a set of interdependent investment dimensions that must be balanced.

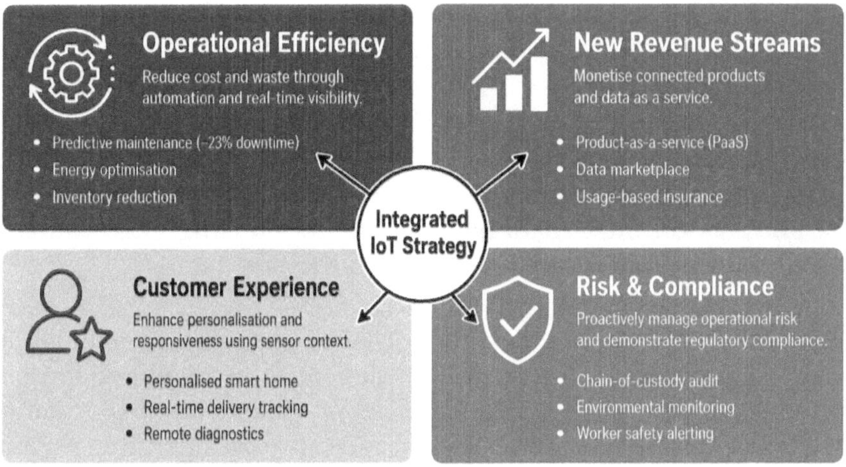

Figure 7.9: The Four Business Dimensions Framework for IoT Value Creation

7.9.1 Technology Dimension

The Technology dimension encompasses all hardware, connectivity, and software platform components of the IoT system. This is the dimension that receives the most attention in technical literature and vendor marketing, and it is the dimension where practitioners typically have the greatest confidence and clarity. Selecting appropriate sensors for the physical environment, choosing connectivity technologies matched to the data rate and power budget requirements, architecting a scalable cloud platform, and implementing security controls are all Technology dimension activities.

The Technology dimension also includes the critical decision of build versus buy: whether to assemble a custom IoT platform from open-source components or to adopt a commercial IoT platform such as PTC ThingWorx, Siemens MindSphere, AWS IoT Core, Microsoft Azure IoT, or Google Cloud IoT. Commercial platforms reduce development time and provide managed infrastructure that scales with deployment, but they introduce vendor lock-in risks and recurring subscription costs that must be factored into long-term business cases. Open-source platforms such as Eclipse IoT, FIWARE Orion, and OpenRemote offer greater flexibility and independence but require internal engineering capability to deploy and maintain.

7.9.2 Data and Analytics Dimension

The Data and Analytics dimension is where the raw sensor data collected by the Technology layer is transformed into the information and insights that drive decisions and actions. This dimension encompasses data architecture (how IoT data is stored, governed, and accessed), analytics engineering (the development of algorithms and models that process the data), and data literacy (the organisational capability to interpret and act on analytical outputs).

A common failure mode in the Data and Analytics dimension is the creation of data silos: organisations that deploy multiple IoT systems in different business units but store their data in incompatible formats on incompatible platforms, preventing cross-domain analysis that might reveal the most valuable insights.

A manufacturing company that stores machine sensor data in an OSIsoft PI historian, quality measurement data in a separate SQL database, and energy consumption data in a utility billing system cannot easily correlate machine operating parameters with quality outcomes and energy consumption to identify the operating regime that simultaneously maximises quality and minimises energy cost. Breaking down these data silos through a unified data lake or common data model is often the highest-value data architecture investment an organisation can make.

7.9.3 Process Dimension

The Process dimension is the most commonly under-estimated in IoT investment planning and the most frequently cited root cause of IoT deployment failure. Deploying IoT sensors and analytics is necessary but insufficient: value is created only when someone or something acts differently because of the IoT data. This requires redesigned processes that integrate IoT data into the workflows through which the organisation makes decisions and delivers services.

Consider predictive maintenance: the technology layer delivers a vibration anomaly alert indicating that a bearing on Pump P-12 is showing early signs of fatigue. For this alert to prevent an unplanned pump failure, the following process chain must function: the alert must be routed to the correct maintenance technician; the technician must have the knowledge to interpret the alert and assess its urgency; the spare part required for the repair must be in the maintenance stores or quickly procurable; the maintenance management system must generate and schedule a work order; and the pump must be available for maintenance within the window between alert generation and projected failure. If any link in this process chain is broken, the IoT investment delivers no value, regardless of the technical quality of the sensor and analytics system.

7.9.4 Organisation Dimension

The Organisation dimension addresses the human, cultural, and governance elements that determine whether an IoT deployment is sustained and scaled beyond its initial pilot phase. IoT deployments require new skills that most organisations do not possess internally at the outset: IoT systems engineers, data engineers, data scientists, and operational technology security specialists are all in high demand and short supply globally. Organisations that plan for training and talent development from the outset of an IoT programme, rather than assuming existing staff will absorb the new capabilities, consistently outperform those that treat workforce development as an afterthought.

Change management is perhaps the most frequently overlooked organisational investment in IoT programmes. Maintenance technicians whose jobs are changing from scheduled time-based routines to condition-based responses triggered by analytics alerts are experiencing a significant change in their work patterns and, potentially, their professional identity. If these changes are not carefully managed, with clear communication of the rationale, adequate training, and recognition of the increased skills now required, resistance to the IoT system and continued reliance on legacy practices can undermine even technically excellent deployments.

Table 7.8: The Four Business Dimensions: Characteristics, Common Failure Modes, and Key Success Factors

Dimension	Core Activities	Common Failure Mode	Key Success Factor
Technology	Sensor selection, connectivity, platform, security	Over-engineering; vendor lock-in; security gaps	Fit-for-purpose selection; security by design
Data and Analytics	Data architecture, analytics models, data governance	Data silos; poor data quality; lack of insight	Unified data model; cross-domain integration
Process	Workflow redesign, alert-to-action integration	Alerts not acted on; process not redesigned	Process map before deployment; accountability
Organisation	Skills, change management, governance, ROI tracking	Talent shortage; change resistance; no ownership	Workforce plan; change champions; executive sponsorship

7.10 Chapter Summary

This chapter has demonstrated that IoT value is generated at the intersection of domain-specific sensing, scalable connectivity, and purposeful data analytics, applied by organisations with the process discipline and workforce capability to act on what their data reveals. Nine application domains have been examined in depth, each illustrating a different facet of this value creation story.

Smart home and building automation have moved from enthusiast projects to mainstream consumer products, with the Matter standard beginning to resolve a decade of ecosystem fragmentation. The Edge Building in Amsterdam and the Samsung SmartThings Matter integration demonstrate the commercial maturity of smart building IoT across both residential and commercial scales. Protocol diversity, from Zigbee and Z-Wave to BLE and Thread, reflects the heterogeneous nature of the domestic environment, while KNX and BACnet continue to anchor commercial building automation.

Smart cities represent IoT at its most ambitious scale, federating transport, utilities, environment, and public safety subsystems through a shared Urban Data Platform. Singapore's Smart Nation programme and Barcelona's Superblocks initiative demonstrate that smart city IoT, when driven by clear policy objectives and rigorous outcome measurement, delivers measurable improvements in urban quality of life, energy efficiency, and environmental conditions. The governance and data sovereignty challenges of smart city data platforms are examined in depth in Chapter 9.

Industrial IoT and Industry 4.0 have generated the most clearly documented return on investment of any IoT application domain, through predictive maintenance, digital factory instrumentation, and the IT/OT convergence that enables analytics to be applied to operational data at production-line granularity. The Siemens Amberg facility and Rolls-Royce TotalCare programme are exemplary cases of how IoT data transforms not just operational efficiency but the fundamental commercial models through which industrial value is exchanged.

Connected healthcare IoT carries the greatest direct human consequence of any application domain. From Abbott FreeStyle Libre continuous glucose monitoring to the NHS Remote Patient Monitoring programme for COVID-19 virtual wards, IoT is enabling a structural shift from episodic clinical encounters to continuous health surveillance. The regulatory complexity of healthcare IoT, spanning FDA SaMD guidance, GDPR Article 9, and HIPAA, demands that data governance and security are designed in from the first architecture decision.

Precision agriculture, environmental monitoring, and smart grid management share the challenge of deploying sensor networks at geographic scale with minimal power and connectivity infrastructure. John Deere's Operations Center, the AirQo network in sub-Saharan Africa, and the Tesla Virtual Power Plant in South Australia each represent a different point on the spectrum from commercial agricultural optimisation to community environmental intelligence to grid-scale energy flexibility. In all three domains, LoRaWAN and NB-IoT provide the long-range, low-power connectivity that makes geographic-scale IoT economically viable.

Retail and logistics IoT, from Amazon Go's autonomous checkout to Maersk's Remote Container Management and Walmart's RFID inventory programme, demonstrate that supply chain visibility at the item level is commercially transformative. Cold chain IoT carries safety and regulatory implications that rival healthcare in their seriousness, particularly for vaccine distribution in low-resource settings where temperature excursions have historically undermined immunisation programme effectiveness.

The brownfield versus greenfield deployment distinction is perhaps the most practically consequential concept in this chapter for the practising engineer. The majority of commercial IoT value in the near term will be generated from brownfield retrofit deployments, because most of the world's revenue-generating infrastructure is already built. Understanding the integration patterns, protocol bridging approaches, and time-to-value dynamics of brownfield IoT is therefore a higher-priority competency for most practitioners than greenfield design skills, though both are essential elements of a complete IoT engineering education.

The Four Business Dimensions framework provides the conceptual anchor for everything in this chapter and for the governance and strategy content that follows in Chapters 8 and 9. Technology alone does not deliver IoT value. Data without analytics culture produces dashboards no one looks at. Analytics without process redesign generates alerts no one acts on. Process redesign without organisational investment produces workflows that revert to legacy practices within months. The chapters that follow examine the security, governance, and future technology dimensions that complete the picture of what it takes to deploy IoT systems that are not just technically sound but operationally sustainable and strategically valuable. Chapter 11 extends this picture to the frontier of machine learning and artificial intelligence integration, examining how techniques such as on-device TinyML inference, federated learning across distributed industrial assets, and reinforcement learning-based control optimisation amplify IoT value across the application domains explored in this chapter.

Part IV

Security, Governance, and Future Directions

Chapter 8

IoT Security: Threats, Mechanisms, and Best Practices

Protecting Devices, Data, and Deployments Across the Full System Lifecycle

Chapter 8 examines IoT security as a fundamental design requirement for connected systems operating across devices, networks, gateways, platforms, and applications. It explains why IoT security differs from conventional IT security, particularly due to constrained hardware, long device lifecycles, physical exposure, heterogeneous protocols, large-scale deployment, and the convergence of operational technology with enterprise systems. The chapter presents a structured vulnerability and threat taxonomy, mapping risks such as weak authentication, insecure firmware, exposed APIs, data interception, device spoofing, denial-of-service attacks, and supply chain weaknesses to the IoT architecture. It also explains key security mechanisms including device identity, authentication, authorisation, encryption, secure boot, PKI, certificate management, OTA updates, and privacy-by-design principles. In addition, the chapter highlights best practices and operational security frameworks required to protect IoT deployments throughout their lifecycle. Overall, this chapter provides the security foundation needed to design trustworthy IoT systems that preserve confidentiality, integrity, availability, privacy, and resilience in real-world deployment environments.

In March 2021, a security researcher scanning the open internet discovered that a default-credential Hikvision IP camera installed in a UK water treatment facility was accessible without authentication. The camera's administrative interface, reachable over port 80 from any IP address on the internet, provided a live view of the facility's control room and, through the same interface, access to the configuration settings of the SCADA terminal visible on screen. The researcher notified the facility and the camera vendor. Subsequent investigation revealed that the device had been in that state for at least 14 months, running firmware from 2018 with three published

CVEs, with its factory-default credentials unchanged since installation.

This was not an unusual incident. It was representative. The UK's National Cyber Security Centre estimated in 2022 that more than 800,000 internet-connected devices in the UK alone were accessible via default or easily guessable credentials. The Shodan search engine, which continuously indexes internet-accessible devices, reports millions of IoT devices globally with exposed management interfaces, unencrypted data streams, and known unpatched vulnerabilities. The Mirai botnet (which in 2016 recruited over 600,000 IoT devices using only factory-default credential exploitation) demonstrated that this exposure is not merely theoretical: it is operationally weaponised, at scale, continuously.

Chapter 8 addresses IoT security with the rigour that the threat environment demands. It begins by explaining why IoT security is different from enterprise IT security — not merely harder, but structurally different in ways that require adapted rather than imported defences. It then presents the four-category vulnerability taxonomy that provides the chapter's analytical framework, examines the technical mechanisms for device identity and authentication, covers encryption and data-in-transit protection, maps the threat landscape from physical attacks through network exploitation to malware, and concludes with the engineering and operational best practices that translate security principles into defensible deployments.

8.1 Why IoT Security is Different

The information security principles underlying IoT security are not new. Confidentiality, integrity, and availability, the CIA triad, have been the organising framework of information security since the 1970s. Cryptographic protocols for authentication and data protection have been maturing since the 1990s. The discipline of threat modelling has produced systematic, repeatable methodologies applicable to any technology domain. The question is not whether these principles apply to IoT, they do, but why their application to IoT is so consistently inadequate, producing the exposure described in the opening scenario with dispiriting regularity.

The answer lies not in the cryptography but in the deployment context. Six structural characteristics of IoT deployments combine to make standard enterprise security approaches insufficient, and understanding these six characteristics is the prerequisite for designing security that actually works.

8.1.1 Resource Constraints

Conventional IT security mechanisms were designed for hardware with abundant computational resources. A server running Transport Layer Security (TLS) with a full certificate chain and an intrusion detection system in parallel has access to gigabytes of memory and gigahertz of multi-core processing power.

A 32-bit microcontroller running at 16 MHz with 2 KB of RAM: a specification representative of billions of deployed IoT devices has a fundamentally different security budget. It can perform symmetric encryption (Advanced Encryption Standard, AES-128) reasonably efficiently. Full asymmetric key exchange (Rivest–Shamir–Adleman, RSA-2048) may take seconds rather than milliseconds, consuming more energy in a single handshake than the device's battery budget for an entire day. Running an intrusion detection system is simply not possible.

Resource constraints force security design choices that do not arise in enterprise IT. The cipher suite must be selected not only for cryptographic strength but for energy cost per bit encrypted. Authentication protocols must be chosen for code size as well as security properties. Certificate validation may need to be simplified or replaced with certificate pinning because full certificate chain validation requires memory that the device does not have. These are not failures of security ambition; they are engineering constraints that must be acknowledged and addressed through design rather than ignored.

DEFINITION: Attack Surface

The total collection of different points (hardware interfaces, software entry points, communication channels, and management interfaces) through which an unauthorised party can attempt to enter, manipulate, or extract data from an IoT system. Security engineering begins with mapping the attack surface; every reduction in attack surface is a security improvement even if no specific vulnerability is known.

8.1.2 Heterogeneity and Scale

Enterprise IT environments, while complex, tend toward homogeneity: a few operating system versions, a manageable set of application platforms, and centralised patch management that can push a security update to every Windows machine in the estate simultaneously. IoT deployments are structurally heterogeneous: thousands of device types from hundreds of manufacturers, running proprietary operating systems, custom firmware, and embedded stacks developed over decades by teams with varying security competence. A large city's smart infrastructure may incorporate IoT devices from 50 or more different vendors, each with its own update mechanism, credential management approach, and vulnerability disclosure practice.

At the scale of typical IoT deployments, tens of thousands to millions of devices, human-administered security management is not feasible. A security team that can maintain security hygiene across 10,000 servers cannot manually manage the firmware versions, credential rotation schedules, and security configurations of 500,000 sensors. Automated, policy-based security management is not an efficiency gain in IoT; it is a fundamental necessity. This automation requirement introduces its own attack surface: a compromised IoT management platform can simultaneously reconfigure or disable the security of every device it manages.

8.1.3 Physical Exposure

Corporate IT assets are physically secured: servers in locked data centres, workstations in access-controlled offices, network equipment in closed cabinets. IoT devices are routinely deployed in publicly accessible locations — streetlights, building facades, agricultural fields, vehicles, hospital wards, retail floors. Physical accessibility fundamentally changes the security model. An attacker with physical access to a device can read flash memory directly by desoldering the storage chip, extract private keys through power analysis of the power supply line, access firmware through exposed Joint Test Action Group (JTAG) debug ports, or simply replace the legitimate device with a malicious clone.

Physical security for IoT requires hardware-level countermeasures: tamper-evident enclosures that make physical intrusion detectable, tamper-detection circuits that erase cryptographic keys if the device casing is opened, potted circuit boards that prevent chip desoldering, and debug interfaces disabled in production firmware. These measures add cost and complexity but are necessary for deployments in environments where physical access cannot be controlled, which is most IoT deployments.

8.1.4 Long Device Lifetimes

Enterprise IT equipment is typically refreshed every three to five years, limiting the window during which a vulnerability discovered after deployment can be exploited before the affected hardware is retired. IoT devices operate on very different economics. Smart meters are designed for 15-year deployments. Industrial sensors are routinely operated for 20 years or more. Medical implants such as pacemakers may be in service for a decade without replacement. A vulnerability discovered seven years after an IoT device's manufacture may affect tens of millions of still-operational devices, running firmware that the original developer may no longer support, on hardware whose manufacturer may no longer exist.

Long device lifetimes create an obligation that is rarely met in practice: the ability to update device security throughout its entire operational life. This requires that the device be designed with an over-the-air (OTA) firmware update capability before it ships, and that the manufacturer commit to providing security patches for the full deployment lifetime. Neither requirement is currently universal. The EU Cyber Resilience Act, discussed further in Section 8.8, addresses this gap by imposing legal obligations on manufacturers of connected products to provide security updates throughout the expected product lifetime.

8.1.5 Safety Criticality

The consequences of security failure differ fundamentally between IT and IoT contexts. Compromising an enterprise mail server results in data loss or exposure: a serious business harm, but not a physical one. Compromising an IoT device in a safety-critical context can result in physical harm or death. The 2021 Oldsmar, Florida water treatment plant attack, in which an attacker remotely increased sodium hydroxide (lye) concentration to 111 times safe levels through a compromised SCADA interface, illustrated how OT-connected IoT can become a mechanism for direct physical harm. The 2017 Triton/TRISIS attack against a Saudi Arabian petrochemical facility targeted the facility's safety instrumented systems, the last line of defence against industrial accidents, demonstrating that adversaries specifically target safety systems to prevent emergency shutdown when initiating destructive attacks.

Key Insight: Why Enterprise Security Playbooks Fail in IoT. IoT's six structural differences from enterprise IT — constrained hardware, physical exposure, long operational lifetimes, absence of user interaction, heterogeneous protocol stacks, and safety-critical consequences — mean that every enterprise security tool and methodology must be re-evaluated before application.

The Mirai botnet compromised over 600,000 devices through unchecked factory-default credentials: a failure that enterprise credential management tooling had no visibility of, because it had no visibility of the IoT estate at all. Security for IoT must be designed at device manufacturing and architecture, not applied retrospectively by network tooling that was designed for a different threat model. Every security property (identity, encryption, access control, update capability) must be specified as a device requirement before the first line of firmware is written.

Safety criticality elevates the security design requirements for industrial, healthcare, and critical infrastructure IoT beyond what commercial risk management alone would justify. When the consequence of a successful attack includes loss of life or mass casualty events, the standard cost-benefit calculus of security investment does not apply. Security is a safety requirement in these contexts, with the regulatory weight and engineering discipline that safety requirements carry in their respective industries.

DEFINITION: Threat Model

A structured analysis identifying the threats applicable to a system, the assets they target, the vulnerabilities they exploit, and the countermeasures appropriate to each. In IoT security engineering, the threat model is the starting point for every security design decision. The STRIDE framework (Spoofing, Tampering, Repudiation, Information Disclosure, Denial of Service, Elevation of Privilege) and the PASTA methodology (Process for Attack Simulation and Threat Analysis) are commonly applied to IoT systems.

The table below formalises the contrast between IT security and IoT security across six dimensions that every IoT security architect should internalise. These are not qualitative differences of degree; they are structural differences that demand adapted rather than imported solutions.

Security Dimension	Enterprise IT	IoT Deployment
Hardware capability	Multi-GHz multi-core processors, GBs of RAM; full cryptographic stack feasible	MHz-range MCUs, KBs of RAM; cipher suites and protocol stacks must be carefully selected for energy and memory budget
Physical access control	Servers and networking equipment in locked, monitored data centres and server rooms	Devices deployed in fields, buildings, streets, vehicles; physical access by adversaries is routinely possible
Device lifetime	3–5 year refresh cycle limits vulnerability exposure window	10–20 year deployment; vulnerabilities discovered years post-manufacture affect millions of operational devices
Fleet homogeneity	Managed OS/application fleet; centralised patch management feasible	Thousands of device types, hundreds of vendors, diverse firmware stacks; uniform patch management impractical

Update frequency	Monthly or more frequent security patches; automated distribution mature	Irregular or absent updates; OTA capability frequently not designed in; no universal update standard
Failure consequences	Data loss, service disruption, financial harm	Physical equipment damage, industrial accidents, healthcare patient harm, critical infrastructure disruption

Table 8.1: Enterprise IT Security Versus IoT Security: Six Structural Differences

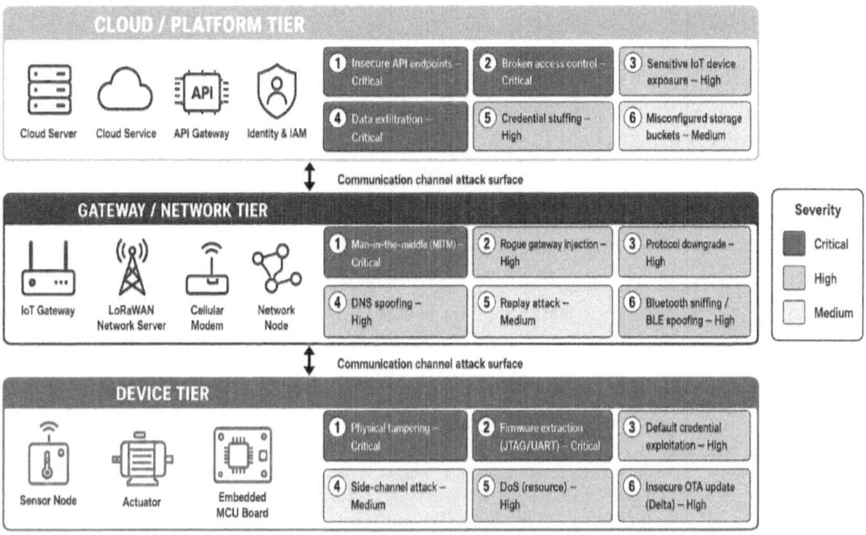

Figure 8.1: IoT Attack Surface: Vulnerability Points Mapped to the Three-Tier Architecture

8.2 IoT Vulnerability Taxonomy: The Four Categories

A vulnerability is a weakness in a system that can be exploited by a threat actor to gain unauthorised access, cause damage, or extract information. Distinguishing vulnerabilities from threats is analytically important: vulnerabilities are properties of the system that can be addressed through design and engineering; threats are attack actions taken by adversaries that exploit those vulnerabilities.

This section catalogues IoT vulnerabilities using the four-category framework that has become the industry standard for structured IoT security assessment. The four categories (Communication, Physical, Software, and Connection Lifecycle) provide a complete and non-overlapping taxonomy that maps every known class of IoT vulnerability to a category amenable to a specific class of remediation.

8.2.1 Communication Vulnerabilities

DEFINITION: Communication Vulnerability

A weakness arising from the communication interfaces and protocols used by IoT devices to transmit data. Communication vulnerabilities expose IoT systems to eavesdropping, man-in-the-middle attacks, message injection, replay attacks, and denial-of-service attacks targeting the communication channel.

Unencrypted data transmission remains one of the most prevalent IoT vulnerabilities, despite being entirely preventable. Early MQTT deployments widely used port 1883 (unencrypted) rather than port 8883 (MQTT over TLS). Many legacy Modbus TCP implementations transmit industrial process data in cleartext over corporate IP networks. Zigbee deployments without mandatory AES-128 link encryption transmit sensor readings that any device within radio range can capture. An attacker with a passive RF receiver and freely available software-defined radio tools can intercept and decode these transmissions without any active attack, simply by listening.

Weak or absent authentication in communication protocols allows device impersonation and rogue device injection. An IoT broker configured to allow anonymous MQTT connections, a common misconfiguration, will accept subscriptions from any device, allowing an attacker to subscribe to all sensor topics and receive a complete stream of sensor readings. The same misconfiguration permits message injection: an attacker can publish forged commands to actuator topics without any credential. This vulnerability has been documented in smart home systems, industrial automation deployments, and building management systems globally.

Protocol-specific vulnerabilities include replay attacks against challenge-response authentication schemes, where a captured legitimate authentication exchange can be retransmitted to gain access at a later time if nonces or timestamps are not correctly implemented. CoAP's stateless architecture, designed to minimise memory requirements on constrained devices, means the protocol has no built-in session concept, making it susceptible to spoofed UDP responses if application-layer authentication is not added.

Bluetooth Classic pairing vulnerabilities in legacy implementations allow an attacker within radio range to inject into or eavesdrop on a paired connection; the KNOB (Key Negotiation of Bluetooth) attack demonstrated in 2019 showed that Bluetooth BR/EDR encryption key length could be forced down to 1 byte through a man-in-the-middle manipulation of the pairing process.

8.2.2 Physical Vulnerabilities

DEFINITION: Physical Vulnerability

A weakness arising from physical accessibility of IoT devices and their hardware interfaces. Physical vulnerabilities are exploitable by an attacker with hands-on access to a deployed device, enabling firmware extraction, credential theft, hardware manipulation, and device replacement.

Exposed debug interfaces are among the most easily exploited physical vulnerabilities. JTAG (Joint Test Action Group) and Universal Asynchronous Receiver-Transmitter (UART) serial debug ports, which engineers use during development to inspect firmware operation and debug software, are frequently left enabled in production devices. An attacker with physical access and a freely available logic analyser (under USD 20) can connect to these interfaces, read and write device memory, extract the complete firmware image, inspect encryption keys stored in memory, and execute arbitrary code on the device processor. In a 2020 study of 40 commercial IoT devices by security firm Senrio, 30 were found to have active UART debug ports accessible without tools beyond a USB-UART adapter.

Firmware extraction enables offline analysis of a device's complete software stack. If the device's flash memory chip uses a standard SPI bus interface, common in cost-optimised IoT designs, a clip-on adapter allows direct reading of the chip contents without desoldering. Extracted firmware can be loaded into a binary analysis tool such as Binwalk, Ghidra, or IDA Pro for static analysis: identifying hardcoded credentials, encryption keys, Application Programming Interface (API) tokens, and exploitable vulnerabilities. The knowledge gained from firmware analysis of a single sample device can be applied to every device in the same product family worldwide.

Side-channel attacks extract cryptographic keys not by breaking the algorithm but by observing physical emissions during cryptographic operations. Simple Power Analysis (SPA) and Differential Power Analysis (DPA) measure the power consumption of a device's power supply line while it performs encryption, exploiting the correlation between power consumption patterns and the bit values of the key being used. Electromagnetic analysis (EMA) similarly extracts information from the electromagnetic emissions of the device's processor. These attacks require physical proximity and specialised equipment but are well within the capability of a nation-state adversary or sophisticated criminal organisation targeting high-value IoT systems.

Physical device replacement, swapping a legitimate device for a malicious clone, is a particularly insidious attack in deployments where devices are geographically distributed and individually unmonitored. A malicious clone can report falsified sensor readings (causing a smart meter to under-report energy consumption, a water quality sensor to mask contamination, or a structural integrity sensor to mask damage), intercept and relay communications (functioning as an undetectable man-in-the-middle), or serve as a persistent implant providing ongoing network access to internal systems. Detection requires cryptographic device identity: a device whose identity is anchored in hardware-protected keys that cannot be cloned.

8.2.3 Software Vulnerabilities

DEFINITION: Software Vulnerability

A weakness in the firmware, operating system, or application software running on an IoT device or its supporting infrastructure. Software vulnerabilities are exploitable without physical access, through communication interfaces, and may affect millions of devices simultaneously when a common firmware version or library is found to be vulnerable.

Unpatched firmware is the most prevalent IoT software vulnerability category globally. The OWASP IoT Attack Surface Areas project and the UK NCSC both report that the majority of successfully compromised IoT devices in documented incidents were running firmware with known, published CVEs (Common Vulnerabilities and Exposures) for which patches were available but had not been applied.

The reasons are structural: no user-accessible update mechanism, no automatic update infrastructure, no lifecycle support commitment from the manufacturer, or simply the organisational failure to apply available patches. The Mirai botnet, to which we return in Section 8.5, required no zero-day exploits; it needed only factory-default credentials and telnet access, vulnerabilities that were neither subtle nor novel.

Insecure default credentials — factory-set usernames and passwords that are identical across all units of a product model and published in the product's user manual are the single most exploited IoT vulnerability in documented incident data. A compiled list of default IoT credentials, maintained collaboratively by security researchers, currently contains over 2,000 known device-model-to-credential mappings. Automated scanning tools attempt all combinations against any IoT device with a management interface reachable over the internet, completing a full credential scan against any single target in seconds.

Buffer overflows and memory corruption vulnerabilities arise from IoT firmware that is predominantly written in C, a language with no automatic memory safety. When a firmware function reads input data into a fixed-size buffer without checking that the input is shorter than the buffer, an attacker can supply input longer than the buffer, overwriting adjacent memory and potentially overwriting the function's return address with an attacker-controlled value, achieving arbitrary code execution.

The Heartbleed vulnerability in OpenSSL, exploitable without authentication, and the Log4Shell vulnerability in Apache Log4j, which affected IoT devices incorporating Java-based management interfaces, demonstrate that third-party library vulnerabilities can propagate across millions of nominally independent IoT devices simultaneously.

Hardcoded credentials — encryption keys, API tokens, and passwords embedded directly in firmware binary rather than loaded from secure configuration at runtime are extractable by any attacker who obtains the firmware image. When the same hardcoded credential is present in every device of a product family, a single firmware extraction compromises authentication for the entire fleet. Hardcoded credentials in IoT firmware have been documented in home routers, IP cameras, industrial controllers, medical devices, and smart home hubs across every major vendor category.

8.2.4 Connection Lifecycle Vulnerabilities

DEFINITION: Connection Lifecycle Vulnerability

A weakness arising from inadequate security management across the full device operational life: from initial provisioning through active operation to decommissioning. Connection lifecycle vulnerabilities include insecure device provisioning, absent deprovisioning procedures, stale credential management, and inadequate management of human access to device systems.

Insecure provisioning is the initial configuration of a device's identity credentials: the assignment of its SIM, the injection of its X.509 certificate, the configuration of its API keys. Provisioning is a high-risk operation because a device's security posture for its entire operational lifetime depends on the integrity of its initial credential configuration. Provisioning workflows that assign credentials over unencrypted channels, that use the same credential for all devices being provisioned in a batch, or that are performed by personnel who retain access to provisioned credentials after the provisioning task is complete all represent lifecycle vulnerabilities exploitable to compromise device identity at the root.

Absent deprovisioning is the failure to revoke and scrub a device's credentials when it is retired, sold, repurposed, or stolen. An IoT device that has been physically removed from service but whose SIM remains active, API keys remain valid, and certificates remain unrevoked is a live attack vector: the device, or its credentials, can be used to access the IoT platform as if it were still a legitimate operational device. In cellular IoT, the GSMA has documented cases of decommissioned devices continuing to generate traffic and incur billing charges for months or years after physical removal, indicating that deprovisioning workflows are frequently absent or inconsistently applied.

Stale credential management encompasses the broader failure to rotate and expire credentials throughout the device operational lifetime. Long-lived API keys that never expire, certificates issued without expiry dates, SIM credentials that are never rotated over a 10-year deployment, all represent accumulating risk. Every day a credential remains valid is another day during which a previously undetected compromise of that credential can be exploited. Credential rotation policies, automated enforcement through connectivity management platforms, and certificate validity periods calibrated to risk exposure are the operational remedies.

Category	Definition	Primary Examples	Primary Remediation
Communication	Weaknesses in protocols and communication interfaces	Unencrypted transmission; unauthenticated MQTT brokers; Bluetooth pairing flaws; replay vulnerabilities	TLS/DTLS encryption; mutual authentication; protocol hardening; certificate-based broker access
Physical	Weaknesses from physical accessibility of hardware	Exposed JTAG/UART ports; accessible flash memory; side-channel key extraction; device replacement	Debug interface disable in production; tamper-detection hardware; hardware security modules; physical monitoring
Software	Weaknesses in firmware, OS, and embedded libraries	Unpatched CVEs; default credentials; buffer overflows; hardcoded API keys; vulnerable open-source libraries	OTA update infrastructure; unique per-device credentials; SAST tools in firmware CI/CD; secure coding standards
Connection Lifecycle	Weaknesses in credential management across device lifetime	Insecure provisioning; absent deprovisioning; non-expiring credentials; stale operator accounts	Secure provisioning workflows; automated deprovisioning; credential rotation policies; CMP lifecycle governance

Table 8.2: IoT Vulnerability Taxonomy: Four-Category Classification with Primary Remediations

8.3 Device Identity: Authentication and Authorisation

Every security function in an IoT system depends on a prior question being correctly answered: is this device who it claims to be, and is it authorised to do what it is requesting? Device identity is the foundation layer of IoT security, and it is the layer most frequently absent or inadequate in real deployments. Without reliable device identity, encryption protects a channel to an unknown endpoint, access control enforces rules for an entity whose identity cannot be verified, and audit trails record actions by actors whose authenticity is uncertain. This section addresses both the cryptographic mechanisms for establishing device identity and the authorisation frameworks for determining what authenticated devices may do.

8.3.1 Foundations of Device Authentication

Authentication in IoT, establishing that a device is who it claims to be, can be achieved through three classes of mechanism: something the device knows (a pre-shared key or password), something the device has (a hardware-bound private key or SIM card), and something the device is (a hardware fingerprint derived from physical unclonable function measurements). The strongest IoT authentication systems combine at least two of these factors, providing defence-in-depth against credential theft.

Pre-shared key (PSK) authentication is the simplest approach: a secret key is programmed into the device at manufacture and is also stored in the IoT platform. When the device connects, it proves knowledge of the PSK without transmitting it (using Hash-based Message Authentication Code (HMAC) or TLS-PSK mode). PSK authentication is computationally efficient and appropriate for the most constrained devices. Its principal weakness is key management at scale: if all devices in a fleet share a single PSK, compromise of any one device's key compromises the entire fleet. Individual per-device PSKs, while secure, require a key management system capable of distributing and tracking thousands of unique keys at manufacture or provisioning time.

DEFINITION: Public Key Infrastructure (PKI)

A system of cryptographic certificates, certificate authorities, and certificate management protocols that enables scalable, verifiable digital identity for IoT devices. In an IoT PKI, each device holds a unique private key (stored in tamper-resistant hardware) and a corresponding X.509 certificate signed by a trusted Certificate Authority (CA). The certificate binds the device's public key to its identity, enabling any system that trusts the CA to verify the device's identity without prior knowledge of that specific device.

PKI-based device authentication is the gold standard for IoT deployments at scale. The device's private key is generated inside a hardware security module (HSM) at manufacture and never leaves the secure hardware; it signs authentication challenges but cannot be extracted. The corresponding X.509 certificate, signed by the IoT operator's CA, contains the device's identity (typically a UUID or hardware serial number), the certificate validity period, and the CA's digital signature.

When the device connects to the IoT platform, Mutual TLS (mTLS) performs a bidirectional certificate exchange: the server presents its certificate (standard TLS), and the device presents its device certificate (the mTLS extension). Both parties verify the other's certificate against their trusted CA list, achieving cryptographically strong mutual authentication.

DEFINITION: Mutual TLS (mTLS)

A configuration of the TLS protocol in which both the connecting client (IoT device) and the server present X.509 certificates for bidirectional authentication. Standard TLS authenticates only the server to the client; mTLS additionally authenticates the client (device) to the server. mTLS is the recommended authentication mechanism for IoT device-to-cloud connectivity where device identity must be cryptographically verifiable.

8.3.2 SIM-Based Identity in Cellular IoT

Cellular IoT deployments have access to an authentication mechanism not available in other connectivity technologies: the SIM card. The SIM is a hardware security module that provides immutable, cryptographically protected device identity at the cellular network level. Every SIM contains an IMSI (International Mobile Subscriber Identity), a globally unique 15-digit identifier, and a secret key (Ki) that is shared with the mobile operator's authentication centre (AuC) and never leaves the SIM in any form.

The 3GPP AKA (Authentication and Key Agreement) protocol, used by all 4G LTE and 5G networks, uses challenge-response cryptography with these keys to authenticate the SIM to the network without ever transmitting the secret key, even the mobile operator cannot extract the Ki from a SIM after manufacture.

For IoT security architects, the SIM's hardware-protected identity provides a layer of device authentication at the network access level that is independent of the application layer's credential system. A cellular IoT device that also uses mTLS for application-layer authentication presents two independent identity proofs: its SIM to the cellular network (providing network-level access control), and its device certificate to the IoT platform (providing application-level access control). This defence-in-depth architecture means that an attacker who compromises the application-layer credential cannot connect unless they also have a valid SIM, and vice versa.

DEFINITION: IMSI (International Mobile Subscriber Identity)

A globally unique 15-digit identifier stored on a SIM card, used by the cellular network to identify and authenticate a cellular subscription. In IoT deployments, the IMSI serves as the primary hardware-level device identity at the network access layer, independently of any application-layer credential the device may also use.

The Connectivity Management Platform (CMP) plays a critical governance role in SIM-based IoT security. The CMP maintains the authoritative registry of which SIM identities (IMSIs) are authorised to connect to the IoT platform, under what data policies, and with access to which services. When a device's SIM should be decommissioned (because the device has been retired, stolen, or compromised) the CMP is the system through which the SIM's connectivity is suspended and its credentials revoked.

The CMP also enforces data volume limits and geographic restrictions that limit the blast radius of a compromised SIM: a SIM with a 1 MB per day data allowance configured to connect only from a specific country cannot be used to exfiltrate large volumes of data or relay traffic from unexpected locations. The full operational role of CMPs is examined in Chapter 9.

8.3.3 Authorisation and Role-Based Access Control

Authentication confirms identity (this device is what it claims to be); authorisation determines what that authenticated identity may do. The two concepts are frequently conflated in IoT designs, with authentication used as the sole gate to full system access. This conflation violates the principle of least privilege: every device should have exactly the permissions required for its function and no more. A temperature sensor that can only read its own telemetry stream cannot be used, even if its credentials are compromised, to issue actuator commands, access other devices' data, or modify platform configuration.

DEFINITION: Role-Based Access Control (RBAC)

An access control model in which permissions are assigned to roles (defined sets of capabilities), and devices or users are assigned to roles rather than receiving permissions directly. RBAC in IoT enables fine-grained access control at scale: a fleet of 10,000 sensors can all be assigned the "sensor-read-write" role, restricting them to publishing telemetry and reading their own configuration, without individually configuring 10,000 permission sets.

Implementing RBAC for IoT devices requires that the IoT platform enforce authorisation checks on every API call and message publication, not just at initial connection. AWS IoT Core's policy engine, Azure IoT Hub's shared access policies, and the MQTT broker's ACL (Access Control List) configuration all provide mechanisms for defining and enforcing device-level permissions.

A well-designed IoT RBAC model defines device roles along two axes: functional role (sensor, actuator, gateway, management agent) and trust level (certified, provisioned, quarantined, decommissioned). A newly connected device that has not completed attestation might be placed in a quarantined role with no access to production data topics until its identity and software integrity have been verified.

CASE STUDY: Certificate-Based Device Identity at Arm Pelion IoT Platform

Global | 2019–Present

Arm's Pelion IoT Platform, used by industrial and enterprise IoT deployments, provides a PKI-based device identity system that illustrates production-scale implementation of the principles in this section. Each device is provisioned at manufacture with a factory-generated X.509 certificate signed by Arm's Pelion CA. The private key is generated inside the device's hardware secure element (a dedicated cryptographic chip with tamper-detection capability) and never leaves the chip in any form.

When a device connects to the Pelion platform, mTLS mutual authentication uses the device certificate to verify identity. The platform returns a session token with the specific permissions associated with that device's provisioned role. A sensor node provisioned as "data-producer" can publish telemetry and read its own configuration but cannot subscribe to actuator topics or access other devices' data. A gateway node provisioned as "relay" can subscribe to child device topics and forward data but cannot modify device configurations.

Certificate lifecycle management is automated: certificates are issued with 2-year validity, and a renewal workflow initiated 30 days before expiry sends a new certificate to the device over a secure channel, with the device's secure element generating a new key pair as part of the renewal. Revocation is handled through the Pelion CRL (Certificate Revocation List) distributed to all brokers, ensuring that a revoked device certificate is refused within minutes of revocation, even if the device attempts to reconnect before its current session expires.

In a 2022 deployment audit of 85,000 devices across a European smart metering programme using Pelion, the customer reported zero successful credential-based intrusions over 18 months of operation, attributable to the combination of hardware-protected keys (preventing credential extraction), mTLS authentication (preventing impersonation), and automated certificate rotation (limiting the value of any credential that might be captured).

8.4 Data Protection in Transit and at Rest

Encrypting IoT communication channels addresses the communication vulnerability category established in Section 8.2: the interception, replay, and manipulation of data traversing unsecured links. Encryption is necessary but not sufficient on its own. The precise architecture of encryption — which layer it is applied at, where keys are held, and how intermediaries are trusted — determines whether it actually protects data from the threats described in Section 8.5. A device sending data over an encrypted link to a broker that re-transmits it in plaintext to a cloud backend has not achieved end-to-end confidentiality: it has achieved hop-by-hop confidentiality, which provides materially weaker guarantees in adversarial environments.

The cryptographic protocols available for IoT transport security span a range from full TLS 1.3 stacks (suitable for gateway devices and cellular IoT modules with adequate memory) to lightweight alternatives for constrained microcontrollers with only kilobytes of RAM. Selecting the appropriate protocol requires matching cryptographic strength to device capability, connectivity technology, and the sensitivity of the data being transmitted.

8.4.1 Transport Layer Security for IoT: TLS and DTLS

DEFINITION: TLS (Transport Layer Security)

The dominant cryptographic protocol for securing TCP-based communications. TLS 1.3 (RFC 8446) is the current standard, removing all cipher suites considered weak and mandating forward secrecy. TLS provides mutual authentication, data confidentiality, and message integrity through a handshake that establishes session keys and then encrypts all subsequent application data.

Source: IETF RFC 8446 (TLS 1.3); GSMA IoT Security Guidelines FS.16

TLS 1.3 is the appropriate transport security protocol for IoT devices communicating over TCP-based application protocols including MQTT, AMQP, and HTTPS. The TLS 1.3 handshake completes in a single round trip (0-RTT mode is available for session resumption), reducing the latency penalty of connection setup, which is significant for battery-powered devices that wake periodically to transmit. The mandatory forward secrecy property of TLS 1.3 ensures that compromise of a device's long-term private key does not retrospectively expose past session data recorded by a passive adversary.

Cipher suite selection for constrained IoT devices favours algorithms with hardware acceleration support. The AES-128-GCM cipher suite, available in hardware on ARM Cortex-M4, -M33, and ESP32 class devices, provides 128-bit symmetric encryption with authenticated encryption and associated data (AEAD). ChaCha20-Poly1305 is the preferred alternative on devices without hardware AES support, as it is highly efficient in software on 32-bit architectures and is included in the TLS 1.3 mandatory cipher suite set.

DEFINITION: DTLS (Datagram Transport Layer Security)

The UDP-based equivalent of TLS, providing authentication, confidentiality, and integrity for connectionless IoT protocols including CoAP and LwM2M. DTLS 1.3 (RFC 9147) adds epoch tracking and replay detection to handle the reordering and loss characteristics of UDP transport. DTLS is the standard security layer for IETF-defined constrained-device application protocols.

Source: IETF RFC 9147 (DTLS 1.3); RFC 7252 (CoAP + DTLS security)

DTLS is the appropriate transport security protocol for devices using UDP-based application protocols. The Constrained Application Protocol (CoAP), widely deployed for sensor data transmission over IPv6 networks including 6LoWPAN and NB-IoT, specifies DTLS as its mandatory security layer. The Lightweight Machine-to-Machine (LwM2M) protocol, the OMA SpecWorks standard for cellular IoT device management, requires DTLS or TLS depending on transport. A DTLS 1.3 session with AES-128-CCM-8 cipher requires approximately 8 KB of RAM on the device, placing it within reach of mid-range Cortex-M3 class microcontrollers.

8.4.2 Link-Layer Versus End-to-End Encryption

The distinction between link-layer and end-to-end encryption is one of the most practically consequential in IoT security architecture, and one of the most frequently overlooked. Link-layer encryption, implemented by protocols such as WPA3 (Wi-Fi), Bluetooth 4.2+ with LE Secure Connections, and IEEE 802.15.4 AES-CCM, encrypts the wireless channel between adjacent nodes. Data is decrypted at each network node it traverses — the access point, the gateway, the cloud broker — and re-encrypted for the next hop. Each node therefore handles plaintext data.

Key Insight: The Intermediary Gap in IoT Encryption. An IoT device transmitting data over an encrypted Wi-Fi link to an MQTT broker that forwards messages to a cloud backend has achieved link-layer confidentiality, not end-to-end confidentiality. If the MQTT broker is hosted on shared infrastructure, operated by a third-party SaaS provider, or is itself compromised, the data is exposed in plaintext at the broker. End-to-end encryption (E2EE), where data is encrypted between the originating device and the final processing application, eliminates this exposure but requires that intermediate brokers and gateways operate only on ciphertext — which limits filtering, routing, and QoS capabilities that depend on message content inspection.

OSCORE (Object Security for Constrained RESTful Environments, RFC 8613) provides end-to-end security for CoAP by encrypting and integrity-protecting CoAP message payloads and sensitive header fields at the application layer, independent of the transport channel. An OSCORE-protected CoAP message can traverse an unencrypted network, a CoAP proxy, or an HTTP-CoAP gateway without being exposed to intermediary nodes. OSCORE uses CBOR Object Signing and Encryption (COSE) with AES-CCM-16-64-128 as the default algorithm, and requires only a shared context (exchanged during EDHOC key agreement or pre-provisioned), making it deployable on Class 1 constrained devices with 10 KB of RAM.

The practical choice between link-layer and end-to-end encryption depends on the trust boundary. When the entire path from device to application backend is operated by a single trusted organisation on dedicated infrastructure, link-layer TLS/DTLS to each hop provides adequate confidentiality with lower complexity and compatibility overhead. When messages transit shared infrastructure, third-party platforms, or multi-vendor intermediaries, end-to-end encryption via OSCORE or application-layer payload encryption (using AES-GCM with per-device keys) is the architecturally correct choice.

8.4.3 Encryption of Data at Rest on IoT Devices

Data protection obligations extend beyond transmission to data stored locally on IoT devices. An IoT device may buffer sensor readings during network outages, store configuration and calibration parameters, hold locally processed inference results, or cache security credentials. All of these represent potential targets for physical extraction attacks (Section 8.2.2), where an adversary reads flash memory directly. Hardware-accelerated AES encryption is available on ARM Cortex-M33 devices (through ARM TrustZone's Secure Partition Manager), on dedicated secure elements (SE050, ATEC-C608B), and through Trusted Platform Modules (TPM) in industrial IoT gateways. File-system-level encryption using eCryptfs or LUKS on Linux-based IoT gateways (Raspberry Pi, i.MX 8M, Yocto-based platforms) provides at-rest protection for data volumes with minimal application-layer changes. For deeply embedded Class 1 devices without an operating system, application-layer encryption of sensitive records before NVM write provides equivalent protection at the cost of explicit key management in firmware. Key management is the critical operational challenge of at-rest encryption. Keys stored in plaintext alongside the data they protect provide no protection against an adversary with physical device access. Cryptographic keys must be stored in hardware-protected storage — a secure element, a TrustZone Trusted Execution Environment (TEE), or OTP fuses — that is not accessible to user-space firmware code and cannot be extracted by standard debug interfaces.

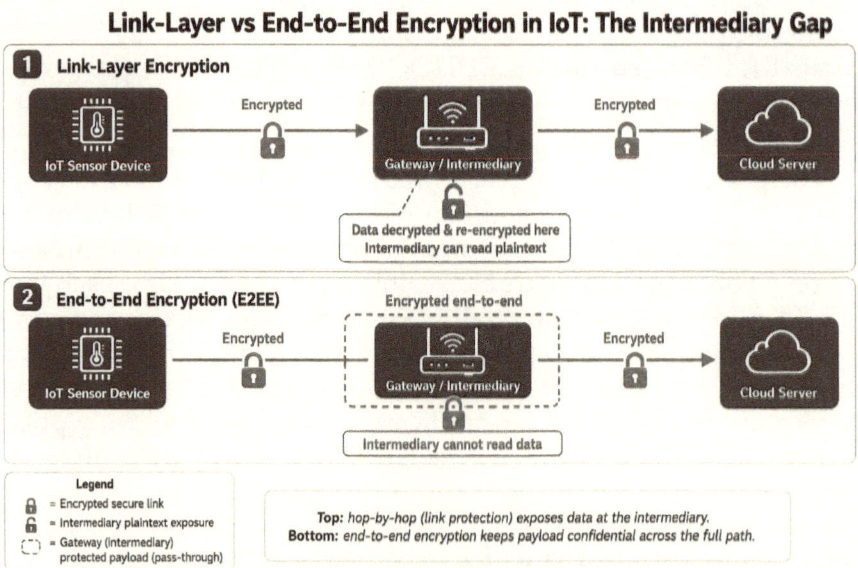

Figure 8.2: Link-Layer vs End-to-End Encryption in IoT: The Intermediary Gap

Table 8.3 — IoT Transport Security Protocols: Scope, Transport, and Device Applicability

Protocol / Mechanism	Transport / Layer	Typical Application Protocols	Approx. Minimum RAM	Forward Secrecy Support
TLS 1.3	TCP transport security	MQTT, AMQP, HTTPS	~20 KB	Yes, mandatory
DTLS 1.3	UDP transport security	CoAP, LwM2M, SNMP	~8 KB	Yes, mandatory
OSCORE	CoAP object security over any transport	End-to-end CoAP protection	~10 KB	Yes, when used with EDHOC
TLS 1.2	TCP transport security	Legacy MQTT and HTTP deployments	~30 KB	Optional, with DHE/ECDHE cipher suites
IEEE 802.15.4 AES-CCM	Link-layer security	Zigbee, Thread, 6LoWPAN	~2 KB	No, link-layer encryption only
WPA3-SAE	Wi-Fi link-layer security	Wi-Fi-based IoT applications	~4 KB	Yes, through per-session key establishment
BLE Secure Connections	BLE link-layer pairing and encryption	GATT, BLE Mesh	~4 KB	Yes, through ECDH key exchange

8.5 IoT Threat Taxonomy: Mapping Attacks to the Vulnerability Landscape

Section 8.2 established a four-category taxonomy of IoT vulnerabilities: communication, physical, software, and connection lifecycle. A vulnerability is a structural weakness in a system. A threat is an actor or event that exploits a vulnerability to cause harm. Understanding threats requires mapping them to the vulnerabilities they exploit, the assets they target, and the impacts they produce. This mapping is the foundation of structured IoT threat modelling and informs both the selection of countermeasures (Sections 8.6 and 8.7) and the security best practices framework (Section 8.8).

The threat taxonomy organises IoT attacks into four categories that mirror the vulnerability taxonomy: network-layer attacks (exploiting communication vulnerabilities), physical and hardware attacks (exploiting physical vulnerabilities), software and firmware attacks (exploiting software vulnerabilities), and lifecycle and supply chain attacks (exploiting connection lifecycle vulnerabilities). This mapping is not absolute — a sophisticated attack such as the Mirai botnet exploited software vulnerabilities (default credentials) to conduct network-layer attacks (DDoS) — but it provides the analytical structure needed for systematic threat assessment.

8.5.1 Network-Layer Attacks: DDoS, Man-in-the-Middle, and Replay

DEFINITION: Distributed Denial of Service (DDoS) Attack

An attack in which a large number of compromised devices simultaneously flood a target network or service with traffic, exhausting its bandwidth or processing capacity and rendering it unavailable to legitimate users. IoT botnets are particularly effective DDoS weapons because of the large number of deployable devices and their typically unrestricted outbound network access.

Source: ENISA Threat Landscape for IoT 2023; Kolias et al. (2017)

Network-layer attacks target communication vulnerabilities: unencrypted channels, unauthenticated brokers, weak pairing mechanisms, and improperly validated certificates. Man-in-the-middle (MitM) attacks position an adversary between an IoT device and its intended communication endpoint. In an IoT context, MitM attacks exploit the absence of mutual TLS authentication: if a device does not verify the server's certificate, it can be redirected to a malicious endpoint that impersonates the legitimate broker or cloud platform. The attacker receives the device's data in plaintext and may issue commands that the device executes as authoritative.

Replay attacks capture legitimate protocol messages — an authentication token, a command frame, an API request — and retransmit them to achieve an action the attacker is not authorised to initiate. IoT protocols without nonce-based message freshness mechanisms (timestamps, sequence numbers, challenge-response) are vulnerable to replay. The MQTT protocol in its default configuration does not include replay protection at the application layer; replay protection must be implemented at the transport layer (via TLS session freshness) or through application-level message sequencing.

DNS amplification and reflection attacks exploit IoT devices with open DNS resolvers or other services that respond to small requests with large responses. An attacker spoofing the source IP address of a victim host sends small queries to thousands of IoT devices whose responses flood the victim with amplified traffic. Mitigations include ingress filtering (BCP38), disabling open recursive DNS on IoT devices, and rate-limiting UDP response generation.

CASE STUDY: Mirai Botnet: The Industrialisation of IoT-Based DDoS

Global | August–October 2016

The Mirai botnet, first identified in August 2016, represents the most consequential IoT security event of the 2010s and remains the canonical case study of what happens when communication and software vulnerabilities are exploited at scale. Mirai was a piece of malware specifically designed to infect Linux-based IoT devices — primarily consumer IP cameras, digital video recorders (DVRs), and home routers — by scanning the public internet for devices with open Telnet ports (port 23) and trying a list of 60 factory-default username/password combinations.

The vulnerability exploited was not a zero-day or a sophisticated cryptographic weakness. It was insecure default credentials (Section 8.2.3) combined with the absence of network segmentation. Devices accessible directly from the internet on port 23, running unchanged factory credentials, accepted Mirai's login attempts and executed the downloaded malware binary. Mirai propagated rapidly because the attack required no human interaction and could scan the entire IPv4 address space in approximately 45 minutes using the compromised device fleet as distributed scanners.

At its peak, Mirai controlled approximately 600,000 compromised devices. In September 2016 it was used to launch the largest DDoS attack recorded at that time against the website of security journalist Brian Krebs, reaching 620 Gbps. In October 2016, a Mirai variant was directed against Dyn, a major DNS infrastructure provider, generating an estimated 1.2 Tbps of traffic and disrupting access to dozens of major internet services including Twitter, Netflix, Reddit, Airbnb, and PayPal for several hours across the US East Coast and Europe.

The lessons of Mirai shaped subsequent IoT security regulation. The UK's Product Security and Telecommunications Infrastructure (PSTI) Act, the EU Cyber Resilience Act, and ETSI EN 303 645 all include provisions directly addressing the Mirai vulnerability class: the prohibition of factory-default credentials that are the same across all devices of a product model, and the requirement for a publicly known vulnerability disclosure policy. The Mirai source code was released publicly in October 2016, and IoT botnet derivatives based on Mirai (Satori, Okiru, Masuta, Reaper) continued to operate and evolve through 2023.

8.5.2 Physical and Hardware Attacks

Physical attacks exploit the physical accessibility of IoT devices — a structural vulnerability category absent from enterprise IT security models where servers are locked in controlled data centres. IoT devices are deployed in publicly accessible locations: utility meters attached to building exteriors, agricultural sensors installed in open fields, industrial sensors on factory floors, and consumer devices in shared living spaces. Physical access enables attacks that are impossible remotely.

Firmware extraction is the most valuable physical attack outcome. An adversary with physical access to a device can attach a Bus Pirate, J-Link, or custom flash reader to the JTAG, UART, or SPI interfaces present on most IoT printed circuit boards and read the complete flash memory contents. The extracted firmware binary can be reverse-engineered using tools including Ghidra, IDA Pro, and binwalk to recover hardcoded credentials, API keys, encryption keys, and proprietary algorithm implementations. The information extracted from one device can then be used to compromise the entire device fleet if credentials are shared across units — the vulnerability identified in the connection lifecycle taxonomy (Section 8.2.4).

Side-channel attacks extract secret information from the physical characteristics of computation rather than from the algorithm itself. Power analysis attacks measure the varying current consumption of a device during cryptographic operations to recover the secret key: the power consumed during AES encryption varies in a statistically detectable way with each bit of the key. Electromagnetic (EM) emission analysis achieves similar results without physical contact, using a near-field probe positioned above the device's processor. These attacks require specialised laboratory equipment but are within reach of well-resourced adversaries targeting high-value IoT deployments.

Device substitution attacks replace a legitimate IoT device with a malicious device that presents the same physical and logical identity. In a supply chain context, counterfeit devices can be inserted before deployment; in an operational context, devices can be physically swapped by an attacker with site access. Without hardware-rooted device attestation (Section 8.6.1), the IoT platform cannot distinguish a legitimate device from a substitution.

8.5.3 Software and Firmware Attacks

Software attacks exploit the vulnerabilities catalogued in Section 8.2.3: unpatched CVEs, default credentials, memory corruption flaws, and hardcoded secrets. They are the most operationally significant threat category because they can be conducted entirely remotely, at scale, and with automated tooling. The attack surface of an IoT device is defined by its externally accessible services: open network ports, published API endpoints, Bluetooth pairing interfaces, and web-based administration panels.

Credential stuffing and brute-force attacks enumerate weak or default credentials on exposed management interfaces. Tools including Shodan, Censys, and ZoomEye continuously scan the public internet and index internet-accessible IoT devices by device type, manufacturer, and open service. An adversary can query these tools to produce a targeted list of devices of a specific make and model, then apply known default credentials from that model's user manual. The OWASP IoT Top Ten consistently lists weak, guessable, or hardcoded passwords as the highest-severity IoT vulnerability category.

CASE STUDY: Oldsmar Water Treatment Plant: Remote Access and Unpatched Software

Oldsmar, Florida, United States | February 2021

In February 2021, an operator at the City of Oldsmar water treatment facility in Florida observed a remote access session on the plant's SCADA system. The remote operator — who was not a legitimate employee — navigated the HMI (Human-Machine Interface) and attempted to increase the sodium hydroxide (lye) concentration in the drinking water supply from the normal level of approximately 100 parts per million to 11,100 parts per million, a level that would have been hazardous to public health. The operator overrode the change immediately, and the plant's downstream pH monitors would have triggered additional alarms before contaminated water reached the distribution network.

The post-incident investigation identified multiple compounding vulnerabilities. The remote access software in use was TeamViewer, configured with a single shared password used by all staff and without multi-factor authentication. The Windows 7 workstations controlling the SCADA system were no longer receiving security updates, as Windows 7 had reached end-of-life in January 2020. The plant's internet connection provided direct access to the operational technology network without a network demilitarisation zone or industrial firewall.

The Oldsmar incident illustrates the convergence of software vulnerabilities (unpatched operating system, shared single-factor credentials), connection lifecycle vulnerabilities (no credential rotation, no access revocation audit), and the absence of network segmentation between IT and OT systems. It demonstrates that the physical consequences of IoT and OT security failures can extend beyond data loss to direct harm to critical infrastructure and public safety. The incident accelerated the development of sector-specific OT security guidance from CISA and the Water Information Sharing and Analysis Centre (WaterISAC), and is cited in ICS-CERT advisories as the reference scenario for water sector security baseline requirements.

8.5.4 Lifecycle and Supply Chain Attacks

Lifecycle and supply chain attacks exploit weaknesses in credential management and device identity across the operational lifetime, from manufacture through decommissioning. They are often the least visible threat category because they may not produce immediately detectable anomalies: a device with a compromised firmware image operates normally while also performing covert exfiltration; a device with non-expiring credentials remains connectable long after its retirement.

Supply chain compromise inserts malicious code or hardware modifications into IoT devices during manufacture or distribution. The risk is structurally elevated in IoT deployments because devices are sourced from global electronics supply chains with limited visibility into firmware provenance, and because devices are often deployed in large quantities with identical firmware images. Secure boot with hardware-rooted chain of trust (Section 8.6.1) is the primary mitigation: a device that will only execute firmware carrying a valid manufacturer signature cannot be compromised at the supply chain level without access to the manufacturer's code-signing private key.

Decommissioning failures leave retired devices connected and authenticated long after their operational role has ended. A cellular IoT device with an active SIM continues to accumulate connectivity charges and represents an exploitable network endpoint. A device whose X.509 certificate has not been revoked can continue to authenticate as a legitimate system participant. The GSMA IoT Security Guidelines mandate explicit device decommissioning workflows, including SIM suspension, certificate revocation via OCSP and CRL, and platform credential scrubbing, as requirements for compliant IoT deployments.

Table 8.4 — IoT Threat Taxonomy: Attack Categories, Exploited Vulnerability Class, and Historical Examples

Threat Category	Exploited Vulnerability Class	Representative Example	Primary Countermeasure
DDoS / Botnet	Software: default credentials	Mirai botnet, 2016, around 600K infected devices	Enforce unique credentials and eliminate default passwords
Man-in-the-Middle	Communication: lack of mutual authentication	Unauthenticated MQTT broker interception	Use mutual TLS and certificate pinning
Replay Attack	Communication: lack of message freshness	Replayed MQTT command message	Use TLS session freshness, timestamps, and nonce-based tokens

Firmware Extraction	Physical: exposed debug interfaces	JTAG flash dump used for key recovery	Disable debug ports and use encrypted flash storage
Side-Channel Attack	Physical: electromagnetic or power leakage	AES key recovery through power analysis	Use secure elements and masked cryptography
Device Substitution	Physical: absence of device attestation	Counterfeit sensor inserted into supply chain	Use hardware root of trust and device attestation
Credential Stuffing	Software: reused or weak credentials	Shodan-indexed camera takeover	Use unique per-device credentials and multi-factor authentication
CVE Exploit	Software: unpatched firmware or legacy systems	Oldsmar water facility incident involving remote access exposure	Maintain OTA updates and structured patch management
Supply Chain Implant	Lifecycle: compromised manufacturing or firmware chain	Backdoored firmware introduced during manufacture	Use secure boot, code signing, and supplier verification
Decommissioning Failure	Lifecycle: incomplete asset retirement	Retired SIM or device identity remains active	Apply explicit deprovisioning and credential revocation workflow

8.6 Security Mechanisms: Secure Boot, PKI, and OTA Updates

The vulnerability and threat analysis in Sections 8.2 through 8.5 defines the problem. This section defines the engineering solutions: the technical mechanisms that, when correctly implemented, address each category of vulnerability and limit the impact of each category of threat. Three mechanisms form the technical foundation of IoT device security: secure boot (which ensures a device only runs authorised software), public key infrastructure (which manages device identity at scale across the full device lifecycle), and over-the-air firmware updates (which maintain security posture over the device operational lifetime). Each mechanism is individually valuable; together they provide the layered defence that makes a device resistant to the most common attack paths.

8.6.1 Secure Boot and the Hardware Root of Trust

DEFINITION: Secure Boot

A security mechanism that ensures an IoT device only executes firmware that has been cryptographically verified as authentic and unmodified before execution begins. Secure boot prevents the execution of tampered firmware (whether modified by a software attack or physically injected through a debug interface), ensuring that even a device whose software has been targeted by an attacker will not run malicious code if its secure boot chain is intact.

The secure boot process operates as a chain of trust, beginning with a component that cannot itself be modified or replaced by software. This component, the hardware root of trust, holds the public key against which the first software stage (the bootloader) is verified. If the bootloader's signature check passes, the bootloader then verifies the signature of the operating system or firmware image before transferring execution to it. If the operating system in turn verifies application code, the chain of trust extends from hardware through every software layer. A signature check failure at any stage halts the boot process, preventing execution of unverified code.

DEFINITION: Hardware Root of Trust (HRoT)

A tamper-resistant hardware component that stores the cryptographic keys and verification code used as the foundation of a device's secure boot chain. Common HRoT implementations include ARM TrustZone (a security extension built into Cortex-A and Cortex-M processors), dedicated secure elements (smart card chips embedded in IoT devices), Trusted Platform Modules (TPM 2.0), and silicon-vendor-specific implementations such as Microchip's CryptoAuthLib and NXP's EdgeLock. The HRoT is physically and logically isolated from the main processor, with keys that cannot be read by software, only used for cryptographic operations inside the secure hardware boundary.

Key Insight: Device Identity Is the Foundation of IoT Security. Every security mechanism in an IoT system — authentication, access control, audit logging, encrypted communication, and certificate revocation — depends on reliable knowledge of which device is communicating.

Without cryptographically verifiable device identity, Transport Layer Security (TLS) encrypts channels to potentially impersonated endpoints; Role-Based Access Control (RBAC) enforces authorisation for entities whose identity cannot be confirmed; and audit logs record actions by unidentifiable actors. Hardware-protected identity, implemented through secure elements, Trusted Platform Modules (TPMs), or ARM TrustZone, provides the immutable foundation that makes all other security properties trustworthy. A deployment that attempts to add device identity retrospectively, after devices are in the field, will find this to be the most expensive retrofit in IoT security.

ARM TrustZone is the most widely deployed HRoT technology in IoT devices because it is integrated into the ARM Cortex-M33 and Cortex-M55 processors used in hundreds of millions of IoT devices. TrustZone partitions the processor into two execution environments: the Normal World (where application firmware runs) and the Secure World (where security-critical code runs, including the secure boot verification, key storage, and cryptographic operations). The Secure World is inaccessible from the Normal World at the hardware level: a compromised application running in the Normal World cannot read or modify Secure World memory, cannot access Secure World keys, and cannot bypass the secure boot chain established in the Secure World.

Rollback protection is a critical extension of secure boot that prevents an attacker from downgrading a device to an older, vulnerable firmware version after a security patch has been applied. Without rollback protection, an attacker who cannot exploit the current firmware version can simply install an older version with known vulnerabilities.

Rollback protection is implemented through a monotonic counter stored in write-once hardware memory (OTP, One-Time Programmable fuses): the firmware version number is stored in OTP, and the bootloader refuses to execute any firmware image whose version number is lower than the stored value. Once a device has been updated to firmware version 3.1, it will never again run version 3.0 or earlier, regardless of what firmware image is presented for installation.

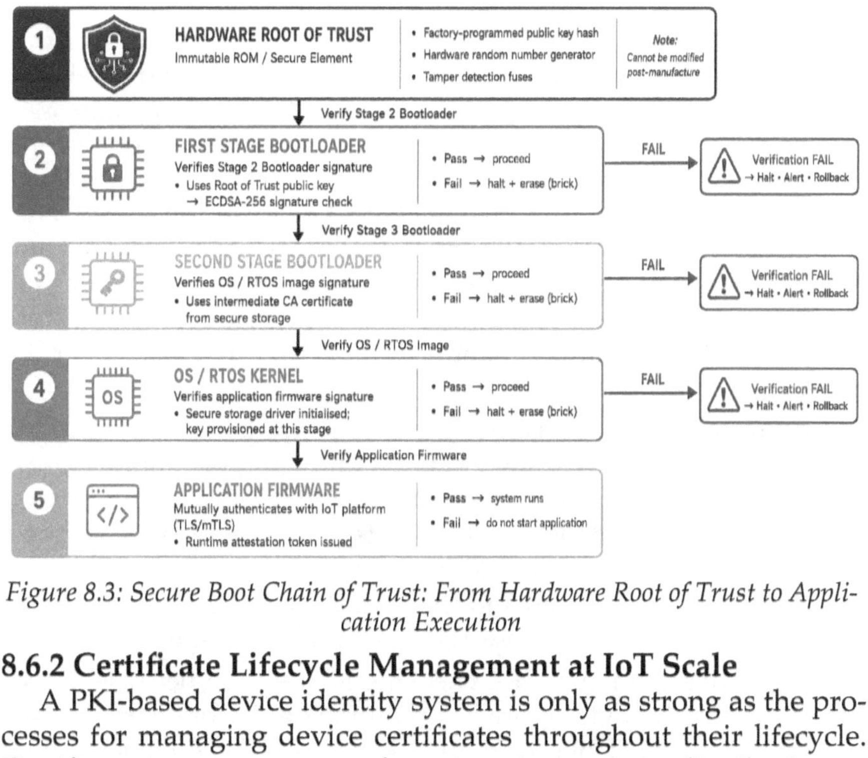

Figure 8.3: Secure Boot Chain of Trust: From Hardware Root of Trust to Application Execution

8.6.2 Certificate Lifecycle Management at IoT Scale

A PKI-based device identity system is only as strong as the processes for managing device certificates throughout their lifecycle. Certificate issuance at manufacturing time, secure distribution to devices, monitoring for certificate expiry, timely renewal, and rapid revocation when a device is compromised or decommissioned are all operational requirements that must be engineered into the system from the outset. At IoT scale, hundreds of thousands or millions of devices, these operations must be automated; manual certificate management is not feasible.

Certificate issuance for IoT devices is most securely performed at the manufacturing stage, when the device's hardware security element can generate a key pair internally and present only the public key for certificate signing. The private key is generated inside the secure element and never leaves it, ensuring that not even the certificate authority or the contract manufacturer has access to the device's private key.

The certificate authority signs the public key with the device's identifying information (serial number, model, batch code) to produce the device certificate, which is loaded into the device's secure storage as part of the manufacturing process. Protocols for this operation include EST (Enrolment over Secure Transport, RFC 7030) and the Lightweight CMP (Certificate Management Protocol) profile for IoT.

The CA hierarchy for IoT deployments follows a standard structure: a root CA whose private key is held in an HSM and used only to sign intermediate CA certificates; one or more intermediate CAs used for day-to-day certificate issuance; and device certificates signed by the intermediate CA. This hierarchy limits the impact of a CA compromise: if an intermediate CA's key is compromised, only certificates signed by that intermediate CA need to be revoked and reissued; the root CA and other intermediate CAs are unaffected. The root CA certificate, embedded in the IoT platform's trust store and in device firmware at manufacture, is the trust anchor for the entire deployment.

Certificate revocation is the emergency mechanism for revoking a device's identity when the device is known to be compromised, lost, stolen, or decommissioned. Two standard revocation mechanisms exist: Certificate Revocation Lists (CRLs), which are periodically published lists of revoked certificate serial numbers that relying parties must download and check, and OCSP (Online Certificate Status Protocol), which allows real-time certificate status queries.

For IoT deployments, CRL checking is preferred because it does not require each device to make an online query for every connection attempt: the IoT platform downloads the CRL and checks it on behalf of connecting devices. CRL validity periods should be short (hours to a day) to limit the window during which a revoked certificate might still be accepted.

8.6.3 Over-the-Air Firmware Updates

DEFINITION: Over-the-Air (OTA) Firmware Update

The remote delivery and installation of firmware updates to IoT devices over a wireless or wired network connection, without requiring physical access to the device. OTA update capability is a fundamental security requirement for IoT devices because it is the mechanism through which security vulnerabilities discovered after deployment can be remediated. Devices without OTA capability cannot be patched and must be physically replaced when vulnerable firmware versions are found: an operationally impractical requirement for large-scale deployments.

The OTA update pipeline itself is a high-value attack target: an attacker who can compromise the firmware delivery infrastructure can push malicious firmware to an entire deployed fleet simultaneously. Securing the OTA pipeline therefore requires the same rigour as securing the devices themselves. The security requirements for OTA are: the firmware image must be signed by the manufacturer's private key; the device must verify this signature before applying the update; the update delivery channel must be encrypted (TLS) to prevent interception and substitution of the firmware image in transit; and rollback protection must prevent an attacker from downgrading the device to a vulnerable previous version by delivering an older (validly signed) firmware image.

The IETF SUIT (Software Updates for Internet of Things) specification, standardised in RFC 9019 and RFC 9124, defines a manifest format and update procedure designed for constrained IoT devices. The SUIT manifest describes the firmware image (its digest, target hardware, minimum version requirement, and installation instructions) and is signed by the manufacturer. The device validates the manifest signature before downloading the firmware image, then validates the image digest before installation. This two-stage validation ensures both authenticity (the manifest was signed by the manufacturer) and integrity (the downloaded image matches the manufacturer's original).

TECHNOLOGY SPOTLIGHT: FOTA at Scale: How Firmware Updates Work Across One Million Devices

Firmware over-the-air (FOTA) updates for large IoT fleets require orchestration infrastructure that goes well beyond simply sending a file to a device. The update must be delivered reliably to devices that may be intermittently connected, running on battery, and operating in environ-

ments where a failed update could cause operational disruption. The FOTA orchestration platform must manage update campaigns across device cohorts, track update status per device, handle retry and failure recovery, and provide rollback capabilities when an update causes unexpected problems.

AWS IoT Device Management Jobs provides a managed FOTA service that illustrates the production requirements. A firmware update campaign is created as an IoT Job, targeting a fleet query (for example: all devices of model X running firmware version 2.x in region Europe). The job is scheduled for progressive rollout: initially 1% of devices, then 10%, then all devices, with automatic rollout pause if the error rate in the initial cohort exceeds a threshold. Each device downloads the firmware in chunks (supporting resumption if interrupted), validates the manifest and image, reports its installation status back to the platform, and triggers a secure reboot to activate the new firmware.

The AWS IoT Jobs approach uses device shadows to track each device's current and desired firmware version. A device that was offline during the initial campaign delivery automatically receives the update when it next connects, because the device shadow records the desired version and the device syncs its state on reconnect. This ensures 100% campaign coverage across fleets with variable connectivity without requiring the platform to track connection events for millions of devices individually.

Delta updates, sending only the changed bytes between firmware versions rather than a complete new image, dramatically reduce the data volume required for FOTA campaigns. For a 1 million device fleet where each device must download a 2 MB firmware update, a delta approach reducing each download to 200 KB saves approximately 1.8 TB of total data transfer, reducing both cost and the energy consumed by each device during the update. The Zephyr RTOS community's MCUboot bootloader and the open-source hawkBit firmware update server are widely used open-source implementations of delta FOTA for constrained IoT devices.

CASE STUDY: Securing the Philips Hue Bridge: From Vulnerability to Remediation

Netherlands / Global | 2020

In February 2020, security researchers at Check Point Research disclosed a critical vulnerability, assigned identifier CVE-2020-6007 (Common Vulnerabilities and Exposures) in the Philips Hue smart lighting system. The vulnerability exploited the Zigbee communication layer between the Hue Bridge (the central hub) and individual Hue light bulbs. An attacker within radio range could exploit the Zigbee touchlink feature to take control of a Hue bulb, force it to send error messages to the bridge, and through a buffer overflow in the bridge's Zigbee stack, achieve remote code execution on the bridge.

Once the bridge was compromised, the attacker could move laterally to the home network to which the bridge was connected, potentially accessing personal devices, files, and credentials. The attack required no authentication credentials and no physical access beyond being within Zigbee radio range (approximately 100 metres in open air) of a Hue bulb.

Signify (the Philips Hue manufacturer) responded by releasing a patched firmware version (1935144040) within 70 days of receiving the disclosure. The patch was delivered automatically via the Hue Bridge's OTA update infrastructure to all connected bridges worldwide. Users who had enabled automatic updates received the patch without any action required. Users with automatic updates disabled received a manual update prompt in the Hue app.

This case demonstrates both the OTA update mechanism working as intended and the critical importance of the update infrastructure being in place before a vulnerability is discovered. Philips had invested in OTA capability for the Hue Bridge from its initial design; without it, remediating CVE-2020-6007 would have required physically replacing hundreds of thousands of bridges rather than pushing a software update. It also illustrates the real-world attack path described in Section 8.5: a Zigbee protocol vulnerability (Communication category) exploited through a software buffer overflow (Software category) to achieve lateral movement through a home network.

8.7 Privacy by Design in IoT Security Architecture

Privacy and security are related but distinct properties of an IoT system. Security protects data from unauthorised access by external actors; it is concerned with preventing the wrong parties from accessing data. Privacy protects individuals from authorised but inappropriate use of their personal data by the system itself, its operators, or its commercial partners; it is concerned with ensuring that even authorised access is appropriate, proportionate, and consented to. Both properties are necessary; neither substitutes for the other. A system with strong security but poor privacy protects data from attackers but not from its own operators' inappropriate use. A system with strong privacy principles but weak security provides no meaningful protection of any kind.

8.7.1 Personal Data in IoT Contexts

The categories of personal data generated by IoT systems are more extensive than is typically appreciated by engineers who have not considered them from a data protection perspective. Location data from GPS-equipped IoT devices or from indoor positioning systems reveals home addresses, places of work, medical appointment locations, and patterns of movement that can expose sensitive lifestyle information.

Biometric data from wearables and healthcare IoT (heart rate patterns, sleep architecture, activity levels, galvanic skin response) can indicate health conditions, stress levels, and physiological states that are among the most sensitive personal information categories under the General Data Protection Regulation (GDPR) Article 9. Smart home usage patterns (when devices are switched on and off, what media is played, when appliances are used) reveal occupancy patterns, household routines, and behavioural information that has been shown in research studies to enable inference of religious practice, employment status, social relationships, and health conditions.

Smart television viewing data is among the most commercially significant personal data generated by consumer IoT. The FTC's 2017 settlement with Vizio required the television manufacturer to pay USD 2.2 million for collecting viewing data from 11 million televisions without adequate consent, and transmitting detailed second-by-second viewing information to data brokers who correlated it with personally identifiable information from other sources. The Vizio case established that automatic content recognition (ACR) in smart TVs constitutes personal data processing under US consumer protection law, and provided the factual foundation for subsequent GDPR guidance on smart TV data processing in European jurisdictions.

8.7.2 The Seven Principles of Privacy by Design Applied to IoT

DEFINITION: Privacy by Design (PbD)

An engineering approach, developed by Ann Cavoukian and codified as a legal requirement by GDPR Article 25, in which privacy protections are embedded into system architecture as default properties rather than added retrospectively as compliance overlays. The seven foundational principles of PbD (proactive protection, privacy as default, privacy embedded into design, full functionality, end-to-end security, visibility and transparency, and respect for user privacy) define a complete framework for privacy-respecting IoT system design.

Translating the seven PbD principles into concrete IoT engineering decisions requires deliberate architectural choices at every system layer. The following treatment maps each principle to its IoT engineering implementation.

Proactive protection means anticipating privacy risks before they materialise rather than responding to breaches after they occur. In IoT engineering terms, this translates to performing a Data Protection Impact Assessment (DPIA) before deploying any system that processes personal data at scale or involving special categories of data. DPIAs, required under GDPR Article 35 for "high risk" processing, systematically identify the data flows, processing purposes, and individuals affected by a system, assess the risks to those individuals' rights and freedoms, and document the technical and organisational measures implemented to address each risk.

Privacy as default means that the most privacy-protective settings are the system's out-of-the-box configuration, not settings that require the user to actively enable them. For a smart home device, this means that cloud synchronisation, voice recording retention, and data sharing with third parties are disabled by default and require explicit opt-in. For an industrial IoT system, it means that the minimum necessary data is transmitted to the cloud by default, with higher-resolution data collection requiring explicit operator configuration. The IoT industry's historical norm, maximising data collection by default and requiring users to opt out is directly contrary to this principle and increasingly contrary to law.

Privacy embedded into design means that privacy protections are structural features of the system architecture rather than configurable add-ons. Edge-tier data minimisation (aggregating or anonymising data before cloud transmission so that personal-level raw data never reaches the cloud), pseudonymisation of device identifiers at the ingestion stage (replacing device IDs with unlinkable pseudonyms before data enters analytics pipelines), and data lake access controls enforcing purpose limitation (preventing analytics queries that access personal data for purposes beyond the original collection purpose) are all examples of structural privacy embeddings.

End-to-end security is both a PbD principle and a security engineering requirement, reflecting that privacy and security are not independent properties. An IoT system whose data is encrypted in transit and at rest, whose access is controlled by role-based policies, and whose audit trail records every access to personal data provides both the security and the accountability that privacy requires. Chapter 8's security mechanisms (TLS, mTLS, OTA updates, secure boot) are as much privacy tools as security tools.

Respect for user privacy operationalises the principle that the individual whose data is being processed is the ultimate stakeholder. In IoT design, this requires user-accessible controls for data access, correction, and deletion; meaningful consent mechanisms that explain data processing in plain language; and transparency about what data is collected, how long it is retained, and with whom it is shared. The EU Data Act's right of access to IoT-generated data, discussed in Chapter 6, is a legislative implementation of this principle applied specifically to connected product data.

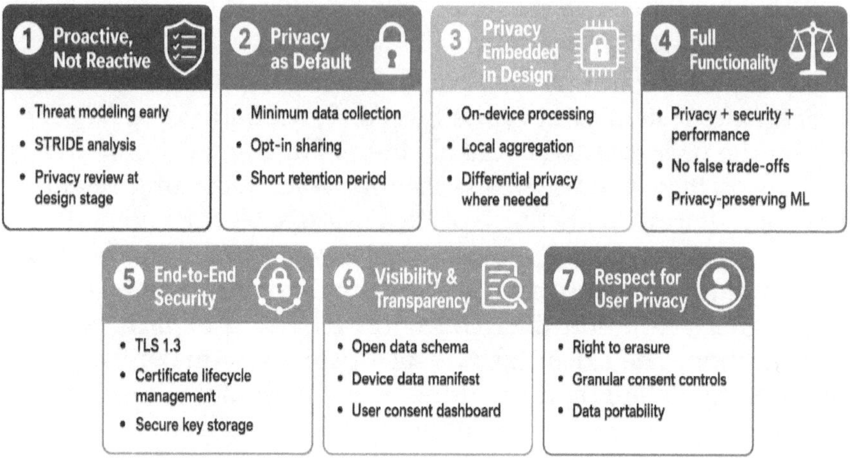

Figure 8.4: The Seven Principles of Privacy by Design: Engineering Implementations for IoT

8.7.3 Data Minimisation in Practice

Data minimisation is the principle of collecting only the personal data actually necessary for the stated processing purpose. It is both a GDPR obligation (Article 5(1)(c)) and a risk management strategy: data that is never collected cannot be stolen, misused, or inadvertently disclosed. In IoT engineering, data minimisation is implemented through decisions at three points in the pipeline: the device (what data to capture at all), the edge tier (what data to transmit to the cloud), and the analytics platform (what data to expose to each query).

At the device tier, data minimisation requires deliberate decisions about sampling rates and sensor activation. A smart energy meter that samples electricity consumption every second and transmits all readings to the cloud creates a high-resolution usage profile that can reveal occupancy patterns, appliance use, and potentially health-related information. The same meter sampling at 30-minute intervals and transmitting only the aggregated reading provides adequate data for billing purposes while dramatically reducing the privacy sensitivity of the transmitted data. The 30-minute aggregation is not a technically inferior design; it is a privacy-by-design choice that meets the functional requirement while minimising personal data generation.

DEFINITION: Differential Privacy

A mathematical framework for releasing statistical results derived from a dataset while providing a formal guarantee that no individual contributor to the dataset can be identified or have their data inferred from the released results. Differential privacy works by adding calibrated random noise to query results before release, with the noise magnitude determined by the privacy budget parameter epsilon (lower epsilon = stronger privacy, more noise).

Apple uses local differential privacy in iOS telemetry collection; Google applies it to COVID-19 mobility reports. For IoT deployments collecting personal data at scale, differential privacy enables population-level analytics, essential for smart city operations and public health monitoring, without exposing individual-level data.

8.8 Security Best Practices and the Seven Keys Framework

Security principles and mechanisms are only effective when translated into consistent engineering and operational practice. This section consolidates the chapter's technical content into two structured reference frameworks: a Security Best Practices Checklist organised by implementation domain, and the Seven Keys to Secure IoT Connectivity framework that provides the capstone synthesis of the chapter's security requirements. Both frameworks are designed to be directly applicable: the checklist as a deployment audit tool, and the Seven Keys as a communication framework for conveying security requirements to non-specialist stakeholders including management, procurement, and regulatory bodies.

8.8.1 Security Best Practices: A Structured Checklist

The best practices below are organised into six implementation domains, reflecting the architecture of an IoT deployment. Each practice maps to one or more vulnerability categories from Section 8.2 and addresses one or more threat categories from Section 8.5.

Practice	Implementation Guidance	Vulnerability Addressed
DEVICE HARDENING		
Disable all debug interfaces in production firmware	JTAG, UART, SWD, and other debug ports must be disabled or physically removed in all production firmware builds. CI/CD pipeline should include automated checks that debug interfaces are disabled before production release.	Physical

Enable secure boot with hardware root of trust	Configure HRoT (TrustZone, secure element, TPM) to anchor the boot chain. Verify signature at each boot stage. Implement rollback protection using OTP monotonic counters.	Physical, Software
Remove all factory-default credentials before shipment	Generate unique, cryptographically random credentials per device at manufacture. Never ship devices with shared or published default passwords. Reject any device configuration tool that sets identical credentials across multiple units.	Software
AUTHENTICATION AND IDENTITY		
Use hardware-protected device certificates for authentication	Generate device private keys inside HSM/secure element at manufacture. Issue X.509 device certificates from a managed IoT CA hierarchy. Deploy mTLS for all device-to-cloud connections.	Communication, Software
Implement unique per-device credentials	Every device must have cryptographically unique credentials. Shared credentials across a device fleet mean one compromise affects all. Use per-device PSK or PKI certificates, never fleet-wide shared secrets.	Communication, Software
Enforce Role-Based Access Control	Define device roles (sensor, actuator, gateway, management) with minimum necessary permissions. Enforce RBAC on the IoT broker and platform API. Review role assignments quarterly.	Connection Lifecycle
Apply multi-factor authentication to management interfaces	All human access to IoT management platforms, CMPs, and device configuration interfaces must require MFA. Service accounts should use certificate-based authentication rather than passwords.	Software, Connection Lifecycle
ENCRYPTION AND COMMUNICATION		
Enforce TLS 1.3 for all device-cloud communications	Disable TLS 1.0, 1.1, and 1.2 on brokers and APIs. Configure cipher suites to AES-128-GCM-SHA256 and ChaCha20-Poly1305 as minimum. Test cipher configuration with SSL Labs or equivalent.	Communication
Implement certificate pinning on devices	Hard-code the hash of the expected server certificate or CA certificate into device firmware. Reject connections presenting unexpected certificates regardless of CA trust.	Communication
Encrypt all data at rest	Sensor data, configuration, and credentials stored on devices or cloud platforms must be encrypted at rest using AES-256. Encryption keys must be stored in HSM or equivalent hardware-protected storage.	Physical, Software
NETWORK ARCHITECTURE		
Segment IoT devices onto dedicated network VLANs	IoT devices must not share a network segment with general-purpose IT systems. Virtual Local Area Network (VLAN) separation limits lateral movement from a compromised IoT device to enterprise systems. Firewall rules should allow only necessary IoT protocol ports.	Communication

Apply IP allowlisting for cloud connections	Configure the IoT platform to accept connections only from known device IP ranges or cellular APN subnets. Reject connection attempts from unexpected IP addresses even if credentials are valid.	Communication
Deploy IoT-specific intrusion detection	Monitor IoT network traffic for anomalous patterns: unusual data volumes, unexpected destination IPs, repeated authentication failures, abnormal protocol usage. Alert on deviations from established baselines.	Communication, Software
LIFECYCLE MANAGEMENT		
Maintain a complete device inventory with firmware versions	Every deployed device must be tracked in a centralised inventory with its model, hardware revision, current firmware version, and last update timestamp. Use this inventory to identify devices running vulnerable firmware versions.	Software, Connection Lifecycle
Implement automated OTA firmware updates with SUIT manifests	Deploy OTA infrastructure capable of delivering signed firmware updates to the full fleet. Sign all firmware with ECDSA P-256. Implement rollback protection. Target 100% fleet coverage for critical security patches within 72 hours of release.	Software
Execute formal deprovisioning procedures	On device retirement, transfer, or loss: revoke the device certificate (CRL/OCSP), suspend the SIM, invalidate API keys, remove the device from the fleet inventory, and perform a remote factory reset if the device is reachable. Document the deprovisioning in the audit trail.	Connection Lifecycle
Rotate credentials on a defined schedule	API keys and certificates should have defined validity periods (certificates: 1-2 years; API keys: 90 days for high-privilege). Automated renewal should trigger before expiry. Alert on any credential approaching expiry without renewal.	Connection Lifecycle
MONITORING AND INCIDENT RESPONSE		
Implement centralised security logging	Aggregate security events (authentication attempts, certificate validations, firmware update results, anomalous traffic) into a centralised Security Information and Event Management (SIEM) platform. Retain logs for a minimum of 12 months. Implement real-time alerting for high-severity events.	All categories
Define and test an IoT incident response playbook	Document the response procedure for each common IoT security incident type: compromised device, mass credential theft, OTA supply chain attack, botnet recruitment. Test the playbook with tabletop exercises annually. Define device quarantine and remote wipe capabilities.	All categories

Table 8.5: IoT Security Best Practices Checklist: Six Implementation Domains

8.8.2 The Seven Keys to Secure IoT Connectivity

The Seven Keys to Secure IoT Connectivity framework synthesises the chapter's security requirements into a structured, communicable summary. Developed from international IoT security standards including European Telecommunications Standards Institute (ETSI) EN 303 645, GSMA IoT Security Guidelines, and National Institute of Standards and Technology (NIST) IR 8259, the Seven Keys provide a complete minimum security specification that can be applied as a procurement requirement, a deployment audit checklist, or a design brief for new IoT systems. Each key maps directly to one or more vulnerability categories from the chapter's taxonomy, ensuring that the framework is grounded in the technical analysis rather than being merely aspirational.

Key	Security Requirement	Technical Control Required	Vulnerability Addressed
Key 1 Secure Device Identity	Every device must have a unique, cryptographically verifiable identity that cannot be fabricated or cloned.	Hardware-protected X.509 device certificate or per-device PSK generated in secure element at manufacture; mTLS for cloud connectivity.	Communication (impersonation); Physical (node cloning)
Key 2 Authenticated Access	All access to IoT devices and management systems must require authentication; anonymous access must be eliminated.	mTLS for device connections; MFA for all human management access; disable Telnet, anonymous MQTT, and all default credentials.	Communication (unauthenticated protocols); Software (default credentials)
Key 3 Encrypted Communication	All data in transit must be encrypted using current protocol standards. Unencrypted channels are not permitted.	TLS 1.3 for TCP communications; DTLS 1.3 for UDP/CoAP; AES-128-GCM minimum cipher suite; certificate pinning on devices.	Communication (unencrypted transmission; Man-in-the-Middle, MITM)
Key 4 Secure Connectivity Management	A Connectivity Management Platform must provide centralised visibility and control over all device communications, enforcing data policies and enabling rapid suspension of compromised devices.	CMP with real-time SIM monitoring; automated anomaly alerting; data volume and geographic controls per SIM; one-click suspension capability.	Connection Lifecycle (stale credentials; absent deprovisioning)
Key 5 Lifecycle Security Governance	Security must be actively maintained across the full device lifecycle from secure provisioning through operation to formal deprovisioning.	Secure manufacturing provisioning workflow; OTA update infrastructure with SUIT manifests; formal deprovisioning procedure with credential revocation.	Software (unpatched firmware); Connection Lifecycle (all sub-categories)
Key 6 Monitoring and Anomaly Detection	Continuous monitoring of device behaviour and communication patterns must detect compromise, misuse, and configuration drift in near-real-time.	SIEM integration for IoT events; baseline profiling per device type; automated alerting on behavioural deviations; audit logging with 12-month retention.	All categories: detection when preventive controls fail

Key 7 Interoperability with Trusted Partners	Third-party connectivity providers, platform vendors, and data processors must meet equivalent security standards; security requirements must be contractually enforced.	Security due diligence process for vendors; contractual security requirements (ISO 27001, GSMA NESAS, ETSI EN 303 645); annual review of partner security posture.	Connection Lifecycle (supply chain; third-party access)

Table 8.6: The Seven Keys to Secure IoT Connectivity: Requirements, Controls, and Vulnerability Map

8.8.3 Regulatory Compliance and Standards Landscape

IoT security is increasingly shaped by mandatory regulatory requirements rather than being left to voluntary best practice. Manufacturers, operators, and service providers in major markets must understand and comply with the following principal regulatory frameworks.

ETSI EN 303 645 is the European standard for consumer IoT security, published in 2020 and referenced by the UK's Product Security and Telecommunications Infrastructure (PSTI) Act 2022 as the benchmark for consumer IoT product security. It defines 13 mandatory provisions including no default passwords, implementing a vulnerability disclosure policy, keeping software updated, securely storing credentials, minimising exposed attack surfaces, ensuring software integrity, ensuring personal data is protected, and ensuring resilience to outages. As of April 2024, the PSTI Act makes compliance with the core provisions of EN 303 645 a legal requirement for consumer IoT devices sold in the UK market, with fines of up to GBP 10 million or 4% of global turnover for violations.

The EU Cyber Resilience Act (CRA, 2024) extends equivalent requirements across the EU market, covering all products with digital elements including IoT devices. The CRA requires security by design, a software bill of materials (SBOM) documenting all software components and their versions, vulnerability reporting to ENISA within 24 hours of discovery, and security updates for the expected product lifetime. The CRA's essential requirements are aligned with ETSI EN 303 645 but extend them in scope and add supply chain transparency requirements through the SBOM mandate.

Regional Example: *National Cybersecurity Frameworks for IoT in the Gulf Cooperation Council.*

The Gulf Cooperation Council states have developed national cybersecurity frameworks that include specific provisions for IoT security, reflecting the region's rapid digital infrastructure expansion and strategic dependence on connected systems in energy, utilities, and smart city de-

ployments. Saudi Arabia's National Cybersecurity Authority (NCA) published dedicated IoT Cybersecurity Controls in 2021, establishing mandatory requirements for organisations deploying IoT in critical national infrastructure — energy generation and distribution, water treatment, and healthcare. The controls mandate unique device credentials at manufacture, mutual TLS authentication for all device-platform communications, and OTA update capability for all externally deployed devices. The UAE's Telecommunications and Digital Government Regulatory Authority (TDRA) issued the UAE IoT Regulatory Policy in 2019 and updated security requirements in 2022, requiring connected consumer devices sold in the UAE marketplace to meet minimum password complexity standards and support security patching — requirements aligned with, and in several provisions exceeding, ETSI EN 303 645. In Oman, the National Computer Emergency Response Team (OCERT) under the Information Technology Authority (ITA) has published IoT security guidance for critical infrastructure operators, with specific attention to operational technology environments in the oil and gas sector. A cross-GCC challenge shared by all member states is the security of legacy operational technology: millions of installed industrial sensors and controllers pre-date IoT security standards and cannot be updated. The Saudi NCA's Industrial Control Systems Security Standard provides a framework for brownfield OT/IoT security that has become a regional reference model.

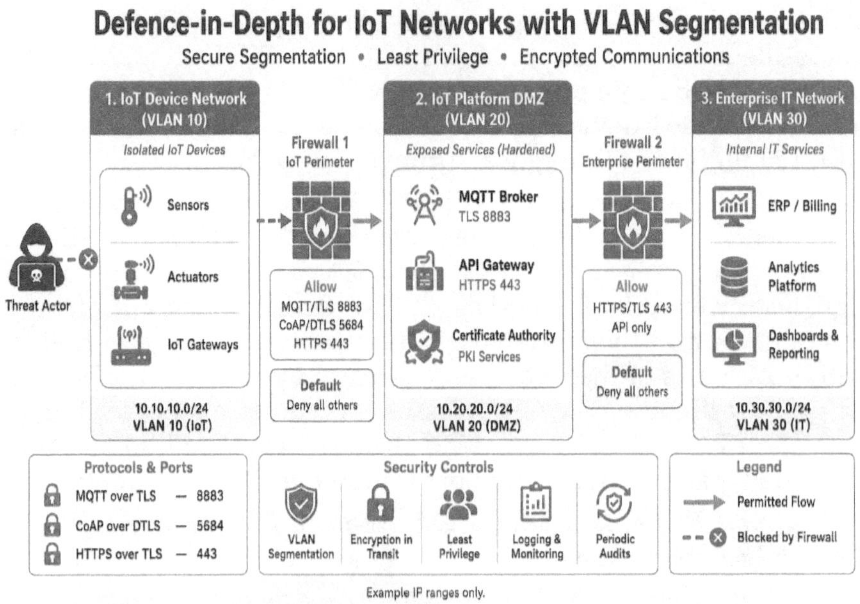

Figure 8.5: IoT Network Segmentation Architecture: VLAN Separation and Defence-in-Depth

NIST IR 8259 (Foundational Cybersecurity Activities for IoT Device Manufacturers) and the associated NIST Cybersecurity Framework Profile for IoT provide the US regulatory reference framework. While not currently mandatory for most commercial IoT devices, NIST IR 8259 is referenced in US Federal procurement requirements and in the FCC's IoT Cybersecurity Labelling Programme launched in 2024, which provides a voluntary "US Cyber Trust Mark" label for consumer IoT devices meeting NIST-defined security criteria. The label programme creates market incentives for security investment even in the absence of a hard legal mandate.

The GSMA IoT Security Guidelines (IG.06) address the specific security requirements of cellular IoT deployments, covering device security, network security, and service security across the end-to-end architecture of a cellular IoT system. The GSMA also publishes the Network Equipment Security Assurance Scheme (NESAS), which provides a security assurance framework for network equipment used in IoT connectivity infrastructure. For cellular IoT operators, NESAS certification of their connectivity infrastructure and adherence to IG.06 for their device and platform deployments represent the industry-standard security baseline.

CASE STUDY: ETSI EN 303 645 in Practice: UK PSTI Act Compliance

United Kingdom | 2024–Present

The UK Product Security and Telecommunications Infrastructure (PSTI) Act 2022 came into force in April 2024, making the core provisions of ETSI EN 303 645 legally binding for consumer IoT devices sold in the UK. The Act covers all consumer connectable products (smart speakers, cameras, televisions, routers, wearables, smart home devices, and similar) and places compliance obligations on both manufacturers and distributors.

The three immediately applicable requirements under the PSTI Act are: unique passwords (no default passwords identical across a product range), a published vulnerability disclosure policy (a publicly accessible URL where security researchers can report vulnerabilities), and a minimum security update period (manufacturers must state the minimum period for which security updates will be provided, with a minimum period of one year required). The Act also creates a regime of investigation, stop-notices, and recall notices for non-compliant products, with financial penalties up to GBP 10 million or 4% of global revenue.

The practical impact on product teams has been significant. Many manufacturers discovered during compliance preparation that their product lines used common passwords across all units, had no formal vulnerability disclosure process, and had no stated end-of-software-support date for any product. The compliance exercise forced a root-and-branch review of product security processes that, for many manufacturers, resulted in the first systematic security design review their products had received.

Market research by the UK's Office for Product Safety and Standards in late 2024 found that compliance rates among products newly introduced to the UK market were significantly higher than among legacy product lines, indicating that manufacturers are internalising security requirements in new product development but struggling to retrofit compliance to existing deployed products. This finding reinforces the core message of this chapter: security must be designed in from the start, not retrofitted after deployment.

8.9 Secure by Design and Software Bill of Materials

Secure by Design means that cybersecurity is treated as a core product requirement from the earliest stages of IoT development, rather than as a corrective activity after deployment. In IoT systems, this includes unique device identity, removal of default passwords, secure boot, signed firmware, encrypted communication, least-privilege access, secure update mechanisms, vulnerability handling, and defined end-of-support policies. This approach is increasingly important because IoT devices may remain deployed for many years in homes, hospitals, factories, cities, vehicles, and critical infrastructure.

A Software Bill of Materials, or SBOM, is a structured list of software components used in a product, including open-source libraries, third-party packages, firmware modules, and version information. For IoT products, an SBOM helps manufacturers, operators, and security teams identify whether a device is affected when a vulnerability is discovered in a component. SBOMs do not make a device secure by themselves, but they improve transparency, vulnerability management, supply-chain security, and long-term maintenance. Together, Secure by Design and SBOM practices support a more accountable and internationally aligned approach to IoT product security.

Professional Checklist: IoT Security Readiness

Before deploying an IoT system, confirm the following:

- *Each device has a unique identity and supports secure authentication.*
- *Default passwords are removed, and credential management follows least-privilege principles.*
- *Data is protected in transit and at rest using appropriate encryption*

and key management.

- *Secure boot, firmware integrity checks, and signed OTA updates are supported where possible.*
- *Network segmentation, monitoring, logging, and incident response procedures are defined.*
- *Vulnerability disclosure, patching responsibility, and end-of-support plans are documented.*

8.10 Chapter Summary

IoT security is not a variant of enterprise IT security made harder by device constraints. It is a structurally distinct discipline whose fundamental differences from IT security — resource-constrained hardware, physical exposure of devices, decade-long operational lifetimes, fleet-scale heterogeneity, and direct physical consequences of failure, require adapted rather than imported defences. The engineer who understands these six structural differences, and who designs security responses to each from the first architectural decision, is working in the right problem frame. The engineer who treats IoT security as "just add TLS" is systematically underestimating the challenge.

The four-category vulnerability taxonomy provides the analytical framework for structured IoT security assessment. Communication vulnerabilities (unencrypted transmission, unauthenticated protocols, protocol-specific weaknesses) are addressed through TLS/DTLS encryption, mutual authentication, and protocol hardening. Physical vulnerabilities (exposed debug interfaces, accessible flash memory, device replacement) are addressed through hardware roots of trust, disabled production debug ports, and tamper-detection hardware.

Software vulnerabilities (unpatched firmware, default credentials, memory corruption, hardcoded keys) are addressed through OTA update infrastructure, unique per-device credentials, secure coding practices, and continuous vulnerability management. Connection lifecycle vulnerabilities (insecure provisioning, absent deprovisioning, stale credential management) are addressed through secure provisioning workflows, formal deprovisioning procedures, and automated credential rotation policies. Most real-world IoT security failures involve at least two of these four vulnerability categories simultaneously, reflecting the systemic nature of IoT security debt.

Device identity is the foundation layer on which every other security function depends. Without reliable, cryptographically verifiable device identity, encryption protects channels to unknown endpoints, access control enforces rules for unverified entities, and audit trails record actions by unidentifiable actors. PKI-based device identity (hardware-protected private keys, X.509 device certificates, mutual TLS) provides scalable, strong device authentication. For cellular IoT, SIM-based identity at the network layer provides an independent hardware-anchored identity proof. Role-based access control maps authenticated identity to authorised capabilities, ensuring that even a compromised device credential cannot be used for actions outside the device's defined role.

Encryption of data in transit is necessary but not sufficient: the difference between link-layer encryption and end-to-end encryption matters when intermediate nodes (gateways, brokers) are themselves potential attack targets. TLS 1.3 with ECDHE key exchange provides forward secrecy; session resumption reduces reconnection overhead for frequently cycling devices. DTLS provides the same security guarantees over UDP for CoAP-based constrained devices. Certificate pinning prevents man-in-the-middle attacks using fraudulently issued certificates. Connectivity resilience (multi-path failover, geographic restrictions, data volume limits) extends security from confidentiality and integrity to availability.

The threat taxonomy maps the attack landscape against the vulnerability taxonomy: physical attacks exploit physical vulnerabilities; network attacks exploit communication vulnerabilities; software attacks and malware exploit software vulnerabilities; operational failures exploit connection lifecycle vulnerabilities. The Mirai botnet, exploiting only default credential vulnerabilities at scale, demonstrated that the most consequential IoT attacks do not require sophisticated techniques, only the exploitation of basic security hygiene failures across large numbers of devices.

The Oldsmar water treatment attack, exploiting unpatched software and shared credentials in an OT environment, demonstrated that the physical consequences of IoT/OT security failure extend to direct risk to human life. The Triton/TRISIS attack, targeting safety instrumented systems to prevent emergency shutdowns, represents the current frontier of adversarial capability against safety-critical IoT infrastructure.

Secure boot and hardware root of trust ensure that a device only executes manufacturer-authorised firmware, preventing the execution of malicious code even if the device is physically accessed or its update mechanism is attacked. Certificate lifecycle management (issuance, distribution, renewal, and revocation) must be automated at scale; manual certificate management is operationally infeasible for deployments larger than a few hundred devices. OTA firmware update capability, secured with SUIT manifest signing, rollback protection, and TLS delivery, is the mechanism through which the long-term security of a deployed fleet is maintained. Without OTA, every subsequently discovered vulnerability requires physical device replacement.

Privacy and security are complementary properties that must both be designed in from the start. Privacy by Design's seven principles provide the architectural framework: data minimisation at the edge reduces the privacy sensitivity of transmitted data; pseudonymisation at ingestion prevents individual identification in analytics pipelines; differential privacy enables population-level insights without individual-level exposure; end-to-end security protects data from all intermediate observers including authorised ones.

The regulatory landscape (ETSI EN 303 645, the UK PSTI Act, the EU Cyber Resilience Act, NIST IR 8259, the GSMA IoT Security Guidelines) is converging on a consistent set of minimum security requirements that are increasingly mandatory rather than voluntary across all major markets.

The Security Best Practices Checklist and the Seven Keys to Secure IoT Connectivity synthesise the chapter's technical content into actionable frameworks. The seven keys, Secure Device Identity, Authenticated Access, Encrypted Communication, Secure Connectivity Management, Lifecycle Security Governance, Monitoring and Anomaly Detection, and Interoperability with Trusted Partners, define the minimum security specification for any defensible IoT deployment. Deployments that satisfy all seven keys across their full operational lifetime have addressed every category of vulnerability identified in this chapter. The operational processes that implement and maintain these keys across device lifecycles are the subject of Chapter 9. The emerging application of machine learning to IoT security (including ML-driven behavioural anomaly detection, adaptive access control, and AI-assisted threat hunting across large IoT estates) is examined in Chapter 11 as part of the broader AI and IoT integration framework.

Chapter 9

IoT System Administration, Connectivity Management, and Governance

Operating and Governing IoT Deployments Across Their Full Lifecycle

Chapter 9 examines the operational, administrative, and governance dimensions required to manage IoT systems at scale. It explains IoT system administration as a specialised discipline that extends beyond traditional IT management because of large device fleets, heterogeneous connectivity, constrained hardware, long deployment lifecycles, distributed ownership, and security-critical operations. The chapter discusses connectivity management platforms, SIM and network lifecycle control, device provisioning, human access management, privileged operations, monitoring, alerting, incident response, and partner coordination. It also presents the Seven Keys framework from an operational administration perspective, showing how authentication, encryption, patching, monitoring, access control, incident readiness, and governance contribute to secure and reliable IoT deployment. In addition, the chapter explores policy, compliance, regulatory expectations, and multi-stakeholder governance models such as SMARTIE for federated IoT environments. Overall, this chapter provides the management and governance foundation needed to operate IoT systems responsibly, securely, and sustainably across enterprise, industrial, public-sector, and smart-city contexts.

In September 2023, a European logistics company operating 12,000 cellular-connected asset trackers across six countries received an automated alert from its connectivity management platform: 340 devices had begun transmitting data at a rate 45 times their established baseline, consuming what would amount to EUR 8,000 in data charges within a single 24-hour period if left unchecked. The alert was generated at 03:17, well outside business hours. Within four minutes, before any human operator had logged in, the platform's automated policy engine had suspended the affected SIMs, restricting their connectivity until an operator could investigate. By 08:30, the operations team had identified the cause: a firmware configuration error in an overnight batch update had enabled continuous high-frequency GPS reporting rather than the intended event-triggered model. A corrected firmware version was deployed to all affected devices by 10:15, and normal operation was fully restored before the first customer delivery of the day.

This scenario illustrates IoT system administration working exactly as it should: automated monitoring detecting an anomaly outside human hours, policy-based containment acting before the problem escalated, human investigation identifying the root cause, and a managed Over-the-Air (OTA) remediation restoring normal service. The entire lifecycle, detection through remediation, completed in seven hours without customer impact. Without a connectivity management platform, without automated alerting rules, and without OTA remediation capability, the same incident would have generated unexpected charges, required manual inspection of each of 340 devices, and potentially taken days to resolve.

Chapter 9 addresses the operational and governance dimension of IoT systems — what happens after deployment. Where Chapter 8 designed the security architecture, Chapter 9 operates it. The chapter is structured in two interconnected halves. The first half (Sections 9.1 through 9.7) addresses operational IoT system administration: the discipline, tools, and processes for managing deployed IoT fleets at scale. The second half (Sections 9.8 and 9.9) addresses institutional IoT governance: the regulatory frameworks, compliance obligations, and architectural approaches for governing IoT systems within legal and organisational boundaries. The connecting thread is the observation that neither technical security nor regulatory compliance survives contact with a fleet of 10,000 devices without operational processes designed to maintain them over years of deployment.

9.1 IoT System Administration as a Discipline

IoT system administration is the operational discipline responsible for managing, maintaining, securing, and governing a deployed IoT system across its full operational lifetime. It is the practice layer that translates the security architecture of Chapter 8, the data governance requirements of Chapter 6, and the regulatory obligations of this chapter into day-to-day operational reality. An IoT system that is well-designed but poorly administered is a security liability that degrades steadily from the moment of deployment: certificates expire without renewal, firmware versions diverge as updates fail to reach some devices, credentials accumulate without rotation, and monitoring alerts pile up unread until a genuine incident is lost in the noise.

DEFINITION: IoT System Administration

The operational discipline responsible for managing, maintaining, securing, and governing a deployed IoT system across its full operational lifetime. IoT system administration encompasses device fleet management, connectivity management, access control, monitoring and alerting, incident response, and compliance reporting. It is distinct from IoT security (which designs protection mechanisms) in that it maintains and operates those mechanisms continuously after deployment.

9.1.1 Why IoT Administration Differs from IT Administration

Traditional IT system administration manages assets that are physically located in controlled environments (data centres, server rooms, offices) accessible for maintenance, with operating systems that support standardised management protocols (SNMP, SSH, WMI). IoT administration faces a fundamentally different environment. Devices are physically distributed across buildings, cities, fields, vehicles, and bodies.

Physical access for maintenance is frequently impractical or economically prohibitive. Operating systems are diverse, proprietary, and often lack standard management interfaces. Device capabilities range from powerful edge servers to microcontrollers with no operating system at all. Connectivity is intermittent, low-bandwidth, and may incur per-byte costs that make chatty management protocols unaffordable.

These differences have three practical consequences for how IoT administration is organised. First, all administration must be remote: every management operation (configuration change, firmware update, credential rotation, deactivation) must be executable over the device's existing communication channel without physical access. This requires that remotability be designed into the device from the outset, not added later.

Second, all administration must be scalable: no IoT operations team can manage 10,000 devices individually. Configuration, updates, and policies must be applied to device groups through policy-based automation, with exceptions escalated to human attention rather than every operation requiring human initiation. Third, all administration must be auditable: every operation performed on a device must generate an immutable log entry, because IoT operations intersect with data protection obligations (General Data Protection Regulation (GDPR) Article 30 processing records), security incident investigations, and contractual Service Level Agreement (SLA) reporting.

9.1.2 Roles in IoT System Administration

Mature IoT operations functions typically organise around four specialised roles, each with distinct responsibilities, tools, and access privileges. These roles may be combined in smaller deployments but should be conceptually distinct even when staffed by the same individuals, because they correspond to different risk profiles and separation-of-duty requirements.

The IoT operations engineer manages the day-to-day health of the device fleet: monitoring connectivity status, managing data usage budgets, coordinating OTA firmware deployments, and responding to operational alerts. The operations engineer needs read-write access to the CMP for device activation, suspension, and configuration, but should not have access to security policy configuration or platform administration functions. This role corresponds to the Device Operator RBAC tier described in Section 9.4.

The IoT security administrator manages access control, security policy enforcement, and incident response. This role configures the APN restrictions, IP allowlists, and anomaly detection rules that determine the fleet's security posture, and leads the investigation and containment process when a security incident is detected. The security administrator needs access to security policy configuration and audit logs but should not have unilateral access to production device configuration (to enforce separation of duty between security oversight and operational change). This role corresponds to the Security Administrator RBAC tier.

The IoT compliance officer is responsible for regulatory reporting, audit evidence collection, and Data Protection Impact Assessment management. This role does not typically need operational access to the CMP but requires read access to usage reports, audit logs, and data processing records sufficient to demonstrate compliance with applicable regulations. In GDPR terms, this role may overlap with or report to the organisation's Data Protection Officer.

The connectivity partner manager is responsible for managing the commercial and technical relationship with MNOs, MVNOs, and other connectivity service providers. This role monitors SLA adherence, manages contract renewals, coordinates incident escalations with carrier NOCs, and governs the data processing agreements that apply to carrier-side data handling. The connectivity partner manager role is often found within procurement or vendor management functions rather than engineering, but requires sufficient technical understanding to interpret CMP reports and assess carrier security posture.

DEFINITION: Fleet Management

The practice of managing a large number of IoT devices as a coordinated group rather than as individual assets, applying configuration changes, firmware updates, security policies, and operational actions at fleet or device-group scale. Fleet management transforms what would be unmanageable individual device operations into scalable policy-driven workflows.

DEFINITION: Zero-Touch Provisioning (ZTP)

A device onboarding approach in which IoT devices are automatically configured with identity credentials, connectivity parameters, and application configuration upon first network contact, without requiring manual per-device intervention by an operator. ZTP enables deployment of large device batches with minimal operational overhead while maintaining security through automated credential injection from a trusted provisioning server. Standardised in IETF RFC 8572 (Secure ZTP) and GSMA SGP.02 for eSIM remote provisioning.

9.2 The Connectivity Management Platform

The Connectivity Management Platform is the operational control plane for cellular IoT deployments. Just as an enterprise IT environment depends on a network management system to provide visibility and control over the network infrastructure, a cellular IoT deployment depends on a CMP to provide visibility and control over the cellular connectivity of every device in the fleet.

Without a CMP, an operator manages cellular IoT devices through carrier billing portals (designed for human account management, not automated fleet operations) with no real-time visibility into device connectivity status, no automated anomaly detection, and no programmatic control over individual device connections. With a CMP, the logistics company in the chapter opening scenario was able to detect and contain a data anomaly affecting 340 devices at 03:17 without waking anyone up.

DEFINITION: Connectivity Management Platform (CMP)

A software platform providing centralised visibility and control over the connectivity lifecycle of SIM-equipped IoT devices. The CMP is positioned between the carrier network and the IoT application platform, providing device inventory management, SIM activation and lifecycle control, real-time data usage monitoring, security policy enforcement, and automated alerting. CMPs connect to carrier networks via GSMA-standardised APIs and expose management capabilities to IoT operators via web dashboards and REST APIs.

9.2.1 Core CMP Functions

A production-grade CMP provides six core operational functions, each addressing a class of management problem that is intractable without centralised platform support.

Device inventory and registry is the CMP's foundational function. The device registry maintains a real-time record of every SIM in the fleet, with attributes including the ICCID (SIM serial number), IMSI (subscriber identity), IMEI (device hardware identifier), current connectivity status (active, suspended, deactivated), current and historical data usage, assigned rate plan, last connection timestamp, and geographic location at cell-tower resolution.

For a fleet of 50,000 devices, this registry is the single source of truth for fleet composition, and its accuracy is a prerequisite for every other CMP function. Without it, operations teams cannot answer the most basic questions: how many of our devices are currently connected? How many are running which firmware version? Which devices have not connected for more than 30 days?

DEFINITION: ICCID (Integrated Circuit Card Identifier)

The unique serial number identifying a SIM card, typically 19 or 20 digits, printed on the SIM card itself and stored in the SIM's memory. The ICCID is the primary identifier used in CMP device registries to track individual SIM-equipped IoT devices. It uniquely identifies the physical SIM card independently of the subscriber identity (IMSI) or device hardware (IMEI).

Connectivity lifecycle management enables the CMP to activate, suspend, and deactivate SIM profiles programmatically, individually or in bulk. Activating 500 new SIMs for a fleet expansion, suspending 200 SIMs for seasonal asset storage, or deactivating the SIMs of decommissioned devices are operations that a CMP can execute in minutes across any number of devices through its Application Programming Interface (API) or batch operation interface. Rate plan management, moving devices between data plans in response to changing usage requirements is handled through the same interface. For global deployments, the CMP manages roaming permissions across carrier networks, controlling which devices are permitted to roam in which countries and under which rate arrangements.

Data usage monitoring and policy enforcement is the function most directly relevant to the chapter-opening scenario. The CMP tracks real-time and historical data usage per device and per fleet segment, enabling operators to detect abnormal consumption patterns before they result in unexpected costs or indicate security compromise. Configurable usage thresholds trigger automated actions: suspending a device that exceeds its monthly data allowance (preventing bill shock), generating an alert when a device's hourly data consumption deviates more than three standard deviations from its rolling 30-day average (a potential indicator of malware, misconfiguration, or data exfiltration), or restricting a device to a limited low-bandwidth mode when it approaches 80% of its monthly allowance.

Security policy enforcement at the network level extends the device-level and application-level security controls of Chapter 8 with network-layer controls. The CMP can restrict each device or device group to communicate only with specific IP addresses or ranges (allowlisting), require that all traffic traverse a private APN rather than the public internet, enforce VPN tunnel requirements, and automatically block devices that have been flagged as compromised by the security monitoring system. Network-level controls provide a defence-in-depth layer that remains effective even when device-level security has been compromised: a device whose credentials have been stolen cannot exfiltrate data to an attacker-controlled server if the CMP's APN restrictions allow only connections to the legitimate IoT platform IP range.

Alerting and event management translates the monitoring data into actionable notifications. CMPs generate alerts when configurable conditions are met: a device goes offline beyond its expected reconnection interval, a device's data usage exceeds a threshold, a SIM is used from an unexpected geographic location, authentication failures occur repeatedly against a device. Alerts are categorised by severity and routed to appropriate recipients: critical security indicators to the on-call security team via PagerDuty, operational alerts to the operations team ticket queue, informational usage reports to management dashboards. Well-designed alerting is specific enough to enable immediate action: not "device offline" but "device ICCID 8944501000000000001 offline since 14:32 UTC, last seen at cell tower ID DE-BER-047, last data transmission 14:27 UTC, average reconnection time for this device type is 4 minutes."

Reporting and audit provides the documentary evidence needed for billing reconciliation, capacity planning, regulatory compliance, and security incident investigation. CMP reports cover: monthly data usage per device and per fleet segment (for billing verification and cost allocation); SIM activation and deactivation history (for asset management); security event logs (for incident investigation and GDPR Article 30 processing records); SLA adherence metrics for carrier partner management. Audit logs, every action performed through the CMP, by whom, at what time, on which SIM, which must be tamper-evident and retained for the period required by applicable regulation and contractual obligation.

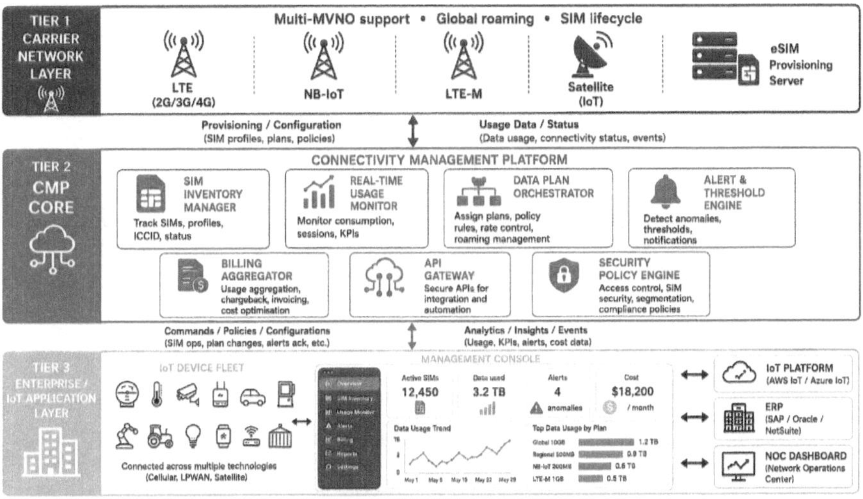

Figure 9.1: Connectivity Management Platform Architecture: Integration Between Carrier Network, CMP, and IoT Platform

9.2.2 CMP Vendor Landscape

The CMP market has evolved through two waves. The first wave, from approximately 2010 to 2018, was dominated by MNO-affiliated platforms. Jasper Wireless, founded in 2004 and acquired by Cisco in 2016, was the most widely deployed independent CMP before its acquisition, and the resulting Cisco IoT Control Center remains the market-leading platform for large enterprise IoT deployments globally. Ericsson Device Connection Platform (DCP) and Nokia WING (Worldwide IoT Network Grid) are the MNO-vendor platforms most commonly deployed by Tier 1 carriers. These platforms provide deep carrier network integration but have historically been less flexible in their API exposure and third-party integration capabilities.

The second wave, from 2018 onwards, has brought independent IoT connectivity management vendors (Aeris, KORE, Eseye) specialising in global multi-carrier management, particularly valuable for IoT deployments spanning multiple countries where no single carrier provides adequate coverage everywhere. These platforms manage relationships with multiple carrier networks simultaneously, presenting a unified management interface to the operator regardless of which carrier network each device is currently using. Twilio's Programmable Wireless (now Twilio Super SIM) brought developer-friendly APIs and consumption-based pricing to the CMP market, making CMP capabilities accessible to smaller IoT deployments that would not qualify for enterprise carrier contracts. In the open-source space, Eclipse Kapua provides CMP-comparable device management and connectivity control capabilities for operators who prefer to run their own platform infrastructure.

Platform	Positioning	Key Strengths	Best Suited For
Cisco IoT Control Center	MNO-affiliated enterprise CMP (formerly Jasper)	Market-leading carrier integrations; advanced policy engine; enterprise-grade SLA	Large enterprise deployments with Tier 1 carrier relationships; 500,000+ device fleets
Ericsson DCP	Carrier-vendor platform for MNO deployments	Deep 5G NR integration; network slicing management; GSMA SGP.02 native	MNO-operated IoT services; private network IoT deployments
KORE / Aeris	Independent global multi-carrier IoT MVNO platforms	Global carrier network aggregation; single API across 700+ networks; flexible rate plans	Multi-country deployments requiring carrier diversity; logistics and asset tracking
Twilio Super SIM	Developer-focused IoT connectivity platform	REST API-first design; consumption pricing; rapid integration; Programmable SIM	Developer-built IoT products; startups; SME IoT deployments up to ~100K devices
Eclipse Kapua	Open-source IoT device management platform	No vendor lock-in; self-hosted; extensible; MQTT and REST APIs	Organisations requiring full platform ownership; private deployment environments

Table 9.1: Connectivity Management Platform Vendor Landscape: Positioning and Use Cases

DEFINITION: APN (Access Point Name)

A gateway identifier that determines which carrier network gateway an IoT device connects to for data services. Private APNs provide a dedicated, isolated network path between IoT devices and the enterprise platform, preventing IoT traffic from traversing the public internet and enabling network-level traffic control and monitoring that is not possible on shared public APNs.

DEFINITION: MVNO (Mobile Virtual Network Operator)

A wireless communications provider that does not own radio spectrum or network infrastructure but resells connectivity services from one or more MNOs under its own brand, rate plans, and management interface.

Many IoT-specialised MVNOs provide global coverage aggregation, purpose-built IoT rate plans (low-volume monthly with overage caps), and CMP platforms tailored to IoT fleet management.

9.3 Device Provisioning and Lifecycle Management

The device lifecycle begins before the device is ever connected. From the moment a device's identity credentials are generated to the moment those credentials are permanently revoked, every stage of the lifecycle carries security implications. Provisioning determines the device's initial security posture. Operational maintenance determines whether that posture is preserved or eroded over years of deployment. Decommissioning determines whether retiring a device creates a lingering security liability or cleanly closes the identity lifecycle. Of the three phases, decommissioning is the most consistently neglected in practice and the most consistently exploited by adversaries.

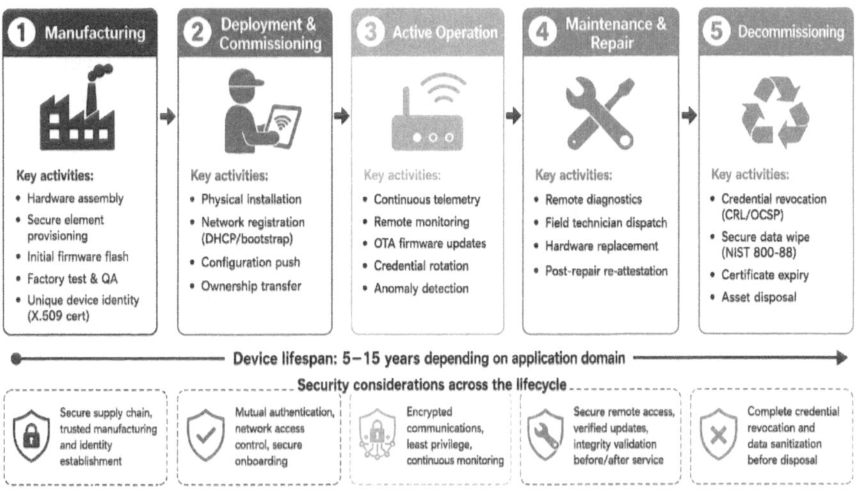

Figure 9.2: IoT Device Lifecycle: Five Phases from Manufacturing to Decommissioning

9.3.1 Provisioning Approaches

Device provisioning is the process of configuring a new IoT device with the identity credentials, connectivity parameters, and application configuration it needs to join the network and begin operating. Provisioning approaches sit on a spectrum from highly manual (secure but unscalable) to fully automated (scalable but requiring careful security design to avoid creating new vulnerabilities in the provisioning pathway itself).

Manual provisioning involves a technician physically connecting to each device (via USB, serial port, or local network) and entering configuration data including credentials, API keys, server addresses, and application parameters. For a deployment of 5 to 50 devices, manual provisioning is entirely reasonable: it is simple, fully auditable, and leaves no automated provisioning infrastructure that itself could become an attack target. For a deployment of 5,000 devices, it is completely impractical: at 15 minutes per device, 5,000 devices require 1,250 technician-hours, equivalent to seven and a half weeks of full-time work, and the per-device cost makes manual provisioning economically prohibitive for any but the highest-value individual assets.

Factory provisioning injects credentials at the manufacturing stage. Before the device leaves the factory, an HSM in the production environment generates a device-unique key pair inside the device's secure element, and the factory provisioning system signs the public key with the manufacturer's CA to produce an X.509 device certificate. The device arrives at the deployment site with its credentials already installed in tamper-resistant hardware, requiring only network activation through the CMP to begin operating. Factory provisioning is the most secure approach: the private key is generated inside the secure element and never handled outside it, but requires a manufacturing-stage Public Key Infrastructure (PKI) integration that smaller manufacturers may find complex to establish.

Zero-touch provisioning enables large-scale automated provisioning without factory-stage credential injection. The device is manufactured with a minimal factory certificate, sufficient to authenticate with the ZTP bootstrap server but not with the production IoT platform. On first network contact, the device authenticates to the ZTP server using the factory certificate, and the ZTP server delivers the device's full operational credentials, configuration, and network parameters over a secure channel. The device installs these credentials and switches to production operation, all without human intervention. IETF RFC 8572 (Secure ZTP) defines the protocol; GSMA SGP.02 provides the equivalent standard for remote eSIM profile provisioning in cellular IoT deployments.

DEFINITION: eUICC (Embedded Universal Integrated Circuit Card)

A hardware component providing SIM functionality in a permanently soldered chip, designed to support remote SIM profile download and operator switching without physical SIM replacement. The eUICC enables a single device design to be deployed globally, with the appropriate local carrier SIM profile loaded remotely after deployment. This is particularly valuable for global logistics, asset tracking, and utility IoT deployments where devices are shipped to different countries and must connect to local carrier networks on arrival. Governed by GSMA SGP.02 (M2M) and SGP.22 (Consumer) standards.

CASE STUDY: Global eUICC Deployment: Remote SIM Provisioning at Maersk

Copenhagen, Denmark | 2021-Present

A.P. Moller-Maersk, the world's largest container shipping company, operates a fleet of 400,000 refrigerated containers (reefers) equipped with IoT sensors for temperature, humidity, and location monitoring. These containers travel to over 130 countries. A critical operational requirement is that each container maintains cellular connectivity at its current geographic location, requiring access to local carrier networks in each country.

Maersk's Remote Container Management programme, first deployed in 2021 at scale, uses eUICC technology to manage carrier connectivity for the global container fleet. Each container's IoT module contains an eUICC that can hold multiple carrier SIM profiles simultaneously, with the active profile switchable remotely via the GSMA SGP.02 remote provisioning protocol. When a container arrives in a new country, the CMP's geographic location awareness triggers an automated profile switch to the local carrier, maintaining connectivity without requiring physical SIM replacement.

The programme eliminated a previous operational requirement to manually swap physical SIM cards when containers transferred between geographic regions: a process that had required shore-based technicians at major ports and frequently resulted in connectivity gaps of 12 to 48 hours. With eUICC remote provisioning, connectivity continuity improved from 87% to 99.3% across the global fleet, measured as the percentage of containers reporting a sensor reading at least every 4 hours.

From a security perspective, the eUICC approach also eliminated the physical SIM card as an attack vector: there are no physical SIM cards that can be removed, copied, or swapped by an adversary with brief physical access to a container. Carrier profile management is conducted exclusively through the CMP and GSMA-standardised remote provisioning protocols, with each profile switch logged in the audit trail.

9.3.2 Operational Phase Management

Once provisioned, devices enter the operational phase, potentially lasting years or decades. The operational phase requires continuous management across three dimensions: software currency (keeping firmware up to date and patched), credential currency (rotating certificates and API keys before expiry and after any suspected compromise), and configuration management (applying parameter changes to adapt device behaviour to changing operational requirements).

OTA configuration management enables IoT operators to change device application parameters (reporting intervals, measurement thresholds, alarm setpoints, server endpoints) without deploying a full firmware update. Configuration changes are typically smaller and faster to deliver than firmware updates, and they can be applied selectively to device subsets based on CMP device group membership.

An energy utility that needs to increase reporting frequency for smart meters during a demand response event can push a configuration change to the affected device group via the CMP in minutes, without requiring a firmware engineering cycle. The configuration delivery channel must be authenticated and encrypted (TLS with device certificate) with the same rigour as any other device communication.

Certificate lifecycle management is the most time-sensitive operational maintenance task. An IoT device whose certificate expires while it is deployed in a remote location with no physical access path is effectively disconnected: it cannot authenticate to the IoT platform and loses the ability to transmit data or receive management commands. Preventing certificate expiry requires: tracking the expiry date of every certificate in the fleet (a function the CMP device registry provides), generating automated alerts when certificates approach their renewal deadline (typically 60 and 30 days before expiry), and executing automated renewal through a certificate management protocol (EST or CMP lite) that delivers new certificates to devices before old ones expire.

Certificate renewals should also be triggered by security events: if a device is reported as physically compromised, its certificate should be revoked and a new one issued immediately, regardless of the original expiry date.

9.3.3 Decommissioning: The Most Neglected Lifecycle Phase

Device decommissioning is the process of permanently retiring an IoT device from service. It is the lifecycle phase most consistently neglected in operational practice and the one that creates the most persistent security liabilities when poorly executed. A decommissioned device with active credentials is not an inactive device; it is an active security vulnerability: a device whose identity the system still trusts, now in the hands of parties unknown.

DEFINITION: Device Decommissioning

The process of permanently retiring an IoT device from service, including the revocation of all associated credentials (SIM deactivation, certificate revocation, API key deletion), the deletion or archival of device data in accordance with the data retention policy, the removal of the device from the fleet inventory, and the physical disposal of the device in compliance with applicable e-waste regulations. Incomplete decommissioning is a connection lifecycle vulnerability that creates persistent exploitable credential exposure.

A complete decommissioning procedure covers five mandatory actions. SIM deactivation and deletion: the device's SIM must be suspended immediately upon decommissioning and permanently deactivated within a short period (typically 30 days, to allow for reinstatement if the decommissioning was made in error). The SIM profile should ultimately be deleted from the carrier network rather than merely suspended, eliminating any possibility of future activation.

Certificate revocation: the device's X.509 certificate must be submitted to the CA for revocation, and the CA's CRL must be updated and distributed to all relying parties. This revocation must be executed before the device leaves the organisation's physical custody, because a device in an uncontrolled environment with a valid certificate is a live identity credential.

API credential revocation: all API keys, OAuth tokens, and other application-layer credentials associated with the device must be deleted from all connected platforms. Credential deletion must be confirmed in audit logs — "marked as deleted" is insufficient if the credential can be recovered from a backup. Device data archival or deletion: all personal data associated with the device must be handled in accordance with the organisation's data retention policy; in GDPR terms, personal data that is no longer needed for its original purpose must be deleted. Physical disposal: the device must be disposed of in compliance with applicable e-waste regulations (the EU WEEE Directive requires proper recycling of electronic waste; secure data destruction standards require that any device containing stored personal data be securely wiped before disposal).

Operationally, decommissioning is best triggered by the asset management system that records the physical device's retirement. Integration between the asset management system and the CMP, so that marking a device as "disposed" in the asset register automatically initiates the SIM deactivation workflow in the CMP, ensures that decommissioning is not forgotten when the device's physical retirement is recorded. Without this integration, the operational reality is that SIM deactivation is initiated only when someone notices unexpected charges, which may be months after the device was physically removed.

9.4 Managing Human Access and Privileged Operations

The device fleet is only as secure as the people who administer it. An over-privileged administrator who can activate, reconfigure, and decommission any device in the fleet is a single point of failure: if their credentials are compromised, the adversary inherits full fleet control. A shared login used by multiple team members produces an audit trail that cannot attribute individual actions to individual people, eliminating the accountability that audit logging is meant to provide. An active account belonging to an employee who left the organisation six months ago is an open door whose existence the organisation may not even be aware of. Human access management for IoT platforms requires the same systematic approach as device access management: minimum necessary privilege, authenticated access, and auditable operations.

9.4.1 Role-Based Access Control for IoT Administration Platforms

The RBAC model for IoT administration platforms defines four roles, arranged in a privilege hierarchy from minimum-access observer to full-access platform administrator. Each role is defined by the operations it may perform, the data it may access, and the authentication requirements it must satisfy.

Role	Permitted Operations	Data Access	Authentication Requirement
Read-Only Observer	View device status, connectivity, usage dashboards, and alerts. No write operations of any kind.	Read-only access to fleet dashboards, device registry, and non-sensitive usage reports. No access to audit logs or security events.	Username + password + MFA (TOTP or hardware key). Session timeout: 8 hours.
Device Operator	Activate, suspend, and deactivate devices; push OTA firmware and configuration updates to assigned device groups; acknowledge and close operational alerts.	Full device registry read/write for assigned groups; usage reports; operational alert queue. No access to security policy configuration or audit logs.	Username + password + MFA (hardware security key required). Session timeout: 4 hours. IP restriction to corporate network or VPN.

Security Administrator	Configure security policies (APN restrictions, IP allowlists, VPN requirements); revoke device credentials; review and export audit logs; lead incident response investigations.	Full security configuration read/write; complete audit log access; security event feeds; SIEM integration. Cannot create or modify user accounts.	Hardware security key (FIDO2) + MFA. Privileged Access Workstation required. Session timeout: 2 hours. All sessions logged to SIEM.
Platform Administrator	Full platform access including user account management, role assignment, API key management, integration configuration, and system configuration.	Unrestricted platform access. Can read all data including complete audit logs and security events.	Hardware security key (FIDO2) + MFA + out-of-band approval for privileged operations (4-eyes principle). Privileged Access Workstation required. All sessions recorded.

Table 9.2: IoT Administration Platform RBAC: Four-Role Hierarchy with Permissions and Authentication Requirements

Multi-tenancy adds a dimension to the RBAC model: in deployments where multiple organisational units or customer tenants share a single CMP instance, role assignments are scoped to tenant boundaries. An operator in Tenant A's Device Operator role can manage Tenant A's devices but has zero visibility into Tenant B's device inventory, configuration, or alerts, even if both tenants are managed by the same IoT platform team. Platform-level roles (Security Administrator, Platform Administrator) that span tenants must be held by a smaller, more carefully governed group than tenant-scoped roles.

Key Insight — Why IoT Administration Cannot Rely on Manual Operations at Scale

Traditional IT administration can tolerate a degree of manual intervention: an experienced administrator can physically access a server, manually configure a device, or inspect a log file on a terminal. IoT administration at scale cannot. When a fleet spans tens of thousands of devices distributed across geographies, time zones, and connectivity networks (each with its own certificate expiry date, firmware version, connectivity status, and role assignment) the operational complexity exceeds human capacity without systematic automation. Connectivity Management Platforms, automated certificate lifecycle management, and policy-based provisioning are not optimisation tools in IoT; they are the minimum viable infrastructure that makes continuous, accountable fleet management operationally possible. An IoT deployment without them is not under-optimised: it is effectively unmanaged.

DEFINITION: Multi-Tenancy

A deployment model in which multiple independent organisations or business units share a single IoT platform instance, with strict data and configuration isolation enforced between tenants by the platform's access control layer. Multi-tenant CMP deployments are common in managed IoT service offerings where a single service provider manages connectivity for multiple enterprise customers.

DEFINITION: Privileged Access Workstation (PAW)

A dedicated, hardened computing device used exclusively for high-privilege administrative operations on IoT management platforms. The PAW is isolated from general-purpose computing (no email, web browsing, or personal applications), reducing the attack surface for credential theft through malware, phishing, or browser exploitation. Required for Security Administrator and Platform Administrator roles in mature IoT operations programmes.

9.4.2 Access Credential Lifecycle Management

Individual named accounts (one account per person, never shared) are the foundational requirement for auditable IoT platform access. Shared accounts destroy the evidentiary value of audit logs: if five people share a login, an audit log entry recording a SIM suspension under that login proves the operation was performed but provides no evidence of who performed it. Beyond accountability, shared accounts mean that when one person leaves the organisation, removing their access requires changing the shared credential and notifying everyone who uses it: a practically unworkable arrangement that frequently results in former employees retaining indefinite access.

Automated de-provisioning on employee offboarding is the most operationally critical access governance control. The common failure mode is not malicious: it is simply that the IoT platform is not included in the standard offboarding checklist that IT runs when an employee leaves. Integrating the CMP user directory with the organisation's identity provider (Active Directory, Okta, Azure AD) via SCIM (System for Cross-domain Identity Management) ensures that when HR marks an employee as departed in the HR system, account deactivation propagates automatically to the CMP and all connected IoT management platforms within minutes, regardless of whether the IT helpdesk ticket includes "CMP access" in its scope.

Session management policies for IoT platforms should be more conservative than for general enterprise applications. Session timeout periods should be short (2 to 8 hours depending on role, as specified in Table 9.2). Concurrent session limits prevent credential sharing by making it impossible for two people to use the same account simultaneously from different IP addresses. IP source restrictions, limiting logins to corporate network addresses or designated VPN endpoints, prevent access from personal devices or unexpected geographies. For Platform Administrator and Security Administrator roles, all session activity should be logged to the enterprise SIEM in real time, providing an additional oversight layer independent of the CMP's own audit trail.

9.5 Monitoring, Alerting, and Incident Response

Security architecture prevents some attacks. Detection and response limits the damage from those that get through. The logistics company in the chapter-opening scenario experienced an incident: a misconfigured firmware update causing runaway data consumption, but it was contained within hours because the monitoring infrastructure detected the anomaly and the automated policy engine acted on it before the cost escalated and before any human operator needed to be woken at 03:17. Every IoT deployment should be designed so that when something goes wrong, the system knows immediately and can respond faster than any human team could. This section describes how that capability is built.

9.5.1 Monitoring: Operational Health and Security

IoT monitoring serves two distinct but overlapping purposes: operational health monitoring (is the device functioning correctly and is it connected?) and security monitoring (is the device behaving as expected, or are there signs of compromise, misuse, or failure?). Both purposes draw from the same data streams (connectivity logs, data usage records, device telemetry, and authentication events) but they apply different analytical lenses and generate different response procedures. The distinction matters because conflating them leads to alert designs that are adequate for one purpose but inadequate for the other.

Device health monitoring tracks the metrics that indicate whether each device is performing its intended function: connectivity status (connected, disconnected, attempting reconnect); time since last heartbeat; current and cumulative data usage against plan; battery level for battery-powered devices; firmware version against the current production release; diagnostic error codes in device-reported telemetry.

For a fleet of 50,000 devices, health monitoring is the mechanism through which an operator knows at any moment that 49,847 devices are connected and healthy, 143 have not reported in more than 48 hours (requiring investigation), 7 have battery levels below 10% (requiring field service dispatch), and 3 are running firmware versions with published CVEs (requiring urgent OTA update deployment).

Security monitoring looks for deviations from expected behaviour that may indicate compromise, misuse, or external attack.

The most operationally significant security monitoring signals are: unusual data volume (a sensor that normally transmits 2 MB per day suddenly transmitting 90 MB, suggestive of data exfiltration or malware activity); communication with unexpected IP addresses or domains (a device contacting an IP address in a known botnet C2 blacklist or a geographic region where the IoT platform has no infrastructure); unusual communication timing patterns (a device that reports every 30 minutes suddenly sending continuous small packets, typical of beaconing malware); repeated authentication failures (indicating credential misuse attempts or a certificate mismatch); and anomalous geographic location (a device whose SIM connects from a different country than the device is deployed in: a strong indicator of SIM cloning or credential theft).

DEFINITION: SIEM (Security Information and Event Management)

A platform that aggregates, normalises, correlates, and analyses security event data from multiple sources including network devices, applications, cloud platforms, and IoT management systems. SIEMs provide the correlated, cross-source view needed to detect complex attack patterns that would be invisible when viewing any single data source in isolation. For IoT deployments, SIEM integration enables correlation of CMP connectivity anomalies with device telemetry anomalies and enterprise IT security events, providing the full attack chain visibility needed for effective incident response.

TECHNOLOGY SPOTLIGHT: Behavioural Baselining for IoT Anomaly Detection

The most effective IoT security monitoring systems do not rely solely on static threshold rules (alert when usage exceeds X MB/day). Static rules are brittle: they generate false positives when device behaviour legitimately changes (a new application version increases reporting frequency) and false negatives when an attack stays below the threshold. Behavioural baselining takes a fundamentally different approach: it learns what normal looks like for each device or device type and alerts on deviations from that learned baseline.

A behavioural baseline for an IoT device captures its normal patterns across multiple dimensions: typical daily data volume (mean and standard deviation over a rolling 30-day window); typical communication timing pattern (hourly buckets showing when the device is most active); typical destination IP addresses and ports; typical message size distribution; and typical geographic location (cell tower IDs or GPS coordinates). When a device's current behaviour deviates significantly from its baseline on multiple dimensions simultaneously, a compound anomaly alert is generated.

AWS IoT Device Defender provides managed behavioural baselining for AWS IoT Core-connected devices, automatically learning device behaviour profiles and generating audit findings and security alerts when devices deviate from established patterns. Cisco's Cyber Vision platform provides equivalent capability for OT and industrial IoT environments, using deep packet inspection of industrial protocols (Modbus, EtherNet/IP, Profinet) to baseline normal device communication patterns and detect intrusions that evade signature-based detection.

The practical benefit is alert quality: a well-tuned behavioural baselining system generates substantially fewer false-positive alerts than static threshold rules while detecting a broader range of abnormal behaviours. In a 2022 evaluation by a European energy utility, deploying AWS IoT Device Defender against a fleet of 35,000 smart meters reduced alert volume by 73% compared to the previous static-threshold alerting system while detecting two genuine incidents (a misconfigured batch update and a compromised testing environment) that the static rules had not flagged.

9.5.2 Alert Design and Operational Governance

An alerting system that generates too many alerts is nearly as dangerous as one that generates too few. Alert fatigue: the progressive desensitisation of operations teams to monitoring notifications due to excessive volume, particularly low-quality or false-positive alerts is one of the most common contributing factors to security incidents that were not detected promptly. Studies of security operations centre performance consistently find that teams receiving more than 500 security alerts per day begin to triage by recency rather than by severity, meaning that alerts generated earlier in the shift are systematically under-investigated. IoT deployments can easily generate thousands of events per day from large fleets; alert design must reduce this to a manageable signal.

DEFINITION: Alert Fatigue

A phenomenon in which security or operations teams become desensitised to monitoring alerts due to excessive volume, particularly from low-quality or false-positive notifications. Alert fatigue causes genuine incidents to be missed or delayed because they are indistinguishable from the noise of routine false positives. Alert fatigue is managed through thresh-

old tuning, behavioural baselining, alert deduplication (grouping related alerts from the same incident into a single notification), and regular alert rule review.

A four-tier severity classification structures alert routing and response time commitments. P1 Critical alerts indicate an active or imminent security incident requiring immediate response regardless of time of day: a device communicating with a known malware C2 server, a mass authentication failure pattern consistent with credential stuffing, or a device accessing network segments it has no legitimate reason to reach. P1 alerts are routed to the on-call security team via PagerDuty or equivalent, with a response time SLA of 15 minutes and an initial containment action SLA of 1 hour.

P2 High alerts indicate a significant operational or security issue that requires same-day response: a device with an active CVE in its firmware version, a certificate expiring within 7 days without renewal in progress, or a device offline beyond its maximum acceptable downtime. P3 Medium alerts enter the operational ticket queue for investigation within 2 business days: data usage approaching the monthly cap, a device firmware version falling two or more versions behind current. P4 Low alerts are informational, batched into a daily digest report: routine usage summaries, upcoming scheduled maintenance windows, quarterly certificate renewal notifications.

Alert routing must be precise: an alert that goes to the wrong person is effectively an alert that goes to no one. P1 security alerts should route to the on-call security administrator, not to the operations team that manages connectivity tickets. A connectivity outage alert should route to the operations engineer with authority to take corrective action, not to a monitoring dashboard that no one checks at 03:17. The alert routing configuration must be reviewed and tested at least quarterly, because team structures, on-call rosters, and contact details change, and an alerting system whose routing is stale will deliver critical alerts to departed employees.

9.5.3 Incident Response Lifecycle

The incident response lifecycle for IoT security events follows the same high-level structure as enterprise IT incident response (Detect, Triage, Contain, Investigate, Remediate, Recover, Post-Incident Review) but the specific tools and actions at each stage are IoT-specific, because the containment and remediation mechanisms available for IoT devices differ fundamentally from those available for servers and workstations.

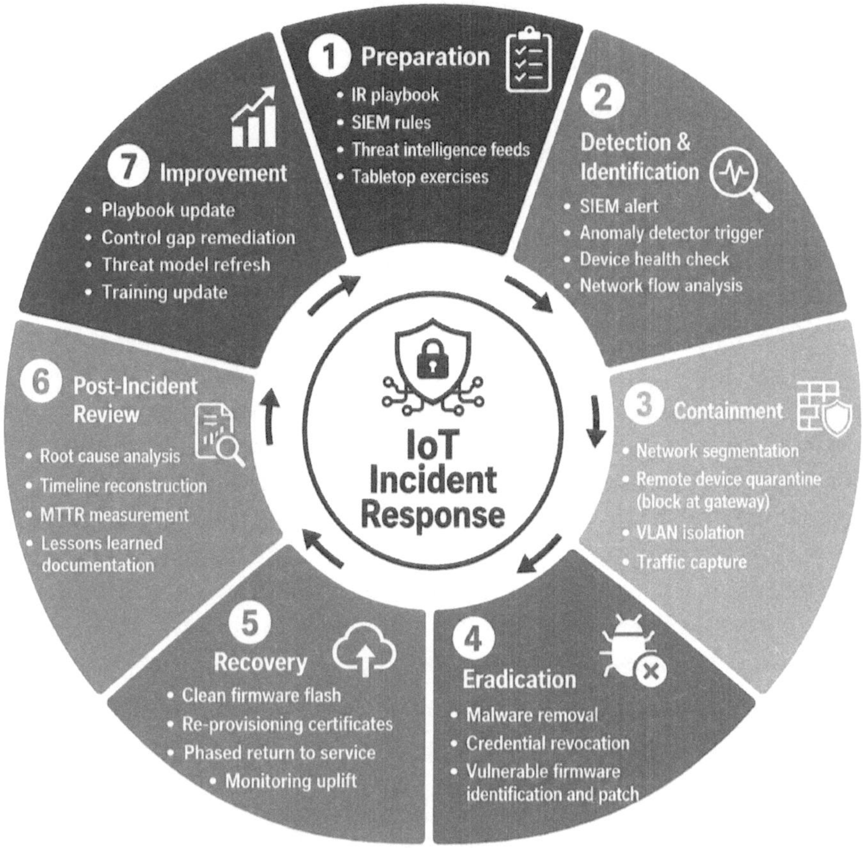

Figure 9.3: IoT Incident Response Lifecycle: Seven Stages from Detection to Post-Incident Review

Detection is triggered by the monitoring infrastructure: a CMP anomaly alert, a SIEM correlation rule, an external threat intelligence feed, or a report from a customer or third party. The detection phase ends when someone in the operations team has confirmed that an alert represents a real event requiring a response, rather than a false positive or a known benign condition.

Triage is the assessment phase: is this a genuine security incident or an operational anomaly? A device transmitting 90 MB in a day when its baseline is 2 MB could be malware exfiltration or a legitimate firmware update received overnight. Triage involves reviewing the device's history, correlating the CMP usage spike with any known operational events (scheduled updates, new software deployments), and applying whatever device-level diagnostic data is available. Triage also assigns a severity classification (P1 through

P4) that determines the response urgency and the personnel who must be involved.

Containment isolates the affected devices or restricts their capabilities to prevent the incident from spreading or causing further damage before the root cause is understood. CMP-based containment actions available to the IoT operations team include: SIM suspension (the device loses cellular connectivity immediately: the most complete containment but also the most operationally disruptive);

APN restriction (the device can only reach a limited set of approved IP addresses, preventing C2 communication while allowing diagnostic heartbeats); data rate throttling (limiting the device to a very low data rate that prevents bulk exfiltration while preserving connectivity for investigation); and geographic restriction (flagging or suspending a SIM that connects from an unexpected geographic location). Containment should be initiated before investigation is complete for P1 incidents: it is better to take a device offline for 30 minutes while the investigation confirms the incident than to leave a compromised device active while the investigation proceeds.

Investigation collects the evidence needed to understand what happened, who was affected, what data may have been accessed or exfiltrated, and whether legal or regulatory reporting obligations have been triggered. Evidence collection for IoT incidents includes: CMP audit logs for all actions taken on affected SIMs; network flow records showing data volumes, destination IPs, and connection timestamps; device diagnostic logs if accessible; carrier NOC records for network-level traffic analysis; and correlation of the IoT incident with enterprise IT security events in the SIEM. Evidence must be preserved in a forensically sound manner before any remediation action that would modify or destroy the evidence: remediation actions (firmware updates, credential resets) will overwrite device state that may be needed for the investigation.

The GDPR 72-hour breach notification clock starts from the point of detection, not from the point of confirmed investigation. If the incident involves personal data of EU residents, the data protection officer must be notified within 72 hours of detection with the information available at that time, with supplementary notifications as the investigation provides additional detail. This regulatory timeline creates pressure to begin the notification process in parallel with the investigation rather than waiting for investigation completion.

Remediation addresses the root cause of the incident. For a firmware vulnerability exploit, remediation involves pushing a patched firmware version to all affected devices via OTA. For compromised credentials, remediation involves revoking the affected certificates, issuing new ones through the automated renewal workflow, and updating the CMP to apply the new credentials. For a misconfigured security policy that allowed unexpected network access, remediation involves correcting the APN restriction rules and auditing other device groups for similar misconfigurations. Remediation should be confirmed by monitoring: verify that the anomalous behaviour has stopped and that normal operation has been restored before closing the incident.

The post-incident review should be conducted within five business days of incident closure while the details are still fresh. The review should answer: what was the root cause? What monitoring or alerting gap allowed the incident to occur or persist? What process or configuration change would prevent recurrence? Were the containment and remediation actions taken at the right speed, with the right tools? The findings should be translated into specific changes: updated alerting rules, improved provisioning process controls, additional documentation, or a recommendation to invest in additional monitoring capability.

9.6 Connectivity Partner Management

An IoT deployment's security posture is only as strong as the weakest link in its connectivity supply chain. The MNO whose network carries device traffic, the MVNO reselling that connectivity, the roaming partners providing coverage in foreign countries, and the third-party platform providing the CMP are all data processors handling traffic that may contain personal data, and all are potential attack vectors. Connectivity partner management is the discipline of ensuring that these external parties meet the security standards required by the deployment and that the contractual, technical, and operational arrangements with them reflect that requirement.

9.6.1 Partner Security Assessment

Partner security assessment should be conducted before entering a connectivity agreement and repeated annually thereafter. The assessment evaluates: data processing agreements (GDPR Article 28 requires a written data processing agreement with every third-party processor; for connectivity partners, this agreement must cover the personal data in transit through the carrier network, the device location data held in carrier systems, and the usage and billing data processed by the CMP);

security certifications (International Organisation for Standardisation (ISO) 27001 for information security management, SOC 2 Type II for cloud service providers, or GSMA NESAS for network equipment vendors); network security capabilities (private APN availability, IPSec VPN support, GSMA-compliant SIM security, DDoS mitigation services); incident notification commitments (the partner must notify you within a defined period, typically 24 to 72 hours, of any security incident affecting your devices or data); and vulnerability disclosure practices (the partner must have a published vulnerability disclosure policy and a track record of timely disclosure and patching).

DEFINITION: GSMA (Global System for Mobile Communications Association)

The industry organisation representing mobile network operators worldwide, responsible for maintaining mobile standards, publishing IoT security guidelines (CLP series), defining remote SIM provisioning standards (SGP.02/SGP.22), and developing the Open Gateway API initiative for standardised access to network capabilities. GSMA membership includes over 1,000 operators and vendor companies. Compliance with GSMA IoT Security Guidelines is the industry standard for evaluating cellular IoT connectivity partner security posture.

The GSMA IoT Security Guidelines, published as a series of complementary documents (CLP.11 for overview, CLP.12 for network operators, CLP.13 for IoT service providers), provide the most widely adopted framework for evaluating and contracting connectivity partner security. They define security requirements across three dimensions: endpoint ecosystem security (device-level controls), network operator security (carrier infrastructure security), and IoT service ecosystem security (platform and application security). When selecting a connectivity partner, verify their claimed compliance with CLP.12 and their published security self-assessment against that standard. The GSMA does not certify compliance, so self-assessment claims should be verified through the contractual audit rights established in the data processing agreement.

9.6.2 Private APNs and Network Architecture

A private APN is the most impactful single network security control available through carrier infrastructure. Where a public

APN routes IoT device traffic through the general public mobile data network (where it is co-mingled with consumer smartphone traffic and traverses the public internet before reaching the IoT platform), a private APN provides a dedicated, isolated network path between the IoT devices and the enterprise platform.

Traffic on a private APN does not traverse the public internet: it travels from the device through the carrier network to a private interconnect (a dedicated IP transit link or an MPLS connection) directly to the enterprise data centre or cloud environment. This eliminates the public internet as a potential interception or injection point for IoT traffic, significantly reducing the attack surface for man-in-the-middle attacks and traffic interception.

DEFINITION: Private APN

A dedicated Access Point Name configured exclusively for a specific enterprise customer, providing an isolated network path between the enterprise's IoT devices and its platform infrastructure without traversing the public internet. Private APNs can be further secured with source IP restrictions (only devices on the private APN can reach the IoT platform backend), enabling network-level access control independent of application-layer authentication.

Static IP allocation for IoT devices on a private APN enables firewall rules to be written against specific device IP addresses, allowing precise network-level access control: device X is permitted to communicate only with IP addresses A, B, and C on specific ports. Combined with CMP-enforced APN restrictions (a device whose SIM is not authorised for the private APN cannot connect to it regardless of any application-layer configuration), this creates a defence-in-depth network architecture where even a device with compromised application-layer credentials cannot reach sensitive platform infrastructure through the normal network path.

9.6.3 SLA Management and Contractual Governance

Service Level Agreements with connectivity partners define the measurable commitments that underpin the operational reliability and security of an IoT deployment.

Relevant SLA metrics for IoT connectivity include: network availability (the percentage of time the private APN is accessible; 99.95% monthly availability is a reasonable enterprise baseline for critical IoT applications, equating to approximately 22 minutes of downtime per month); incident response time (P1 security incidents acknowledged within 15 minutes and initial investigation commenced within 1 hour); data usage reporting latency (real-time or near-real-time CMP updates, critical for anomaly detection; 15-minute reporting intervals are the minimum for meaningful security monitoring); and SIM activation processing time (bulk activations completed within 4 hours, critical for deploying new device batches without operational delay).

Regular SLA reviews (quarterly for critical connectivity infrastructure, annually for secondary providers) should review performance against contracted SLAs using CMP-generated reports as the primary evidence base. Performance gaps should be escalated through the contractual governance structure defined in the connectivity agreement. For carriers with persistent SLA underperformance, the contractual review is the mechanism through which remediation commitments and, ultimately, contract termination decisions are made. The value of detailed CMP reporting (precise uptime measurements, incident timestamps, response time records) is that it converts SLA reviews from negotiations about perception into reviews of documented facts.

CASE STUDY: Multi-Carrier IoT Connectivity at Jaguar Land Rover *Coventry, UK | 2020-Present*

Jaguar Land Rover's connected vehicle programme, which provides over-the-air software updates, remote diagnostics, and real-time fleet telematics for its global vehicle fleet, illustrates the connectivity partner management challenges of a truly global IoT deployment. JLR's connected vehicles operate in over 100 countries, requiring cellular connectivity with adequate coverage and appropriate regulatory compliance in each market.

Rather than establishing bilateral agreements with 100+ national carriers, JLR works with a small number of global IoT MVNO partners (including Eseye) who aggregate connectivity from hundreds of carrier networks into a single commercial relationship and a single management API. The MVNO continuously selects the optimal network for each vehicle based on signal quality, latency, and cost, with automatic failover between networks when coverage degrades. This multi-network approach improved connected vehicle connectivity from 91% (with a single-carrier approach) to 99.4% across the global fleet.

From a governance perspective, the multi-MVNO model concentrates data processing agreement obligations at the MVNO level rather than requiring JLR's legal team to negotiate GDPR-compliant DPAs with 100+ national carriers in different legal jurisdictions. The MVNO assumes re-

sponsibility for ensuring that its carrier relationships comply with the data protection standards specified in the JLR-MVNO master agreement, and JLR's annual security reviews are conducted with the MVNO rather than with each underlying carrier.

Security policy enforcement uses private APNs in each major regional hub (EU, North America, Asia Pacific), with vehicle traffic on each regional APN restricted to the JLR connected services platform infrastructure in that region. This architecture satisfies GDPR data residency requirements for EU customer data (EU vehicle data stays within EU infrastructure) while maintaining the operational simplicity of a unified global CMP.

9.7 The Seven Keys: An Operational Administration Perspective

The Seven Keys to Secure IoT Connectivity were introduced in Chapter 8, Section 8.8, as a security-focused summary of the technical controls required for a defensible IoT deployment. In this chapter, they are revisited from an operational administration perspective: not what each key requires technically (Chapter 8's domain) but how an IoT administrator operationalises each key and maintains compliance with it throughout the deployment lifetime.

The distinction is significant. A key is technically implemented once, at system design time. A key is operationally maintained continuously, as the fleet evolves, as devices age, as the threat landscape changes, and as personnel and processes are updated. The administrative operationalisation of each key is the practice that keeps a technically sound deployment secure over years of operation.

Key	Technical Requirement (Ch.8)	Operational Administration Actions (Ch.9)	KPI / Audit Evidence
Key 1 Secure Device Identity	Hardware-protected X.509 certificate; unique per-device credentials; mTLS authentication	Maintain complete CMP device registry with certificate expiry dates; automate certificate renewal 60 days before expiry; revoke credentials within 24 hours of decommissioning; conduct quarterly inventory reconciliation	% of fleet with valid certificates; mean days between decommission and credential revocation; inventory discrepancy count
Key 2 Authenticated Access	mTLS for devices; MFA for humans; RBAC; no default credentials	Enforce MFA for all CMP logins; SCIM integration for automated offboarding; monthly access review; quarterly RBAC audit against current role assignments; test all human accounts with MFA bypass attempt	MFA adoption rate (target: 100%); mean time to offboard departed employee; % accounts with appropriate role assignment

Key 3 Encrypted Communication	TLS 1.3; DTLS 1.3; AES-128-GCM; certificate pinning	Monthly CMP report of devices using deprecated TLS versions; private APN enforcement for sensitive segments; quarterly certificate chain validation scan; alert on new device connections using unencrypted channels	% fleet on TLS 1.3; number of devices on deprecated protocols; private APN adoption for critical segments
Key 4 Secure Connectivity Management	CMP deployment; data usage baselines; automated suspension rules; APN restrictions	Define and maintain device type usage baselines; review and tune anomaly detection rules monthly; test automated suspension policies quarterly; verify CMP-to-SIEM alert routing monthly	Alert false positive rate; mean time to detect anomaly; automated containment action rate vs manual intervention rate
Key 5 Lifecycle Security Governance	Secure provisioning; OTA updates; formal decommissioning; credential rotation	Execute provisioning checklist for every new device batch; weekly firmware currency report against current production version; quarterly decommissioning audit (verify all retired devices have revoked credentials); automate certificate renewal workflow	% fleet on current firmware; mean days to patch after CVE publication; % decommissioned devices with confirmed credential revocation
Key 6Monitoring and Anomaly Detection	SIEM integration; baseline profiling; P1-P4 alert categories; audit logging	Monthly alert rule review with false positive analysis; quarterly red-team exercise against monitoring detection capability; review and update incident response playbook annually; verify 12-month audit log retention monthly	Mean time to detect (MTTD); mean time to respond (MTTR) by severity; alert volume trend; false positive rate
Key 7 Trusted Partner Interoperability	Partner security DPAs; GSMA IG.06 compliance; contractual security requirements	Annual partner security review with GSMA CLP.12 checklist; verify DPA currency before each contract renewal; participate in GSMA Open Gateway adoption planning; conduct partner SLA review quarterly	DPA compliance rate (target: 100%); partner security review completion rate; SLA adherence score per partner

Table 9.3: The Seven Keys to Secure IoT Connectivity: Operational Administration Actions and KPIs

The KPI column of Table 9.3 is not merely decorative. IoT security is only measurable if it is measured, and measurement requires defined metrics with regular collection and review. An IoT operations programme that cannot report the percentage of its fleet running current firmware, the mean time to detect anomalies, and the time taken to revoke credentials after device decommissioning is an operations programme that cannot demonstrate its own effectiveness to management, auditors, or regulators. The Seven Keys operational KPIs provide the minimum measurement framework for a mature IoT operations programme, supplemented by deployment-specific metrics appropriate to the domain.

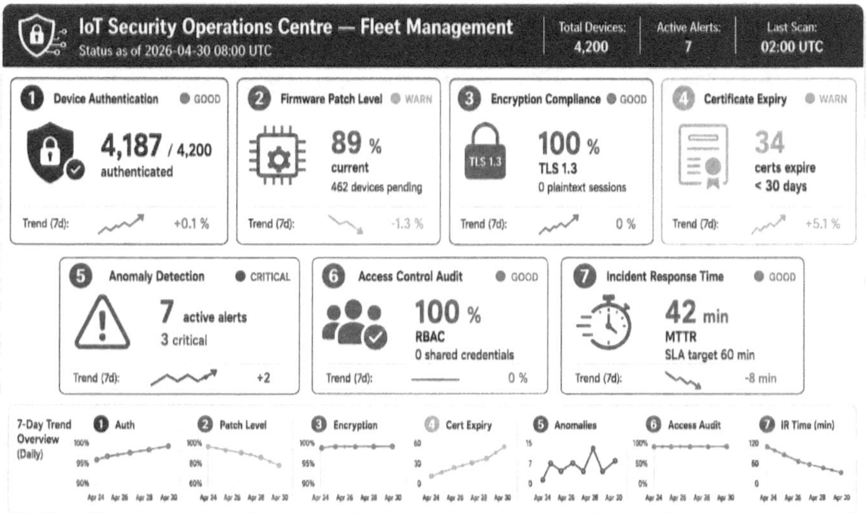

Figure 9.4: Seven Keys Operational Dashboard: KPI Status Visualisation for IoT Fleet Security Posture

9.8 IoT Governance: Policy, Compliance, and Regulatory Frameworks

IoT governance is the institutional framework within which IoT system administration operates. Where the preceding sections of this chapter address operational practices (how to manage a fleet, how to respond to incidents, how to govern human access) IoT governance addresses the policy and regulatory context that determines which operational practices are legally required, which are good practice, and which are prohibited. An IoT operations programme that is technically excellent but governance-naive will eventually encounter a regulatory requirement it has not designed for, a data subject exercising rights the system cannot fulfil, or a breach notification deadline it cannot meet. Building governance requirements into IoT system design from the outset, rather than discovering them during a regulatory audit, is the professional standard this chapter advocates.

DEFINITION: IoT Governance

The policies, processes, standards, and institutional arrangements that determine how IoT systems are designed, deployed, operated, and retired within legal, ethical, and organisational boundaries. IoT governance encompasses regulatory compliance (GDPR, CRA, NIS2, sector-specific regulations), internal policy frameworks (data classification, access control policies, incident response procedures), and standards adherence (ETSI EN 303 645, GSMA IoT Security Guidelines, IEC 62443). Governance is the framework within which security and privacy are mandated and enforced.

9.8.1 The Governance-Security-Privacy Triangle

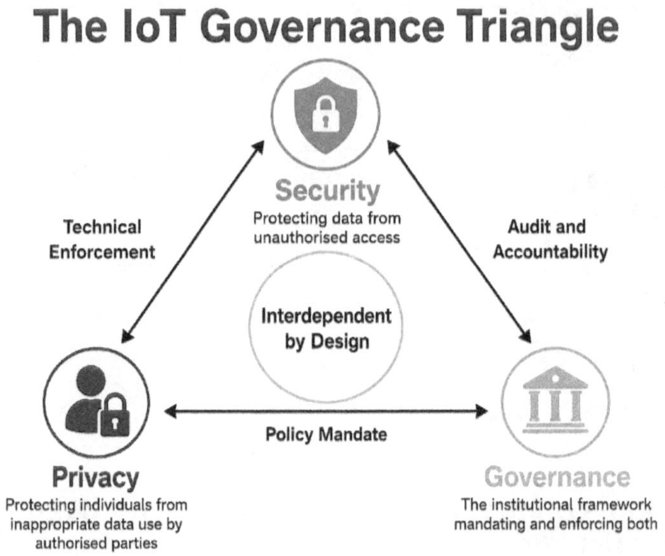

Figure 9.5: The IoT Governance Triangle: Security, Privacy, and Governance as Interdependent Architectural Properties

Three properties that IoT systems must exhibit are frequently discussed independently but are structurally interdependent: security (protecting data from unauthorised access), privacy (protecting individuals from inappropriate use of their data by authorised parties), and governance (the institutional framework that mandates and enforces both). Each requires the other two to be effective. Security without governance is uncoordinated: individual teams implement security controls without a common standard, producing heterogeneous security postures across the organisation that are difficult to audit and easy to exploit at their weak points.

Privacy without security is aspirational: privacy policies that are not backed by technical security controls are promises that can be broken by any attacker who can access the unprotected data. Governance without security and privacy is bureaucratic: documentation and compliance exercises that do not correspond to the actual security and privacy properties of the deployed systems.

The practical implication of this interdependence is that the governance framework for an IoT deployment must be designed in concert with its security architecture and data governance architecture, not as a separate compliance layer applied afterwards. When the Data Protection Impact Assessment for a smart city surveillance system identifies that facial recognition data is a special category under GDPR Article 9, that finding must drive architectural decisions (where is the data stored, how is it protected, who can access it, when is it deleted) that are enforced by technical controls, not merely documented in a risk register while the system continues to process the data without those controls.

Key Insight — Designing the Governance Triangle: Security, Privacy, and Accountability Cannot Be Sequential

A recurring failure in IoT deployments is the sequential design approach: engineers build the security architecture, legal teams map privacy requirements onto it, and compliance functions overlay a governance documentation framework. This sequence guarantees misalignment. Security architectures built without privacy requirements cannot satisfy the data-protection-by-design mandate of GDPR Article 25. Privacy frameworks implemented without security enforcement remain aspirational policies rather than enforceable technical constraints. Governance frameworks retrofitted to an existing architecture require expensive remediation or permanently accept residual non-compliance. The governance triangle (security, privacy, and accountability) must be co-designed from the requirements phase, with each element shaping the others before a single technical specification is committed to paper.

9.8.2 GDPR Compliance for IoT Operations

The General Data Protection Regulation imposes specific operational obligations on organisations that deploy IoT systems processing personal data of EU residents. The six processing principles examined in Chapter 6 (Section 6.8) are the architectural obligations; the following are the operational obligations that IoT administrators and compliance officers must maintain continuously.

Data subject rights impose response obligations on IoT operators. The right of access (Article 15) requires the ability to produce, on request, all personal data held about an individual across all IoT data stores — device telemetry, usage logs, location history, and audit records. For IoT systems with distributed data stores (device-local storage, edge tier databases, cloud data lakes), fulfilling a subject access request requires a data mapping that knows where every category of personal data is held.

The right to erasure (Article 17) requires deletion of personal data when the subject requests it and no legitimate continuing processing basis exists: a technically non-trivial operation in a distributed IoT data architecture where data may be replicated across multiple storage tiers, and where some data may be embedded in aggregate analytics outputs rather than in individually identifiable records. The right to data portability (Article 20) requires that personal data be exportable in a structured, machine-readable format, directly relevant to the EU Data Act's mandate for access to IoT device-generated data.

DEFINITION: Data Protection Impact Assessment (DPIA)

A structured process required by GDPR Article 35 for processing operations likely to result in high risk to individuals' rights and freedoms. DPIAs are mandatory for large-scale processing of location data, biometric data, data from connected devices in public spaces, and systematic monitoring of publicly accessible areas, all categories directly applicable to IoT. A DPIA identifies the data flows, processing purposes, and individuals affected; assesses the risks; and documents the technical and organisational measures implemented to address each risk.

Data Protection Impact Assessments are mandatory for IoT deployments involving large-scale sensor networks in public spaces, biometric data collection (including facial recognition), continuous location tracking, and health monitoring. The DPIA must be completed before the processing begins, not as a retrospective documentation exercise after the system is deployed. GDPR Article 36 requires that where a DPIA indicates a high residual risk that cannot be mitigated by the data controller alone, the competent supervisory authority must be consulted before the processing proceeds. This consultation obligation is frequently overlooked in smart city IoT deployments, where large-scale public sensor networks are deployed without prior supervisory authority engagement.

Breach notification under GDPR Article 33 requires that the competent supervisory authority be notified within 72 hours of becoming aware of a personal data breach, not 72 hours after the breach is confirmed or fully investigated, but 72 hours after becoming aware that it may have occurred. For IoT security incidents involving personal data (a compromised smart meter network, a hacked health monitoring system), the 72-hour clock starts from the point of detection, not investigation.

The notification must include: the nature of the breach, the approximate number of individuals affected, the categories of data involved, the likely consequences, and the measures taken or proposed to address the breach. If the breach is likely to result in high risk to individual rights and freedoms, Article 34 requires notification to the affected individuals as well, without undue delay.

The Data Protection Officer is mandatory for public authorities, organisations that carry out large-scale systematic monitoring of individuals (smart city surveillance IoT), and organisations that process special categories of data (health IoT) at large scale. The DPO must be involved in all matters relating to IoT data processing: reviewing DPIAs, advising on lawful processing bases, acting as the point of contact for supervisory authorities, and monitoring compliance with GDPR obligations. The DPO must be independent, not subject to instructions from the organisation regarding the exercise of their tasks, and must have adequate resources to carry out their role effectively.

9.8.3 Sector-Specific IoT Regulatory Obligations

Beyond the horizontal data protection framework of GDPR, IoT deployments in specific sectors are subject to vertical regulatory requirements that impose additional design, operational, and reporting obligations. The following examines the principal sector-specific frameworks.

Healthcare IoT is regulated by the EU Medical Device Regulation (MDR, Regulation 2017/745) for devices that perform a medical function, and by the FDA's cybersecurity guidance for Software as a Medical Device (SaMD) in the US. The EU MDR classifies many connected health monitoring devices as medical devices requiring conformity assessment before market placement. HIPAA in the US requires that connected health monitoring devices used in healthcare contexts implement specific administrative, physical, and technical safeguards for protected health information, with breach notification requirements and penalty structures that parallel but differ from GDPR. The FDA's cybersecurity guidance (2023 "Cybersecurity in Medical Devices: Quality System Considerations and Content of Premarket Submissions") now requires a software bill of materials (SBOM) and a cybersecurity management plan as part of premarket submissions for connected devices.

Industrial IoT and critical infrastructure IoT are regulated by the EU NIS2 Directive (Directive 2022/2555), which replaces the original NIS Directive and significantly expands the scope of critical infrastructure cybersecurity obligations. NIS2 covers energy, transport, banking, financial market infrastructure, health, drinking water, waste water, digital infrastructure, information and communications technology (ICT) service management, public administration, and space sectors, essentially every domain where IoT is deployed in critical infrastructure roles.

Operators of essential services in these sectors must implement risk management measures including incident handling, business continuity, supply chain security, network security, and access control. The IEC 62443 standard series provides the most widely adopted technical framework for industrial IoT security, defining requirements for industrial automation and control system components, systems, and the organisations that operate them.

The EU Cyber Resilience Act (CRA, 2024) is the most significant recent addition to the IoT regulatory landscape, extending mandatory security requirements to IoT device manufacturers and importers. The CRA requires security by design for all products with digital elements, including IoT devices; a software bill of materials documenting all software components; vulnerability disclosure within 24 hours of discovery to the European Union Agency for Cybersecurity (ENISA); security updates for the expected product lifetime; and a conformity assessment process demonstrating compliance before market placement.

Regional Example — GCC Data Protection Laws and IoT Governance: PDPL, UAE Decree-Law 45/2021, and National Frameworks

Gulf Cooperation Council member states have enacted national data protection legislation that directly governs IoT deployments. Saudi Arabia's Personal Data Protection Law (PDPL, Royal Decree M/19, September 2021, effective September 2023) establishes consent requirements, data subject rights, breach notification obligations, and restrictions on cross-border data transfers broadly aligned with GDPR, with specific provisions for automated processing and IoT-generated personal data. The UAE Federal Decree-Law No. 45 of 2021 on Personal Data Protection imposes a 72-hour breach notification obligation, mandatory Data Protection Impact Assessments for high-risk processing, and data localisation requirements that directly affect IoT cloud architecture decisions in smart city, healthcare, and financial services deployments. Oman's National Centre for Information Security (NCSI) IT Governance Framework and the Telecommunications Regulatory Authority's IoT Service Regulation require licensed IoT service providers to maintain documented device management procedures, incident response plans, and data handling policies compliant with national standards aligned with ISO/IEC 27001 principles. Across the GCC, the convergence of national data protection laws with IoT-specific regulatory instruments is establishing a multi-layered compliance environment that IoT operators must navigate at both the device architecture and operations management levels, making governance-by-design not merely a profes-

sional best practice but a legal obligation.

The CRA's requirements are aligned with ETSI EN 303 645 but broader in scope and backed by enforcement mechanisms including CE marking requirements and market surveillance, with penalties up to EUR 15 million or 2.5% of global annual turnover for non-compliance. For IoT device manufacturers, the CRA transforms security from a differentiating feature to a legal prerequisite for EU market access.

IoT Domain	Primary EU Framework	Primary US Framework	Key Obligation	Non-compliance Consequence
Consumer IoT (all categories)	EU Cyber Resilience Act (2024); ETSI EN 303 645; UK PSTI Act 2022	NIST IR 8259; FCC IoT Cyber Trust Mark (voluntary)	Security by design; unique passwords; vulnerability disclosure; security updates for product lifetime	CRA: up to EUR 15M or 2.5% global turnover; PSTI: up to GBP 10M or 4% global turnover
IoT Personal Data Processing	GDPR (EU) 2016/679; EU Data Act 2023	CCPA/CPRA (California)	DPIA for high-risk processing; 72-hour breach notification; data subject rights fulfilment; DPO for large-scale monitoring	GDPR: up to EUR 20M or 4% global turnover per infringement
Healthcare IoT	EU MDR Regulation 2017/745; GDPR Article 9	FDA SaMD cybersecurity guidance; HIPAA Security Rule	Conformity assessment for medical devices; SBOM for connected medical devices; PHI safeguards; breach notification	MDR: market withdrawal; HIPAA: up to USD 1.9M per category of violation per year
Industrial / Critical Infrastructure IoT	NIS2 Directive 2022/2555; IEC 62443	NIST CSF 2.0; CISA ICS-CERT guidelines	Risk management measures; incident reporting within 24 hours; supply chain security; business continuity	NIS2: up to EUR 10M or 2% global turnover for essential service operators
Smart City / Public Sector IoT	GDPR Article 35 (DPIA); FIWARE/NGSI-LD technical standards; NIS2 for critical infrastructure	FTC enforcement action precedents; local government cybersecurity frameworks	DPIA before deployment of public surveillance; supervisory authority consultation for high-risk processing	GDPR enforcement action; potential processing prohibition order
Connected Vehicles	UNECE WP.29 Regulation 155 (cybersecurity); GDPR (location data)	NHTSA cybersecurity best practices; SAE J3061	Cybersecurity management system; software update management system; vulnerability monitoring throughout vehicle lifecycle	UN Regulation 155: vehicle type approval denial; recall obligation for deployed vehicles

Table 9.4: IoT Governance Framework Mapping: Regulatory Requirements by Application Domain

9.8.4 IoT Standards Bodies and Their Governance Roles

The IoT standards landscape involves multiple organisations with complementary but sometimes overlapping roles, each producing standards that shape different aspects of IoT governance. ISO/IEC Joint Technical Committee 1 (JTC 1) Subcommittee 41 produces the core IoT vocabulary (ISO/IEC 20924), reference architecture (ISO/IEC 30141), and security guidelines (ISO/IEC 27400) that provide the international consensus baseline for IoT governance across all sectors. ETSI produces the consumer-facing security standard EN 303 645 (now referenced in EU law) and the Coordinated Vulnerability Disclosure standard TS 103 838. IETF produces the protocol-level standards that underpin IoT communications security: TLS 1.3, DTLS 1.3, CoAP, OSCORE, SUIT manifests, and SZTP, all of which are directly relevant to the security mechanisms described in Chapter 8.

The oneM2M international standards body produces the oneM2M standard for IoT service layer interoperability, providing a common framework for data models, APIs, and security in IoT deployments that must interoperate across different device platforms and cloud services. oneM2M Release 4 (2020) introduced end-to-end security enhancements specifically addressing multi-hop IoT architectures. International Telecommunication Union (ITU)-T Focus Group on IoT (FG-IoT) produced foundational smart city and IoT governance frameworks that inform national policy in many jurisdictions, particularly in Asia-Pacific and Latin America. The GSMA, as discussed throughout this chapter, provides the operational standards (remote SIM provisioning, IoT security guidelines, Open Gateway APIs) most directly relevant to the administration practices described in Sections 9.1 through 9.7.

Professional Checklist: IoT Governance Readiness

Before operating an IoT system at scale, confirm the following:

- *Ownership of devices, data, platforms, access rights, and operational responsibilities is clearly assigned.*
- *Policies exist for provisioning, configuration, monitoring, updates, decommissioning, and audit trails.*
- *Compliance obligations related to privacy, cybersecurity, safety, and sector-specific regulation are identified.*
- *Third-party vendors, connectivity providers, and cloud services are governed through clear agreements.*
- *Data sharing, consent, retention, and cross-border transfer requirements are addressed.*

- *Governance review is repeated periodically as technology, regulation, and risk conditions change.*

9.9 SMARTIE: A Reference Architecture for Multi-Stakeholder IoT Governance

The governance principles, access control models, and privacy-by-design requirements described in the preceding sections are not merely theoretical constructs; they can be implemented in real platform architectures. The SMARTIE project (Secure and sMArT platfoRms for rEsilient IoT Ecosystems), an EU Horizon 2020 research initiative concluded in 2016, provides one of the most thoroughly documented reference architectures for privacy-preserving, multi-stakeholder IoT governance.

While the project's specific implementation is now a historical reference point, its architectural principles remain current, have been independently validated in subsequent deployments, and are directly applicable to the governance challenges discussed in this chapter. SMARTIE is examined here not as a prescriptive standard but as an instructive case study in how governance requirements translate into architectural decisions.

DEFINITION: SMARTIE

The Secure and sMArT platfoRms for rEsilient IoT Ecosystems project, an EU Horizon 2020-funded research initiative (Grant Agreement 609062, 2013-2016). SMARTIE developed a reference architecture for secure, privacy-preserving IoT platforms supporting multi-stakeholder smart city applications, with particular focus on attribute-based access control, distributed trust, and data anonymisation at the platform level. The project consortium included universities, SMEs, and industry partners from Spain, the UK, Italy, and other EU member states.

9.9.1 SMARTIE Architecture and Design Motivations

SMARTIE was motivated by a governance problem specific to smart city IoT deployments: data is generated by sensors owned and operated by different city departments, utilities, and private companies, but its analytical value is greatest when data from multiple sources can be correlated and queried together. A traffic management authority that can correlate its vehicle count data with the electricity utility's smart meter data and the transit authority's passenger count data has far more analytical power than any single organisation can achieve alone. But data sharing across organisational boundaries raises governance challenges: who has the right to access whose data? Under what conditions? For what purposes? And how can these rights be enforced technically, not just contractually?

The SMARTIE architecture addresses this challenge through a layered platform that separates data ownership from data access. Data contributors (city departments, utilities, private sensor operators) retain ownership of and control over their data. The SMARTIE platform enforces their access policies but does not centralise data ownership. Authorised consumers (city applications, researchers, citizens) access data through policy-enforced APIs that evaluate the consumer's attributes against the data owner's access policy before returning any data. This federated trust model contrasts with the centralised trust model used in most commercial IoT platforms, where the platform operator is implicitly trusted with all data and enforces access policies on behalf of data owners, creating a single point of trust failure if the platform operator is compromised or acts contrary to data owners' interests.

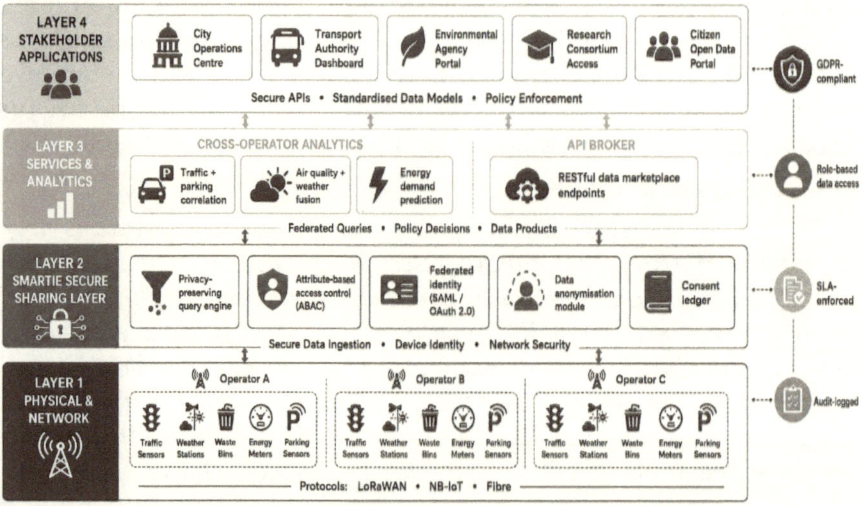

Figure 9.6: SMARTIE Architecture: Federated Multi-Stakeholder IoT Platform with Attribute-Based Access Control

9.9.2 Attribute-Based Access Control in SMARTIE

DEFINITION: Attribute-Based Access Control (ABAC)

An access control model in which access decisions are made by evaluating attributes of the requesting subject (user or application), the target resource (data or device), the requested action, and the environmental context (time, location, network) against an access policy defined by the resource owner. ABAC is more expressive than RBAC: while RBAC grants access based on role membership, ABAC can enforce fine-grained conditions such as "a researcher from an accredited institution may access aggregate air quality data for academic purposes during business hours, but not raw individual sensor readings or data from locations within 100 metres of a residential building."

SMARTIE's ABAC implementation uses the XACML (eXtensible Access Control Markup Language) standard for expressing and evaluating access policies. The XACML architecture defines four functional components: the Policy Decision Point (PDP), which evaluates access requests against applicable policies and returns permit or deny decisions; the Policy Enforcement Point (PEP), which intercepts data access requests and enforces the PDP's decisions; the Policy Information Point (PIP), which provides the attribute values needed for policy evaluation (for example, verifying that a requesting researcher's university has a current data sharing agreement); and the Policy Administration Point (PAP), where data owners define and manage their access policies.

The practical benefit of ABAC over RBAC for multi-stakeholder IoT platforms is expressiveness. A city transport authority's data access policy might specify: "city planning department staff may access aggregate vehicle count data grouped by 15-minute intervals and 100-metre road segments (not individual vehicle tracks) for transport modelling purposes; academic researchers with a signed data use agreement may access the same aggregate data for publications; no party may access data that could identify individual vehicle movements or be combined with license plate data." RBAC cannot express these conditions within a single role definition; ABAC evaluates them as a policy statement that applies to any request meeting the specified criteria.

9.9.3 Data Anonymisation and Privacy Architecture

SMARTIE's approach to privacy protection applies anonymisation at the ingestion point, when data first enters the platform from the sensor network, rather than at the point of query. This architectural choice has a critical implication: the platform never holds personal-level raw data, only anonymised aggregates. A query that attempts to access personal-level data cannot retrieve it because the data does not exist in the platform in that form, not because a query filter prevents access to it. The difference between "the policy prevents you from accessing this data" and "this data does not exist at this resolution" is significant: the former protects against authorised users with misconfigured permissions, but the latter protects against both misconfigured access control and platform operator curiosity.

The anonymisation techniques applied by SMARTIE at ingestion include spatial aggregation (replacing precise GPS coordinates with grid-level or zone-level location codes that cannot be used to identify individual movements), temporal aggregation (replacing second-resolution timestamps with 15-minute interval codes that cannot be correlated with other data sources to identify individuals), and k-anonymisation (suppressing data records where fewer than k individuals contributed to the aggregate, preventing inference about the few individuals whose data would dominate a small-sample aggregate). These techniques are applied as configurable parameters in the data ingestion pipeline, with each data stream having anonymisation parameters specified by the data owner in their access policy configuration.

The SMARTIE privacy architecture also addresses the re-identification risk that arises when multiple anonymised data streams are correlated. A transport dataset anonymised to 100-metre road segments may be benign in isolation, but correlated with a retail checkout dataset anonymised to 15-minute intervals and a cellular network dataset anonymised to cell-tower resolution, it may permit re-identification of individual movement patterns.

SMARTIE's federated data model partially addresses this through the ABAC policy evaluation: a research application requesting access to three data streams simultaneously must satisfy the access policies of all three data owners, and any data owner whose policy prohibits cross-stream correlation can block the combined query. Full re-identification risk management across fully anonymised datasets remains an open research challenge that the chapter's readers will encounter in their own deployments.

9.9.4 Lessons from SMARTIE for Contemporary Deployments

SMARTIE was completed in 2016, a decade before this book's publication. In the intervening decade, the smart city IoT landscape has changed enormously: LoRaWAN, NB-IoT, and 5G have matured; commercial IoT platforms including Azure IoT Hub, AWS IoT Core, and ThingsBoard have reached enterprise scale; GDPR has come into force; and the EU Data Act has extended data portability rights to IoT-generated data. Despite these changes, three architectural lessons from SMARTIE remain directly transferable to contemporary deployments.

First, data owner-controlled access policies scale better than platform-centralised access control. In the most widely deployed commercial IoT platforms, the platform operator configures access policies on behalf of data owners: a trusted intermediary model that requires every data owner to trust the platform operator's configuration of their policies. As deployments grow to span multiple organisations with different data sensitivity levels and different regulatory obligations, this centralised trust model becomes a governance bottleneck and a single point of failure. SMARTIE's federated policy model, where each data owner directly controls their own access policy configuration in a standardised format (XACML), scales to arbitrarily many data owners without increasing the platform operator's trusted role.

Second, anonymisation must be applied at the ingestion point, not retrospectively. A platform that collects raw personal data and then applies anonymisation at query time is a platform that stores personal data, with all the GDPR storage limitation, data minimisation, and access control obligations that entails. Applying anonymisation at ingestion, as SMARTIE does, means the platform never stores personal data, eliminating a significant class of regulatory obligation and dramatically reducing the impact of a platform data breach.

Third, governance frameworks must be defined before the technical platform is built. SMARTIE's consortium spent significant effort before the technical implementation phase establishing the data sharing agreements, access policy vocabulary, and privacy requirements that the platform's technical architecture would need to enforce. In commercial smart city deployments, the most common governance failure is the opposite: the technical platform is built first (because engineers start work before lawyers and policy makers), and the governance framework is retrofitted to the existing technical architecture rather than the architecture being designed to enforce the governance requirements. Retrofitting governance onto a deployed IoT platform is expensive, slow, and frequently incomplete, exactly the situation the principle of privacy by design, and the DPIA requirement of GDPR Article 35, are designed to prevent.

CASE STUDY: Amsterdam Smart City Data Platform: SMARTIE Principles in Practice

Amsterdam, Netherlands | 2018-Present

Amsterdam's Urban Data Platform, developed by the Amsterdam Economic Board and Gemeente Amsterdam, implements many of the SMARTIE architectural principles in a production smart city deployment that has served as a reference implementation for the EU FIWARE smart city initiative. The platform aggregates IoT data from city sensors across transport, energy, environment, and public space domains, serving both city operational systems and a public open data API.

The platform's access control model uses a multi-tier approach that reflects the SMARTIE federated principle: each city department retains administrative control over the access policies for its own data streams, configuring which categories of consumers (city departments, accredited researchers, commercial partners, general public) may access which data at which resolution. The platform enforces these policies through a centralised API gateway but does not override them: a department that specifies that its camera network data is restricted to internal city use cannot have that restriction overridden by another department's administrator.

Anonymisation is applied at the ingestion pipeline: raw sensor data including GPS coordinates, timestamp sequences, and identification codes is processed through configurable anonymisation transforms before storage in the data platform. The public open data API exposes only pre-anonymised aggregate data. Direct access to less-anonymised data is available only to authorised city departments through an authenticated API endpoint with full audit logging. This architecture allowed Amsterdam to publish a significant volume of urban sensing data as open data while satisfying the DPA (Dutch Data Protection Authority)'s requirements for public surveillance data processing.

The platform has been in production operation since 2018, processing data from over 12,000 city IoT sensors and serving approximately 400 registered data consumers. In 2022, the platform was assessed against the GDPR requirements by an independent auditor and found fully compliant, with the audit report specifically citing the anonymisation-at-ingestion architecture as a model for other European municipalities seeking to deploy urban IoT platforms while meeting GDPR obligations.

9.10 Chapter Summary

This chapter has examined the two interdependent operational disciplines that determine whether an IoT deployment succeeds beyond its pilot phase: system administration and connectivity governance. The two disciplines share a common premise: that IoT devices, unlike conventional IT endpoints, cannot be managed reactively; they require structured, automated, and policy-driven oversight from the moment a SIM is activated to the moment a device is securely decommissioned.

Section 9.1 framed IoT system administration as a distinct profession, contrasting its fleet-scale, heterogeneous, and often physically inaccessible character with classical IT operations. Four core roles were identified (connectivity partner manager, IoT operations engineer, IoT security administrator, and IoT compliance officer) and the concept of Zero Touch Provisioning was introduced as the operational ideal toward which modern platforms converge.

Section 9.2 dissected Connectivity Management Platforms, explaining how CMPs abstract the underlying Mobile Network Operator infrastructure and expose lifecycle APIs covering SIM activation, data-plan assignment, real-time diagnostics, and multi-carrier failover. The comparative analysis of Cisco Jasper, Ericsson DCP, KORE Wireless, Twilio Super SIM, and Eclipse Kapua illustrated the spectrum from hyperscaler commercial offerings to open-source community platforms.

Section 9.3 traced the full device lifecycle from factory provisioning through operational management to secure decommissioning. The eUICC/eSIM standard and GSMA SGP.02 were shown to be fundamental enablers of over-the-air profile switching, with Maersk's global container-tracking deployment serving as a concrete demonstration of the operational benefits at scale.

Section 9.4 addressed human access governance, establishing a four-role RBAC model appropriate for IoT management platforms and explaining how multi-tenancy, Privileged Access Workstations, and SCIM-based automated offboarding combine to reduce the insider-threat surface across large operator organisations.

Section 9.5 covered monitoring, alerting, and incident response. Behavioural baselining using machine-learning tools such as AWS IoT Device Defender was contrasted with threshold-based alerting, and a four-tier severity taxonomy (P1–P4) was linked to a structured incident lifecycle that explicitly incorporates the GDPR 72-hour breach notification clock.

Section 9.6 examined the management of connectivity partners, showing how operators must conduct structured GSMA assessments, negotiate SLA commitments with measurable KPIs, and implement private APN isolation to maintain both performance and security across multi-carrier environments. The Jaguar Land Rover Connected Car programme illustrated multi-carrier management at automotive scale.

Section 9.7 applied the Seven Keys to Securing IoT framework as an operational lens, mapping each key to concrete KPIs and platform-level admin actions, and presenting an operational dashboard architecture that consolidates fleet health, security posture, and connectivity metrics into a single management surface.

Section 9.8 broadened the scope to IoT governance, charting the regulatory landscape that operators must navigate: GDPR's operational obligations (data subject rights, DPIA, breach notification,

DPO appointment), the EU Cyber Resilience Act's secure-by-design mandate, NIS2 essential-service requirements, IEC 62443's defence-in-depth model for industrial systems, and the emerging regulatory expectations in the medical-device and smart-city domains. The governance framework mapping table provided a cross-domain reference linking healthcare, smart city, automotive, industrial, consumer IoT, and logistics deployments to their primary regulatory instruments.

Section 9.9 examined the SMARTIE research project as a reference architecture for privacy-preserving IoT data management. SMARTIE's use of ABAC and XACML policies, anonymisation at the point of ingestion, federated data storage, and transparent audit trails demonstrated how fine-grained governance can be implemented without sacrificing the analytics utility that motivates IoT deployments in the first place. The Amsterdam Smart City case study grounded these architectural principles in a real governance programme.

Together, the operational and governance themes of this chapter establish a foundation for the application chapters that follow. Every vertical deployment examined in Chapters 4, 5, and 10 rests on the platform capabilities, lifecycle disciplines, and regulatory frameworks introduced here. The emerging application of machine learning to IoT operations, including ML-driven anomaly detection for fleet security monitoring, AI-assisted access policy optimisation, and automated governance compliance checking, representing a rapidly developing frontier that builds directly on the platform architectures described in this chapter; these developments are examined in Chapter 11. Competent IoT governance is not a constraint on innovation; it is the condition that makes large-scale, trusted IoT deployment possible.

Chapter 10

Emerging Trends in IoT: AIoT, Digital Twins, 5G, Edge AI, Blockchain, and Green IoT

Chapter 10 examines the emerging technologies and future directions that are reshaping the next generation of IoT systems. It explores the convergence of IoT with artificial intelligence, digital twins, 5G and next-generation connectivity, edge AI, blockchain, sustainability, and green computing. The chapter explains how AIoT enables connected devices and platforms to move beyond data collection toward intelligent sensing, prediction, automation, and autonomous decision-making. It also discusses digital twin architectures, 5G-enabled IoT service models, embedded machine learning, decentralized trust mechanisms, and sustainable IoT design practices. In addition, the chapter highlights the societal, ethical, environmental, and technological challenges that must be addressed as IoT becomes more intelligent, distributed, and deeply integrated into critical infrastructure. Overall, this chapter provides a forward-looking perspective on how IoT is evolving into a more intelligent, secure, sustainable, and adaptive foundation for future digital ecosystems.

Opening Scenario: The Factory That Thinks

The automated vehicle component plant outside Lyon has been operating for thirty-seven years, but the facility that existed in 2020 bears little resemblance to the one running in 2025. The assembly lines still produce the same outputs (ADAS sensors, camera modules, and electric vehicle power management units) but the intelligence governing those lines has been transformed by a convergence of technologies that were theoretical when the plant was built.

On the factory floor, 1,400 IoT sensors stream vibration, temperature, current draw, and cycle-time data across a private 5G network. Latency from sensor measurement to control-system response is under 2 milliseconds: a figure that would have required dedicated fibre hardwiring a decade ago. A digital twin of every assembly cell runs in parallel on an edge server cluster adjacent to the production floor, ingesting live telemetry and continuously updating a physics-based simulation model of each machine. When the twin's simulation diverges from the live measurement by more than a calibrated threshold, the system flags an anomaly before any physical fault has occurred.

The anomaly detection itself runs not in the cloud but on STM32 microcontrollers embedded in each motor drive unit. A TinyML vibration classifier: a 47-kilobyte neural network quantised to 8-bit integer weights, runs inference at 500 Hz, consuming 12 milliwatts. When the classifier detects the spectral signature of bearing wear, it raises a flag in the device shadow before transmitting a compact alert payload to the plant MQTT broker. The classifier was trained on eighteen months of vibration data using the Edge Impulse platform, deployed via Over-the-Air (OTA) update to all 340 motor units in a single maintenance window.

Every sensor reading, every anomaly flag, every maintenance action, and every component batch record is written to a permissioned Hyperledger Fabric blockchain. The plant's Tier 1 automotive customers, who require traceability of every component in a vehicle safety system, can query the ledger directly through a customer portal, verifying the complete manufacturing provenance of any serial number without relying on the plant's own reporting. When a production quality audit is triggered, the auditor does not request records from the plant; they query the immutable ledger.

The plant's energy management system is governed by a Green IoT framework that monitors energy consumption at the cell level, correlates consumption with production output to compute a joules-per-unit metric, and schedules energy-intensive processes for off-peak hours when the grid carbon intensity is lowest. Rooftop photovoltaic panels, combined with 240 solar-harvesting wireless sensor nodes (no battery replacement in four years of operation), have reduced the facility's Scope 2 carbon emissions by 31% since 2021.

None of these technologies operates in isolation. The 5G network provides the low-latency backplane the digital twin requires. The digital twin provides the context that makes TinyML anomaly flags meaningful. The blockchain provides the trust infrastructure that makes the sensor data commercially actionable for customers. The Green IoT framework makes the entire system economically and environmentally sustainable at scale.

This is not science fiction. Every technology described in this scenario is either deployed in industrial facilities today or is in late-stage pilot. Chapter 10 explains each of them: what they are, how they work, where they are applied, and how they connect to the IoT foundations the preceding nine chapters have established. The reader who reaches this chapter has studied the protocols that carry the sensor data, the architectures that organise it, the security mechanisms that protect it, and the governance frameworks that govern its use. The question this chapter answers is: where does that knowledge lead next?

10.1 Introduction: The Evolving IoT Landscape

The nine chapters that precede this one have built a comprehensive foundation for understanding and practising IoT engineering. Chapter 1 established what IoT is and why it matters. Chapters 2 through 5 provided the engineering toolkit: hardware, architecture, protocols, and the design methodology that assembles them into deployable systems. Chapters 6 and 7 examined how IoT data is managed, processed, and applied across industrial and commercial domains. Chapters 8 and 9 addressed the security threats, protection mechanisms, governance frameworks, and regulatory requirements that make IoT deployments trustworthy and legally compliant.

Chapter 10 looks forward. Its purpose is not to introduce a new foundational framework but to show the directions in which the foundations already laid are being extended and to equip the reader to engage with those extensions as a practitioner, not merely as an observer. The six technology themes addressed in this chapter are not speculative research proposals. They are active engineering disciplines with deployed systems, published standards, commercial platforms, and measurable industrial impact. What makes them emerging is the pace and scale at which they are being integrated into mainstream IoT architectures. The mathematical and algorithmic foundations of the machine learning methods deployed across these themes including neural network architectures, training methodology, model compression theory, and federated optimisation are examined in rigorous depth in Chapter 11.

The pace of IoT innovation reflects a compounding dynamic. According to IoT Analytics (2025), the number of connected IoT devices reached about 21.1 billion in 2025 and is forecast to reach around 39 billion by 2030: a near-doubling in five years. But the raw device count understates the transformation: where the first wave of IoT connectivity was largely passive (sensors transmitting data for human interpretation), the emerging wave is active and autonomous.

McKinsey Global Institute (2023) estimates that more than 60% of new IoT deployments planned for 2025 to 2027 include on-device AI capabilities. The Gartner Hype Cycle for Emerging Technologies (2024) places Digital Twins in the early Slope of Enlightenment, past peak hype, entering productive industrial deployment. Edge AI and TinyML are approaching the Plateau of Productivity.

This chapter addresses six transformative technology domains. Section 10.2 examines AIoT, the convergence of artificial intelligence and IoT, including on-device inference via TinyML and privacy-preserving federated learning.

Section 10.3 covers Digital Twins: their architecture, lifecycle, and industrial adoption across manufacturing, infrastructure, and healthcare. Section 10.4 explains how 5G's three service categories and network slicing architecture transform what is possible for IoT at scale. Section 10.5 provides technical depth on Edge AI and embedded machine learning: model compression, hardware platforms, and the complete training-to-deployment toolchain. Section 10.6 evaluates blockchain and distributed ledger technologies as IoT trust infrastructure, with an honest assessment of their limitations alongside their genuine utility. Section 10.7 addresses Sustainability and Green IoT: the engineering practices that reduce the environmental footprint of large-scale IoT deployments. Section 10.8 closes the chapter and the textbook with a reflective treatment of societal, ethical, and technological horizons, including a technology roadmap to 2030.

10.2 AIoT: Convergence of Artificial Intelligence and IoT

Artificial Intelligence of Things, AIoT, describes the integration of AI capabilities directly into IoT systems: not AI applied to IoT data after the fact, in a separate cloud analytics pipeline, but AI embedded in the IoT architecture itself, from the microcontroller at the sensor node to the edge server at the gateway to the cloud platform managing the fleet. The convergence is driven by three simultaneous developments: the maturation of lightweight neural network architectures that run on constrained hardware; the reduction in cost and energy consumption of inference-capable processors; and the accumulation of large IoT datasets that provide the training signal for practical industrial models.

10.2.1 What is AIoT?

AIoT is distinguished from IoT with cloud analytics in a fundamental architectural respect: the AI inference (the execution of a trained model to classify, predict, or detect) runs within the IoT system, at or near the source of the data, rather than in a separate machine learning platform that receives IoT data as its input.

This distinction has practical consequences for latency (inference at the edge takes microseconds; a cloud round-trip takes tens to hundreds of milliseconds), bandwidth (an edge classifier that reduces a 10 kHz vibration stream to a one-bit anomaly flag eliminates the need to transmit 80 MB/hour of raw data per sensor), privacy (data that is classified at the device does not need to leave the device, reducing exposure to interception and retention risks), and reliability (an AIoT device continues making inferences during cloud connectivity outages).

DEFINITION: AIoT (Artificial Intelligence of Things)

The integration of artificial intelligence capabilities, particularly machine learning inference, directly into IoT system architectures, enabling IoT devices and edge nodes to perform intelligent sensing, classification, prediction, and autonomous actuation without cloud round-trips. AIoT ranges from TinyML inference on microcontrollers to federated learning across distributed IoT fleets.

Source: Seng, J.K.P. et al. (2022), IEEE Internet of Things Journal

10.2.2 AIoT Application Patterns

Predictive maintenance is the most commercially mature AIoT application pattern. A machine learning model trained on historical sensor data from operating equipment learns the normal signature of healthy operation and can detect the subtle deviations that precede failure: the spectral shift in a bearing's vibration signature weeks before it produces audible noise; the gradual increase in motor current that indicates developing rotor imbalance; the temperature excursion pattern that correlates with lubricant degradation. Deployed on an edge device or gateway co-located with the monitored equipment, the model provides early warning with the latency and availability profile that industrial maintenance schedules require.

Anomaly detection is a generalisation of predictive maintenance: rather than learning the signature of a specific failure mode, an anomaly detector learns the distribution of normal operation and flags departures from that distribution without needing labelled examples of the specific fault. Autoencoder neural networks and one-class classifiers are the most common architectures for IoT anomaly detection because they can be trained on normal data alone, which is abundant, without requiring the large labelled fault datasets that supervised classifiers need.

Natural language control is an emerging AIoT pattern enabled by the deployment of small transformer models on edge processors: an IoT device equipped with a microphone and an on-device keyword spotting or intent classification model can respond to natural language commands without transmitting audio to a cloud speech recognition service. This pattern is particularly relevant in healthcare (hands-free operation in clinical environments), manufacturing (voice-commanded equipment adjustments without touching a control panel), and accessibility applications.

10.2.3 On-Device AI: TinyML

TinyML is the discipline of deploying trained machine learning models on microcontrollers with kilobytes of RAM and milliwatts of power consumption. The name reflects the constraint: models that run on tiny hardware, consuming tiny energy budgets. The TinyML Foundation (2023) estimated that 250 million TinyML-capable devices shipped in 2022, with projections exceeding two billion by 2030. The economic driver is clear: a microcontroller with inference capability costs pennies more than one without it, but the intelligence it enables can eliminate the need for a cloud analytics subscription, reduce bandwidth consumption, and provide real-time response that cloud latency cannot match.

The TinyML pipeline begins with model training on a full-capability machine learning platform (TensorFlow, PyTorch) using representative IoT sensor data. Training produces a floating-point model that may have hundreds of thousands of parameters and megabytes of weight data, far too large for a microcontroller's flash. The model is then compressed through a pipeline of transformations:

Quantisation converts the model's weight and activation representations from 32-bit floating-point (FP32) to 8-bit integer (INT8). An FP32 weight requires 4 bytes; its INT8 equivalent requires 1 byte: a 4-fold reduction in model size with typically less than 2% accuracy degradation for well-trained models. Post-training quantisation (PTQ) is the simplest approach: the trained FP32 model is converted after training using a calibration dataset to determine the optimal scaling factors. Quantisation-aware training (QAT) simulates the quantisation error during training itself, generally yielding better accuracy for models that must be quantised aggressively.

Pruning removes connections (weights) from the neural network that have magnitude below a threshold, replacing them with zeros. A pruned model may have 50-90% of its weights set to zero; if stored in sparse format, this reduces memory footprint and can accelerate inference on hardware that supports sparse matrix operations. Unstructured pruning removes individual weights; structured pruning removes entire neurons or filters, which provides better hardware acceleration because it reduces actual computation rather than just storing zeros.

Knowledge distillation trains a small student model to mimic the behaviour of a large teacher model. Rather than compressing the teacher directly, distillation trains the student using the teacher's output probability distributions (soft labels) as training targets, in addition to the ground truth labels. The student learns a more general representation than it would from hard labels alone, achieving accuracy closer to the teacher than a small model trained from scratch could achieve.

The compressed model is then deployed to the target microcontroller using a framework such as TensorFlow Lite Micro (TFLM), which provides a runtime interpreter with no operating system dependencies, a binary footprint of approximately 20 KB, and support for a growing library of neural network operators. The CMSIS-NN library from ARM provides optimised INT8 convolution and fully-connected layer implementations for Cortex-M processors, providing 4-8x inference speedup over unoptimised implementations on the same hardware.

10.2.4 Federated Learning for IoT

Federated learning (FL) addresses a fundamental tension in AIoT: training accurate machine learning models requires large datasets, but IoT sensor data is often too sensitive or too voluminous to centralise. In a traditional ML pipeline, all training data is collected in a central server and the model is trained there. In federated learning, the model is trained locally on each device using its own data; only the model updates (gradients or weight differences), not the raw data, are transmitted to a central aggregation server, which combines them to produce an improved global model, and distributes the updated model back to all participating devices.

The privacy benefit is significant: raw sensor data (patient vital signs, industrial process data, energy consumption patterns that imply household occupancy) never leaves the originating device. The bandwidth benefit is also substantial: transmitting a model update of kilobytes is orders of magnitude less expensive than transmitting the training dataset of megabytes or gigabytes. Google's Gboard

(2017) demonstrated federated learning at scale on consumer smartphones; the FATE (Federated AI Technology Enabler) and Flower frameworks have since extended FL to IoT edge deployments.

IoT-specific challenges for federated learning include device heterogeneity (devices with different sensor configurations and processing capabilities must contribute to the same global model), communication constraints (LoRaWAN's low data rate makes model update transmission impractical — FL is better suited to Wi-Fi and 5G-connected IoT gateways than to constrained LPWAN end nodes), and stragglers (slow or intermittently connected devices that delay global aggregation rounds). Asynchronous FL algorithms and model compression techniques for the update payloads are active research areas addressing these challenges.

10.2.5 AIoT Architecture: The Perception-Inference-Action Loop

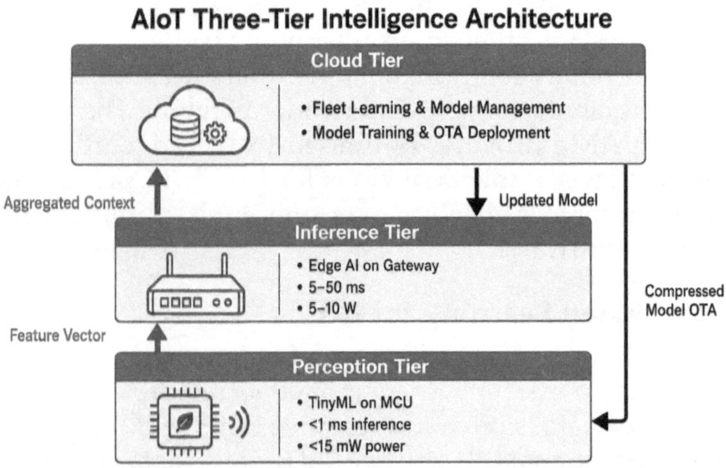

Figure 10.1: The AIoT Three-Tier Inference Architecture: Perception, Inference, and Cloud Tiers with Distributed Intelligence

The AIoT system architecture builds on the IoT functional layers established in Chapter 3 and extended in Chapter 5's functional view, adding intelligence at each tier. At the perception tier, sensors equipped with on-device pre-processing (low-pass filtering, feature extraction) produce not raw measurements but feature vectors, compact representations that contain the information the inference model needs. At the inference tier (which may be on the device itself for TinyML deployments, on the gateway for larger models, or in the cloud for the most complex analyses), the trained model produces a classification, prediction, or anomaly score. At the action tier, the inference output triggers an actuation command, an alert, a dashboard update, or an entry in the audit log.

The three-tier inference distribution creates an architectural pattern that the factory scenario illustrates precisely: the TinyML bearing classifier runs at the perception tier (on the STM32 in the motor drive unit), classifying each 500 Hz vibration sample and producing a compact flag. The digital twin's simulation model runs at the gateway tier, correlating flags from multiple sensors into a component-level health score. A fleet-level predictive maintenance model runs in the cloud, correlating health scores across the entire plant to optimise the maintenance schedule. Each tier performs the inference most appropriate to its computational capability and data access.

Key Insight — The AIoT Principle: Intelligence at Every Tier, Not Concentrated in the Cloud

The defining shift that AIoT represents is not the application of AI to IoT data: that has existed since the first rule-based alarm threshold. The defining shift is the distribution of intelligence: machine learning inference running on the same microcontrollers that sample the sensor, on the gateways that aggregate the data, and in the cloud platform that manages the fleet, each tier contributing the intelligence it is best positioned to execute. TinyML inference at the perception tier eliminates round-trip latency for real-time control. Gateway-tier inference aggregates context that no single device can observe alone. Cloud-tier learning provides the training data scale and computational depth that embedded inference cannot. Together, they produce an IoT system that is not merely connected but genuinely intelligent at its periphery, capable of acting without waiting for the cloud to respond.

10.2.6 AIoT Application Domains

Table 10.1 compares AIoT applications across six industrial and consumer domains, mapping each to the AI technique, inference tier, hardware platform, and latency requirement. The table illustrates the breadth of AIoT deployment and the diversity of hardware and algorithm choices that different requirements impose.

Application	AI Technique	Inference Tier	Hardware Platform	Latency Req.	Domain
Predictive maintenance (industrial motors)	Vibration anomaly detection (autoencoder, CNN)	Device (MCU)	STM32H7 + CMSIS-NN	Less than 10 ms	Factory automation, IIoT

Keyword spotting (smart speaker)	Temporal CNN CRNN	Device (MCU)	Arduino Nano 33 BLE Sense	Less than 100 ms	Consumer electronics, accessibility
Fall detection (wearable)	Accelerometer classifier (decision tree + CNN)	Device (MCU)	nRF52840 + TF Lite Micro	Less than 50 ms	Healthcare, elderly care
Visual inspection (manufacturing QA)	Object detection (MobileNet SSD)	Edge gateway	NVIDIA Jetson Nano	Less than 100 ms	Manufacturing, logistics
Fleet anomaly detection (predictive analytics)	LSTM time-series forecasting	Cloud + FL aggregation	Cloud GPU + FL server	Minutes (batch)	Automotive, smart grid
Energy demand forecasting (smart grid)	LSTM + federated learning	Gateway + cloud	Raspberry Pi 4 + cloud	Hours (daily forecast)	Utilities, smart city

Table 10.1: AIoT Application Patterns: Technique, Hardware, and Latency

TECHNOLOGY SPOTLIGHT: Tech Spotlight: Edge Impulse — From Sensor Data to Deployed TinyML Model

Edge Impulse is a cloud-based development platform that provides an end-to-end pipeline for TinyML model development: data collection from real IoT sensors, signal processing block design, neural network architecture selection and training, performance benchmarking against target hardware, and one-click deployment to over 60 supported boards including the Arduino Nano 33 BLE Sense, STM32 Discovery boards, and Raspberry Pi. The platform is free for individual developers and academic use.

A vibration anomaly detector for a pump motor can be developed on Edge Impulse in four steps: (1) collect 10-second vibration samples from the ADXL345 accelerometer in normal and fault conditions using the Edge Impulse data forwarder; (2) design a spectral analysis signal processing block that computes FFT features; (3) train a fully-connected neural network classifier with INT8 quantisation; (4) deploy as an Arduino library. The resulting model binary is typically 20-80 KB and runs at 10-100 Hz on a Cortex-M4 processor.

Edge Impulse's model testing tools report not only accuracy on the validation set but also RAM usage, flash usage, and inference latency on the target hardware, essential information for the constrained resource budget of a TinyML deployment. The platform also supports continuous learning: as production devices encounter novel data, samples can be automatically flagged for labelling and retraining, closing the model lifecycle loop.

10.3 Digital Twins: Concepts, Architecture, and Applications

A digital twin is a dynamic, continuously updated virtual model of a physical asset, system, or process that mirrors the physical entity's state, behaviour, and lifecycle in real time. The concept was first formalised by Michael Grieves at the University of Michigan in 2002, describing a virtual product model that maintained synchronisation with its physical counterpart throughout the product lifecycle.

NASA applied the concept operationally in space mission management: the Apollo 13 crisis response used a physical simulacrum of the spacecraft on the ground, what would today be called a digital twin, to model options for returning the damaged spacecraft safely. Industrial adoption accelerated dramatically after 2015, driven by the availability of IoT connectivity for continuous telemetry, cloud computing for model hosting, and edge computing for real-time synchronisation.

DEFINITION: Digital Twin

A dynamic virtual representation of a physical asset, system, or process that is synchronised with the physical entity through real-time IoT data streams, enabling simulation, analysis, prediction, and remote control of the physical entity via its digital counterpart. Digital twins exist at multiple scales: component level (a bearing), asset level (a wind turbine), system level (a production line), and ecosystem level (a city).

Source: Grieves, M. (2014); ISO 23247-1:2021

10.3.1 The Digital Twin Lifecycle

The digital twin lifecycle has five phases that operate continuously throughout the physical asset's operational life. Creation is the initial construction of the twin model from design data (CAD drawings, engineering specifications, physics equations governing the asset's behaviour), historical operational data, and any calibration measurements taken at installation. The creation phase produces a model that represents the asset's expected normal behaviour, its baseline.

Synchronisation is the continuous process of updating the twin's state with real-time IoT telemetry from the physical asset. For a wind turbine twin, synchronisation involves ingesting rotor speed, blade pitch angle, generator output, nacelle vibration, and weather station data at update rates from one second (for control-relevant parameters) to one minute (for slower thermal parameters). Synchronisation latency: the delay between a physical state change and its reflection in the twin is a critical performance parameter, typically measured in milliseconds for industrial control applications and seconds for monitoring applications. This is where IoT data pipelines of the kind studied in Chapter 6 are directly applied: the twin is, architecturally, a structured consumer of IoT time-series data.

Simulation is the execution of the twin's physics model to predict future states, test what-if scenarios, and explore operating conditions that cannot safely be tested on the physical asset. A manufacturing digital twin can simulate the effect of increasing line speed by 15% on component quality and equipment stress, providing the data for a production optimisation decision without risking a real production run. A structural twin of a bridge can simulate the stress distribution under projected traffic loads or flood conditions, informing maintenance scheduling without waiting for an actual overload event.

The Insight phase applies analytics and machine learning to the synchronised twin data to extract conclusions that are not visible in raw telemetry: component health scores, remaining useful life estimates, process efficiency metrics, and anomaly flags. The twin's value as an analytical substrate lies in its integration of multiple sensor streams into a coherent physics-informed context: a vibration anomaly flag is more actionable when the twin's model can localise it to a specific bearing in a specific shaft based on the transmission path of the vibration signal.

The Action phase closes the loop: twin-derived insights trigger physical actions, either through automated control systems (the twin adjusts a parameter, which the control system enacts on the physical asset) or through human decision-making supported by twin visualisation. The factory scenario at the chapter opening illustrates the action phase: when the twin flags a divergence from expected behaviour, a maintenance recommendation is generated and dispatched to the maintenance scheduling system before any physical fault occurs.

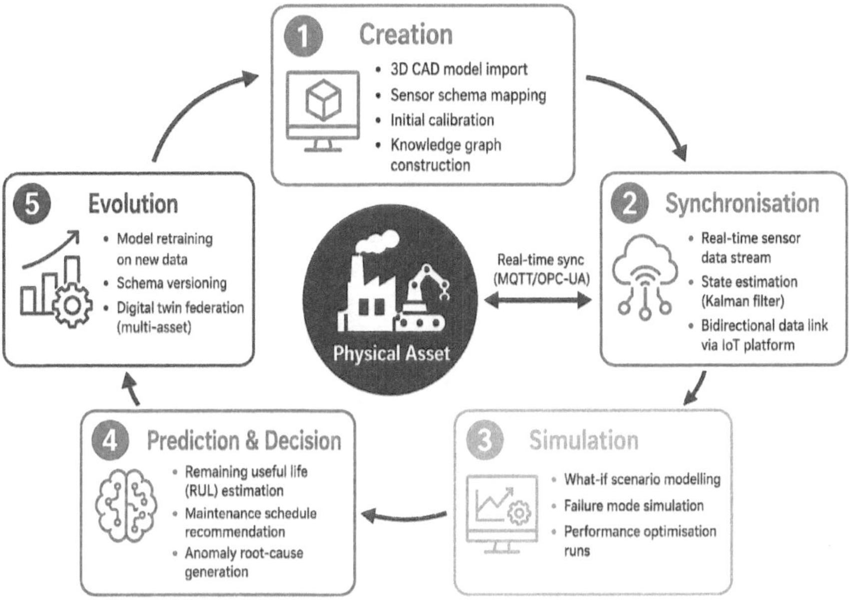

Figure 10.2: Digital Twin Lifecycle

10.3.2 Digital Twin Architecture

The architecture of a digital twin system has four layers. The Physical Asset Layer contains the real-world equipment instrumented with IoT sensors: the source of all telemetry that feeds the twin. Sensor selection and placement for digital twin applications are governed by the twin's model requirements: the model must be observable, meaning that the sensors must provide sufficient information to determine the model state. Chapter 2's sensor and hardware platform content is directly applicable here: the same selection criteria (accuracy, interface, power consumption) apply, with the additional requirement that sensor sampling rates are matched to the twin's update frequency.

The Connectivity and Ingestion Layer provides real-time data delivery from the physical asset to the twin model. For industrial twins requiring sub-second synchronisation, this layer uses protocols examined in Chapter 4: OPC UA (the industrial automation standard for machine data exchange), MQTT with QoS 1 or 2, and DDS (Data Distribution Service) for highest-throughput applications. For infrastructure twins with relaxed latency requirements (minutes to hours), standard LPWAN and cellular IoT protocols suffice.

The Twin Model Layer hosts the virtual representation of the asset: a combination of physics-based models (differential equations describing mechanical, thermal, or electrical behaviour),

data-driven models (neural networks trained on historical operational data), and knowledge models (rule bases encoding engineering expertise about failure modes and maintenance procedures). Industry platforms provide managed hosting and model tooling for this layer: Azure Digital Twins (Microsoft) uses a DTDL (Digital Twins Definition Language) JSON-LD schema for asset models and provides a graph-based twin topology service; AWS IoT TwinMaker provides a spatial scene composer for 3D asset model integration; NVIDIA Omniverse provides photorealistic real-time simulation for complex physical systems including robotics and autonomous vehicles.

The Analytics and Visualisation Layer presents twin state and insights to human operators and automated systems. Grafana dashboards (Chapter 6) are widely used for time-series metrics; 3D visualisation environments (Unity, NVIDIA Omniverse) provide immersive representations of complex spatial assets; custom web applications expose twin APIs to maintenance management systems and ERP platforms.

10.3.3 Industry Applications

Smart manufacturing is the most mature Digital Twin application domain. Siemens' MindSphere platform hosts digital twins of production equipment across hundreds of factories globally, enabling predictive maintenance, line optimisation, and virtual commissioning of new equipment before physical installation. A virtual commissioning workflow creates the twin before the machine is installed, validates the control software against the simulated machine, and arrives at physical installation with a pre-validated configuration, reducing commissioning time by 30-50% in published case studies. The factory scenario at this chapter's opening represents a deployed instance of this pattern.

Smart infrastructure twins extend the concept to city-scale systems. Singapore's Virtual Singapore platform, one of the world's most ambitious city-scale digital twin projects, integrates building information models, utility network data, environmental sensor feeds, and population mobility patterns into a unified 3D city model used for urban planning, emergency response simulation, and infrastructure maintenance scheduling. Smaller-scale infrastructure twins are deployed for individual assets: bridge structural twins monitor strain gauge data and correlate it with traffic load models to predict remaining structural life; water network twins identify pressure anomalies that indicate leaks before they cause service disruption.

Healthcare digital twins represent an emerging frontier. Patient-level twins, models of individual patient physiology calibrated with wearable IoT data are being developed for personalised treatment optimisation in cardiac care, diabetes management, and post-surgical rehabilitation. The European Union (EU)-funded Living Heart project demonstrated that a patient-specific cardiac twin built from MRI imaging and wearable ECG data could predict drug response more accurately than population-average models. Regulatory and ethical frameworks for patient-level digital twins are still developing, with the EU AI Act and the General Data Protection Regulation (GDPR)'s requirements for explainability and consent presenting both challenges and an opportunity to establish trustworthy AI-assisted clinical practice.

10.3.4 Digital Twin Platform Comparison

Table 10.2 compares the four dominant commercial Digital Twin platforms across the specification dimensions most relevant to IoT integration decisions.

Platform	Model Schema	Connectivity/Data	Scale	Cost Model	Best Fit
Azure Digital Twins (Microsoft)	DTDL (JSON-LD) knowledge graph	IoT Hub, Event Hubs, ADX, Azure ML	Global Azure regions; Auto-scale	Consumption-based; per query and event	Enterprise IoT; cross-asset topology modelling; Teams integration
AWS IoT TwinMaker (Amazon)	Custom entity-component schema	IoT Core, Kinesis, Timestream, S3	Global AWS regions; Auto-scale	Per data connector and scene query	3D spatial scene integration; Grafana plugin; AWS ecosystem
NVIDIA Omniverse (NVIDIA)	USD (Universal Scene Description)	Isaac Sim, Replicator; GPU compute clusters	On-premise or cloud GPU clusters	Enterprise licence; GPU infrastructure cost	Photorealistic simulation; robotics and factory twins; AI training data synthesis
Siemens MindSphere (Siemens)	Asset model (JSON) + OPC UA integration	MindConnect; IoT hub; MindAnalytics	Siemens cloud; AWS/ Azure hosted	Per-asset subscription volume discounts;	Industrial OT/ IT integration; Native Siemens equipment support

Table 10.2: Digital Twin Platform Comparison: Azure DT, AWS TwinMaker, NVIDIA Omniverse, Siemens MindSphere

10.4 5G and Next-Generation Connectivity for IoT

5G New Radio (NR) is not simply a faster version of 4G LTE. Its architectural innovations, three distinct service categories with fundamentally different performance profiles, network slicing for workload isolation, massive MIMO for spatial multiplexing, and ultra-dense deployment at millimetre-wave frequencies, enable IoT use cases that were technically impossible on 4G infrastructure. Understanding 5G's IoT relevance requires understanding not just its peak data rates (which attract consumer marketing attention) but its latency, density, and reliability characteristics, which are the parameters that matter for industrial and massive-scale IoT.

This section complements the protocol discussion in Chapter 4, which covered LPWAN technologies (LoRaWAN, NB-IoT, LTE-M) as constrained end-node connectivity. 5G does not replace these: LoRaWAN and NB-IoT remain the appropriate choice for battery-powered, low-data-rate IoT end nodes. 5G provides the high-performance tier for applications that those technologies cannot serve, and the backhaul and core network infrastructure over which NB-IoT and LTE-M also operate in Release 17 non-terrestrial network configurations.

10.4.1 5G NR Technical Architecture

5G NR (3GPP Release 15, 2018, with significant IoT extensions in Releases 16-17) operates across three frequency bands. Sub-1 GHz bands (600-900 MHz) provide wide-area coverage comparable to 4G LTE, with the same penetration characteristics, appropriate for NB-IoT and LTE-M integration in 5G core networks.

Mid-band frequencies (1-6 GHz, particularly the 3.4-3.8 GHz band used extensively in Europe and Asia) provide the practical 5G deployment sweet spot: coverage radii of 1-3 km combined with peak data rates of 100-1,000 Mbps. Millimetre-wave bands (24-100 GHz) provide peak data rates exceeding 10 Gbps but with coverage radii of 100-300 m and severe sensitivity to obstruction, appropriate for dense indoor deployments (stadiums, factories, campuses) where many access points are pre-installed but not for wide-area coverage.

The 5G core network (5GC) uses a service-based architecture (SBA): each core network function (authentication, session management, mobility management, policy) is exposed as a microservice with a RESTful HTTP/2 Application Programming Interface (API). This architecture enables the network functions to be deployed as software containers on commercial off-the-shelf hardware, operated by cloud-native DevOps tools, and orchestrated with Kubernetes, transforming the mobile network from a hardware appliance into a software platform. For IoT, the SBA enables network slicing: the dynamic allocation of virtual network instances with guaranteed performance parameters to specific IoT workloads.

10.4.2 The Three 5G Service Categories and IoT Implications

3GPP defines three service categories for 5G NR, each addressing a distinct set of use cases with different performance trade-offs.

eMBB, enhanced Mobile Broadband, is the service category that dominates 5G consumer marketing: peak data rates of 10-20 Gbps with typical user-experienced rates of 100-1,000 Mbps. Its IoT relevance lies in applications that require continuous high-bandwidth video or sensor streaming: high-resolution surveillance cameras (4K at 30 fps requires 15-20 Mbps per stream), augmented reality maintenance assistance (a technician views a live AR overlay of machine documentation superimposed on the physical equipment, requiring 25+ Mbps and sub-50 ms latency to avoid motion sickness), and connected vehicles transmitting camera and lidar data to edge processing infrastructure.

URLLC, Ultra-Reliable Low Latency Communications, is the service category specifically designed for mission-critical IoT. URLLC targets end-to-end latency of under 1 millisecond and reliability of 99.9999% (one packet loss per million transmissions).

These parameters are qualitatively different from any prior wireless technology and enable closed-loop industrial control applications that previously required dedicated wired fieldbus connections: robot arm synchronisation in collaborative manufacturing (where a millisecond delay could cause a collision), autonomous guided vehicle (AGV) fleet control in logistics warehouses, remote surgical robotics (where control latency directly affects clinical outcome), and power grid protection relay coordination (where URLLC replaces dedicated fibre links between substations).

mMTC, massive Machine-Type Communications, addresses the density extreme of IoT: connecting up to one million devices per square kilometre with low power consumption and low data rates. 5G mMTC incorporates and extends the 4G NB-IoT and LTE-M standards, providing a cellular path for the same battery-powered, infrequently-transmitting sensor nodes that LoRaWAN serves in unlicensed spectrum. The advantage of cellular mMTC over LoRaWAN is operator-managed coverage, guaranteed quality of service, and integration with the same SIM provisioning and billing infrastructure used for smartphones, simplifying large-scale fleet deployment across national and international boundaries.

10.4.3 Network Slicing for IoT

Network slicing is the 5G capability that enables a single physical network infrastructure to simultaneously support multiple isolated virtual network instances, each with its own performance characteristics, security posture, and management domain.

A hospital deploying 5G can define three slices on the same physical infrastructure: a URLLC slice for surgical robotics and patient monitoring alarms (guaranteed sub-1 ms latency, isolated from all other traffic); an eMBB slice for radiology image streaming and visitor Wi-Fi calling offload; and an mMTC slice for the building's environmental sensors, asset tracking tags, and smart-lighting controllers. Each slice is logically isolated: a security compromise of the visitor eMBB slice cannot affect the URLLC surgical slice.

For IoT system designers, network slicing provides a contractual quality-of-service guarantee that shared public networks cannot offer. An automotive manufacturer's private 5G URLLC slice for robot control can be provisioned with a latency SLA of 0.5 ms, a reliability SLA of 99.9999%, and a bandwidth reservation of 500 Mbps, parameters that are committed in the network service contract and enforced by the 5G core's traffic management. This transforms wireless connectivity from a best-effort medium into an engineering component with quantified, contractual performance characteristics.

10.4.4 Private 5G Networks

Private 5G networks — dedicated 5G NR deployments within a campus, factory, port, or hospital, operated by the enterprise rather than a public mobile operator are the fastest-growing 5G segment for industrial IoT. The private network operator controls the spectrum (licensed locally or through a spectrum sharing arrangement), the base stations, the 5G core, and the network slicing configuration. Data remains on-premises, addressing data sovereignty and latency requirements simultaneously. Equipment from Nokia (NDAC), Ericsson, Siemens (private 5G solutions), and dedicated enterprise 5G vendors such as Celona and Emnify enables deployment without mobile operator involvement.

Regional Example — GCC 5G-IoT and AIoT Deployment: NEOM, e& Smart Factory, and Vision 2030 Digital Infrastructure

Gulf Cooperation Council member states are among the world's most active deployers of 5G-enabled IoT and AI-powered smart infrastructure. Saudi Arabia's NEOM development, the planned linear city in the Tabuk region, has committed to a 5G-native connectivity architecture with a real-time digital twin of the entire 170 km city corridor, fed by embedded IoT sensors managing energy distribution, traffic flow, environmental quality, and utility infrastructure. Saudi Aramco has deployed AI-native predictive maintenance across its oil and gas facilities, with digital twins of compressor trains and pipeline segments enabling condition-based maintenance scheduling that has reduced unplanned downtime by measurable margins across its upstream operations. In the UAE, e& (formerly Etisalat) launched commercial private 5G network services for industrial IoT customers in 2022, delivering URLLC-grade connectivity for autonomous guided vehicle navigation and robotic assembly applications in electronics manufacturing. Dubai's Roads and Transport Authority has integrated AIoT-powered traffic management across 14,000 km of monitored road network, using edge AI inference at intersection cameras to dynamically optimise signal timing in real time. These deployments illustrate how the GCC's Vision 2030 and UAE Vision 2031 frameworks, which prioritise AI and IoT as foundational technologies for economic diversification are translating strategic intent into operational infrastructure at scale.

Port of Antwerp, Europe's second-largest container port, deployed one of the world's earliest industrial private 5G networks in 2021. The network supports autonomous crane operation, AGV fleet management, and container sensor data collection across 80 km of quayside. The URLLC slice supports the sub-10 ms control latency required for autonomous crane positioning; the mMTC slice manages 12,000 container temperature and humidity sensors on refrigerated cargo. The private network replaced a mix of Wi-Fi and 4G that could not simultaneously satisfy the latency and density requirements of the full IoT deployment.

10.4.5 5G IoT Service Category Comparison

Service Category	Data Rate	Latency	Reliability	Key Characteristic	IoT Use Cases
eMBB (enhanced Mobile Broadband)	100 Mbps - 10 Gbps	10-50 ms	Moderate	High bandwidth	Video surveillance, AR maintenance, connected vehicles, remote monitoring
URLLC (Ultra-Reliable Low Latency)	1-100 Mbps	Less than 1 ms	99.9999% (6 nines)	Deterministic control	Industrial robot control, autonomous AGV, remote surgery, grid protection

mMTC (massive Machine-Type Comms)	1-100 kbps	Seconds to minutes	99.9%	Ultra-low power; high density	Smart meters, agricultural sensors, asset tracking, building automation

Table 10.3: 5G Service Categories: eMBB, URLLC, and mMTC IoT Comparison

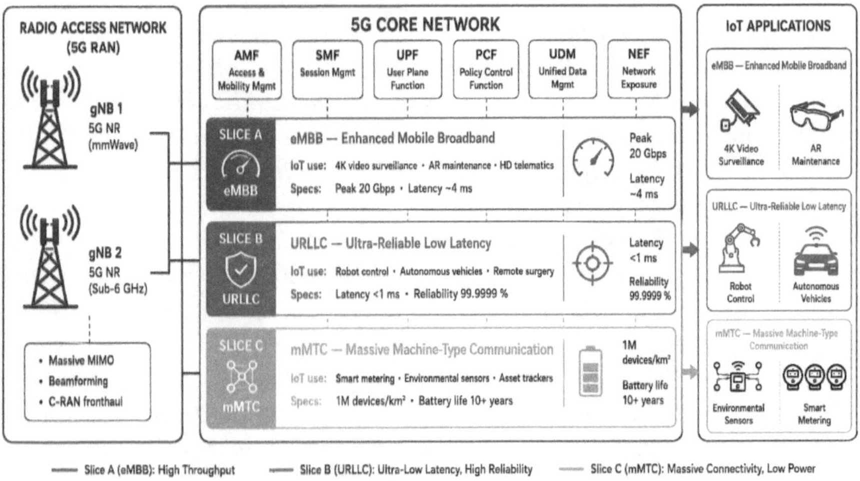

Figure 10.3: 5G-IoT integration architecture

10.4.6 6G: The Next Horizon

Research and early standardisation work on 6G, the successor to 5G, is already underway at 3GPP, the International Telecommunication Union (ITU), and major national research programmes in the EU (Hexa-X), the US (Next G Alliance), South Korea, and China. Commercial 6G deployments are targeted for 2030. While specifications are not yet finalised, several 6G design objectives are well-established in the research literature and are directly relevant to IoT.

Terahertz (THz) communication uses frequency bands from 100 GHz to 10 THz, enabling data rates of 100 Gbps to 1 Tbps, three orders of magnitude beyond 5G eMBB. Coverage radius is extremely limited (10-100 m) due to atmospheric absorption, confining THz to indoor ultra-dense deployments: immersive extended reality, holographic communication, and industrial micro-environments requiring massive data throughput over short distances.

AI-native networking is the most transformative 6G design principle: AI is embedded in the network itself, not applied on top of it. Base stations use AI models to predict channel conditions, pre-position data, and allocate resources without waiting for traditional signalling exchanges. Semantic communications, where the network transmits the meaning of a message rather than its bits, reduces bandwidth requirements for AI inference results by transmitting only semantically relevant changes. For IoT, an AI-native 6G network would automatically adapt its resource allocation to the dynamically changing demands of a heterogeneous IoT deployment, without the manual network slicing configuration that 5G requires.

10.5 Edge AI and Embedded Machine Learning

Edge AI refers to the execution of machine learning inference on devices at or near the source of data (IoT gateways, embedded processors, and microcontrollers) rather than in a centralised cloud platform. TinyML is the extreme end of this spectrum: trained neural network models executing on microcontrollers with kilobytes of RAM and milliwatts of power consumption. Both disciplines address the same fundamental problem: as the number and capability of IoT sensors grow, the cost and latency of transmitting all sensor data to the cloud for AI processing becomes the binding constraint on AI-enabled IoT systems. Moving inference to the edge dissolves that constraint.

Section 10.2 introduced the concepts of TinyML and model compression in the AIoT context. This section provides the technical depth that an IoT practitioner needs to implement Edge AI: the model compression pipeline in detail, the hardware platform selection decision, the toolchain from training environment to deployed firmware, and the operational challenges that distinguish a production edge AI deployment from a laboratory demonstration.

10.5.1 Why Edge AI?

The case for edge AI rests on four engineering arguments that are relevant at different points in the IoT design decision. Latency is the most compelling argument for real-time control applications: a cloud round-trip from an industrial sensor to a cloud inference endpoint and back takes 20-200 ms depending on network conditions; edge inference on the same MCU that drives the sensor takes microseconds to milliseconds. For the vibration anomaly classifier in the chapter's opening scenario, a 200 ms cloud latency would mean 100 vibration samples have been collected and discarded before the first inference result arrives: the system cannot react to a transient event. On-device inference at 500 Hz classifies every sample in real time.

Privacy and data sovereignty are the second argument. Raw sensor data from industrial production lines, patient monitors, or residential energy systems contains information that manufacturers, healthcare providers, and individuals may be legally or commercially required to keep on-premises. An edge classifier that reduces a raw audio stream to a yes/no keyword detection result transmits only the result, not the audio, and eliminates both the privacy risk and the regulatory complexity of transmitting identifiable audio to a cloud service.

Bandwidth and cost are the third argument, particularly for high-rate sensor streams. An accelerometer sampling at 10 kHz produces 1.2 MB/hour of raw data per sensor. A factory with 300 such sensors produces 360 MB/hour of raw telemetry, approximately 8.6 GB/day, which at typical cloud data ingestion pricing represents a substantial recurring cost. An on-device classifier that reduces this to a 10-byte status packet every minute reduces the data volume by a factor of more than 10,000.

Resilience is the fourth argument: edge inference continues during cloud connectivity outages. In the agricultural deployment of Chapter 5, an edge AI classifier for crop stress detection running on the Raspberry Pi gateway would continue operating through internet outages that would disable a cloud-dependent inference service. For critical applications (infrastructure monitoring, medical devices, industrial safety systems) this offline operational capability is not a convenience feature; it is a safety requirement.

10.5.2 The Edge AI Pipeline: Training in the Cloud, Inference at the Edge

The standard Edge AI development pipeline separates the training environment from the inference environment: training occurs on full-capability hardware (GPU servers, cloud ML platforms) with access to large labelled datasets and standard ML frameworks; inference executes on the constrained edge device using a compressed, optimised version of the trained model.

Data collection and labelling is the pipeline's most labour-intensive phase and the most consequential for model quality. IoT sensor data must be labelled with ground-truth class information: for a vibration anomaly detector, this means collecting vibration samples under both normal operation and known fault conditions (bearing wear, imbalance, misalignment) and labelling each sample with its class. Data quality at this stage determines the ceiling on model accuracy, with no amount of architectural sophistication can compensate for poorly labelled training data.

Model training on the collected and labelled dataset produces a floating-point model. The architecture choice must consider not only accuracy but the ultimate deployment target: models that will run on Cortex-M4 microcontrollers should be designed as small convolutional neural networks (CNNs) or fully-connected networks with at most a few thousand parameters, rather than deep residual networks with millions of parameters that are computationally intractable on MCU hardware even after quantisation.

The compression pipeline (quantisation, pruning, distillation, introduced in Section 10.2.3) reduces the trained model to a form deployable on the target hardware. The TensorFlow Lite converter and ONNX Runtime optimiser both automate this pipeline given the trained model and a calibration dataset. The output is a .tflite or .onnx model file containing INT8 weights and operator specifications.

Deployment packages the compressed model into a C array embedded in the device firmware, compiled with the TensorFlow Lite Micro runtime. The runtime provides an interpreter that loads the model, allocates a tensor arena (a static RAM buffer for intermediate activations), and executes inference given an input tensor. The tensor arena size, the primary RAM consumer of TinyML inference, must be calculated and verified against the target device's available RAM during the development phase, before production assembly.

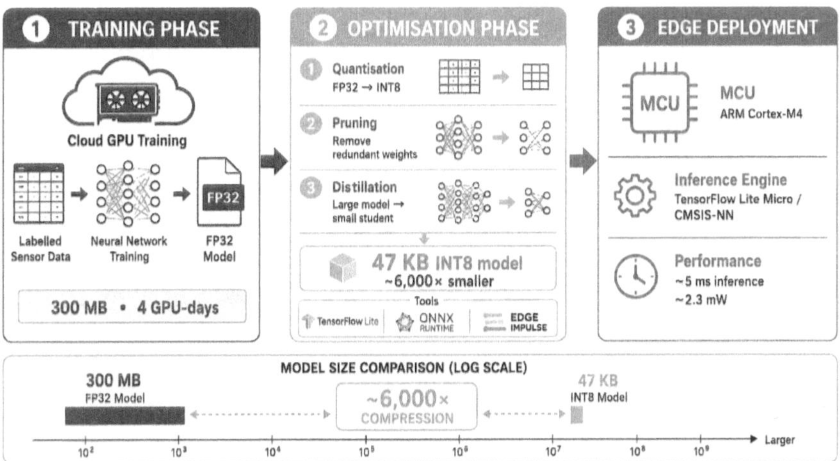

Figure 10.4: Edge AI development pipeline

10.5.3 Hardware Platforms for Edge AI

Hardware platform selection for Edge AI follows the constraint hierarchy established in Chapter 2, with model complexity and inference throughput requirements added as first-tier constraints alongside power budget.

The Arduino Nano 33 BLE Sense is the entry-level TinyML reference platform: a Nordic nRF52840 Cortex-M4F at 64 MHz with 256 KB RAM and 1 MB flash, augmented with an onboard 9-axis IMU (LSM9DS1), microphone (MP34DT05), temperature/humidity/pressure sensor (HTS221, LPS22HB), and colour/proximity sensor (APDS9960). The sensor suite makes it a single-board laboratory for audio keyword spotting, gesture recognition, colour classification, and anomaly detection without external hardware. INT8 inference latency for a small CNN (50-100 KB model) is approximately 5-50 ms on the Cortex-M4F, sufficient for audio (inference at keyword detection rate) and motion classification applications.

STM32 microcontrollers from STMicroelectronics are the dominant choice for production TinyML deployments. The STM32H7 series (Cortex-M7 at 480 MHz, 1 MB RAM, 2 MB flash) with ST's Cube.AI toolchain provides an integrated flow from Keras model import to optimised C code generation with CMSIS-NN acceleration. ST's CubeAI benchmarks demonstrate ResNet-8 inference at 15 ms on the STM32H747: a meaningful capability for real-time classification of audio and vibration signals. The STM32L4 series (ultra-low-power, 1.1 microampere stop mode) enables TinyML on battery-powered nodes with stringent power budgets.

The NVIDIA Jetson Nano represents the opposite end of the edge AI spectrum: a 128-core Maxwell GPU with 4 GB LPDDR4 RAM, capable of running full computer vision models (YOLO, ResNet-50, SSD-MobileNet) at 30+ fps with power consumption of 5-10 W. Jetson Nano is appropriate for edge AI applications that require vision-based classification, object detection, or pose estimation: quality inspection cameras, autonomous robot perception, or the gateway tier of a Digital Twin system aggregating visual sensor data from multiple cameras. Its power profile precludes battery operation but makes it viable for mains-powered gateway or edge server installations.

10.5.4 Worked Example: Vibration Anomaly Detector on STM32

The factory scenario's TinyML bearing classifier can be developed using the following steps, applicable to any vibration-based anomaly detection deployment. An ADXL345 accelerometer is connected to the STM32 SPI bus and sampled at 3.2 kHz. A 1-second window of 3,200 samples is acquired. A preprocessing block computes a 128-point FFT of the X-axis acceleration, producing 64 frequency bins covering 0-1.6 kHz: the frequency range where bearing fault signatures typically appear (at the bearing defect frequencies

BPFI, BPFO, BSF, and FTF, which depend on bearing geometry and shaft speed).

The 64-bin spectral feature vector is the input to a small fully-connected neural network with two hidden layers (64 and 32 neurons) and a three-class softmax output (Normal, Bearing Fault, Imbalance). Trained on 4,000 labelled 1-second windows from a test rig with seeded faults, the FP32 model achieves 96.4% validation accuracy. Post-training INT8 quantisation reduces the model from 52 KB to 14 KB with 95.1% accuracy. Deployed via ST Cube.AI to the STM32H743 with CMSIS-NN acceleration, inference takes 3.8 ms, well within the 1-second window acquisition time. The sensor, preprocessing, and inference together consume 18 mW, compatible with a 500 mAh battery providing over 27 hours of continuous operation.

10.5.5 Challenges: Model Staleness and Production Operations

A TinyML model trained on historical data will degrade in accuracy as the physical environment evolves: a bearing anomaly detector trained on a specific motor will produce false positives when the motor is replaced with a different model that has a different normal vibration signature; an agricultural crop stress classifier trained on one growing season's data may not generalise to the next season's different crop variety or pest pressure. Model staleness is not a theoretical concern; it is the primary operational challenge of production TinyML deployments.

Addressing model staleness requires a continuous learning infrastructure: a data collection pipeline that logs edge inference inputs and outputs (with sampling to avoid flooding the system), a labelling workflow for collecting ground truth on flagged samples, a retraining trigger (scheduled or accuracy-threshold-based), and an OTA update mechanism that pushes the retrained model to deployed devices. This lifecycle management infrastructure is as important as the model itself for production deployments, and must be designed into the system architecture from the beginning; it cannot be retrofitted after deployment without significant rework of the data pipeline and device management components.

10.6 Blockchain for IoT: Trust, Transparency, and Decentralisation

At the heart of many IoT deployment challenges lies a trust problem. In a system involving hundreds of organisations (device manufacturers, platform providers, system integrators, data consumers, regulatory authorities) who controls the IoT data that flows between them?

Who guarantees that a temperature reading recorded at a pharmaceutical warehouse was actually measured at that location at that time, and was not subsequently altered? Who enforces the contractual obligation that a logistics provider delivers a package within the temperature range specified in the smart contract? In traditional systems, trust is centralised: a database operated by a trusted third party. Blockchain offers an alternative: trust through mathematics, distributed among all participants, without any single controlling authority.

DEFINITION: Blockchain

A distributed ledger technology in which records (transactions) are grouped into cryptographically linked blocks forming an append-only chain. Each block's header contains the hash of the previous block, making the chain tamper-evident: altering any historical record invalidates all subsequent blocks. Consensus mechanisms (Proof of Work, Proof of Stake, or permissioned BFT algorithms) ensure that all participants agree on the canonical chain without a central authority.

Source: Nakamoto, S. (2008); Buterin, V. (2014)

10.6.1 Blockchain Fundamentals

A blockchain is a distributed ledger, a database replicated across multiple independent nodes, in which records are organised into blocks linked by cryptographic hashes. Each block contains a set of transactions (data entries), a timestamp, and the SHA-256 hash of the preceding block. The hash linkage makes the chain tamper-evident: altering any transaction in any block changes that block's hash, invalidating the hash stored in the next block, which then requires recomputation of every subsequent block: a computationally infeasible task when the chain is long and the network is large.

A consensus mechanism ensures that all nodes in the network agree on which blocks are valid and in what order.

Proof of Work (PoW), used by Bitcoin, requires the proposing node to solve a computational puzzle (finding a nonce that makes the block header hash below a target value) before the block is accepted. PoW's security comes from its energy cost: an attacker who wishes to rewrite history must control more than 50% of the network's total hashing power, economically prohibitive on large public chains. Proof of Stake (PoS), used by Ethereum since 2022, selects block validators in proportion to the amount of cryptocurrency they have staked as collateral, consuming far less energy than PoW while providing equivalent or better security under most attack models.

Permissioned blockchains, used in most enterprise IoT applications, replace PoW and PoS with Byzantine Fault Tolerant (BFT) consensus algorithms (Practical BFT, Raft, PBFT variants) that require network participants to be pre-approved. Hyperledger Fabric uses this model: organisations join a permissioned network, each operating one or more validator nodes; a consensus algorithm achieves finality (irreversible confirmation) within seconds rather than the 10-60 minutes required by public PoW chains. Permissioned blockchains sacrifice the open participation of public chains for performance, throughput, and the ability to manage identity and access control, properties that enterprise IoT deployments require.

10.6.2 The Trust Gap in Multi-Party IoT Deployments

The value proposition of blockchain for IoT is most clearly seen in multi-party deployments where participants do not fully trust each other's systems. Consider a pharmaceutical cold-chain involving a manufacturer in Germany, a logistics provider transporting through the UAE, a customs authority in Oman, and a hospital pharmacy in Muscat. The manufacturer requires proof that the drug shipment was maintained between 2 and 8 degrees Celsius throughout transit. The logistics provider asserts compliance through its own telemetry system. But the hospital pharmacy has no independent way to verify that the telemetry system was not selectively edited, malfunctioned silently, or simply reported compliance parameters that the physical containers did not achieve.

A blockchain-anchored IoT architecture addresses this by writing each sensor reading (timestamped, signed by the sensor's private key, and hashed with the previous reading) to a distributed ledger accessible to all parties.

The temperature record is not in any one party's database; it is on an immutable chain that no single party controls. The hospital pharmacy can verify the complete temperature history of the shipment from manufacture to delivery by querying the ledger directly, without trusting the logistics provider's reporting. The customs authority can verify transit time and handling conditions from the same ledger. The manufacturer can automate release of payment to the logistics provider through a smart contract that executes only when the ledger confirms continuous cold-chain compliance.

10.6.3 IOTA: Distributed Ledger for Constrained IoT Devices

Traditional blockchain architectures face a fundamental constraint in IoT contexts: transaction fees. Bitcoin and Ethereum charge a per-transaction fee (gas, in Ethereum's terminology) that can range from cents to tens of dollars depending on network congestion. An IoT sensor that writes a temperature reading every 15 minutes would incur thousands of dollars per year in transaction fees on a public blockchain, economically absurd for a USD 20 sensor.

IOTA addresses this with a fundamentally different data structure: the Tangle, a directed acyclic graph (DAG) rather than a linear blockchain. In the Tangle,

each new transaction validates two previous transactions by computing their proof-of-work, embedding the validation in the new transaction's structure. There is no miner or validator collecting fees: the work of validation is distributed across all participants. The result is feeless micro-transactions, each IoT sensor reading can be anchored to the Tangle without any transaction cost, making IOTA economically viable for high-frequency IoT data logging. IOTA's Chrysalis (2021) and Stardust (2022) protocol updates introduced coloured tokens for asset tracking and a smart contract layer, significantly expanding the protocol's IoT applicability.

10.6.4 Smart Contracts for IoT Automation

A smart contract is a self-executing program stored on a blockchain that automatically enforces the terms of an agreement when predefined conditions are met, without requiring any trusted intermediary. Ethereum's Solidity language is the most widely used smart contract platform; Hyperledger Fabric uses Go or JavaScript chaincode.

For IoT, smart contracts create a powerful automation primitive: IoT sensor data triggers financial, operational, or access-control consequences automatically and irreversibly. The pharmaceutical cold-chain example illustrates this: a Hyperledger Fabric smart contract defines the terms of the logistics agreement (drug manufacturer, logistics provider, receiving hospital) and the conditions for payment: continuous temperature compliance (2-8 degrees Celsius) from dispatch to delivery. As each IoT temperature reading is written to the ledger by the sensor's gateway, the smart contract evaluates it against the compliance condition.

When the final delivery event is recorded and all readings are within range, the contract automatically releases payment to the logistics provider's digital wallet. No invoice, no payment approval process, no dispute about whether the temperature data is accurate: the ledger is the single source of truth, and the contract executes on it automatically.

CASE STUDY: Case Study: Blockchain Cold-Chain for Vaccine Logistics — Kenya

Nairobi, Kenya, 2023

A UNICEF-supported vaccine logistics programme in Kenya deployed a Hyperledger Fabric blockchain to anchor cold-chain telemetry for vaccine shipments from Nairobi's cold storage hub to 47 county health facilities across the country. Each transport unit carried an IoT temperature logger (TempTale 4 Ultra, Sensitech) with a cellular modem writing signed temperature readings to the Hyperledger network at 10-minute intervals.

Before blockchain deployment, the programme's cold-chain assurance relied on paper temperature logs submitted by logistics providers: a process that produced compliance rates of 97% on paper despite field observations suggesting actual compliance was significantly lower. After blockchain deployment, immutable telemetry records became the basis for compliance certification. In the first six months, verified cold-chain excursions (temperature above 8 degrees Celsius for more than 30 consecutive minutes) were identified in 8% of shipments, previously undetected under the paper reporting system. Affected vaccine batches were quarantined before distribution rather than after administration.

A smart contract automatically released payment to approved logistics providers within 24 hours of compliant delivery confirmation, reducing the previous 45-day payment cycle to near-instantaneous settlement. The reduction in payment delay improved logistics provider participation in the programme by 34% in the first year.

10.6.5 Blockchain for IoT: Platform Comparison and Challenges

Table 10.4 compares four blockchain platforms across the dimensions most relevant to IoT deployment decisions. The comparison illustrates that no single platform dominates across all dimensions: the choice depends on whether the deployment requires open participation or permissioned access, feeless micro-transactions or general-purpose smart contracts, and how constrained the participating IoT devices are.

Platform	Consensus	Throughput	Energy Cost	IoT Suitability	Primary IoT Use Case
Bitcoin	Proof of Work (Nakamoto consensus)	7 TPS	Very high (PoW energy)	Very poor (No smart contracts; high fees)	Value storage; provenance anchoring for high-value assets only
Ethereum (post-Merge)	Proof of Stake (Gasper)	15-30 TPS (~100k with L2)	Low-moderate (PoS)	Moderate (smart contracts; gas fees variable)	Supply chain audit; DeFi IoT integration; open ecosystems
Hyperledger Fabric	Permissioned BFT (Raft / PBFT)	2,000-20,000 TPS	Very low (no mining)	Good (no fees; chaincode; identity management)	Enterprise IoT; cold chain; manufacturing audit; healthcare
IOTA (Tangle)	DAG-based (Coordicide)	Feeless; high throughput	Very low (lightweight PoW per tx)	Excellent (feeless micro-tx-;Data Marketplace)	High-frequency sensor logging; IoT data marketplace; machine economy

Table 10.4: Blockchain Platforms for IoT: Comparison (Bitcoin, Ethereum, Hyperledger Fabric, IOTA)

An honest assessment of blockchain for IoT must acknowledge its genuine limitations alongside its utility. Block confirmation latency: the time between a transaction being submitted and being irreversibly confirmed, ranges from seconds (Hyperledger Fabric) to minutes (Ethereum) to hours (Bitcoin), and is incompatible with real-time IoT control applications; blockchain is a record-keeping and audit technology, not a control protocol.

Scalability remains a challenge for public chains: even with Layer 2 solutions, Ethereum's transaction throughput is orders of magnitude below what a fleet of millions of IoT devices writing every sensor reading would require. Protocol heterogeneity between different blockchain platforms creates interoperability challenges in supply chains that cross multiple organisations using different Distributed Ledger Technology (DLT) implementations. And the oracle problem: the challenge of ensuring that off-chain data (such as IoT sensor readings) introduced to the blockchain is authentic — means that blockchain does not eliminate trust requirements: it shifts them from trusting the database to trusting the data ingestion oracle that writes sensor readings to the ledger.

Blockchain for IoT is best understood as a complementary layer to the security mechanisms studied in Chapter 8 and the governance frameworks studied in Chapter 9. It provides tamper-evident audit trails and multi-party trust for specific high-value IoT data streams where the cost of blockchain integration is justified by the value of the trust guarantee. It does not replace TLS, device authentication, access control, or governance frameworks; it adds a layer of decentralised verifiability on top of them.

10.7 Sustainability and Green IoT

The global IoT device fleet has reached about 21.1 billion connected devices and is forecast to reach around 39 billion by 2030. Each of these devices was manufactured, consumes energy during operation, and will eventually become electronic waste.

At scale, the environmental footprint of this fleet is not negligible: the production of a typical IoT sensor node requires rare earth elements, emits approximately 0.5-2 kg of CO_2 equivalent in manufacturing (depending on the manufacturing location and semiconductor complexity), and, if battery-powered, generates a maintenance logistics burden that involves periodic travel to remote field sites to replace depleted cells. Aggregated across tens of billions of connected devices, these impacts become significant at both the enterprise and planetary scale.

Green IoT is the engineering and policy discipline that addresses this challenge. It encompasses low-power design to reduce operational energy consumption, energy harvesting to eliminate battery replacement, circular economy principles to extend device operational life and reduce manufacturing waste, and carbon accounting methods to measure, report, and improve the lifecycle environmental footprint of IoT deployments. Sustainability and engineering quality are aligned rather than in tension: the duty cycling, sleep mode management, and energy harvesting techniques that reduce environmental impact also reduce battery replacement cost, extend deployment lifetime, and reduce total cost of ownership. A Green IoT design is typically also a better-engineered design.

10.7.1 The IoT Carbon Footprint

The carbon footprint of an IoT deployment has three components. Embodied carbon is the CO_2 equivalent emitted during the manufacture of the device and its components — silicon wafer production, PCB fabrication, battery cell production, and enclosure moulding. For a typical constrained IoT sensor node, embodied carbon ranges from 0.5 to 2 kg CO_2e depending on processor complexity and battery size. For a Raspberry Pi gateway with its more complex System-on-Chip (SoC) and DRAM, embodied carbon is estimated at 10-30 kg CO_2e. Across a 40-node AgroSense deployment (Chapter 5), embodied carbon is approximately 40-80 kg CO_2e, roughly equivalent to a single return flight of 400 km.

Operational carbon is the CO2 equivalent of the electricity consumed during the device's operational life, determined by the device's average power consumption and the carbon intensity of the electricity supply. A sensor node consuming 65 microamperes average at 3.7 V draws 240 microwatts, consuming 2.1 Wh per year. At the global average grid carbon intensity of approximately 450 g CO2e/kWh (IEA, 2023), this represents approximately 0.95 g CO2e per year per node — negligible in operational terms relative to embodied carbon. For mains-powered gateways and edge servers, operational carbon dominates: a Raspberry Pi 4 consuming 5 W continuously draws 43.8 kWh per year, producing 20 kg CO2e annually at average grid intensity.

End-of-life carbon encompasses both the emissions from device disposal and the avoided emissions from recovery of materials through recycling. Electronic waste (e-waste) is the world's fastest-growing waste stream: the UN Global E-waste Monitor (2024) reported 62 million tonnes of e-waste generated in 2023, of which only 22% was formally recycled. IoT devices, particularly those with soldered batteries and non-standardised connectors are especially difficult to disassemble and recycle, contributing disproportionately to the unrecycled fraction.

10.7.2 Low-Power Design as a Sustainability Tool

The low-power design principles studied in Chapter 2 — duty cycling, sleep modes, radio power management, peripheral power gating — are Green IoT's most powerful tools because they directly reduce the operational energy consumption that dominates lifecycle carbon for long-lived deployments. The numerical example from Chapter 2 is worth revisiting in a sustainability frame: an nRF52840 node with 1.57 microampere average current consumes 13.75 mWh per year — while a naive design that keeps the radio and processor active continuously would consume 29,200 mWh per year. The duty-cycled design reduces operational energy by a factor of 2,127 — and eliminates the logistics, cost, and carbon of battery replacement entirely when combined with a small solar harvester.

Adaptive sampling is a Green IoT technique that extends duty cycling from the hardware level to the application level: rather than sampling at a fixed rate regardless of what the sensor is observing, the node reduces its sampling rate when the measured value is stable and increases it when rapid change is detected. An environmental sensor in an empty office building might report temperature every hour at night and every 5 minutes during occupied hours; a soil moisture sensor might sample every 2 hours on overcast days and every 30 minutes on hot, sunny days when evapotranspiration is highest. Adaptive sampling reduces average current consumption, data transmission volume, and cloud storage cost simultaneously.

10.7.3 Energy Harvesting for Battery-Free IoT

Energy harvesting (generating power from ambient sources (solar, thermoelectric, piezoelectric, RF)) is Green IoT's most transformative technology because it eliminates the battery replacement logistics that dominate the operational cost and carbon footprint of large-scale, widely-distributed IoT deployments. Chapter 2 introduced the principal harvesting sources and their output characteristics. This section examines the systems design implications of deploying harvesting at scale.

The AgroSense deployment from Chapter 5 provides the sustainability calculation directly. Each of 40 sensor nodes carries a 2W solar panel and a 3,000 mAh LiPo buffer battery. The average node current is approximately 170 microamperes at the 15-minute LoRaWAN reporting duty cycle; the solar panel in Rajasthan generates approximately 400 mAh/day at minimum winter insolation. Daily solar harvest exceeds daily consumption by a factor of approximately 90, providing indefinite operation with substantial weather margin. The alternative, replacing primary batteries annually across a 40-node field deployment, which would require a field technician to travel to 40 GPS-located field sites annually, generating approximately 120 kg CO2e in travel emissions and 40 kg of spent primary battery waste per year. The solar-powered design eliminates both.

Ericsson's Connected Mangroves initiative demonstrates energy harvesting IoT at environmental monitoring scale: autonomous sensor nodes monitoring mangrove forest health in Indonesia and Sri Lanka use solar harvesting and LoRaWAN transmission to provide continuous habitat data for conservation scientists, operating without any field maintenance for over three years. The programme demonstrates that Green IoT and environmental monitoring applications are particularly well-aligned: the same remote, access-constrained environments that make battery replacement expensive are typically rich in solar or wind energy for harvesting.

10.7.4 Circular Economy Principles for IoT

The circular economy applies three design principles to IoT hardware that can dramatically reduce manufacturing waste and embodied carbon: repairability, modularity, and standardisation.

Repairability by design requires that IoT devices be designed for field repair rather than field replacement. The EU's Right to Repair Directive (2023) establishes repairability as a consumer right for a broad class of electronics, and the methodology is directly applicable to IoT hardware: replaceable batteries (not soldered), user-accessible firmware update ports, documented repair procedures, and spare part availability commitments. The IPC-2591 Connected Factory Exchange standard for industrial IoT includes repairability scoring as a design quality metric.

Modular hardware separates the communication module from the sensing payload, allowing the higher-value radio module to be reused when a sensor fails, and allowing a sensing module to be upgraded without replacing the entire node. The Arduino MKR form factor and the Feather ecosystem (Adafruit) both implement this modularity: the processor and radio board is standardised; add-on sensor shields can be swapped independently. Industrial IoT platforms from Phoenix Contact and Wago implement modular I/O architectures that allow individual sensor channels to be replaced without powering down the entire field device.

Standardised interfaces (including standardised connector types, standard programming interfaces (JTAG, USB-C), and interoperable communication protocols) reduce the risk that a device becomes obsolete because its proprietary interface is no longer supported. The IoT device longevity problem is partly a standards fragmentation problem: devices become non-functional not because their sensing elements have failed, but because the cloud platform they depend on has been discontinued, or because the proprietary gateway software has not been updated to support a newer operating system. Open protocol standards (MQTT, CoAP, Matter, LwM2M) and open platform architectures significantly extend the practical operational lifetime of IoT hardware, reducing the replacement cadence and the associated embodied carbon.

10.7.5 Green IoT Standards and Frameworks

Several standards bodies have developed Green IoT frameworks that provide measurement methods and design guidance for sustainable IoT deployments. ITU-T Recommendation L.1024 (2022) defines energy efficiency metrics for IoT networks, establishing standardised measurement methods for device-level energy consumption and network-level energy efficiency that allow comparison across different IoT architectures and deployments.

ETSI EN 303 470 extends the ETSI EN 303 645 consumer IoT security framework with sustainability provisions, including energy consumption reporting and battery replacement cycle disclosure requirements. The ITU-T Focus Group on AI for Autonomous and Assisted Driving has extended lifecycle assessment (LCA) methodology to IoT deployments, providing guidance on how to account for embodied carbon, operational carbon, and end-of-life impacts in a standardised, comparable way.

10.8 The Road Ahead: Societal, Ethical, and Technological Horizons

The six technology themes addressed in Sections 10.2 through 10.7 are not just engineering advances. They are reshaping the relationship between digital systems and the physical world, between organisations and the data they generate, and between technology and the societies it serves. The closing section of this chapter, and of the textbook, addresses the human dimensions of these developments: the societal implications of pervasive IoT infrastructure, the ethical questions raised by AI-driven autonomous systems, the privacy challenges of increasingly intelligent sensing environments, and the quantum and connectivity technologies that will shape the next decade.

10.8.1 Societal Dimensions of Pervasive IoT

Smart city IoT deployments (sensor networks monitoring traffic, air quality, noise, water, energy, and crowd dynamics) represent some of the most ambitious and impactful IoT applications in deployment today. Singapore, Amsterdam, Dubai, and Songdo (Korea) have invested substantially in city-scale IoT infrastructure.

The governance question that accompanies these investments is as important as the technical question: who controls the city's IoT data? Who decides what is measured, how long data is retained, and who can access it? Amsterdam's Smart City programme has developed an explicit Data Governance Framework addressing these questions, establishing citizen data rights, open data publication requirements for non-sensitive city sensor data, and privacy impact assessments for new sensor deployments. This framework represents a model for the governance dimension of smart city IoT that complements the technical governance mechanisms studied in Chapter 9.

Digital inclusion, ensuring that IoT technology's benefits are accessible across all socioeconomic strata and geographies is a central challenge for policy makers and engineers alike. The AgroSense deployment in Chapter 5 illustrates both the potential and the tension: precision agriculture IoT can transform the productivity of smallholder farmers, but only if the system is designed for their specific constraints, modest technology budget, non-English literacy, intermittent connectivity, and reliance on feature phones rather than smartphones. Engineers who design IoT systems without explicit consideration of the end users' context and capabilities routinely produce systems that serve wealthy, technically literate users and exclude the populations who could benefit most.

The right to disconnect: the principle that individuals should be able to opt out of IoT monitoring in their homes, workplaces, and public spaces without penalty is an emerging dimension of digital rights policy. As IoT sensors become embedded in shared infrastructure (office buildings, public transport, retail spaces), individuals may find themselves under continuous monitoring in environments where they have no practical means of opting out. The EU's AI Act, which requires human oversight of high-risk AI systems and prohibits certain forms of biometric surveillance, addresses part of this concern; a broader legal framework for the right to disconnect in IoT-instrumented environments is an active policy debate in multiple jurisdictions.

10.8.2 Ethical Dimensions of AIoT

The deployment of AI inference within IoT systems creates ethical responsibilities that extend beyond the technical performance of the model. When an AIoT system makes an autonomous decision (opening a valve, triggering a maintenance alert, denying access, or flagging a person as a security risk) the decision affects real people in the physical world. The engineering responsibility for that decision is shared between the model designer, the system architect, the deployment organisation, and the regulatory framework within which the system operates.

Key Insight — Engineering Ethics in AIoT: Every Automated Decision Executes a Design Assumption

When a TinyML model on a wearable classifies a patient's heart rhythm as normal, it is executing an assumption embedded in its training data: that 'normal' means 'resembles the training distribution'. If that distribution was drawn from one demographic, the model's elevated error rate on another demographic is not a statistical anomaly; it is an engineering choice made implicitly at the data collection stage. When a predictive maintenance model schedules downtime, it executes an assumption about what precursor failure looks like. When an AIoT irrigation controller opens a valve, it executes an assumption about what water-stressed soil looks like. Every automated decision in an AIoT system is the execution of assumptions built into the training pipeline by the engineer who designed it. The responsibility for those assumptions, and for their consequences on the people and systems they affect — does not transfer to the algorithm.

Algorithmic bias in AIoT systems arises when training data does not represent the full distribution of conditions the deployed model will encounter. A predictive maintenance model trained on vibration data from new equipment may perform poorly on older equipment with different baseline signatures, producing false alarms that damage trust in the system, or missing faults in the equipment most at risk of failure. A health monitoring wearable trained predominantly on data from one demographic group may be less accurate for others. The solution is not simply to collect more data; it is to define the target population and operating conditions in the requirements specification (Step 1 of the design methodology), and to evaluate model performance explicitly across all relevant subgroups before deployment.

Transparency in AIoT decision-making requires that automated decisions be explainable to affected stakeholders: a farmer whose irrigation system has not opened a valve should be able to understand why; a maintenance engineer whose AIoT system has scheduled an unplanned maintenance intervention should be able to see the sensor evidence that triggered the decision.

Explainable AI (XAI) techniques (SHAP values, LIME, attention visualisation) are being extended to the constrained model architectures used in TinyML, though full explainability at the microcontroller level remains an active research area. The EU AI Act's explainability requirements for high-risk AI systems provide a regulatory baseline that will drive practical XAI adoption in IoT deployments across European jurisdictions and, through global market access requirements, internationally.

10.8.3 Privacy and Surveillance in IoT Environments

The convergence of pervasive sensing (cameras, microphones, motion detectors, biometric sensors embedded in public and private spaces), edge AI inference (real-time person identification, behaviour classification, emotional state estimation), and low-latency 5G connectivity creates an unprecedented surveillance capability that challenges both legal frameworks and social norms. The same technology stack that enables a smart city to optimise traffic flow also enables a government to track the movements of every citizen in real time.

The privacy-preserving techniques studied in Chapters 8 and 9 (data minimisation, differential privacy, federated learning, anonymisation) are the engineering responses to this challenge. But engineering solutions alone are not sufficient when the legal and institutional framework permits surveillance at scale. The EU AI Act's prohibition on real-time biometric identification systems in public spaces (with narrow law enforcement exceptions), and its classification of predictive policing and social scoring as prohibited AI practices, represent the most comprehensive legal framework yet enacted for constraining AI-enabled IoT surveillance. The IoT engineer operating in this environment must understand not only the technical capability of the systems they build but the legal and ethical boundaries within which those systems may operate.

10.8.4 Quantum Computing and Post-Quantum Cryptography for IoT

Quantum computing: the use of quantum mechanical phenomena such as superposition and entanglement to perform computations that are intractable for classical computers, poses a fundamental threat to the cryptographic foundations of IoT security. Shor's algorithm, executable on a sufficiently powerful quantum computer, can factor large integers and solve discrete logarithm problems in polynomial time, breaking RSA, ECDSA, and ECDH, the asymmetric cryptographic algorithms that underpin TLS, X.509 certificates, and LoRaWAN key exchange as studied in Chapters 4 and 8.

A cryptographically relevant quantum computer capable of breaking current 2048-bit RSA keys is not yet built, but the National Institute of Standards and Technology (NIST) timeline for post-quantum cryptography standardisation reflects a consensus that cryptographic migration must begin now, given the long operational lifetimes of IoT devices and the harvest-now-decrypt-later attack threat.

NIST published its first post-quantum cryptography (PQC) standards in August 2024: FIPS 203 (ML-KEM, lattice-based key encapsulation), FIPS 204 (ML-DSA, lattice-based digital signatures), and FIPS 205 (SLH-DSA, hash-based signatures). These algorithms are designed to be secure against both classical and quantum computers. Implementing PQC on constrained IoT devices is a significant engineering challenge: ML-KEM public keys are approximately 1.2 KB (versus 65 bytes for an ECC P-256 public key) and key generation is computationally more expensive. Research groups at TU/e (Netherlands) and ARM Research have demonstrated ML-KEM and ML-DSA implementations on Cortex-M4 microcontrollers with acceptable performance, and the Mbed TLS and wolfSSL libraries both have PQC implementations in active development for embedded deployment.

Quantum sensing: the use of quantum mechanical effects to measure physical quantities with precision exceeding classical limits is a separate quantum technology with direct IoT relevance. Quantum gravimeters (sensing gravitational field variations with sub-nanometre precision) are being developed for underground infrastructure mapping and resource exploration. Quantum magnetometers (nitrogen-vacancy centres in diamond) offer room-temperature magnetic field sensitivity 100-1,000 times better than classical Hall effect sensors, with applications in medical imaging, navigation in GPS-denied environments, and non-destructive testing of structural integrity. These are longer-horizon applications, but they represent the direction in which the sensing frontier of IoT is moving.

10.8.5 IoT Technology Roadmap 2025-2030

Figure 10.5 presents a technology adoption roadmap for the six themes of this chapter and their enabling infrastructure, mapping each technology's expected trajectory from current state (2025) to mainstream deployment (2030) and indicating the key milestones that will mark each transition.

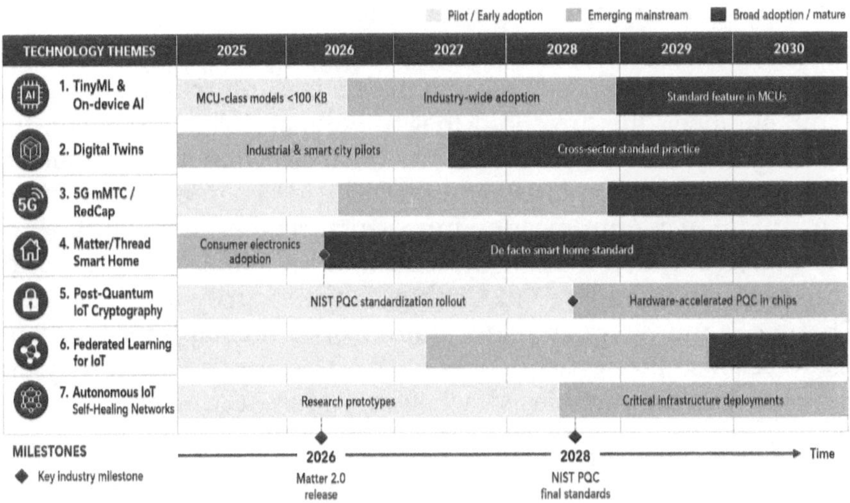

Figure 10.5: IoT Technology Roadmap 2025–2030

10.8.6 Closing Reflection: The IoT Engineer's Responsibility

The textbook opened with Kevin Ashton's 1999 coinage of the phrase 'Internet of Things' in a presentation to Procter and Gamble about RFID supply chain tracking: a specific, practical problem and a specific, practical solution. Twenty-five years later, the concept he named has expanded into an infrastructure layer that touches almost every domain of human activity: the water we drink is monitored by networked sensors; the buildings we work in are managed by connected control systems; the food we eat moves through IoT-instrumented supply chains; the vehicles we travel in are increasingly autonomous participants in connected transportation systems.

The technologies in this chapter — AI that makes IoT systems intelligent, digital twins that make them self-aware, 5G that makes them real-time, edge AI that makes them autonomous, blockchain that makes them trustworthy, and Green IoT principles that make them sustainable, accelerate this trajectory.

Each of these technologies extends what IoT systems can do and where they can operate, and each of them shifts more decision-making authority from humans to machines. The autonomous valve controller in the AgroSense deployment decides when to irrigate without waiting for human instruction. The predictive maintenance system in the factory scenario schedules maintenance before the human maintenance manager has been informed of the fault. The smart contract in the pharmaceutical cold-chain releases payment without a human approving the invoice.

This shift creates genuine engineering responsibility. Every autonomous decision an IoT system makes was, ultimately, designed by an engineer: the threshold that triggers an irrigation event, the anomaly score that schedules a maintenance action, the compliance rule that governs a payment contract. The IoT engineer is not merely a builder of communication infrastructure; they are a designer of automated decision-making systems that act in the physical world. The design methodology of Chapter 5, the security architecture of Chapter 8, and the governance frameworks of Chapter 9 exist precisely because the consequences of these decisions (when they are wrong, when they are biased, when they are insecure, or when they are ungoverned) are real and can be serious.

The ten chapters preceding this one have equipped the reader with the technical foundations, the design discipline, and the governance awareness to build IoT systems that are not only functional but trustworthy, not only efficient but fair, and not only innovative but sustainable.

The technology roadmap to 2030 presents extraordinary opportunity: a world in which precision agriculture reduces water consumption in water-scarce regions; in which predictive maintenance extends the operational lifetime of critical infrastructure; in which healthcare IoT delivers monitoring and early warning to patients who previously had no access to continuous care; in which energy management systems reduce the carbon intensity of cities and industries. These are not inevitable outcomes; they are design choices. They are the choices that the engineers and practitioners who read this book will make, in the systems they build, for the communities they serve.

The blank page that Aisha faced in Chapter 5 was the beginning of a design process. This chapter is the beginning of a career. The IoT field is still being shaped. The engineer who understands its foundations, masters its methodology, respects its constraints, and keeps its societal implications in view has a important contribution to make, not just to the technology, but to the world it will increasingly govern.

10.9 Chapter Summary

Chapter 10 has mapped the trajectory of IoT from its current deployed state to the emerging horizon of 2030, treating six transformative technology domains with the depth that the foundational knowledge accumulated across the preceding nine chapters makes possible. Each section has introduced a technology, explained its architecture and mechanisms, grounded it in deployed case studies, and connected it explicitly to the protocols, platforms, security mechanisms, and governance frameworks studied earlier in the book. The chapter opened with the Lyon plant scenario — a deployed industrial IoT system in which AIoT, digital twins, 5G, TinyML, blockchain, and Green IoT are all operational simultaneously — demonstrating that the emerging technologies are not independent novelties but a convergent system.

Section 10.2 examined AIoT: the convergence of artificial intelligence and IoT. The defining characteristic of AIoT is architectural: AI inference runs within the IoT system, at the device, gateway, or edge tier, rather than in a separate cloud analytics platform. The primary AIoT application patterns (predictive maintenance, anomaly detection, and natural language control) were examined alongside the TinyML technology stack that enables inference on microcontrollers with kilobytes of RAM and milliwatts of power.

The three model compression techniques (quantisation (FP32 to INT8), pruning (low-weight connection removal), and knowledge distillation (student-teacher training)) were explained as the pipeline that bridges full-scale cloud training and constrained edge deployment. Federated learning was introduced as the privacy-preserving approach to distributed IoT model training, transmitting model updates rather than raw sensor data. Table 10.1 compared AIoT applications across six domains, mapping each to its inference tier and hardware platform.

Section 10.3 addressed Digital Twins — dynamic virtual models of physical assets synchronised through real-time IoT telemetry. The five-phase digital twin lifecycle (Creation, Synchronisation, Simulation, Insight, Action) was examined, with particular emphasis on the synchronisation phase's dependence on the IoT data pipelines studied in Chapter 6, and on the Action phase's use of the actuation and control mechanisms studied in Chapter 2. Industry applications in smart manufacturing (Siemens MindSphere), smart infrastructure (Singapore Virtual Singapore), and healthcare were surveyed. Table 10.2 compared the four dominant platform options (Azure Digital Twins, AWS IoT TwinMaker, NVIDIA Omniverse, and Siemens MindSphere) across model schema, connectivity, scalability, cost model, and best-fit application.

Section 10.4 explained why 5G matters specifically for IoT through its three service categories: eMBB (enhanced Mobile Broadband (high bandwidth for video and AR applications), URLLC (Ultra-Reliable Low Latency Communications) sub-1 ms latency for industrial control and autonomous systems), and mMTC (massive Machine-Type Communications, one million devices per square kilometre for dense sensor deployments).

Network slicing was introduced as the 5G architectural capability that provides contractual quality-of-service guarantees for IoT workloads on shared infrastructure. Private 5G campus networks were presented as the fastest-growing segment for industrial IoT, with the Port of Antwerp deployment as a detailed example. The section concluded with an outlook to 6G: terahertz bands, AI-native networking, and semantic communications targeting deployment around 2030.

Section 10.5 provided technical depth on Edge AI and TinyML, extending the AIoT concepts of Section 10.2 with the practical implementation detail that a deploying engineer requires. The four engineering arguments for edge inference (latency, privacy, bandwidth, and resilience) were examined, followed by a step-by-step description of the Edge AI development pipeline from data collection through model training, compression, and firmware deployment. Hardware platform selection across the Arduino Nano 33 BLE Sense (entry TinyML), STM32 family (production deployment), and NVIDIA Jetson Nano (GPU-accelerated edge vision) was examined with concrete inference performance benchmarks. A worked example: a vibration anomaly detector for bearing fault classification on STM32H743 with CMSIS-NN acceleration, achieving 3.8 ms inference at 18 mW, demonstrated the complete pipeline. The Tech Spotlight on Edge Impulse provides a practical entry point to TinyML development.

Section 10.6 evaluated blockchain and distributed ledger technologies as IoT trust infrastructure. The trust gap problem in multi-party IoT deployments, where no single party controls the data but all parties need to trust its integrity was identified as blockchain's primary value proposition for IoT. IOTA's Tangle architecture was examined as the feeless distributed ledger most suited to high-frequency IoT sensor logging. Smart contracts on Hyperledger Fabric were demonstrated through the pharmaceutical cold-chain payment automation example, and validated through the Kenya vaccine logistics case study.

Table 10.4 compared Bitcoin, Ethereum, Hyperledger Fabric, and IOTA across consensus mechanism, throughput, energy cost, and IoT suitability. The section concluded with an honest treatment of blockchain's genuine limitations — confirmation latency, scalability, the oracle problem — and positioned it as a complementary layer to, not a replacement for, the security and governance mechanisms studied in Chapters 8 and 9.

Section 10.7 addressed Sustainability and Green IoT, framing the environmental responsibility of IoT engineering as aligned with, rather than in tension with, engineering quality. The three-component IoT carbon footprint model (embodied, operational, end-of-life) was quantified with reference to the sensor platforms studied in Chapter 2. The AgroSense deployment from Chapter 5 was revisited as a Green IoT example: solar-harvested sensor nodes eliminating both battery replacement logistics and annual battery waste, with the sustainability benefit calculated in concrete numbers.

Circular economy principles (repairability, modularity, and standardised interfaces) were examined as design practices that extend IoT device operational lifetime and reduce embodied carbon. Green IoT standards from ITU-T (L.1024) and ETSI (EN 303 470) were referenced as the regulatory baseline for sustainable IoT deployment.

Section 10.8 closed this chapter with a reflective treatment of societal, ethical, and technological horizons. The governance of smart city IoT, the challenge of digital inclusion, the algorithmic bias risks of AIoT decision-making, and the privacy implications of pervasive intelligent sensing were addressed with the intellectual honesty that these complex issues require. Quantum computing's threat to current IoT cryptography and the NIST post-quantum cryptography standards (FIPS 203, 204, 205, published August 2024) were presented as an active engineering migration challenge.

The IoT Technology Roadmap to 2030 (Figure 10.5) synthesised the chapter's six technology tracks into a unified timeline. The closing reflection emphasised the IoT engineer's responsibility as a designer of autonomous decision-making systems that act in the physical world, and the opportunity to use that responsibility in service of human benefit.

Chapter 11

AI and Machine Learning with IoT

Chapter 11 examines the integration of Artificial Intelligence and Machine Learning with IoT as a major step toward intelligent, adaptive, and autonomous connected systems. It explains how AI enhances IoT by enabling pattern recognition, prediction, anomaly detection, optimisation, automation, and decision support across device, gateway, edge, and cloud layers. The chapter discusses the major types of IoT data used in AI/ML, common machine learning techniques, AIoT architecture, model development pipelines, deployment locations, and practical implementation models. It also highlights important technologies and platforms supporting AI-enabled IoT, including TinyML, edge AI, cloud ML services, federated learning, and intelligent dashboards. Through real-world case studies such as industrial predictive maintenance and smart campus energy management, the chapter demonstrates how AI transforms raw sensor data into actionable intelligence and operational value. In addition, it addresses the benefits, challenges, risks, security, privacy, ethical, and governance concerns associated with AI-enabled IoT. Overall, this chapter provides a future-oriented framework for understanding how IoT evolves from connected sensing infrastructure into intelligent systems capable of learning, adapting, and supporting autonomous decision-making.

Opening Scenario: The Bearing That Warned Its Operators

A bearing on the main drive shaft of a food-processing conveyor at a facility in the Sohar Industrial Port, Oman, develops a surface fatigue crack. The defect is invisible to plant operators and generates no unusual sound. Yet three accelerometers mounted on the bearing housing are recording vibration spectra every 100 milliseconds, and a trained machine learning model running on a local edge gateway has been monitoring the frequency signature at 43 Hz with growing concern for the past eighteen hours.

At 03:47 on a Tuesday morning, the model's anomaly score crosses the critical threshold. An alert is dispatched automatically to the maintenance supervisor's mobile dashboard, flagging the bearing as requiring immediate inspection before the day shift begins. The supervisor examines the reading, cross-references it with historical failure data visualised on the same dashboard, and schedules an emergency bearing replacement for 05:30. The faulty bearing is swapped out in ninety minutes. The production line runs at full capacity from the start of the shift.

Without the AI-enabled monitoring system, the bearing would likely have failed mid-shift, triggering an emergency shutdown of the entire conveyor, contaminating product in progress, and requiring multi-hour repair under production pressure. The estimated cost of an unscheduled bearing failure on this line is approximately 40,000 US dollars in downtime, waste, and emergency maintenance. The cost of the scheduled replacement is approximately 800 US dollars.

This scenario captures the central value of combining the Internet of Things with Artificial Intelligence. IoT provides the persistent, structured, real-time window into the physical world: the sensors, the connectivity, and the data pipelines. AI provides the cognitive layer that transforms that data into foresight and action. Building on the AIoT and Edge AI concepts introduced in Chapter 10, this chapter provides the foundational understanding, practical implementation models, and real-world case studies needed to design, deploy, and govern AI-enabled IoT systems.

11.1 Introduction to AI and ML in the Context of IoT

Artificial Intelligence (AI) is the field of computer science concerned with building systems that can perform tasks which would normally require human intelligence: reasoning, pattern recognition, planning, language understanding, and decision-making. AI is not a single technology but a broad family of techniques that includes rule-based expert systems, probabilistic models, and, most prominently today, machine learning. The goal of AI is to produce systems that sense their environment, process information about it, and take actions that maximise the likelihood of achieving a defined objective.

Machine Learning (ML) is the subfield of AI in which systems learn from data rather than being programmed with explicit rules. An ML system is trained on a dataset of examples, identifies statistical patterns in that data, and builds a model that can make predictions or decisions when presented with new, unseen inputs. ML is particularly powerful in domains where the rules governing behaviour are too complex, too numerous, or too dynamic to encode manually, which is precisely the situation in most IoT environments.

It is important to distinguish between several related terms. Data Analytics involves descriptive and diagnostic analysis of historical data to understand what happened and why. Machine Learning extends this to predictive and prescriptive analysis, learning models that forecast future events or recommend actions. Deep Learning (DL) is a subset of ML that uses multi-layer neural networks capable of learning hierarchical feature representations; it excels at image, audio, and complex time-series data. Artificial Intelligence is the broadest term, encompassing all of these together with planning, reasoning, and autonomous decision-making capabilities.

IoT systems are uniquely well-suited to AI and ML for three reasons. First, they generate enormous volumes of time-stamped, structured data from sensors that monitor continuous physical processes (exactly the kind of data on which ML models thrive). Second, they operate at scales of thousands of devices, millions of readings per day, which make manual monitoring and rule-based management practically impossible. Third, many IoT use cases inherently require prediction, optimisation, or anomaly detection rather than simple threshold alerting, which only AI can deliver reliably.

The relationship between IoT and AI is symbiotic. IoT provides AI with high-fidelity, real-time data from the physical world — data about machines, environments, people, vehicles, and infrastructure that AI systems could not otherwise access. AI provides IoT with the intelligence to extract meaning from that data and translate it into decisions and actions that the IoT infrastructure can then execute through its actuators, dashboards, and automation systems. Neither alone achieves what both together make possible.

As introduced in Chapter 10, the integration of AI and IoT has given rise to the concept of AIoT, the Artificial Intelligence of Things, in which intelligence is distributed not only in cloud analytics platforms but throughout the IoT architecture itself: in edge servers, gateways, and increasingly in the sensor nodes and microcontrollers at the very periphery of the network. This chapter examines the AI and ML foundations that underpin AIoT, and provides the practical knowledge needed to build, deploy, and govern AI-enabled IoT systems.

Key Insight: IoT and AI as Complementary Capabilities

IoT connects the physical world to digital systems, providing the continuous, structured, real-time data that AI needs to learn and act. AI and ML enable IoT systems to move beyond monitoring and alerting into prediction, classification, optimisation, and autonomous decision-making.

Together, they form the foundation of intelligent connected systems.

11.2 How AI Complements IoT

Raw IoT data (streams of numbers from temperature sensors, accelerometers, flow meters, and cameras) does not by itself generate value. Value is created when patterns in that data are identified, interpreted, and acted upon. Without AI, IoT systems are limited to reactive threshold alerting: when a reading exceeds a fixed limit, an alarm is raised. This approach misses subtle patterns, generates large numbers of false positives, and cannot anticipate events before they occur. AI fundamentally changes what is possible.

The first and most direct contribution of AI to IoT is pattern recognition at scale. An ML model trained on months of vibration data from an industrial motor can learn what normal operation looks like across dozens of operating conditions, different loads, temperatures, speeds, and ages. When a new vibration signature appears that deviates from any known normal condition, the model flags it regardless of whether the reading exceeds any fixed threshold. This capability, known as unsupervised anomaly detection, is far more sensitive and specific than threshold-based alerting.

AI also enables predictive capability, foresight about events that have not yet occurred. Supervised learning models trained on historical data that includes labelled failure events can learn to recognise the precursor signatures of failure and predict its occurrence hours or days in advance. This predictive maintenance capability, demonstrated in the opening scenario, transforms maintenance from a reactive, costly, disruptive activity into a planned, efficient, and safe one.

Beyond prediction, AI supports autonomous decision-making in IoT systems. A reinforcement learning model governing a smart traffic system does not merely predict congestion; it continuously adjusts signal timings to minimise queue lengths and average journey times across the entire network, learning from the outcomes of every decision it makes. Similarly, an AI system controlling a building's HVAC does not simply respond to current temperature readings but anticipates occupancy patterns and weather changes to optimise energy use proactively.

AI also makes IoT systems substantially more reliable by reducing false positives and false negatives. Rule-based systems must choose between sensitivity (low thresholds that catch every real event but also generate many false alarms) and specificity (high thresholds that reduce false alarms but miss real events). ML models can learn the multivariate context of events, combining multiple sensor streams to achieve both high sensitivity and high specificity simultaneously. A pressure anomaly that co-occurs with elevated temperature and unusual vibration has a very different significance from a pressure spike in isolation.

The practical applications of AI-complemented IoT are extensive. In manufacturing, predictive maintenance reduces unscheduled downtime. In agriculture, AI analyses soil moisture, weather forecasts, and crop-growth models to generate precision irrigation recommendations that reduce water usage. In healthcare, AI running on wearable IoT devices detects arrhythmias, falling events, and abnormal activity patterns in real time, enabling interventions before clinical deterioration occurs. In smart cities, AI optimises traffic flow, waste collection routes, and energy distribution continuously, reducing both cost and environmental impact.

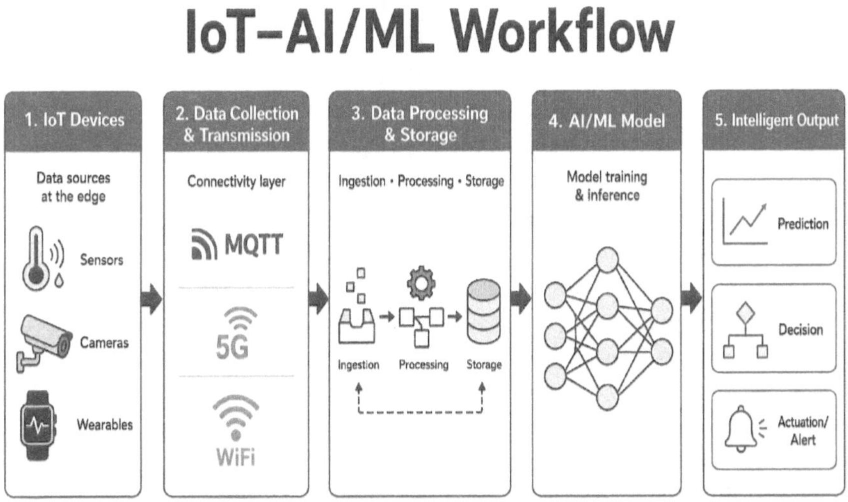

Figure 11.1: Relationship Between IoT, Data, AI/ML, and Intelligent Action

11.3 Types of IoT Data Used in AI/ML

AI and ML models can only be as good as the data they are trained on, and IoT environments produce data of many different types, each with distinct characteristics, quality challenges, and requirements for pre-processing. Understanding the data landscape is a prerequisite for selecting appropriate AI/ML methods and designing effective data pipelines. The primary categories of IoT data are described below, together with their typical sources and the AI/ML approaches for which they are most suitable.

Time-series sensor data is the most common category in IoT. It consists of sequences of numerical measurements taken at regular or irregular intervals — temperature readings every minute, vibration samples at 1,600 Hz, power consumption every 15 seconds. Time-series data has temporal structure that must be preserved and exploited; models such as Long Short-Term Memory networks (LSTMs), temporal convolutional networks, and classical forecasting methods are designed specifically for this structure. Event-driven data, by contrast, records discrete occurrences (a door opened, a button pressed, a fault triggered) and is more naturally handled by classification or association rule models.

Unstructured data types, including images, video, and audio, are increasingly common in AI-enabled IoT applications. Industrial cameras generate image streams for defect detection; security cameras provide video for intruder detection and crowd analytics; microphones capture acoustic signatures for equipment health monitoring and keyword spotting. These data types require Deep Learning approaches (Convolutional Neural Networks (CNNs) for images and spectrograms, recurrent models for audio sequences) and typically demand substantially more computational resources than tabular sensor data. Location data from GPS trackers, indoor positioning systems, and cellular network triangulation is valuable for fleet management, asset tracking, and spatial analytics, where clustering and route optimisation algorithms are most applicable.

Across all data types, IoT data presents characteristic quality challenges that must be addressed before training AI models. Missing values arise when sensors fail, lose connectivity, or are temporarily out of range. Noise from electrical interference, mechanical vibration, or analogue conversion errors introduces spurious readings. Calibration drift causes systematic bias that changes gradually over time. Class imbalance is a particularly severe problem in fault detection: failure events may occur only a handful of times per year in a dataset of millions of normal readings, making it difficult to train supervised models with adequate sensitivity. Effective AI/ML in IoT therefore requires robust data preprocessing pipelines (validation, imputation, normalisation, and denoising) before model training begins.

Table 11.1 summarises the major types of IoT data, their typical sources, the AI/ML methods best suited to each type, and representative application examples.

IoT Data Type	Example Source	Suitable AI/ML Method	Example Application
Time-series sensor data	Industrial machine sensors, smart meters	Regression, LSTM, anomaly detection	Predictive maintenance, energy forecasting
Event data	Smart access systems, alarms, PLCs	Classification, rule-based AI	Security monitoring, occupancy control
Location data	GPS vehicle trackers, indoor BLE tags	Clustering, route optimisation	Fleet management, asset tracking
Image and video data	Industrial cameras, security systems	CNN, computer vision, object detection	Defect detection, intruder identification
Audio data	Industrial microphones, smart speakers	Spectrogram + CNN, RNN	Machine fault detection, voice commands
Vibration data	Accelerometers on rotating equipment	FFT analysis, anomaly detection	Bearing failure prediction, structural health
Environmental data	Weather, air quality, soil sensors	Time-series forecasting, regression	Smart agriculture, HVAC optimisation
Energy consumption data	Smart meters, sub-meters	Regression, forecasting, clustering	Demand response, energy efficiency
Device health and log data	IoT gateways, routers, edge nodes	Anomaly detection, classification	Network intrusion detection, fault prediction
Health sensor data	Wearables, medical IoT devices	Classification, anomaly detection	Patient risk alerts, fall detection

11.4 AI/ML Techniques Commonly Used in IoT

IoT applications span a wide range of problem types: prediction, classification, anomaly detection, clustering, control optimisation, and natural language interaction. No single AI or ML technique is suitable for all of these. This section surveys the principal AI/ML families most commonly applied in IoT systems, explaining how each works, where it is most effective, and what IoT problems it is best suited to address.

11.4.1 Supervised Learning

Supervised learning involves training a model on a labelled dataset: a collection of input examples, each paired with the correct output. The model learns the mapping from inputs to outputs and can then apply that mapping to new, unlabelled inputs. There are two main types: classification, in which the output is a discrete category (for example, normal, warning, or critical); and regression, in which the output is a continuous numerical value (for example, predicted temperature or remaining useful life in hours).

In IoT contexts, supervised classification is used extensively for fault detection and condition monitoring. A model trained on labelled vibration data from a motor (with readings annotated as normal, misalignment, bearing wear, or imbalance) can classify the condition of any new motor from its vibration signature alone. Supervised regression is applied to energy demand forecasting, where a model trained on historical consumption data, weather data, and occupancy data learns to predict future energy demand with sufficient accuracy to inform purchasing, scheduling, and grid management decisions.

The main limitation of supervised learning in IoT is the requirement for labelled training data. Labelling is straightforward for normal operating conditions, which are abundant, but rare and expensive for failure conditions. A manufacturing plant may experience only a handful of bearing failures per year. Collecting sufficient labelled failure data to train a reliable classifier typically requires months or years of operation, or access to historical datasets from similar deployments. Techniques such as transfer learning, data augmentation, and synthetic data generation are used to mitigate this problem.

11.4.2 Unsupervised Learning

Unsupervised learning trains models on unlabelled data, discovering inherent structure (patterns, groupings, and anomalies) without explicit guidance from human-annotated examples. The two most important unsupervised learning families in IoT are clustering and anomaly detection. Clustering algorithms, such as k-means and DBSCAN, group similar observations together; they are used to segment IoT devices by usage pattern, identify building zones with similar energy behaviour, or group vehicle routes by traffic characteristics.

Anomaly detection is particularly valuable in IoT because normal operating conditions are abundant and well-understood, while failures are rare and diverse. Unsupervised anomaly detection models learn what normal looks like by training exclusively on normal data, then flag any observation that deviates significantly from the learned normal distribution. Approaches include Isolation Forest, Local Outlier Factor, autoencoders, and one-class Support Vector Machines (SVMs). Because these methods do not require labelled failure data, they can be deployed on new equipment or in new environments where historical failure records do not yet exist.

A practical advantage of unsupervised anomaly detection in IoT is its ability to detect novel failure modes, faults that have never been seen before and therefore could not have been represented in a labelled training set. This is important in IoT security, where new attack patterns emerge continuously, and in industrial IoT, where equipment may exhibit failure modes that are unique to a specific installation or operating environment.

11.4.3 Deep Learning

Deep Learning uses neural networks with many layers, each of which learns progressively more abstract representations of the input data. The power of deep learning lies in its ability to learn feature representations automatically from raw data, without requiring the domain expert to specify which features matter. For images, a Convolutional Neural Network (CNN) learns to detect edges, textures, shapes, and finally objects across successive layers. For sequential data, recurrent architectures such as Long Short-Term Memory (LSTM) networks learn temporal dependencies across time steps of any length.

CNNs have become the dominant approach for image-based IoT applications: visual inspection systems that detect surface defects in manufactured parts, smart camera systems that identify vehicle types or pedestrian behaviour, and drone-based agricultural imaging systems that assess crop health. LSTMs and their variants are the primary tools for IoT time-series modelling: predicting remaining useful life of equipment, forecasting energy demand, and detecting anomalies in multivariate sensor streams. Their ability to capture long-range temporal dependencies makes them substantially more accurate than classical statistical methods for complex, non-stationary IoT signals.

Transformer architectures, originally developed for natural language processing, have more recently been applied to time-series forecasting and multivariate sensor analysis. Transformers use self-attention mechanisms to model dependencies between time steps directly, without the sequential computation bottleneck of recurrent models, making them efficient on modern parallel hardware. For IoT applications with long time-series and complex cross-sensor dependencies, such as smart grid load forecasting or building energy management — transformers are increasingly competitive with LSTMs.

The principal limitation of deep learning in IoT is computational cost. Training deep models requires substantial data and processing power, typically in the cloud. Deploying them at the edge requires model compression techniques (quantisation, pruning, and knowledge distillation) that reduce model size and inference cost at some accuracy cost. The TinyML discipline, discussed in Section 11.7.4, addresses the challenge of running useful deep learning models on the severely constrained microcontrollers found at the IoT edge.

11.4.4 Reinforcement Learning

Reinforcement Learning (RL) trains an agent to take actions in an environment so as to maximise a cumulative reward signal over time. Unlike supervised learning, RL does not learn from labelled examples; instead, the agent explores the action space, receives feedback in the form of rewards or penalties, and gradually learns a policy, a mapping from states to actions, that maximises long-term reward. RL is particularly appropriate for sequential decision problems in dynamic environments where the optimal action depends on the current state of the system.

In IoT, RL is applied to smart traffic signal control, where the agent adjusts signal timings based on current queue lengths and arrival rates to minimise average vehicle wait time across the network. It is used in building energy management, where the agent learns policies for HVAC scheduling that balance occupant comfort against energy cost. Industrial robots controlled by RL agents can adapt their behaviour in real time to variations in workpiece position, material properties, and tool wear. The main challenge of RL in IoT is the need for either a high-fidelity simulation environment for safe training or a very long and potentially unsafe exploration phase in the real system.

11.4.5 Generative AI and IoT

Generative AI, particularly Large Language Models (LLMs), is beginning to find practical roles in AI-enabled IoT systems. LLMs can generate natural language explanations of sensor alerts, translate technical anomaly reports into plain-language summaries for non-specialist operators, and act as conversational interfaces through which operators can query IoT dashboards using natural language questions such as "Which machines showed anomalous behaviour in the last 24 hours?" or "What is the predicted energy consumption for tomorrow?".

Generative AI also enables automated maintenance report generation, where sensor data and diagnostic model outputs are synthesised into structured written reports that would previously have required manual analyst time. In smart factory environments, LLM-based assistants can guide maintenance technicians through repair procedures, drawing on equipment manuals, historical maintenance records, and current diagnostic data simultaneously.

The application of Generative AI to IoT requires careful governance. IoT systems often control physical actuators (valves, motors, switches, heating elements) whose incorrect operation can cause safety incidents, equipment damage, or process failures. An LLM that generates incorrect maintenance instructions, misinterprets a sensor alert, or recommends an inappropriate control action can have consequences that extend well beyond the digital domain. Generative AI should therefore be used in IoT primarily as an interface and explanation layer, with all control actions validated by deterministic safety logic before execution. Chapter 11's governance discussion in Section 11.12 addresses these constraints in detail.

Table 11.2 provides a consolidated overview of the principal AI/ML techniques used in IoT applications, their primary purposes, representative IoT examples, and typical deployment locations.

AI/ML Technique	Main Purpose	IoT Example	Deployment Location
Linear regression	Continuous value prediction	Energy demand forecasting from smart meters	Cloud or edge
Decision tree / Random forest	Classification and regression	Equipment condition classification (normal/warning/critical)	Edge or gateway
Support vector machine	Binary and multi-class classification	Network intrusion detection in IoT traffic	Cloud
k-means / DBSCAN clustering	Grouping similar observations	Device behaviour profiling, zone segmentation	Cloud
Isolation forest	Anomaly detection without labels	Sensor fault detection, security anomaly flagging	Edge or gateway
LSTM (deep learning)	Sequential data and time series	Vibration-based failure prediction, demand forecasting	Edge or cloud
CNN (deep learning)	Image and spectrogram analysis	Visual defect detection, acoustic fault classification	Edge server or cloud
Reinforcement learning	Sequential control optimisation	Smart traffic signal control, HVAC scheduling	Edge or cloud

11.5 AIoT: Artificial Intelligence of Things

AIoT, Artificial Intelligence of Things, refers to the architectural integration of AI capabilities into IoT systems at every tier of the network, from cloud analytics platforms down to edge servers, gateways, and device-level microcontrollers. The concept was introduced and explored in Chapter 10 in the context of emerging IoT trends; this section provides a deeper analysis of what distinguishes AIoT from conventional IoT, how the AIoT architecture is structured, and why the distributed intelligence model it embodies is increasingly the design standard for modern IoT systems.

Conventional IoT systems — collect, transmit, store, and report. Sensors generate data, connectivity infrastructure transports it to a central platform, the platform stores and displays it, and human operators interpret it and take action. The intelligence is entirely human, and the IoT system is a data-collection and communication infrastructure. AIoT systems: sense, infer, decide, and act. Intelligence is embedded within the system itself, distributed across its tiers in accordance with the latency, bandwidth, power, and privacy requirements of each application. Human operators shift from data interpreters to exception handlers, intervening only when the AI requests guidance or when a decision exceeds the system's autonomous authority.

The AIoT architecture spans four tiers. At the device tier, TinyML models run on microcontrollers embedded in sensors and actuators, performing keyword spotting, gesture recognition, and simple anomaly detection at the point of measurement, with no network connectivity required. At the gateway tier, lightweight inference models aggregate and analyse streams from multiple devices, performing classification and rule-based decisions for the local environment. At the edge tier, more powerful edge servers run computationally intensive inference tasks (deep learning image analysis, multivariate time-series models, digital twin simulation) close to the data source, with single-digit millisecond response times. At the cloud tier, large foundation models are trained, fleet-wide analytics are performed, and long-term patterns are analysed to generate updated models that are pushed back down to lower tiers.

This distributed intelligence architecture has several important implications for system design. Model management becomes a critical operational concern: models at all four tiers must be versioned, validated, and updated in a coordinated way. Data privacy is substantially improved because sensitive data can be analysed locally, with only aggregated or anonymised results transmitted to higher tiers. Resilience is enhanced because local tiers continue to operate intelligently even when connectivity to higher tiers is unavailable. Energy efficiency is improved because local inference avoids the power cost of transmitting raw data to the cloud for processing.

The distinction between IoT and AIoT is not merely a difference in capability; it is a difference in the nature of the system. An IoT system is a measurement and communication infrastructure. An

AIoT system is an autonomous intelligent agent distributed across physical space, capable of continuous learning, adaptive decision-making, and coordinated action without continuous human supervision. As sensor costs fall, edge computing power increases, and TinyML techniques mature, the AIoT architecture is becoming the expected standard for new IoT deployments across industry, healthcare, transport, and smart infrastructure.

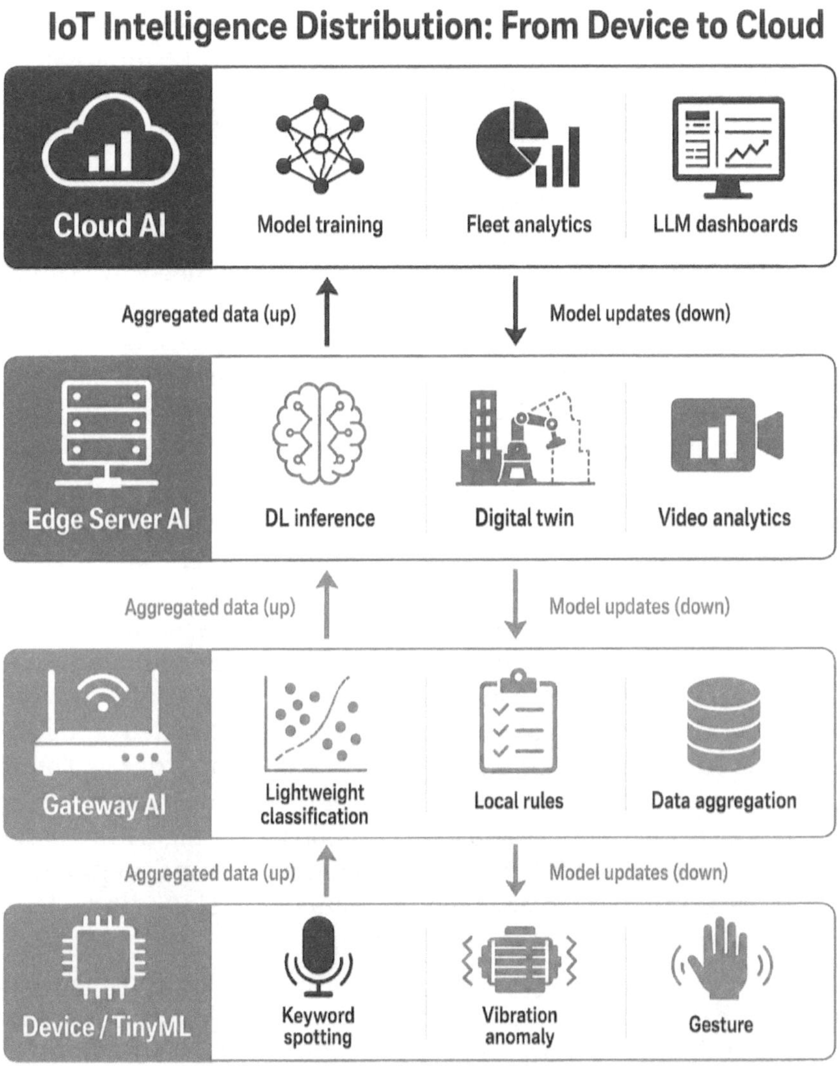

Figure 11.2: AIoT Architecture Across Device, Gateway, Edge, and Cloud Layers

11.6 AI/ML Development Pipeline for IoT Systems

Deploying AI/ML in an IoT system is not a single-step process of selecting and running a model. It requires a structured end-to-end pipeline that spans problem definition, data collection and preparation, model development, deployment, and ongoing monitoring. This pipeline must be designed from the outset to address the specific constraints of IoT environments: limited labelled data, resource-constrained deployment targets, real-time latency requirements, and the need for continuous adaptation as the physical environment changes. The following twelve-step pipeline describes the standard workflow for AI/ML development in IoT systems.

The pipeline begins with problem definition (Step 1): specifying precisely what the AI system must do, what inputs it will have, what outputs it must produce, and what the acceptable performance criteria are. This is followed by identifying sensors and data sources (Step 2), determining which physical quantities need to be measured and at what resolution and frequency. Data collection (Step 3) is often the most time-consuming phase, requiring weeks or months of instrumented operation to accumulate sufficient data across all relevant operating conditions, including the rare fault conditions that supervised models must learn to recognise.

Data cleaning and preprocessing (Step 4) addresses missing values, noise, outliers, and calibration inconsistencies. Labelling (Step 5) is required for supervised models; in IoT this typically involves annotating time-series segments by cross-referencing sensor data with maintenance logs, operator reports, and inspection records. Feature selection and engineering (Step 6) transforms raw sensor readings into the input variables most predictive of the outcome of interest; this may involve statistical features extracted from time windows (mean, variance, kurtosis, FFT coefficients), derived quantities (vibration RMS, power factor), or learned representations from deep models. Model selection (Step 7) chooses the algorithm family most appropriate for the problem type, data volume, deployment constraints, and performance requirements. Model training (Step 8) fits the selected model to the training data.

Validation and testing (Step 9) evaluates model performance on held-out data not used during training, using appropriate metrics for the problem type: accuracy, precision, recall, and F1 score for classification; mean absolute error and root mean square error for regression; area under the receiver operating characteristic curve for anomaly detection. Deployment (Step 10) packages the validated model for the target runtime environment — cloud API, edge server container, TensorFlow Lite file for mobile/gateway, or TF Lite for Microcontrollers binary for an MCU. Performance monitoring (Step 11) tracks model accuracy and operational behaviour in production, detecting model drift and data distribution shifts. Retraining and improvement (Step 12) completes the cycle by updating the model periodically with new data or when performance falls below acceptable thresholds.

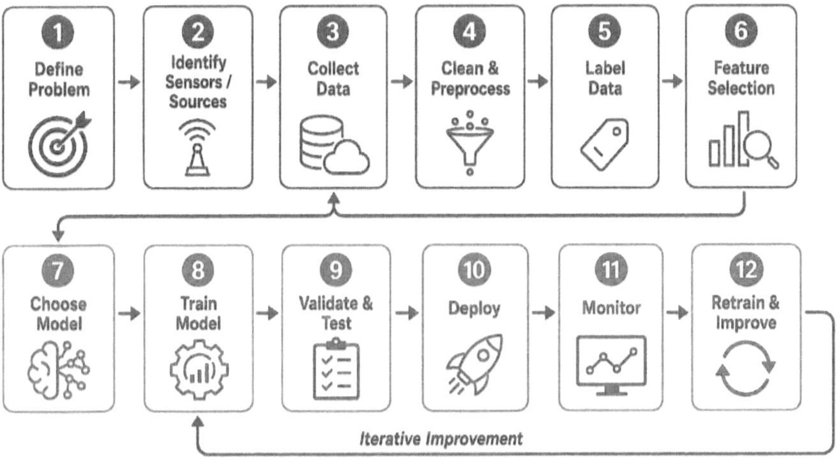

Figure 11.3: AI/ML Pipeline for IoT Applications

Practical Note: IoT Model Evaluation Must Go Beyond Accuracy

In IoT, model accuracy alone is insufficient. A model deployed at the edge must also satisfy latency requirements (response within milliseconds or seconds), memory constraints (fitting within device RAM and flash storage), power budgets (inference energy per prediction), bandwidth limits (avoiding unnecessary data transmission), privacy obligations (processing sensitive data locally), and reliability standards (operating correctly in the presence of sensor noise, missing values, and communication interruptions). These operational requirements must be specified in Step 1 and used to evaluate candidate models in Step 9.

11.7 Where AI Runs in IoT: Cloud, Edge, Gateway, and Device

One of the most consequential design decisions in an AI-enabled IoT system is where the AI inference runs, in a remote cloud data centre, at a local edge server, in an IoT gateway, or on the device itself. This decision affects latency, bandwidth consumption, privacy, energy consumption, resilience, and cost. In practice, many AIoT systems distribute inference across multiple tiers, routing different decisions to the tier best suited for their requirements.

11.7.1 Cloud AI

Cloud AI performs inference and analytics on servers in remote data centres, accessed via the internet or a private WAN connection. Its principal advantage is essentially unlimited computational power, making it suitable for training large models, running complex analytics on large datasets, and executing inference tasks that require more memory or computation than any local device can provide. Long-term historical analysis, fleet-wide pattern mining, and training of foundation models for downstream deployment are all cloud-appropriate tasks.

The limitations of cloud AI are significant for many IoT use cases. Round-trip latency to a cloud endpoint is typically 20 to 200 milliseconds, which is too slow for applications requiring sub-10-millisecond responses, such as industrial safety systems, real-time motor control, or emergency vehicle preemption in smart traffic management. Bandwidth costs can be substantial when raw sensor streams, particularly video or high-frequency vibration data, must be transmitted continuously. And data privacy regulations, discussed in Chapter 8, increasingly restrict the transmission of sensitive health, financial, or personal data to remote servers, favouring on-premises or edge processing.

11.7.2 Edge AI

Edge AI performs inference on servers or workstation-class computing hardware located physically close to the IoT devices whose data it processes — on the factory floor, in the telecommunications cabinet, in the hospital ward, or in the roadside cabinet. Edge AI reduces round-trip latency to single-digit milliseconds, eliminates the bandwidth cost of transmitting raw data to the cloud, and keeps sensitive data within a controlled local environment. NVIDIA Jetson series edge AI modules, Intel NUC edge servers, and purpose-built edge AI appliances from industrial automation vendors are representative hardware platforms.

Edge AI is the preferred deployment target for computationally intensive real-time inference tasks: deep learning-based visual defect detection on a manufacturing line, pedestrian and vehicle detection in smart city camera networks, real-time speech recognition in industrial voice-command systems, and medical image analysis in point-of-care diagnostic devices. Because edge servers have meaningful compute budgets (8–32 GB RAM, GPU or neural processing unit acceleration), they can run models of practical complexity without the accuracy compromises required by gateway or device deployment.

11.7.3 Gateway AI

IoT gateways, devices that aggregate data from multiple sensors and forward it to higher tiers of the network, increasingly incorporate lightweight AI capabilities. A gateway running a small classification or anomaly detection model can filter, prioritise, and pre-process data from dozens of connected sensors before transmitting only relevant events or aggregated features to the edge or cloud, substantially reducing bandwidth consumption and cloud processing costs. In smart building systems, a gateway AI can manage basic HVAC and lighting control rules locally, maintaining comfort and efficiency even when the cloud platform is temporarily unreachable.

11.7.4 TinyML

TinyML: the deployment of trained ML inference models on microcontrollers and ultra-low-power processors, representing the extreme end of the distributed intelligence spectrum. TinyML models run within the memory and power budgets of devices such as the Arduino Nano 33 BLE Sense (256 KB RAM), the ESP32, and the STM32 series of microcontrollers, consuming milliwatts or less. This enables intelligent sensing without any network connectivity: a vibration sensor node can detect its own anomaly and transmit only the alert rather than the full waveform; a keyword-spotting microphone can wake a larger system only when a trigger word is detected; a wearable can perform fall detection and cardiac rhythm classification on-device, preserving patient privacy.

The key enabling technologies for TinyML are model quantisation (reducing weight precision from 32-bit floats to 8-bit integers), pruning (removing low-importance model weights), knowledge distillation (training a small student model to replicate the behaviour of a large teacher model), and efficient neural architecture design (MobileNet, EfficientNet-Lite). Frameworks including TensorFlow Lite for Microcontrollers and Edge Impulse provide the toolchain for training, compressing, and deploying models to MCU targets. The TinyML domain is evolving rapidly, with increasingly capable models being deployed on progressively smaller and lower-power hardware.

Table 11.3 compares Cloud AI, Edge AI, Gateway AI, and TinyML across the key dimensions relevant to IoT deployment decision-making.

Deployment Level	Processing Location	Strengths	Limitations	Example Use Case
Cloud AI	Remote data centre	Powerful models, large-scale training, unlimited storage, complex analytics	High latency, bandwidth cost, privacy risk, internet dependency	Fleet analytics, model training, LLM-assisted dashboards
Edge AI	Local edge server near devices	Low latency, reduced bandwidth, good privacy, GPU acceleration available	Higher hardware cost, physical deployment and management required	Industrial defect detection, smart camera inference, medical imaging
Gateway AI	IoT gateway device	Aggregates multiple sensor streams, reduces cloud traffic, local resilience	Limited memory and compute, models must be compact	Smart building automation, agricultural monitoring, edge alerting
TinyML	MCU/ sensor node	Ultra-low power, offline operation, real-time response, inherent privacy	Very limited model size, quantised accuracy, restricted toolchain	Keyword spotting, gesture recognition, vibration anomaly on battery devices

11.8 Technologies, Tools, and Platforms for AI-Enabled IoT

AI-enabled IoT development draws on a broad ecosystem of hardware platforms, software frameworks, and cloud services. Understanding this ecosystem is essential for practitioners designing and implementing AIoT solutions. The following overview describes the major categories and the most widely used tools within each, organised to support technology selection across the full IoT-to-AI stack.

At the hardware level, the choice of platform determines the AI capability available at each tier. For TinyML and gateway deployment, the Arduino Nano 33 BLE Sense integrates an IMU, microphone, and BLE radio on a board with 256 KB RAM and runs TensorFlow Lite for Microcontrollers; it is widely used for educational TinyML projects and lightweight sensor-based inference. The ESP32 family supports Wi-Fi, Bluetooth, and sufficient compute for simple edge inference tasks, making it suitable for battery-powered IoT nodes with local AI capabilities. The Raspberry Pi 4 provides Linux-based edge computing with 4–8 GB RAM, suitable for gateway and lightweight edge AI tasks. For computationally intensive edge AI, the NVIDIA Jetson Nano and Jetson Orin Nano provide GPU-accelerated inference (0.5–40 TOPS) in compact, embedded form factors designed for industrial, robotics, and smart city deployments.

On the software side, Python is the universal language of AI/ML development, supported by the scientific computing stack of NumPy, Pandas, and Matplotlib. Scikit-learn provides efficient implementations of classical ML algorithms (random forest, SVM, isolation forest, k-means) and is the standard tool for tabular IoT data analysis. TensorFlow and Keras offer a comprehensive deep learning framework for training CNNs, LSTMs, and transformer models. TensorFlow Lite and TensorFlow Lite for Microcontrollers provide the inference runtimes for edge and MCU deployment. Edge Impulse is a dedicated end-to-end platform for TinyML that automates data collection, signal processing, model training, quantisation, and deployment to over 50 embedded hardware targets. PyTorch is widely used in research and is increasingly adopted for production edge AI deployment. For IoT data pipeline management, Node-RED provides a visual flow-programming interface for routing sensor data between MQTT brokers, databases, ML inference endpoints, and dashboards; InfluxDB provides time-series storage optimised for IoT sensor data; and Grafana provides configurable real-time visualisation.

Cloud and IoT platform integration is provided by services including AWS IoT Core (device management, message routing, and integration with AWS SageMaker for model training and deployment), Azure IoT Hub combined with Azure Machine Learning, ThingsBoard (an open-source IoT platform with rule engine and analytics capabilities), and HiveMQ (an MQTT broker designed for high-throughput industrial IoT deployments). These platforms abstract the complexity of device registration, authentication, message routing, and integration with ML services, enabling development teams to focus on application logic and model development rather than infrastructure management.

Table 11.4 provides a reference overview of tools and platforms across the AI-enabled IoT development stack. This table is intended as a practical guide for technology selection; the appropriate choices for any specific project depend on deployment tier, budget, team skills, and regulatory constraints.

Tool / Platform	Category	Main Use	Suitable Application
Arduino Nano 33 BLE Sense	Embedded hardware	TinyML prototyping on MCU	Gesture recognition, vibration anomaly, keyword spotting
ESP32	Embedded hardware	Edge inference on battery IoT nodes	Environmental monitoring, local alerting
Raspberry Pi 4	Edge compute hardware	Lightweight Linux-based edge AI	Smart home gateway, lightweight CV, Node-RED host

NVIDIA Jetson Nano / Orin Nano	Edge AI hardware	GPU-accelerated edge inference	Industrial vision, robotics, smart city cameras
Python	Programming language	AI/ML model development and deployment	All AI/ML IoT applications
Scikit-learn	ML library	Classical ML algorithms	Classification, regression, clustering, anomaly detection
TensorFlow / Keras	Deep learning framework	Neural network training and evaluation	Time-series, image, NLP IoT models
TensorFlow Lite	Deployment framework	Inference on mobile and edge devices	Edge AI deployment on Raspberry Pi, Android, Jetson
TF Lite for Microcontrollers	Embedded ML library	TinyML inference on MCUs	Arduino, STM32, ESP32 on-device inference
Edge Impulse	TinyML platform	End-to-end TinyML pipeline	Gesture, vibration, audio TinyML on embedded targets
PyTorch	Deep learning framework	Research and custom model development	Custom deep models, federated learning research
Node-RED	Flow-based programming	IoT data pipeline integration	Data routing, MQTT integration, alert logic
InfluxDB + Grafana	Time-series DB and visualisation	IoT sensor data storage and dashboarding	Industrial monitoring, smart building analytics
AWS IoT Core + SageMaker	Cloud IoT and ML platform	End-to-end IoT-ML workflow in AWS	Industrial IoT, fleet management, predictive maintenance
Azure IoT Hub + Azure ML	Cloud IoT and ML platform	End-to-end IoT-ML workflow in Azure	Smart building, connected health, manufacturing AI

11.9 How to Use AI in IoT: Practical Implementation Models

The implementation of AI in IoT follows several recurring patterns, each suited to a different combination of data type, inference requirement, deployment environment, and operational context. The five models described below represent the most common IoT-AI integration patterns encountered in practice. Each model is described in terms of its data source, AI/ML method, deployment location, output, and primary benefit.

Model 1: Sensor Data + Cloud ML. In this model, IoT sensors transmit time-series readings to a cloud platform where ML models are trained and served. Example: a smart energy management system for a commercial building collects data from sub-meters, occupancy sensors, weather stations, and HVAC controllers. A cloud-hosted gradient boosting regression model trained on twelve months of historical data predicts next-day energy consumption with sufficient accuracy to enable automated demand response and tariff optimisation. The output is a 24-hour energy demand forecast delivered to the building management system at midnight. The primary benefit is substantial energy cost reduction without requiring edge compute infrastructure.

Model 2: Sensor Data + Edge ML. In this model, ML inference runs on an edge server or gateway co-located with the IoT devices. Example: a factory deploys accelerometers on twenty motor-pump assemblies. Vibration data is sampled at 1,600 Hz and streamed to an edge server running an LSTM-based anomaly detection model. The model scores every 10-second vibration window in real time, generates an alert when the anomaly score exceeds the threshold, and logs all scores locally for trend analysis. The output is a real-time condition score for each asset, available with 50-millisecond latency. The primary benefit is early fault detection with no dependency on internet connectivity, protecting the production process from both equipment failures and network outages.

Model 3: Camera + Computer Vision. IoT cameras integrated with computer vision models enable automated visual inspection, security monitoring, and spatial analytics. Example: a food-processing facility deploys eight cameras above the packaging line. Each camera feed is processed by a CNN-based defect detection model running on an edge AI appliance. The model classifies each unit as pass or fail in real time, triggers a rejection actuator for defective units, and logs all defect images with timestamps for quality audit purposes. The output is a per-unit quality decision with sub-100-millisecond latency. The primary benefit is consistent, fatigue-free inspection quality at the speed of the production line.

Model 4: Wearable IoT + Health Prediction. Health IoT wearables generate continuous physiological data that AI models can analyse to detect clinical events, predict deterioration, and support remote patient monitoring. Example: a hospital deploys wearable patches on sixty post-operative patients. Each patch measures heart rate, respiratory rate, SpO2, skin temperature, and movement continuously. A classification model on the hospital's edge server analyses the multivariate stream for each patient and generates an early warning score every 30 seconds. When the score indicates high deterioration risk, a bedside alert and nurse station notification are generated automatically. The primary benefit is earlier clinical intervention, reducing adverse outcomes and intensive care admissions.

Model 5: Smart Agriculture + Predictive Analytics. Soil, weather, and crop-condition IoT sensors combined with ML forecasting models enable precision agriculture at scales impractical with manual observation. Example: a date palm plantation in the Batinah coast of Oman deploys soil moisture sensors, tensiometers, and weather stations across a 50-hectare site. A regression model trained on three years of soil, weather, and crop-growth data generates daily irrigation recommendations for each field zone, specifying volume and timing. The model incorporates a three-day weather forecast to avoid irrigating before rain and adjusts recommendations based on current crop growth stage. The primary benefit is a 25–35% reduction in water consumption with equivalent or improved crop yield, critical in a water-scarce region. These water savings figures are well-supported by regional research: peer-reviewed studies of sensor-guided drip and subsurface irrigation for date palm across Oman, Saudi Arabia, and the UAE document water-use reductions of 27–64% relative to conventional surface irrigation, and 25–50% relative to unoptimised drip systems, under comparable arid climatic conditions. The conservative 25–35% range cited here reflects optimised-drip-to-precision-scheduled-drip comparisons and is consistent with FAO guidance on regulated deficit irrigation for Phoenix dactylifera in arid zones (FAO Irrigation and Drainage Paper 56; Al-Ghobari et al., Biosystems Engineering, 2021).

These five models are not mutually exclusive. Advanced IoT deployments commonly combine multiple patterns, edge ML for real-time anomaly detection, cloud ML for long-range forecasting and model retraining, computer vision for quality assurance, and health prediction for workforce safety monitoring — within a unified AIoT architecture. The design challenge is to allocate each inference task to the tier that best satisfies its latency, bandwidth, privacy, and accuracy requirements, as discussed in Section 11.7.

11.10 Benefits of AI and ML in IoT

The integration of AI and ML into IoT systems delivers benefits that span operational performance, economic efficiency, safety, sustainability, and governance. This section consolidates the principal categories of benefit, with explanations and examples drawn from the application domains discussed throughout this chapter.

The most immediately quantifiable benefits are operational: predictive maintenance reduces unscheduled downtime and repair costs; real-time decision-making enables automated responses to events that previously required human intervention; and edge intelligence reduces the latency of critical decisions from minutes or hours (human response time) to milliseconds (algorithmic response time). These operational improvements translate directly into cost savings, quality improvements, and capacity increases that are measurable and attributable to the AI investment.

Safety benefits are equally significant. AI systems that continuously monitor environmental and equipment conditions can detect hazardous situations (gas leaks, structural anomalies, cardiac arrhythmias, fire precursors) earlier and more reliably than threshold-based alerting systems or periodic human inspection. In industrial environments, this translates into reduced injury rates and avoided catastrophic failures. In healthcare, early warning systems based on continuous AI monitoring have been shown to reduce cardiac arrest rates and intensive care admissions. In smart infrastructure, AI-driven structural health monitoring enables maintenance intervention before failure rather than after.

Sustainability benefits derive primarily from AI's ability to optimise resource consumption. Smart irrigation systems reduce water usage by 25–35% compared to schedule-based irrigation. AI-optimised HVAC systems reduce building energy consumption by 15–25% compared to rule-based control. Smart grid management using AI demand forecasting reduces peak load and the need for fossil-fuel peaker plants. As IoT deployments scale to billions of devices, even modest per-device efficiency gains accumulate to substantial aggregate environmental impact reductions.

Finally, AI-enabled IoT creates new governance capabilities. Automated audit logging of AI decisions, with timestamps and input data records, enables regulatory compliance monitoring and post-incident investigation at a level of detail and completeness impossible with human-operated systems. Anomaly detection applied to the IoT network itself detects compromised devices, unusual data exfiltration, and protocol violations, supporting the cybersecurity monitoring requirements described in Chapter 8. These governance benefits are becoming increasingly important as regulatory frameworks for AI-enabled systems, including the EU AI Act and sector-specific frameworks for healthcare and critical infrastructure, impose new requirements on AI decision auditability and human oversight.

Benefit	Explanation	Example
Predictive maintenance	Detects equipment faults before failure occurs, enabling planned intervention	Bearing failure prediction in a manufacturing line
Real-time decision-making	Enables instant automated responses to sensor events faster than human reaction	Emergency valve shutoff on pressure anomaly detection
Automation and autonomy	Reduces continuous human monitoring requirements	Automated greenhouse climate control based on sensor fusion

Reduced latency	Edge AI enables sub-second decisions without cloud round-trip	Traffic signal optimisation using roadside edge inference
Better resource utilisation	AI optimises energy, water, and material allocation dynamically	Smart irrigation reducing water usage by 25-35%
Energy efficiency	Models predict and minimise energy consumption proactively	HVAC demand-response reducing building energy by 15-25%
Improved safety	Detects hazardous conditions and triggers protective actions automatically	Gas leak detection triggering ventilation before alarm threshold
Reduced operational cost	Fewer breakdowns, less waste, and lower maintenance expenditure	Predictive maintenance halving unscheduled downtime costs
Better user experience	Personalised, responsive, intelligent service delivery	Adaptive smart home environments responding to occupant patterns
Sustainability	Reduces waste, energy consumption, and carbon footprint	Green IoT energy management across smart city infrastructure
Smarter governance	AI-generated audit logs and automated compliance monitoring	Regulatory reporting in smart grid and healthcare IoT
Scalable intelligence	Consistent model behaviour deployed across thousands of devices	Fleet-wide firmware anomaly detection across global device deployments

11.11 Challenges and Risks of AI/ML with IoT

The benefits of AI-enabled IoT are real and substantial, but so are the challenges. Many IoT AI deployments fail not because the AI algorithms are inadequate but because the data pipelines, system integration, operational constraints, and governance frameworks are insufficiently designed. Understanding these challenges is essential for practitioners planning AI/ML deployments in IoT environments.

Data quality and availability are the most common root causes of poor AI performance in IoT. Sensors fail, communication links drop, clocks drift, and calibration degrades, all producing missing, noisy, and biased data that undermines model accuracy. Labelling difficulty is particularly acute: the failure events that supervised models must learn to recognise are rare by definition, and the historical records needed to label them are often incomplete, inaccurate, or unavailable. Semi-supervised learning, transfer learning from related domains, and synthetic data generation using physics-based simulation are practical mitigations, but none fully substitutes for high-quality labelled data from the target deployment environment.

Model drift: the degradation of model accuracy over time as the real-world distribution of inputs changes is an inherent challenge of AI in dynamic IoT environments. Seasonal changes alter energy demand patterns. Equipment ages and changes its vibration signature. Operational processes evolve. A model that was accurate at deployment may become unreliable within months without monitoring and retraining. Addressing model drift requires continuous performance monitoring infrastructure and automated or semi-automated retraining pipelines, capabilities that add complexity and operational cost to the AI system.

Resource constraints at the IoT edge (limited memory, restricted compute, and finite battery capacity) impose hard limits on the size and complexity of models that can run locally. Model compression techniques mitigate but do not eliminate this constraint. In some cases, the model that fits within the device budget is not sufficiently accurate for the application, and the deployment must fall back to a higher, more capable tier, accepting the latency and bandwidth costs that entails. Physical safety risks are the most serious category of risk in AI-enabled IoT. Systems that control actuators (motors, valves, ventilation systems, medical infusion pumps) can cause injury, equipment damage, or process failures if their AI makes an incorrect decision. Unlike software bugs in a desktop application, an incorrect actuation command in an industrial or medical IoT system can have immediate, irreversible physical consequences.

Important Point: AI Decisions in IoT Act on the Physical World

AI-enabled IoT systems do not only generate recommendations; they execute actions: opening valves, adjusting motor speeds, administering drug doses, releasing emergency locks, switching power circuits. Model errors, adversarial inputs, distribution shift, and unforeseen edge cases can therefore produce safety incidents, financial losses, or irreversible physical damage. Every AI-enabled IoT system whose outputs affect physical actuators must incorporate validated fail-safe logic, human-in-the-loop oversight for high-consequence decisions, comprehensive testing under edge-case conditions, and continuous post-deployment monitoring with defined performance thresholds and fallback modes.

Table 11.5 summarises the principal challenges of AI/ML in IoT deployments and the mitigation strategies most commonly used to address them.

Challenge	Description	Mitigation Strategy
Poor data quality	Sensor noise, missing values, calibration drift, and communication failures corrupt training data	Data validation pipelines, sensor fusion, anomaly filtering, and imputation strategies

Labelling difficulty	Failure events are rare and expensive to label; historical records are often incomplete	Semi-supervised learning, transfer learning, synthetic data from physics simulation
Model drift	Accuracy degrades as real-world distributions change over time	Continuous monitoring dashboards, automated retraining pipelines, drift detection algorithms
Resource constraints	Edge MCUs and gateways have limited memory, compute, and power budgets	Quantisation, pruning, knowledge distillation, efficient architecture design (TinyML)
Privacy risks	IoT data often contains sensitive personal, commercial, or operational information	Federated learning, on-device processing, data minimisation, differential privacy
Cybersecurity threats	AI models and inference pipelines may be attacked via adversarial inputs or model poisoning	Adversarial robustness testing, model integrity verification, secure deployment pipelines
Bias in AI models	Training data may not represent all operating conditions, populations, or failure modes	Diverse and representative training data, fairness audits, regular revalidation
Physical safety risks	AI errors in actuator control can cause injury, equipment damage, or process failures	Fail-safe design, human-in-the-loop for critical decisions, comprehensive edge-case testing

11.12 Security, Privacy, Ethics, and Governance in AI-Enabled IoT

The integration of AI into IoT systems creates a new and distinct governance challenge. Conventional IoT governance, as discussed in Chapter 9, addresses device lifecycle management, access control, firmware integrity, and data stewardship. AI-enabled IoT adds a further layer of concern: the behaviour of autonomous systems that make consequential decisions, the fairness and transparency of those decisions, the privacy implications of AI-driven data analysis, and the accountability structures required when things go wrong. This section addresses the governance requirements specific to AI-enabled IoT.

Secure data collection and transmission remain foundational. The data that AI models consume must be protected from tampering, injection, and exfiltration using the device authentication, encrypted transmission, and network segmentation measures described in Chapter 8. In AI-enabled systems, these requirements are heightened because compromised data does not merely produce incorrect readings; it can corrupt model behaviour, inject adversarial inputs that cause systematic misclassification, or poison retraining datasets in ways that persist long after the attack itself is remediated. Adversarial robustness: the resilience of AI models to inputs deliberately crafted to cause misclassification is an active area of research and must be incorporated into the security testing of AI-enabled IoT systems with safety-critical outputs.

Privacy-preserving AI techniques are increasingly important as IoT deployments intersect with personal data. Federated Learning (FL) is a particularly relevant approach: rather than centralising raw sensor data for model training, FL trains models locally on each device or edge node, sharing only model weight updates, which do not contain raw personal data, with a central aggregation server. FL enables AI model improvement across a fleet of devices without the privacy risks of data centralisation. Applications include training healthcare wearable models without sharing patient physiological data, and training smart building energy models without revealing occupancy patterns.

Explainable AI (XAI) is the discipline of producing AI model outputs that can be understood, interpreted, and justified by human stakeholders. In IoT contexts, XAI is important for operator trust (operators are more likely to act on AI alerts they can understand), regulatory compliance (the EU AI Act requires explanations for high-risk AI decisions), and audit trail requirements (incident investigation requires understanding why a particular automated action was taken). Techniques such as SHAP (SHapley Additive exPlanations) and LIME (Local Interpretable Model-agnostic Explanations) can attribute model predictions to specific input features, enabling engineers to explain why a model flagged a particular sensor reading as anomalous.

Human oversight is a governance requirement that must be explicitly designed into AI-enabled IoT systems, particularly those whose outputs affect safety-critical actuators. The appropriate level of human oversight depends on the consequence severity and the model's demonstrated reliability. Low-consequence, high-reliability decisions, such as adjusting HVAC setpoints within a narrow range, may be delegated fully to the AI system. High-consequence decisions, such as initiating an emergency shutdown of a production line or adjusting a medication dosage, which should require human confirmation even when the AI system is operating correctly, providing a check on both model errors and unexpected situational factors the model was not designed to handle.

Bias detection and fairness auditing are necessary in IoT applications that affect people. A predictive maintenance model trained on data from well-maintained, newer equipment may perform poorly on older or less-maintained assets, systematically under-predicting failures in facilities with lower maintenance standards. A healthcare monitoring model trained predominantly on data from one demographic may have lower sensitivity for other demographics.

Governance frameworks must require periodic fairness audits that evaluate model performance disaggregated by relevant subgroups, and mandate retraining or supplementation when performance disparities are identified.

Audit trails and compliance monitoring must capture not only raw sensor data but AI model decisions, confidence scores, and the actions those decisions triggered. Immutable, timestamped audit logs, ideally stored on tamper-evident infrastructure, are required for post-incident investigation, regulatory inspection, and continuous performance monitoring. Compliance with sector-specific AI regulations, including the EU AI Act (which classifies many IoT AI applications as high-risk), the GDPR requirements for automated decision-making, and Oman's National Cybersecurity Strategy obligations, must be built into system design from the outset rather than retrofitted after deployment.

Responsible AIoT requires that the governance principles described above be operationalised, not merely stated as policy. This means designating human roles responsible for AI system performance (AI system owners), establishing clear escalation paths for AI alerts that require human judgment, defining the conditions under which an AI system must be taken offline for retraining or replacement, and maintaining documentation that enables any AI decision to be traced back to its input data, model version, and configuration state. As AIoT systems become more autonomous and more consequential, the governance frameworks governing them must evolve in parallel with the technology.

Professional Checklist: AIoT Deployment Readiness

Before deploying AI-enabled IoT, confirm the following:

- The AI model has a clear operational purpose and is trained on relevant, representative, and quality-checked data.
- The location of AI execution, such as device, gateway, edge, or cloud, matches latency, privacy, energy, and cost constraints.
- Model accuracy, drift, bias, explainability, and failure behaviour are monitored after deployment.
- Human oversight is available for high-impact decisions affecting safety, privacy, finance, health, or public services.
- Security controls protect sensor data, model files, inference results, APIs, and dashboards.
- Governance records document model version, training data source, update history, and accountability.

11.13 Real-World Case Study 1: Predictive Maintenance in Industrial IoT

Case Study 11.1: AI-Based Predictive Maintenance in a Smart Factory

Background: A mid-sized manufacturer of precision engineering components operates a facility with 200 CNC machining centres, 60 conveyor motors, and 35 industrial compressors. The plant had historically operated on a time-based preventive maintenance schedule, replacing bearings, seals, and drive belts at fixed intervals regardless of their actual condition. This approach resulted in two categories of cost: unnecessary maintenance of components that were still in good condition, and unexpected failures of components that degraded faster than the standard interval predicted. Over three years, unscheduled downtime averaged 340 hours per year, at an average cost of 120,000 US dollars per year. These figures are consistent with published manufacturing benchmarks: industry surveys report 300–360 hours of unplanned downtime per year as the median for discrete manufacturing facilities (MaintainX Industry Report, 2024; Deloitte Smart Manufacturing Study, 2023). A cost per hour of production stoppage in the range of USD 300–500 is typical for precision component machining environments with moderate labour and overhead intensity — at USD 353 per hour, the USD 120,000 annual cost figure presented here falls at the mid-point of that range for a 340-hour annual stoppage duration.

Sensors deployed: Each monitored asset was instrumented with a triaxial accelerometer (vibration, 1,600 Hz sampling), a surface-mounted thermocouple (bearing temperature), and a clamp-on current transformer (electrical load current). A total of 880 sensor channels were connected to 44 local edge gateways, each managing 20 channels. All gateways communicated with a central edge server over the plant's industrial Ethernet network. Sensor data was stored in an InfluxDB time-series database with a 90-day rolling window on the edge server and 36-month archival storage in cloud object storage.

AI/ML method: An LSTM-based anomaly detection model was trained on six months of historical sensor data from each asset type, using only data from periods confirmed by maintenance logs as fault-free. The model learned the multivariate normal vibration signature of each asset class across its full range of operating loads and temperatures. A separate random forest classifier was trained on a smaller labelled dataset of confirmed fault signatures (bearing wear, misalignment, imbalance, and lubrication failure) generated by combining historical data with synthetic data from physics-based simulation of bearing degradation. The anomaly detection model generates a continuous anomaly score; the classifier is invoked when the anomaly score exceeds a threshold to provide a specific fault hypothesis.

Deployment architecture: Sensor data is processed locally on each edge gateway (anomaly score computation for 20 channels in under 10 milliseconds). Edge gateways transmit only the anomaly scores and metadata, not the full waveforms, to the central edge server over the plant network. The central server runs the random forest classifier and maintains the asset health dashboard. When an asset's anomaly score exceeds the warning threshold for three consecutive 10-minute windows, a maintenance alert is generated and pushed to the maintenance supervisor's mobile application via MQTT over the plant Wi-Fi network.

Results: In the twelve months following deployment, the system issued 47 maintenance alerts, of which 41 corresponded to genuine developing faults confirmed on inspection (87% precision). Six alerts were false positives caused by transient load variations not represented in the training data. The system missed two failures that occurred within 4 hours of an anomaly score first exceeding the normal range, insufficient time for the alert-to-intervention cycle. Unscheduled downtime fell from 340 hours per year to 58 hours per year, a reduction of 83%. Planned maintenance cost increased slightly as the frequency of bearing and seal replacements rose, but total maintenance cost (planned plus unscheduled) fell by 34%.

Technical challenges: The most significant technical challenge was the variation in vibration signatures between nominally identical assets arising from differences in installation, age, and local operating environment. A model trained on data from one CNC machining centre performed poorly when applied to another of the same model. This required training a separate model per asset class and investing in per-asset calibration periods of four to eight weeks before each model reached reliable accuracy. Data labelling was the second major challenge: the maintenance database contained only 23 confirmed bearing failure events across three years, insufficient to train a supervised classifier directly. Synthetic data generation using the SKF bearing degradation model was used to augment the labelled dataset to 340 events, substantially improving classifier performance.

Governance considerations: All AI alerts are logged with the asset identifier, timestamp, anomaly score, fault hypothesis, sensor readings, and model version number. No asset is taken offline based on an AI alert alone; a maintenance technician performs a brief on-site inspection before scheduling a planned repair. This human-in-the-loop requirement adds 30–90 minutes to the intervention cycle but has been essential for maintaining operator trust in the system and for catching the small number of false positives that would otherwise cause unnecessary production interruptions.

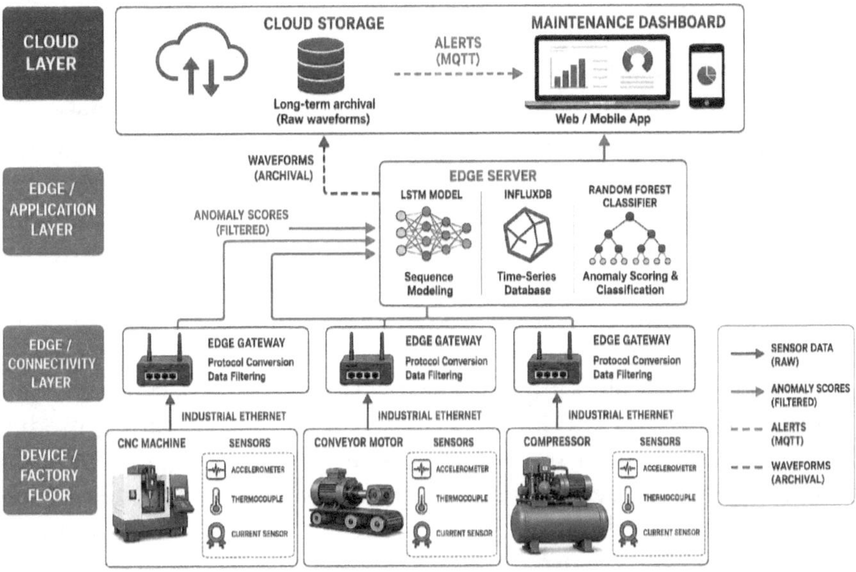

Figure 11.4: Predictive Maintenance Architecture Using AI and IoT

11.14 Real-World Case Study 2: Smart Campus AI-IoT Energy Management

Case Study 11.2: AI-Enabled Smart Campus Energy and Occupancy Management

Background: A university campus in the GCC region operates 42 buildings (lecture halls, laboratories, offices, student accommodation, and a sports complex) with a combined floor area of approximately 180,000 square metres. Energy consumption is dominated by air conditioning, which accounts for 65–75% of total building energy use in a climate where outdoor temperatures regularly exceed 40°C during the academic year. The campus had historically operated HVAC systems on fixed time schedules (systems on at 07:00, off at 22:00) regardless of actual occupancy or outdoor conditions. This approach resulted in significant energy waste: lecture halls air-conditioned to full capacity for classes of five students, offices cooled for two hours after the last occupant left, and laboratories maintained at laboratory temperature during extended public holidays.

Sensors deployed: The smart campus instrumentation comprised occupancy sensors (passive infrared and CO2-based) in all 1,840 rooms, smart electricity sub-meters at building and floor level (15-minute interval data), temperature and humidity sensors at 3,680 points, outdoor weather stations at four campus locations, and access-control readers at 340 entry points providing secondary occupancy signals. All sensor data was transmitted over the campus Wi-Fi and wired Ethernet infrastructure to a central IoT platform using MQTT over TLS. Aggregated time-series data was stored in InfluxDB with a 5-year retention policy.

Data pipeline and AI/ML approach: Two AI models were developed. The first, an occupancy prediction model, was a gradient boosting classifier trained on twelve months of historical occupancy sensor data combined with the academic timetable and access-control records. The model predicts room occupancy 30 minutes in advance with 89% accuracy, enabling HVAC pre-conditioning to begin 20–25 minutes before predicted occupancy, achieving comfortable temperature at the start of occupancy without the energy cost of maintaining temperature continuously when rooms are empty. The second model, an energy demand forecasting model, was an LSTM trained on historical energy consumption, weather data, and occupancy predictions. It generates 24-hour ahead forecasts for each building, enabling proactive load management and integration with the campus solar generation forecast.

Deployment architecture: Both models run on a campus edge server connected to the central IoT platform. The occupancy prediction model generates setpoint recommendations for each room's HVAC controller every 15 minutes, transmitted via the BACnet building automation protocol. The energy demand forecast is generated daily at midnight and published to the campus energy management dashboard and the demand response interface with the grid operator. Campus operators review AI recommendations on a dashboard but can override any setpoint recommendation manually. Override events are logged and used as labelled feedback for model improvement.

Outcomes: In the twelve months following full deployment, the campus achieved a measured reduction of 22% in total electricity consumption, equivalent to a cost saving of approximately 1.4 million US dollars per year at the prevailing electricity tariff. IoT-enabled smart building deployments at universities in cooling-intensive climates consistently report energy reductions of 20–34%, with the upper end achieved where HVAC represents more than 60% of site energy — a condition met by most GCC campuses operating in extreme ambient temperatures (Aldossari et al., Smart Cities, 2023; MDPI Sustainability, 2025). The USD 1.4 million annual saving reflects a campus electricity bill of approximately USD 6.4 million per year at prevailing GCC commercial tariffs, consistent with published consumption data for major regional universities operating air-conditioned floor areas of 150,000 m² or more. Carbon emissions attributable to campus electricity consumption fell by an equivalent proportion. Occupant comfort surveys conducted before and after deployment showed no statistically significant change in reported satisfaction with thermal comfort, confirming that the energy savings were achieved through waste elimination rather than comfort compromise.

Privacy and governance considerations: Occupancy sensor data was handled with care. Individual room-level occupancy data is not stored beyond 72 hours; only aggregated statistics used for model training are retained. The access-control reader data used as a secondary occupancy signal is processed in a privacy-preserving manner — door-open events are converted into occupancy probability estimates without retaining individual identity records beyond the building security retention policy of 30 days. All AI-generated HVAC setpoints are within the range approved by the campus facilities team; the AI cannot command temperatures below 18°C or above 26°C in any occupied space. The academic and facilities governance committee approved the AI deployment, its privacy framework, and the override policy before commissioning.

Campus Smart Building AIoT Architecture

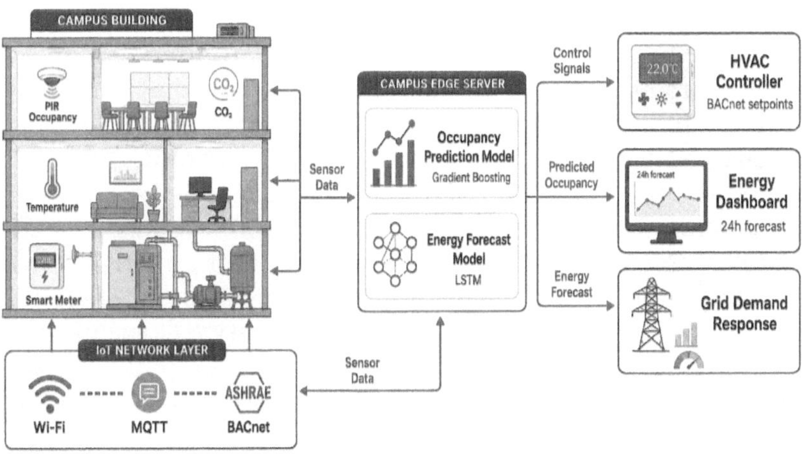

Figure 11.5: AI-IoT Architecture for Smart Campus Energy Management

Regional Example: AI-IoT for Energy and Smart Campus Innovation in the GCC

Several GCC institutions and government programmes are pioneering AI-enabled smart campus and smart building deployments. Sultan Qaboos University and the National University (NU) in Oman are among the regional institutions exploring IoT-based energy management as part of Oman Vision 2040 sustainability commitments. In Saudi Arabia, KAUST (King Abdullah University of Science and Technology) operates a smart campus platform integrating IoT sensor networks, AI analytics, and renewable energy systems. The NEOM project has embedded AI-enabled building management as a core infrastructure requirement for its planned city developments. Across the Gulf, the DEWA's smart grid programme integrates IoT smart meters and digital utility infrastructure across millions of electricity and water metering points. These regional deployments demonstrate that AI-IoT energy management is not merely a technology pilot but an operational reality delivering measurable environmental and economic benefits aligned with GCC sustainability agendas.

11.15 Future Directions of AI and ML with IoT

The convergence of AI and IoT is still in its early stages. The systems operating today (predictive maintenance platforms, smart building controllers, precision agriculture systems) represent the first generation of AIoT. The next generation will be substantially more autonomous, more adaptive, and more deeply integrated with the physical world. The trends described in this section are likely to define AI-enabled IoT over the next five to ten years, though the pace of development in both AI and IoT hardware makes precise timelines difficult to forecast.

AI-native IoT systems will move beyond retrofitting AI onto existing IoT architectures towards designing systems in which intelligence is a first-class architectural principle from the outset. AI-native sensors will embed inference capability (anomaly detection, event classification, feature extraction) directly in the sensor silicon, transmitting only processed information rather than raw data. AI-native connectivity protocols will incorporate intelligent routing, quality-of-service management, and protocol adaptation based on network conditions and data content. AI-native cloud platforms will automatically manage the full model lifecycle (data ingestion, training, compression, deployment, monitoring, and retraining) without manual intervention.

Autonomous IoT agents will go beyond executing predefined control algorithms to engage in goal-directed, self-improving behaviour. LLM-assisted IoT interfaces will enable operators to interact with complex AI-IoT systems through natural language (querying system state, requesting analyses, and issuing high-level operational directives) reducing the specialist expertise required to operate advanced IoT systems. Digital twins with integrated AI will move from static simulation to living predictive models: continuously updated from real-time sensor streams, used for predictive maintenance and operational optimisation, and capable of simulating the consequences of proposed operational changes before they are implemented on the physical system.

Federated Learning at scale will enable AI model improvement across fleets of millions of IoT devices without centralising sensitive data, addressing the privacy constraints that currently limit the use of personal and commercial sensor data for model training. TinyML will continue to extend the capability boundary of on-device intelligence, models that today require a Raspberry Pi will run on an ESP32; models that today require an ESP32 will run on an Arduino Nano. Neuromorphic computing chips, which process information using spike-based neural networks inspired by biological brains, promise further orders-of-magnitude improvements in the energy efficiency of on-device AI, making continuous intelligence feasible in the most severely power-constrained IoT nodes.

6G networks, expected in the early 2030s, will provide latencies below 1 millisecond and data rates sufficient to support real-time transmission of high-resolution sensor streams currently too bandwidth-intensive for wireless transmission. This will extend the reach of edge AI and open new categories of AI-enabled IoT applications, surgical robotics over wireless networks, cooperative autonomous vehicle systems with sub-millisecond coordination, and immersive mixed-reality industrial interfaces overlaying AI analysis on live sensor data. AI-enabled networks will also optimise their own operation, using ML models to manage spectrum allocation, beam forming, and network slicing dynamically in response to real-time traffic patterns.

Green AI for sustainable IoT is an emerging discipline concerned with the environmental cost of AI itself. Training large deep learning models consumes substantial energy: a single large language model training run has been estimated to emit as much CO2 as a transatlantic flight. Deploying AI at scale across billions of IoT devices requires that inference be computationally efficient, not merely accurate. Green AI research focuses on more efficient model architectures, hardware-aware neural architecture search, and the use of TinyML techniques to minimise inference energy at every tier. The goal is AI-enabled IoT that improves sustainability not only by optimising the systems it manages but by being efficient in its own resource consumption.

The development of responsible and explainable AIoT (systems that are transparent, auditable, fair, and governed by appropriate human oversight) is perhaps the most important future direction of all. As AIoT systems take on increasingly consequential roles in healthcare, critical infrastructure, transportation, and public services, the governance frameworks, regulatory requirements, and professional norms that govern them must evolve in parallel with the technology. The engineers and practitioners who design and deploy the next generation of AI-enabled IoT systems will bear substantial responsibility for ensuring that the intelligence they embed in the physical world is used safely, fairly, and in service of human well-being.

11.16 Chapter Summary

This chapter has examined the convergence of Artificial Intelligence and Machine Learning with the Internet of Things: a convergence that transforms IoT from a data-collection and monitoring infrastructure into an intelligent, adaptive, and increasingly autonomous platform for physical-world decision-making. The opening scenario of a bearing failure predicted and prevented by an edge-deployed LSTM model illustrated the practical value that this convergence delivers; the subsequent sections provided the conceptual foundations, technical methods, and governance frameworks needed to design and deploy AI-enabled IoT systems competently and responsibly.

AI and ML transform IoT by providing the cognitive layer that connected sensing alone cannot provide. Supervised learning enables prediction and classification; unsupervised learning enables anomaly detection without labelled failure data; deep learning handles image, audio, and complex time-series data; reinforcement learning supports sequential control optimisation; and generative AI is beginning to create natural language interfaces for IoT system management. No single technique is appropriate for all IoT problems: the selection of AI/ML method must be driven by the data type, the problem structure, the deployment constraints, and the performance requirements of the specific application.

AI in IoT can run at four distinct tiers of the network architecture: in the cloud for powerful training and fleet-wide analytics; at the edge for low-latency, privacy-preserving inference close to the data source; in gateways for lightweight local aggregation and classification; and on devices themselves using TinyML for ultra-low-power, offline intelligence at the sensor node. Modern AIoT systems distribute intelligence across all four tiers, routing each decision to the tier best suited to its requirements, managing the resulting model lifecycle with systematic versioning, monitoring, and retraining pipelines.

The development of an AI/ML system for IoT requires a structured twelve-step pipeline spanning problem definition, data collection, preprocessing and labelling, model selection and training, validation, deployment, and continuous monitoring. The most common causes of AI failure in IoT deployments are not algorithmic but operational: poor data quality, insufficient labelled training data, model drift, and inadequate post-deployment monitoring. Success requires investment in the data infrastructure and operational processes that support the AI system throughout its lifecycle, not merely in the model development phase.

The benefits of AI-enabled IoT (predictive maintenance, real-time autonomous decision-making, energy efficiency, improved safety, sustainability, and scalable governance) are well-evidenced across manufacturing, healthcare, smart cities, agriculture, and building management. The case studies presented in Sections 11.13 and 11.14 illustrate both the magnitude of these benefits and the design and governance considerations required to realise them in practice. The challenges (data quality, labelling difficulty, model drift, resource constraints, privacy risks, and physical safety implications) are equally real and must be addressed with equal rigour.

The governance of AI-enabled IoT systems requires security, privacy, explainability, human oversight, bias detection, and audit capabilities that go beyond conventional IoT governance. The EU AI Act, GDPR, sector-specific regulations for healthcare and critical infrastructure, and national frameworks such as Oman's National Cybersecurity Strategy are increasingly codifying these requirements into law. Engineers and practitioners designing AI-enabled IoT systems must treat responsible governance not as an optional add-on but as a core design requirement alongside accuracy, latency, and energy efficiency.

Looking forward, the trajectory of AI-enabled IoT points towards systems that are more autonomous, more adaptive, more energy-efficient, and more deeply integrated with both the physical world and the governance frameworks that mediate human society. The practitioners who understand both the technical foundations and the ethical dimensions of this integration will be best placed to design systems that deliver its benefits while managing its risks, and to contribute to the responsible development of the intelligent connected world that IoT and AI together are building.

The convergence of IoT and AI marks an important transition in the history of computing: from systems that merely observe the physical world to systems that can interpret, learn, predict, and respond to it. The future of IoT will not be measured only by the number of connected devices, but by the quality of intelligence, trust, security, sustainability, and human value built into those connections. As AI becomes embedded across devices, gateways, edge servers, cloud platforms, and enterprise applications, IoT systems will increasingly support safer industries, smarter cities, more efficient energy systems, resilient healthcare, sustainable agriculture, and more responsive public services. However, this future must be designed with responsibility. Every intelligent connected system must be engineered with privacy, transparency, accountability, cybersecurity, and human oversight as core principles, not afterthoughts.

This book has presented the Internet of Things as a complete technological ecosystem: from sensors and actuators to protocols, architectures, data platforms, applications, security, governance, emerging technologies, and AI-enabled intelligence. The journey from foundational IoT concepts to advanced AIoT systems reflects the direction in which modern digital infrastructure is moving. The reader who understands these foundations will be prepared not only to use IoT technologies, but to design, secure, manage, govern, and improve them for real-world impact. As the connected digital world continues to evolve, the true promise of IoT will lie in building systems that are intelligent enough to act, secure enough to trust, sustainable enough to scale, and human-centred enough to serve society responsibly.

References

3GPP. (2022). Technical Report 21.917: Release 17 description; summary of work items. 3rd Generation Partnership Project.

Abadi, M., Barham, P., Chen, J., and others. (2016). TensorFlow: A system for large-scale machine learning. Proceedings of the 12th USENIX Symposium on Operating Systems Design and Implementation (OSDI), 265-283.

Al-Fuqaha, A., Guizani, M., Mohammadi, M., Aledhari, M., & Ayyash, M. (2015). Internet of Things: A survey on enabling technologies, protocols, and applications. IEEE Communications Surveys and Tutorials, 17(4), 2347-2376.

Amazon Web Services. (2023). AWS IoT Core Developer Guide. Amazon Web Services. https://docs.aws.amazon.com/iot/latest/developerguide/

Analog Devices. (2022). ADXL345: Small, Thin, Low Power, 3-Axis +/-16g Accelerometer with High Resolution (13-Bit) Measurement. Analog Devices Datasheet Rev. G.

Antonakakis, M., April, T., Bailey, M., Bernhard, M., Bursztein, E., Cochran, J., & Durumeric, Z. (2017). Understanding the Mirai botnet. Proceedings of the 26th USENIX Security Symposium, 1092-1110.

Apache Software Foundation. (2023). Apache Flink Documentation: Stream Processing. Apache Software Foundation. https://flink.apache.org/docs/

Apache Software Foundation. (2023). Apache Kafka Documentation. Apache Software Foundation. https://kafka.apache.org/documentation/

Arduino. (2023). Arduino documentation: LMIC LoRaWAN library reference. https://docs.arduino.cc

ARM Ltd. (2021). ARM TrustZone Technology for Cortex-M Processors: Technical Reference Manual. ARM Ltd, Cambridge, UK.

Ashton, K. (2009). That 'Internet of Things' thing. RFID Journal, 22 June 2009. https://www.rfidjournal.com/that-internet-of-things-thing

Atzori, L., Iera, A., & Morabito, G. (2010). The Internet of Things: A survey. Computer Networks, 54(15), 2787-2805.

Baldini, G., Pricopi, L., Fovino, I. N., & Steri, G. (2020). A survey of techniques for the identification of mobile phones using the physical fingerprints of the built-in components. IEEE Communications Surveys and Tutorials, 22(3), 1471-1528.

Bauer, M., Boussard, M., Bui, N., and others. (2013). IoT Reference Architecture. IoT-A Project Deliverable D1.5. European Commission FP7.

Blackstock, M., & Lea, R. (2014). IoT interoperability: A hub-based approach. Proceedings of the 4th International Conference on the Internet of Things (IoT 2014). MIT Press.

Bormann, C., Castellani, A. P., & Shelby, Z. (2012). CoAP: An application protocol for billions of tiny internet nodes. IEEE Internet Computing, 16(2), 62-67.

Bormann, C., Ersue, M., & Keranen, A. (2014). Terminology for Constrained-Node Networks. IETF RFC 7228. Internet Engineering Task Force.

Borthakur, D. (2007). The Hadoop Distributed File System: Architecture and Design. Apache Software Foundation.

Boswarthick, D., Elloumi, O., & Hersent, O. (Eds.). (2012). M2M Communications: A Systems Approach. Wiley.

BSRIA. (2023). World Smart Homes Market 2023. BSRIA Ltd, Bracknell, UK.

Buterin, V. (2014). A next-generation smart contract and decentralised application platform. Ethereum White Paper. https://ethereum.org/whitepaper/

Cavoukian, A. (2009). Privacy by Design: The 7 Foundational Principles. Information and Privacy Commissioner of Ontario, Canada.

Cerwall, P., Jonsson, P., Moller, R., Blystad, S., & Brahme, R. (2016). Ericsson Mobility Report. Ericsson AB.

Check Point Research. (2020). Lights Off! Hack of Philips Smart Bulbs (CVE-2020-6007). Check Point Software Technologies, Tel Aviv. https://research.checkpoint.com

Chen, M., Mao, S., & Liu, Y. (2014). Big data: A survey. Mobile Networks and Applications, 19(2), 171-209.

Chintapalli, S., Dagit, D., Evans, B., Farivar, R., Graves, T., Holderbaum, M., Liu, W., Nusbaum, C., Patil, K., Peng, B. J., & Poulosky, P. (2016). Benchmarking Streaming Computation Engines: Storm, Flink and Spark Streaming. 2016 IEEE International Parallel and Distributed Processing Symposium Workshops. IEEE.

CISA. (2021). Advisory AA21-042A: Compromise of U.S. Water Treatment Facility. Cybersecurity and Infrastructure Security Agency, Washington DC.

Cisco Systems. (2023). Cisco Jasper Control Center: Platform Overview. https://www.cisco.com/c/en/us/products/wireless/jasper.html

Connectivity Standards Alliance. (2022). Matter Specification v1.0. https://csa-iot.org/developer-resource/specifications-download-request/

Dean, J., & Ghemawat, S. (2008). MapReduce: Simplified data processing on large clusters. Communications of the ACM, 51(1), 107-113.

Deloitte / BREEAM. (2016). The Edge: Amsterdam. Building Research Establishment Environmental Assessment Method Outstanding Rating. BRE Global.

Deng, L., Li, G., Han, S., Shi, L., & Xie, Y. (2020). Model compression and hardware acceleration for neural networks: A comprehensive survey. Proceedings of the IEEE, 108(4), 485-532.

Dimitrov, D. V. (2016). Medical Internet of Things and Big Data in Healthcare. Healthcare Informatics Research, 22(3), 156-163.

Dohler, M., & Watteyne, T. (2016). IoT protocols for a smart and connected world. IEEE Communications Magazine, 54(9), 14-15.

Dwork, C., & Roth, A. (2014). The algorithmic foundations of differential privacy. Foundations and Trends in Theoretical Computer Science, 9(3-4), 211-407.

ENISA. (2020). Guidelines for Securing the Internet of Things: Secure Supply Chain for IoT. European Union Agency for Cybersecurity. https://www.enisa.europa.eu

Ericsson. (2022). Ericsson Device Connection Platform: Technical Documentation. https://www.ericsson.com/en/portfolio/digital-services/iot-accelerator

Ericsson. (2023). Ericsson Mobility Report, November 2023. Ericsson AB. https://www.ericsson.com/en/reports-and-papers/mobility-report

Ericsson. (2024). Ericsson Mobility Report, June 2024. Ericsson AB. https://www.ericsson.com/en/reports-and-papers/mobility-report

Espressif Systems. (2023). ESP-IDF Programming Guide v5.1. https://docs.espressif.com/projects/esp-idf/

Espressif Systems. (2023). ESP32 Series Datasheet v4.2. Espressif Systems Co., Ltd.

ETSI. (2011). Machine-to-machine communications (M2M): Functional architecture. ETSI TS 102 690, V1.1.1.

ETSI. (2020). ETSI EN 303 645 v2.1.1: Cyber Security for Consumer Internet of Things -- Baseline Requirements. European Telecommunications Standards Institute.

European Commission. (2020). FIWARE NGSI-LD API Specification. OpenAPI Initiative.

European Commission. (2022). Proposal for a Regulation on Horizontal Cybersecurity Requirements for Products with Digital Elements (Cyber Resilience Act). COM(2022) 454 final.

European Commission. (2023). EU Data Act: Regulation (EU) 2023/2854 of the European Parliament and of the Council. Official Journal of the European Union, L 2023/2854.

European Commission. (2023). Regulation on the Right to Repair. Directive (EU) 2023/1734. Official Journal of the European Union.

European Parliament and Council. (2016). Regulation (EU) 2016/679 (General Data Protection Regulation). Official Journal of the European Union, L 119, 1-88.

European Parliament and Council. (2017). Regulation (EU) 2017/745 on Medical Devices (MDR). Official Journal of the European Union, L 117, 1–175.

European Parliament and Council. (2022). Directive (EU) 2022/2555 (NIS2 Directive). Official Journal of the European Union, L 333, 80–152.

European Parliament. (2024). Cyber Resilience Act: Regulation (EU) 2024/2847. Official Journal of the European Union.

FAO. (2022). The State of Food and Agriculture 2022: Leveraging Automation in Agriculture. Food and Agriculture Organisation of the United Nations, Rome.

Fernandez-Carames, T. M., & Fraga-Lamas, P. (2018). A review on the use of blockchain for the Internet of Things. IEEE Access, 6, 32979-33001.

Ferrandez-Pastor, F. J., Garcia-Chamizo, J. M., Nieto-Hidalgo, M., Mora-Pascual, J., & Mora-Martinez, J. (2016). Developing ubiquitous sensor network platform using Internet of Things: Application in precision agriculture. Sensors, 16(7), 1141.

Fielding, R. T., & Taylor, R. N. (2002). Principled design of the modern Web architecture. ACM Transactions on Internet Technology, 2(2), 115-150.

Fielding, R., & Reschke, J. (2014). Hypertext Transfer Protocol (HTTP/1.1): Message Syntax and Routing. RFC 7230. IETF.

Firework Analytics. (2017). Vizio Smart TV Settlement: Analysis of FTC Enforcement Action. Electronic Frontier Foundation.

Gartner. (2024). Hype Cycle for Emerging Technologies 2024. Gartner, Inc.

Garza, P., Grimaudo, L., & Ruffo, G. (2021). Federated Learning of IoT Time-Series for Predictive Maintenance. IEEE Internet of Things Journal, 8(18), 14030-14040.

Gentry, C. (2009). A fully homomorphic encryption scheme. PhD Dissertation. Stanford University.

Google Cloud. (2023). Google Cloud IoT Core Decommission Notice and Migration Guide. Google LLC. https://cloud.google.com/iot-core/docs/migrate-overview

Gould, K. (2021). Energy Harvesting for Industrial IoT: A Practical Guide. Texas Instruments Application Report SLAA901A.

Grafana Labs. (2023). Grafana documentation: InfluxDB data source and dashboard design guide. https://grafana.com/docs/

Grieves, M. (2014). Digital twin: Manufacturing excellence through virtual factory replication. White Paper. Florida Institute of Technology.

GSMA. (2016). IoT Security Guidelines Overview Document (CLP.11). GSM Association.

GSMA. (2017). GSMA SGP.02 v3.2: Remote Provisioning Architecture for Embedded UICC Technical Specification. GSM Association.

GSMA. (2019). GSMA CLP.14: IoT Device Connection Efficiency Guidelines. GSM Association.

GSMA. (2020). SGP.02: Remote Provisioning Architecture for Embedded UICC Technical Specification v4.1. GSMA.

GSMA. (2022). GSMA IoT Security Guidelines: Endpoint Ecosystem IG.06 Version 3.0. GSMA, London.

GSMA. (2022). GSMA IoT Security Guidelines: Overview Document IG.01 Version 3.0. GSMA, London.

Gubbi, J., Buyya, R., Marusic, S., & Palaniswami, M. (2013). Internet of Things (IoT): A vision, architectural elements, and future directions. Future Generation Computer Systems, 29(7), 1645-1660.

Guinard, D., & Trifa, V. (2016). Building the Web of Things: With examples in Node.js and Raspberry Pi. Manning Publications.

Hanes, D., Salgueiro, G., Grossetete, P., Barton, R., & Henry, J. (2017). IoT Fundamentals: Networking Technologies, Protocols, & Use Cases for the Internet of Things. Cisco Press.

Harber, A. (2020). Maersk and the NotPetya Attack: Lessons for Global Logistics Cyber Resilience. MIT Sloan Management Review.

IDC. (2023). IDC's Global DataSphere Forecast, 2023-2027. International Data Corporation, Framingham, MA.

IEA. (2023). Electricity 2023: Analysis and forecast to 2025. International Energy Agency. https://www.iea.org/reports/electricity-2023

IEA. (2023). Empowering Buildings: The Role of Data and Digitalisation in Efficient Building Energy Systems. International Energy Agency, Paris.

IEC. (2018). IEC 62443-3-3:2013/AMD1:2018 — Security for Industrial Automation and Control Systems. International Electrotechnical Commission.

IEC. (2022). IEC 62443-4-2:2019 Security for Industrial Automation and Control Systems: Technical Security Requirements for IACS Components. International Electrotechnical Commission, Geneva.

IEEE. (2020). IEEE Standard for Low-Rate Wireless Networks (IEEE Std 802.15.4-2020). Institute of Electrical and Electronics Engineers.

IEEE. (2021). IEEE Std 802.15.4e-2012 Amendment: Medium Access Control (MAC) Amendments for Industrial Applications. Incorporated in 802.15.4-2015.

IETF. (2004). RFC 3768: Virtual Router Redundancy Protocol (VRRP). IETF.

IETF. (2010). RFC 5905: Network Time Protocol Version 4. IETF.

IETF. (2011). RFC 6282: Compression Format for IPv6 Datagrams over IEEE 802.15.4-Based Networks. IETF.

IETF. (2012). RFC 6347: Datagram Transport Layer Security Version 1.2. IETF.

IETF. (2012). RFC 6550: RPL: IPv6 Routing Protocol for Low-Power and Lossy Networks. IETF.

IETF. (2014). RFC 7252: The Constrained Application Protocol (CoAP). IETF.

IETF. (2015). RFC 7641: Observing Resources in the Constrained Application Protocol. IETF.

IETF. (2019). RFC 7643: System for Cross-domain Identity Management: Core Schema. Internet Engineering Task Force.

IETF. (2019). RFC 8572: Secure Zero Touch Provisioning (SZTP). Internet Engineering Task Force. https://datatracker.ietf.org/doc/rfc8572/

IETF. (2019). RFC 8613: Object Security for Constrained RESTful Environments (OSCORE). IETF.

IETF. (2020). RFC 8949: Concise Binary Object Representation (CBOR). Internet Engineering Task Force.

IETF. (2021). RFC 9030: An Architecture for IPv6 over the Time-Slotted Channel Hopping Mode of IEEE 802.15.4 (6TiSCH). Internet Engineering Task Force.

IETF. (2022). RFC 9019: A Firmware Update Architecture for Internet of Things. Internet Engineering Task Force.

IETF. (2022). RFC 9124: A Manifest Information Model for Firmware Updates in Internet of Things (IoT) Devices. Internet Engineering Task Force.

IETF. (2022). RFC 9147: The Datagram Transport Layer Security (DTLS) Protocol Version 1.3. IETF.

IHL Group. (2022). Retailers and the Ghost Economy: How Out-of-Stocks Cost Retailers. IHL Group Research Report.

Industrial Internet Consortium. (2019). Industrial internet Reference Architecture v1.9. IIC:PUB:G1:V1.90.

Industrial Internet Consortium. (2019). The Industrial Internet of Things Volume G1: Reference Architecture, version 1.9. IIC.

InfluxData. (2023). InfluxDB 3.0 Architecture Documentation. InfluxData Inc. https://docs.influxdata.com/

InfluxData. (2023). InfluxDB v2 Documentation: Data elements and API reference. https://docs.influxdata.com

IoT Analytics. (2023). State of IoT -- Spring 2023. IoT Analytics GmbH.

IoT Analytics. (2025). Number of connected IoT devices growing 14% to 21.1 billion. IoT Analytics GmbH.

IoT Analytics. (2024). State of IoT — Spring 2024. IoT Analytics GmbH.

IOTA Foundation. (2023). IOTA 2.0: the Coordicide solution. https://wiki.iota.org

Islam, S. M. R., Kwak, D., Kabir, M. D. H., Hossain, M., & Kwak, K. S. (2015). The Internet of Things for healthcare: A comprehensive survey. IEEE Access, 3, 678-708.

ISO. (2021). ISO 23247-1:2021: Automation systems and integration, Digital twin framework for manufacturing, Part 1: Overview and general principles. International Organisation for Standardisation.

ISO/IEC. (2018). ISO/IEC 30141: Internet of Things (IoT) -- Reference Architecture. International Organisation for Standardisation.

ISO/IEC/IEEE. (2018). ISO/IEC/IEEE 29148:2018: Systems and software engineering, Life cycle processes, Requirements engineering. International Organisation for Standardisation.

ITU-T. (2012). ITU-T Recommendation Y.2060: Overview of the Internet of Things. International Telecommunication Union.

ITU-T. (2012). Recommendation Y.2060: Overview of the Internet of Things. International Telecommunication Union, Geneva.

ITU-T. (2015). Focus Group on Smart Sustainable Cities: An Overview of Smart Sustainable Cities and the Role of ICT. ITU-T FG-SSC, Geneva.

ITU-T. (2016). ITU-T Recommendation Y.4000/Y.2060: Overview of the Internet of Things (Revised). International Telecommunication Union.

ITU-T. (2022). Recommendation ITU-T L.1024: Energy efficiency metrics and measurement methods for IoT networks. International Telecommunication Union.

Jaguar Land Rover. (2021). Connected Car Technologies: Telematics and Over-the-Air Updates. JLR Technical Whitepaper.

John Deere. (2023). Operations Center Platform Overview. Deere and Company, Moline, IL.

Kamara, S., & Lauter, K. (2010). Cryptographic cloud storage. Financial Cryptography and Data Security, LNCS 6054, 136–149.

Kamilaris, A., & Prenafeta-Boldu, F. X. (2018). Deep learning in agriculture: A survey. Computers and Electronics in Agriculture, 147, 70-90.

Keoh, S., Kumar, S., & Tschofenig, H. (2014). Securing the Internet of Things: A standardization perspective. IEEE Internet of Things Journal, 1(3), 265-275.

Kleppmann, M. (2017). Designing Data-Intensive Applications. O'Reilly Media, Sebastopol, CA.

Kolias, C., Kambourakis, G., Stavrou, A., & Voas, J. (2017). DDoS in the IoT: Mirai and other botnets. Computer, 50(7), 80–84.

Kolias, C., Kambourakis, G., Stavrou, A., & Voas, J. (2017). DDoS in the IoT: Mirai and other botnets. Computer, 50(7), 80-84.

Kreps, J., Narkhede, N., & Rao, J. (2011). Kafka: A distributed messaging system for log processing. Proceedings of the NetDB Workshop at VLDB 2011.

Langner, R. (2011). Stuxnet: Dissecting a cyberwarfare weapon. IEEE Security and Privacy, 9(3), 49-51.

Langner, R. (2017). Triton: How it Disrupted Safety Systems and Changed the Threat Landscape. Langner Communications, Hamburg.

Lim, B., & Zohren, S. (2021). Time-series forecasting with deep learning: A survey. Philosophical Transactions of the Royal Society A, 379(2194), 20200209.

Liu, V., Parks, A., Talla, V., Gollakota, S., Wetherall, D., & Smith, J. R. (2013). Ambient backscatter: Wireless communication out of thin air. ACM SIGCOMM Computer Communication Review, 43(4), 39-50.

Lom, M., Pribyl, O., & Svitek, M. (2016). Industry 4.0 as a part of smart cities. 2016 Smart Cities Symposium Prague. IEEE.

LoRa Alliance. (2020). LoRaWAN Specification v1.0.4. LoRa Alliance Technical Committee.

Lu, Y. (2017). Industry 4.0: A survey on technologies, applications and open research issues. Journal of Industrial Information Integration, 6, 1-10.

Maersk. (2022). Remote Container Management: Technical Overview. A.P. Moller-Maersk, Copenhagen.

Maxim Integrated. (2019). DS18B20: Programmable Resolution 1-Wire Digital Thermometer. Maxim Integrated Products Datasheet.

McKinsey Global Institute. (2015). The Internet of Things: Mapping the value beyond the hype. McKinsey and Company.

McKinsey Global Institute. (2020). The Internet of Things: Catching Up to an Accelerating Opportunity. McKinsey and Company.

McKinsey Global Institute. (2023). The Internet of Things: Catching up to an accelerating opportunity. McKinsey and Company.

McMahan, H. B., Moore, E., Ramage, D., Hampson, S., & Agarwal, A. (2017). Communication-efficient learning of deep networks from decentralized data. Proceedings of the 20th International Conference on Artificial Intelligence and Statistics (AISTATS).

Merenda, M., Porcaro, C., & Iero, D. (2020). Edge machine learning for AI-enabled IoT devices: A review. Sensors, 20(9), 2533.

Microchip Technology. (2021). ATECC608B: CryptoAuthentication Device Datasheet. Microchip Technology Inc.

Microsoft Azure. (2023). Azure IoT Hub Developer Guide. Microsoft Corporation. https://docs.microsoft.com/en-us/azure/iot-hub/

Microsoft Azure. (2024). Azure Digital Twins documentation. https://docs.microsoft.com/azure/digital-twins

Minerva, R., Biru, A., & Rotondi, D. (2015). Towards a definition of the Internet of Things (IoT). IEEE internet Initiative, 1(1), 1-86.

MITRE Corporation. (2023). ATT&CK for Industrial Control Systems. MITRE Corporation, McLean, VA. https://attack.mitre.org/matrices/ics/

Nakamoto, S. (2008). Bitcoin: A peer-to-peer electronic cash system. https://bitcoin.org/bitcoin.pdf

NHS England. (2022). NHS Long Term Plan: Digital and Technology Investment Framework. NHS England, London.

NIST. (2019). NIST SP 800-82 Rev. 2: Guide to Industrial Control Systems (ICS) Security. National Institute of Standards and Technology.

NIST. (2020). NIST Interagency Report 8259: Foundational Cybersecurity Activities for IoT Device Manufacturers. National Institute of Standards and Technology.

NIST. (2021). NIST Special Publication 1500-201: Framework for Cyber-Physical Systems Volume 1, Overview. National Institute of Standards and Technology.

NIST. (2021). NIST Special Publication 800-207: Zero Trust Architecture. National Institute of Standards and Technology.

NIST. (2024). FIPS 203: Module-Lattice-Based Key-Encapsulation Mechanism Standard. National Institute of Standards and Technology.

NIST. (2024). FIPS 204: Module-Lattice-Based Digital Signature Standard. National Institute of Standards and Technology.

Node-RED Project. (2023). Node-RED documentation. OpenJS Foundation. https://nodered.org/docs/

Nordic Semiconductor. (2023). nRF52840 Product Specification v1.8. Nordic Semiconductor ASA.

OASIS. (2012). AMQP Version 1.0. OASIS Standard.

OASIS. (2013). eXtensible Access Control Markup Language (XACML) Version 3.0. OASIS Standard. https://docs.oasis-open.org/xacml/3.0/xacml-3.0-core-spec-os-en.html

OASIS. (2019). MQTT Version 5.0. OASIS Standard. Committee Specification 01, 07 March 2019.

OMA SpecWorks. (2020). Lightweight Machine to Machine Technical Specification Core v1.2. Open Mobile Alliance.

Omega Engineering. (2022). The Temperature Handbook: A Reference Guide to Temperature Measurement. Omega Engineering Inc.

OMG. (2015). Data Distribution Service Specification v1.4. Object Management Group.

oneM2M. (2021). oneM2M TS-0001 Release 4: Functional Architecture. oneM2M Partnership Project.

oneM2M. (2023). oneM2M Technical Specification TS-0001: Functional Architecture, Release 5. oneM2M Partnership Project.

OpenJS Foundation. (2023). Node-RED: Low-code programming for event-driven applications. https://nodered.org

OWASP Foundation. (2023). OWASP IoT Attack Surface Areas Project. Open Web Application Security Project Foundation. https://owasp.org/www-project-internet-of-things/

Patel, K. K., & Patel, S. M. (2016). Internet of Things: IOT definition, characteristics, architecture, enabling technologies, applications and future challenges. International Journal of Engineering Science and Computing, 6(5), 6122-6131.

Perera, C., Zaslavsky, A., Christen, P., & Georgakopoulos, D. (2014). Sensing as a service model for smart cities supported by Internet of Things. Transactions on Emerging Telecommunications Technologies, 25(1), 81–93.

Perrig, A., Stankovic, J., & Wagner, D. (2004). Security in wireless sensor networks. Communications of the ACM, 47(6), 53-57.

Popovski, P., Trillingsgaard, K. F., Simeone, O., & Durisi, G. (2018). 5G wireless network slicing for eMBB, URLLC, and mMTC: A communication-theoretic view. IEEE Access, 6, 55765-55779.

Pulver, G. (2019). Hands-On MQTT Programming with Python. Packt Publishing.

Qin, Y., Sheng, Q. Z., Falkner, N. J. G., Dustdar, S., Wang, H., & Vasilakos, A. V. (2016). When things matter: A survey on data-centric Internet of Things. Journal of Network and Computer Applications, 64, 137-153.

Rani, S., Babbar, H., Coleman, S., Sikandar, A., & Singh, A. (2021). Green Internet of Things (G-IoT): A review on energy-efficient protocols and architectures for IoT. IEEE Access, 9, 164530-164547.

Raspberry Pi Foundation. (2023). Raspberry Pi 4 Model B Datasheet. https://www.raspberrypi.com/products/raspberry-pi-4-model-b/

Reyna, A., Martin, C., Chen, J., Soler, E., & Diaz, M. (2018). On blockchain and its integration with IoT: Challenges and opportunities. Future Generation Computer Systems, 88, 173-190.

Rolls-Royce Holdings. (2022). Annual Report and Accounts 2022. Rolls-Royce Holdings plc, London.

Roman, R., Zhou, J., & Lopez, J. (2013). On the features and challenges of security and privacy in distributed Internet of Things. Computer Networks, 57(10), 2266-2279.

Rose, K., Eldridge, S., & Chapin, L. (2015). The Internet of Things: An overview -- Understanding the issues and challenges of a more connected world. Internet Society White Paper.

Roth, A., & Roughgarden, T. (2010). Interactive privacy via the median mechanism. Proceedings of the 42nd ACM Symposium on Theory of Computing. ACM.

Rouse, J. W., Haas, R. H., Schell, J. A., & Deering, D. W. (1974). Monitoring vegetation systems in the Great Plains with ERTS. Proceedings of the Third ERTS Symposium, NASA SP-351, 309-317.

Salama, M., Hassanien, A. E., & Fahmy, A. A. (2019). IoT Data Management for Healthcare Applications. Springer, Cham.

Samsung SmartThings. (2023). SmartThings Matter Integration Technical Documentation. Samsung Electronics.

Seng, J. K. P., Ang, K. L. M., & Hines, A. (2022). Artificial Intelligence of Things (AIoT): A survey. IEEE Internet of Things Journal, 9(11), 8454-8467.

Sensirion AG. (2021). SCD30 Sensor Module for CO2, Humidity and Temperature. Sensirion Datasheet.

Sethi, M., & Sarangi, S. R. (2017). Internet of Things: Architectures, protocols, and applications. Journal of Electrical and Computer Engineering, 2017, 1-25.

Shelby, Z., & Bormann, C. (2009). 6LoWPAN: The Wireless Embedded Internet. Wiley.

Shelby, Z., Hartke, K., & Bormann, C. (2014). The Constrained Application Protocol (CoAP). IETF RFC 7252.

Shoushtari, M., & Gressier-Soudan, E. (2020). Energy management for IoT battery life optimisation. IEEE Internet of Things Journal, 7(8), 7412-7427.

Silicon Labs. (2022). Z-Wave Protocol Overview and SDK 7.x Technical Reference. Silicon Labs.

Singapore Housing Development Board. (2022). HDB Smart Town and Smart Estate Initiatives: Building Smart, Liveable Towns. Housing Development Board, Singapore.

SMARTIE Project Consortium. (2015). SMARTIE Deliverable D2.2: Privacy and Security Architecture. EU FP7 Project 609062. http://www.smartie-project.eu

SMARTIE Project Consortium. (2016). SMARTIE Deliverable D5.3: Final Integration and Validation Report. EU FP7 Project 609062.

Srinivasa Rao, B. S., Vyas, K., & Maheswar, R. (2018). Internet of Things: Architecture, protocols and applications. In R. Maheswar and others (Eds.), IoT and Its Applications. CRC Press, Boca Raton.

Srinivasa, K. G., Siddesh, G. M., & Hanumantha Raju, S. (2018). Internet of Things: Technological perspectives and practical applications. CRC Press. [Primary source for the ten-step IoT Design Methodology.]

STMicroelectronics. (2023). STM32L4+ Series Ultra-low-power ARM Cortex-M4 MCU. STMicroelectronics Product Overview and Datasheet.

Tao, F., Sui, F., Liu, A., Qi, Q., Zhang, M., Song, B., & Nee, A. Y. C. (2018). Digital twin-driven product design, manufacturing and service with big data. International Journal of Advanced Manufacturing Technology, 94(9-12), 3563-3576.

Taylor, S. J., & Letham, B. (2018). Forecasting at scale. The American Statistician, 72(1), 37-45.

Tesla Energy. (2022). South Australia Virtual Power Plant: Technical and Commercial Evaluation. Tesla Inc, Palo Alto, CA.

Texas Instruments. (2022). DRV8833 Dual H-Bridge Motor Driver Datasheet. Texas Instruments Inc.

Texas Instruments. (2023). BeagleBone Black System Reference Manual Rev. C.1. BeagleBoard.org Foundation.

ThingsBoard Inc. (2023). ThingsBoard IoT Platform Documentation. ThingsBoard Inc. https://thingsboard.io/docs/

TinyML Foundation. (2023). State of TinyML Market Report 2023. https://www.tinyml.org

Tuballa, M. L., & Abundo, M. L. (2016). A review of the development of Smart Grid technology. Renewable and Sustainable Energy Reviews, 59, 710-725.

Tucker, C. J. (1979). Red and photographic infrared linear combinations for monitoring vegetation. Remote Sensing of Environment, 8(2), 127-150.

Twilio. (2023). Twilio Super SIM: Multi-Network IoT Connectivity. https://www.twilio.com/en-us/iot/super-sim

UK Department for Energy Security and Net Zero. (2023). Smart Meters: Economic Impact Assessment 2023. HMSO, London.

UK Government. (2022). Product Security and Telecommunications Infrastructure (PSTI) Act 2022. His Majesty's Stationery Office, London.

UN Global E-waste Monitor. (2024). The Global E-waste Monitor 2024. International Telecommunication Union / UN University.

US FTC. (2017). In the Matter of VIZIO, Inc.: Consent Order. Federal Trade Commission, Washington DC.

Vegetronix Inc. (2022). VH400 soil moisture sensor datasheet and application note. Vegetronix Inc. https://www.vegetronix.com/Products/VH400/

Verbraeken, J., Wolting, M., Katzy, J., Kloppenburg, J., Verbelen, T., & Rellermeyer, J. S. (2020). A survey on distributed machine learning. ACM Computing Surveys, 53(2), 1-33.

Verdouw, C., Sundmaeker, H., Tekinerdogan, B., Conzon, D., & Montanaro, T. (2019). Architecture framework of IoT-based food and farm systems: A multiple case study. Computers and Electronics in Agriculture, 165, Article 104939.

Vermesan, O., & Friess, P. (Eds.). (2014). Internet of Things: From research and innovation to market deployment. River Publishers.

Viegas, V., Pereira, J. M. D., & Girao, P. S. (2012). Measuring temperature with resistance temperature detectors. IEEE Instrumentation and Measurement Magazine, 15(2), 54-60.

W3C. (2020). Web of Things (WoT) Architecture. W3C Recommendation, 9 April 2020. https://www.w3.org/TR/wot-architecture/

Wang, A., Iyer, V., Talla, V., Smith, J. R., & Gollakota, S. (2017). LoRa backscatter: Enabling the vision of ubiquitous connectivity. Proceedings of ACM IMWUT, 1(3), 105.

Warden, P., & Situnayake, D. (2019). TinyML: Machine learning with TensorFlow on Arduino and ultra-low power microcontrollers. O'Reilly Media.

Weiser, M. (1991). The computer for the 21st century. Scientific American, 265(3), 94-104.

Whitmore, A., Agarwal, A., & Da Xu, L. (2015). The Internet of Things: A survey of topics and trends. Information Systems Frontiers, 17(2), 261–274.

WHO. (2022). Ambient Air Quality Database 2022. World Health Organisation, Geneva.

Wiliot. (2023). Wiliot IoT Pixel: Ambient-Powered Bluetooth Tags. https://www.wiliot.com

Winter, T., Thubert, P., Brandt, A., Hui, J., Kelsey, R., Levis, P., & Vasseur, J. (2012). RPL: IPv6 Routing Protocol for Low-Power and Lossy Networks. RFC 6550. IETF.

World Economic Forum. (2020). Internet of Things guidelines for sustainability. WEF White Paper. https://www.weforum.org

Wortmann, F., & Flüchter, K. (2015). Internet of Things: Technology and value added. Business & Information Systems Engineering, 57(3), 221–224.

Wurm, J., Jin, Y., Liu, Y., Hu, S., Heffner, K., Rahman, F., & Tehranipoor, M. (2016). Introduction to cyber-physical system security: A cross-layer perspective. IEEE Transactions on Multi-Scale Computing Systems, 3(3), 215-227.

Zaharia, M., Chowdhury, M., Franklin, M. J., Shenker, S., & Stoica, I. (2010). Spark: Cluster computing with working sets. Proceedings of the 2nd USENIX Workshop on Hot Topics in Cloud Computing.

Zanella, A., Bui, N., Castellani, A., Vangelista, L., & Zorzi, M. (2014). Internet of Things for smart cities. IEEE Internet of Things Journal, 1(1), 22–32.

Zhang, Z. K., Cho, M. C. Y., Wang, C. W., Hsu, C. W., Chen, C. K., & Shieh, S. (2014). IoT security: Ongoing challenges and research opportunities. Proceedings of the 7th IEEE International Conference on Service-Oriented Computing and Applications, 230-234.

Zhao, K., & Ge, L. (2013). A survey on the Internet of Things security. In Proceedings of the 9th International Conference on Computational Intelligence and Security, pp. 663-667. IEEE.

Zhou, W., Jia, Y., Peng, A., Zhang, Y., & Liu, P. (2019). The effect of IoT new features on security and privacy: New threats, existing solutions, and challenges yet to be solved. IEEE Internet of Things Journal, 6(2), 1606-1616.

Ziegler, J. G., & Nichols, N. B. (1942). Optimum settings for automatic controllers. Transactions of the ASME, 64(8), 759-768.

Zigbee Alliance. (2015). Zigbee Specification Revision 22, Version 1.0. Connectivity Standards Alliance.

Appendix 1:

Glossary of Terms

6LoWPAN (IPv6 over Low-Power Wireless Personal Area Networks). An IETF adaptation layer (RFC 4944, RFC 6282) that compresses IPv6 and UDP headers to fit within the 127-byte IEEE 802.15.4 frame, enabling full IPv6 addressability on constrained IoT devices. IPHC compression reduces the 40-byte IPv6 header to as few as 2 bytes.

A

ABAC (Attribute-Based Access Control). An access control model in which authorisation decisions are computed dynamically from the attributes of the subject, resource, action, and environment, enabling fine-grained, context-sensitive policies that RBAC alone cannot express.

Accelerometer. A MEMS inertial sensor that measures acceleration along one, two, or three orthogonal axes by detecting the displacement of a proof mass suspended by micro-fabricated spring structures. Used in IoT for activity recognition, fall detection, tilt sensing, and vibration monitoring. The ADXL345 and MPU-6050 are widely deployed examples.

Acceptance Testing. The final level of IoT system testing in which the complete deployed system is validated against the original requirements with end users as the test audience. Acceptance testing verifies not only technical function but usability, workflow fit, and satisfaction of non-functional requirements including latency, accuracy, and availability.

Actuator. A device that converts a digital signal or electrical input into a physical action, operating a motor, opening a valve, switching a relay, or adjusting a lighting level. Actuators form the IoT effector layer, enabling autonomous physical responses to sensor-derived decisions.

ADC (Analogue-to-Digital Converter). An electronic component or peripheral that converts a continuously variable analogue voltage into a discrete digital value represented as an N-bit integer. Resolution (N bits) and sampling rate (samples per second) are the primary specifications. Most microcontrollers include a built-in successive-approximation ADC (SAR ADC) with 10-12 bit resolution.

Advanced Metering Infrastructure (AMI). A system of smart electricity and gas meters with two-way communication capability, enabling half-hourly consumption data, remote reading, time-of-use tariffs, and demand response programmes. AMI is the foundational IoT layer of smart grid infrastructure.

AIoT (Artificial Intelligence of Things). The architectural integration of machine learning inference capabilities into IoT systems at the device, gateway, or edge tier. AIoT enables autonomous classification, prediction, and actuation without cloud round-trips, providing latency, privacy, bandwidth, and resilience advantages over cloud-only AI deployments.

Alert Fatigue. The desensitisation of operations teams caused by an excessive volume of low-fidelity alarms, which increases the risk that genuine security or reliability events are overlooked. Addressed through machine-learning-assisted threshold tuning and alert correlation.

Algorithmic Bias. Systematic errors in AI model outputs arising from unrepresentative training data or flawed model design, producing predictions that are less accurate or less fair for particular subgroups of the target population. In AIoT, algorithmic bias can cause predictive maintenance models trained on new equipment to miss faults in older equipment, or health monitoring models trained on one demographic to be less accurate for others.

AMQP (Advanced Message Queuing Protocol). An OASIS standard (v1.0) TCP-based messaging protocol providing enterprise-grade features including transactions, routing rules, and dead-letter queues. Used at the gateway-to-platform and platform-to-platform tiers of industrial IoT architectures rather than directly on constrained devices.

Anomaly Detection. The identification of data points, events, or observations that deviate significantly from the expected pattern in a dataset. In IoT, anomaly detection algorithms running at the edge or cloud can identify equipment faults, cyberattack signatures, or sensor malfunctions in real time.

API-First Design. A software engineering practice in which API contracts: the complete interface specifications for every service boundary in a system are defined, reviewed, and formally agreed before any implementation begins. API-first design prevents integration crises caused by independently developed components with incompatible interface assumptions.

APN (Access Point Name). A configurable gateway identifier on a mobile network that determines how a SIM-equipped device routes its data traffic. Private APNs create logically isolated network paths for IoT fleets, preventing devices from traversing the public internet.

Architectural Reference Model (ARM). A normative framework defining the high-level structure, major components, interfaces, and design principles of a system class without specifying implementation details.

Attack Surface. The total collection of different points through which an unauthorised party can attempt to enter, manipulate, or extract data from an IoT system, including hardware interfaces, software entry points, communication channels, and management interfaces.

B

Batch Processing. A data processing paradigm in which accumulated data is processed as a discrete group (batch) at scheduled intervals rather than continuously as data arrives. Batch processing trades real-time insight for higher throughput and simpler error recovery, and remains appropriate for IoT use cases where latency tolerance exceeds the batch interval.

Big Data. Data sets characterised by high Volume, Velocity, & Variety that exceed the processing capacity of conventional database systems. IoT is one of the primary generators of big data, producing continuous time-series streams from millions of sensors that require specialised time-series databases and stream-processing architectures.

Bill of Materials (BoM). A structured list of all hardware components, quantities, unit costs, and specifications required to build an IoT system. In the ten-step methodology, the BoM is produced in Step 8 and every line item must be traceable to a requirement. The BoM is the primary output used for procurement, production, and cost estimation.

BLE (Bluetooth Low Energy). A short-range wireless standard (Bluetooth 4.0+, governed by the Bluetooth SIG Core Specification) optimised for ultra-low-power operation. BLE uses 40 advertising channels and data channels across the 2.4 GHz ISM band; connection intervals from 7.5 ms to 4 seconds; and a peak receive current of 4-8 mA with sub-microampere sleep current. Primary IoT uses: wearables, proximity beacons, building sensors, & Thread/Matter-over-BLE commissioning.

Blockchain. A distributed ledger in which records are grouped into cryptographically linked, append-only blocks. Tampering with any historical record invalidates all subsequent blocks. Consensus mechanisms (Proof of Work, Proof of Stake, or permissioned BFT) ensure all nodes agree on the canonical chain without a central authority.

Body Area Network (BAN). A network of wearable, on-body, or implantable sensors communicating over short-range wireless links (typically BLE or IEEE 802.15.6) to aggregate physiological measurements and forward them to a cloud health platform via a smartphone gateway.

Botnet. A network of internet-connected devices infected with malicious software operating under remote command and control, used collectively for large-scale attacks such as distributed denial-of-service. IoT devices are disproportionately recruited due to default credentials, unpatched firmware, and permanent internet connectivity.

Brownfield IoT Deployment. Integration of IoT capabilities into existing infrastructure not originally designed for IoT connectivity, requiring protocol bridging, retrofit sensor attachments, and data normalisation middleware.

C

CBOR (Concise Binary Object Representation). An IETF-standardised binary data serialisation format (RFC 8949) derived from JSON's data model but encoded in binary. CBOR is optimised for IoT and constrained environments, offering 50 to 70 percent size reduction over equivalent JSON with minimal encoding complexity.

Certificate Pinning. A security technique in which an IoT device is hard-coded with the hash of the expected server certificate or CA certificate, rejecting any connection presenting a different certificate regardless of CA trust. Prevents man-in-the-middle attacks using fraudulently issued certificates.

Cloud Computing. A model for delivering on-demand, scalable computing resources (compute, storage, networking, and managed services) over the internet on a pay-per-use basis. Cloud computing is the IoT data processing backbone, providing the horizontal scalability that on-premises infrastructure cannot economically deliver for large device fleets.

CMDB (Configuration Management Database). A repository that records the authoritative attributes of every managed asset, including firmware version, assigned policies, network identifiers, and physical location. Serves as the single source of truth for fleet-wide compliance reporting.

CMP (Connectivity Management Platform). A software platform, provided by an MNO or independent operator, that exposes APIs for activating, configuring, monitoring, and terminating SIM-based connectivity at fleet scale. Examples include Cisco Jasper, Ericsson DCP, & Twilio Super SIM.

CoAP (Constrained Application Protocol). A lightweight web transfer protocol designed for constrained IoT devices. It operates over UDP, implements the RESTful interaction model of HTTP, and is standardised in IETF RFC 7252.

Cold Chain. The temperature-controlled supply chain required for perishable goods, vaccines, and pharmaceuticals. IoT enables continuous real-time monitoring at every stage, replacing periodic manual checks that may miss damaging temperature excursions.

Common Service Entity (CSE). The core architectural component of the oneM2M standard. Present at each node type, the CSE provides standardised IoT service functions including device registration, data management, access control, and subscription and notification.

Concept Drift. The gradual change in the statistical relationship between input features and target variables in a deployed machine learning model, caused by changes in the underlying system being modelled (equipment ageing, process changes, seasonal variation). Concept drift degrades model accuracy over time and necessitates periodic retraining.

Conceptual Design. The first phase of the ten-step IoT Design Methodology, comprising Steps 1 through 3: Purpose and Requirement Specification, Process Specification, & Domain Model. The conceptual design phase is entirely technology-agnostic; it clarifies the problem before any solution is proposed.

Connection Lifecycle Vulnerability. A weakness arising from inadequate security management across the full device operational lifetime, including insecure provisioning, absent deprovisioning, non-expiring credentials, and stale operator access management.

Constraint (Requirements Engineering). A requirement that specifies a non-negotiable boundary on the design: a fixed condition that cannot be relaxed through trade-off analysis. Examples include budget limits, regulatory requirements, physical environment restrictions, and technology exclusions. Constraints must be identified in Step 1 before any design work begins.

CRA (Cyber Resilience Act). European Union Regulation adopted in 2024 that mandates security-by-design, vulnerability disclosure, and mandatory OTA update capability for all products with digital elements sold in the EU market, including IoT devices.

CSMA/CA (Carrier Sense Multiple Access with Collision Avoidance). The medium access control mechanism used by IEEE 802.15.4. A device listens for channel activity before transmitting and backs off for a random period if the channel is busy, reducing collision probability in multi-device networks.

Cyber-Physical System (CPS). A system in which computational processes and physical processes are tightly integrated through sensors, actuators, and communication networks. Industrial IoT sensor networks are the sensing and communication infrastructure of CPSs.

D

Data Lake. A centralised storage repository that holds large amounts of raw data in its native format until it is needed, supporting schema-on-read access patterns. Data lakes built on object storage are the dominant architecture for long-term retention of diverse IoT data types including telemetry, images, audio, and log files.

Data Lakehouse. A data architecture combining the cost-effectiveness and scalability of a data lake with the transactional reliability, data versioning, and query performance of a traditional data warehouse. Implemented using table formats such as Apache Iceberg or Delta Lake over object storage. The leading architecture for IoT data at enterprise scale.

Data Lineage. The documented record of the origin, movement, transformation, and consumption of data through an IoT system. Data lineage enables impact analysis when data quality issues are discovered, supports regulatory accountability requirements, and accelerates debugging of analytics discrepancies.

Decommissioning. The structured end-of-life process for an IoT device, encompassing certificate revocation, credential wiping, SIM deactivation, CMDB removal, and physical disposal in compliance with data protection and environmental regulations.

Demand Response. A utility programme enabling grid operators to coordinate reductions or shifts in electricity consumption by IoT-connected loads (thermostats, EV chargers, industrial equipment) during periods of high demand or constrained supply.

Design Verification Test (DVT). A structured set of pass/fail tests applied to a prototype to validate that the physical design meets its requirements before volume production begins. The DVT checklist covers power budget, radio range, data format, sensor accuracy, and environmental protection, and serves as the gate between prototype and production assembly.

Differential Privacy. A mathematical framework for quantifying and limiting the privacy loss incurred when a dataset is used for analysis. Differential privacy adds calibrated statistical noise to query results, providing a formal guarantee that the presence or absence of any individual's data cannot be reliably inferred from published aggregates.

Digital Factory. A manufacturing environment in which every machine, conveyor, product, and worker is a data-generating node in an interconnected IoT system, enabling real-time quality control, predictive maintenance, and production optimisation.

Digital Twin. A dynamic virtual representation of a physical asset, system, or process, synchronised through real-time IoT telemetry and used for simulation, insight generation, and remote control. Digital twins operate across scales from individual components to city-level systems, enabling predictive maintenance, process optimisation, and virtual commissioning.

DODAG (Destination-Oriented Directed Acyclic Graph). The tree-shaped routing topology constructed by RPL, rooted at the 6LoWPAN Border Router. Every node selects a preferred parent based on an Objective Function minimising Expected Transmission Count, orienting all traffic efficiently toward the network root.

Domain Model. A conceptual model (Step 3) that identifies the real-world entities in an IoT system's operational domain (physical entities (devices), digital entities (data records, configurations), and actor entities (users, external systems)) and maps their relationships and multiplicities. The domain model reveals implicit design requirements not surfaced in requirements interviews.

DPIA (Data Protection Impact Assessment). A structured risk analysis mandated by GDPR Article 35 whenever processing is likely to result in high risk to individuals. Required for large-scale IoT deployments processing location, health, or behavioural data at scale.

DPO (Data Protection Officer). An individual mandated by GDPR Article 37 for controllers whose core activities involve large-scale systematic monitoring or processing of sensitive data. The DPO advises on DPIA requirements and acts as the supervisory authority contact point.

DTLS (Datagram Transport Layer Security). A TLS adaptation for UDP-based transports (RFC 6347 for v1.2, RFC 9147 for v1.3) that adds explicit sequence numbers, a cookie-based DoS prevention mechanism, and handshake message fragmentation. The recommended secure transport for CoAP and other constrained IoT protocols.

Duty Cycle. In power management, the fraction of time a device or radio is in its active (powered) state versus its total operating period. A 1% radio duty cycle means the transmitter is active for 1% of each reporting interval and off for 99%. Minimising duty cycle is the primary mechanism for achieving multi-year battery life in constrained IoT end nodes.

E

Edge Computing. The practice of processing data close to the source (at an IoT gateway, a local server, or on the device itself) rather than transmitting all data to a central cloud platform. Edge computing reduces latency, bandwidth consumption, and cloud processing cost by performing analytics and inference locally.

Edge Inference. The execution of trained machine learning models on edge hardware for real-time prediction without cloud connectivity. Enables applications with millisecond latency requirements (quality inspection, safety interlocks) that cannot tolerate the round-trip time to a cloud inference endpoint.

eMBB (Enhanced Mobile Broadband). One of three 5G NR service categories, providing peak data rates of 10-20 Gbps and typical user rates of 100-1,000 Mbps. IoT applications include high-resolution surveillance cameras, AR maintenance assistance, and connected vehicle sensor data streaming. Distinct from URLLC (low latency) and mMTC (high density).

Embodied Carbon. The CO2 equivalent emitted during the manufacture of a device, including semiconductor fabrication, PCB assembly, battery production, and enclosure manufacturing. For IoT sensor nodes, embodied carbon is typically 0.5-2 kg CO2e; for single-board computers, 10-30 kg CO2e. A component of the lifecycle carbon footprint alongside operational and end-of-life carbon.

Enabling Technologies. The set of previously independent technology trajectories (RFID, sensors and actuators, cloud computing, big data analytics, AI/ML, and wireless connectivity) whose simultaneous maturation in the 2010s created the conditions for IoT's rapid expansion. Each technology is necessary but not sufficient on its own; their interdependence defines the IoT technology ecosystem.

End-to-End Encryption (E2EE). Encryption applied between the originating IoT device and the final destination application, ensuring no intermediate node can read the plaintext. Contrasts with link-layer encryption, which protects individual communication hops but leaves data visible at intermediate nodes.

ETSI EN 303 645. The European standard for consumer IoT security, defining 13 mandatory provisions including no default passwords, vulnerability disclosure policy, and minimum software update periods. Referenced by the UK PSTI Act 2022 as the legal baseline for consumer IoT security.

EUI-64 (Extended Unique Identifier, 64-bit). An IEEE standard 64-bit hardware address composed of a 24-bit OUI (assigned to the manufacturer) and a 40-bit extension. Used as the native link-layer address in IEEE 802.15.4 and Bluetooth networks, and as the basis for IPv6 interface identifier generation in 6LoWPAN (SLAAC). LoRaWAN DevEUI is an EUI-64 assigned at device manufacture.

eUICC / eSIM. Embedded Universal Integrated Circuit Card: a hardware SIM soldered onto a device PCB whose operator profile can be switched over the air without physical SIM swap. Governed by GSMA SGP.02 (M2M) and SGP.22 (consumer) specifications.

F

Federated Learning. A machine learning approach in which multiple devices or servers collaboratively train a shared model without sharing raw training data. Each participant trains locally and shares only model gradient updates with a central aggregation server. Enables IoT ML where data privacy, sovereignty, or commercial sensitivity prevents centralisation.

Fog Computing. A layer of distributed computing infrastructure positioned between edge devices and cloud data centres, providing intermediate compute, storage, and networking capabilities. Fog nodes (typically small servers or capable gateways) aggregate data from multiple edge nodes and perform analytics requiring cross-device correlation.

Forward Secrecy (Perfect Forward Secrecy). A property of key exchange protocols ensuring that compromise of long-term session keys does not enable decryption of previously recorded communications, achieved through ephemeral key exchange (ECDHE). Mandatory in TLS 1.3 for all cipher suites.

Functional Block. A modular, self-contained capability unit within an IoT platform that encapsulates a specific function (such as device management or analytics) and communicates with other blocks through defined interfaces.

Functional Requirement. A requirement that specifies an observable behaviour or capability of the system; what it must do. Functional requirements are technology-agnostic and must be verifiable by test, demonstration, or inspection. Distinct from non-functional requirements (how well the system does something) and constraints (what limits the design).

G

Geofencing. A virtual perimeter around a real-world geographic area. When an IoT-tracked asset crosses the boundary, an automated event such as an alert, action, or log entry is triggered by the IoT platform.

Green IoT. The engineering and policy discipline addressing the environmental footprint of IoT deployments through low-power design, energy harvesting, circular economy hardware principles, and lifecycle carbon accounting. Green IoT principles are aligned with engineering quality: designs that minimise energy consumption also reduce cost and extend battery life.

Greenfield IoT Deployment. Design and construction of an IoT-enabled system from the ground up, with IoT connectivity as a first-class design constraint, enabling standardised protocols, security by design, and optimal hardware selection.

GSMA. The Global System for Mobile Communications Association: the international trade body representing mobile network operators. Publishes the SGP.02 eUICC M2M specification, the CLP Connected Living Programme guidelines, and the IoT Security Guidelines that underpin industry best practice.

H

H-Bridge. An electronic circuit consisting of four switching elements (transistors or MOSFETs) arranged in an H configuration that allows the polarity of voltage applied to a load (typically a DC motor) to be reversed, enabling bidirectional rotation. Combined with PWM, an H-bridge provides both direction and speed control of DC motors in IoT actuation applications.

Hardware Root of Trust (HRoT). A tamper-resistant hardware component storing the cryptographic keys used as the foundation of a device secure boot chain. Implementations include ARM TrustZone, dedicated secure elements, and TPM 2.0. The HRoT is physically isolated from the main processor with keys inaccessible to software.

Homomorphic Encryption. A cryptographic technique enabling computations to be performed on encrypted data without first decrypting it, such that the decrypted computation result is identical to performing the same computation on the plaintext. Enables cloud analytics on sensitive IoT data (healthcare, financial) without exposing raw data to the analytics platform.

Horizontal Architecture. An IoT platform design in which shared infrastructure supports multiple application domains simultaneously, as opposed to the siloed, application-specific vertical architecture of M2M systems.

Hyperledger Fabric. A permissioned blockchain framework hosted by the Linux Foundation that uses BFT consensus, achieves

2,000-20,000 TPS, and charges no transaction fees. Designed for enterprise IoT deployments requiring identity management, access control, and chaincode (smart contract) execution within a known set of participating organisations.

I

ICCID (Integrated Circuit Card Identifier). A globally unique 19–20 digit identifier embedded in every SIM card, used by CMPs as the primary key for managing individual SIM records including activation state, data consumption, and assigned tariff plan.

IEC 62443. An international standard series for industrial automation and control system cybersecurity. Defines Security Levels (SL 0–4) and a defence-in-depth zone-and-conduit model applicable to IIoT deployments in energy, manufacturing, and critical infrastructure.

IEEE 802.15.4. The IEEE PHY/MAC standard for low-rate wireless personal area networks, operating at 250 kbps in the 2.4 GHz band with AES-128 CCM* link-layer security. The foundational standard for Zigbee, Thread, 6LoWPAN, & WirelessHART.

IIoT (Industrial Internet of Things). The application of IoT technology to industrial environments (manufacturing, energy, mining, logistics, and utilities) with emphasis on predictive maintenance, process optimisation, and operational technology integration. IIoT deployments have stricter latency, reliability, and safety requirements than consumer IoT.

IMSI (International Mobile Subscriber Identity). A globally unique 15-digit identifier stored on a SIM card, used by the cellular network to identify and authenticate a cellular IoT device at the network access layer, independently of any application-layer credential.

Industrial IoT (IIoT). Application of IoT technologies to industrial and manufacturing environments, characterised by extreme reliability requirements, real-time control integration, industrial-grade hardware, and integration with OT systems including SCADA, PLCs, MES, and ERP.

InfluxDB. An open-source time-series database specifically designed for high-write-throughput storage and retrieval of time-stamped metrics and events. Widely used as the primary IoT telemetry store in conjunction with Grafana for visualisation. The InfluxDB line protocol is a common IoT data ingest format.

Information Model. Step 4 of the ten-step methodology: a precise specification of every data item the IoT system collects, stores, transmits, or derives, including data type, unit, range, accuracy, update frequency, and retention policy. The information model is the shared data vocabulary for all development teams and the foundation for the MQTT payload schema, database schema, and API response format.

Integration Testing. The second level of IoT system testing, validating the end-to-end data flow between real hardware and software components: sensor to gateway to cloud to database to user interface. Integration testing measures actual latency, packet loss rate, and data format fidelity under realistic conditions with a small number of deployed nodes.

IoT Application. A software system that consumes data from IoT devices, applies domain-specific logic, and delivers an output modifying the physical or informational environment. May be human-in-the-loop or fully automated.

IoT Ecosystem. The multi-stakeholder value chain that delivers IoT deployments, comprising device and component manufacturers, connectivity providers, platform vendors, system integrators, application developers, end users, and regulators. Value is only created when all tiers of the ecosystem function correctly and interoperate.

IoT Functional View. Step 6 of the ten-step methodology: a technology-agnostic logical architecture diagram organising the system's services into the standard IoT functional layers (Sensing and Actuation, Connectivity, Processing, Application, User Interface). The functional view shows what components exist and how they connect without naming specific products.

IoT Levels. A six-level taxonomy classifying IoT deployments by their data processing location, networking architecture, and intelligence distribution. Level 1 (single device, local action) to Level 6 (distributed multi-tier system with intelligence at every tier). The taxonomy guides technology selection by clarifying where computation, storage, and intelligence should reside in a given deployment.

IoT-A. The Internet of Things Architecture project, an EU FP7-funded initiative that produced a comprehensive Architectural Reference Model comprising Domain, Information, Functional, Communication, & Security sub-models.

IOTA (Tangle). A distributed ledger based on a directed acyclic graph (DAG) rather than a linear blockchain. Each transaction validates two previous transactions, distributing the validation work across all participants. The result is feeless micro-transactions, making IOTA economically viable for high-frequency IoT sensor data logging where per-transaction blockchain fees would be prohibitive.

IPHC (IP Header Compression). The 6LoWPAN compression scheme defined in RFC 6282 that reduces a standard 40-byte IPv6 header to as few as 2 bytes by eliding fields that can be inferred from link-layer context. NHC (Next Header Compression) similarly compresses UDP headers from 8 bytes to 4 bytes.

ITU-T Y.2060: An ITU Telecommunication Standardization Sector Recommendation published in 2012 providing the first internationally agreed definition of the Internet of Things and a four-layer reference model.

K

Kappa Architecture. A data processing architecture that uses a single replayable event stream (typically Apache Kafka) as the system of record, processing both real-time and historical data through the same stream processing engine. Eliminates the batch/speed duality of Lambda Architecture at the cost of requiring the stream processor to handle all reprocessing requirements.

Knowledge Distillation. A model compression technique in which a small student neural network is trained to mimic the output probability distributions of a large teacher model, rather than being trained from scratch on ground-truth labels alone. Knowledge distillation produces compact models with accuracy closer to the teacher model than small models trained from scratch can achieve, and is part of the TinyML compression pipeline for edge deployment.

L

Lambda Architecture. A data processing architecture with three layers: a batch layer that processes complete historical data for high accuracy, a speed layer that processes recent data with low latency, and a serving layer that merges results from both. Provides both real-time and historical analytical views but requires maintaining two codebases.

Logical Design. The second phase of the ten-step IoT Design Methodology, comprising Steps 4 through 6: Information Model, Service Specification, & IoT Functional View. The logical design phase defines what data the system handles and what services it provides, in a technology-agnostic manner that bridges the conceptual design and physical implementation.

LoRaWAN. The network protocol and system architecture standard built on Semtech's LoRa chirp-spread-spectrum modulation, maintained by the LoRa Alliance. Uses a star-of-stars topology with transparent gateways and a centralised Network Server, achieving 2-15 km range at 0.3-50 kbps with AES-128 dual-key encryption.

LPWAN (Low-Power Wide Area Network). A category of wireless network technology characterised by low power consumption, long range (2-15 km), and low data rate (0.3-50 kbps). LoRaWAN, Sigfox, NB-IoT, and LTE-M are the primary LPWAN technologies. Suited for battery-powered sensors deployed across large geographic areas where higher-bandwidth connectivity is uneconomical.

LwM2M (Lightweight Machine-to-Machine). The OMA standard (v1.2) for constrained IoT device management, built on CoAP/DTLS. Defines a hierarchical Object/Instance/Resource data model and four interfaces (Bootstrap, Registration, Device Management, Information Reporting) for complete device lifecycle management.

M

M2M (Machine-to-Machine). A predecessor paradigm to IoT involving bilateral communication between machines using proprietary protocols and point-to-point network connections. Distinct from IoT in its reliance on proprietary vendor stacks, absence of internet-standard protocols, and inability to scale to ecosystem-level integration across multiple systems and platforms.

Matter. An open-source IoT interoperability standard developed by the Connectivity Standards Alliance (formerly Zigbee Alliance) and supported by Apple, Google, Amazon, Samsung, and over 200 other companies. Released in 2022, Matter defines a common application layer for smart home devices, enabling products from different manufacturers to work together without proprietary integration.

MEMS (Micro-Electro-Mechanical Systems). A manufacturing technology that fabricates microscopic mechanical structures on silicon wafers, enabling sensors (accelerometers, gyroscopes, pressure sensors, microphones) to be produced as integrated circuits at coin-cell size and cent-level cost. MEMS cost reduction is the primary enabler of dense IoT sensor deployment.

Mirai Botnet. An IoT botnet first identified in 2016 that infected approximately 600,000 devices by exploiting factory-default Telnet credentials. Used to launch DDoS attacks reaching 1.2 Tbps against DNS provider Dyn, disrupting internet services across North America. Its publicly released source code spawned numerous active variants.

mMTC (Massive Machine-Type Communications). One of three 5G NR service categories, targeting connection density of up to one million devices per square kilometre with low power consumption and low data rates. Incorporates and extends 4G NB-IoT and LTE-M for cellular coverage of battery-powered IoT sensors. Suited for smart meters, agricultural sensors, and building automation at national scale.

Model Quantisation. An optimisation technique that reduces the precision of neural network weights and activations from 32-bit floating point to lower-precision formats (typically 8-bit integers), reducing model size and inference compute requirements with typically less than 1% accuracy loss. Essential for deploying ML models on constrained edge hardware.

MoSCoW Prioritisation. A requirement prioritisation method in which each requirement is classified as Must Have (non-negotiable for deployment), Should Have (important but not critical), Could Have (desirable if budget and time permit), or Won't Have (explicitly deferred). MoSCoW prevents scope creep by establishing clear tiers of requirement importance at the start of the design process.

MQTT (Message Queuing Telemetry Transport). An OASIS standard (v5.0) broker-centric publish-subscribe protocol over TCP. Defines three QoS levels (at-most-once, at-least-once, exactly-once) and a 2-byte fixed header. The de facto standard for cloud-connected IoT telemetry; must be deployed over TLS on port 8883 for internet-accessible brokers.

Mutual TLS (mTLS). A TLS configuration in which both the connecting client (IoT device) and the server present X.509 certificates for bidirectional authentication. The recommended authentication mechanism for IoT device-to-cloud connectivity where device identity must be cryptographically verifiable.

MVNO (Mobile Virtual Network Operator). A provider that offers mobile connectivity services by reselling capacity leased from one or more MNO infrastructure owners. Many IoT CMPs operate as MVNOs to deliver multi-carrier SIM products with a single management interface.

N

NB-IoT (Narrowband IoT). A 3GPP-standardised LPWAN technology operating within licensed cellular spectrum (LTE bands) using a 200 kHz channel. Provides longer range than standard LTE, enhanced indoor penetration, and device power consumption optimised for battery operation via PSM (Power Saving Mode) and eDRX (Extended Discontinuous Reception). Suited for fixed or slowly-moving IoT devices requiring nationwide coverage.

NDIR (Non-Dispersive Infrared). A gas measurement technique that quantifies gas concentration by the attenuation of infrared light at the molecule's characteristic absorption wavelength. Highly selective (measures only the target gas), accurate (typically 30-50 ppm CO2), and long-lived (no electrochemical degradation). The SCD30 and MH-Z19B are widely used NDIR CO2 sensors in IoT indoor air quality applications.

NDVI (Normalised Difference Vegetation Index). A spectral index (NIR - Red) / (NIR + Red) quantifying vegetation health from remote sensing data. Used in UAV-based crop monitoring to detect stress, disease, and yield potential.

NETCONF/YANG. The IETF network configuration protocol (RFC 6241) paired with YANG data modelling language (RFC 7950). Used for programmatic configuration of industrial IoT gateways and network infrastructure devices; RESTCONF (RFC 8040) provides a RESTful variant over HTTPS.

Network Slicing. A 5G core network capability that creates multiple isolated virtual network instances on a single physical infrastructure, each with independently configured performance parameters (latency, reliability, bandwidth, density). Network slicing enables a single 5G deployment to simultaneously serve URLLC industrial control, eMBB video streaming, and mMTC sensor networks with contractual quality-of-service guarantees for each.

NFC (Near Field Communication). A short-range (under 10 cm) wireless communication standard (ISO/IEC 18092) operating at 13.56 MHz, derived from high-frequency RFID technology. Used in contactless payment, access control, and device pairing. Enabled by passive tags that harvest energy from the reader field, requiring no battery.

NIS2 Directive. EU Directive 2022/2555 on the security of network and information systems, expanding the scope of NIS1 to include additional sectors and introducing stricter incident reporting obligations and board-level accountability for cybersecurity risk.

Non-Functional Requirement. A requirement that specifies a quality attribute of the system; how well it must perform its functions. Non-functional requirements include accuracy, availability, latency, battery life, security level, and maintainability. They are often the requirements most commonly discovered to have been inadequately specified only after deployment.

O

oneM2M. A global IoT standards partnership of eight SDOs (seven founding partners in 2012: ARIB, ATIS, CCSA, ETSI, TIA, TTA, TTC; with TSDSI joining in 2015) developing technical specifications for a horizontal service layer that abstracts device diversity and enables cross-domain IoT application development.

OPC-UA (OPC Unified Architecture). An industrial IoT communication standard (IEC 62541) providing a vendor-neutral, platform-independent data model for industrial equipment, enabling IT/OT convergence by abstracting diverse field-level protocols into a unified interface accessible over IP networks.

Operational View. Step 7 of the ten-step methodology: the physical deployment specification showing device locations, wireless link topology, radio link budget analysis, environmental ratings (IP code, temperature range), power sources, and maintenance access requirements. The operational view translates the functional architecture into a real-world installation plan.

OSCORE (Object Security for Constrained RESTful Environments). An IETF application-layer security scheme (RFC 8613) for CoAP that encrypts payload and sensitive header options end-to-end, independent of the transport layer. Unlike DTLS, OSCORE survives hop-by-hop proxying, making it the preferred security choice in multi-hop IoT architectures.

OT/IT Convergence. The integration of operational technology (machine control, SCADA, PLCs) with information technology (enterprise software, cloud analytics) enabled by IIoT, creating new capabilities for data-driven operations management but also expanding the OT cybersecurity attack surface.

OTA Firmware Update. The remote delivery and installation of firmware updates to IoT devices over a network connection without physical access. A fundamental security requirement enabling remediation of post-deployment vulnerabilities. Must be secured with manufacturer digital signatures, TLS delivery, and rollback protection.

OTAA (Over-the-Air Activation). The LoRaWAN join procedure in which a device derives fresh session keys (NwkSKey, AppSKey) per join using a Join Request/Accept exchange with the Network Server. Provides forward secrecy and is strongly preferred over ABP for production deployments.

P

PAW (Privileged Access Workstation). A hardened, dedicated computing environment used exclusively for privileged administrative operations on IoT management platforms. Minimises attack surface by prohibiting general browsing, email, and untrusted application execution.

Peltier Device (TEC). A solid-state thermoelectric device that transports heat between its two faces when direct current flows through it (Peltier effect), or generates voltage when a temperature gradient exists across it (Seebeck effect). Used as a thermal actuator in pharmaceutical cold-chain, optical component stabilisation, and portable cooling applications. Coefficient of performance is 0.3-0.7, lower than compressor refrigeration but with no moving parts.

Physical Design. The third phase of the ten-step IoT Design Methodology, comprising Steps 7 through 10: Operational View, Device and Component Integration, Application Development, & Testing, Deployment, & Iteration. Physical design produces specific hardware choices, software implementations, test plans, and deployment procedures.

Physical Vulnerability. A weakness arising from physical accessibility of IoT devices, enabling firmware extraction, key recovery through debug interfaces or side-channel analysis, and malicious device replacement. Addressed through hardware security modules, disabled production debug ports, and tamper-detection.

PID Controller. A feedback control algorithm that adjusts a control output to minimise the error between a measured process variable and a desired setpoint, using three terms: Proportional (correction proportional to current error), Integral (correction proportional to accumulated past error, eliminating steady-state offset), & Derivative (correction proportional to error rate of change, reducing overshoot). Standard control strategy for temperature, speed, and position regulation in IoT actuator systems.

PIR (Passive Infrared Sensor). A motion detector that measures changes in infrared radiation emitted by warm bodies (humans, animals) in its field of view. Passive, requires no emitted signal. Inexpensive (under USD 1 for HC-SR501 module), low power (under 50 microamperes in monitor mode), and widely deployed for occupancy detection in smart building and security IoT applications.

Post-Quantum Cryptography (PQC). Cryptographic algorithms designed to be secure against attacks from both classical and quantum computers. NIST published the first PQC standards in August 2024 (FIPS 203 ML-KEM, FIPS 204 ML-DSA, FIPS 205 SLH-DSA), based on lattice and hash-based mathematical problems that are believed to be resistant to Shor's algorithm. PQC migration is required for IoT systems with long operational lifetimes.

Precision Agriculture. Use of IoT sensors, satellite remote sensing, and variable-rate application technology to manage field-level spatial variability in crop and soil conditions, optimising input use and reducing environmental impact.

Predictive Maintenance. A maintenance strategy using continuous IoT sensor monitoring to detect early signatures of equipment degradation, enabling maintenance to be scheduled before failure occurs, reducing unplanned downtime and maintenance costs.

Privacy by Design (PbD). An engineering approach in which privacy protections are embedded into system architecture as default properties, codified as a legal requirement by GDPR Article 25. The seven foundational principles include proactive protection, privacy as default, privacy embedded into design, and end-to-end security.

Process Specification. Step 2 of the ten-step methodology: a dynamic description of the system's operational behaviour, expressed as a process flow diagram showing triggers, data flows, decision points, and actions on both the device side and the platform side. Process specification exposes exception paths (connectivity loss, sensor fault, database unavailable) that informal design approaches routinely miss.

Protocol Buffers (Protobuf). A binary data serialisation format developed by Google that uses a schema definition language (proto3) to generate efficient encode/decode code for target programming languages. Protobuf messages are typically 3 to 10 times smaller than equivalent JSON and encode/decode 5 to 10 times faster, making them a leading choice for high-volume IoT telemetry.

PRU (Programmable Real-time Unit). A deterministic RISC co-processor integrated into the Texas Instruments Sitara AM335x/AM57x SoCs (as the PRU-ICSS — Programmable Real-time Unit and Industrial Communication Subsystem). The PRU executes at 200 MHz without OS scheduling latency, enabling microsecond-precision GPIO control and implementation of industrial fieldbus protocols (EtherCAT, PROFIBUS) in the BeagleBone Black platform.

Pruning. A neural network compression technique that removes connections (weights below a magnitude threshold) from a trained model. Unstructured pruning removes individual weights; structured pruning removes entire neurons or filters. Pruned models stored in sparse format reduce memory footprint; structured pruning additionally reduces computation, improving inference speed on hardware with sparse matrix support.

Publish-Subscribe. An asynchronous messaging pattern in which publishers send messages to named topics managed by a broker, and subscribers receive messages from their registered topics without direct publisher-subscriber awareness.

Purpose Statement. The one-paragraph output of Step 1 that answers three questions: what does the system do, for whom does it do it, and what value does it create? A well-formed purpose statement is concrete enough to be testable and abstract enough to remain valid as implementation details change. It names the problem, not the solution.

PWM (Pulse-Width Modulation). A digital technique for controlling the average power delivered to a load by varying the duty cycle of a fixed-frequency square wave. The average output voltage equals duty_cycle x supply_voltage. PWM is the standard mechanism for MCU control of DC motor speed, LED brightness, servo position, heater power, & Peltier TEC drive current in IoT actuation applications.

Q

QoS (Quality of Service). In MQTT: three delivery guarantee levels (0 = at-most-once, 1 = at-least-once, 2 = exactly-once). In DDS: a rich policy system of over 20 configurable parameters governing reliability, deadline, liveliness, and ownership for data-centric real-time communication.

Quantisation. A model compression technique that reduces the numerical precision of neural network weights and activations from 32-bit floating-point (FP32) to 8-bit integer (INT8) or lower. INT8 quantisation reduces model size by 4x with typically less than 2% accuracy degradation for well-trained models, and enables faster inference on hardware with INT8 multiply-accumulate units. The primary enabling technique for TinyML.

R

RBAC (Role-Based Access Control). An access control model in which permissions are assigned to roles and roles are assigned to users. In IoT management platforms, a four-role hierarchy (Observer, Device Operator, Security Admin, & Platform Admin) is a common baseline.

Remote Patient Monitoring (RPM). Use of IoT devices to collect and transmit patient health data from outside clinical settings, enabling continuous physiological monitoring and earlier clinical intervention than episodic appointment-based care.

Request-Response. A synchronous communication pattern in which a client initiates an exchange by sending a request to a server and waits for a corresponding response before proceeding.

RFC 7228 Device Classes. Three device classes defined by IETF RFC 7228 based on available RAM: Class 0 (less than 10 KB RAM; cannot run IP stack; requires gateway proxy), Class 1 (approximately 10 KB RAM; can run 6LoWPAN/CoAP), Class 2 (50+ KB RAM; can run full TCP/TLS stack). The classification guides protocol selection for constrained IoT deployments.

RFID (Radio Frequency Identification). A technology that assigns digital identities to physical objects via radio: an RFID reader emits radio waves; a tag attached to the object responds with a unique identifier. Passive UHF RFID (860-960 MHz, ISO 18000-63) is the dominant standard for supply chain and logistics IoT. Inspired the original coinage of the term Internet of Things by Kevin Ashton in 1999.

RPL (Routing Protocol for Low-Power and Lossy Networks). The IETF routing protocol (RFC 6550) for constrained IPv6 mesh networks. Builds a Destination-Oriented Directed Acyclic Graph rooted at the 6LoWPAN border router using an Objective Function that minimises Expected Transmission Count. Uses the Trickle algorithm to minimise control message overhead.

RTD (Resistance Temperature Detector). A precision temperature sensor whose electrical resistance changes predictably with temperature according to the metal's resistivity-temperature coefficient. PT100 (100 ohms at 0 degrees Celsius, platinum) is the most common; Class A PT100 provides accuracy of plus/minus 0.15 degrees Celsius at 0 degrees Celsius. RTDs require Wheatstone bridge excitation or precision constant-current sourcing with 4-wire (Kelvin) connection to eliminate lead resistance errors.

RTPS (Real-Time Publish Subscribe Protocol). The wire protocol underlying DDS, used for peer-to-peer participant discovery and data exchange without a central broker. RTPS multicast enables automatic discovery of DDS publishers and subscribers on a network, eliminating broker dependency in real-time industrial IoT systems.

S

SBC (Single-Board Computer). A complete computer on a single printed circuit board: processor, RAM, storage interface, networking, and I/O. In IoT, SBCs (Raspberry Pi, BeagleBone Black) serve as gateways and edge endpoints, running full Linux operating systems and providing the processing capability, memory, and software ecosystem needed for protocol bridging, local analytics, and cloud connectivity management.

SCIM (System for Cross-domain Identity Management). An open standard protocol (RFC 7643/7644) for automating the provisioning and deprovisioning of user accounts across identity providers and service platforms, enabling automated offboarding when staff leave an IoT operations team.

Secure Boot. A mechanism ensuring an IoT device only executes firmware cryptographically verified as authentic and unmodified before execution begins. Implemented through a chain of trust anchored in the hardware root of trust, with signature verification at each boot stage.

Seebeck Effect. The generation of a voltage proportional to a temperature gradient across a junction of two dissimilar conductors or semiconductors. The basis of thermocouple temperature sensing and thermoelectric energy harvesting. The Seebeck coefficient (microvolts per Kelvin) is the primary material parameter for thermocouple and harvester design.

Sensor. A device that converts a physical quantity (temperature, pressure, acceleration, light, gas concentration) into an electrical signal that can be processed by a digital system. Sensors form the IoT perceptual layer: the interface through which digital systems observe the physical world. Sensor miniaturisation via MEMS technology has been the primary enabler of dense IoT deployment.

Service Specification. Step 5 of the ten-step methodology: a catalogue of all services the IoT system provides, each with a complete interface contract defining the communication protocol, endpoint or topic address, payload format, and quality-of-service requirement. Service contracts must be agreed before implementation begins (API-first principle).

SIEM (Security Information and Event Management). A platform that aggregates, normalises, and correlates log and telemetry data from across an IT/OT environment to enable real-time threat detection, compliance reporting, and forensic investigation. Ingests IoT device telemetry alongside network flow and platform audit logs.

Signal Conditioning. The analogue processing chain between a raw transducer output and the ADC input: typically comprising amplification (bringing millivolt transducer signals to ADC full-scale range), filtering (removing aliasing noise above the Nyquist frequency and rejecting power-line interference), and offset correction (removing DC bias). Instrumentation amplifiers (INA128, AD8221) are the standard component for high-gain, high-CMRR amplification of differential transducer signals.

SLAAC (Stateless Address AutoConfiguration). An IPv6 mechanism (RFC 4862) by which a device autonomously constructs its globally unique IPv6 address from a network-advertised prefix and its EUI-64 interface identifier. Eliminates DHCP server dependency, which is particularly valuable in large-scale IoT deployments.

Smart City. A municipality that uses IoT technology to instrument and optimise urban infrastructure (traffic management, public lighting, waste collection, water systems, air quality monitoring) at city scale. Smart cities are IoT systems of systems, integrating multiple independently operated subsystems into a unified operational platform, presenting the most complex integration and governance challenges in the IoT domain.

Smart Contract. A self-executing program stored on a blockchain that automatically enforces the terms of an agreement when predefined on-chain conditions are met, without requiring a trusted intermediary. In IoT applications, smart contracts enable automated payment release when IoT sensor data confirms contractual compliance (e.g., temperature range in cold-chain logistics) and automated access control or device operation tied to verifiable sensor events.

SMARTIE. A European FP7 research project that produced a reference architecture for privacy-preserving IoT data sharing. Key contributions include an ABAC/XACML policy engine, anonymisation at the point of data ingestion, and a federated data storage model that keeps personal data within national boundaries.

Software Vulnerability. A weakness in firmware, operating system, or embedded libraries running on an IoT device. Includes unpatched CVEs, default credentials, buffer overflows, and hard-coded API keys. The most exploited vulnerability category in documented IoT security incidents.

Solenoid Valve. An electromechanically operated valve that uses a solenoid coil to drive a ferromagnetic plunger, opening or closing fluid flow (water, gas, compressed air). Classified as normally open (NO, flow when de-energised) or normally closed (NC, blocked when de-energised), determining fail-safe behaviour on power loss. Widely used in IoT irrigation, HVAC, and pharmaceutical cold-chain systems.

Spreading Factor (SF). A LoRaWAN parameter (SF7 to SF12) that controls the ratio between chip rate and symbol rate. Higher spreading factors increase link budget (and range) at the cost of reduced data rate and increased airtime. SF12 provides maximum range (approximately 15 km rural) at minimum data rate (approximately 0.3 kbps).

Stepper Motor. An electric motor that divides a full rotation into a fixed number of discrete angular steps (typically 200 per revolution for 1.8-degree step angle), controlled by sequential energisation of stator coils. Achieves precise open-loop position control by counting pulses without a position encoder. Used in IoT for 3D printing, CNC valve actuation, infusion pumps, and laboratory automation.

Streaming Analytics. The application of analytical computations to data in motion, processing each event or micro-batch as it arrives rather than querying stored historical data. Streaming analytics platforms such as Apache Flink and Apache Kafka Streams enable real-time aggregation, anomaly detection, and event-driven alerting on IoT telemetry streams.

SUIT (Software Updates for Internet of Things). An IETF standard (RFC 9019, RFC 9124) defining a manifest format and update procedure for constrained IoT firmware updates. The SUIT manifest describes the firmware image, is signed by the manufacturer, and is validated by the device before download and installation, providing authenticated, integrity-protected OTA updates.

Sybil Attack. An attack in which a single malicious entity creates multiple false identities in a distributed network, corrupting routing tables and consensus mechanisms in IoT mesh networks. Countermeasures include hardware-rooted identity, resource testing, and geographic validation.

T

Thing Description. A W3C WoT standard document format (JSON-LD) providing a machine-readable description of an IoT device properties, actions, events, and communication endpoints, enabling automated device discovery and composition.

Threat Model. A structured analysis identifying the threats applicable to a system, the assets they target, the vulnerabilities they exploit, and the countermeasures appropriate to each. The STRIDE framework and PASTA methodology are commonly applied to IoT systems as the starting point for security design.

Time-Series Database (TSDB). A database system optimised for storing, retrieving, and processing time-stamped data sequences. TSDBs use time-aware compression algorithms (delta-of-delta, Gorilla float compression), time-indexed storage layouts, and time-range query optimisations to achieve write throughputs and query latencies orders of magnitude better than general-purpose databases for IoT telemetry workloads.

TimescaleDB. A time-series database built as a PostgreSQL extension, combining the time-series performance of purpose-built TSDBs with the full SQL compatibility and ecosystem of PostgreSQL. TimescaleDB is particularly suited to IoT deployments requiring complex relational queries that join time-series telemetry with metadata stored in relational tables.

TinyML. The deployment of trained machine-learning inference models on microcontrollers with kilobytes of RAM and milliwatts of power consumption. Frameworks including TensorFlow Lite for Microcontrollers and Edge Impulse enable keyword recognition, gesture detection, and anomaly detection at the device edge, eliminating cloud round-trips for inference.

TLS (Transport Layer Security). The dominant cryptographic protocol for securing TCP-based communications. TLS 1.3 (RFC 8446) is the current standard, mandating forward secrecy, a 1-RTT handshake, and a fixed set of strong cipher suites. MQTT over TLS (port 8883) is the standard secure configuration for cloud-connected IoT devices.

TR-069 (CWMP). The Broadband Forum's CPE WAN Management Protocol, used for managing consumer IoT devices and home gateways via an Auto Configuration Server over HTTPS/SOAP. Legacy but widely deployed; superseded by TR-369 (USP) in new deployments.

Traceability. The property of a design in which every physical component, implementation choice, and test criterion can be traced back through the chain of models and specifications to a specific requirement, and ultimately to the system's purpose statement. Traceability makes a design auditable, defends design decisions against scope creep, and enables targeted iteration when operational data reveals performance gaps.

TSCH (Time-Slotted Channel Hopping). An IEEE 802.15.4e MAC-layer enhancement that schedules all transmissions in a repeating time-slot frame and hops the radio frequency each slot according to a pseudo-random sequence. TSCH simultaneously achieves very low radio duty cycle, deterministic bounded latency, and frequency-diverse interference resilience. The basis of 6TiSCH (RFC 9030) for industrial IPv6 mesh IoT networks.

U

Ubiquitous Computing. A computing paradigm articulated by Mark Weiser in 1991, describing a future in which computation is distributed across many small, inexpensive, embedded devices and recedes into the physical environment, becoming transparent to users. Ubiquitous computing is widely regarded as the conceptual predecessor of the Internet of Things.

Urban Data Platform (UDP). A shared data infrastructure aggregating IoT sensor streams from multiple city subsystems, normalising them into a common data model (such as NGSI-LD), enforcing data governance policies, and exposing data through standardised APIs to authorised applications.

URLLC (Ultra-Reliable Low Latency Communications). One of three 5G NR service categories, providing end-to-end latency below 1 millisecond and reliability of 99.9999% (six nines). URLLC enables IoT applications previously requiring dedicated wired connections: industrial robot synchronisation, autonomous guided vehicle control, remote surgical robotics, and power grid protection relay coordination.

V

V2X (Vehicle-to-Everything). A communications paradigm in which vehicles exchange real-time data with other vehicles (V2V), roadside infrastructure (V2I), pedestrians (V2P), and network services (V2N) to improve safety, traffic efficiency, and autonomous driving capability. V2X represents the convergence of IoT, 5G cellular, and automotive engineering.

Vertical Architecture. An IoT or M2M system design in which hardware, network, and software components are dedicated to a single application domain and are not shared with or accessible to other domains.

Virtual Commissioning. A digital twin technique in which the control software for a new piece of equipment or production line is developed and validated against the digital twin model before the physical equipment is installed. Virtual commissioning reduces physical commissioning time by 30-50% by arriving at installation with pre-validated software, and eliminates the risk of control algorithm errors being discovered during live production.

Virtual Power Plant (VPP). A cloud-based IoT platform that aggregates and coordinates the generation, storage, and consumption capabilities of distributed energy resources including rooftop solar, home batteries, and EV chargers, operating them collectively as a dispatchable grid asset.

W

W3C WoT (Web of Things). A W3C standardisation initiative that defines semantic interoperability for IoT devices through the Thing Description (TD) specification: a JSON-LD metadata format describing a device's properties, actions, events, and protocol bindings. A WoT-compliant device can be automatically integrated by any platform that understands the Thing Description standard, without custom driver development.

WebSocket. A standardised network protocol providing full-duplex, persistent communication channels over a single TCP connection, used in IoT contexts implementing the Exclusive Pair communication model.

X

X.509 Certificate: A digital document binding a public key to an identity (device ID, domain name, or organisation), signed by a trusted Certificate Authority. The standard mechanism for device identity in PKI-based IoT authentication; used in mTLS to verify both device and server identity in every connection.

XACML (eXtensible Access Control Markup Language). An OASIS standard XML-based policy language and evaluation framework for expressing and enforcing attribute-based access control decisions. Used in the SMARTIE architecture to represent fine-grained data-sharing policies that can be audited, versioned, and exchanged between platforms.

Z

Z-Wave. A proprietary sub-GHz (868/908 MHz) mesh protocol for home automation, controlled by Silicon Labs. Classic Z-Wave supports 100 kbps, four-hop mesh, and up to 232 nodes; Z-Wave Long Range extends support up to 4000 nodes in star topology when supported by the controller and devices. AES-128 S2 security applies across both variants. Mandatory certification ensures cross-vendor interoperability; primary use cases are residential security, smart locks, and thermostats.

Zero Touch Provisioning (ZTP). A device onboarding methodology, formalised in IETF RFC 8572, in which a new device automatically bootstraps its configuration, certificates, and connectivity settings upon first power-up without requiring manual operator intervention.

Zigbee. A complete mesh networking and application protocol stack built on IEEE 802.15.4 PHY/MAC, maintained by the Connectivity Standards Alliance. Operates at 250 kbps in the 2.4 GHz band, supports up to 65,000 nodes, and provides AES-128 security at both network and link key levels. Primary use cases are smart home and commercial building automation.

www.ingramcontent.com/pod-product-compliance
Lightning Source LLC
Chambersburg PA
CBHW031334230926
51848CB00002B/232